Proceedings

Fifth International Symposium on High-Performance Computer Architecture

HPCA

Proceedings

Fifth International Symposium on High-Performance Computer Architecture

January 9 – 13, 1999

Orlando, Florida

Sponsored by

IEEE Computer Society
Technical Committee on Computer Architecture

IEEE
COMPUTER
SOCIETY

Los Alamitos, California

Washington   •   Brussels   •   Tokyo

IEEE Computer Society Order Number PR00004
ISBN 0-7695-0004-8
ISBN 0-7695-0006-4 (microfiche)
Library of Congress Number 98-88211

Additional copies may be ordered from:

IEEE Computer Society
Customer Service Center
10662 Los Vaqueros Circle
P.O. Box 3014
Los Alamitos, CA 90720-1314
Tel: + 1-714-821-8380
Fax: + 1-714-821-4641
E-mail: cs.books@computer.org

IEEE Service Center
445 Hoes Lane
P.O. Box 1331
Piscataway, NJ 08855-1331
Tel: + 1-732-981-1393
Fax: + 1-732-981-9667
mis.custserv@computer.org

IEEE Computer Society
Ooshima Building
2-19-1 Minami-Aoyama
Minato-ku, Tokyo 107
JAPAN
Tel: + 81-3-3408-3118
Fax: + 81-3-3408-3553
Tokyo.ofc@computer.org

Editorial production by Regina Spencer Sipple

Cover art production by Alex Torres

Printed in the United States of America by The Printing House

QA
76
.9
.A73
I566
1999

Table of Contents

Panel Session I

Controversial Panel
    Organizer: *Yale Patt, University of Michigan, Ann Arbor*

Keynote Address II

Software and HPCA
    Speaker: *Ken Kennedy, Rice University*

Session 4: Instruction Scheduling & Speculation

Session 5A: Cache Coherence

Session 5B: SMP Clusters

Preface

Welcome to the 5th International Symposium on High-Performance Computer Architecture. HPCA has quickly become one of the most visible and prestigious conferences in the field of Computer Architecture and a lot of credit goes to the steering committee for their vision in realizing the need for such a meeting. Their dedication and effort helped in filling such a void.

This year, a total of 117 papers were submitted. Out of these, 24 regular papers and 13 short papers were selected. The selection procedure was rigorous and a great deal of effort was expended in ensuring fairness: an average of 4.3 reports were received for each submission and none received fewer than three reports. In fact, many papers had as many as six reviews. The Program Committee met at the beginning of October and examined each manuscript individually before making a decision. The referees and program committee members deserve a lot of thanks for this hard work: they have made possible the superlative program you will now enjoy. We have three outstanding keynote speakers: Bill Wulf, the President of the National Academy of Sciences; Ken Kennedy of Rice University; and B. Ramakrishna Rau of H.P. Labs. We are also fortunate to have a controversial panel being organized by Yale Patt of the University of Michigan. Another panel on storage is being planned by A. L. Narasimha Reddy of Texas A & M University. In addition, the technical program of this meeting is preceded by what we believe will be five stimulating workshops as follows: the Fifth Annual Workshop on Computer Education is being organized by David Kaeli and Bruce Jacobs; the Third Workshop on Communication, Architecture, and Applications for Network-based Parallel Computing (CANPC '99) is being organized by Anand Sivasubramaniam and Mario Lauria; Multithreaded Execution Architecture and Compilation is being organized by Dean M. Tullsen and Guang Gao; Parallel Computing for Irregular Applications is being organized by Jacques Chassin de Kergommeaux, Yves Denneulin and Thierry Gautier; and the Workshop on Computer Architecture Evaluation using Commercial Workloads is being organized by Russell Clapp, Ashwini Nanda, and Josep Torrellas.

A technical meeting of this size would have not been possible without help from many volunteers. Jie Wu did more than his share in the role of Local Arrangements Chair and he took several trips to Orlando in search of a perfect location. Anand Sivasubramaniam did a superb job as the Publicity Chair and Yuanyuan Yang, our Finance/Registration Chair made every efforts to make the registration process as smooth as possible. Chungta-Cheng performed an outstanding job as webmaster for the paper submission and refereeing. We are also grateful to the Workshop organizers. We would like to thank the IEEE Computer Society staff for all of the cooperation and help we received. Thanks are also due to University of Cincinnati and to the University of Southern California for their support.

We want to encourage students' participation and this year, for the first time, we plan to have at least 10 student travel awards. We look forward to your participation and discussion in making this an intellectually stimulating meeting that will serve as a leading forum for the Architecture community. We would appreciate receiving your comments and suggestions on all aspects of the program.

By the way, on Tuesday evening, there will be a business meeting of the IEEE Computer Society Technical Committee and everyone is invited to attend.

We thank you for your participation and wish you a nice stay in Orlando.

Jean-Luc Gaudiot
Program Chair
gaudiot@ampere.usc.edu

Dharma P. Agrawal
General Chair
dpa@ececs.uc.edu

Organizing Committee

Steering Committee

Dharma P. Agrawal, *University of Cincinnati*
Jean-Loup Baer, *University of Washington*
Laxmi Bhuyan, *Texas A&M / NSF*
Kai Hwang, *USC / Hong Kong*
Yale Patt, *University of Michigan*

General Chair

Dharma P. Agrawal, *University of Cincinnati*

Program Committee Chair

Jean-Luc Gaudiot, *USC*

Program Committee

David Abramson, *Monash University*
Nader Bagherzadeh, *UC Irvine*
Laxmi Bhuyan, *Texas A&M / NSF*
Wim Bohm, *Colorado State*
Luc Bouge, *ENS Lyon*
Tom Conte, *NC State*
Kemal Ebcioglu, *IBM TJ Watson*
Guang R. Gao, *University of Delaware*
Vinod Kathail, *HP Laboratories*
Kai Hwang, *USC / Hong Kong*
David R. Kaeli, *Northeastern*
Daniel Litaize, *Universite de Toulouse*

Ashwini Nanda, *IBM TJ Watson*
Yale Patt, *University of Michigan*
David Patterson, *UC Berkeley*
Andre Seznec, *IRISA / INRIA*
Mike Shebanow, *HAL Computer Systems*
Jim Smith, *University of Wisconsin-Madison*
Guri Sohi, *University of Wisconsin-Madison*
Josep Torrellas, *UIUC*
Mateo Valero, *UPC-Barcelona*
Sudhakar Yalamanchili, *Georgia Tech*
Qing Yang, *University of Rhode Island*
Tse-Yu Yeh, *Intel*

Workshop/Tutorial Chair

Bernard Lecussan, *ONERA / CERT and SupAero*

Local Arrangements Chair

Jie Wu, *Florida Atlantic*

Finance/Registration Chair

Yuanyuan Yang, *University of Vermont*

Publications Chair

Alex Eichenberger, *NC State*

Publicity Chair

Anand Sivasubramaniam, *Penn State*

List of Referees

Abe, Shigeo
Abraham, Santosh
Adve, Sarita
Agrawal, Dharma
Albonesi, Dave
Albuz, Elif
Al-Mouhamed, Mayez
Altman, Erik
Amaral, Jose Nelson
Anik, Sadun
Arvind
Ayguade, Eduard
Badia, Rosa M.
Baer, Jean-Loup
Bagherzadeh
Banerjia, Sanjeev
Barroso, Luiz Andre
Barton, Charles
Basu, Sujoy
Bechennec, Jean-Luc
Beck, Noah
Beivide, Ramon
Benkner, Siegfried
Bhuyan, Laxmi
Bic, Lubomir
Blumrich, Matthias
Bohm, Wim
Bose, Pradip
Brown, Aaron
Brown, Andrea C. A-D
Bruck, J.
Burkhard, Walt
Burns, Jim
Butler, Mike
Calder, Brad
Chang, Po-Yung
Chappell, Robert
Chen, Chien
Chen, William
Chen, Ying
Cheng, Chung-Ta
Ching, Li Kuan
Choi, Yungho
Chou, Chien-Chun
Chow, Paul
Cintra, Marcelo
Clark, Douglas
Coelho, Fabien
Cohen, Willim
Collard, Jean Francois
Conway, Patrick

Corbal, Jesus
Cosnard, Michel
Cox, Alan
Darte, Alain
Das, Chita R.
Davidson, Edward
Desoli, Guiseppe
Desprez, Frederic
Diderich, Claude G.
Drach, N.
Drach-Temam, Nathalie
Draper, Bruce A.
Duato, Jose
Dubey, Pradeep K.
Dubois, Michel
Ebcioglu, Kemal
Egan, Greg
Eichenberger, Alexandre,
Eickemeyer, Richard
Eisenbeis, Christine
Eknath
Etiemble, Daniel
Evers, Marius
Falsafi, Babak,
Farrens, Matthew
Feautrier, Paul
Feo, John
Filali
Fleury, Eric
Flynn, Mike
Friendly, Dan
Fu, Chao-ying
Fu, John
Gebis, Joseph
Gefflaut, Alain
Geiger, Thomas
Golbus, Jason
Gonzalez, Antonio
Gornish, Eddie
Goshima, Masahiro
Gottlieb, Allan
Govindarajan, R.
Gribstad, Ben
Gupta, Manish
Gupta, Shail Aditya
Gurd, John
Gyllenhaal, John C.
Hall, Mary
Hameurlain, Abdelkader
Hammes, Jeffrey
Hassan, Mahbub

He, Xubin
Hill, Mark D.
Hily, Sbastien
Hiromoto, Robert
Hu, Yiming
Huang, Michael Wei
Hum, Herbert
Hung, Shih-Hao
Hurson, A.R.,
Hutsell, Brian
Hwang, Kai
Iftode, Liviu
Iyer, Ravi
Jegou, Yvon
Jennings, Matthew D.
Jiang, Hong
Jin, Hai
Johnson, Teresa
Joseph, Doug
Jouppi, Norman P.
Juan, Toni
Kaeli, David
Kailas, Krishnan
Kalamatianos, John
Kathail, Vinod
Kavi, Krishna
Kaxiras, Stefanos
Keeton, Kimberley
Kim, Chinhyun
Kim, Mike
Kim, Sangwook
Klauser, Artur
Kling, Ralph
Ko, Seok Bum
Kodama, Yuetsu
Kontothanassis, Leonidas
Krishnan, Venkata
Kumar, Mohan
Kuskin, Jeffrey
Lang, Tomas
Larin, Sergei
Lecussan
Lenoski, Daniel,
Li, Cheng
Lin, X
Litaize, Daniel
Loic, Prylli
Lovett, Thomas D.
Lu, Mi
Luick, David
Luk, Chi-Keung

Maciunas, Kevin J.
Maheshwari, Piyush
Mahlke, Scott A.
Mantripragada, Srinivas
Maquelin, Olivier
Marquez, Andres
Martin, David
Martinez, Jose F.
Martonosi, Margaret
May, Phil
Mehaut, Jean-Francois
Meleis, Waleed
Melhem, Rami
Mendelson, Avi
Michael, Maged
Modi, Harit
Mohapatra, Prasant
Mongenet, Catherine
Moreno, Jaime
Mori, Shin-ichiro
Morin, Christine
Moudgill, Mayan
Mudge, Trvor
Muntz, R.
Mzoughi, Abdelaziz
Najjar, W.
Nakra, Tarun
Nanda, Ashwini,
Nemirovsky, Mario
Newburn, Chris J.
Ni, Nan
Nishikawa, Hiroaki
Norris, Cindy
Nowatzyk, Andreas G.
O'Brien, K.
Olariu, Stephan
Oppenheimer, David
Ortega, Daniel
Ozer, Emre
Panda, D.K.
Pande, Santosh
Pastor, Enric
Patel, Sanjay J.
Patterson, David
Patterson
Pedram, Massoud
Peir, Jih-Kwon
Pellegrini, Francois
Petrini, Fabrizio
Pfister, Gregory

Pierce, Jim
Pinkston, Timothy M.
Pinter, Schlomit
Pirvu, Marius
Pollock, Lori
Pontius, Mark
Pouzet, Marc
Prez, Ivn Martel
Puig, Fermin
Qiu, B
Quach, Nhon
Racunas, Paul
Raghavendra, C.S.
Ranganathan, Parthasarathy
Rau, B. Ramakrishna
Rencuzogullari, Umit
Rezaei, Mehran
Rigault
Rinker, Robert
Robert, Yves
Robinson, John
Rochange, Christine
Roman, Jean
Rosu, Marcel-Catalin
Rubin, Norm
Sainrat, Pascal
Saouter, Yannick
Saxena, Nirmal
Scheideler, Christian
Schimmel, David E.
Schlansker, Michael
Schreiber, Rob
Schwiebert, Loren,
Scott, Michael L.
Seznec, A-T. Nguyyendre
Sha, Edwin
Shebanow, Mike
Shen, Hong
Shin, Chulho
Shirazi, Behrooz
Siegel, H.J.
Silberman, Gabby
Singh, Jaswinder Pal
Sinharoy, Balaram
Sivasubramaniam, Anand
Smith, Jim
Snelling, David
Snider, Greg
Snir, Marc
Sodani, Avinash

Soffa, Mary Lou
Sohn, Andrew
Sreedhar, V.C.
Srinivasan, Viji
Stark, Jared
Steinberg, Jesse
Stenstrom, Per
Strumpen, Volker
Stunkel, Craig
Suginuma, Koji
Tang, Xinan
Temam, Olivier
Thomas, Randi
Toburen, Mark
Torrellas, Josep
Trichina, Elena
Tsai, Jenn-Yuan
Tubella, Jordi
Tvrdik, Pavel
Uhlig, Richard
Uht, Gus
Vai, M. Michael
Vaidya, Aniruddha S
Vanneschi, Marco
Vartanian, Alexis
Vincent, Jean-Marc
Vinyals, Victor
Vollmer, Jrgen
Vranesic, Z.
Wang, C.L.
Wang, Jian
Wang, Jianchao
Wang, San-Yuan
Wills, Scott
Wilson, Kenneth M.
Worley, Patrick
Wu, Jie
Xu, Lihao
Yalamanchili, Sudhakar
Yang, Qing
Yang, Yuanyuan
Yates, Robert Kim
Yeh, Chihsiang
Yeh, Tse-Yu
Zahir, Rumi
Zhang, Chihong
Zhang, Ye
Zhu, Yingchun
Zwaenepoel, Willy

Keynote Address I

Computing and Policy — Are We Fumbling the Future Again?

William Wulf

National Academy of Engineers

Session 1

Performance Enhancements

Global Context-Based Value Prediction[1]

Tarun Nakra, Rajiv Gupta and Mary Lou Soffa
Department of Computer Science
University of Pittsburgh
{nakra,gupta,soffa}@cs.pitt.edu

Abstract

*Various methods for value prediction have been proposed to overcome the limits imposed by data dependencies within programs. Using a value prediction scheme, an instruction's computed value is predicted during the fetch stage and forwarded to all dependent instructions to speed up execution. Value prediction schemes have been based on a **local context** by predicting values using the values generated by the **same** instruction. This paper presents techniques that predict values of an instruction based on a **global context** where the behavior of **other** instructions is used in prediction. The global context includes the path along which an instruction is executed and the values computed by other previously completed instructions. We present techniques that augment conventional last value and stride predictors with global context information. Experiments performed using path-based techniques with realistic table sizes resulted in an increase in prediction of 6.4-8.4% over the current prediction schemes. Prediction using values computed by other instructions resulted in a further improvement of 7.2% prediction accuracy over the best path-based predictor.*

1 Introduction

The efficiency of modern architectures is highly dependent on the amount of parallelism extracted both by the compiler and the hardware. The barriers to parallelism are the dependencies that exist between instructions of a program. These dependencies are classified as 1) *control dependencies*, arising from conditional branches in a program, and 2) *data dependencies*, arising from the flow of data between instructions.

To overcome the limitations imposed by control dependencies, branch outcomes are predicted and instructions are executed speculatively. Current branch predictors have been shown to accurately predict more than 98% of the branches [9].

Data dependencies existing between the instructions are more prevalent than control dependencies. To overcome these dependencies, it is possible to perform speculation on data as well. The data speculation could be performed based on the storage addresses [5, 10] or data values [7]. Recent studies on predicting data values have shown that the benefits of value prediction have significant potential for performance improvement [7, 12, 13]. Moreover, studies performed to observe the patterns of values computed by an instruction have found that instructions demonstrate locality of data values [8]. The sequences that occur in certain patterns are easier to predict than others. Typically, the patterns of values include:

(1) Constant values - these are the easiest to predict by always predicting the same constant value. Constant values have been shown to occur often in benchmark programs [8].

(2) Values differing by a stride - these usually occur in case of loop induction variables or variables that are dependent on induction variables.

(3) Other sequences - these include sequence of values that differ by non-constant strides. This category is the hardest to predict.

The techniques that perform prediction based on a local context of an instruction include **last value prediction** in which the value predicted is the one that was computed in the last execution of that instruction. Previous work using last value prediction indicates successful prediction for 40-50% of the dynamic instruction instances [7]. Another technique is **stride prediction**, which predicts values to be the sum of the last computed value of the same instruction and a stride. Stride prediction has been compared with last value prediction and shown to improve the prediction performance significantly [4]. In other work, **finite context method** (FCM) predictors are proposed that

[1]Partially supported by National Science Foundation Grant CCR-9808590 and a grant from Hewlett Packard to the University of Pittsburgh

predict values based on previously observed patterns of values [12]. The recent history of values computed by an instruction is matched with previous value history of the instruction. The next value of the instruction is predicted to be the next value in the previous pattern. These predictors have been shown to improve the accuracy of last value and stride predictors by as much as 20% . However, this is an upper bound since the study uses unbounded history table sizes. Also, **hybrid predictors** [14] have been proposed that attempt to detect sequences that are composition of stride and non-stride sequences. Due to their complexity, the FCM predictor and the proposed hybrid predictors do not have efficient implementations.

This paper proposes techniques that associate a more global context with an instruction to help predict its value. This global context association is analogous to branch prediction performed by correlating with other branches [15] and has not been considered for value prediction before. Two types of global contexts are considered.

- **Path information (branch history):** Different values for an instruction are predicted along different paths within a program. Branch history is used to separate the different paths. In the work by Lipasti[6], branch history is used to either select instructions for prediction, or predict input operands for estimating data dependencies. However, branch history is not involved in the actual prediction of computed values.

- **Values produced by recently completed instructions:** Values are predicted by using the correlation between values produced by instructions close to each other within the dynamic instruction stream.

Consider the code sequence shown in Figure 1. Instructions 8, 9 and 10 in block 5 compute three address values from previously defined base and offset values. $Addr_a$ depends on a base value that has either the value Y or X, depending on whether the condition $Condition_1$ evaluates to true or false, while the offset value is fixed at 10 for all loop iterations. $Addr_b$ uses a base value that is fixed for all loop iterations and an offset that is incremented by either 1 or 2, depending on the outcome of $Condition_1$. Finally, $Addr_c$ depends on base and offset values, both of which are different for the two paths within the loop.

Let us now consider the prediction of these values, assuming the *true, false, false* sequence of outcomes for $Condition_1$ repeats itself. The conventional last value and stride predictors would not work in this case. It

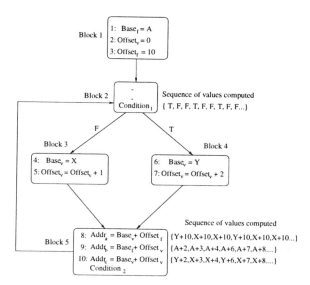

Figure 1. Example

is possible to perform prediction using the FCM or the hybrid predictor by maintaining the patterns of values. However, new patterns of values would be generated often and the number of patterns generated would be large. Thus, frequent mispredictions can be expected.

It is possible to predict these values using control flow information. Consider the sequence of values computed by instruction 8 as shown in the figure. We can predict the next value by looking at the most recent outcome of $Condition_1$. If $Condition_1$ evaluates to false/true, the next value will be the last value of instruction 8 along the false/true branch (i.e., $Y+10/X+10$).

Consider the sequence of values computed by instruction 9. We notice that this sequence is similar to a stride sequence. In case the true branch is taken, the stride is 2; otherwise it is 1. Thus, the next value can be predicted from the stride pattern of the offset occurring along a path.

Finally, the computed value of instruction 10 depends on base and offset values, both of which depend on the control path taken from block 2 to block 5. In this case, it is possible to perform prediction by remembering both the last value and the stride values for each incoming path.

In all the above cases, we can perform the prediction for any arbitrary sequence of branch outcomes. Values of an instruction along different paths are stored separately and branch history is used to predict the value on the current path. In this example, a branch history composed of the last two branches is sufficient for correct prediction. In general, outcomes from several branches may be required.

Let us modify basic block 5 in the example as shown

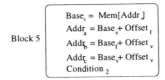

Figure 2. Modified block 5 of example

in Figure 2. The assignment to base value $Base_v$ is moved from blocks 3 and 4 to block 5. This value is now loaded from a memory location whose address, $Addr_v$, may be different for different iterations of the loop. In this case, the value of $Addr_a$ may not be predictable using path information since a different value can be produced for separate iterations of the loop along the same path. However, this value can be predicted as the sum of the loaded value of $Base_v$ and $Offset_f$. This implies that we can predict the value of $Addr_a$ by correlating it with the value loaded by a previous instruction. Essentially, we need to capture the dependence occurring between the instruction computing $Base_v$ and the one using this value. Notice that the values that were predicted using path information could also be predicted using value correlation. For example, values of $Addr_b$ and $Addr_c$ can be predicted by correlating them with the value of instruction computing $Offset_v$.

In this paper, we present prediction techniques that combine the use of branch history with last value and stride predictors. Also, a technique that predicts values based on the correlations between instructions is developed. The predictors resulting from these techniques were experimentally evaluated and compared with conventional predictors.

The rest of the paper is organized as follows. Sections 2 and 3 present the new prediction schemes based on path information. Section 4 presents a prediction scheme that uses correlation between instructions. Each prediction scheme is evaluated by doing a performance comparison with the conventional prediction schemes. The conclusions are presented in Section 5.

2 Path-based Last Value Prediction

Our first scheme, Path-based Last Value (PLV) Prediction, extends the last value predictor by storing the most recent values of an instruction for different branch histories. The history of recent branch outcomes is maintained and used, along with the instruction address, to predict the next value of the instruction. For the example in Figure 1, two different values of $Addr_a$ are stored and then, based on the path followed, the

appropriate value computed on that path is predicted.

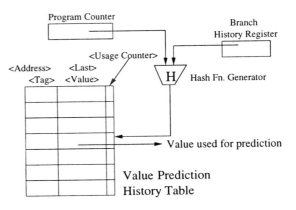

Figure 3. Per path Last value Predictor Microarchitecture

The implementation of this predictor is depicted in Figure 3. The components of the predictor are as follows:

Branch History Register (BHR): This register is similar to the history registers used in branch prediction techniques [9]. The register stores the most recent branch outcomes. After each branch is evaluated, the entire history contents are shifted left by one bit and the least significant bit is set/reset depending on whether the branch was taken/not taken. The number of paths that can be represented is limited by the size of the register.

Value Prediction History Table (VPHT): This table stores the values of instructions for different branch histories. It differs from the value prediction table proposed in [7] in that this table may store several values computed by an instruction for different branch histories. The table is set-associative and accessed using the instruction address and BHR bits. Each entry stores the predicted value and a usage counter for performing replacement. The counter is a saturating counter incremented after every correct prediction and decremented upon a misprediction. Whenever an entry needs to be replaced, the one with the lowest counter value is selected for replacement.

Hash Function Generator : The VPHT is accessed using both the address of the instruction and the history register. This unit performs the hashing of the two for indexing into the VPHT. For instruction i and BHR's value b, the function used is

$$f_1(i,b) = ((Addr(i) << Size(BHR)) + b) \bmod Size(VPHT)$$

where $Addr(i)$ denotes the address value of instruction i, $Size(BHR)$ and $Size(VPHT)$ give the total number of distinct entries in buffer BHR and VPHT respectively. This function maps an instruction within a segment of

Benchmark	Input set	Instrns. analyzed
Unix Utilities		
diff	4K C files	5.4M
gawk	parse 250K input	6.9M
grep	search 1.28M file	20.9M
SPEC INT 95 programs		
li	train.lsp	125.3M
perl	primes.in	10.3M
ijpeg	vigo.ppm	1282.4M
go	2stone9.in	397.1M
SPEC FP 95 programs		
applu	applu.in	147.1M
fpppp	natoms.in	112.5M
swim	swim.in	176.8M
wave5	wave5.in	934.5M

Table 1. Description of benchmarks

the VPHT of size $2^{Size(BHR)}$. Within each segment, different branch histories for the same instruction are mapped to different entries of the table. This function is easy to implement in hardware and all experimental results presented in this paper are based upon this function.

For each instruction, the predictor computes the index in the VPHT by hashing the instruction's address bits with the current branch history contents. If the index maps to a valid entry, the corresponding value is used for prediction. After execution, the computed value is compared with the predicted one. Upon a misprediction, the instruction using the predicted value is squashed and re-issued with the correct value. Upon the instruction's completion, its last value information for the current branch history is updated in the VPHT.

The performance of the PLV predictor was analyzed using trace-driven simulations and instrumenting the code to perform the prediction. The experimental framework consisted of an instruction-set simulator SHADE [2], a code instrumentation tool from SUN Microsystems, which simulates the SPARC (Versions 8 and 9) instruction sets. The instructions of the benchmarks were instrumented to record the instruction values and branch histories. Performance was analyzed by executing the traces generated by the instrumented code over the PLV predictor's simulated microarchitecture on a 64-bit SPARC Ultra-2 processor running SunOS 5.5.1. The benchmarks were compiled using the SUN Workshop C Compiler, Version 4.2 with the -O option, and run until completion. The data input to the benchmarks is described in Table 1. Only the integer instructions were analyzed in the benchmarks. Since previous work [7] shows that floating point instructions exhibit value prediction patterns similar to those of integer instructions, similar performance is expected for floating point instructions.

We implemented the PLV predictor and compared

its performance with the performance of the last value predictor and the FCM predictor. The FCM predictor was implemented as a two-level table, with tables of both levels having the same size. The first level table entries consisted of an address tag and partial values from the last three instances of the instruction. The address tag along with the stored values are hashed to a second table storing predicted values for the instruction. The hashing function used performs exclusive-OR on the most significant bits of the stored values.

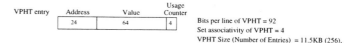

Figure 4. Table entry line for PLV predictor

For each scheme, we performed experiments for different table sizes. The different sizes of the VPHT in PLV predictor are shown in Figure 4. Each entry is 4-way set associative. Since it is possible that some of the programs require only a small branch history and others require greater path information, we ran our experiments for three different branch history depths, last 2, 4 and last 8 branches. It was observed that for smaller table sizes a small branch history performed best since larger branch histories result in significant aliasing. Overall the branch history size of 2 produced the best results as compared with the other history sizes and therefore we selected this number for all our experiments.

Performance comparison of the PLV predictor with the last value and the FCM predictors, for same number of entries per table, is shown in Figure 5. The figure shows the percentage of analyzed instructions that were successfully predicted. The first bar for each benchmark shows the result of applying the FCM technique. The second and third bars show results of applying the last value technique and PLV prediction technique respectively. From the comparisons, it can be seen that the FCM method did not match up to the other techniques for realistic table sizes. This is due to the large number of patterns that need to be stored, resulting in frequent collisions within the tables. Also, the PLV predictor outperforms the conventional predictors for most of the cases. For a 256 entry VPHT, there is slight degradation in performance in cases of *ijpeg*, *swim* and *wave5*, as compared to last value prediction. The degradation can be attributed to the aliasing problem, apparent for smaller table sizes, since we need to store several values for different branch histories for an instruction. With an increase in the number of entries, the aliasing is reduced and a considerable

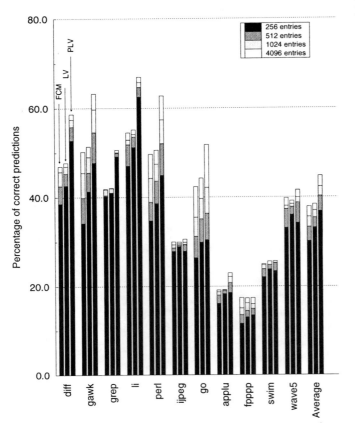

Figure 5. Performance of FCM vs. Last value vs. PLV Predictors in Percentage Predictions

performance improvement is observed. The average performance improvement over last value prediction is 6.4% for the table size of 4096 entries. For larger table sizes, this improvement is higher for larger branch history but this is not apparent from the results shown which use a fixed branch history size throughout.

In the above experiments, the branch history and predictor table state are updated immediately after the values are available. In a real machine, this update may take a few cycles, in which case the instruction is not allowed to execute immediately. In order to take these extra cycles into account, we ran the benchmarks using a delayed update of 2 cycles as an estimate of the extra cycles needed for an update. This resulted in reduction in prediction accuracy in the range of 2-7% in case of both the conventional and new prediction schemes. The reduction in accuracy is due to the VPHT remaining inconsistent after executing an instruction for 2 cycles, when the table would be updated by the instruction's value. However, the average performance improvement decreased only by a fraction of a percentage indicating the improvement for the pro-

posed predictors was not impacted severely by delayed updates.

3 Per-Path Stride Prediction

We also developed two prediction schemes that improve stride prediction by incorporating path information. The first of these two schemes, Per-Path Stride (PS) prediction, stores different stride values for an instruction along different paths. The extension of stride prediction is analogous to extending last value prediction within the PLV predictor. Path information can be useful for stride prediction when a loop variable is updated by different amounts along different paths within a loop. In the example of Figure 1, the variable $Offset_v$ demonstrates this characteristic. While the strides are stored separately for different branch histories, the last value is stored globally for all the strides. The table storing the strides is accessed using the instruction address and branch history bits.

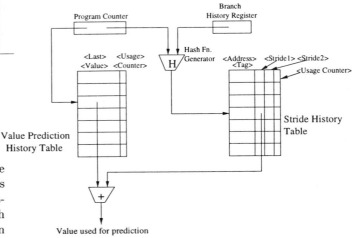

Figure 6. Per-path Stride Predictor Microarchitecture

The components of the predictor are shown in Figure 6. Besides using the components of the PLV predictor, this scheme makes use of an additional table, the **Stride History Table(SHT)**. The SHT stores the stride values for different execution histories of an instruction. It is accessed by hashing the address bits and the branch history register value. The stride update policy used here is the **two-delta policy** [3]. In this policy, the stride gets updated only if the difference between the two most recent values of an instruction occurs twice in a row. To implement this policy, two strides are stored for an instruction. The first one stores the difference between the last two values computed by the instruction while the other stride stores the value being used for prediction. The latter value is updated when the first stride has the same value twice in a row.

For each analyzed instruction, the predictor uses its lower (k bits) to map to the VPHT. The last value of the instruction is obtained from this table. Simultaneously, the address bits are hashed with the branch history to map to the SHT. This mapping accesses the stride used for the instruction and current branch history. The sum of the two values is used to predict the next value. Similar to the PLV scheme, the correctness of the prediction is checked after execution of the instruction is completed, and the update of the last value and stride is performed following completion.

The second path-based stride predictor scheme combines the previous two proposed schemes by maintaining a last value for each path, as well as a stride value for each path. This scheme, Per-Path Stride Per-Path Last Value (PS-PLV) prediction, is used to handle conditions such as that of $Addr_c$ in the example of Figure 1, whose value depends on operands evaluated differently along different paths. The implementation is shown in Figure 7. It is similar to the PLV predictor with the exception that each entry in the VPHT now also contains a stride value.

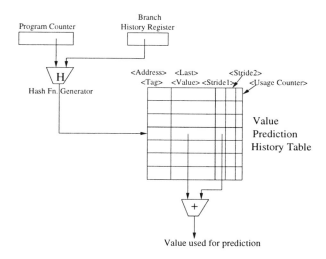

Figure 7. Per-path Stride Per-path Value Predictor Microarchitecture

Each instruction is hashed to index the VPHT based on its address and branch history. This table stores the last value as well as the strides for each branch history. A single access results in accessing both the values to be used for prediction. These values get updated during the completion stage of the instruction, as in the previous methods.

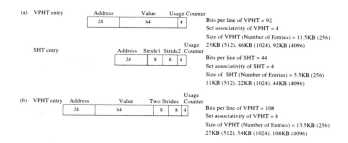

Figure 8. Table entry lines for (a) PS predictor (b) PS-PLV Predictor

The configurations of PS and PS-PLV predictors that were used are shown in Figure 8. They were implemented and compared with conventional stride predictors. The performances of the PS and PS-PLV predictors are shown in Figure 9. For each benchmark, the first bar shows the result of applying conventional stride prediction. The second and third bars show results of applying the PS and PS-PLV prediction techniques respectively. The fourth bar shows the result of applying a hybrid predictor that combines the PS and PS-PLV prediction techniques. Details of this hybrid predictor are provided below. Similar to the study for the PLV predictor, we chose a branch history size of 2 for our analysis. From the figure, we observe that the PS predictor almost always outperforms the conventional stride predictor (except for the benchmark *fpppp* which has a marginal degradation in performance). The PS-PLV predictor also gives a better performance when compared to the conventional stride predictor for most of the cases. However, the performance improvement is less than with PS predictor. Overall, the PS predictor shows an average improvement of 8.4% for 4096 entries while the PS-PLV predictor improves performance by an average of 6.9%.

From the above results, we infer that the PS predictor improves conventional prediction significantly. Notice that both PS and PS-PLV prediction schemes would be able to capture different sets of prediction cases (as illustrated by the example of Section 1). Hence a hybrid predictor that uses both these prediction schemes would potentially give an additive improvement in performance. Such a hybrid predictor was implemented involving both the PS and PS-PLV prediction mechanisms. The method used for prediction was based on a confidence mechanism associated with the instruction. The confidence mechanism used was a 4-bit counter value that was updated depending on which prediction mechanism performed correctly on the instruction. The performance of such a predictor is shown in Figure 9. The improvement in performance over conventional stride prediction for 256 entries was

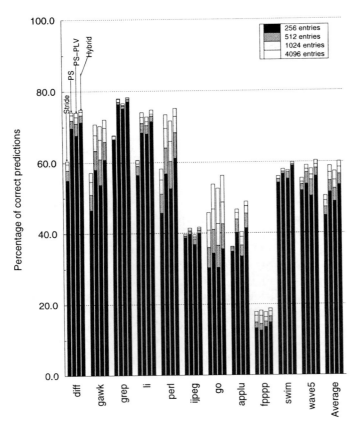

Figure 9. Performance of Stride vs. PS vs. PS-PLV vs. Hybrid Predictors in Percentage Predictions

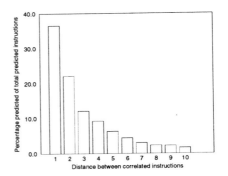

Figure 10. Percentage predicted vs. Distance between correlation

shown to predict $Addr_a$. However, using simply the last instruction will not allow us to predict $Addr_b$ and $Addr_c$ in this case. In order to correlate with a previous instruction value, we need to store values generated by a number of previously completed instructions. The correlation is detected by selecting an instruction from these instructions and using its value to predict the current instruction's value. However, the issue here arises as to which instruction to select out of the recently completed instructions.

We performed experiments to observe the detectable correlation with recently completed instructions, the results of which are presented in Figure 10. From this figure, we notice that 37% of the instructions are cor-

10.4% and was 2% over the best path-based stride predictor. The main issue to be explored in implementing a hybrid predictor of this form is to select which predictor to use every time a prediction is to be made.

The performances of all the predictors were reduced by 3-8% when the the predictors were implemented with a delayed update. However, the performance improvements of the new predictors were reduced marginally.

4 Path and Instruction-based Value Prediction

It is possible that information other than path information may be useful in predicting an instruction value. This was demonstrated in the example when $Base_v$ was moved to block 5 in Figure 2, and $Addr_a$ could no longer be predicted using path history. A scheme that performs prediction of the value of an instruction by correlating it with the value computed by the previous instruction in the instruction sequence was

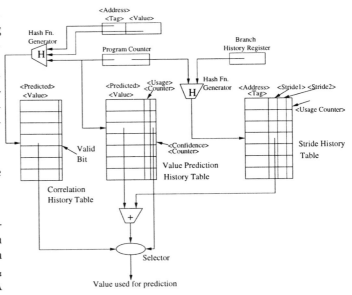

Figure 11. Per-Stride Previous Instruction-based Predictor Microarchitecture

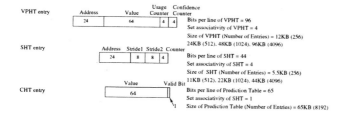

Figure 12. Table entry lines for PS-PI Predictor

rectly predictable due to their correlation with the immediately preceding instruction appearing in the dynamic sequence. Therefore, to maintain simplicity of the predictor we choose to correlate the instruction to be predicted with the immediately preceding instruction.

Prediction using instruction correlation is able to capture prediction cases that are independent of paths. Hence, we implemented a hybrid predictor that performs prediction using instruction correlation in conjunction with the PS predictor. The PS predictor was chosen as part of the hybrid predictor since it produced the best performance of the path based predictors. The new predictor, **Per-Path Stride Per-Instruction (PS-PI)**, attempts to predict the instruction value using either path information or the previous instruction's value. The prediction component that is selected, each time an instruction is predicted, is based on a confidence mechanism. Each entry of the VPHT has a 4-bit confidence counter whose value is incremented whenever the PS component makes a correct prediction and decremented when the instruction-based component predicts correctly. The value of this counter is used to decide which prediction component to use for predicting the next value of the instruction. In case the instruction does not have an entry in the VPHT, the instruction-based component is used for prediction.

The implementation of the PS-PI predictor is shown in Figure 11. The left half of the figure depicts the previous-instruction-based component of the predictor. It uses a table, **Correlation History Table (CHT)**, which stores values that are predicted using correlation with previously computed values. In order to perform such correlation, the address and value computed by the last instruction are always saved and used (along with the program counter) to map to the entry storing the predicted value in the table. The right half of the figure shows the PS component described in the last section. The selector chooses one of the two values predicted based on the confidence counter value in the VPHT.

The size of the CHT was fixed at 8K entries. We analyzed the performance of previous-instruction-based correlation by comparing the PS-PI predictor with the PS predictor using the experimental design described in Section 2.1. The results are depicted in Figure 13. The first bar shows the result of applying the PS predictor and the second bar shows the result of applying the PS-PI predictor. We observe that the improvement is significant for all benchmarks. The average improvement is 7.2% for table sizes of 256 entries and similar performance for other table sizes.

When the predictor was modified to incorporate delayed update of branch history and tables as discussed in the last two sections, the prediction accuracy of all the predictors was reduced in the range of 2-8.5%. However, the degradation in performance improvement over PS predictor was less than 2%.

5 Conclusions

From our experiments, a number of conclusions can be drawn.

(1) Path information is helpful in performing prediction of data values of instructions. Three

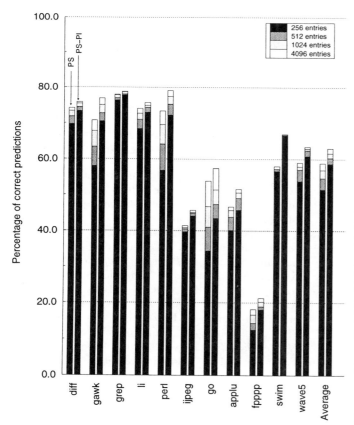

Figure 13. Performance of PS vs. PS-PI Predictors in Percentage Predictions

novel schemes have been proposed for performing value prediction sensitive to path information. The first scheme, PLV predictor, improves the last value prediction by as much as 15% for some benchmarks and 6.4% on average. The other two proposed predictors, PS and PS-PLV, extend the stride predictors. The PS prediction scheme shows an improvement exceeding 15% for some benchmarks and 8.4% on average. For PS-PLV prediction, the improvement exceeds 13% for some benchmarks and 6.9% on average. The PS and PS-PLV stride predictors are combined in a hybrid predictor, which improves prediction accuracy by 10.4% over convention stride prediction and by 2% over the best path-based predictor.

(2) Prediction based on correlating instruction values can produce additional benefits over path-based predictors. The proposed previous-instruction-based prediction scheme is incorporated within a hybrid predictor, PS-PI. Analysis of the PS-PI predictor indicates that this method can capture several cases of instruction values that are not predictable by path-based predictors. The percentage of instructions of this kind exceeds 15% for some benchmarks and 7.2% on an average.

(3) Significant performance improvement is attainable with a simple hardware scheme and realistic table sizes. The proposed prediction schemes provide improvement over the conventional last value and stride predictors for limited number of entries per table. The FCM predictor does not match up to these predictors for the table sizes under consideration. We have shown that each of the proposed schemes would require very simple hardware for implementation.

(4) Delaying update of information as is done in real microarchitecture does not affect the performance significantly. We performed experiments by updating branch history a few cycles after the branch outcome is available. In an attempt to give a more realistic view of the performance, we performed experiments by updating branch history 2 cycles after the branch outcome is available. Results indicate that the degradation in performance due to delayed update is minimal.

References

[1] T. F. Chen and J. L. Baer. A performance study of software and hardware data prefetching schemes. *Proceedings of the 21st International Symposium on Computer Architecture*, pages 223–232, April 1994.

[2] R. F. Cmelik and D. Keppel. Shade: A fast instruction set simulator for execution profiling. *Tech. Rep. TR-93-12, Sun Microsystems Laboratories*, July 1993.

[3] R. J. Eickemeyer and S. Vassiliadis. A load instruction unit for pipelined processors. *IBM Journal of Research and Development*, pages 547–564, 1993.

[4] F. Gabbay and A. Mendelson. Speculative execution based on value prediction. *EE Department TR#1080, Technion - Israel Institute of Technology*, November 1996.

[5] D. M. Gallagher, W. Y. Chen, S. A. Mahalke, J. C. Gyllenhaal, and W. W. Hwu. Dynamic memory disambiguation using the memory conflict buffer. *Proceedings of the 6th International Conference on Architectural Support for Programming Languages and Operating Systems*, pages 183–193, October 1994.

[6] M. H. Lipasti. Value locality and speculative execution. *Ph.D. Thesis, Department of Electrical and Computer Engineering, Carnegie Mellon University*, May 1997.

[7] M. H. Lipasti and J. P. Shen. Exceeding the dataflow limit via value prediction. *Proceedings of the 29th Annual ACM/IEEE International Symposium on Microarchitecture*, pages 226–237, December 1996.

[8] M. H. Lipasti, C. B. Wilkerson, and J. P. Shen. Value locality and load value prediction. *Proceedings of the 7th International Conference on Architectural Support for Programming Languages and Operating Systems*, pages 138–147, October 1996.

[9] S. McFarling. Combining branch predictors. *Tech. Rep. DEC WRL TN-36*, pages 281–290, June 1993.

[10] A. Moshovos and G. Sohi. Streamlining inter-operation memory communication via data dependence prediction. *Proceedings of the 30th Annual ACM/IEEE International Symposium on Microarchitecture*, pages 235–245, December 1997.

[11] S. T. Pan, K. So, and J. T. Rahmeh. Improving the accuracy of dynamic branch prediction using branch correlation. *Proceedings of the 5th International Conference on Architectural Support for Programming Languages and Operating Systems*, pages 76–84, October 1992.

[12] Y. Sazeides and J. E. Smith. The predictabilty of data values. *Proceedings of the 30th Annual ACM/IEEE International Symposium on Microarchitecture*, pages 248–258, December 1997.

[13] Y. Sazeides, S. Vassiliadis, and J. E. Smith. The performance potential of data dependence speculation and collapsing. *Proceedings of the 29th Annual ACM/IEEE International Symposium on Microarchitecture*, pages 238–247, December 1996.

[14] K. Wang and M. Franklin. Highly accurate data value prediction using hybrid predictors. *Proceedings of the 30th Annual ACM/IEEE International Symposium on Microarchitecture*, pages 281–290, December 1997.

[15] T. Y. Yeh and Y. N. Patt. Alternate implementation of two-level adaptive branch prediction. *Proceedings of the 19th International Symposium on Computer Architecture*, pages 124–134, May 1992.

Dynamically Exploiting Narrow Width Operands to Improve Processor Power and Performance

David Brooks and Margaret Martonosi
Dept. of Electrical Engineering
Princeton University
{dbrooks, martonosi}@ee.princeton.edu

Abstract

In general-purpose microprocessors, recent trends have pushed towards 64-bit word widths, primarily to accommodate the large addressing needs of some programs. Many integer problems, however, rarely need the full 64-bit dynamic range these CPUs provide. In fact, another recent instruction set trend has been increased support for sub-word operations (that is, manipulating data in quantities less than the full word size). In particular, most major processor families have introduced "multimedia" instruction set extensions that operate in parallel on several sub-word quantities in the same ALU.

This paper notes that across the SPECint95 benchmarks, over half of the integer operation executions require 16 bits or less. With this as motivation, our work proposes hardware mechanisms that dynamically recognize and capitalize on these "narrow-bitwidth" instances. Both optimizations require little additional hardware, and neither requires compiler support.

The first, power-oriented, optimization reduces processor power consumption by using aggressive clock gating to turn off portions of integer arithmetic units that will be unnecessary for narrow bitwidth operations. This optimization results in an over 50% reduction in the integer unit's power consumption for the SPECint95 and MediaBench benchmark suites. The second optimization improves performance by merging together narrow integer operations and allowing them to share a single functional unit. Conceptually akin to a dynamic form of MMX, this optimization offers speedups of 4.3%-6.2% for SPECint95 and 8.0%-10.4% for MediaBench.

1. Introduction

As high-end processor word widths have made the shift from 32 to 64 bits, there has been an accompanying trend towards efficiently supporting subword operations. Subword parallelism, in which multiple 8- or 16-bit operations are performed in parallel by a 64-bit ALU, is supported in current processors via instruction set and organizational extensions. These include the Intel MMX [1], HP MAX-2 [2], and Sun VIS [3] multimedia instruction sets, as well as vector microprocessor proposals such as the T0 project [4].

All of these ideas provide a form of SIMD (single instruction-multiple data) parallel processing at the word level. These instruction set extensions are focused primarily on enhancing performance for multimedia applications. Such applications perform large amounts of arithmetic processing on audio, speech, or image samples which typically only require 16-bits or less per datum.

The caveat to this type of processing is that thus far these new instructions are mainly used only when programmers hand-code kernels of their applications in assembler. Little compiler support exists to generate them automatically, and the compiler analysis is limited to cases where programmers have explicitly defined operands of smaller (i.e., char or short) sizes.

This paper proposes hardware mechanisms for dynamically exploiting narrow width operations and sub-word parallelism without programmer intervention or compiler support. By detecting "narrow bitwidth" operations dynamically, we can exploit them more often than with a purely-static approach. Thus, our approach will remain useful even as compiler support improves.

In this paper we provide two optimizations that take advantage of the core "narrow width operand" detection that we propose. The first idea watches for small operand values and exploits them to reduce the amount of power consumed by the integer unit. This is accomplished by an aggressive form of clock gating. Clock gating has previously been shown to significantly reduce power consumption by disabling certain functional units if instruction decode indicates that they will not be used [5]. The key difference of our work is to apply clock gating based on operand values. When the full width of a functional unit is not required, we can save power by disabling the upper bits. With this method we show that the amount of power consumed by the integer execution unit can be reduced by 54.1% for the SPECint95 suite with little additional hardware.

The second proposed optimization improves performance by dynamically recognizing, at issue time, opportunities for packing multiple narrow operations into a single ALU. With this method the SPECint95 benchmark suite shows an average speedup of 4.3%-6.2% depending on the processor configuration. The MediaBench suite showed an average speedup of 8.0%-10.4%.

The primary contributions of this work are three-fold: a detailed study of the bitwidth requirements for a wide-range of benchmarks, and two proposals for methods to exploit narrow width data to improve processor power consumption and performance. In Section 2 we further discuss the motivations for our work and place it in the context of prior work in multimedia instruction sets, power savings, and other methods of using dynamic data.

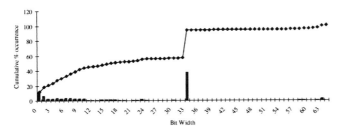

Figure 1 – Bitwidths for SPECint95 on 64-bit Alpha.

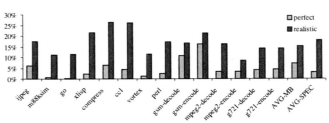

Figure 2 – Percentage of instructions whose operand precision changes from less than 16-bit to greater than 16-bit over a single program run.

Section 3 describes the experimental methodology used to investigate our optimizations. Section 4 details the power optimization technique based on clock gating for operand size and presents results on its promise. In Section 5, we describe the method for dynamically packing narrow instructions at issue-time. Finally, Section 6 concludes and discusses other opportunities to utilize dynamic operand size data in processors.

2. Motivations and Past Work

2.1 Application Bitwidths

In this study we show that a wide range of applications have small operand sizes. Figure 1 illustrates this by showing the cumulative percentage of integer instructions in SPECint95 in which both operands are less than or equal to the specified bitwidth. (Section 3 will discuss the Alpha compiler and SimpleScalar simulator used to collect these results.) Roughly 50% of the instructions had both operands less than or equal to 16-bits. We will refer to these operands as narrow-width; an instruction execution in which both operands are narrow width is said to be a "narrow-width operation". Since this chart includes address calculations, there is a large jump at 33 bits. This corresponds to heap and stack references. (Larger programs than SPEC might have this peak at a larger bitwidth.) The data demonstrate the potential for a wide range of applications, not just multimedia applications, to be optimized based on narrow-width operands. While other such work, e.g. protein-matching codes [6], required algorithm or compiler changes, we focus here on hardware-only approaches.

2.2 Observing Narrow Bitwidth Operands

The basic tenet behind both of the optimizations proposed here is that when operations are performed with narrow-width operands, the upper bits of the operation are unneeded. For example, when adding 17, a 5-bit number, to 2, a 2-bit number, the result is 19, a 5-bit number. Only the lower five bits are needed to perform the computation. To decrease power dissipation, clock gating can disable the latch for the unneeded upper bits. Alternatively, to improve performance, we propose

"operation packing", in which we issue and execute several of these narrow operations in parallel within the same ALU. In either case, the crux in exploiting narrow-width operands, however, lies in recognizing them and modifying execution. Sections 4 and 5 will discuss hardware approaches for tagging result operands as "narrow-width" as they are produced, and for storing these tags along with source operands as we stage subsequent instructions waiting for issue.

2.3 Disadvantages of Static Compiler Analysis

Part of the motivation for this work was the fact that *static* analysis of input operand sizes has several disadvantages. Most importantly there are many cases where it is impossible to know what the true operand bitwidths (as opposed to the declared operand sizes) will be until run-time. Actual operand sizes depend very much on the input data presented. Operand sizes for particular instructions can also vary over the program run even with the same input data, which makes the task of the compiler even more difficult.

Figure 2 shows the percentage of PC values where operand width changes as the instruction is executed repeatedly within a single run. In particular, the figure shows how often an instruction fluctuates from having less than 16-bit operands to greater than 16-bit operands as it executes repeatedly within a single program run.

With perfect branch prediction, the instruction operand sizes are far more predictable than with realistic branch prediction. This is because with perfect branch prediction only the true execution path is seen. With imperfect branch prediction, uncommon paths, like error conditions, may be executed (but not committed) if the branch predictor points that way. Along these paths, operand statistics may be markedly different. Compile time analysis must conservatively analyze all potential paths to ensure that operations can truly be packed. This may include uncommon error conditions and other extreme cases. As a result, the compiler runs into much of the same diverse operand values as seen by imperfect branch prediction.

Overall, compiler dataflow analysis for operand sizes must be conservative about possible operand values.

Table 1 – Baseline configuration of simulated processor.

Parameter	Value
Processor Core	
RUU size	80 instructions
LSQ (ld/store queue) size	40
Fetch Queue Size	8 instructions
Fetch width	4 instructions/cycle
Decode width	4 instructions/cycle
Issue width	4 instructions/cycle (out-of-order)
Commit width	4 instructions/cycle (in-order)
Functional units	4 Integer ALUs (performing arithmetic, logical, shift, memory, branch ops), 1 integer multiply/divide
Branch Prediction	
Branch Predictor	Combining: 4K 2-bit selector, 12-bit history; 1K 3-bit local predictor, 10-bit history; 4K 2-bit global predictor, 12-bit history
BTB	2048-entry, 2-way
Return-address stack	32-entry
Mispredict penalty	2 cycles
Memory hierarchy	
L1 data-cache	64K, 2-way (LRU), 32B blocks, 1 cycle latency
L1 instruction-cache	64K, 2-way (LRU), 32B blocks, 1 cycle latency
L2	Unified, 8M, 4-way (LRU), 32B blocks, 12-cycle latency
Memory	100 cycles
TLBs	128 entry, fully associative, 30-cycle miss latency

Programmer hints about operand sizes can aid the compiler. It is unrealistic, however, to assume that programmers will provide these hints on codes other than small multimedia kernels.

From Figure 1 it is clear that many opportunities exist to exploit narrow width data for subword parallelism and aggressive clock gating. Searching for subword parallelism in applications is somewhat analogous to the search for instruction-level parallelism (ILP) in applications. In the late 80s and early 90s, most general purpose superscalar microprocessors were statically scheduled, and the compiler was responsible for uncovering ILP in programs. Current microprocessors implement aggressive dynamic scheduling techniques to uncover more ILP. This evolution was necessary to feed the wider-issue capabilities of these processors. In a similar manner, more subword parallelism can be uncovered with the dynamic approaches we propose than if one relies solely on compiler techniques.

There has been other work in specializing for particular operand values at runtime. The PowerPC 603 includes hardware to count the number of leading zeros of input operands to provide an "early out" for multicycle integer multiply operations. This can reduce the number of cycles required for a multiply from five for 32-bit multiplication to two for an 8-bit multiplication [7]. At a higher level, value prediction seeks to predict result values for certain operations and speculatively execute additional instructions based on these predicted operand values [8].

Finally, there has also been other work in exploiting narrow bitwidth operations. Razdan and Smith propose a hardware-programmable functional unit which augments the base processor's instruction set with additional instructions that are synthesized in configurable hardware at compile time [9]. Since all synthesized instructions must complete in a single cycle, bitwidth analysis is performed at compile time to highlight sequences of narrow-width operations that are the best candidates for implementation.

3. Methodology

3.1 Simulator

We used a modified version of SimpleScalar's [10] *sim-outorder* to collect our results. SimpleScalar provides a simulation environment for modern out-of-order processors with speculative execution. The simulated processor contains a unified active instruction list, issue queue, and rename register file in one unit called the reservation update unit (RUU). The RUU is similar to the Metaflow DRIS (deferred-scheduling, register-renaming instruction shelf) [11] and the HP PA-8000 IRB (instruction reorder buffer) [12]. Separate banks of 32 integer and floating point registers make up the architected register file and are only written on commit. Table 1 summarizes the important features of the simulated processor. The baseline configuration parameters are roughly those of a modern out-of-order processor.

The changes made to the simulator for this study are localized to the issue and decode stages. In decode, bitwidths are calculated for dynamic data and stored in the reservation station entry to be used during the issue stage. In the issue stage, this data is used to decide if instructions can be issued and executed in parallel based on the data from the decode stage. These changes reflect the simulator implementation; Section 4 discusses how they would be implemented in an actual processor.

3.2 Benchmarks

A goal of this study is to demonstrate and exploit the prevalence of narrow-width operations even in applications outside the multimedia domain. For this reason we evaluate the SPECint95 suite of benchmarks as well as several benchmarks from the MediaBench suite [13]. We have compiled the benchmarks using the DEC *cc* compiler with the following SPEC optimization options: -migrate -std1 -O5 -ifo -non_shared. In particular, the -O5 setting, along with numerous other optimizations, provides vectorization of some loops on 8-bit and 16-bit data (char and short).

Table 2 – SPECint95 Benchmarks

Benchmark	Inputs	Warm Up Instructions
ijpeg	vigo.ppm	824M
m88ksim	dhrystone	26M
go	9stone21	926M
xlisp	All xlisp inputs	271M
compress	bigtest.in	2576M
gcc	cccp.i	221M
vortex	persons.1k	2451M
perl	scrabble game	601M

Table 3 – MediaBench Benchmarks

Benchmark	Description
gsm-encode	Audio and speech encoding with the GSM standard
gsm-decode	Audio and speech decoding with the GSM standard
mpeg2encode	MPEG digital compressed format encoding
mpeg2decode	MPEG digital compressed format decoding
g721encode	Voice compression using the G.721 standard
g721decode	Voice decompression using the G.721 standard

For this study we wanted to use the reference inputs for the SPECint95 suite. The test or training inputs are unsuitable because our data-specific optimizations might be unfairly helped by smaller data sets. Using reference inputs, the SPECint95 benchmarks run for billions of instructions, which, if simulated fully, would lead to excessively long execution times. Thus we use a methodology similar to that described by Skadron et al. [14]. We warm up architectural state using a fast-mode cycle-level simulation that updates only the caches and branch predictors during each cycle. The warmup period

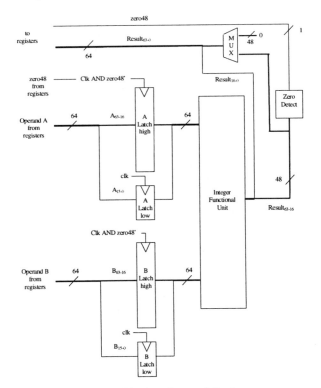

Figure 3 – Clock gating architecture.

also avoids the effects of smaller operand sizes that are prevalent within program initialization. Using Skadron et al.'s results identifying representative program sections based on cache and branch prediction statistics, we then simulate a 100 million instruction window using the detailed simulator. Table 2 lists the reference input that we have chosen for the SPECint95 benchmarks, and the number of instructions for which we warm up the caches and branch predictor. Table 3 describes the applications chosen from the MediaBench suite. For the MediaBench suite, *gsm*, *g721*, and *mpeg2-decode* were run to completion while *mpeg2-encode* was simulated for 100 million instructions after a 500M instruction warmup period.

4. Power Optimizations

4.1 Clock Gating

Dynamic power dissipation is the primary source of power consumption in CMOS circuits. In CMOS circuits, dynamic power dissipation occurs when changing input values cause their corresponding output values to change. Only small leakage currents exist as long as inputs are held constant. Clock gating has been used to reduce power by disabling the clock and thereby disabling value changes on unneeded functional units. In static CMOS circuits, disabling the clock on the latch that feeds the input operands to functional units essentially eliminates dynamic power dissipation. Power consumption on the critical clock lines is also saved because the latch itself is disabled. In dynamic or domino CMOS circuits, the same effect can be obtained by disabling the clocks that control the pre-charge and evaluate phases of the circuit.

Currently most work on clock gating has used the decoded opcode to decide which units can be disabled for a particular instruction. For example, *nop*'s allow most of the units to be disabled since no result is being computed. As another example of opcode-based clock gating, consider an "add byte" instruction. Since the opcode *guarantees* that only the lower part of the adder is needed, the top part of the functional unit is disabled.

4.2 Proposed Architecture

We propose and quantify a more aggressive clock gating approach. At run-time, the hardware determines instances when, based on the input operands, the upper bits of an operation are not needed; in those cases, it disables the upper portion of the functional unit. Key differences from prior approaches are that (1) our approach is operand-based, not opcode-based, and (2) our approach is dynamic, not static. (One could, of course, use our method *in addition to* prior opcode-based approaches.) Different program runs, or even different

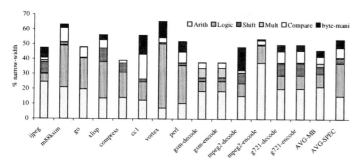

Figure 4 – Operations with both operands 16-bits or less.

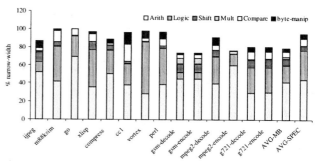

Figure 5 – Operations with both operands 33-bits or less.

executions of the same instruction, dissipate different amounts of power depending on the operands seen.

Figure 3 is a diagram of our proposed implementation. This unit recognizes that the upper bits of both input operands are zeros. For example, in an addition operation, if both input operands have all zeros in their top 48 bits, these bits do not have to be latched and sent to the functional units. We already know that the result of this part of the addition will be zero, and thus zeros can be multiplexed onto the top 48 bits of the result bus, rather than computed via the adder. In this architecture the low 16 bits are always latched normally. The high 48 bits are selectively latched based on a signal that accompanies the input operand from the reservation station. This signal, called *zero48* in Figure 3, denotes that the upper 48-bits are all zeros and is created by zero detection logic when the result was computed. Since some operands come directly from the cache, there must also be a zero-check during load instructions. We believe such zero-detects are already performed in some processors; for example, to recognize divide-by-zero exceptions early. However, in some processors it may not be possible to perform zero-detects on incoming loads, and in these cases the hardware will not recognize an opportunity to gate the clock. For the SPECint95 suite, 13.1% of power saving instructions have one or more operands that come directly from a load instruction; these are the instructions that would be missed if zero-detect were omitted on loads. The percentages for the media benchmarks are much lower at 1.5%.

In order for any power saving technique to be useful, it must save more power than it consumes. In our technique the new power dissipated is mainly in the zero-detection logic and in widening the mux onto the result bus. The primary power savings stems from selectively clock-gating the functional units based on the results of the zero-detection logic. In the following subsections we evaluate these costs and benefits in more detail.

4.3 Bitwidth Analysis of Benchmarks

The success of our approach relies on the frequent occurrence of narrow bitwidth operands. Figure 4 shows, for each benchmark, the percentage and type of operations whose input operands are both less than or equal to 16-bits. (Both operands must be small in order for the clock gating to be allowed.) The breakdown by operation type is another important metric. Intuitively, disabling the upper bits on an adder or multiplier will save more power than turning off the upper bits on the less power-hungry logical functions. Figure 4 shows that for most benchmarks arithmetic and logical operations dominate the number of narrow-width operations. In most of the benchmarks multiplies are rather infrequent although they do account for 6% of the narrow-width operations in *gsm*.

Recall that Figure 1 illustrated how address calculations result in many operations with bitwidths of 33. Figure 5 emphasizes this point. From this data it makes sense to include a second control signal for clock gating of operands that are 33-bits or less. The zero detect logic can be shared so that the extra hardware requirements are minimal. This modification is also useful for optimizing the multiplication of two 16-bit numbers. In these cases a 32-bit result can occur, so the 33-bit mux onto the result bus would be used.

In the Alpha architecture that we considered in this study, the fundamental datum is the 64-bit quadword. Quadword integers are represented with a sign bit occupying the most significant bit [15]. Numbers are expressed in two's complement form, which simplifies arithmetic operations. The techniques presented in this paper rely on determining when data requires less than the full word width of the machine. For positive numbers, this can be accomplished by performing a zero detect on the high order bits. For negative numbers in the two's complement representation, leading 1's signify the same thing that leading 0's do for positive number – essentially unneeded data. Thus a ones detect must be performed in parallel with the zero detect computation to detect narrow bitwidth negative numbers.

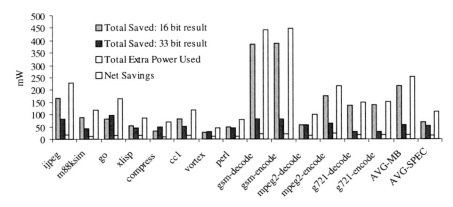

Figure 6 – Net power saved by clock gating at 16 and 33 bits. Total extra used is the amount used by zero detection and muxing. Net savings denotes the amount saved at 16 bits plus the amount saved at 33 bits minus the amount used. Numbers are per cycle.

4.4 Power Results

The amount of power that is saved by our approach depends on both the type and frequency of narrow width operations. In order to quantify the amount of power saved, we use previously-reported research to estimate the amount of power that various functional units use [16, 17, 18]. From these sources we obtain power estimates assuming dynamic logic and relatively fast carry look-ahead adders. We assume that the multiplier is pipelined with its power usage scaling linearly with the operand size. Table 4 summarizes the values that we have assumed for different size devices. The functional units in current high-end microprocessors are likely to use even more power, but detailed numbers are not yet available in the literature. For this analysis though, the important factor is the ratio of the respective functional units to each other.

Figure 6 summarizes the amount of power saved and expended per cycle. We arrived at these numbers by determining the amount of power saved and expended per instruction executed and multiplying by the average issue rate. These results include all loads, stores, branches, and other integer execution unit instructions that are not part of the set of instructions that our optimization applies to. Among the SPECint95 benchmarks, our technique saves the most power for *ijpeg* and *go*. *Ijpeg* has a large number of narrow-width arithmetic operations. *Go* includes a large number of address calculations and is helped the most by adding the extra signal to detect 33-bit operations. The

media benchmarks tend to save even more power than the SPECint95 benchmarks. This is primarily because of the larger number of arithmetic operations. *GSM*, in particular, has a relatively large number of narrow bitwidth multiply operations. The amount of power used by the zero detection circuitry is small and nearly constant for all benchmarks. In no case does the amount of power used for zero detection exceed the amount of power saved.

Figure 7 shows the total amount of power that is saved by the integer unit with our optimization. For the baseline system, we assume that all operations use the amount of power that a 64-bit device would use. (We assume basic clock gating in which, for example, multipliers are turned off for add instructions and vice versa.) For the SPECint95 benchmark suite, the average power consumption of the integer unit was reduced by 54.1%. For the media benchmarks, the reduction was 57.9%.

While a 50-60% power reduction seems exceptional, it is important to note that the integer unit's contribution to total power varies depending on the CPU. In some high-end CPUs much of the power is spent on clock distribution and control logic, and thus the integer unit represents only about 10% of the power dissipation [19]. In such a processor, our optimizations will lead to 5-6% power reductions on average. As control is streamlined, either in DSPs or via explicitly-parallel instruction computing

Device	32-bit	48-bit	64-bit
Adder (CLA)	105	158	210
Booth Multiplier	1050	1580	2100
Bit-Wise Logic	5.8	8.7	11.7
Shifter	4.4	6.6	8.8
Zero-Detect	--	4.2	--
Additional Muxes	--	3.2	--

Table 4 – Estimated power consumption of functional units at 3.3V and 500Mhz (mW).

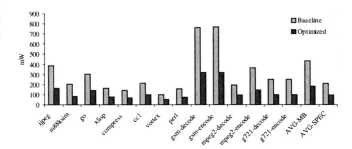

Figure 7 – Power usage of integer unit (per cycle).

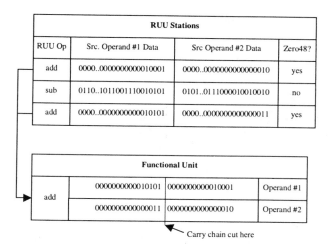

Figure 8 – Packing two add instructions with narrow operand widths.

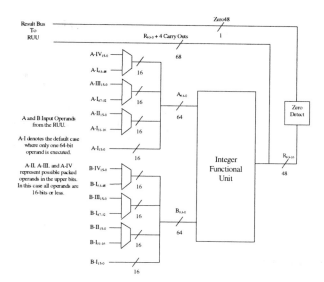

Figure 9 – Datapath Modifications.

(EPIC) as in future Intel processors [20], the integer unit is a larger factor in the processor's total power dissipation, as much as 20-40%. In these cases, the total power savings from our technique will approach 20%. In all processors, our approach promises a relatively easy way to prune power from the integer unit where this is important. We also note that our power savings estimates are somewhat conservative. The clock gating technique also reduces the switch capacitance seen by the clock distribution network, and this can lead to a further power reduction. Although this effect can be significant, it cannot be quantified without a chip floorplan.

5. Operation Packing

In this section, we present a technique to increase performance by exploiting dynamic data values. As with the prior technique, this relies on dynamically recognizing zeros in the upper bits of the input operands to take advantage of the unused upper bits in the functional units. Since the power optimization involves clock gating functional units and the performance optimization involves executing instructions in parallel, only one technique can be used at a time. However, because the techniques share a common hardware base, one could implement both and choose between them. For example, one could use thermal sensory data to have the processor switch between the two techniques, depending on current thermal or performance concerns. Related but simpler approaches are already found in commercial processors; for example, the IBM/Motorola PPC750 is equipped with an on-chip thermal assist unit and temperature sensor which responds to thermal emergencies by controlling the instruction fetch rate through I-cache throttling [21].

5.1 Background

Multimedia instruction sets define new instructions to perform a common operation on several subwords in parallel. For example, the Parallel Add instruction in HP-MAX performs four parallel additions on the 16-bit subwords that reside in the two specified 64-bit source registers. Few hardware changes are necessary to support these additional instructions; only the carry chain between the 16-bit chunks must be handled differently. Figure 8 demonstrates how two add instructions in the RUU, both with narrow operand widths, can be packed together at issue time into one functional unit. In this example, there are three instructions in the RUU: an add with source operand values of 17 and 2, a sub with source operands that are larger than 16-bits, and another add with source operands of 21 and 3. In this case, the two add instructions both have narrow width operands, so a single 64-bit adder can perform the two additions in parallel. The hardware built into ALUs for multimedia instruction sets will automatically stop the carry at 16-bit boundaries.

In machines with multimedia extensions, programmers or (less frequently) compilers statically generate code using multimedia instructions. As previously discussed, there are several shortcomings to this method. For those reasons, this section introduces an approach that is akin to dynamically generating multimedia instructions. In this study, we focus on merging narrow integer operations into parallel sub-word operations as currently supported by multimedia instruction set extensions. This is a subset of the operations that we explore in Section 4 and consists of the arithmetic, logical, and shift operations. For example, we do not attempt to pack multiply operations, although in some implementations this would be possible.

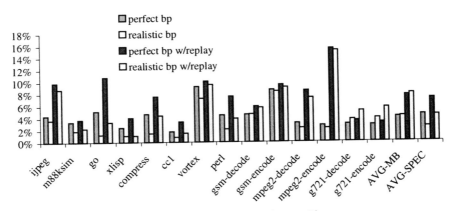

Figure 10 – Speedup due to operation packing.

5.2 Proposed Architecture

Figure 9 is a diagram of the proposed changes to the datapath. The most notable changes to the datapath are the additional muxes which move data from the low 16 bits of the source RUU stations onto the higher 16-bit paths of the source operand bus. In addition, 4 extra lines are needed on the result bus for the carry-out that could result when two 16-bit operands are added. These additional carry-out lines are needed because most multimedia instruction sets provide a form of saturating arithmetic which, upon overflow of two 16-bit values, sets the result to the maximum 16-bit value, namely 0xFFFF. In addition, the reservation stations must be modified. The additional hardware needed here includes muxes which reverse the effect of the above; data in the higher 16-bit subwords of the result bus are muxed into the low 16-bit boundaries to be written back to the result reservation station. It should be noted that much of this "additional" muxing hardware most likely already exists in processors with multimedia instruction sets. For example, the HP MAX-2 instruction set includes instructions to select any field in a source register and right-align it in the target register. Instructions also exist to select a right-aligned field from the source register and place it anywhere in the target register.

Our core idea is similar to the power optimization discussed in the last section. Each entry in the reservation update unit (RUU) stores an extra bit for each operand indicating that the size of the operand is 16-bits or less. These fields are updated when operands are computed and stored in the RUU buffers. Using these fields, the issue logic can recognize opportunities to pack narrow width operations together to share one integer ALU in the same way that the multimedia instructions do. In order for two operations to be packed, three things must occur. First both instructions must have satisfied their data dependencies and be ready to issue. Second, both

instructions must have narrow width operands. Finally, they must perform the same operation.

The issue logic issues ready instructions from the RUU using its normal algorithm. In most processors, this algorithm issues the oldest instructions in the RUU which are ready to issue. However, when operations are issued in which both operands are 16-bits or less, an opportunity for packing exists. The issue logic must keep track of which issuing instructions are available for packing. If other instructions that perform the same operations are available to issue and have narrow-width operands, these instructions can be packed. The issue logic will set the appropriate muxes to issue the packed instructions in parallel.

After the instructions issue, they execute in the same fashion as packed instructions do in the multimedia instruction sets. When execution completes, the result operands share the result bus and are sent back to their respective RUU station as well as RUU stations awaiting the results as input operands. This optimization opens up machine issue bandwidth and integer ALUs available for certain integer executions. Much of the required multiplexing hardware already exists within processors designed with multimedia instruction sets. These processors also have functional units that are designed to disable the carry chain at 16-bit intervals. The primary hardware cost for this optimization is in the increased complexity of the logic that decides when packed instructions can issue. Handling negative numbers adds additional complexity to the issue logic.

5.3 Replay Packing: Speculating on Operand Size

The architecture in Section 5.2 is designed to pack operations together to be executed in parallel when both input operands are less than 16-bits. The requirement that both input operands be less than 16-bit excludes a large number of arithmetic operations used for memory addressing, loop incrementing, etc. In these cases, one of the input operands may be very large, while the other is

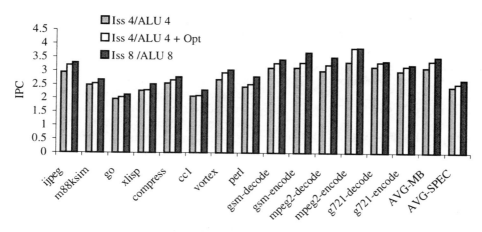

Figure 11 – IPC for the baseline system, the optimized system, and an 8-issue system.

quite small. If one operand is large and the other is small, in most arithmetic operations only the lower bits of the result will change. However, in some cases, the carry will ripple all the way down to the higher bits. In practice, this happens relatively infrequently. Based on this observation, we propose an extension to the architecture in Section 5.2 that allows operands to be packed if only one of the two input operands is less than 16-bits. In most cases there will be no overflow from the 16-bit addition, and the high 48-bits of the larger source operand can be muxed into the destination RUU station. However, in the rare cases that there is overflow from the 16-bit addition, the instruction can be squashed and subsequently re-issued as a full-width instruction. Such a situation could be handled by "replay traps", which are already available for other reasons in the Alpha 21264 and other CPUs.

5.4 Operation Packing Results

In this section we present the results for the speedup with and without replay packing. We have considered two configurations: The first configuration is exactly the same as the baseline configuration discussed in Section 3.1. The second configuration increases the decode bandwidth from four instructions per cycle to eight instructions per cycle. The increased decode bandwidth causes the RUU to fill up faster giving more opportunities for packing.

Figure 10 shows the percent speedup over the baseline system in the configuration with the decode width of four. In this chart, we include results for both perfect and the combining predictor. In most cases moving from perfect to realistic branch prediction shows a performance degradation, because it reduces the number of useful instructions that are ready to issue each cycle. We can see that *go*, notorious for its poor branch prediction, is affected the most. *Ijpeg* and *vortex*, on the other hand, see little difference in the speedup between perfect and the realistic predictor. The average speedup across SPECint95 was 7.1% for perfect branch prediction and 4.3% with the

realistic predictor. As one might expect, the multimedia benchmarks performed better than SPECint95. Here better branch prediction led to only a small difference in speedup between perfect and realistic predictors. In fact, *g721* had higher speedup with realistic branch prediction, due to speculative execution. Speculative instructions that will eventually be squashed still get executed until the branch is resolved; packing them with other instructions can increase effective issue bandwidth. The average speedup for the media benchmarks was 7.6% with perfect branch prediction and 8.0% with the combining predictor.

We also studied the packing optimization with 8-wide decode. As expected, the optimization performs better with increased decode bandwidth, because the RUU is filled with more useful instructions which have the potential to be packed, issued, and executed in parallel. Most of the benchmarks show a 2-3% increase in speedup with the increased decode bandwidth. The average speedup for SPECint95 was 9.9% for perfect branch prediction and 6.2% with the combining predictor. The multimedia benchmarks performed better as well, but not as significantly as SPECint95. This is because multimedia applications have many loop-oriented arithmetic operations with few data dependencies. This gives them a larger pool of usable instructions even with the smaller decode bandwidth. The average speedup for the media benchmarks was 10.3% with perfect branch prediction and 10.4% with the realistic predictor.

As previously mentioned, the proposed optimization increases the effective issue bandwidth and number of integer ALUs by packing several instructions and issuing and executing them in parallel. Thus, it is useful to compare our optimization to a machine that simply has more issue and execution bandwidth. Figure 11 compares instructions per cycle (IPC) for three different configurations, all with combining branch prediction and decode and commit width of four. The first is the baseline machine with issue width of 4 and 4 integer ALUs. The second is the baseline machine augmented with our operation packing optimizations. The third machine is the baseline machine with an issue width of 8 and 8 integer ALUs. *Ijpeg* and *vortex*, as well as many of the media benchmarks, come very close to achieving the same IPC as the more costly 8-issue/8-ALU implementation.

6 Conclusions and Future Work

Increased interest in support for sub-word parallelism motivated this work on value-specific power and performance optimizations in current microprocessors. Prior use of multimedia-style operation packing has required significant programmer intervention. Compile-time analysis is constrained by the fact that the operand range may vary over the course of a program run depending on the input data. In addition, the compiler must conservatively analyze all potential paths taken. Our work notes that certain uncommon paths may have different operand size characteristics than the typical path through programs.

Thus, in order to augment compile-time analysis, we present two techniques to *dynamically* exploit low bitwidth data. The first reduces power in integer execution units with aggressive clock gating, after determining that the upper portion of functional unit is not needed. The second increases performance by dynamically recognizing opportunities to issue multiple narrow width instructions to the same functional unit to be executed in parallel. The mechanisms we discuss could be extended to other optimizations as well, such as reducing power in the floating point units or in the cache memories.

A key characteristic of our current proposals is that they require only a small amount of hardware and no compiler intervention. More broadly, they represent a step towards implementing operand-value-based optimization strategies throughout processors.

Acknowledgments
We thank Saman Amarasinghe, Douglas W. Clark, and the reviewers for their helpful comments on early paper drafts. Research support includes funds from DARPA DABT63-97-C-1001, NSF MIP-97-08624, and a donation from Intel Corp. Brooks is supported by an NSF Graduate Research Fellowship, and Martonosi by an NSF CAREER Award.

References

[1] A. Peleg and U. Weiser. MMX Technology Extension to the Intel Architecture. *IEEE Micro*, vol.16, no.4, p. 42-50.

[2] R. Lee. Subword parallelism with MAX-2. *IEEE Micro*, vol.16, no.4, p. 51-9.

[3] M. Tremblay et al. The Visual Instruction Set (VIS) in UltraSPARC. *Proc. COMPCON* 1995, p. 462-469.

[4] Asanovic K., Kingsbury B., Irissou B., Beck J., and Wawrzynek J. T0: A Single-Chip Vector Microprocessor with Reconfigurable Pipelines. *Proc. 22nd European Solid-State Circuits Conference*, Sep., 1996.

[5] R. Gonzalez and M. Horowitz. Energy Dissipation in General Purpose Microprocessors. *IEEE Journal of Solid-State Circuits*, vol.31, no.9, p. 1277-84.

[6] Alpern, B., L. Carter, and K. S. Gatlin. Microparallelism and High-Performance Protein Matching. *SuperComp.95*

[7] G. Gerosa, et al. A 2.2W, 80 MHz Superscalar RISC Microprocessor. *IEEE Journal of Solid-State Circuits*, vol. 29, no. 12, p. 1440-54.

[8] M. Lipasti, J.P. Shen. The performance potential of value and dependence prediction. *Proc. 3rd International Euro-Par Conference*. p. 1043-52

[9] R. Razdan and M. Smith. A High-Performance Microarchitecture with Hardware-Programmable Functional Units. *Proc. of Micro 27*. p. 1-9. Nov 1994.

[10] D. Burger, T.M. Austin, and S. Bennett. Evaluating future microprocessors: the SimpleScalar tool set. TR-1308, Univ. of Wisconsin-Madison CS Dept., July 1996.

[11] V. Popescu, M. Schultz, J. Spracklen, G. Gibson, B. Lightner, and D. Isaman. The Metaflow architecture. *IEEE Micro*, p. 10-13, 63-73, June 1991.

[12] D. Hunt. Advanced performance features of the 64-bit PA-8000. In *CompCon '95*, p. 123-128, Mar. 1995.

[13] C. Lee, M. Potkonjak, and W. H. Mangione-Smith, MediaBench: A Tool for Evaluating Multimedia and Communications Systems. *Proc. of Micro 30*, 1997.

[14] K. Skadron, et al. A Quantitative Evaluation of Branch Prediction's Impact on Instruction-Window Size and Cache Size. Princeton Univ. CS Dept. TR-578-98.

[15] D. Bhandarkar. Alpha Implementations and Architecture – Complete Reference and Guide. Digital Press, 1996.

[16] R. Zimmermann and W. Fichtner. Low-Power Logic Styles: CMOS Versus Pass-Transistor Logic. In *IEEE Journal of Solid State Circuits*, vol. 32, no. 7, p. 1079-90.

[17] M. Borah, R. Owens, M. Irwin. Transistor Sizing for Low Power CMOS Circuits. *IEEE Trans. on CAD for Integrated Circuits and Systems*, vol. 15, no. 6, p. 665-71.

[18] P. Ng, P. Balsara, D. Steiss: Performance of CMOS Differential Circuits. *IEEE Journal of Solid State Circuits*, vol. 31, no. 6, p. 841-846.

[19] M. Gowan, L. Biro, D. Jackson. Power Considerations in the Design of the Alpha 21264 Microprocessor. *Proc. 35th Design Automation Conference*. p. 726-731. June, 1998.

[20] C. Dulong. The IA-64 architecture at work. *IEEE Computer*, vol. 31, no. 7, p. 24-32.

[21] H. Sanchez *et al*. Thermal management system for high performance PowerPC microprocessors. *Proc. COMPCON 1997*, Feb. 1997.

Improving the Accuracy vs. Speed Tradeoff for Simulating Shared-Memory Multiprocessors with ILP Processors *

Murthy Durbhakula, Vijay S. Pai, Sarita Adve
Department of Electrical and Computer Engineering
Rice University
Houston, Texas 77005
{murthy|vijaypai|sarita}@rice.edu

Abstract

Previous simulators for shared-memory architectures have imposed a large tradeoff between simulation accuracy and speed. Most such simulators model simple processors that do not exploit common instruction-level parallelism (ILP) features, consequently exhibiting large errors when used to model current systems. A few newer simulators model current ILP processors in detail, but we find them to be about ten times slower. We propose a new simulation technique, based on a novel adaptation of direct execution, that alleviates this accuracy vs. speed tradeoff.

We compare the speed and accuracy of our new simulator, DirectRSIM, with three other simulators – RSIM (a detailed simulator for multiprocessors with ILP processors) and two representative simple-processor based simulators. Compared to RSIM, on average, DirectRSIM is 3.6 times faster and exhibits a relative error of only 1.3% in total execution time. Compared to the simple-processor based simulators, DirectRSIM is far superior in accuracy, and yet is only 2.7 times slower.

1. Introduction

Shared-memory multiprocessors are a fast growing segment of the high performance computing and server market. Simulation is the most widely used technique to evaluate new shared-memory architectures. Recent advances in processor architecture, however, force a re-evaluation of current shared-memory simulation methodology. Current processors aggressively exploit instruction-level paral-

lelism (ILP) through techniques such as multiple issue, out-of-order issue, non-blocking loads, and speculative execution. Most shared-memory simulation studies, however, use a much simpler model of the processor, assuming single-issue, in-order issue, blocking loads, and no speculative execution. We refer to the two types of processors as *ILP processors* and *simple processors* respectively.

Pai et al. showed that using current simple-processor based simulators to model ILP-processor based systems can give large and application-dependent errors (over 100% error in execution time in some cases) [9]. Unfortunately, the more accurate previous ILP-processor based simulators are much slower: we find an average slowdown of 9.7X.

The higher speed of simple-processor based simulators comes from the inherent benefits of a less complex processor, as well as from several speed enhancing techniques developed for such simulators. Direct execution is one such widely used technique that has previously relied on simple-processor features such as blocking loads, in-order issue, and no speculation [2, 3, 7].

This paper presents a novel adaptation of direct execution to substantially speed up simulation of shared-memory multiprocessors with ILP processors, without much loss of accuracy. We have developed a new simulator, DirectRSIM, based on our new technique. We evaluate the accuracy and speed of DirectRSIM by comparing it with RSIM, a state-of-the-art detailed ILP-processor based shared-memory simulator, as well as two representative simple-processor based direct execution simulators. For a variety of system configurations and applications, and using RSIM as the baseline for accuracy, we find:

- DirectRSIM, on average, is 3.6X faster than RSIM with an error in execution time of only 1.3% (range of -3.9% to 2.2%).

- Simple-processor based simulators remain an average of 2.7X faster than DirectRSIM. However, this addi-

---
*This work is supported in part by an IBM Partnership award, Intel Corporation, the National Science Foundation under Grant No. CCR-9410457, CCR-9502500, CDA-9502791, and CDA-9617383, and the Texas Advanced Technology Program under Grant No. 003604-025. Sarita Adve is also supported by an Alfred P. Sloan Research Fellowship and Vijay S. Pai by a Fannie and John Hertz Foundation Fellowship.

23

tional speed comes at a high cost, with average error in execution time of 46% (range of 0% to 128%) with the best simple-processor model, and average error of 137% (range of 9% to 438%) with the most common model.

Our results suggest a reconsideration of the appropriate simulation methodology for shared-memory systems. Earlier, the order-of-magnitude performance advantage of the simple-processor based simulators over RSIM made a compelling argument for their use in spite of their potential for large errors. It is not clear that those errors are still justifiable given only a 2.7X performance advantage relative to DirectRSIM.

2. Background

2.1. Direct execution with simple processors

Direct execution is a widely used form of execution-driven simulation, and has been shown to be accurate and fast for modeling shared-memory systems with simple processors [2, 3, 7].

Direct execution decouples functional and timing simulation. Functional simulation generates values (for registers and memory) and control flow, while timing simulation determines the number of cycles taken by the simulated execution. Direct execution achieves high speed in two ways. First, for functional simulation, it directly executes the application on the host. Second, timing for non-memory instructions is determined mostly by static analysis. The application is instrumented to convey this analysis to the memory timing simulator. Previous direct execution shared-memory simulators assume in-order issue and no speculation since they cannot model the effects of out-of-order issue statically and they view only one basic block at a time. With the exception of the Wisconsin Wind Tunnel II [7], these simulators also assume single-issue processors. Timing for memory references is modeled in detail, and is the most expensive part of the simulation.

For memory simulation, the application is usually instrumented to invoke the timing simulator on each memory reference, as these are the only points of interaction between the processors. When an application process invokes the timing simulator on a load, its functional simulation is suspended until the timing simulator completes the entire simulation of the load, thereby modeling only blocking loads. Stores are either modeled as blocking or non-blocking. In the non-blocking case, direct execution of the store's process may be resumed as soon as the appropriate simulation events for the store are scheduled (but not necessarily completed). The timing simulator can process these events asynchronously with respect to the store's process because, unlike a load, later instructions of the process do not depend on the completion of the store.

2.2. Simulators for ILP shared-memory systems

RSIM [8] and SimOS with the MXS processor simulator [10] are two previous shared-memory simulators that model ILP processors explicitly and in detail. They use straightforward execution-driven simulation, interpreting every instruction and simulating its effects on the complete processor pipeline and memory system in software.

Researchers have also used simple-processor based simulators to model ILP-processor based shared-memory systems using certain approximations. The most common approximation is to simply simulate a system with a simple processor to approximate a system with an ILP processor with the same clock speed (referred to as *Simple*). Other studies have sped up the clock rate of the simulated simple processor to model the benefits of ILP [5]. Pai et al. showed that the best previously used approximation is to speed up the processor clock cycle and L1 cache access time by a factor equal to the ILP processor's peak instruction issue rate (i) [9] (referred to as *Simple-ix*). They found that Simple-*ix* was reasonably accurate for some applications, but exhibited large errors in others. The key source of inaccuracy was that simple-processor based simulators do not model the impact of non-blocking loads (specifically, the overlapping of multiple load misses with each other).

3. Direct execution with ILP shared-memory multiprocessors

There are two problems with using previous direct execution techniques for ILP-processor based shared-memory systems:

Values for non-blocking loads. After a non-blocking load invokes the timing simulator, its direct execution process must be allowed to proceed before its timing simulation completes. This is required so that the direct execution process can generate later instructions for the timing simulator to execute in parallel with the load. However, the value that the load will return in the simulated architecture is unknown until the load's timing simulation is complete; this value depends on writes to the same location by other processors before the load reaches memory in the simulated architecture. Thus, the first problem is that the simulator must decide what value to return when a load occurs in the direct execution while it is incomplete in the timing simulation, and what action to take when the direct execution reaches a later instruction dependent on such a load.

Timing simulation of ILP features. The second problem is that a simple static analysis is insufficient to determine the impact of ILP features (such as out-of-order issue, speculative execution, and non-blocking loads) on the execution time of CPU instructions and on the time at which a memory instruction can be issued (or when it stalls the processor). Previous direct execution techniques do not directly provide a way to account for these features.

Sections 3.1 and 3.2 discuss our solutions to the above problems. Section 3.3 describes the detailed implementation of our technique in DirectRSIM.

3.1. Values for non-blocking loads

We focus on a release consistent architecture. For ease of explanation, we assume that synchronization accesses are identified to the simulator.

When a synchronization load invokes the timing simulator, it is treated as a blocking load as in previous direct execution simulators. When invoked by a data load, the timing simulator starts processing all instructions executed since its last invocation as described in Section 3.2. The timing simulator may return control to the direct execution before the load completes at (or even issues to) the memory hierarchy. The load returns the current value for the accessed memory location at the time of the direct execution, based on the following insight.

If the load does not form a data race with a store from another process in the simulated execution, the load and store will be executed in the same order in the direct execution as in the simulated execution. A load that is not part of a data race (a non-race load) must be separated from any conflicting store by a chain of synchronization releases and acquires; these synchronization accesses are ordered as in previous direct execution simulators and enforce the necessary orderings among non-race accesses. Thus, for a non-race load, the value at the time of the direct execution can be safely returned and used by dependent instructions.

For a race load, the value returned may be different from the one that would be returned in the simulated architecture. This value would be legal for release consistency, but may not be possible on the simulated architecture. Since data races are generally rare in parallel programs, we expect this issue to not have a significant impact. Further, a system that obeys the data-race-free consistency model (which requires identifying data races for a guarantee of sequential consistency) and blocks on race loads can naturally be simulated with our technique without any error (by simply blocking on the race loads).

3.2. Timing simulation of ILP features

Like previous direct execution simulators, our technique performs the functional simulation directly on the host machine and invokes the timing simulator only on memory references. Unlike previous uses of direct execution, the application is instrumented to record the path taken by the direct execution since the previous invocation of the timing simulator by the same process. The timing simulator simulates the timing for this path with the goal of providing the best accuracy and performance possible.

A naive timing simulator would simply replicate the features of detailed simulators such as RSIM, modeling the register state, pipeline stages, and all instruction effects in detail. Instead, our timing simulator improves performance relative to RSIM in three ways. First, direct execution allows the timing simulator not only to avoid instruction emulation, but also to make use of the values determined in direct execution to speed up several parts of simulation (e.g., register renaming and memory disambiguation).

Second, we approximate some parts of the processor simulation, motivated by previous work that shows that the key characteristic in determining shared-memory multiprocessor performance is the behavior of the memory system and its interaction with the processor [9]. Our most significant approximation is that we do not simulate speculated execution paths that are mispredicted. This approximation does not preclude modeling other effects of speculation; e.g., we keep track of branch prediction tables and stall instruction fetch on a mispredicted branch as the processor waits for the branch to be resolved. The simulation speed benefits of this approximation cannot be exploited by detailed simulators such as RSIM since RSIM does not know if a prediction is correct until the prediction is actually resolved in the simulated execution. The timing simulator of DirectRSIM has this information at the time the prediction is made, based on the values generated by the direction execution.

Third, with direct execution, the different application processes execute asynchronously in the simulation. In contrast, RSIM's processor and cache simulation, due to its detailed nature, is inherently a cycle-by-cycle simulation in which all processors and caches proceed in lockstep (Section 4.3). We improve performance of our timing simulation by further increasing the asynchrony in our system, partly by exploiting the features described above. The next section provides further details.

3.3. Implementation of DirectRSIM

DirectRSIM implements the direct execution methodology described in Sections 3.1 and 3.2. It consists of an application instrumentation mechanism (Section 3.3.1) and a timing simulator (Section 3.3.2).

3.3.1 Application code instrumentation

The instrumentation code calls the timing simulator on each memory reference and provides it with the execution path to be processed. The path is represented as ranges of contiguous program-counter values traversed by the direct execution since the last invocation of the timing simulator. For this purpose, the instrumentation code marks each unconditional branch or taken path of a conditional branch as ending a program-counter range and starting a new range. We currently instrument the application assembly code, but could also use the more general methods of executable-editing or dynamic binary translation.

3.3.2 Timing simulator

The timing simulator consists of three main parts: the event-driven simulation engine, the multiprocessor memory system simulator, and the processor simulator. The event-driven simulation engine and multiprocessor memory system simulator are common to all our simulators, and are described in more detail in Section 4. The processor simulator is the key feature that sets DirectRSIM apart. Upon entry, the DirectRSIM processor simulator processes the execution path provided by the instrumentation code, attempting to bring each instruction from the path into its instruction window.

Key functionality, data structures, and simulation clocks. The key work done by the processor simulator is: (1) keeping track of true dependences and structural hazards, and determining when instructions complete or when loads and stores can be issued based on these dependences[1], (2) retiring instructions from the instruction window at appropriate times based on the above completion times, (3) maintaining branch prediction tables, and (4) memory forwarding (i.e., if a load is ready to issue while a previous store to the same location is pending, then the store's value is forwarded to the load).

The key data structures in the processor simulator are (1) a structure analogous to the reorder buffer or instruction window of an ILP processor, (2) a load queue and a store queue to track memory accesses that need to be issued, (3) a structure to track outstanding stores, hashed on their addresses for efficient forwarding (4) the branch prediction table, and (5) a structure for tracking structural hazards for functional units.

The memory system and event-driven simulation engine of DirectRSIM provide a global view of time in the system. However, unlike RSIM, the processors are not required to be in lockstep with the global clock when performing internal actions. Each processor is allowed to maintain local views of the clock that run ahead of the global clock, as long as it synchronizes with the global clock before issuing any instruction to the memory system. The completion timestamps of individual instructions are one type of localized clock. Additionally, each processor simulator has two other views of time: a fetch time and a retire time. Instructions are marked with the value of the fetch time when they are

fetched into the window, and the processor retires instructions from the head of its instruction window according to the value of the retire time (as further explained below).

Instruction issue and completion. As the processor simulator brings instructions into its simulated instruction window, it tags non-memory instructions with their completion times, if known. The completion time for an instruction is known as long as it is not directly or indirectly data dependent on any incomplete loads. For such an instruction, the completion timestamp depends on its latency and the availability of a functional unit. The latter is approximated by tracking the future use of functional units by instructions whose completion times are already known; it is possible that some instructions with unknown completion times may interfere with the current instruction, but this effect is not modeled. If an instruction's completion time is not immediately known, it is attached to the instructions on which it is dependent; its completion timestamp will be set upon completion of these instructions.

For a load instruction, the processor simulator calculates a timestamp for the time when the load is ready to issue (if known), and inserts it in the load queue in issue time order. If the issue time is not known (due to dependencies on incomplete loads), then the load is attached to the instructions on which it is dependent and inserted into the load queue on completion of these instructions. When the global simulation time catches up with the issue time of a load, the processor simulator checks to see if the load can be forwarded from a previous store. This check is efficient since addresses for all previous stores are immediately known through direct execution, and can be stored and matched through a hash table. If there is no forwarding, an event is scheduled for issuing the load to the memory system. On forwarding, a completion time is marked for the load.

As with most current processor simulators, to ensure precise interrupts, a store instruction is marked ready for issue only when it reaches the top of the instruction window. At this time, the store will be inserted in the store queue with an issue timestamp equal to the current retire time. When the global time catches up with the issue time, an event for the issue of the store is scheduled.

Instruction fetch and retirement. Instruction fetching continues until either the instruction window or the load queue or the store queue fills up, or all instructions executed by the functional simulator since the last timing simulator invocation are processed, or there is a misspeculation. In the misspeculation case, instruction fetching continues once the misspeculation penalty is determined. In the case that the instruction window is full, the processor simulator tries to retire the first set of instructions. Retirement is an entirely local action; the head of the instruction window can always be retired unless it is an incomplete load. The processor's retire clock is possibly updated based on the com-

---

[1] These dependences are the primary reason for DirectRSIM's processor model. Although previous work has shown that the Simple-*ix* model (Section 2.2) can predict the CPU component of execution time reasonably well for the applications studied [9], we do not use its processor model because its policy of simply speeding the CPU clock based on issue rate would allow multiple non-blocking loads to be issued even if there was a dependence from one to the next.

pletion time of the retiring instruction and the number of instructions that have already retired at that time relative to the processor's peak retire rate.

Suspending and resuming processor simulation. A processor's simulation (and its corresponding direct execution process) is suspended when its instruction window is full, it cannot retire any further instructions, and no other loads or stores can be issued (either because they are dependent on other loads, or because the cache ports are full, or because the global time has not caught up with their issue time yet). At this point, the processor stalls in a state waiting for an action that will allow progress on any of the above situations. A processor's direct execution may be resumed once all of its directly executed instructions so far have been entered in its instruction window.

4. Evaluation Methodology

4.1. Simulated architectures

We model CC-NUMA shared-memory multiprocessors. Cache coherence is maintained through an invalidation-based MESI directory coherence protocol. Each system node includes one processor, a two-level write-back cache hierarchy, part of the system's distributed physical memory and directory, a network interface, and a split-transaction bus connecting the different components of the node. All nodes are connected by a two-dimensional mesh network. Contention is modeled at all resources in the processor, memory hierarchy, bus, and network.

The base processor incorporates aggressive features such as multiple issue, out-of-order issue, non-blocking loads and stores, speculative execution, and register renaming. Since most previous direct execution simulators model only single cycle functional unit latencies, we assume the same. Both caches are non-blocking and use miss status holding registers (MSHRs) to store state for outstanding accesses. The L1 and L2 cache sizes follow the methodology of Woo et al. [13] for our application input sizes (described in Section 4.2). All primary working sets in these applications fit in the L1 cache, while the secondary working sets do not fit in the L2 cache. Currently, a perfect instruction cache and TLB are modeled since the application suite is known to have a small instruction cache and TLB miss ratio. Figure 1 summarizes the key system parameters for our base system. Results for five variations of the base system are also reported, as described in Section 5.

4.2. Applications

We study 5 applications – FFT, LU, and Radix from SPLASH-2 [13], MP3D from SPLASH [12], and Erlebacher from the Rice parallel compiler group [1]. A few changes have been made to the original SPLASH-2 codes

ILP processor and cache parameters	
Processor speed	500MHz
Maximum fetch/decode/retire rate	4
Instruction issue window	64 entries
Functional units	4 integer arithmetic
	4 floating point
	4 address generation
Branch speculation depth	8
Memory unit size	32 entries
Cache line size	64 bytes
L1 cache (on-chip)	Direct mapped, 16 K
L2 cache (off-chip)	4-way associative, 64 K
L1 request ports	2
L2 request ports	1
Number of MSHRs at L1 and L2	8
Representative contentionless latencies	
L1 cache hit	1 cycle
L2 cache hit	10 cycles
Local memory	85 cycles
Nearest remote memory	182 cycles
Farthest remote memory	262 cycles
Nearest cache to cache transfer	210 cycles
Farthest cache to cache transfer	309 cycles

Figure 1. Base system parameters. The number of processors varies by application, as described in Section 4.2 and Figure 2.

Application	Input Size	Processors
Erlebacher	64x64x64 cube, block 8	16
FFT	65536 points	16
LU	256x256 matrix, block 8	8
Radix	512K keys, max: 512K, 1024	8
Mp3d	50000 particles	8

Figure 2. Application input sizes and number of simulated processors.

for better performance. In LU, one loop nest is interchanged to cluster read misses closer together, thereby increasing their overlap with each other and improving performance in a system with ILP processors [9]. A similar change is applied to two loop nests in FFT. For better load balance, we use flags instead of barriers for synchronization in LU.

Figure 2 lists the input data sizes (chosen so that the simulations complete in reasonable time) and the number of processors simulated for each application (based on the scalability of the application for the input size used).

4.3. Simulators

We compare DirectRSIM with RSIM (the only publicly available detailed ILP-processor based shared-memory simulator), and Simple and Simple-*ix* (two representative simple-processor based direct execution simulators). RSIM and DirectRSIM directly model the ILP processor described in Section 4.1. Simple and Simple-*ix* use a simple-processor model to approximate the ILP processor, using previous direct execution methodology (Section 2). We chose these two simple-processor approximations since they are the most widely used and the best reported such approximations respectively [9]. Recall that to model the 500 MHz 4-way base ILP processor, Simple-4x models a 2 GHz single-issue processor. To ensure that the performance of our simple-processor based simulators is representative of the state-of-the-art, we compared Simple to the recently released Wisconsin Wind Tunnel-II (a simple-processor based direct execution simulator) and found the speed of the two simulators to be comparable [4].

The differences between our four simulators are limited to the processor model and its interaction with the cache hierarchy. The memory system simulation in all simulators uses nearly identical code. It is based on an event-driven simulation engine [2], where events for the simulated system modules are scheduled by inserting them on a central event queue, and are triggered by a central driver routine.

A few differences between RSIM and the other simulators arise because of the inherent differences between detailed and direct execution based simulation. The direct execution simulators use user-level lightweight processes to provide the register and stack state needed by each simulated processor for direct execution. Each activation of a process incurs the overhead of a lightweight context-switch. RSIM does not use lightweight processes, as it simulates all register and stack state in software. Instead, it uses a special event that occurs every cycle and examines the state of each processor, L1 cache, and L2 cache, scheduling any external events triggered by these parts of the system in the event queue. Effectively, RSIM simulates the processors and caches on a cycle-by-cycle basis, since in a detailed ILP processor simulation it can be expected that some processor or cache will have some event scheduled every cycle.

Additionally, the direct execution simulators optimize L1 cache hits whenever the cache is guaranteed to have ports available and not be stalled for resources such as MSHRs. In these cases, the processor simulator itself accounts for the impact of the hit on execution time without forwarding the request to the L1 cache module. The processor may, however, still have to stall to allow the global simulation clock to catch up with the issue time of such an access. RSIM issues all hits to the caches, consistent with its cycle-by-cycle detailed simulation policy.

4.4. Metrics

The accuracy of a direct execution simulator is evaluated based on the execution time it reports for the simulated application (excluding initialization), relative to the time reported by RSIM. Since all simulators use nearly identical code for the memory system, the discrepancy in simulated execution times occurs solely due to the level of detail in the processor models. To gain further insight, we also report three components of the execution time – CPU time, memory stall time, and synchronization stall time – calcu-

lated as in previous work [9, 10].

To determine simulator performance, the elapsed (wall-clock) time is measured for each simulation when run on an unloaded single 250MHz UltraSPARC-II processor of a Sun Ultra Enterprise 4000 server with 1GB memory and 1MB L2 cache. The simulators were all compiled using the Sun C 4.2 compiler with the highest practical level of optimization. The time spent in the initialization phase of the application is not included, since this time is not reported in the simulated execution time and can be sped up in various ways orthogonal to the rest of the simulation methodology.

5. Results on simulator accuracy

5.1. Base system configuration

Figure 3 shows the simulated execution time and its components reported by each simulator for each application on the base system configuration, normalized to that for RSIM. The number above each bar in the figure gives the percentage error in total execution time relative to RSIM. Numbers shown at the side of a bar represent the breakup of the total error among the three components of execution time.

Figure 3 shows that DirectRSIM reports overall simulated execution time very close to RSIM on all our applications, with a maximum error of 2.2%. This is a striking improvement over the best previous approximation of Simple-4x, which sees an execution time error of 87% for LU and 25% to 33% on three other applications studied. The Simple simulator sees much larger errors, ranging from 47% to 271%.

The differences between the four simulators arise from their abilities to capture the benefits that ILP provides to the various components of execution time. As discussed in [9], ILP reduces the CPU component of execution time by issuing multiple instructions at a time and by issuing instructions out of order. ILP reduces the memory component primarily by overlapping multiple long latency memory operations with each other, or also by overlapping memory latency with CPU instructions. ILP can also increase the memory component by increasing contention for resources or by changing an access pattern. Synchronization time is negligible for all our applications, and is not discussed further.

As reported by Pai et al. [9], the Simple model cannot capture the effects of ILP on either the CPU or memory stall component of execution time. Simple-4x models much of the benefit for the CPU component (because its clock speed is increased by a factor equal to the issue width of the processor). Most of the errors seen by Simple-4x are in the memory stall component, primarily because Simple-4x does not allow multiple read misses to overlap with each other. Thus, this method cannot properly capture

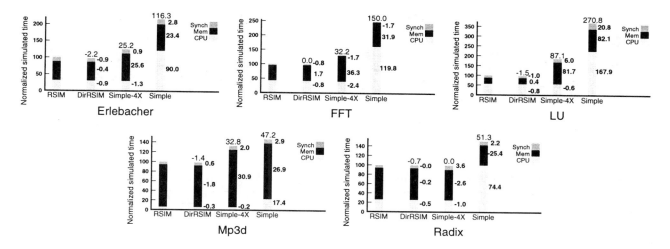

Figure 3. Simulator accuracy for the base system.

Config.	Difference from the base configuration
Lat. x2	Roughly twice the local and remote memory latencies.
Lat. x3	Three times the local memory latency, and a minimum contentionless remote-to-local latency ratio of 3:1.
ILP+	Processor is twice as aggressive, with double the instruction issue width, instruction window size, processor memory unit size, functional units, branch-prediction hardware, cache ports, and MSHRs.
ILP++	Same as ILP+, but with four times the instruction window size, memory unit size, and MSHRs as the base.
C. net	Constant-latency 50-cycle network instead of a 2-D mesh network.

Figure 4. Variations on base configuration.

ILP-specific improvements in the memory stall component of execution time. DirectRSIM models the impact of ILP in both CPU and memory stall components of execution time, and provides a closer and more consistent approximation to the functionality of detailed execution-driven simulators.

5.2. Other system configurations

Figure 4 summarizes the variations on the base system configuration studied in this section. These configurations are intended to capture future trends towards higher processor clock speeds, larger remote to local memory latency ratios, aggressive processor microarchitectures, and aggressive network configurations. In the ILP+ and ILP++ configurations, Simple-8x is used rather than Simple-4x.

Figures 5(a), (b), and (c) show the percentage errors in total execution time relative to RSIM as seen by Direct-RSIM, Simple-ix, and Simple respectively for the various system configurations (the first row in the tables repeats the data of the base configuration shown in Figure 3). Di-

	Erle.	FFT	LU	Mp3d	Radix	Avg.
Base	-2.2	0.0	-1.5	-1.4	-0.7	1.2
Lat. x2	-1.6	-1.5	-2.0	-0.7	0.0	1.2
Lat. x3	-0.7	2.2	-0.7	0.0	-0.3	0.8
ILP+	-2.8	0.2	-3.5	-3.9	-0.8	2.2
ILP++	0.7	-1.2	-2.4	-0.9	-0.8	1.2
C. net	-1.5	-0.8	-1.6	-0.5	-0.5	1.0
Avg.	1.6	1.0	1.9	1.2	0.5	1.3

(a) % error in execution time for DirectRSIM relative to RSIM

	Erle.	FFT	LU	Mp3d	Radix	Avg.
Base	25.2	32.2	87.1	32.8	0.0	35.5
Lat. x2	27.5	35.0	109.0	31.9	3.6	41.4
Lat. x3	27.6	38.4	90.5	23.3	2.0	36.4
ILP+	31.4	50.0	122.4	58.6	4.0	53.3
ILP++	69.8	58.8	127.8	98.2	10.1	72.9
C. net	23.1	29.7	84.7	28.1	3.6	33.8
Avg.	34.1	40.7	103.6	45.5	3.9	45.5

(b) % error in execution time for Simple-ix relative to RSIM

	Erle.	FFT	LU	Mp3d	Radix	Avg.
Base	116.3	150.0	270.8	47.2	51.3	127.1
Lat. x2	77.7	99.5	232.4	38.8	22.7	94.2
Lat. x3	54.5	73.4	147.6	25.8	9.1	62.1
ILP+	156.3	227.8	425.1	78.2	68.0	191.1
ILP++	231.2	247.1	437.8	122.8	77.8	223.3
C. net	110.6	145.8	264.9	38.3	55.9	123.1
Avg.	124.4	157.3	296.4	58.5	47.5	136.8

(c) % error in execution time for Simple relative to RSIM

Figure 5. Simulator accuracy for all configurations. (Averages are over absolute values of the errors.)

rectRSIM continues to see very low errors, with an average of 1.3% and a maximum of 3.9%. In contrast, the errors with Simple-ix remain high for most of the applications, and continue to vary widely, ranging from 0% to 128%, with an average of 46%. The errors seen with Sim-

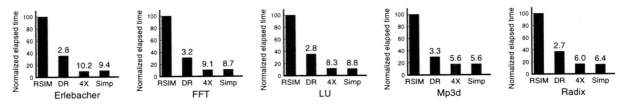

Figure 6. Simulator performance for the base system. DR=DirectRSIM, 4X=Simple-4X, Simp=Simple.

ple are even higher, ranging from 9% to 438%, averaging 137%. As with the base configuration, most of the error with Simple-*ix* comes from the memory component, while the error with Simple comes from both the CPU and the memory component [4]. As expected, the errors are greatest in the applications with the most read miss overlap. This application characteristic becomes even more important for systems with future aggressive processors (e.g., ILP+ and ILP++), as seen by the increase in error with Simple and Simple-*ix* for these configurations.

In conclusion, DirectRSIM achieves significantly greater and more reliable accuracy than Simple-*ix* or Simple in a variety of current and future multiprocessor configurations.

5.3. Applicability to architectural studies

So far, we have evaluated the simulators based on their ability to predict absolute execution times and the fraction of time stalled for memory. The latter is particularly important for a large class of architectural studies that target the memory stall component.

In some architectural studies, accurately modeling relative gains of an optimization may be more important than accurately modeling absolute execution time. We evaluate DirectRSIM and Simple-4x on the base configuration for their ability to predict the benefits of an example optimization. Recall that our version of LU has been optimized with a loop interchange to increase the overlap of read misses with each other. We compare the reduction in execution time due to this optimization reported by the simulators. We find that RSIM reports a reduction of 26%. DirectRSIM closely follows RSIM showing a reduction of 23%. In contrast, Simple-4x reports no reduction in execution time, as it does not model the benefits of read miss overlap. Therefore, unlike DirectRSIM, Simple-4x is unable to predict the benefits of the optimization.

6. Results on simulator performance

6.1. Overall performance

Figure 6 graphically depicts the elapsed times for the four simulators in the base configuration for each application, normalized to the time for RSIM. The number above the bars for DirectRSIM, Simple-*ix*, and Simple are the

	Erle.	FFT	LU	Mp3d	Radix	Avg.
Base	2.8	3.2	2.8	3.3	2.7	3.0
Lat. x2	3.3	3.9	3.0	4.8	3.2	3.6
Lat. x3	3.7	3.8	3.5	5.9	4.8	4.3
ILP+	3.8	4.4	3.1	3.7	3.2	3.6
ILP++	2.9	4.2	3.2	5.0	3.7	3.8
C. net	3.1	3.3	3.0	4.4	2.7	3.3
Avg.	3.3	3.8	3.1	4.5	3.4	3.6

(a) Speedup of DirectRSIM over RSIM

	Erle.	FFT	LU	Mp3d	Radix	Avg.
Base	3.6	2.8	3.0	1.7	2.2	2.7
Lat. x2	3.3	2.8	2.8	1.6	2.5	2.6
Lat. x3	3.0	3.8	2.6	2.1	2.7	2.8
ILP+	3.2	2.7	2.9	1.6	2.2	2.5
ILP++	4.0	2.8	3.0	1.6	2.9	2.9
C. net	3.6	3.1	3.3	2.0	3.0	3.0
Avg.	3.4	3.0	2.9	1.8	2.6	2.7

(b) Speedup of Simple-*ix* over DirectRSIM

	Erle.	FFT	LU	Mp3d	Radix	Avg.
Base	10.2	9.1	8.3	5.6	6.0	7.8
Lat. x2	10.9	10.9	8.3	7.8	8.0	9.2
Lat. x3	11.2	14.5	9.2	12.6	12.8	12.1
ILP+	12.1	11.6	9.1	6.0	7.3	9.2
ILP++	11.7	11.7	9.5	8.2	10.8	10.4
C. net	11.0	10.1	9.8	8.9	8.0	9.6
Avg.	11.2	11.3	9.0	8.2	8.8	9.7

(c) Speedup of Simple-*ix* over RSIM

Figure 7. Simulator performance for all configurations.

speedups achieved by those simulators over RSIM. Since the elapsed times for Simple and Simple-*ix* are similar in all cases and since Simple gives much larger errors, we do not discuss the performance of Simple any further. Figure 7 tabulates speedup for each pair of simulators, for all configurations in Figure 4. As reference for absolute performance, RSIM simulates an average of 20,000 instructions per second for the base configuration (more data appears in [4]).

Simple-*ix* gives the best elapsed time, with an average speedup of 9.7 over RSIM. DirectRSIM has some additional overheads from processor simulation, but still sees an average speedup of 3.6 over RSIM. Of particular interest are the increases in DirectRSIM speedup for the longer-latency configurations, which represent future configurations with faster processor speeds. DirectRSIM profits by switching from a largely cycle-driven simulator to a purely event-driven simulator, and so is less sensitive to future increases in system latencies than RSIM. DirectRSIM also sees higher speedups in ILP+ and ILP++ by effectively targeting the more expensive processor simulation component seen by these aggressive microarchitectures.

Most notably, the performance advantage of Simple-ix is reduced to an average of 2.7X compared to DirectRSIM. The competitive performance of DirectRSIM indicates that the performance benefits of simple-processor based simulators may no longer be enough to justify their large inaccuracies in modeling current and future multiprocessor systems.

6.2. Detailed analysis of DirectRSIM's performance

To further understand the reasons for the performance differences among the simulators, Figure 8 depicts their execution profiles for LU on the base configuration as reported by `prof` (with monitoring turned on only during the parallel phase of the application). The other applications show similar profiles. The function calls of the simulators are divided according to the logical tasks they perform. From the bottom to the top of each bar, these tasks are instruction fetch and decode (including dependence checking), instruction retirement, processor memory unit simulation, functional unit management, cache simulation, cycle-driven simulation management, instruction emulation, direct-execution, event-driven simulation management, context switching among lightweight processes, and other tasks (e.g., memory and network simulation, and branch speculation). Not all tasks are present in all simulators.

DirectRSIM vs. RSIM. DirectRSIM improves performance relative to RSIM primarily by reducing the time spent simulating instruction fetch and decode, instruction retirement, the processor memory unit, and functional unit management. DirectRSIM's knowledge of values and addresses through direct execution enables more efficient register renaming and management of store-to-load forwarding, respectively. The provision to allow internal processor actions to proceed ahead of the global clock enables more efficient instruction fetching and retirement. The instruction dependence checking for issue is sped by the use of timestamps. Functional unit management is sped by the structure to approximately track future functional unit utilizations.

DirectRSIM also spends less time than RSIM in cache simulation by not simulating accesses that are known to hit in the L1 cache without contention. Among the remaining components of elapsed time (accounting for less than 20% of RSIM's total time), DirectRSIM eliminates the cycle-driven controller, but adds a component to handle context-switching and also increases event-driven simulation overhead. DirectRSIM avoids the overhead of instruction em-

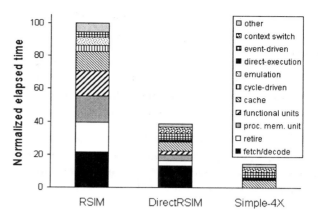

Figure 8. Components of elapsed time.

ulation (about 4% of RSIM time) and replaces it with a smaller component in direct execution. In the "other" category, DirectRSIM also uses values computed in direct execution to reduce the cost of mispredicted branches.

DirectRSIM vs. Simple-4x. As expected, most of DirectRSIM's overhead relative to Simple-4x stems from its processor simulation features. It also sees slightly more overhead in memory hierarchy simulation (due to increased resource contention from non-blocking reads).

7 Related Work

Section 2 reviewed the previous shared-memory simulation techniques most relevant to this paper. Additionally, sampling [10] and parallelization [7] are used to speed up shared-memory simulation. Both techniques are orthogonal to ours and can be used in conjunction with DirectRSIM.

Dynamic binary translation is sometimes used to speed up simulation [10] (as an alternative to direct execution). For our purposes, this technique can also be seen as a form of direct execution as it also decouples functional and timing simulation and executes most of the translated application directly on the host. Hence, the techniques presented in this paper can also be applied to dynamic binary translation.

Effectively, DirectRSIM's timing simulator acts as a trace-driven simulator operating on the trace of instructions executed since its last invocation by the same process. DirectRSIM, however, is still execution-driven because the simulated application's execution path is affected by the dynamic ordering of synchronization accesses and contention. In the uniprocessor case, however, DirectRSIM effectively becomes a trace-driven simulator.

Concurrently, Krishnan and Torrellas have proposed a method similar to ours for direct-execution for ILP multiprocessors [6]. They do not discuss the potential for error (or solutions) when using values of non-blocking loads in direct execution. They also do not assess the accuracy of their simulator or compare performance with detailed simulation. Their performance comparison with a previous simple-processor simulator is done without memory system simulation, and shows slowdowns of 24–29X.

Schnarr and Larus concurrently developed a direct execution simulator for uniprocessors with ILP processors [11]. They simulate mispredicted paths and also propose instruction-window memoization. The use and/or benefits of some of their techniques for shared-memory multiprocessors are unclear (e.g., speculative stores and memoization). Further, their approach focuses on accurate microarchitectural simulation. We allow approximations, since we focus on accurate memory simulation in a multiprocessor with only as much emphasis on microarchitectural simulation as needed for correct memory simulation.

8 Conclusions

This paper presents a new simulation technique for shared-memory multiprocessors with ILP processors that combines the speed advantages of simple-processor based simulators with the accuracy of detailed ILP-processor based simulators. Our technique is based on a novel adaptation of direct execution. First, it allows a data load to proceed in direct execution even before its simulation has completed at the memory system. Second, it provides an efficient timing simulator that accounts for aggressive ILP features such as multiple issue, out-of-order issue, and non-blocking loads.

DirectRSIM, our implementation of the new technique, sees an average of 1.3% error (maximum of only 3.9%) in simulated execution time relative to RSIM for all studied applications and configurations. At the same time, Direct-RSIM sees a speedup of 3.6 over RSIM. In contrast, the best current simple-processor based simulation methodology sees large and variable errors in execution time, ranging from 0% to 128%, and averaging 46%. The most commonly used simple-processor based simulation methodology sees errors ranging from 9% to 438%, averaging 137%. Despite its superior accuracy, DirectRSIM sees only a factor of 2.7X slowdown compared to current simple-processor based simulators. Although the performance advantage of simple-processor based simulators is still significant, it may no longer be enough to justify their high errors. Our results, therefore, suggest a reconsideration of simulation methodology for evaluating shared-memory systems.

In the future, several features supported in other simulators can be added to DirectRSIM to further improve its performance and/or functionality. Examples include parallelization, sampling, instrumentation through executable editing or binary translation, instruction cache, TLB, and full simulation of system calls. We are not aware of any fundamental problems in incorporating such support for DirectRSIM. Finally, if desired, we believe that support for simulating mispredicted paths could also be incorporated.

Acknowledgments

We thank Jim Larus and Parthasarathy Ranganathan for valuable comments on earlier versions of this paper.

References

[1] V. S. Adve et al. An Integrated Compilation and Performance Analysis Environment for Data Parallel Programs. In *Proc. Supercomputing '95*, December 1995.

[2] R. G. Covington et al. The Efficient Simulation of Parallel Computer Systems. *Intl. Journal in Computer Simulation*, 1:31–58, January 1991.

[3] H. Davis, S. R. Goldschmidt, and J. Hennessy. Multiprocessor Simulation and Tracing Using Tango. In *Proc. Intl. Conf. on Parallel Processing*, pages II-99–II107, 1991.

[4] M. Durbhakula, V. S. Pai, and S. V. Adve. Improving the Speed vs. Accuracy Tradeoff for Simulating Shared-Memory Multiprocessors with ILP Processors. Technical Report 9802, Department of Electrical and Computer Engineering, Rice University, April 1998. Revised November 1998.

[5] C. Holt, J. P. Singh, and J. Hennessy. Application and Architectural Bottlenecks in Large Scale Distributed Shared Memory Machines. In *Proc. 23rd Intl. Symp. on Computer Architecture*, pages 134–145, May 1996.

[6] V. Krishnan and J. Torrellas. A Direct-Execution Framework for Fast and Accurate Simulation of Superscalar Processors. In *Proc. Parallel Architectures and Compilation Techniques*, October 1998.

[7] S. S. Mukherjee et al. Wisconsin Wind Tunnel II: A Fast and Portable Parallel Architecture Simulator. In *Workshop on Performance Analysis and Its Impact on Design*, June 1997.

[8] V. S. Pai, P. Ranganathan, and S. V. Adve. RSIM Reference Manual version 1.0. Technical Report 9705, Department of Electrical and Computer Engineering, Rice University, August 1997.

[9] V. S. Pai, P. Ranganathan, and S. V. Adve. The Impact of Instruction Level Parallelism on Multiprocessor Performance and Simulation Methodology. In *Proc. Intl. Symp. on High Performance Computer Architecture*, pages 72–83, 1997.

[10] M. Rosenblum et al. Using the SimOS Machine Simulator to Study Complex Computer Systems. *ACM Transactions on Modeling and Computer Simulation*, 1997.

[11] E. Schnarr and J. Larus. Fast Out-Of-Order Processor Simulation Using Memoization. In *Proc. 8th Intl. Conf. on Architectural Support for Programming Languages and Operating Systems*, pages 283–294, October 1998.

[12] J. P. Singh, W.-D. Weber, and A. Gupta. SPLASH: Stanford Parallel Applications for Shared-Memory. *Computer Architecture News*, 20(1):5–44, March 1992.

[13] S. C. Woo et al. The SPLASH-2 Programs: Characterization and Methodological Considerations. In *Proc. 22nd Intl. Symp. on Computer Architecture*, pages 24–36, June 1995.

Memory Hierarchy Considerations
for Fast Transpose and Bit-Reversals

Kang Su Gatlin and Larry Carter*
Department of Computer Science and Engineering, UCSD
9500 Gilman Drive, La Jolla, CA, 92093-0114

Abstract

This paper explores the interplay between algorithm design and a computer's memory hierarchy. Matrix transpose and the bit-reversal reordering are important scientific subroutines which often exhibit severe performance degradation due to cache and TLB associativity problems. We give lower bounds that show for typical memory hierarchy designs, extra data movement is unavoidable. We also prescribe characteristics of various levels of the memory hierarchy needed to perform efficient bit-reversals. Insight gained from our analysis leads to the design of a near optimal bit-reversal algorithm.

This Cache Optimal Bit Reverse Algorithm (COBRA) is implemented on the Digital Alpha 21164, Sun Ultrasparc 2, and IBM Power2. We show that COBRA is near optimal with respect to execution time on these machines and performs much better than previous best known algorithms.

1 Introduction

In many scientific computations, it is not the arithmetic operations but rather the movement of data among main memory, TLB (the translation lookaside buffer), cache, and registers that limits the performance. To achieve high performance, programs must be tuned to make efficient use of the target machine's memory hierarchy.[1]

This paper explores the interplay between algorithm design and a computer's memory hierarchy. We look at two important data-reorderings transformations, transpose and bit-reversal. Matrix transpose is heavily used in many applications areas, especially in linear algebra and computational

fluid dynamics. The practical importance of the bit-reversal lies in its role for the Fast Fourier Transform (FFT). FFT's consume a significant fraction of cycles on many large computers [9]. A major component of some FFT algorithms (e.g. Pease's algorithm) is the bit-reversal reordering. Other "self-ordering" FFT algorithms have been developed expressly to avoid the costly bit-reversal computation. They have a disadvantage of requiring more memory, and still may not avoid memory hierarchy problems [19].

As is well-known, naive implementations of these reorderings are slow, and loop transformations (tiling or blocking) can greatly improve performance. Here, we explore in depth a harder issue that often arises: when the array dimensions are large powers of two, there can be extreme cache and TLB associativity problems.

We show that there are tradeoffs to be made for good performance, and for most modern computers the tradeoffs favor making efficient use of cache over TLB and registers. We also prescribe memory hierarchy space characteristics necessary to perform these reorderings efficiently. Lastly we present a new bit-reversal reordering algorithm that is optimal with respect to cache and near optimal with respect to TLB. The algorithm is implemented on three architectures (the Digital Alpha 21164, the Sun Ultrasparc 2, and the IBM Power2) and achieves near optimal performance compared to our analytical model. This performance is better than any other bit-reversal algorithm we know of.

An outline of the papers follows: In the next section we define transpose and bit-reversal array reorderings, and show how they can exhibit Murphy's Law, where every cache and TLB problem that can occur, does occur. In section 3, we explore the relationship between such "Murphy" reorderings and the memory hierarchy. We also describe our Cache Optimal Bit-Reversal Algorithm (COBRA). The performance of COBRA is given in section 4, and a comparison to the lower bounds in section 5.

---

*{kgatlin, carter}@cs.ucsd.edu.

[1]This tuning can sometimes be performed by a compiler or optimizing preprocessor, but most often it is done by hand.

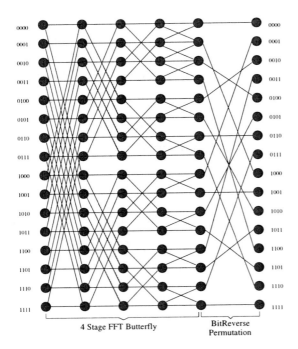

0000
0001
0010
0011
0100
0101
0110
0111
1000
1001
1010
1011
1100
1101
1110
1111

0000
0001
0010
0011
0100
0101
0110
0111
1000
1001
1010
1011
1100
1101
1110
1111

4 Stage FFT Butterfly — BitReverse Permutation

Figure 1. The "standard" picture of an FFT, followed by the bit-reversal reordering.

2 Reorderings and Murphy's Law

We consider copying a source array X into a distinct destination array Y in some permuted order.[2] *Transpose*, when X is $M \times N$ and Y is $N \times M$, is defined by the pseudocode:

```
Transpose(X, Y):
    for i = 0 to M-1
        for j = 0 to N-1
            Y[j,i] = X[i,j]
```

To define the bit-reversal reordering, we need some preliminary definitions. X and Y are arrays of length N, where $N = 2^n$. Given an n-bit long binary string a representing the index of an element in X or Y, let a' denote the *reversal* of a. For instance, if $n = 5$ and $a = 00010$, then $a' = 01000$, i.e. the reverse of the 5-bit representation of 2 is 8. The bit-reversal reordering of array X to array Y is defined as:

```
Bit-Reversal(X, Y):
    for i = 0 to N-1
        Y[i'] = X[i]
```

The position that an element is placed in the destination array is referred to as that element's *final position*. The final position of each array element is the reversal of the index representing its location in the source array.

We will represent the concatenation of two binary strings a and b by ab, and denoting the number of bits in a binary string a as $|a|$. Thus if $a = 001$ and $b = 1001$ then $ab = 0011001$ and $|ab| = 7$. Note that if $c = ab$ then $c' = b'a'$.

The role of the bit-reversal reordering in the FFT is shown in figure 1. The four stages of the standard 16-point butterfly network go from left to right, and the final stage is a 16-element bit-reversal reordering. This reordering places the data in the right locations so that repeated applications of the FFT will correctly swap between the time and frequency domains.

When the arrays being transposed or bit-reversed are significantly larger than the computer's cache, it is well-known that the performance of the simple programs given above is severely degraded. The memory references on one of the arrays[3] jump around so much that most or all references to that array are cache misses. For transpose, the problem can be ameliorated by "blocking" or "tiling" the computation. For instance, if the matrix is processed as a sequence of, say, 20×20 submatrices, then the relevant submatrices of both X and Y may stay resident in cache during the processing of each submatrix, if things go right. Unfortunately Murphy's Law [13] asserts things will not go right.

Understanding why Murphy's Law often holds requires a short digression into computer architecture. All computers move data between main memory and cache in blocks, called *cachelines*, of L_{cache} contiguous elements. L_{cache} is typically between 4 and 64 (measured in 4-byte array elements) depending on the computer's architecture. Furthermore, all caches are *k-way set associative* for some small value of k (typically 1, 2, or 4, depending on the architecture). This restricts what memory addresses[4] can be in cache at any particular time. Suppose the cache holds C elements. If a is the index of an element written as a binary string, we can write $a = tso$ where $|o| = \lg L_{cache}$ and $|s| = \lg(C/k) - |o|$. (lg is log-base-2.) The *offset* o gives the displacement of the element from the beginning of its cacheline, s is called the *set* of the element's cacheline, and t is the *tag*. The restriction imposed by k-way set associativity is that for any value of s, at most k cachelines from set s can be in cache at one time.

---

[2] The results of this paper are equally applicable to *in-place* reorderings, where X and Y are the same array.

[3] For Bit-Reversal, it is the Y array. For Transpose, it depends on whether the arrays are in row- or column-major order.

[4] A further complication is that some caches use *virtual* addresses and some use *physical* addresses to determine the mapping into cache. The discussion assumes a virtually-addressed cache. We note that the same problems can (and do) arise for physical-addressed caches.

A problematic scenario is that, firstly, for each cacheline of the X array, the final positions of its L_{cache} elements are in distinct cachelines all in the same associativity set and, secondly, for each cacheline of Y, the initial positions in X of these elements are in distinct cachelines of the same associativity set.[5] When this happens, we say we have a *Murphy* reordering (see Figure 2).

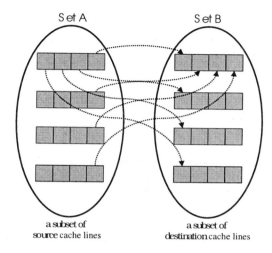

Figure 2. Visualization of how a source cache line from a given set A maps all elements to distinct destination cache lines in set B. It also shows that for a given cache line in set B all elements are mapped from distinct source cache lines in set A.

For Murphy reorderings, it is difficult to achieve spatial locality, that is, to use all the data brought into cache. Ideally, when a cacheline of X is brought into cache, we would copy all L_{cache} elements to their final positions. But this will entail at least $L_{cache} - k$ cache misses in Y.[6] To reduce the number of cache misses, we will develop algorithms that use a cache-resident *buffer* to hold elements temporarily.

Murphy reorderings are surprisingly common in practice. Many arrays have dimensions that are large powers of two. For a $N \times N$ matrix X, if N is a multiple of C/k, then transposing X is Murphy.[7] For example, a 16 KByte 1-way set associative cache, or a 64 KByte 4-way set associative

cache, transpose will be Murphy when N is any multiple of 4096 (recall our assumption of 4-byte "elements").[8] Matrices of this size ($4096^2 \times 4\text{Bytes} = 64\text{MB}$) are not uncommon in scientific simulations.

Three-dimensional matrices exacerbate the problem. Transposing a "small" $64 \times 64 \times 64$ matrix to interchange the x-axis with the z-axis is Murphy for the above-mentioned caches. This can be seen by thinking of the address of X(i,j,k), where i, j, and k are 6-bit binary strings, as the 18-bit string ijk. The elements of a cacheline of X all have the same value of i and j. Their final positions are of the form kji; and thus have the identical 12 low-order address bits, forcing them to be in the same set in many caches.

Bit-reversal reorderings are even worse. For instance, suppose $L_{cache} = 16$. If we write the index of an element as abc where a and c are 4 bits long, we see that the 16 elements in a cacheline, which only differ in their value for |c|, will have final positions c'b'a' whose indices differ only in the first 4 bits. A bit-reverse reordering will be Murphy whenever the array is at least $16/k$ times larger than the cache.

We have focused on cache associativity, but similar problems arise for TLB associativity. Pages of memory are typically at least 4KBytes, so the bits of an address that determine the TLB associativity set are further to the left than those determining the cache set. Consequently, a square matrix transpose problem needs to be unreasonably large to be "TLB-Murphy", but even modest-sized bit-reversals will be TLB-Murphy.

2.1 Related Work

In recent years, bit-reversal reorderings have been extensively studied. In Alan Karp's excellent survey [11], thirty bit-reversal reordering programs are compared, including Karp's own program which he calls the *Hybrid* method. In his experiments on a variety of computers, *Hybrid* is always competitive with the best algorithm and a large majority of the time is *the* best performing algorithm. For this paper, we will use *Hybrid* as our performance reference point.

One technique used to ameliorate cache associativity problems of Murphy reorderings is to introduce padding [17], for instance by storing a matrix in an array whose lead-

---

[5]We do not require that the associativity set of the source cachelines be the same as the associativity set of the corresponding destination cachelines, thought that would make things even worse!

[6]Another caveat: some caches are not *write-allocated*. In such a cache, writing to a memory location that isn't in cache don't bring the cacheline into cache. This avoids the cache miss penalty on Y, but writing directly to memory is slower than writing to cache. There is no free lunch.

[7]Yet another caveat: We assume that our arrays are aligned on cacheline and page boundaries. If not, the problems may not quite satisfy our definition of being Murphy, but the problems won't be any easier.

[8]Even though increasing the associativity results in *smaller* problems being Murphy, this does not imply that fewer problems occur with direct-mapped or low-associativity caches. Reorderings that are "nearly-Murphy" cause problems too, and these problems are usually most severe on direct-mapped caches.

ing dimension is a little larger than a power of two. This can help, but care must be taken (particularly with three-dimensional arrays) that the amount of padding between adjacent matrix elements isn't a multiple of a moderate-sized power of two. Furthermore, introducing padding into a bit-reversal problem (such as for an FFT) involves complicated programming and extra overhead.

Another technique in the literature to address cache associativity problems is to have a compiler copy data (remapping) [12] [20]. The techniques presented in these papers can not properly remap the data for a Murphy reordering such as the bit-reversal. Many other techniques used to reduce the impact of cache associativity problems require either the support of the OS or hardware [10] [5].

In terms of modeling multi-level memories, notable works include the Red-Blue Pebble Game [8]. This game's neglect of the spatial structure of memory makes it inapplicable to array permutations (as data is not reused). Floyd's two level model [7] adds spatial considerations, but the smaller of the two levels is limited to only two blocks in his analysis of transpose. Aggarwal and Vitter extend the work of [7] allowing the smaller level to hold more than two blocks. This two-level model allows one to permute data in the small memory module at no cost. This model is appropriate for disk-memory systems, where the cost of moving data from the disk drive overwhelms the cost of computation at the processor level. Our interest though lies with in-core algorithms. For arrays in main memory, the cost of moving data from memory to cache, for instance, has the same order of magnitude as moving data from cache to registers. Modeling this accurately enough to determine the constants requires a hierarchical model of memory.

In the Block Transfer model of hierarchical memory [1], copying a block of consecutive locations takes one unit of time per element, after an initial access time that is a function of the source and target locations. There are results for a variety of smooth access time cost functions. Unfortunately, there is no obvious way to translate these asymptotic analyses to specific results for the step-wise functions that occur in practice.

The Memory Hierarchy model [2] represents memory as a sequence of progressively smaller modules, where the ith module can hold k_i blocks of size b_i. Transferring a block between a module and the next larger module requires time t_i. If $k_i \geq b_i$ for each module and $t_i = b_i$ (i.e., the busses are all unit-bandwidth), Transpose of "nicely-aligned" arrays requires only $(2 + \epsilon)N$ cycles (where ϵ depends on the exact model, but is very small). Unfortunately, the assumption that $k_i \geq b_i$ doesn't hold for Murphy reorderings. Further, many computers cannot overlap communication as required by the model.

Savage [18] presents a multilevel pebble game and briefly suggests an extension that can model block moves, but his results don't apply to the issues we address in this paper.

3 Murphy Reorderings

In this section we explore the relationship between the performance of Murphy reordering algorithms and architectural parameters.

3.1 Model

Our machine model has an infinite memory, a K_{TLB}-way set associative TLB with each entry representing a L_{TLB}-sized page; a K_{cache}-way set associative cache of size C, where each line hold L_{cache} array elements; and R registers. All capacities are measured in 4-byte elements. Both the TLB and cache are read/write allocate. We assume, for simplicity, that the source and destination arrays begin on cacheline and page boundaries.

We say that an algorithm has an *L-efficiency*, denoted E_L, of $\frac{1}{e}$ if, on average, each datum is brought into level L e times. An algorithm is *L-efficient* iff $E_L = 1.0$. This notion of efficiency is applicable to all levels of the memory hierarchy (ie $E_{cache}, E_{TLB}, E_{reg}$).

3.2 Cache-Efficient Murphy Reorderings

We show that to perform a cache-efficient Murphy reordering, a *buffer* must be used. A buffer is temporary storage, residing in registers and/or cache. For a reordering to be cache-efficient, given a block of the source array is in cache, all of its L_{cache} elements must be moved either to the destination array or into the buffer before the cacheline can be evicted. The following theorem gives a lower bound on the size of the buffer needed to achieve cache-efficiency.

Theorem 1 *If $L_{cache} > 2K_{cache}$ in the machine model described above, then performing a Murphy reordering of a source array X to a destination array Y requires a buffer of size at least $L_{cache}(L_{cache} - 2K_{cache})$ elements to be cache-efficient.*[9]

---

[9]A "hidden" assumption is that all array elements are incompressible atomic units.

Proof:

During the execution of the reordering program, each cacheline of Y will be brought into cache (only once, by cache-efficiency) and then evicted. Let f be the very first cacheline from the destination array that is evicted, say at time T. Since f is filled with L_{cache} elements in their final position when it is evicted, the cachelines of X holding elements whose final positions are in f must have been loaded some time before time T. Since the reordering is Murphy, there are L_{cache} distinct such cachelines and all are in the same associativity set. Therefore (at most) K_{cache} can be in cache at time T. Let E be the set of (at least) $L_{cache} - K_{cache}$ cachelines of X that have an element in f but which have been evicted before time T.

Where can the $L_{cache}(L_{cache} - K_{cache})$ elements that began in E be? Since the reordering is cache-efficient, they must have been copied somewhere. By the Murphy assumption, all elements in E have final positions in cachelines in the same associativity set as f, and at most K_{cache} such lines can be in cache at time T. This accounts for at most $L_{cache}K_{cache}$ elements of E. Further, since f is the *first* cacheline of the destination array to be evicted, no other elements can be in their final positions. Thus, the remaining $L_{cache}(L_{cache} - 2K_{cache})$ elements must be in the buffer. $\diamondsuit$

The assumption that $L_{cache} > 2K_{cache}$ is usually met in practice, due to the dual pressures of making the cache associativity small (one- to four-way) to reduce access times, and making the line length large to enhance spatial locality [16]. Table 1 illustrates this for the three architectures of our study.

Buffer requirements			
	Power2	Ultrasparc2	Alpha 21164
L_{cache}	32	8	16
K_{cache}	4	1	3
Buffer size	768	48	192

Table 1. Cache parameters measured in 4-Byte elements, and required buffer sizes for a cache-efficient algorithm. For the Ultrasparc2 and Alpha, data are for the L2 cache.

From the above theorem, we draw several conclusions:

- *Most architectures cannot support a Murphy reordering that is both cache-efficient and register-efficient.* To be register efficient, the buffer would have to reside entirely in the set of registers. Table 1 illustrates that this is unachievable with the usual set of 32 registers.

- *Most architectures have enough room in cache for a buffer that satisfies Theorem 1.* The "wide cache principle" [15], which says a cache should have at least as many cachelines as it has elements in a cacheline, is met on all modern microprocessors. It ensures the cache can hold at least $(L_{cache})^2$ elements.

3.3 TLB Efficiency

This situation for TLB's is quite different. The identical proof, substituting "TLB" for "cache" gives:

Corollary 1 *If $L_{TLB} > 2K_{TLB}$, then a TLB-efficient Murphy reordering requires a buffer (residing in TLB and/or registers[10]) of size at least $L_{TLB}(L_{TLB} - 2K_{TLB})$ elements. In other words, it must have at least $L_{TLB} - 2K_{TLB}$ entries.*

This requirement is unrealistic. All operating systems have L_{TLB} of at least 1024, but the TLBs have a relatively modest number of entries. In fact, even if the TLB were fully associative, it would need over $1024/3$ entries to satisfy above requirement. In Figure 3 we plot the minimum buffer sizes for cache- and TLB-efficient algorithms. For the range of associativities plotted, associativity plays a minor role.

3.4 COBRA: Cache-optimal Bit-reverse Algorithm

In creating an optimal reordering algorithm, our first concern is to focus on the worst bottleneck, that is, to reduce the amount of data movement where the bandwidth is most limited. Table 2 estimates the bandwidths for three systems. The data in this table is from the cited references along with the Lmbench website (www.bitmover.com/lmbench). It shows that the bandwidth is most restricted between memory and (L2) cache, and that TLB efficiency is of the least concern. Since, as we have shown, an algorithm cannot be both cache- and register-efficient, we choose to optimize for cache-efficiency.

In the following, C is the cache capacity, L is a "blocking parameter", and array indices will be written in the form abc where a and c are $\lg L$ bits long. The algorithm we present is based on two facts:

---

[10]If a cache were virtually-tagged, so that a cache hit didn't involve a TLB lookup, then the buffer could reside in cache. However, large caches in modern processors are physically tagged, making this impossible.

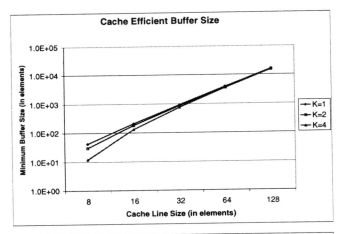

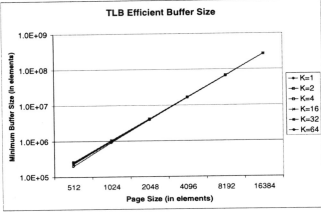

Figure 3. The minimum buffer sizes required for cache- or TLB-efficient algorithm, given various reasonable associativities.

Bandwidth in elements/cycle			
Memory Hierarchy	Power2 66 MHz	Ultrasparc2 300 MHz	Alpha 21164 200 MHz
Mem $\Rightarrow$ TLB	68.27	102.3	81.92
Mem $\Rightarrow$ L2	n.a.	0.20	0.32
Mem/L2 $\Rightarrow$ L1	1.78	1.14	1.00
L1 $\Rightarrow$ Reg	2.00	1.00	2.00

Table 2. Bandwidth (in 4-Byte elements per cycle) of various levels of the memory hierarchy on several architectures.

1. An aligned block of L contiguous elements from the source array, which have indices $abc, ab(c + 1), ab(c + 2), ..., ab(c + L - 1)$, map to destination array positions $c'b'a', (c + 1)'b'a', (c + 2)'b'a', ..., (c + L - 1)'b'a'$.

Note that the destination array positions all have $b'a'$ as the least significant bits and differ only in the most significant bits.

2. Similarly, a block of contiguous destination array positions $abc, ab(c + 1), ab(c + 2), ..., ab(c + L - 1)$ come from source array positions $c'b'a', (c + 1)'b'a', (c + 2)'b'a', ..., (c + L - 1)'b'a'$.

Each of the source array positions all have $b'a'$ as their least significant bits and differ only in the uppermost bits.

Given these two properties, our algorithm (in an attempt to preserve *cache-efficiency*) loads EVERY source block (L source blocks total) that maps to the same set of L destination blocks. This requires two basic steps. (1) We write these L blocks to a contiguous buffer space in cache. (2) We then write this buffer space to the appropriate L destination locations, one cacheline at at a time.

There are two requirements involved in choosing the blocking parameter L, which defines the size of a and c:

- $|a| = |c| \geq \lg L_{cache}$. This rule ensures that we read and write full cachelines.

- $|ac| \leq \lg C$. This rule ensures that the buffer can fit in cache.

In the algorithm of Figure 4, `bitrev()` is a function call, while `bittable[]` is a reference to a small (L-element) look-up table. Notice that the algorithm always accesses the destination and source arrays using unit stride. The buffer, which is completely in cache, has unit stride in the first loop and a constant sized stride in the second loop (minimizing address arithmetic).

3.4.1 TLB Behavior With COBRA

In the previous section we showed that our algorithm for bit-reversal reordering is *cache-efficient*, but we made no explicit mention of TLB performance. And as we saw in the previous section a corresponding *TLB efficient* algorithm is overly ambitious on modern machines due to the storage requirements imposed by it.

Thus while our algorithm is *cache efficient* it is not *TLB efficient*, but the TLB performance is not much worse than the

```
#define ACBITS 6
#define ACSIZE 64
lgn = log(n);
lgdiff = lgn - ACBITS;
stepsize = 1 << lgdiff;
sizeofb = n >> (2*ACBITS);

for(b=0;b<sizeofb;b++) {
    brev = bitrev(b, logn(sizeofb));
    bshift = b << ACBITS;
    brevshift = brev << ACBITS;
    Xpoint = &X[bshift];
    for(a=0;a<SIZE;a++,Xpoint+=stepsize) {
        arev = bittable[a];
        buffpoint = &buffer[arev << ACBITS];
        for(c=0;c <ACSIZE;c+=4) {
            ftemp0 = Xpoint[c];
            ftemp1 = Xpoint[c+1];
            ftemp2 = Xpoint[c+2];
            ftemp3 = Xpoint[c+3];
            buffpoint[c] = ftemp1;
            buffpoint[c+1] = ftemp2;
            buffpoint[c+2] = ftemp3;
            buffpoint[c+3] = ftemp4;
    } }
    for(c=0;c<ACSIZE;c++) {
        Ypoint = &Y[(bittable[c] <<
        (lgnminus)) | brevshift];
        Xpoint = &buffer[c];
        for(arev=0;arev<ACSIZE;
        arev+=8,Xpoint+=(ACSIZE*8)) {
            ftemp0 = Xpoint[0];
            ftemp1 = Xpoint[ACSIZE];
            ftemp2 = Xpoint[2*ACSIZE];
            ftemp3 = Xpoint[3*ACSIZE];
            ftemp4 = Xpoint[4*ACSIZE];
            ftemp5 = Xpoint[5*ACSIZE];
            ftemp6 = Xpoint[6*ACSIZE];
            ftemp7 = Xpoint[7*ACSIZE];
            Ypoint[arev] = ftemp0;
            Ypoint[arev+1] = ftemp1;
            Ypoint[arev+2] = ftemp2;
            Ypoint[arev+3] = ftemp3;
            Ypoint[arev+4] = ftemp4;
            Ypoint[arev+5] = ftemp5;
            Ypoint[arev+6] = ftemp6;
            Ypoint[arev+7] = ftemp7;
} } }
```

Figure 4. Main loop of the COBRA algorithm.

the theoretical best TLB performance for a *cache efficient algorithm* (see Section 5).

In performing a *Murphy reordering* with COBRA, if $|a|$ and $|c|$ are selected such that $|a| = |c|$ and $|ac| = \lg C$ then $|a| = |c| = \frac{\lg C}{2}$. Thus every $\sqrt{C}$ elements we record two TLB misses (one on the source and one from destination array) giving $\frac{\sqrt{C}}{2}$ elements reordered per TLB miss with the COBRA algorithm. [11]

See table 4 for a comparison of efficiencies of the *implemented* COBRA algorithm versus what we analytically predicted COBRA would achieve on various machines.

4 Performance

We implemented and experimented with the COBRA algorithm on three processors, the Digital Alpha 21164 (300MHz) [4] [21], the Sun Ultrasparc 2 (200MHz) [14] and the IBM Power2 (RS6000/590) (66MHz) [22].

The IBM Power2 we used was a single node of an SP2. It has a 4-way set associative 128KByte primary data cache, with cacheline length of 128 bytes. The data cache miss penalty is 18 cycles and it is write-allocate. The TLB has 512 2-way set associative entries, each page being 4KBytes with a 15 cycle miss penalty.

The Sun Ultrasparc 2 has a direct mapped 16KByte L1 data cache, with cachelines consisting of two 16 byte sub-blocks. The L1 data cache is read allocate with a 2 cycle latency with a 6 cycle miss penalty (serviced by L2 cache). L2 cache is off-chip with 47 cycle miss penalty if data must be serviced from main memory. The TLB has 64 fully associative entries with 8KByte pages.

The DEC Alpha 21164 (a single node of a T3E) has a direct mapped 8KByte L1 data cache with each cacheline being 32 bytes. It also has a 3-way set associative 96KByte secondary unified (data plus instruction) cache with each cacheline being 64 bytes.[12] The L1 cache miss (serviced from L2) has a 6 cycles miss penalty and is read-allocate. The L2 cache miss goes to memory (no L3 cache on this machine) and suffers a 80 cycle cache miss penalty and is write-allocate. The TLB has 64 fully-associative entries with each page being 8KB.

The COBRA algorithm, being a cache efficient algorithm, has $E_{cache} = 1.0$. The register efficiency of COBRA is

---

[11]We can actually reorder $\sqrt{\frac{8C}{27}}$ elements per TLB miss with a derivative of COBRA, but this uses a more complex algorithm which, due to added overhead, doesn't improve execution time.

[12]L2 cachelines are programmable as either 32 or 64 bytes.

$E_{reg} = 0.5$ due to the fact that we must store the data into the buffer then load the data back out later. The TLB efficiency of COBRA, as discussed in the previous section, is $E_{TLB} = \frac{2^{|a|}}{L_{TLB}}$.

For COBRA on the Power2 we got the best performance if we let $|a| = |c| = 6$. Thus we are loading two cachelines at a time and it requires a buffer space of 16KB. The Power2 has a much larger cache, but as it turns out little to no improvement is found making $|a|, |c|$ larger since with $|a| = |c| = 6$ the cost of the TLB misses is still amortized out rather effectively.

With Digital Alpha 21164 and Ultrasparc2 we achieved the best performance with $|a| = |c| = 5$. In this case we are loading four cachelines at a time and requires a buffer space of 4KB. For all three architectures we followed $|ac| \leq \frac{\lg C}{2}$. As a general rule of thumb we suggest that this conservative estimate of how large to make the buffer should be followed, since other data will also occupy cache (such as the lookup tables).

From Table 3 we see that COBRA achieves about 5 cycles per element on the Power2 compared to 4 cycles analytically predicted (to analytically predict the runtimes of CO-BRA we used the theorems that will be cited in Section 5 coupled with the heuristic that communication can not be overlapped). The one cycle difference we see as minor and attribute to unaccounted cache misses (due to the bit-reverse lookup table) and program overhead (such as loop overhead and address arithmetic).

On the Digital Alpha 21164 COBRA achieves 19 cycles per element versus the 13 cycles per element predicted. This 6 cycle difference also appears attributable to unaccounted cache misses (this affect is amplified due to the unified L2 cache and the high cost of an L2 cache miss) and program overhead.

On the Ultrasparc2 COBRA gets about 13 cycles per element versus the 12 cycles per element predicted. Again we attribute this minor difference to program overhead.

On all three architectures our algorithm outperformed the *Hybrid* code, which was selected as a benchmark of performance as it was consistently the best or a top performing reordering algorithm in [11]. On the Power2 COBRA outperforms *Hybrid* by nearly a factor of 2 on large arrays, on the 21164 by a factor of 4 on large arrays, and by a factor of 3 on large arrays for the Ultrasparc2. See Table 5.

The algorithm we present moves data from a source array to a distinct destination array. An inplace version (a single array for the source and destination) requires only slight mod-

Efficiency of COBRA		
	Simulated	Predicted
IBM Power2		
L1 Cache	0.99	1.00
TLB	0.06	0.18
DEC Alpha 21164		
L1 Cache	0.78	1.00
L2 Cache	0.99	1.00
TLB	0.02	0.03
Sun Ultrasparc2		
L1 Cache	0.88	1.00
L2 Cache	0.99	1.00
TLB	0.03	0.03

Table 4. The efficiency of various levels of the memory hierarchy, comparing simulations of COBRA using the Acme Cache Simulator, to our analytical predictions of COBRA.

ifications and achieves comparable levels of performance.[13]

5 Near-optimality of COBRA

In our companion paper [6], we prove several theorems that can be used to give a lower bound on the efficiency of Murphy reorderings. They don't give as tight a bound on the buffer size as the theorem of this paper, but they provide lower bounds on the total number of cache misses in a register-efficient algorithm and *vice versa*. In particular, the following are proven:

Theorem 2 *Any register-efficient Murphy reordering of N-element arrays on a computer with R registers and a cache with K-way set associativity must have at least $N/(K + \frac{\sqrt{1+8R}-1}{4})$ cache misses.*

Theorem 3 *Any cache-efficient Murphy reordering of N-element arrays on a computer with R registers, a cache with K-way set associativity, and cache lines of length L has an*
$$E_{reg} \leq \frac{1}{2 - \frac{2K + \frac{\sqrt{1+8R}-1}{2}}{L}}.$$

Theorem 4 *Any cache-efficient Murphy reordering of N-element arrays on a computer where cache and registers have a total capacity of C elements and the TLB of has pages of size L_{TLB} and associativity K_{TLB} has $E_{TLB} \leq \frac{K_{TLB} + \frac{\sqrt{1+8C}-1}{2}}{L_{TLB}}$*

---

[13]In our experience, it outperform the out-of-place version.

-	IBM Power2	Digital Alpha 21164	Sun Ultrasparc 2
-	in cycles/element		
Lower bound for $E_{reg} = 1$ algorithm	6.81	18.09	12.31
Lower bound for $E_{cache} = 1$ algorithm	3.20	13.05	9.06
COBRA predictions	4.03	13.26	10.93
Actual COBRA performance	5.34	19.4	12.8

Table 3. Theoretical lower bound on performance, along with predicted COBRA execution times and the measured execution time. All values are in cycles per element, and are for arrays of 2^{20} elements.

BitReverse on Various Machines in cycles per element											
Algorithm	Size of BitReverse (2^n)										
-	12	13	14	15	16	17	18	19	20	21	22
IBM Power2											
Hybrid	3.49	3.30	3.34	6.46	6.31	6.26	6.48	10.62	10.66	10.35	10.29
COBRA	4.47	4.83	4.80	4.67	4.42	4.29	4.43	4.62	5.34	5.31	5.28
DEC Alpha											
Hybrid	21.6	24.5	43.4	55.9	58.2	58.3	89.5	92.3	93.7	-	-
COBRA	17.9	18.4	18.9	18.5	19.0	19.2	19.4	19.3	19.4	-	-
Sun Ultrasparc2											
Hybrid	8.4	9.4	9.7	9.6	10.4	11.5	22.2	26.2	37.7	38.2	37.0
COBRA	8.2	7.3	6.5	6.5	6.7	8.1	11.4	13.2	12.8	12.9	12.9

Table 5. The performance of computing a BitReversal reordering on the Power2 590, Ultrasparc2, and the Alpha 21164 for COBRA and Karp's Hybrid algorithm. Table entries are the total number of cycles for the entire reordering divided by the number of elements in the BitReversed array.

Using these theorems, we can calculate a lower bound on the theoretically-optimal performance that a register-efficient or a cache-efficient algorithm can achieve. These figures are given in the first two lines in Table 3, along with the actual runtimes. They show that COBRA performs better (on the Power 2) than is possible for any register-efficient algorithm, justifying our choice to focus on cache-efficiency. We also see that COBRA only misses the lower bound for a cache-efficient algorithm by about 50%.

6   Conclusion

In this paper we examined *Murphy reorderings*, a class of array permutations that are especially difficult on associative memory hierarchies. In developing high-performance algorithms for Murphy reorderings, one must optimize for the memory-to-cache bottleneck. Unfortunately, this forces us to have a less than optimal implementation for other levels of the memory hierarchy. This is due to two factors: set-associative caches ill-suited aspect ratios of TLB's. Trade-offs are unavoidable, but with care a good algorithm can still result.

We presented an algorithm (COBRA) based on our insights and showed its performance is near-optimal. We compared COBRA to best prior algorithm and its performance on the IBM Power2, Sun Ultrasparc2, and Digital Alpha 21164 is superior.

As future work, we hope to incorporate COBRA into an FFT program. It has been shown [2] that the four-step FFT [3] runs in O(N lg N lg lg N) on the PMH model of computation due to the transposes data reorderings that are done. However, there is an O(N lg N) algorithm on that model, which requires a fast bit-reversal. We hope this theoretical difference will translate to observable increased performance.

7   Acknowledgements

We would like to thank Alan Karp for supplying us the source code of the *Hybrid* algorithm.

References

[1] A. Aggarwal, A. Chandra, and M. Snir. Hierarchical memory with block transfer. In *Proc. of 28th Symposium on Foundations of Comp. Sci.*, pages 204–216, Oct. 1987.

[2] B. Alpern, L. Carter, E. Feig, and T. Selker. The uniform memory hierarchy model of computation. *Algorithmica*, 12(2-3), August-September 1994.

[3] D. Bailey. Ffts in external or hierarchical memory. *The Journal of Supercomputing*, 4:23–35, 1990.

[4] B. Benschneider. An overview of the alpha axp 21164 microprocessor. In *Proc. of 38th Midwest Symposium on Circuits and Systems*, volume 2, pages 1131–4, Rio de Janeiro, Brazil, Aug. 1995.

[5] B. Bershad, D. Lee, T. Romer, and B. Chen. Avoiding conflict misses dynamically in large direct-mapped caches. In *Proc. of ASPLOS-VI*, San Jose, Oct. 1994.

[6] L. Carter and K. Gatlin. Towards an optimal bit-reversal permutation program. In *Proc.of FOCS '98*, Nov. 1998.

[7] R. Floyd. Permuting information in idealized two-level storage. *Complexity of Computer Computations*, pages 105–109, 1972.

[8] J.-W. Hong and H. Kung. I/o complexity: The red-blue pebble game. In *Proc. of 13th. Symposium on Theory of Comp.*, May 1981.

[9] J. Johnson and R. Johnson. Challenges of computing the fast fourier transform. In *DARPA Conference*, June 1997.

[10] N. Jouppi. Improving direct-mapped cache performance by the addition of a small fully-associative cache and prefetch buffers. In *Proc. of 17th International Symposium on Computer Architure*, Seattle, May 1990.

[11] A. Karp. Bit reversals on uniprocessors. *SIAM Review*, 38(1):1–26, Mar. 1996.

[12] M. Lam, E. E. Rothberg, and M. E. Wolf. The cache performance of blocked algorithms. In *ASPLOS-IV*, Apr. 1991.

[13] R. A. J. Matthews. The science of murphy's law. *Scientific American*, Apr. 1997.

[14] S. Microsystems. The ultrasparc processor – technology white paper. http://www.cs.wisc.edu/mscalar/simplescalar.html.

[15] N. Mitchell, L. Carter, and J. Ferrante. A compiler perspective on architectural evolution. In *Workshop on Interation Between Compilers and Computer Architecture*, Feb. 1997.

[16] D. A. Patterson and J. L. Hennessey. *Computer Architecture A Quantitative Approach*. Morgan Kaufmann, San Mateo, 1990.

[17] G. Rivera and C. Tseng. Eliminating conflict misses for high performance architectures. In *Proc. of ICS '98*, Melbourne, Australia, July 1998.

[18] J. Savage. Extending the hong-kung model to memory hierarchies. In *Proceedings from COCONN '95*, volume LNCS 959, pages 270–281, Springer Verlag, 1995.

[19] P. Swarztrauber. Fft algorithms for vector computers. *Parallel Computing*, 1:45–63, 1984.

[20] O. Teman, E. D. Granston, and W. Jalby. To copy or not to copy: A compile-time technique for assessing when data copying should be used to eliminate cache conflicts. In *Proc. of SuperComputing '93*, Nov. 1993.

[21] C. Weib. Dec alpha hardware overview. http://wwwbode.informatik.tu-muenchen.de/Par/arch/cache/rb2d/dec.html.

[22] S. White and S. Dhawan. Power2: The next generation of the risc system/6000 family. *PowerPC and POWER2: Technical Aspects of the New IBM RISC System/6000*, IBM SA23-2737, 1994.

Session 2

Simultaneous Multithreading

Instruction Recycling on a Multiple-Path Processor

Steven Wallace   Dean M. Tullsen   Brad Calder

Department of Computer Science and Engineering
University of California, San Diego
{swallace,tullsen,calder}@cs.ucsd.edu

Abstract

Processors that can simultaneously execute multiple paths of execution will only exacerbate the fetch bandwidth problem already plaguing conventional processors. On a multiple-path processor, which speculatively executes less likely paths of hard-to-predict branches, the work done along a speculative path is normally discarded if that path is found to be incorrect. Instead, it can be beneficial to keep these instruction traces stored in the processor for possible future use.

This paper introduces instruction recycling, *where previously decoded instructions from recently executed paths are injected back into the rename stage. This increases the supply of instructions to the execution pipeline and decreases fetch latency. In addition, if the operands have not changed for a recycled instruction, the instruction can bypass the issue and execution stages, benefiting from* instruction reuse. *Instruction recycling and reuse are examined for a simultaneous multithreading architecture with multiple path execution. It is shown to increase performance by 7% for single-program workloads and by 12% on multiple-program workloads.*

1 Introduction

Modern processors spend much of their time doing repetitious tasks — fetching the same instructions and executing them over and over again, sometimes even with the same operand values. This is true of speculative processors, which may execute an instruction down a speculative path, throw it away, and execute the same instruction down the correct path which has merged with the previous incorrect path. This is even more evident in processors capable of executing along multiple speculative paths [17, 5, 16, 7, 1, 18], where the same instantiation of an instruction may be executed by several threads or virtual processors. The fetch unit is highly repetitious on any iterative task, even on a non-speculative processor; but much more so on a multiple-path processor.

Modern processors exploit these recurrent instructions via caches; the instruction cache avoids memory access by the fetch unit, and the data cache saves the data for re-executed loads with the same address. However, all other stages of execution are repeated, even if the inputs of an instruction are unchanged. This paper examines a technique for recycling previously-fetched instructions back through the processor, saving fetch and decode bandwidth in the worst case, and execution resources and latency in the best case. Recycled instructions can augment the instructions coming through the normal fetch path, which is typically hampered by branch and cache line boundary fetch limitations. This increases the bandwidth of instructions into the machine in three ways. It increases the raw bandwidth into the processor by merging recycled instructions with fetched instructions. It increases fetch parallelism, as instructions from more contexts can be introduced into the machine in a single cycle. Third, recycled instructions re-enter the processor in the form of a trace, bypassing branch and cache line boundaries.

Although many of the techniques examined in this paper will also work for more conventional speculative processors, we study them within the context of a multiple-path processor. These techniques apply to most of the multiple-path architectures recently proposed, but our baseline architecture is derived from our Threaded Multipath Execution (TME) architecture described in [18]. A TME processor uses idle hardware contexts on a simultaneous multithreading (SMT) [14, 15] processor to execute down both paths at conditional branch points, potentially eliminating the branch misprediction penalty. Our study [18] showed that performance can be increased by creating threads in hardware to execute instructions down both paths of certain hard-to-predict conditional branches. TME differs from other multiple-path architectures by also allowing multiple programs to be sharing the processor via SMT.

Other techniques that have been proposed to preserve instruction cache and execution bandwidth are the Trace Cache [10] and the Reuse Buffer [12]. The Trace Cache only bypasses the instruction cache, as all instructions still use all pipeline stages, including fetch. The Reuse Buffer does not bypass the fetch unit, but does bypass the execution stages for instructions whose operands have not changed.

Unlike those mechanisms, we modify existing structures to enable recycling, which minimizes the cost of additional storage. We recycle the instructions directly from the active lists (similar to a reorder buffer) in the TME architecture. In addition, we examine recycling in an environment (multiple-path execution) where the incidence of redundant fetch and execution is much higher than traditional single-thread processors.

Instruction recycling and reuse increase single-program performance over TME by 7% on average. With multiple programs running, where TME has been shown to be less effective, recycling and reuse achieve a 12% increase (for four programs running on an eight-context processor) by easing the contention for fetch resources.

This paper is organized as follows. We describe the multiple-path architecture on which this research is based in Section 2. The additional hardware to permit instruction recycling is given in Section 3. Our evaluation methodology is described in Section 4, and Section 5 presents our performance results for a number of different architectural alternatives. Section 6 describes related research, and Section 7 summarizes our results.

2 Threaded Multiple Path Execution

A simultaneous multithreading processor allows multiple threads of execution to issue instructions to the functional units each cycle. This can provide significantly higher processor utilization than conventional superscalar processors or traditional multithreaded processors, which also use multiple hardware contexts (program counters, registers) to boost throughput and latency-tolerance. The ability to combine instructions from multiple threads in the same cycle allows simultaneous multithreading to not only hide latencies, but also to more fully utilize the issue width of a wide superscalar processor.

Threaded multi-path execution extends SMT by using unused contexts to execute both paths of conditional branches. As a result, the processor resources can be more fully utilized, and the probability of executing the correct path is increased. By executing both paths of the branch, TME can eliminate the branch misprediction penalties for hard to predict branches [18].

The register renaming and mapping hardware of an SMT/TME processor is particularly relevant to this discussion. Register renaming takes place via a register mapping scheme (similar to the MIPS R10000 [19]) extended for simultaneous multithreading and TME as shown in Figure 1. Each instruction that writes a register removes a physical register from the free list and writes a new mapping to the mapping table. When that instruction commits from the end of an active list, it frees the physical register used by the previous mapping. Each context has its own active list so that

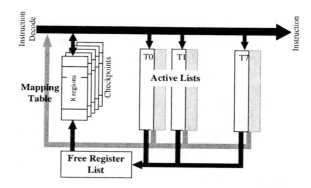

Figure 1: The register mapping scheme for an SMT/TME processor (black data paths), with additions to support recycling (gray paths).

instructions can commit independent of the progress of other threads.

Each context also requires its own mapping region to translate its own set of logical registers, so the mapping table of an 8-context SMT/TME processor has 8 mapping regions as shown in Figure 1. Mapping tables in existing processors are shadowed by *checkpoints*, which are snapshots of the table taken when a branch was encountered. The active list in a conventional processor contains the physical register mapping that will be freed if this instruction retires. In the SMT/TME processor, the active list also contains that instruction's new mapping, which will be freed if the instruction gets squashed. This is necessary because instructions in different threads get squashed independently.

The following terms are used to describe the behavior of the TME architecture: *Primary-path thread* — the thread that has taken the predicted path through the code; *alternate-path thread* — a thread that is executing an unpredicted path through the code; *idle context* — a context that is not executing any thread; *spare context* — a context that is partitioned to a primary thread to be used for alternate path execution; *fork a branch* — take both paths of a branch; *spawn a thread* — create an alternate-path thread.

To effectively follow both paths of a single branch, we must be able to quickly duplicate the register state of the executing context to an idle context. A TME processor has a single shared physical register file, so we can duplicate register state simply by duplicating the first context's register map. The TME architecture does this via the *Mapping Synchronization Bus* (MSB) [18]. The MSB partitions the register map into groups of contexts. Each group includes one primary thread and zero to seven alternate contexts available to spawn alternate paths. All idle threads within a partition are kept in sync with the primary thread using the MSB, so that they are available for spawning immediately.

TME only spawns alternate threads off of branches in the primary thread. Candidate branches are selected based on branch confidence prediction methods [6]. When a branch that spawned an alternate path is found to be mispredicted, the alternate path thread becomes the primary thread, and all idle threads use the MSB to re-synchronize with the new primary thread. See [18] for a complete description of TME.

Results in [18] show that (1) TME achieved significant speedups when a single (low branch accuracy) program was running, (2) TME does not degrade the performance of SMT when multiple programs are running, and (3) TME provides the most benefit for programs with low branch prediction accuracy. It does not degrade the performance of programs with high branch prediction accuracy, because branch confidence controls the spawning of alternate paths.

TME provides performance advantage when there are idle resources, but it provides diminishing returns in performance as more primary threads (programs or software threads) are executed. In this situation, there is insufficient fetch bandwidth to adequately serve all primary and alternate paths, so the latter starve.

3 Hardware Support for Instruction Recycling

The active lists on a TME processor already contain predicted traces of fetched instructions. In this section, we show how these traces can be exploited by recycling them into the processor to provide higher instruction bandwidth. Recycling saves fetch bandwidth, bypasses fetch limitations (branches and cache lines), and can allow the reuse of instruction values to eliminate instruction latencies.

To enable instruction recycling and reuse, we need to (1) preserve instruction information in the processor and keep it around as long as possible, (2) detect when a thread should stop fetching and begin gathering instructions through recycling, (3) have a mechanism for identifying instructions that need not be re-executed, and (4) have additional datapaths to reinsert instructions back into the processor. In Figure 1, the gray regions represent additions to the register renaming architecture of a TME processor to support instruction recycling. These include additional information stored in the active list to reconstruct each instruction (this includes the decoded opcode and physical and logical register operands) and a new datapath from the active lists to the rename path to inject those instructions back into the processor.

3.1 Managing Spare Contexts to Maximize Recycling Availability

In TME, a spawned path is always squashed (i.e., active list cleared, register mappings freed) as soon as a correctly predicted branch is resolved. However, with recycling, we want to delay the squashing of alternate-path threads as long as possible to maximize the opportunity to recycle instructions. In the recycle architecture, a context can be either active or inactive. An *active* context is currently executing either the primary or an alternate path. An *inactive* context has finished executing, but the active list and registers have not been freed, making it available for recycling. We will only see *idle* contexts (not available for recycling) at startup. Normally, contexts will be kept inactive until just before they are reclaimed for TME spawning.

In the TME/Recycle architecture, a primary path has a number of spare contexts associated with it for executing alternate paths. When a correctly-predicted branch is resolved, the corresponding alternate thread (if there is one) stops executing, but it is not squashed, allowing the architecture to use the instructions for recycling — the thread becomes inactive. The current register map of the newly inactive thread is then checkpointed, and the mapping is resynchronized with the primary path. The re-synchronization allows the spare context to be spawned for TME immediately when another low confidence branch is encountered. Upon encountering a low-confidence branch, the architecture identifies the least-recently-used inactive context and reclaims it, squashing the instructions in the active list and freeing the registers.

Under TME, we can have several alternate paths that start at the same instruction, corresponding to various instantiations of the same low-confidence branch. We would like to minimize this duplication. We would rather preserve contexts to fork other branches, creating more unique starting points for recycling. Therefore, instead of creating many alternate paths with the same start point, we can *re-spawn* the existing inactive context, when one already exists with that start address. Re-spawning re-executes the instructions in the inactive thread through the *recycling* data paths, making it active again. Since recycling is used to provide the initial instructions down the alternative path, fetch bandwidth is saved when re-spawning. Therefore, re-spawning maintains the benefits of TME, but with much less contention for fetch resources compared to regular TME.

3.2 Identifying Merge Points

To determine when instructions from a context can be recycled, we need to identify *merge points*, where the current path has merged with another path that is available for recycling. In particular, we want to determine when the primary (most likely) path has merged with another path (that may or may not still be active). Most often, the merge point is the first instruction of the alternate context. For example, if the alternate path begins at a branch target because the primary path predicted the branch not taken, the paths will most likely merge in the future when the branch is later taken (or predicted taken).

To identify merge points the program counter (PC) of the first instruction in the active list is stored with each hardware context. The current PC that is used to fetch instructions for the primary path is used to search the merge PCs of its spare contexts and its own hardware context for a match. If a match is found with an alternate path thread, subsequent instructions will come from the alternate active list once the prior fetched instructions for that thread have cleared the rename stage. If a match is found with the primary path hardware context, we will be recycling instructions from the primary path thread, back into its own active list. The recycling frees the fetch unit to begin fetching from other threads, or perhaps even further downstream for the same thread.

Since backward branches are common from loops in programs, we also record the target address of the *last* backwards branch for each context. It is searched along with the first PC as a possible merge point. These are the only two possible merge points for a particular context that we consider. If another backwards branch is detected, it overwrites the previous backward branch merge point. Also, if an instruction is inserted into the active list which overwrites the first instruction of a backwards branch merge point, then the merge point is invalidated. Hence, only loops smaller than the current active lists are able to benefit from the backward branch recycling.

3.3 Recycled Datapath

To enable recycling, an extra datapath is needed from the active lists back through the renaming logic to be able to reintroduce this data into the pipeline. A recycled instruction is read from the originating active list, makes a new pass through register renaming, writes into a (potentially different) active list, and (if not marked for reuse) into the instruction queue for execution. Recycled instructions, at a minimum, bypass the fetch and decode stages (Figure 2). Reused instructions can bypass the queue and execution (and surrounding) stages as well.

Instructions which are recycled and instructions which are fetched and decoded need to be merged in the rename stage. We give highest priority to instructions from the fetched paths, filling in empty slots with recycled instructions. The only constraint is that program order is maintained for a thread that has instructions from both sources, which may involve blocking instructions either trying to recycle or coming from the decode stage.

Instruction fetch priority of a thread is determined by the number of instructions in the pipeline. This is identical to the ICOUNT fetch scheme used by Tullsen, et al. [14] (with the same modifications for TME recommended in [18]), except when instructions are recycled. In this case, the number of instructions recycled is added immediately to the instruction counter used for fetching priority. When multiple threads want to recycle, a separate instruction counter is used to determine the priority of those threads for insertion into the rename stage. This counter uses the number of instructions in the rename and queue stages only.

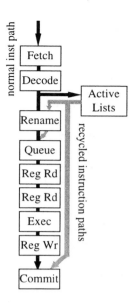

Figure 2: Instruction recycling allows instructions to bypass parts of the processor pipeline.

We assume no expansion of the rename stage to accommodate the two paths, which is 16 instructions wide in the processor we simulate.

3.4 Recycling Instructions

When a merge point is detected, the processor begins recycling instructions from the corresponding active list. Fetching immediately continues from where recycling will complete. This is enabled by saving the PC of the instruction after the last instruction in the active list, which will become the new fetch target. The branch prediction previously used for the recycled instructions can be used. The global history register used for branch prediction is then updated with that prediction. Alternatively, when the instructions are read from the active list, if the branch prediction differs, recycling can stop and fetching continues on the newly predicted path. For this paper, we use the latter method. The former method still requires one more branch prediction per cycle than normal SMT/TME, because in the event that the predicted fetch point for a thread is a merge point, we would like to be prepared to use the fetch opportunity for other threads that cycle. The latter method requires even higher prediction throughput and should be considered an aggressive approach.

Each cycle, when the primary thread prepares to fetch, it will compare its fetch PC (and following addresses) with the merge points of itself and its alternate contexts. Also, each thread that fetches will also compare its PC with its own backward-branch merge point. If the match is on the initial PC, then there is no need to fetch from the instruction cache for this thread, and another thread is sought for fetching. In the case a match is found in the middle of a fetch block, instructions are fetched up to the matching instruction, and recycling begins after it.

3.5 Instruction Reuse

For some recycled instructions, execution can also be by-passed. If none of the operands of a recycled instruction have been changed, and the instruction was actually executed, the old computed value can be *reused* [12]. We accomplish this by re-using the old register mapping (writing it into the new mapping table entry) instead of re-mapping the instruction. Subsequent instructions, either fetched or recycled, then use the value already in the register. Reuse for backward branch recycling is not allowed, given the way we track register changes for re-use detection. Reuse is only allowed for alternate to primary thread recycling.

Instructions can be reused more than once, but this complicates register and context reclaiming — in particular, we need to ensure we do not free a register (by squashing a context in preparation for spawning) which another context is still accessing due to re-use of the register mapping. We do not free the registers used by a recyclable active list until (1) TME wants to use the context to spawn a new path, and (2) all other reuses of instructions in this path by the primary path have completed. To implement this, we assume each alternate path keeps track of the last reuse by its primary path. When the primary path commits a result, it checks to see if it is the last reuse among alternate paths and clears any matches. Then the alternate path will be able to free all its registers when it is used again to fork off a low-confidence branch.

In order to determine if a register has changed since an instruction was executed, a new structure is introduced. A *written* bit-array of contexts indexed by logical registers is used. When a new path is started on a context, the column of register bits for that context is reset. When the *primary* context makes a new instance of a register, then the row of context bits for that register is set. As a result, when an operand of a recycled instruction is checked during the renaming, the corresponding bit for that register and context is looked up in the array. If it is reset, then it has not been changed. If it is set, then it has been changed and the instruction cannot be reused.

We assume that load operations can be reused if the source register, and thus the address, has not been changed and there are no intervening stores to the same address. A Memory Disambiguation Buffer (MDB) can be used to keep track of loads whose values can be reused. The MDB provides hardware support to determine if a load instruction's address has been overwritten since the last time the load was executed. The MDB is used to store the load PC and the effective addresses. When subsequent stores are executed, it searches the MDB for its effective address. If the store finds its address in the MDB, the load PC and address are removed from the MDB. When recycling the load PC, if it is still located in the MDB, then we can reuse its value. Otherwise, the load has to be re-executed.

4 Evaluation Methods

All of our results are obtained using execution-driven simulation of a multiple-thread processor running Alpha executables. The simulator models a simultaneous multithreading processor extended for threaded multipath execution and recycling, as described in Section 3. Instruction latencies are based on the DEC Alpha 21264.

Our workload consists of eight of the SPEC95 benchmarks. Six of the programs are integer benchmarks (compress, gcc, go, lisp, perl, and vortex) and two are floating point (su2cor and tomcatv). Although most of the SPEC95 floating point programs do not benefit from TME due to high branch prediction accuracy, there is potential for benefit from recycling due to primary-path to primary-path recycling. All of the benchmarks were compiled with the DEC cc (version 5.2) and f77 (version 4.1) compilers with full optimization (-O5 -om).

We will look at recycling both with single-thread workloads and multiple-thread workloads (multiple single-thread applications running simultaneously). For the multi-thread workloads, the results shown consist of the average of eight permutations of the benchmarks that weight each of the benchmarks evenly in the results.

4.1 Baseline Architecture Model

We evaluate instruction recycling in the context of a future-generation 16-wide SMT/TME processor with 8 hardware contexts. It has the ability to fetch eight sequential instructions from each of two different threads each cycle. Those instructions, after decoding and register renaming, find their way to one of two 64-entry instruction queues. Instructions are issued to the functional units (6 floating point, 12 integer, 8 of which also can do load-store operations) when their register operands are ready. This is an aggressive design, but exposes many of the problems future processors will exhibit. We also examine more conservative architectures in Section 5.3.

The simulated memory hierarchy has 64KB direct-mapped instruction and data caches, a 256 KB 4-way set-associative on-chip L2 cache, and a 4 MB off-chip cache. Cache line sizes are all 64 bytes. The on-chip caches are all 8-way banked. Throughput as well as latency constraints are carefully modeled at all levels of the memory hierarchy. Conflict-free miss penalties are 6 cycles to the L2 cache, another 12 cycles to the L3 cache, and another 62 cycles to memory.

Branch prediction is provided by a decoupled branch target buffer (BTB) and pattern history table (PHT) scheme [2].

We use a 256-entry BTB, organized as four-way set associative. The 2K x 2-bit PHT is accessed by the XOR of the lower bits of the address and the global history register [9, 20]. Return destinations are predicted with a 12-entry return stack (per context).

The assumed processor has a 9-stage pipeline, with a minimum 7-cycle branch misprediction penalty. We assume each register file (fp and integer) has enough registers to store the logical registers of the eight contexts (when all eight contexts are being used), plus 100 more for register renaming. This is the same number used in many previous SMT studies, even though recycling (and the larger machine) puts additional pressure on the renaming registers.

5 Results

This section examines the performance of instruction recycling and reuse, examines policies for fetch and execution after a context becomes inactive, and considers the effectiveness of recycling techniques on some alternate architectures.

5.1 Recycling, Reusing and Respawning

The baseline instruction recycling architecture extends the previously described SMT/TME architecture by saving executed instructions in the active list even after the thread becomes inactive, and enables their injection into the architecture. This eliminates refetching and in some cases reexecution of the instruction, and significantly increases fetch bandwidth.

Figures 3 and 4 show the performance for the default SMT and TME architectures and recycling with and without re-spawning and reuse. The architectural parameters shown are as follows:

- **SMT** This is the base simultaneous multithreading architecture. It can only exploit inter-thread parallelism when there are multiple threads running.

- **TME** Threaded multiple-path execution can exploit parallelism between multiple paths in the same instruction stream, but puts high demand on the fetch and execution units for the occasional benefit of a mispredicted branch. The rest of the results all include TME and one or more of the following optimizations.

- **REC** Recycling. Instructions from alternate paths, inactive threads, or even the primary thread, can be merged at the rename stage with fetched instructions. (This does not include the Reuse and Re-spawn options.)

- **RU** Reuse. Recycled instructions from inactive threads whose operands are unchanged are not dispatched to the instruction queue. Rather, the old result is reused.

- **RS** Re-spawning of identical paths. The REC result suffers from the design decision to not spawn threads with an identical start address as an existing alternate or inactive thread. This increases the number of unique merge points available for recycling, but decreases opportunities for TME. The RS architecture re-spawns an inactive thread that matches the start address of a path TME wants to spawn. But it is re-spawned via recycling, without consuming fetch bandwidth.

In single-program execution, recycling is effective any time TME is effective, although in one case recycling alone (without reuse) actually under-performs TME (compress). That is also the program where we get the largest benefit from reuse. Reuse, on average, increases performance by about 2%. Re-spawning provides speedup in about half of the applications (about 2% increase on average over REC). The best combination (REC/RS/RU) had an average 7% improvement over TME.

For multiple programs, the benefits of recycling go up significantly, just as the benefits of TME (over SMT) are dropping. With multiple programs, competition for the fetch unit is high, rendering TME ineffective while magnifying the importance of fetch-conservation through recycling. Instruction reuse is not as important, only increasing performance by about half a percent on average. Re-spawning still provides a 2% increase in performance. With the best configuration, performance is improved by 12% over normal TME with four programs running.

Table 1 lists recycling statistics. The first two columns show the percentage of all instructions (including squashed ones) inserted into the rename stage that were recycled and reused, respectively. *Branch Miss Cov* gives the percentage of mispredicted branches that were successfully covered by speculatively forking. The next three columns give the percentage of forked paths used successfully by TME, recycled, or respawned at least once, relative to the total number of branches forked. *Merges Per Alt Path* gives the average number of merges from a given recycled alternate path before it was deleted (this does not include backward branch merges). Finally, *Back Merges* is the percentage of all merges that were from backward branches.

From Table 1 we can see that the level of recycling is generally very high. 17-61% (average of 33% for one thread) of all forked (spawned) paths are used for recycling, and 9-56% (average, 27% for one thread) of instructions introduced into the machine come from recycling. 6% of instructions introduced into the machine are actually reused. As the number of programs increases, reliance on alternate to primary recycling and reuse goes down, while reliance on primary to primary backward branch recycling goes up. This is due to a decrease in the number of alternate contexts available to hold

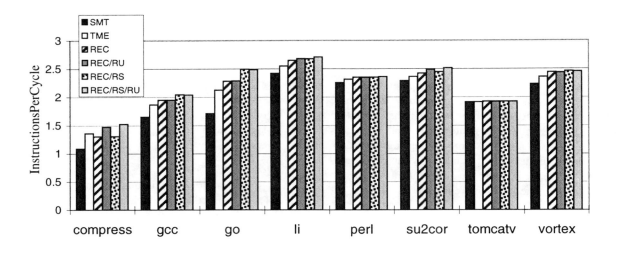

Figure 3: Performance of recycling with reuse and respawning for individual programs.

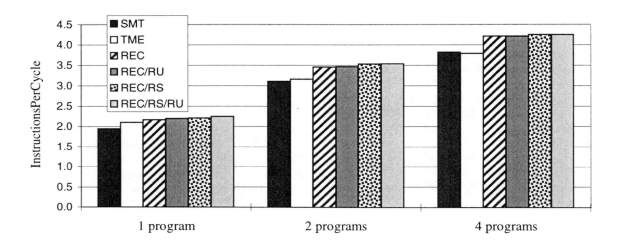

Figure 4: Average Performance of Recycling with Reuse and Respawning when running 1, 2 and 4 programs at once.

recyclable instructions per program, and explains the lower importance of reuse with multiple programs in Figure 4.

In addition, TME still does a good job at covering mispredicted branch paths with an average coverage of 67% for four program and 72% for single program results.

5.2 Recycling Fetch Limits

With recycling, instructions can be useful even after the branch is resolved that identifies the instructions as on the wrong-path. That may even be true for instructions that have not been fetched or executed yet along this path. We examine continuing fetch and/or execution after the path becomes inactive, up to various cutoff points (in total number of instructions). The danger in stopping immediately is that a context

with just one or two instructions does not have enough instructions to enable effective recycling, yet that context can inhibit future spawning of threads. The danger in fetching too long is that we occupy fetch bandwidth for instructions that may have a low likelihood of being used.

Figure 5 shows results for the following policies:

- stop 8, 16, 32 — stop immediately when the branch is resolved and the context becomes inactive. In addition, it does not allow TME to ever follow an alternate path for more than 8, 16, or 32 instructions.

- fetch 8, 16, 32 — do not issue any more instructions for execution after branch resolution, but continue fetching up to the total 8, 16, or 32 instruction limit.

| Program | % Instrs | | % Branch Miss Cov | % Forks | | | Merges Per Alt Path | % Back Merges |
	Recycle	Reuse		TME	Recyc	Respawn		
compress	55.9	14.2	66.5	18.3	61.1	25.8	1.9	57.3
gcc	22.4	7.8	80.1	17.1	28.4	4.4	1.6	35.2
go	24.3	10.3	84.6	20.3	26.7	3.5	1.5	41.1
li	31.9	5.7	81.8	19.9	41.0	12.6	2.3	47.5
perl	9.0	1.4	92.4	11.3	17.2	3.8	1.8	76.1
su2cor	32.0	4.2	78.5	11.9	34.7	8.8	1.9	41.9
tomcatv	25.1	0.5	3.5	0.4	28.7	17.9	1.2	17.8
vortex	13.7	3.8	85.2	22.3	22.0	3.7	1.7	35.5
1 prog avg	26.8	6.0	71.6	15.2	32.5	10.1	1.7	44.1
2 progs avg	24.5	4.7	77.5	20.4	26.1	4.2	1.5	57.2
4 progs avg	22.0	2.6	66.6	29.1	13.2	0.9	1.1	80.4

Table 1: Recycling Statistics

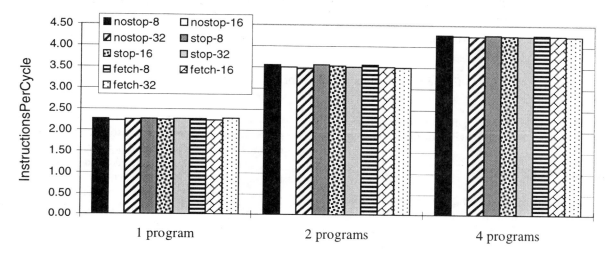

Figure 5: Effects of different recycling fetch limits.

- nostop 8, 16, 32 — continue fetching up to a total of 8 to 32 instructions, and send all of those instructions to the instruction queue to be scheduled for execution.

Although the results indicate this is not a major performance factor, a fetch limit of 8 instructions for an alternate thread achieves some performance gain over fetching more. Most of the performance savings appears to be achieved in the first block of instructions and fetching more blocks results in using too much fetch bandwidth relative to the return received. Stopping immediately after resolution worked well for most programs; however, the results indicate that all of the policies provide acceptable performance.

5.3 Performance for Limited Resource Architectures

Our architecture has assumed an aggressive processor which can fetch 16 instructions from 2 threads each cycle and execute as many as 18 in a cycle. We now examine the performance of recycling, respawning and reuse (we'll call the combination recycling for brevity) with three less aggressive

architectures. We will examine three new processor design points. We will look at the same 18 functional-unit processor, but with reduced fetch bandwidth, allowing only one thread to fetch up to eight consecutive instructions per cycle (this is the big.1.8 result, the baseline is big.2.16). We will also look at two machines about half the size (with half the functional units and half the cache and instruction queue sizes as our baseline processor) and the eight-instruction fetch bandwidth filled by one (the small.1.8 result) or two threads (the small.2.8 result). These machines correspond closely to the processors in [14, 18].

For multiple programs, recycling improves performance over TME and SMT for all architecture configurations. Recycling supplies the larger architecture with primary and alternate instructions effectively and it greatly benefits from the additional instructions. For the smaller architecture, recycling improves the performance of 1.8 fetching so that a more complicated 2.8 fetching mechanism becomes less necessary.

While recycling is effective for all of these architectures, it is most effective when the fetch unit is least able to fill

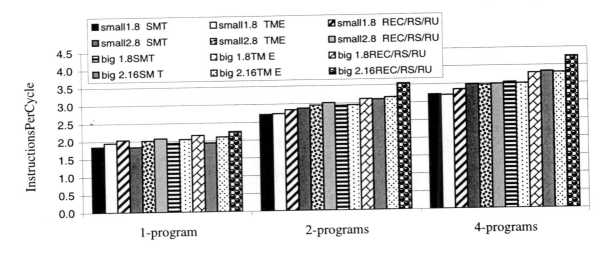

Figure 6: Instruction recycling for different fetch bandwidths.

the fetch bandwidth — the 1.8 fetch scheme for the small machine, and the 2.16 fetch scheme for the big machine.

6   Related Work

There have been several studies describing architectures that can follow multiple paths through execution concurrently [17, 5, 16, 7, 1, 18]. All of these multiple path architectures create a scenario of high redundancy in the processor, which can be exploited with instruction recycling.

The Speculative Multithreaded (SM) processor [8], and the Multiscalar processor [13] are two speculative architectures that allow aggressive loop-based speculation. If all the hardware contexts are executing similar paths in the loop, these architectures could benefit from instruction recycling. The Speculative Multithreaded processor can take advantage of this in its fetch scheme, since each thread context has its own rename stage. In SM, only one thread context is allowed to fetch from the cache at a time, but the instructions are broadcast to all the thread contexts. Therefore, if other contexts are waiting on the same instructions they will also benefit from the fetch.

In our TME/Recycle architecture, we use the active lists as small caches of instruction traces. This provides a similar effect to a trace cache [10]. A trace cache collects traces of instructions, allowing those instructions to be placed in the processor at a higher rate than they can be fetched from the instruction cache, fetching multiple basic blocks per cycle. However, there are key differences between the recycling architecture and trace caches. The trace cache design does not allow the trace-path instructions and the instruction-cache path instructions to be introduced into the machine in the same cycle — in a multithreaded environment, recycling benefits from the increased parallelism of bringing instruc-

tions from multiple sources and multiple threads into the processor in a single cycle. Also, the recycling architecture requires much less additional hardware storage than a large trace cache, both because it takes advantage of some data that is already in the active list, but also because we only keep a few traces that prove to be beneficial (those that are not used are quickly reclaimed). The recycling architecture is also unique in its ability to construct useful traces along paths not yet (or not recently) taken.

Smotherman and Franklin [11] propose a decoded instruction cache to address the complexity of decoding CISC instructions. That cache can operate as a trace cache, holding non-contiguous instructions, but also can reduce the fetch latency when it hits, like recycling. Our proposed recycling architecture differs from that work in all the aspects listed in the previous paragraph.

Sodani and Sohi [12] use the reuse buffer to identify instructions which do not need to be re-executed because their operands have not changed. Our technique for identifying instructions that can be reused is similar to their S_n technique. In fact, their approach to reuse is more general than the one examined in our paper, and may provide a higher rate of reuse in some cases, but at a cost of more specialized hardware to store values. Their scheme concentrates on reuse and does not seek to reduce fetch bandwidth. We are also examining reuse in the context of a very different architecture, one that aggressively executes down low confidence paths, providing higher opportunities for reuse.

The Memory Disambiguation Buffer we describe to record which load values can be reused is similar to the Memory Conflict Buffer (MCB) proposed by Gallagher et. al. [4]. The MCB provides a hardware solution with compiler support to allow load instructions to speculatively execute before stores. The addresses of speculative loads are stored with a conflict bit in the MCB. All potentially ambiguous stores probe the MCB and set the conflict bit if the store address matches the address of a speculative load. Another approach for memory disambiguation was proposed by Franklin and Sohi [3], called the Address Resolution Buffer (ARB). The ARB directs memory references to bins based on their address and uses the bins to enforce a temporal order among references to the same address.

7 Summary

This paper presents a new architecture to enable instruction recycling and reuse. We examine the performance of this new approach in the presence of threaded multiple path execution and simultaneous multithreading. The TME architecture naturally creates traces of instructions that can be moved, through recycling, at high rates and low latency back into execution. Instruction re-use increases the gain by bypassing nearly the entire pipeline for instructions whose operands have not changed. Thread re-spawning allows multiple-path execution to rely more heavily on recycling for creating alternate paths. This greatly reduces the contention for fetch bandwidth that previously rendered TME ineffective with multiple programs.

The results show that instruction recycling achieves an average 11% improvement over SMT and an average 7% improvement over TME when there is one primary thread. With multiple primary threads, instruction recycling achieves an average improvement of 12%. We found that conservative approaches to TME and recycling, stopping after 8 instructions down an alternate or inactive path, perform very well. We also show that recycling is effective on a variety of architectures, from 8-wide to 16-wide.

Acknowledgments

We would like to thank the anonymous reviewers for their useful comments. This work was funded in part by NSF grant No. CCR-980869, NSF CAREER grants No. CCR-9733278 and No. MIP-9701708, and a Digital Equipment Corporation external research grant No. US-0040-97.

References

[1] P.S. Ahuja, K. Skadron, M. Martonosi, and D.W. Clark. Multi-path execution: Opportunities and limits. In *International Conference on Supercomputing*, July 1998.

[2] B. Calder and D. Grunwald. Fast and accurate instruction fetch and branch prediction. In *21st Annual International Symposium on Computer Architecture*, pages 2–11, April 1994.

[3] M. Franklin and G. S. Sohi. ARB: A hardware mechanism for dynamic reordering of memory references. *IEEE Transactions on Computers*, 46(5), May 1996.

[4] D.M. Gallagher, W.Y. Chen, S.A. Mahlke, J.C. Gyllenhaal, and W.W. Hwu. Dynamic memory disambiguation using the memory conflict buffer. In *Sixth International Conference on Architectural Support for Programming Languages and Operating Systems*, 1994.

[5] T.H. Heil and J.E. Smith. Selective dual path execution. Technical Report http://www.engr.wisc.edu/ece/faculty/smith_james.html, University of Wisconsin - Madison, November 1996.

[6] E. Jacobsen, E. Rotenberg, and J.E. Smith. Assigning confidence to conditional branch predictions. In *29th Annual International Symposium on Microarchitecture*, pages 142–152. IEEE, December 1996.

[7] A. Klauser, A. Paithankar, and D. Grunwald. Selective eager execution on the polypath architecture. In *25th Annual International Symposium on Computer Architecture*, pages 250–259, June 1998.

[8] P. Marcuello, A. Gonzalez, and J. Tubella. Speculative multithreaded processors. In *International Conference on Supercomputing*, July 1998.

[9] S. McFarling. Combining branch predictors. Technical Report TN-36, DEC-WRL, June 1993.

[10] E. Rotenberg, S. Bennett, and J.E. Smith. Trace cache: a low latency approach to high bandwidth instruction fetching. In *29th Annual International Symposium on Microarchitecture*, pages 24–34. IEEE, December 1996.

[11] M. Smotherman and M. Franklin. Improving cisc instruction decoding performance using a fill unit. In *28th Annual International Symposium on Microarchitecture*, November 1995.

[12] A. Sodani and G.S. Sohi. Dynamic instruction reuse. In *24th Annual International Symposium on Computer Architecture*, pages 194–205, June 1997.

[13] G.S. Sohi, S.E. Breach, and T.N. Vijaykumar. Multiscalar processors. In *22nd Annual International Symposium on Computer Architecture*, pages 414–425, June 1995.

[14] D.M. Tullsen, S.J. Eggers, J.S. Emer, H.M. Levy, J.L. Lo, and R.L. Stamm. Exploiting choice: Instruction fetch and issue on an implementable simultaneous multithreading processor. In *23nd Annual International Symposium on Computer Architecture*, pages 191–202, May 1996.

[15] D.M. Tullsen, S.J. Eggers, and H.M. Levy. Simultaneous multithreading: Maximizing on-chip parallelism. In *22nd Annual International Symposium on Computer Architecture*, pages 392–403, June 1995.

[16] G. Tyson, K. Lick, and M. Farrens. Limited dual path execution. Technical Report CSE-TR 346-97, University of Michigan, 1997.

[17] A. Uht and V. Sindagi. Disjoint eager execution: An optimal form of speculative execution. In *28th Annual International Symposium on Microarchitecture*, pages 313–325. IEEE, December 1995.

[18] S. Wallace, B. Calder, and D.M. Tullsen. Threaded multiple path execution. In *25th Annual International Symposium on Computer Architecture*, pages 238–249, June 1998.

[19] K.C. Yeager. The MIPS R10000 superscalar microprocessor. *IEEE Micro*, 16(2), April 1996.

[20] T.-Y. Yeh and Y. Patt. Alternative implementations of two-level adaptive branch prediction. In *19th Annual International Symposium on Computer Architecture*, pages 124–134, May 1992.

Supporting Fine-Grained Synchronization on a Simultaneous Multithreading Processor

Dean M. Tullsen
Dept. of Computer Science and Engineering
University of California, San Diego
tullsen@cs.ucsd.edu

Jack L. Lo
Transmeta Corporation
Santa Clara, CA
jlo@transmeta.com

Susan J. Eggers, Henry M. Levy
Dept. of Computer Science and Engineering
University of Washington
{eggers,levy}@cs.washington.edu

Abstract

This paper proposes and evaluates new synchronization schemes for a simultaneous multithreaded processor. We present a scalable mechanism that permits threads to cheaply synchronize within the processor, with blocked threads consuming no processor resources. We also introduce the concept of lock release prediction, which gains an additional improvement of 40%. Overall, we show that these improvements in synchronization cost enable parallelization of code that could not be effectively parallelized using traditional techniques.

1. Introduction

The performance of a multiprocessor's synchronization mechanisms determine the granularity of parallelism that can be exploited on that machine. Synchronization on a conventional multiprocessor carries a high cost due to the hardware levels at which synchronization and communication must occur (e.g., main memory). As a result, compilers and programmers must decompose parallel applications in a coarse-grained way in order to reduce synchronization overhead.

This paper examines *fine-grained* synchronization on a simultaneous multithreaded (SMT) processor — a processor in which the CPU can issue instructions from multiple threads in a single cycle [10, 9]. Multithreaded processors provide an opportunity to greatly *decrease* synchronization cost, because the communicating threads are *internal* to a single processor. While previous work has shown the benefits of SMT on parallel workloads [6, 7], those studies relied on traditional synchronization mechanisms, ignoring the potential advantages (and problems) of synchronizing in an SMT CPU.

A simultaneous multithreading processor differs from a conventional multiprocessor in several crucial ways that influence the design of SMT synchronization: (1) Threads on an SMT processor compete for all fetch and execution resources each cycle. Synchronization mechanisms (e.g., spin locks) that consume *any* shared resources without making progress, can impede other threads. (2) Data shared by threads is held closer to the processor, i.e., in the thread-shared L1 cache; therefore, communication is dramatically faster between threads. Synchronization must experience a similar increase in performance to avoid becoming a bottleneck. (3) Hardware thread contexts on an SMT processor share functional units. This opens the possibility of communicating synchronization and/or data much more effectively than through memory.

This paper presents a scalable synchronization mechanism for SMT that permits threads to cheaply synchronize within the processor, with blocked threads consuming no processor resources. The basic mechanism, blocking *acquire* and *release*, is a hardware implementation of traditional software synchronization abstractions, implemented with a thread-shared hardware *lock box*. The lock box is a simple hardware mechanism that enables the transfer of memory-based locks between threads on the same processor in just a few cycles. This latency can be further reduced by a new technique called *lock-release prediction*, which minimizes the cost of restarting a blocked thread.

Our results show an order of magnitude improvement in the granularity of parallelism made available with this new synchronization, relative to synchronization on conventional shared-memory multiprocessors. We demonstrate that it is sufficiently lightweight to permit parallelization of new codes that could not previously be parallelized.

2. Synchronization Mechanisms

In this section, we begin with a brief description of existing synchronization mechanisms. We then present our goals for synchronization in SMT processors and describe the new mechanism that we evaluate in this paper.

2.1. Review of Existing Synchronization Schemes

A number of different synchronization mechanisms exist in commercial or research multiprocessors, both conventional and multithreaded. Most common are *spin locks*, such as `test-and-set`. While `test-and-set` modifies memory, optimizations typically allow the spinning to take place in the local cache to reduce bus traffic. More recently, *Lock-Free synchronization* has been widely studied [4] and is included in modern instruction sets, e.g., the DEC Alpha's load-locked (`ldl_l`) and store-conditional (`stl_c`) (collectively, LL-SC). Rather than achieve mutual exclusion by preventing multiple threads from entering the critical section, lock-free synchronization prevents more than one thread from successfully writing data and exiting the critical section.

The Tera [2] and Alewife [1] machines rely on *full/empty (F/E) bits* associated with each memory block. F/E bits allow memory access and lock acquisition with a single instruction, where the full/empty bit acts as the lock, and the data is returned only if the lock succeeds.

The M-Machine [5], attaches full/empty bits to registers. Synchronization among threads on different clusters or even within the same cluster is achieved by a cluster-local thread explicitly setting a register to empty, after which a write to the register by another thread will succeed, setting it to full. Keckler et al. [5] provide a good description of these mechanisms in a study with similar goals to ours. We do not consider register full/empty bits to be sufficient in themselves for SMT synchronization. Differences between the M-machine and SMT result in the different directions taken by our two studies: (1) the M-machine is a message-passing multicomputer, so its synchronization mechanisms do not have to scale to a shared-memory MP; and (2) no single execution unit is shared by all threads, so the M-Machine cannot use execution-unit-based synchronization. The CRAY X-MP also introduced shared registers for synchronization, but with the synchronization bits decoupled from the data registers.

2.2. Goals for SMT Synchronization

This section identifies the desired goals for SMT synchronization. These goals are motivated by the special properties of an SMT processor, as described in Section 1. Given these properties, synchronization on an SMT processor should be:

(1) *High Performance*. High performance implies both high throughput and low latency. Full/empty bits on main memory provides high throughput but high latency.

(2) *Resource-conservative*. Both spin locks and lock-free synchronization consume processor resources while waiting for a lock, either retrying or spinning, waiting to retry. To be resource-conservative on a multithreaded processor, stalled threads must use *no* processor resources.

(3) *Deadlock-free*. We must avoid introducing new forms of deadlock. SMT shares the instruction scheduling unit among all executing threads and could deadlock if a blocked thread fills the instruction queue, preventing the releasing instruction (from another thread) from entering the processor.

(4) *Scalable*. The same primitives should be usable to synchronize threads on different processors and threads on the same processor, even if the performance differs. Full/empty bits on registers are not scalable.

None of the existing synchronization mechanisms presented in Section 2.1 meets all of these goals when used in the context of SMT.

2.3. A Mechanism for Blocking SMT Synchronization

Here we present a design for SMT synchronization that meets our criteria. It uses hardware-based blocking locks. A thread that fails to acquire a lock blocks and frees all resources it is using except the hardware context itself. A thread that releases a lock upon which another is blocked causes the blocked thread to be restarted. The actual primitives consist of two instructions:

Acquire(lock) – This instruction acquires a memory-based lock. The instruction does not complete execution until the lock is successfully acquired; therefore, it appears to software like a test-and-set that never fails.

Release(lock) – This instruction writes a zero to memory if no other thread in the processor is waiting for the lock; otherwise, the next waiting thread is unblocked and memory is not altered.

These primitives look familiar, not because they are common hardware primitives, but because they are common software interfaces to synchronization (typically implemented with spinning locks). For the SMT processor, we implement these primitives directly in hardware.

The synchronization instructions are implemented with a small processor structure associated with a single functional unit. The structure, which we call a *lock-box*, has one entry per context (per hardware-supported thread). Each entry contains: the address of the lock, a pointer to the lock instruction that blocked and a valid bit.

When a thread fails to acquire a lock (a read-modify-write of memory returns nonzero), the lock address and instruction id are stored in that thread's lock-box entry, and the thread is flushed from the processor after the lock instruction. When another thread releases the lock, hardware performs an associative comparison of the released address against the lock-box entries. On finding the blocked thread, the hardware allows the original lock instruction to complete, allowing the thread to resume, and invalidates the blocked thread's lock-box entry. A release for which no thread is waiting is written to memory.

The acquire instruction is restartable. Because it never commits if it does not succeed, a thread that is context-switched out of the processor while blocked for a lock will always be restarted with the program counter pointing to the acquire or earlier.

Flushing a blocked thread from the instruction queue (and pre-queue pipeline stages) is critical to preventing deadlock. The mechanism needed to flush a thread is the same mechanism used after a branch misprediction on an SMT processor. We can prevent starvation of any single thread without adding information to the lock box simply by always granting the lock to the thread id that comes first (including wrap-around) after the id of the releasing thread.

The entire mechanism is scalable (i.e., it can be used between processors), as long as a release in one processor is visible to a blocked thread in another. We discuss several ways that this could be accomplished in [11].

3. Characterizing Synchronization Efficiency

Using a detailed trace-driven simulator, we compare several alternative synchronization mechanisms on an SMT architecture. The simulator executes unmodified Alpha object code using emulation-based, instruction-level simulation techniques. It models the execution pipelines, memory hierarchy, TLBs, and branch prediction logic of an 8-issue SMT processor. More details of the processor and memory system model are given in [11].

In this section we define an efficiency metric for synchronization and use it to evaluate the speed of different synchro-

```
single-threaded:
for (i = 0; i < N; i++)
    A[i+1] = A[i] + independent_computation
parallelized:
(for each thread)
for (i = threadId; i < N; i += numThreads)
    temp = independent_computation
    acquire(lock[threadId])
    A[i+1] = A[i] + temp
    release(lock[nextId])
```

Figure 1. Our synchronization efficiency test

nization schemes. Our vehicle for expressing the metric is a loop containing a mix of loop-carried dependent (serial) computation and independent (parallel) computation, that can represent a wide range of loops or codes with different mixes of serial and parallel work (Figure 1). Our efficiency metric is the *ratio* of parallel-to-serial computation at which the threaded version of the loop begins to outperform a single-threaded version. The amount of independent computation (work that contains no loop-carried dependences in the i loop) is varied by enclosing it in a loop that iterates between 1 and 128 times. Each iteration of the independent computation loop does a load (a cache hit), a floating-point multiply and and a floating point add. The result is then added to A[i] in the critical section.

In Figure 2 *Single-thread* is the performance of the serial version of the loop, which defines the break-even point. *SMT-block* is the base SMT synchronization with blocking acquires using the lock-box mechanism. *SMT-ll/sc* uses the lock-free synchronization currently supported by the Alpha. To implement the ordered access in the benchmark, the acquire primitive is implemented with load_locked and store_conditional and the release is a store instruction. *SMP-** each use the same primitives as SMT-block, but force the synchronization (and data sharing) to occur at different levels in the memory hierarchy. This mimics the synchronization and communication performance of systems with contexts less tightly coupled than on an SMT, such as a typical shared-memory multiprocessor (SMP-Mem), a tightly-coupled cluster of processors sharing an off-chip cache (SMP-L3), and a single-chip multiprocessor with a shared secondary cache (SMP-L2). Synchronization within a processor is more than an order of magnitude more efficient than synchronization in memory. The break-even point for parallelization is about 5 computations for SMT-block, and over 80 for memory-based synchronization. Thus, an SMT processor will be able to exploit opportunities for parallelism that are an order of magnitude finer than those needed on a traditional multiprocessor, even if the SMT processor is using existing synchronization primitives (e.g., the lock-free LL-SC).

However, blocking synchronization does outperform lock-free synchronization; for this benchmark the primary factor is not resource waste due to spinning, but the *latency* of the synchronization operation. We observed the critical path through successive iterations of the for loop when the independent

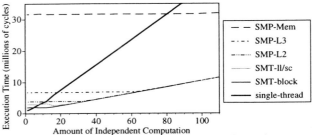

Figure 2. The speed of synchronization configurations.

computation is small and performance is dominated by the loop-carried calculation. In that case the critical path becomes the locked (serial) region of each iteration. For the lock-free synchronization, the critical path is at least 20 cycles per iteration [11]. A key component is the branch misprediction penalty when the thread finally acquires the lock and the LL-SC code stops looping on lock failure. For blocking SMT synchronization, the critical path through the loop is 15 cycles. This time is dominated by the restart penalty (to get a blocked thread's instructions back into the CPU).

In summary, fine-grained synchronization, when performed close to the processor, changes the available granularity of parallelism by an order of magnitude. We will examine this potential in more detail later using common program loops. Those loops, like our efficiency benchmark, will put the speed of synchronization on the critical performance path. The following optimization reduces that critical path length.

Faster Synchronization Via Speculative Restart. The restart penalty for a blocked acquire assumes that the blocked thread is not restarted until the corresponding release instruction retires. It then takes several cycles to fetch the blocked thread's instruction stream into the processor. While the release cannot perform until it retires (or is at least guaranteed to retire), it is possible to speculatively restart the blocked thread earlier; the thread can begin fetching and even execute instructions that are not dependent on the acquire.

In Figure 3, we show the results of speculatively restarting a blocked thread as soon as the release is seen by the decode unit. A history based on thread ID and PC is used to predict which thread will be released by a given instruction. Speculatively restarting a thread before the releasing instruction retires reduces the critical path from 15 cycles to nine cycles (when the prediction is correct), lowering the break-even point to about 3 iterations of the independent loop (Figure 3).

4. Case Studies in Parallelization With Fast Synchronization

Any program traditionally regarded as parallel has achieved performance in the face of relatively high-cost synchronization, and should run well with any of the synchronization mechanisms we have considered. However, efficient fine-grain parallelism will create a new class of "parallel" programs. The size of that new class, and their exact performance, will in large part be determined by the speed of the synchronization

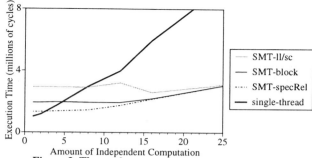

Figure 3. The performance of speculative restart.

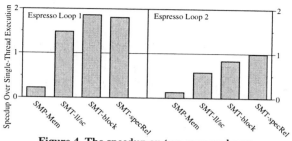

Figure 4. The speedup on two *espresso* loops.

mechanism. Because this type of fine-grain parallelism is not available on existing systems, we have access to no compiler which can identify and transform code appropriately. Thus we have identified some potential code by hand to use as case studies. Although we hand-insert synchronization in these loops, we do so at the source level, and do not otherwise alter the code significantly (except for obvious compiler transformations, like a reduction in one case). For much more detail on how the loops were parallelized, see [11].

We examine five loops that a standard parallel compiler would not parallelize: the two most important loops in *espresso* and three of the Livermore loops. These loops are significant exactly because of the compiler's assumption that parallelizing would not be worthwhile. We attempt to parallelize these loops across 8 threads using our fine-grained SMT synchronization mechanism, and report the success stories and one less-than-successful effort.

Espresso. For the SPEC benchmark *espresso* and the input file ti.in, a large part of the execution time is spent in two loops in the routine *massive_count*.

The first loop is a doubly-nested loop with both ordered and un-ordered dependences across the outer loop. The first dependence in this loop is a pointer that is incremented until it points to zero (the loop exit condition). The second dependence is a large array of counters which are conditionally incremented based on individual bits of calculated values.

Figure 4 (Loop 1) shows that both SMT versions perform well; however, there is little performance difference with speculative restart because collisions on the counters are unpredictable (thus restart prediction accuracy is low). With LL-SC, ordered access to the pointer must use software versions of `acquire` and `release`. The atomic incrementing of counters is more tailor-made for lock-free synchronization; however, there are still enough collisions to create some wasted computation. Memory-based synchronization clearly cannot overcome the high cost of synchronization and communication.

The second component of *massive_count* is a single loop primarily composed of many nested `if` statements with some independent computation. The loop has four scalar dependences for which we must preserve original program order (shared variables are read and conditionally changed) and two updates to shared structures that need not be ordered.

The performance of the blocking synchronization was disappointing (Figure 4, loop 2). Further analysis uncovered several contributing factors. (1) The single-thread loop already has significant ILP. (2) Most of the shared variables are in registers in the single-thread version, but must be stored in memory for parallelization. (3) The locks constrained the efficient scheduling of memory accesses in the loop. (4) The branches are highly correlated from iteration to iteration, allowing our branch predictor to do very well for serial execution; however, much of this correlation was lost when the iterations went to different threads. Despite all this, choosing to parallelize this loop still would not hurt performance given our fast synchronization mechanisms.

With LL-SC, the ordered accesses had to be protected in the same manner as the blocking synchronization, but with software acquire and release. For the unordered variables, they were each updated atomically using LL-SC. The overall performance was poor due to spinning for contested locks.

Livermore Loops. Unlike most of the Livermore Loops, loops 6, 13, and 14 are not parallelized by, for example, SUIF, because they each contain cross-iteration dependencies. These loops have a reasonable amount of code that is independent, however, and should be amenable to parallelization, given fine-grained synchronization.

Loop 6 is a doubly-nested loop that reads a triangular region of a matrix. The inner loop accumulates a sum. While parallelization of this loop (Figure 5, Loop 6), does not make sense on a conventional multiprocessor, it becomes profitable with standard SMT synchronization, and more so with speculative restart support. Later in this section, we'll show a trivial change to get much better performance. LL-SC performs poorly due to the high overhead of threads spinning at the barrier around the reduction for the sum.

Loop 13 has only one cross-iteration dependence, the incrementing of an indexed array, which happens in an unpredictable, data-dependent order. Although it is not necessary to preserve the order of these updates, we chose to do so because (1) these loops are very uniform, and (2) the performance of the speculative restart prediction is better with a forced ordering. *Loop 13* achieves more than double the throughput of single-thread execution with SMT synchronization and the speculative restart optimization. Here LL-SC also performs well, since the only dependence is a single unordered atomic update. This can be done with a single `ldl_l`, `stl_c` pair.

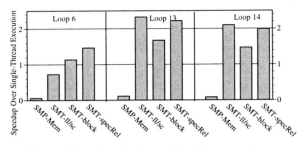

Figure 5. Speedup for three of the Livermore loops.

Loop 14 is actually three loops, which are trivial to fuse. This maximizes the amount of parallel code available to execute concurrently with the serial portion. The serial portion is two updates to another indexed array, like *Loop 13*.

Figure 6 shows that different numbers of threads were appropriate for different loops and different SMT synchronization mechanisms. *Loop 6*, which only achieved a small speedup with 8 threads, had linear speedup with two, then fell off. Performance on *Loops 13* and *14* only improves beyond 2 threads with speculative restart. These results indicate that (1) it is important to choose the level of parallelism carefully and (2) the optimal choice of threads is dependent on the loop and the underlying synchronization mechanism.

For the five loops examined (two from espresso, three from livermore), none of which could be parallelized on a convention multiprocessor, fine-grained synchronization enabled significant parallel speedups on four and no speedup or slowdown on one. In each case, parallelization created execution paths that made the speed of synchronization critical to the performance of the code, as all were sensitive to the exact mechanism used.

5. Related Work

Section 2.1 described other multithreaded architectures and multithreaded synchronization mechanisms. Other work which is related to this study follows.

Pai, et al. [8] describe a synchronization buffer for multiprocessors of single-threaded processors. The synchronization buffer is an off-chip structure which holds lock addresses from executing lock instructions. It retries the lock so that software does not have to loop. They do not block the thread, nor do they associate releases with locks in their structure.

Bradford and Abraham [3] propose hardware-implemented semaphores which block a thread waiting for a semaphore. They compare this scheme with spin-waiting and OS-implemented blocking synchronization.

6. Summary

We have proposed a new synchronization mechanism based on a simple hardware structure called a lock box, tailored specifically for an SMT processor. This mechanism (1) maximizes synchronization efficiency by ensuring that threads waiting on synchronization consume no execution resources, and (2) minimizes synchronization latency by using lock-

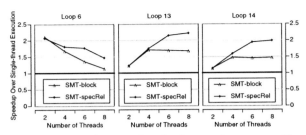

Figure 6. Blocking synchronization performance with varying number of threads.

release prediction to resume blocked threads with no restart delay.

Acknowledgments

This work was funded by NSF CAREER grant MIP-9701708, NSF grant MIP-9632977, UC MICRO grant 97-018, and a DEC external research grant US-0040-97. Joel Emer and Rebecca Stamm contributed ideas and insight to this project.

References

[1] A. Agarwal, J. Kubiatowicz, D. Kranz, B.-H. Lim, D. Yeung, G. D'Souza, and M. Parkin. Sparcle: An evolutionary processor design for large-scale multiprocessors. *IEEE Micro*, June 1993.

[2] R. Alverson, D. Callahan, D. Cummings, B. Koblenz, A. Porterfield, and B. Smith. The Tera computer system. In *International Conference on Supercomputing*, June 1990.

[3] J. Bradford and S. Abraham. Efficient synchronizatin for multithreaded processors. In *Workshop on Multithreaded Execution Architecture and Compilation*, January 1998.

[4] M. Herlihy. A methodology for implementing highly concurrent data objects. In *Symposium on Principles and Practices of Parallel Programming*, March 1990.

[5] S. Keckler, W. Dally, D. Maskit, N. Carter, A. Chang, and W. Lee. Exploiting fine-grain thread level parallelism on the MIT multi-alu processor. In *International Symposium on Computer Architecture*, June 1998.

[6] J. Lo, S. Eggers, J. Emer, H. Levy, S. Parekh, R. Stamm, and D. Tullsen. Converting thread-level parallelism into instruction-level parallelism via simultaneous multithreading. *ACM Transactions on Computer Systems*, August 1997.

[7] J. Lo, S. Eggers, H. Levy, S. Parekh, and D. Tullsen. Tuning compiler optimizations for simultaneous multithreading. In *International Symposium on Microarchitecture*, December 1997.

[8] V. Pai, P. Ranganathan, S. Adve, and T. Harton. An evaluation of memory consistency models for shared-memory systems with ilp processors. In *International Conference on Architectural Support for Programming Languages and Operating Systems*, 1996.

[9] D. Tullsen, S. Eggers, J. Emer, H. Levy, J. Lo, and R. Stamm. Exploiting choice: Instruction fetch and issue on an implementable simultaneous multithreading processor. In *International Symposium on Computer Architecture*, May 1996.

[10] D. Tullsen, S. Eggers, and H. Levy. Simultaneous multithreading: Maximizing on-chip parallelism. In *International Symposium on Computer Architecture*, June 1995.

[11] D. Tullsen, J. Lo, S. Eggers, and H. Levy. Supporting fine-grained synchronization on a simultaneous multithreading processor. Technical Report CS98-587, UCSD, June 1998.

The Synergy of Multithreading and Access/Execute Decoupling

Joan-Manuel Parcerisa and Antonio González
Departament d'Arquitectura de Computadors
Universitat Politècnica de Catalunya - Barcelona (Spain)
Email: {jmanel,antonio}@ac.upc.es

Abstract

This work presents and evaluates a novel processor microarchitecture which combines two paradigms: access/ execute decoupling and simultaneous multithreading. We investigate how both techniques complement each other: while decoupling features an excellent memory latency hiding efficiency, multithreading supplies the in-order issue stage with enough ILP to hide the functional unit latencies. Its partitioned layout, together with its in-order issue policy makes it potentially less complex, in terms of critical path delays, than a centralized out-of-order design, to support future growths in issue-width and clock speed.

The simulations show that by adding decoupling to a multithreaded architecture, its miss latency tolerance is sharply increased and in addition, it needs fewer threads to achieve maximum throughput, especially for a large miss latency. Fewer threads result in a hardware complexity reduction and lower demands on the memory system, which becomes a critical resource for large miss latencies, since bandwidth may become a bottleneck.

1. Introduction

Dynamic scheduling is a latency tolerance technique that can hide much latency of memory and functional units. However, as memory latencies and issue widths continue to grow in the future, dynamically scheduled processors will need larger instruction windows. As reported in [4], the hardware complexity of some components in the critical path that determines the clock cycle time may prevent centralized architectures to scale up to faster clock frequencies. Therefore, several architectures have been proposed recently, either in-order or out-of-order, which address this problem by partitioning critical components of the architecture and/or providing less complex scheduling mechanisms [6, 1, 3, 4, 9]. This work focuses on one of these partitioning strategies: the access/execute paradigm [5], which was first proposed for early scalar architectures to provide them with dual issue and a limited form of dynamic scheduling that is especially oriented to tolerate memory latency.

On the other hand, simultaneous multithreading has been shown to be an effective technique to boost ILP [8]. In this paper, we analyze its potential when implemented on a decoupled processor.

We show in this study that the combination of decoupling and mulithreading takes advantage of their best features: while decoupling is a simple but effective technique for hiding high memory latencies with a reduced issue complexity, multithreading provides enough parallelism to hide functional unit latencies and keep them busy. In addition, multithreading also helps to hide memory latency when a program decouples badly. However, since decoupling hides most memory latency, few threads are needed to achieve a near-peak issue rate. This is an important result, since having few threads reduces the memory pressure, which is a major bottleneck in multithreading architectures, and reduces the hardware cost and complexity.

The rest of this paper is organized as follows. Section 2 quantifies the latency hiding effectiveness of decoupling. Section 3 describes and evaluates a multithreaded decoupled architecture. Section 4 summarizes the main conclusions.

2. Latency Hiding Effectiveness of Decoupling

Since the interest of decoupling is closely related to its ability to hide memory latencies without resorting to other more complex issue mechanisms, we have first quantified such ability for a wide range of L2 cache latencies, from 1 to 256 cycles. We have evaluated a 4-way issue, single-threaded, decoupled architecture with 4 general purpose functional units and a 2-port L1 data cache. The latencies and other architectural parameters are those of Figure 2.

The baseline single-threaded decoupled architecture consists of two superscalar decoupled processing units: the Address Processing unit (AP) and the Execute Processing unit (EP). Precise exceptions are supported by means of a reorder buffer, a graduation mechanism, and a register renaming map table. The Instruction Queue in the EP allows the AP to execute ahead of the EP, providing the necessary slippage between them to hide the memory latency, and the Store Address Queue allows loads to bypass stores. For

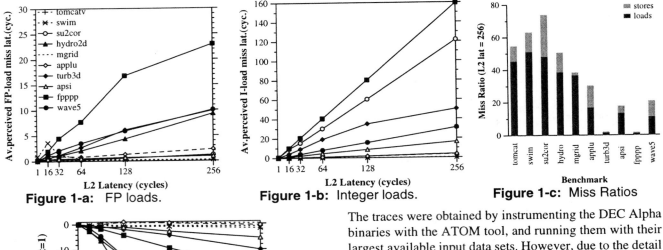

Figure 1-a: FP loads.

Figure 1-b: Integer loads.

Figure 1-c: Miss Ratios

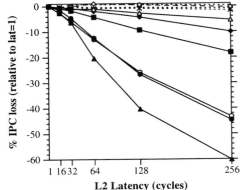

Figure 1-d: Impact of latency on performance.

these experiments, the sizes of all the architectural queues and physical register files are scaled up proportionally to the L2 latency.

The instruction stream, which is based on the DEC Alpha ISA, is dynamically split: instructions are dispatched to either the AP or the EP following a simple steering mechanism based on their data type (int or fp), except for memory instructions, which are all sent to the AP. Although this rather simplistic scheme mostly benefits to numerical programs, it still provides a basis for our study which is mainly focused on the latency hiding potential of decoupling and its synergy with multithreading. Techniques to decouple integer codes can be found elsewhere [5].

Since one of the main arguments for the decoupled approach is the reduced issue logic complexity, each thread issues instructions in-order within each processing unit. It may be argued that in-order processors have a limited potential to exploit ILP. However, current compiling techniques can extract much ILP and thus, the compiler can pass this information to the hardware instead of using runtime schemes (this is the approach that emerging EPIC architectures take [2]).

The experiments consisted of a set of trace driven cycle-by-cycle simulations of the SPEC FP95 benchmark suite.

The traces were obtained by instrumenting the DEC Alpha binaries with the ATOM tool, and running them with their largest available input data sets. However, due to the detail of the simulations, we only run 100M instructions of each benchmark, after skipping the initial start-up phase.

In addition to the IPC, we have also measured separately the average "perceived" latency of integer and FP load misses, i.e., the average number of stall cycles of instructions that use data from a previous uncompleted load. Since we are interested in the particular benefit of decoupling, independently of the cache miss ratio, this average does not include load hits.

The perceived latency of FP load misses measures the EP stalls caused by misses, and reveals the "decoupled behavior" of a program, i.e., the amount of slippage of the AP with respect to the EP. As shown in Figure 1-a, except for *fpppp*, more than 96% of the FP load miss latency is always hidden. The perceived latency of integer load misses measures the AP stalls caused by misses, and it depends on the ability of the compiler to schedule integer loads ahead of other dependent instructions. As shown in Figure 1-b, *fpppp*, *su2cor*, *turb3d* and *wave5* are the programs that experience the largest integer load miss stalls.

Regarding the impact of the L2 latency on performance (see Figure 1-d), although programs such as *fpppp* or *turb3d* perceive much load miss latency, they are hardly performance degraded due to their extremely low miss ratios (see Figure 1-c). The most performance degraded programs are those with both high perceived miss latency and significant miss ratios: *hydro2d*, *wave5* and *su2cor*.

To summarize, performance is little affected by the L2 latency when either it can be hidden efficiently (*tomcatv*, *swim*, *mgrid*, *applu* and *apsi*), or when the miss ratio is low (*fpppp* and *turb3d*), but it is seriously degraded for programs that lack both features (*su2cor*, *wave5* and *hydro2d*). The hidden miss latency of FP loads depends on the degree of program decoupling, while that of integer loads relies exclusively on the static instruction scheduling.

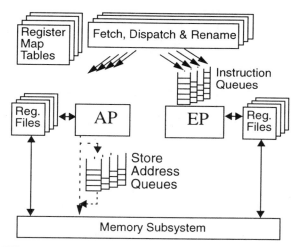

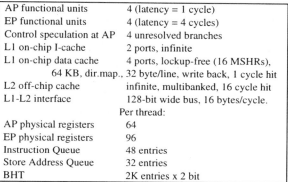

AP functional units	4 (latency = 1 cycle)
EP functional units	4 (latency = 4 cycles)
Control speculation at AP	4 unresolved branches
L1 on-chip I-cache	2 ports, infinite
L1 on-chip data cache	4 ports, lockup-free (16 MSHRs),
64 KB, dir.map.,	32 byte/line, write back, 1 cycle hit
L2 off-chip cache	infinite, multibanked, 16 cycle hit
L1-L2 interface	128-bit wide bus, 16 bytes/cycle.
	Per thread:
AP physical registers	64
EP physical registers	96
Instruction Queue	48 entries
Store Address Queue	32 entries
BHT	2K entries x 2 bit

Figure 2: Scheme and main parameters of the multithreaded decoupled processor

3. A Multithreaded Decoupled Architecture

A multithreaded decoupled architecture (Figure 2) supports multiple hardware contexts, each executing in a decoupled mode. The fetch and dispatch stages - including branch prediction and register map tables - and the register files and queues are replicated for each context. The issue logic, functional units and caches are shared by all the threads. Up to 8 instructions from different threads can be issued per cycle to 8 general purpose functional units. All the threads are allowed to compete for each of the 8 issue slots each cycle, and priorities among them are round-robin (similar to the *full simultaneous issue* scheme reported in [8]). Each cycle, only two threads have access to the I-cache, and each of them can fetch up to 8 consecutive instructions (or up to the first taken branch). The two chosen threads are those with less instructions pending to be dispatched (similar to the RR-2.8 with I-COUNT schemes, reported in [7]).

Early experiments revealed that in a single-threaded architecture most of the wasted issue slots are caused by true data dependences between EP register operands, due to the

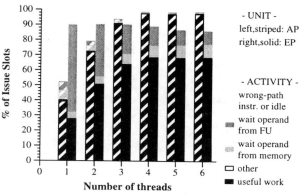

Figure 3: issue slots breakdown

restricted ability of the in-order issue model to exploit ILP. Therefore, as far as decoupling hides memory latency and multithreading supplies enough amounts of parallelism to remove the remaining stalls, we expect important synergistic effects between these two techniques in a hybrid architecture.

For the experiments in this section, the multithreaded decoupled architecture parameters are those in Figure 2. The simulator is fed with independent threads. Each thread consists of a sequence of traces from all SpecFP95 programs, in a different order for each thread.

3.1. Sources of Wasted Issue Slots

The first column pair in Figure 3 represents the case of a single thread, showing that the major bottleneck is caused by the EP functional units latency, as discussed above. When two more contexts are added, multithreading drastically reduces these stalls in both units, and produces a 2.31 speed-up (from 2.68 IPC to 6.19 IPC). Since with 3 threads the AP functional units are nearly saturated (90.7%), negligible speed-ups are obtained by adding more contexts (6.65 IPC is achieved with 4 threads).

Note that although the AP almost achieves its maximum throughput, the EP functional units are not saturated due to the load imbalance between the AP and the EP. Therefore, the effective peak performance is reduced by 15%, from 8 to 6.8 IPC. This problem could be addressed with a different issue width in each processor unit, but this is beyond the scope of this study.

Another important remark is that when the number of threads is increased, the combined working set is larger, and the miss ratios increase progressively, putting higher demands on the external bus bandwidth. On average, there are more pending misses, which increases the effective load miss latency, and the EP stalls caused by *waiting operands from memory* (Figure 3). However, in the AP, since integer loads are much less frequent than fp loads, the ad-

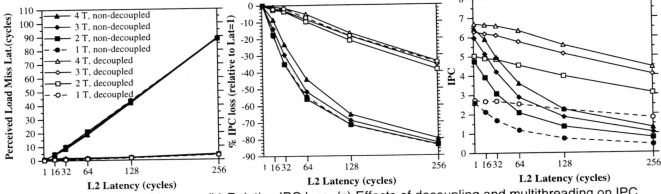

Figure 4: (a) Perceived latency. (b) Relative IPC loss. (c) Effects of decoupling and multithreading on IPC.

ditional parallelism provided by multithreading eliminates almost all of this kind of stalls.

3.2. Latency Hiding Effectiveness

Multithreading and decoupling are two different approaches to tolerate high memory latencies. We have run some experiments to quantify the latency tolerance of a multithreaded decoupled processor for 1 to 4 threads. In addition, some other experiments are also carried out to reveal the contribution of each mechanism to the latency hiding effect. They consist of a set of identical runs on a degenerated version of our multithreaded architecture where the instruction queues are disabled (i.e. a non-decoupled multithreaded architecture).

Figure 4-a shows the average perceived load miss latency, when varying L2 latency from 1 to 256 cycles for the 8 configurations (combinations of 1 to 4 threads with/without decoupling). This metric expresses the average number of cycles that an instruction that uses a load value cannot issue although there is a free issue slot. It can be seen that decoupling hides almost all memory latency, even when it is very high, whereas multithreading helps very little.

Figure 4-b shows the corresponding relative performance loss (with respect to the 1-cycle L2 latency) of each of the 8 configurations. Notice that this metric compares the tolerance of these architectures to memory latency, rather than their absolute performance. Several conclusions can be drawn from these graphs. First, it is shown that when the L2 memory latency is increased from 1 to 32 cycles, the decoupled multithreaded architecture experiences performance drops of less than 4%, while the performance degradation observed in all non-decoupled configurations is greater than 23%. Even for a huge memory latency of 256 cycles, the performance loss of the decoupled configurations is lower than 39% while it is greater than 79% for the non-decoupled configurations.

Second, multithreading provides some additional latency tolerance improvement, especially in the non-decoupled

configurations, but it is much lower than that provided by decoupling.

Some other conclusions can be drawn from Figure 4-c. While multithreading raises the performance curves, decoupling makes them flatter. In other words, while the main effect of multithreading is to provide more parallelism, the major contribution to memory latency tolerance, which is related to the slope of the curves, comes from decoupling, and this is precisely the specific role that decoupling plays in this hybrid architecture.

3.3. Reduction in Hardware Contexts

Multithreading is a powerful mechanism that highly improves the processor throughput, but it has a cost: it needs a considerable amount of hardware resources. We have run some experiments that illustrate how decoupling reduces the required number of hardware contexts.

We have measured the performance of several configurations having from 1 to 7 contexts, for a decoupled multithreaded architecture and a non-decoupled multithreaded architecture (Figure 5, solid lines). While the decoupled configuration achieves the maximum performance with just 3 or 4 threads, the non-decoupled configuration needs 6 threads to achieve similar IPC rates.

Multithreading is usually claimed to be able to sustain a high processor throughput, even in systems with a high memory latency. Since hiding a longer latency may require a higher number of contexts and this has a strong negative impact on the memory performance, the reduction in hardware context requirements obtained by decoupling may become a key factor when L2 memory latency is high. To illustrate this fact, we have run a similar experiment for 1 to 16 contexts and a L2 memory latency of 64 cycles. As shown in Figure 5 (dotted lines), while the decoupled architecture achieves the maximum performance with just 4 or 5 threads, the non-decoupled architecture cannot reach a similar performance with any number of threads, because it would need so many that they would saturate the external

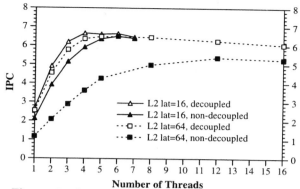

Figure 5: Decoupling reduces hardware contexts and avoids external bus saturation

L2 bus: the average bus utilization is 89% for 12 threads, and 98% for 16 threads. Moreover, note that the decoupled architecture requires just 3 threads to achieve about the same performance as the non-decoupled architecture with 12 threads. Thus, decoupling significantly reduces the amount of thread-level parallelism required to reach a certain level of performance.

To summarize, decoupling and multithreading complement each other to hide memory latency and increase throughput with reduced amounts of thread-level parallelism and low issue logic complexity.

4. Summary and Conclusions

In this paper we have analyzed the synergy of multithreading and access/execute decoupling. A multithreaded decoupled architecture takes advantage of the latency hiding effectiveness of decoupling, and the potential of multithreading to exploit ILP. We have analyzed the most important factors that determine its performance and the synergistic effect of both paradigms.

A multithreaded decoupled architecture hides efficiently the memory latency: the average perceived load miss latency is less than 5 cycles in the worst case (with 4 threads and a L2 latency of 256 cycles). We have also found that, for L2 latencies lower than 32 cycles, their impact on the performance is quite low: less than 4% IPC loss, relative to the 1-cycle latency scenario, and it is quite independent of the number of threads. On the other hand, this impact is greater than a 23% IPC loss if decoupling is disabled. This latter fact points out that decoupling is the main contributor to memory latency tolerance.

The architecture reaches maximum performance with very few threads, significantly less than in a non-decoupled architecture. The number of simultaneously active threads supported by the architecture has a significant impact on the hardware chip area and complexity, which may compromise the clock cycle.

Reducing the number of threads also reduces the cache conflicts and the required memory bandwidth, which is usually one of the potential bottlenecks of a multithreaded architecture. We have shown that if decoupling is disabled, the external L2 bus bandwidth becomes a bottleneck when the miss latency is 64 cycles, which prevents the processor from achieving the maximum performance for any number of threads.

In summary, we can conclude that decoupling and multithreading techniques complement each other to exploit parallelism and to hide memory latency. A multithreaded decoupled processor obtains its maximum performance with few threads, has a reduced issue logic complexity, and it is hardly performance degraded by a wide range of L2 latencies. All of these features make it a promising alternative for future increases in clock speed and issue width.

Acknowledgements

This work has been supported by grant CYCIT TIC98-0511 and the ESPRIT Project MHAOTEU (EP24942).

References

[1] K.I.Farkas, P.Chow, N.P.Jouppi, Z.Vranesic. The Multi-cluster Architecture: Reducing Cycle Time Through Partitioning. In *Proc of the Micro-30*, Dec. 1997

[2] L. Gwennap. Intel, HP Make EPIC Disclosure. *Microprocessor Report*, 11(14), Oct. 1997.

[3] G.A.Kemp, M.Franklin. PEWs: A Decentralized Dynamic Scheduler for ILP Processing. In *Proc. of the ICPP*. 1996, v.1, pp 239-246.

[4] S. Palacharla, N.P. Jouppi, and J.E. Smith. Complexity-Effective Superscalar Processors. In *Proc of the 24th. ISCA*, 1997, pp 1-13.

[5] S.S.Sastry, S.Palacharla, J.E.Smith. Exploiting Idle Floating-Point Resources For Integer Execution. In *Proc. of the PLDI*. Montreal, 1998.

[6] J.E. Smith. Decoupled Access/Execute Computer Architectures. *ACM Trans. on Computer Systems*, 2 (4), Nov. 1984, pp 289-308.

[7] G.S.Sohi, S.E.Breach, and T.N.Vijaykumar. Multiscalar Processors. In *Proc. of the 22nd ISCA*. 1995, pp 414-425.

[8] D.M. Tullsen, et al. Exploiting Choice: Instruction Fetch and Issue on an Implementable Simultaneous Multithreading Processor. In *Proc. of the 23rd. ISCA*. 1996, pp 191-202.

[9] D.M. Tullsen, S.J. Eggers, and H.M. Levy. Simultaneous Multithreading: Maximizing On-Chip Parallelism. In *Proc. of the 22nd. ISCA*. 1995, pp 392-403.

[10] Y.Zhang, G.B.Adams III. Performance Modelling and Code Partitioning for the DS Architecture. In *Proc. of the 25th. ISCA*, Jun. 1998, pp 293-304.

Out-Of-Order Execution May Not Be Cost-Effective on Processors Featuring Simultaneous Multithreading*

Sébastien Hily
Intel Microcomputer Research Lab
shily@ichips.intel.com

André Seznec
IRISA/INRIA
seznec@irisa.fr

Abstract

To achieve high performance on a single process, superscalar processors now rely on very complex out-of-order execution. Using more and more speculative execution (e.g. value prediction) will be needed for further improvements.

On the other hand, most operating systems now offer time-shared multiprocess environments. For the moment most of the time is spent in a single thread, but this should change, as the computer will perform more and more independent tasks. Moreover, desktop applications tend to be multithreaded. A lot of users should then be more concerned with the performance throughput on the workload than with the performance of the processor on a single process.

Simultaneous multithreading (SMT) is a promising approach to deliver high throughput from superscalar pipelines. In this paper, we show that when executing 4 threads on an SMT processor, out-of-order execution induces small performance benefits over in-order execution. Then, for application domains where performance throughput is more important than ultimate performance on a single application, SMT combined with in-order execution may be a more cost-effective alternative than ultimate aggressive out-of-order superscalar processors or out-of-order execution SMT.

1 Introduction

During the last few years, the design trend for general purpose microprocessors has been to track the ultimate single process performance. Current microprocessor architectures are relying on very aggressive hardware mechanisms to execute instructions out-of-order. Such mechanisms enhance an application execution by looking for independent instructions to issue. The ability of a processor to free itself from the sequential model imposed by the applications has thus become a key feature determining the level of

performance. Further increase of the performance of singlethreaded superscalar architectures will depend on even more aggressive techniques, such as load and value predictions , multiple basic block fetching and possibly other forms of speculative execution. This will further increase the design complexity and may lead to longer and longer design and test cycles. Moreover, besides the high level of complexity reached by the implementation, the effective performance observed on general-purpose processors remains relatively low compared to their peak performance.

On the other hand, most of the desktop computers or workstations run multitasked operating systems (e.g.: Windows95, WindowsNT, Unix). While previously multithreaded workloads were limited to a scientific environment or to databases, now, a conventional PC running Windows95 has around 20 threads created before the user launches any application. Even if for the moment the main CPU activity is limited to usually a single task, this will change as the user will be willing to play a game while downloading a file or to print data and process a worksheet while writing a report. In the near future more and more desktop applications should then be able to take advantage of hardware support for parallel execution.

Such hardware support on a uniprocessor may be provided by Simultaneous Multithreading (SMT). SMT is a new concept of processor for achieving high throughput [8, 9]. It relies on the availability of independent instructions, from several simultaneously active threads, to enhance ILP. Compared to an on-chip multiprocessor, in an SMT microprocessor the active threads share the hardware resources, in particular, instruction and data caches may be shared. This gives SMT a significant performance advantage [9], especially when the number of threads decreases. When only one thread is available, it can use most of the processor to execute. An SMT single-chip processor can be built adapting an existing superscalar

---

*This work was done while the first author was with IRISA

architecture, thus limiting the design and test cycle. Two alternatives exist for the design of the superscalar pipeline architecture: in-order execution and out-of-order execution.

In [9], Tullsen et al. chose an in-order pipeline for their SMT architecture. Their model overlooked several aspects of the architecture, specially the memory hierarchy. In their following study [8], they shifted to a more accurate out-of-order pipeline. The model proposed by Goossens and Vu [1] aiming at a short cycle is limited to in-order execution. To our knowledge, no studies comparing performance of in-order and out-of-order executions have been undertaken when several threads are available simultaneously.

In this article, we investigate the respective performance of both types of implementation in an SMT processor. Our study shows that, while ultimate single process performance requires out-of-order execution, high-throughput microprocessors may rely on in-order execution and SMT. When executing 4 threads, in-order execution is shown to be nearly as effective as out-of-order execution.

The remainder of this paper is organized as follows. Section 2 gives a short presentation of the methodology and the simulated architectures. In Section 3, we compare the respective performance of the two types of pipelines. Finally, Section 4 presents a summary of this study.

2 Experimental framework

A trace-driven simulation model has been used in this study. Our simulator is based on the Sparc V7 instruction set and has been built from Spy [5]. Our benchmark set is composed of the Spec95 applications compiled with the standard -O2 optimization on a Sparcstation 20.

2.1 Methodology

We have undertaken simulations for various workloads constituted of 1, 2 or 4 distinct applications of Spec95. It was shown in [3] that with a conventional memory hierarchy, more than 4 threads would not be cost-effective, even when using an ultimately aggressive out-of-order execution. For each of the simulations, the memory hierarchy is initialized by executing 10 millions of instructions per active thread. The simulation stops as soon as one of the threads has executed 20 millions of instructions.

2.2 Simulated architectures

For the simulations, a 7-stage integer pipeline has been used (Fig. 2). First, instructions are fetched from the memory into an instruction buffer. There is one buffer per thread. The instructions available in

the buffers can then be fed into the pipeline according to the priorities given to the active threads. The highest priority is granted to the thread having the least instructions in the static part of the pipeline[8].

Figure 2: Integer pipeline

During every cycle, up to 8 instructions are read from the buffers. If only one thread is available, it should be able to fill all slots in the execution pipeline. Fig. 1 shows the two simulated architectures, the first, featuring in-order execution, the second, out-of-order execution. A more detailed description of the architectures can be found in [4].

In-order execution (Fig. 1A) One 32-entry instruction queue is associated with each thread. During every cycle, queues are scanned to find instructions to issue to the functional units. The same priority rule as described for instruction fetch is used for instruction selection in the queues. Instructions from a queue are issued in-order until there is a resource conflict, a data hazard or a branch. The following queue in the priority order is then selected. Each thread has access to 32 integer registers and 32 floating-point registers.

Out-of-order execution For out-of-order execution (Fig. 1B), after the decoding, the instructions wait in reservation stations for their operands and functional units. During every cycle, any fireable instruction can be executed irrespective of the program order. Out-of-order execution relies on register renaming with 64 physical integer registers and 64 physical floating-point registers per thread [6]. Each reservation station has 16 entries.

Common features These two architectures rely on a shared branch prediction mechanism (12-bit gshare PHT and 512-entry BTB) and a shared memory hierarchy (split 32 Kbytes L1 caches, 1Mbytes 4-way L2 cache). Two branch predictions on two different threads can be made during each cycle. The two levels of caches are non-blocking. Both architectures have 4 ALU, 3 load/store units, 2 branch units and 3 undifferentiated floating-point units. All functional units are fully pipelined. The execution phase takes one cycle for an integer instruction and three cycles for a floating point. A memory access is done in one cycle when hitting in the cache. The writeback phase assumes no conflicts on the result buses. For the out-of-order architecture, we do not simulate in-order retirement.

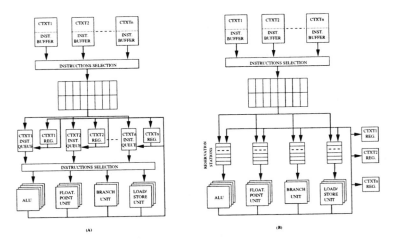

Figure 1: Architectures featuring in-order execution (A) and out-of-order execution (B)

3 In-order versus out-of-order executions

In this section, we evaluate the respective performance of architectures issuing instructions in-order or out-of-order when several threads are executed simultaneously. More details can be found in [4].

Figure 3 shows the average performance for architectures featuring 1, 2 or 4 simultaneous threads and executing instructions either in-order (dark bar) or out-of-order (light bar). In the first graphic, only the pipeline is simulated; branch predictions and the first-level caches were assumed perfect. In the second graphic, pipeline and branch prediction are simulated but the accesses to caches remain ideal. In the third graphic, a real memory hierarchy is simulated with the pipeline, but the branch prediction is perfect. In the fourth graphic, the complete processor is simulated, i.e. the pipeline, the branch prediction and the memory hierarchy. The ratio of in-order performance versus out-of-order performance is illustrated by dots.

Complete simulation The fourth graphic shows that despite our aggressive design, when a single thread is available, the average performance exhibited by in-order execution is relatively weak (1.3 IPC). Out-of-order execution allows a significant performance gain, with an IPC of 2.3. In-order execution offers only 54% of the out-of-order performance.

As the number of threads increases, the throughput improves significantly. For out-of-order execution, the IPC is multiplied by 1.5 for 2 threads and 2 for 4 threads. For in-order execution, the IPC is multiplied by 1.86 for 2 threads and 3 for 4 threads. Hence the gap between out-of-order and in-order executions decreases. For 4 threads (respectively 2 threads), in-order execution allows to reach 85% (resp. 66%) of

the IPC observed for out-of-order execution. The large performance advantage offered by out-of-order execution on singlethreaded workload shrinks when several threads are executed on an architecture featuring SMT. This can be explained by several converging reasons: in the in-order pipeline, the opportunity to find independent instructions to fire increases when several threads are executing in parallel. In the out-of-order pipeline, the speculative execution of instructions which will be later canceled consumes resources potentially useful for the execution of valid instructions from the other threads.

Impact of memory hierarchy and branch prediction In order to measure the respective impact of the memory hierarchy and the branch prediction on performance, we ran three complementary sets of simulations assuming either perfect or effective models of caches and branch predictor.

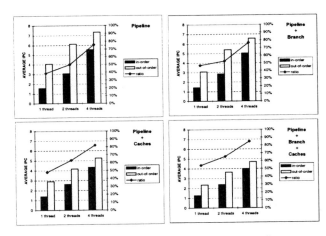

Figure 3: Average performance impact of memory hierarchy and branch prediction for 1, 2 or 4 threads with in-order or out-of-order execution

Figure 3 shows that the saturation of caches leading to conflict and capacity misses and the limited accuracy of branch prediction clearly impairs performance :

- Branch mispredictions results in a high performance loss, especially in out-of-order execution: out-of-order execution favors the speculative execution of "less likely to be useful" instructions. The impact of a misprediction however weakens as the number of threads increases. First, less advance is made on execution by the running threads and fewer instructions are executed speculatively. At second when a misprediction is detected on a thread, the pipeline continue to execute instructions from the other threads. The pipeline is then very rarely empty.

- The impact of the memory hierarchy is far more important. Unlike in branch mispredictions, the penalty of a cache miss will be potentially "paid" by all the threads because it consumes memory bandwidth and may delay any subsequent cache miss either from its thread or from another. For example for 4 threads, the average drop in performance induced by the cache misses is higher than 25%.

The combined negative impact of the bad predictions and the cache misses is however very dependent on the type of the pipeline and on the number of threads. Thus, when instructions execute in-order, this negative impact increases as the number of threads grows; the loss in the IPC is 19% for one thread and reaches 28% for four threads. For out-of-order execution, this is the opposite with a decreasing impact when the number of threads increases; the loss in the IPC is 42% for one thread and falls to 36% for four threads, mainly due to a lower impact of mispredictions on the performance. Despite this, simultaneous multithreading offers a strong gain in performance, as the IPC reaches an average of 4 for in-order execution, and 4.7 for out-of-order execution.

4 Summary

In this paper, we have investigated the respective performance offered by two types of architectures both featuring up to 4 threads simultaneously but one issuing instructions in-order and the other out-of-order.

On a single thread, in-order execution suffers from a 46 % performance gap compared with out-of-order execution. However, if 4 threads are available for execution, the performance gap is only around 15% in average when the same number of pipeline stages and the same clock cycle are assumed for in-order and out-of-order execution. Moreover, many of our assumptions for simulations were optimistic when considering out-of-order execution: same minimum pipeline length for in-order and out-of-order execution, same

clock speed, etc. Then on real implementations, the small performance advantage of out-of-order execution will be lower, and may even not exist if higher clock speed is achieved with in-order execution.

We have also shown that imperfect branch prediction and memory hierarchy have a high impact on the performance. The use of multithreading decreases the impact of the branch prediction: fewer instructions are involved by a single misprediction. On the other hand, use of multithreading increases the stress on the memory hierarchy generating more cache misses and more memory traffic.

For users concerned by ultimate performance on a single process, out-of-order execution will be needed. On the other hand, if operating systems and applications continue to evolve to more and more thread and process level parallelism, then more and more users will be more concerned with throughput rather than with ultimate single process performance. Then for those users, our study has established that processors featuring SMT and in-order execution will be sufficient. Even when only 2 threads are available, an SMT architecture featuring in-order execution will outperform a singlethreaded superscalar architecture relying on out-of-order execution.

References

[1] B. Goossens and D. T. Vu. On-chip multiprocessing. In *Lecture Notes in Computer Science. Euro-Par'96*, vol. 2, Aug. 96.

[2] S. Hily and A. Seznec. Branch Prediction and Simultaneous Multithreading. In *PACT'96*, oct. 96.

[3] S. Hily and A. Seznec. Standard Memory Hierarchy Does Not Fit Simultaneous Multithreading. In *MTEAC'98*, Colorado State Univ. Tech. Report CS-98-102, Jan. 98, http://www.cs.colostate.edu/ ftp-pub/TechReports/1998/mteac98.html

[4] S. Hily and A. Seznec. Out-Of-Order Execution May Not Be Cost-Effective on Processors Featuring Simultaneous Multithreading. Technical report PI-1179, IRISA, March 1998. ftp://ftp.irisa.fr:/techreports/1998/PI-1179.ps.gz

[5] G. Irlam. Spa package. http://www.base.com/gordoni/spa.html, 1994.

[6] M. Johnson. *Superscalar Microprocessor Design*. Prentice Hall, 1991.

[7] LSI LOGIC. *SPARC Architecture Manual (v 7)*.

[8] D. M. Tullsen et al. . Exploiting Choice: Instruction Fetch and Issue on an Implementable Simultaneous Multithreading Processor. *23th ISCA*, May 96.

[9] D. M. Tullsen et al. . Simultaneous Multithreading: Maximising On-Chip Parallelism. *22nd ISCA*, June 95.

Session 3

Memory Systems

Impulse: Building a Smarter Memory Controller

John Carter, Wilson Hsieh, Leigh Stoller, Mark Swanson†, Lixin Zhang,
Erik Brunvand, Al Davis, Chen-Chi Kuo, Ravindra Kuramkote,
Michael Parker, Lambert Schaelicke, Terry Tateyama

Department of Computer Science   †Intel Corporation
University of Utah   Dupont, WA
Salt Lake City, UT

Abstract

Impulse is a new memory system architecture that adds two important features to a traditional memory controller. First, Impulse supports application-specific optimizations through configurable physical address remapping. By remapping physical addresses, applications control how their data is accessed and cached, improving their cache and bus utilization. Second, Impulse supports prefetching at the memory controller, which can hide much of the latency of DRAM accesses.

In this paper we describe the design of the Impulse architecture, and show how an Impulse memory system can be used to improve the performance of memory-bound programs. For the NAS conjugate gradient benchmark, Impulse improves performance by 67%. Because it requires no modification to processor, cache, or bus designs, Impulse can be adopted in conventional systems. In addition to scientific applications, we expect that Impulse will benefit regularly strided, memory-bound applications of commercial importance, such as database and multimedia programs.

1. Introduction

Since 1985, microprocessor performance has improved at a rate of 60% per year. In contrast, DRAM latencies have improved by only 7% per year, and DRAM bandwidths by only 15-20% per year. The result is that the relative performance impact of memory accesses continues to grow. In addition, as instruction issue rates continue to increase, the demand for memory bandwidth increases proportionately (and possibly even superlinearly) [7, 12]. For applications that do not exhibit sufficient locality, these trends make it increasingly hard to make effective use of the tremendous processing power of modern microprocessors. It is an unfortunate fact that many important applications (e.g., sparse matrix, database, signal processing, multimedia, and CAD applications) do not exhibit such high degrees of locality. In the Impulse project, we are attacking this problem by designing and building a memory controller that is more powerful than conventional ones.

The Impulse memory controller has two features that are not present in current memory controllers. First, the Impulse controller supports an optional extra stage of address translation: as a result, data can have its addresses remapped *without copying*. This feature allows applications to control how their data is accessed and cached, in order to improve bus and cache utilization. Second, the Impulse controller supports prefetching at the memory controller, which reduces the effective latency to memory. Prefetching at the memory controller is important for reducing the latency of Impulse's address translation, and is also a useful optimization for non-remapped data.

The novel feature in Impulse is the addition of another level of address translation at the memory controller. The key insight exploited by this feature is that unused "physical" addresses can undergo translation to "real" physical addresses at the memory controller. An unused physical address is a legitimate address, but one that is not backed by DRAM. For example, in a system with 4GB of physical address space with only 1GB of installed DRAM, there is 3GB of unused physical address space. We call these unused addresses *shadow addresses*, and they constitute a *shadow address space* that is mapped to physical memory by the Impulse controller. By giving applications control (mediated by the OS) over the use of shadow addresses, Impulse supports application-specific optimizations that restructure data. Using Impulse requires modifications to software: applications (or compilers) and operating systems. Using Impulse does not require any modification to other hardware (either processors, caches, or buses).

As a simple example of how Impulse memory remapping can be used, consider a program that accesses the diagonal

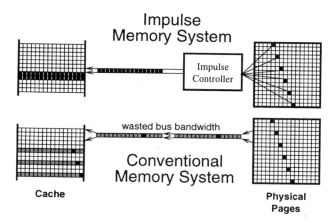

Figure 1. Using Impulse to remap the diagonal of a dense matrix into a dense cache line. The black boxes represent data on the diagonal, whereas the gray boxes represent non-diagonal data.

elements of a matrix A. The physical layout of part of the data structure A is shown on the right-hand side of Figure 1. On a conventional memory system, each time the processor accesses a new diagonal element (e.g., A[i][i]), it must request a full cache line of contiguous physical memory. On modern systems, a cache line contains 32–128 bytes of data, of which the program accesses only a single word. Such an access is shown in the bottom of Figure 1.

On an Impulse memory system, an application can configure the memory controller to export a dense shadow space alias that contains just the diagonal elements, and have the OS map a new set of virtual addresses to this shadow memory. The application can then access the diagonal elements via the new virtual alias. Such an access is shown in the top half of Figure 1. The details of how Impulse performs the remapping is described in Section 2.1.

Remapping the array diagonal to a dense alias results in several performance benefits. First, the processor achieves a higher cache hit rate, because several diagonal elements are loaded into the caches at once. Second, the processor consumes less bus bandwidth, because non-diagonal elements are not sent over the bus. Finally, the processor makes more effective use of cache space, because the non-diagonal elements are not sent. In general, the flexibility that Impulse supports allows applications to customize addressing to fit their needs.

The second important feature of the Impulse memory controller is that it supports prefetching. We include a small amount of SRAM on the Impulse memory controller to store data prefetched from the DRAM's. For non-remapped data, prefetching is useful for reducing the latency of se-

quentially accessed data. We show that controller-based prefetching of non-remapped data performs as well as a system that uses simple L1 cache prefetching. For remapped data, prefetching enables the controller to hide the cost of remapping: some remappings can require multiple DRAM accesses to fill a single cache line. With both prefetching and remapping, an Impulse controller greatly outperforms conventional memory systems.

In recent years, a number of hardware mechanisms have been proposed to address the problem of increasing memory system overhead. For example, researchers have evaluated the prospects of making the processor cache configurable [25, 26], adding computational power to the memory system [14, 18, 24], and supporting stream buffers [13, 16]. All of these mechanisms promise significant performance improvements; unfortunately, most require significant changes to processors, caches, or memories, and thus have not been adopted in current systems. Impulse supports similar optimizations, but its hardware modifications are localized to the memory controller.

We simulated the impact of Impulse on two benchmarks: the NAS conjugate gradient benchmark and a dense matrix-matrix product kernel. Although this paper only evaluates two scientific kernels, we expect that Impulse will be useful for optimizing non-scientific applications as well. Some of the optimizations that we describe are not conceptually new, but the Impulse project is the first system that will provide hardware support for them in general-purpose computer systems. For both benchmarks, the use of Impulse optimizations significantly improved performance compared to a conventional memory controller. In particular, we found that a combination of address remapping and controller-based prefetching improved the performance of conjugate gradient by 67%.

2. Impulse Architecture

To illustrate how the Impulse memory controller (MC) works, we describe in detail how it can be used to optimize the simple diagonal matrix example described in Section 1. We describe the internal architecture of the Impulse memory controller, and explain the kinds of address remappings that it currently supports.

2.1. Using Impulse

Figure 2 illustrates the address transformations that Impulse performs to remap the diagonal of a dense matrix. The top half of the figure illustrates how the diagonal elements are accessed on a conventional memory system. The original dense matrix, A, occupies three pages of the virtual address space. Accesses to the diagonal elements of A are translated into accesses to physical addresses at the

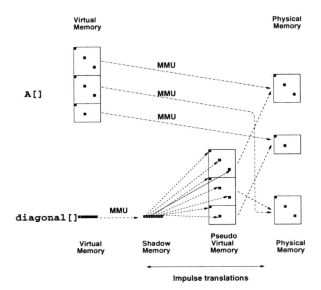

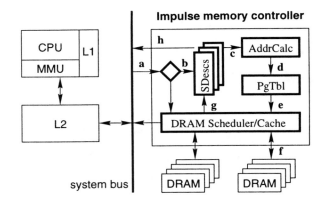

Figure 3. The Impulse memory architecture. The arrows indicate how data flows within an Impulse memory system.

Figure 2. Using Impulse to remap memory: The translation on the top of the figure is the standard translation performed by an MMU. The translation on the bottom of the figure is the translation performed on an Impulse system. The processor translates virtual aliases into what it thinks are physical addresses; however, these physical addresses are really *shadow addresses*. The Impulse MC maps the shadow addresses into *pseudo-virtual addresses*, and then to physical memory.

processor. Each access to a diagonal element loads an entire cache line of data, but only the diagonal element is accessed, which wastes bus bandwidth and cache capacity.

The bottom half of the figure illustrates how the diagonal elements of A are accessed using Impulse. The application reads from a data structure that the OS has remapped to a shadow alias for the matrix diagonal. When the processor issues the read for that alias over the bus, the Impulse controller gathers the data in the diagonal into a single cache line, and sends that data back to the processor. Impulse supports prefetching of memory accesses, so that the latency of the gather can be hidden.

The operating system remaps the diagonal elements to a new alias, diagonal, as follows:

1. The application allocates a contiguous range of virtual addresses large enough to map the diagonal elements of A, and asks the OS to map it through shadow memory to the actual elements. This range of virtual addresses corresponds to the new variable diagonal. To improve L1 cache utilization, an application can allocate virtual addresses with appropriate alignment and offset characteristics.

2. The OS allocates a contiguous range of shadow ad-

dresses large enough to contain the diagonal elements of A. The operating system allocates shadow addresses from a pool of physical addresses that do not correspond to real DRAM addresses.

3. The OS downloads to the memory controller a mapping function from the shadow addresses to offsets within *pseudo-virtual memory space*. An address space that mirrors virtual space is necessary to be able to remap data structures that are larger than a page. We use a pseudo-virtual space in order to save address bits. In our example, the mapping function involves a simple *base* and *stride* function — other remapping functions supported by the current Impulse model are described in Section 2.3.

4. The OS downloads to the memory controller a set of page mappings for pseudo-virtual space for A

5. The OS maps the virtual alias diagonal to the newly allocated shadow memory, flushes the original address from the caches, and returns.

Currently, we have modified application kernels by hand to perform the system calls to remap data; we are exploring compiler algorithms similar to those used by vectorizing compilers to automate the process. Both shadow addresses and virtual addresses are system resources, so the operating system must manage their allocation and mapping. We have designed a set of system calls that allow applications to use Impulse without violating inter-process protection.

2.2. Hardware

Figure 3 illustrates Impulse's memory architecture, including the internal organization of the memory controller (MC). The major functional units of the MC are:

72

- a small number of shadow space descriptors (SDesc) - currently we model eight despite needing no more than three for the applications we simulated,

- a simple ALU that remaps shadow addresses to pseudo-virtual addresses (AddrCalc), based on information stored in shadow descriptors,

- logic to perform page-grained remapping of pseudo-virtual addresses to physical addresses backed by DRAM (PgTbl), and

- a DRAM scheduler that will optimize the dynamic ordering of accesses to the actual DRAM chips.

In Figure 3, an address first appears on the memory bus (**a**). This address can be either a physical or a shadow address. If it is physical, it is passed directly to the DRAM scheduler. Otherwise, the matching shadow descriptor is selected (**b**). The remapping information stored in the shadow descriptor is used to translate the shadow address into a set of pseudo-virtual addresses using a simple ALU (AddrCalc) (**c**). Pseudo-virtual addresses are necessary for Impulse to be able to map data structures that span multiple pages. These addresses are translated into real physical addresses (**d**) using a page table (an on-chip TLB backed by main memory), and passed to the DRAM scheduler (**e**). The DRAM scheduler orders and issues the reads (**f**), and sends the data back to the shadow descriptors (**g**). Finally, the appropriate shadow descriptor assembles the data into cache lines and sends it over the bus (**h**).

An important design goal of Impulse is that it should not slow down accesses to non-shadow physical memory, because not all programs will utilize Impulse's remapping functions. Even programs that do remap data will probably contain significant numbers of references to non-remapped data. Therefore, our design tries to avoid adding latency to "normal" accesses to memory. In addition, the Impulse controller has a 2K buffer for prefetching non-remapped data using a simple one-block lookahead prefetcher. As we show in Section 4, using this simple prefetch mechanism at the controller is competitive with L1 cache prefetching.

Because accesses to remapped memory require a potentially complex address calculation, it is also important that the latency of accesses to remapped memory be kept as low as possible. Therefore, the Impulse controller is designed to support prefetching. Each shadow descriptor has a 256-byte buffer that can be used to prefetch shadow memory.

We also expect that the controller will be able to schedule remapped memory accesses so that the actual DRAM accesses will occur in parallel. We are designing a low-level DRAM scheduler designed to exploit locality in parallelism between DRAM accesses. First, it will reorder word-grained requests to exploit DRAM page locality. Second, it will schedule requests to exploit bank-level parallelism.

Third, it will give priority to requests from the processor over requests that originate in the MC. The design of our DRAM scheduler is not yet complete. Therefore, the simulation results reported in this paper assume a simple scheduler that issues accesses in order.

2.3. Software Interface

The initial design for Impulse supports several forms of shadow-to-physical remapping:

- *Direct mapping*: Impulse allows applications to map a shadow page directly to a physical page. By remapping physical pages in this manner, applications can recolor physical pages without copying as described in Section 3.1. In another publication we have described how direct mappings in Impulse can be used to form superpages from non-contiguous physical pages [21].

- *Strided physical memory*: Impulse allows applications to map a region of shadow addresses to a strided data structure. That is, a shadow address at offset *soffset* on a shadow region is mapped to a pseudo-virtual address *pvaddr* + *stride* * *soffset*, where *pvaddr* is the starting address of the data structure's pseudo-virtual image. By mapping sparse, regular data items into packed cache lines, applications reduce their bus bandwidth consumption and the cache footprint of the data. An example of such an optimization, tile remapping, is described in Section 3.2.

- *Scatter/gather using an indirection vector*: Impulse allows applications to map a region of shadow addresses to a data structure through an indirection vector. That is, a shadow address at offset *soffset* in a shadow region is mapped to a pseudo-virtual address *pvaddr* + *stride* * *vector[soffset]*. By mapping sparse, indirectly addressed data items into packed cache lines, applications reduce their bus bandwidth consumption, the cache footprint of the data, and the number of loads they must issue. An example of this optimization for conjugate gradient is described in Section 3.1.

In order to keep the controller hardware simple and fast, Impulse restricts the remappings. For example, in order to avoid the necessity for a divider in the controller, strided mappings must ensure that a strided object has a size that is a power of 2. Also, we assume that an application (or compiler/OS) that uses Impulse ensures data consistency through appropriate flushing of the caches.

3. Impulse Optimizations

In this section we describe how Impulse can be used to optimize two scientific application kernels: sparse matrix-

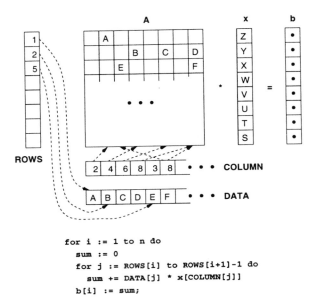

```
for i := 1 to n do
  sum := 0
  for j := ROWS[i] to ROWS[i+1]-1 do
    sum += DATA[j] * x[COLUMN[j]]
  b[i] := sum;
```

Figure 4. Conjugate gradient's sparse matrix-vector product. The matrix A is encoded using three dense arrays: DATA, ROWS, and COLUMN. The contents of A are in DATA. ROWS[i] indicates where the ith row begins in DATA. COLUMN[i] indicates which column of A the element stored in DATA[i] comes from.

vector multiply (SMVP) and dense matrix-matrix product. We apply two techniques to optimize SMVP: vector-style scatter/gather at the memory controller and no-copy physical page coloring. We apply a third optimization, no-copy tile remapping, to dense matrix-matrix product.

3.1. Sparse Matrix-Vector Product

Sparse matrix-vector product is an irregular computational kernel that is critical to many large scientific algorithms. For example, most of the time in conjugate gradient [3] or in the Spark98 earthquake simulations [17] are spent performing SMVP.

To avoid wasting memory, sparse matrices are generally encoded so that only non-zero elements and corresponding index arrays are stored. For example, the Class A input matrix for the NAS Conjugate Gradient kernel (CG-A) is 14,000 by 14,000, and contains only 2.19 million non-zeroes. Although sparse encodings save tremendous amounts of memory, sparse matrix codes tend to suffer from poor memory performance, because data must be accessed through indirection vectors. When we ran CG-A on an SGI Origin 2000 processor (which has a 2-way, 32K L1 cache and a 2-way, 4MB L2 cache), the L1 cache hit rate was only 63%, and the L2 cache hit rate was only 92%.

Sparse matrix-vector product is illustrated in Figure 4.

Each iteration multiplies a row of the sparse matrix A with the dense vector x. This code performs poorly on conventional memory systems, because the accesses to x are both indirect (via the COLUMN index vector) and sparse. When x is accessed, a conventional memory system will fetch a cache line of data, of which only one element is used. Because of the large sizes of x, COLUMN, and DATA and the sparse nature of accesses to x during each iteration of the loop, there will be very little reuse in the L1 cache. Each element of COLUMN or DATA is used only once, and almost every access to x results in an L1 cache miss. A large L2 cache can provide reuse of x, if physical data layouts can be managed to prevent L2 cache conflicts between A and x. Unfortunately, conventional systems do not typically provide mechanisms for managing physical layout.

Scatter/gather. The Impulse memory controller supports scatter/gather of physical addresses through indirection vectors. Vector machines, such as the CDC STAR-100 [11], have provided scatter/gather capabilities in hardware, but such mechanisms have been provided at the processor. Because Impulse allows scatter/gather to occur at the memory, it can be used to reduce memory traffic over the bus. In addition, Impulse will allow conventional CPU's to take advantage of scatter/gather functionality.

The CG code on Impulse would be:

```
setup x', where x'[k] = x[COLUMN[k]]
for i := 1 to n do
  sum := 0
  for j := ROWS[i] to ROWS[i+1]-1 do
    sum += DATA[j] * x'[j]
  b[i] := sum
```

The first line asks the operating system to allocate a new region of shadow space, map x' to that shadow region, and have the memory controller map the elements of the shadow region x'[k] to the physical memory for x[COLUMN[k]]. After the remapped array has been set up, the code accesses the remapped version of the gathered structure (x') rather the original structure (x).

This optimization improves the performance of sparse matrix-vector product in two ways. First, spatial locality is improved in the L1 cache. Since the memory controller packs the gathered elements into cache lines, the cache lines contain 100% useful data, rather than only one useful element each. Second, fewer memory instructions need to be issued. Since the read of the indirection vector (COLUMN[]) occurs at the memory controller, the processor does not need to issue the read. Note that the use of scatter/gather at the memory controller reduces temporal locality in the L2 cache. The reason is that the remapped elements of x' cannot be reused, since all of the elements have different addresses.

Page recoloring. The Impulse memory controller supports dynamic physical page recoloring through direct remapping of physical pages. Physical page recoloring changes the physical addresses of pages so that reusable data is mapped to a different part of a physically-addressed cache than non-reused data By performing page recoloring, conflict misses can be eliminated. On a conventional machine, physical page recoloring is expensive to exploit. (Note that virtual page recoloring has been explored by other authors [5].) The cost is in copying: the only way to change the physical address of data is to copy the data between physical pages. Impulse allows pages to be recolored *without copying*.

For sparse matrix-vector product, the x vector is reused within an iteration, while elements of the DATA, ROW, and COLUMN vectors are used only once each in each iteration. As an alternative to scatter/gather of x at the memory controller, Impulse can be used to physically recolor pages so that x does not conflict in the L2 cache with the other data structures. For example, in the CG-A benchmark, x is over 100K bytes: it would not fit in most processors' L1 caches, but would fit in many L2 caches. Impulse can be used to remap x to pages that occupy most of the physically-indexed L2 cache, and can remap DATA, ROWS, and COLUMNS to a small number of pages that do not conflict with x. In effect, we can use a small part of the L2 cache as a stream buffer [16] for DATA, ROWS, and COLUMNS.

3.2. Tiled Matrix Algorithms

Dense matrix algorithms form an important class of scientific kernels. For example, LU decomposition and dense Cholesky factorization are dense matrix computational kernels. Such algorithms are "tiled" (or "blocked") in order to increase their efficiency. That is, the iterations of tiled algorithms are reordered so as to improve their memory performance. The difficulty with using tiled algorithms lies in choosing an appropriate tile size [15]. Because tiles are non-contiguous in the virtual address space, it is difficult to keep them from conflicting with each other (or with themselves) in the caches. To avoid conflicts, either tile sizes must be kept small (which makes inefficient use of the cache), or tiles must be copied into non-conflicting regions of memory (which is expensive).

Impulse provides another alternative to removing cache conflicts for tiles. We use the simplest tiled algorithm, dense matrix-matrix product, as an example of how Impulse can be used to improve the behavior of tiled matrix algorithms. Assume that we want to compute $C = A \times B$. We want to keep the current tile of the C matrix in the L1 cache as we compute it. In addition, since the same row of the A matrix is used multiple times to compute a row of the C matrix, we would like to keep the active row of A in the L2 cache.

Impulse allows base-stride remapping of the tiles from non-contiguous portions of memory into contiguous tiles of shadow space. As a result, Impulse makes it easy for the OS to virtually remap the tiles, since the physical footprint of a tile will match its size. If we use the OS to remap the virtual address of a matrix tile to its new shadow alias, we can then eliminate interference in a virtually-indexed L1 cache. First, we divide the L1 cache into three segments. In each segment we keep a tile: the current output tile from C, and the input tiles from A and B. When we finish with one tile, we remap the virtual tile to the next physical tile by using Impulse. In order to maintain cache consistency, we must purge the A and B tiles and flush the C tiles from the caches whenever they are remapped. As Section 4.2 shows, these costs are minor.

4. Performance

We have performed a preliminary simulation study of Impulse using the Paint simulator [20]: it models a variation of a 120 MHz, single-issue, HP PA-RISC 1.1 processor running a BSD-based microkernel, and a 120 MHz HP Runway bus. The 32K L1 data cache is non-blocking, single-cycle, write-back, write-around, virtually indexed, physically tagged, and direct mapped with 32-byte lines. The 256K L2 data cache is non-blocking, write-allocate, write-back, physically indexed and tagged, 2-way set-associative, and has 128-byte lines. Instruction caching is assumed to be perfect. A hit in the L1 cache has a minimum latency of one cycle; a hit in the L2 cache, seven cycles; an access to memory, forty cycles. The TLB's are unified I/D, single-cycle, and fully associative, with a not-recently-used replacement policy. In addition to the main TLB, a single-entry micro-ITLB holding the most recent instruction translation is also modeled. Kernel code and data structures are mapped using a single *block TLB* entry that is not subject to replacement.

In our experiments we measure the performance benefits of using Impulse to remap physical addresses, as described in Section 3. We also measure the benefits of using Impulse to prefetch data. When prefetching is turned on for Impulse, both shadow and non-shadow accesses is prefetched. As a point of comparison, we compare controller prefetching against a form of processor-side prefetching: hardware next-line prefetching into the L1 cache, such as that used in the HP PA 7200 [8]. We show that controller prefetching is competitive with this simple form of processor-side prefetching, and that a combination of controller- and cache-based prefetching is best.

In the following sections we show how Impulse's remappings can be used to support optimizations on sparse matrix-vector product (SMVP) and dense matrix-matrix product. Scatter/gather remapping improves the L1 cache performance of SMVP. Alternatively, page remapping can be used to recolor the physical pages of SMVP data for the L2 cache. Finally, base-stride remapping can be used to remap

	Standard	Prefetching		
		Impulse	L1 cache	both
Conventional memory system				
Time	2.81	2.69	2.51	2.49
L1 hit ratio	64.6%	64.6%	67.7%	67.7%
L2 hit ratio	29.9%	29.9%	30.4%	30.4%
mem hit ratio	5.5%	5.5%	1.9%	1.9%
avg load time	4.75	4.38	3.56	3.54
speedup	—	1.04	1.12	1.13
Impulse with scatter/gather remapping				
Time	2.11	1.68	1.51	1.44
L1 hit ratio	88.0%	88.0%	94.7%	94.7%
L2 hit ratio	4.4%	4.4%	4.3%	4.3%
mem hit ratio	7.6%	7.6%	1.0%	1.0%
avg load time	5.24	3.53	2.19	2.04
speedup	1.33	1.67	1.86	1.95
Impulse with page recoloring				
Time	2.70	2.57	2.39	2.37
L1 hit ratio	64.7%	64.7%	67.7%	67.7%
L2 hit ratio	30.9%	31.0%	31.3%	31.3%
mem hit ratio	4.4%	4.3%	1.0%	1.0%
avg load time	4.47	4.05	3.28	3.26
speedup	1.04	1.09	1.18	1.19

Table 1. Simulated results for the NAS Class A conjugate gradient benchmark, with various memory system configurations. Times are in billions of cycles; the hit ratios are the number of loads that hit in the corresponding level of the memory hierarchy divided by total loads; the average load time is the average number of cycles that a load takes; the speedup is the "Conventional, no prefetch" time divided by the time for the system being compared.

dense matrix tiles into contiguous shadow addresses.

4.1. Sparse Matrix-Vector Product

To evaluate the performance benefits that Impulse enables, we use the NAS Class A conjugate gradient benchmark as our benchmark for sparse matrix-vector product. Table 1 illustrates the performance of an Impulse system on that benchmark, under various memory system configurations. In the following two sections we evaluate the performance of scatter/gather remapping and page recoloring, respectively. Note that our use of "L2 cache hit ratio" uses the total number of loads (not the total number of L2 cache accesses) as the divisor to make it easier to compare the effects of the L1 and L2 caches on memory accesses.

Scatter/gather The first and second parts of Table 1 show that the use of scatter/gather remapping on CG-A im-

proves performance significantly. If we examine the performance without prefetching, Impulse improves performance by 1.33, because it increases the L1 cache hit ratio dramatically. The extra cache hits are due to the fact that accesses to the remapped vector x′ now fetch several useful elements of x at a time. In addition to the increase in cache hits, the use of scatter/gather reduces the total number of loads issued, since the indirection load occurs at the memory. The reduction in the total number of loads outweighs the fact that scatter/gather increases the average cost of a load: almost one-third of the cycles saved are due to this factor. Finally, despite the drop in L2 cache hit ratio, using scatter/gather still improves performance.

The combination of scatter-gather remapping and prefetching is even more effective in improving performance: the speedup is 1.67. Prefetching improves the effectiveness of scatter/gather: the average time for a load drops from 5.24 cycles to 3.53 cycles. Even though the cache hit ratios do not change, CG-A runs significantly faster because Impulse hides the latency of the memory system.

While controller-based prefetching was added to Impulse primarily to hide the latency of scatter/gather operations, it is useful on its own. Without scatter/gather support, controller-based prefetching improves performance by 4%, compared to the 12% performance improvement that can be achieved by performing a simple one-block-ahead prefetching mechanism at the L1 cache. However, controller-based prefetching requires no changes to the processor core, and thus can benefit processors with no integrated hardware prefetching. Controller-based prefetching improves performance by reducing the effective cost of accessing DRAM when the right data is fetched into the controller's 2-kilobyte SRAM prefetch cache.

Page recoloring The first and third sections of Table 1 show that the use of page recoloring improves performance on CG-A. We color the vectors x, DATA, and COLUMN so that they do not conflict in the L2 cache. The multiplicand vector x is reused during SMVP, so it is most important to keep it in the L2 cache. Therefore, we color it to occupy the first half of the L2 cache. We want to keep the two other large data structures, DATA and COLUMN, from conflicting as well. As a result, we divide the second half of the L2 cache into two quadrants and then color DATA and COLUMN so that they each occupy one of these quadrants.

Without prefetching, the speedup of using page recoloring is 1.04. The improvement occurs because we remove one fifth of the original memory references hit in the L2 cache with Impulse. With the addition of prefetching at the controller, the speedup increases to 1.09. Page recoloring consistently reduces the cost of memory accesses. When comparing controller prefetching with L1 cache prefetching, the effects are similar to those with scatter/gather. Controller prefetching alone is about half as effective as either

L1 cache prefetching or the combination of the two.

Although page recoloring does not achieve as great a speedup as scatter/gather remapping, it does provide useful speedups. In addition, page recoloring can probably be applied in more applications than scatter/gather (or other fine-grained types of remappings).

4.2. Dense Matrix-Matrix Product

This section examines the performance benefits of tile remapping for matrix-matrix product, and compares the results to software tile copying. Because Impulse places alignment restrictions on remapping, remapped tiles must be aligned to L2 cache line boundaries, which adds the following constraints to our matrices:

- Tile sizes must be a multiple of a cache line. In our experiments, this size is 128 bytes. This constraint is not overly limiting, especially since it makes the most efficient use of cache space.

- Arrays must be padded so that tiles are aligned to 128 bytes. Compilers can easily support this constraint: similar padding techniques have been explored in the context of vector processors [6].

Table 2 illustrates the results of our tiling experiments. The baseline is the conventional no-copy tiling. Software tile copying and tile remapping both outperform the baseline code by more than 95%, unsurprisingly. The improvement in performance is primarily due to the difference in caching behavior: both copying and remapping more than double the L1 cache hit rate. As a result, the average memory access time is approximately one cycle! Impulse tile remapping is slightly faster than tile copying: the system calls for using Impulse, and the associated cache flushes/purges, are faster than copying tiles.

Note that this comparison between conventional and Impulse copying schemes is conservative for several reasons. Copying works particularly well on matrix product, because the number of operations performed on a tile is $O(n^3)$, where $O(n^2)$ is the size of a tile. Therefore, the overhead of physical copying is fairly low. For algorithms where the reuse of the data is lower (or where the tiles are larger), the relative overhead of copying will be greater. In addition, our physical copying experiment avoids cross-interference between active tiles in both the L1 and L2 cache. Other authors have found that the performance of copying can vary greatly with matrix size, tile size, and cache size [22]. Because Impulse remaps tiles without copying, we expect that tile remapping using Impulse will not be sensitive to cross-interference between tiles. Finally, as caches (and therefore tiles) grow larger, the cost of copying grows, whereas the cost of tile remapping does not.

| | Standard | Prefetching | | |
		Impulse	L1 cache	both
Conventional memory system				
Time	2.57	2.51	2.58	2.52
L1 hit ratio	49.0%	49.0%	48.9%	48.9%
L2 hit ratio	43.0%	43.0%	43.4%	43.5%
mem hit ratio	8.0%	8.0%	7.7%	7.6%
avg load time	6.37	6.18	6.44	6.22
speedup	—	1.02	1.00	1.02
Conventional memory system with software tile copying				
Time	1.32	1.32	1.32	1.32
L1 hit ratio	98.5%	98.5%	98.5%	98.5%
L2 hit ratio	1.3%	1.3%	1.4%	1.4%
mem hit ratio	0.2%	0.2%	0.1%	0.1%
avg load time	1.09	1.08	1.06	1.06
speedup	1.95	1.95	1.95	1.95
Impulse with tile remapping				
Time	1.30	1.29	1.30	1.28
L1 hit ratio	99.4%	99.4%	99.4%	99.6%
L2 hit ratio	0.4%	0.4%	0.4%	0.4%
mem hit ratio	0.2%	0.2%	0.2%	0.0%
avg load time	1.09	1.07	1.09	1.03
speedup	1.98	1.99	1.98	2.01

Table 2. Simulated results for tiled matrix-matrix product. Times are in billions of cycles; the hit ratios are the number of loads that hit in the corresponding level of the memory hierarchy divided by total loads; the average load time is the average number of cycles that a load takes; the speedup is the "Conventional, no prefetch" time divided by the time for the system being compared. The matrices are 512 by 512, with 32 by 32 tiles.

All forms of prefetching performed approximately equally well for this application. Because of the effectiveness of copying and tile remapping, prefetching makes almost no difference. When the optimizations are not being used, controller prefetching improves performance by about 2%. L1 cache prefetching actually hurts performance slightly, due to the very low hit rate in the L1 cache — the effect is that prefetching causes too much contention at the L2 cache.

5. Related Work

A number of projects have proposed modifications to conventional CPU or DRAM designs to overcome memory system performance: supporting massive multithreading [2], moving processing power on to DRAM chips [14], building programmable stream buffers [16], or developing configurable architectures [26]. While these projects show promise, it is now almost impossible to prototype non-traditional CPU or cache designs that can perform as well as commodity processors. In addition, the performance of processor-in-memory approaches are handicapped by the optimization of DRAM processes for capacity (to increase bit density) rather than speed.

We briefly describe the most closely related architecture research projects. The Morph architecture [26] is almost entirely configurable: programmable logic is embedded in virtually every datapath in the system. As a result, optimizations similar to those that we have described are possible using Morph. The primary difference between Impulse and Morph is that Impulse is a simpler design that current architectures can take advantage of.

The RADram project at UC Davis is building a memory system that lets the memory perform computation [18]. RADram is a PIM ("processor-in-memory") project similar to IRAM [14], where the goal is to put processors close to memory. The Raw project at MIT [24] is an even more radical idea, where each IRAM element is almost entirely reconfigurable. In contrast to these projects, Impulse does not seek to put an entire processor in memory, since DRAM processes are substantially slower than logic processes.

Several researchers have proposed different forms of hardware to improve the performance of applications that access memory using regular strides (vector applications, for example). Jouppi proposed the notion of a stream buffer [13], which is a device that detects strided accesses and prefetches along those strides. McKee et al. [16] proposed a programmable variant of the stream buffer that allows applications to explicitly specify when they make vector accesses. Both forms of stream buffer allow applications to improve their performance on regular applications, but they do not support irregular applications.

Yamada [25] proposed instruction set changes to support combined relocation and prefetching into the L1 cache. Because relocation is done at the processor in his system, no bus bandwidth is saved. In addition, because relocation is done on virtual addresses, the utilization of the L2 cache cannot be improved. With Impulse, the utilization of the L2 cache can directly be improved; the operating system can then be used to improve the utilization of the L1 cache.

A great deal of research has gone into prefetching into the cache [19]. For example, Chen and Baer [9] describe how a prefetching cache can outperform a non-blocking cache. Fu and Patel [10] describe how cache prefetching can be used to improve the performance of caches on vector machines, which is somewhat related to Impulse's scatter/gather optimization. Although our research is related, cache prefetching is orthogonal to Impulse's controller prefetching. In addition, we have shown that con-troller prefetching can outperform simple forms of cache prefetching.

One memory-based prefetching scheme, described by Alexander and Kedem [1], can improve the performance of some benchmarks significantly. They use a prediction table to store up to four possible predictions for any given memory address. All four predictions are prefetched into SRAM buffers. The size of their prediction table is kept small by using a large prefetch block size.

Finally, the Impulse DRAM scheduler that we are designing has goals that are similar to other research on dynamic access ordering. McKee et al. [16] show that reordering of stream accesses can be used to exploit parallelism in multi-bank memories, as well as locality of reference in page-mode DRAM's. Valero et al. [23] show how reordering of strided accesses on a vector machine can be used to eliminate bank conflicts. On Impulse, the set of addresses to be reordered will be more complex: for example, the set of physical addresses that is generated for scatter/gather is much more irregular than strided vector accesses.

6. Conclusions

The Impulse project is attacking the memory bottleneck by designing and building a smarter memory controller. The Impulse controller requires no modifications to the CPU, caches, or DRAM's, and it has two forms of "smarts":

- The controller supports application-specific physical address remappings. This paper demonstrates that several simple remapping functions can be used in different ways to improve the performance of two important scientific application kernels.

- The controller supports prefetching at the memory. The paper demonstrates that controller-based prefetching performs as well as simple next-line prefetching in the L1 cache.

Both of these features can be used to improve performance. The combination of these features can result in good speedups: using scatter/gather remapping and prefetching improves performance on the NAS conjugate gradient benchmark by 67%. Speedups should be greater on superscalar machines (our simulation model was single-issue), because non-memory instructions will be effectively cheaper. That is, on superscalars, memory will be even more of a bottleneck, and Impulse will therefore be able to improve performance even more.

Flexible remapping support in the Impulse controller can be used to support a variety of optimizations. Although our simulation study has only examined two scientific kernels, the optimizations that we have described should be usable across a variety of memory-bound applications. In addition, despite the fact that we use conjugate gradient as our application for two optimizations, we are not comparing optimizations: the two optimizations are usable on different sets of different applications.

In previous work [21], we have shown that the Impulse memory remappings can be used to dynamically build superpages and reduce the frequency of TLB faults. Impulse can create superpages from non-contiguous user pages: simulations show that this optimization improves the performance of five SPECint95 benchmark programs by 5-20%.

Finally, an Impulse memory system will be useful in improving system-wide performance. For example, Impulse can improve messaging and interprocess communication (IPC) performance. A major chore of remote IPC is collecting message data from multiple user buffers and protocol headers. Impulse's support for scatter/gather can remove the overhead of gathering data in software, which should significantly reduce IPC overhead. The ability to use Impulse to construct contiguous shadow pages from non-contiguous pages means that network interfaces need not perform complex and expensive address translation. Finally, fast local IPC mechanisms, such as LRPC [4], use shared memory to map buffers into sender and receiver address spaces, and Impulse could be used to support fast, no-copy scatter/gather into shared shadow address spaces.

7. Acknowledgments

We thank Sally McKee, Massimiliano Poletto, and Llewellyn Reese for comments on drafts of this paper, and Chris Johnson for his assistance in providing us information on conjugate gradient.

References

[1] T. Alexander and G. Kedem. Distributed prefetch-buffer/cache design for high performance memory systems. In *Proc. of the Second HPCA*, pp. 254–263, Feb. 1996.

[2] R. Alverson, D. Callahan, D. Cummings, B. Koblenz, A. Porterfield, and B. Smith. The Tera computer system. In *Proc. of the 1990 ICS*, pp. 272–277, Amsterdam, The Netherlands, June 1990.

[3] D. Bailey et al. The NAS parallel benchmarks. TR RNR-94-007, NASA Ames Research Center, Mar. 1994.

[4] B. Bershad, T. Anderson, E. Lazowska, and H. Levy. Lightweight remote procedure call. In *Proc. of the 12th SOSP*, pp. 102–113, Litchfield Park, AZ, Dec. 1989.

[5] B. Bershad, D. Lee, T. Romer, and J. Chen. Avoiding conflict misses dynamically in large direct-mapped caches. In *Proc. of the 6th ASPLOS*, pp. 158–170, Oct. 1994.

[6] P. Budnik and D. Kuck. The organization and use of parallel memories. *ACM Trans. on Computers*, C-20(12):1566–1569, 1971.

[7] D. Burger, J. Goodman, and A. Kagi. Memory bandwidth limitations of future microprocessors. In *Proc. of the 23rd ISCA*, pp. 78–89, May 1996.

[8] K. Chan, C. Hay, J. Keller, G. Kurpanek, F. Schumacher, and J. Zheng. Design of the HP PA 7200 CPU. *Hewlett-Packard Journal*, 47(1):25–33, February 1996.

[9] T.-F. Chen and J.-L. Baer. Reducing memory latency via non-blocking and prefetching caches. In *Proc. of the 5th ASPLOS*, pp. 51–61, Oct. 1992.

[10] J. Fu and J. Patel. Data prefetching in multiprocessor vector cache memories. In *Proc. of the 18th ISCA*, pp. 54–65, Toronto, Canada, May 1991.

[11] R. Hintz and D. Tate. Control Data STAR-100 processor design. In *IEEE COMPCON*, Boston, MA, Sept. 1972.

[12] A. Huang and J. Shen. The intrinsic bandwidth requirements of ordinary programs. In *Proc. of the 7th ASPLOS*, pp. 105–114, Oct. 1996.

[13] N. Jouppi. Improving direct-mapped cache performance by the addition of a small fully associative cache and prefetch buffers. In *Proc. of the 17th ISCA*, pp. 364–373, May 1990.

[14] C. E. Kozyrakis et al. Scalable processors in the billion-transistor era: IRAM. *IEEE Computer*, pp. 75–78, Sept. 1997.

[15] M. S. Lam, E. E. Rothberg, and M. E. Wolf. The cache performance and optimizations of blocked algorithms. In *Proc. of the 4th ASPLOS*, pp. 63–74, Santa Clara, CA, Apr. 1991.

[16] S. McKee et al. Design and evaluation of dynamic access ordering hardware. In *Proc. of the 10th ACM ICS*, Philadelphia, PA, May 1996.

[17] D. R. O'Hallaron. Spark98: Sparse matrix kernels for shared memory and message passing systems. TR CMU-CS-97-178, CMU, Oct. 1997.

[18] M. Oskin, F. T. Chong, and T. Sherwood. Active pages: A model of computation for intelligent memory. In *Proc. of the 25th ISCA*, pp. 192–203, Barcelona, Spain, June 27–July 1, 1998.

[19] A. Smith. Cache memories. *ACM Computing Surveys*, 14(3):473–530, Sept. 1982.

[20] L. Stoller, R. Kuramkote, and M. Swanson. PAINT: PA instruction set interpreter. TR UUCS-96-009, Univ. of Utah CS Dept., Sept. 1996.

[21] M. Swanson, L. Stoller, and J. Carter. Increasing TLB reach using superpages backed by shadow memory. In *Proc. of the 25th ISCA*, June 1998.

[22] O. Temam, E. D. Granston, and W. Jalby. To copy or not to copy: A compile-time technique for assessing when data copying should be used to eliminate cache conflicts. In *Proc. of SC '93*, pp. 410–419, Portland, OR, Nov. 1993.

[23] M. Valero, T. Lang, J. Llaberia, M. Peiron, E. Ayguade, and J. Navarro. Increasing the number of strides for conflict-free vector access. In *Proc. of the 19th ISCA*, pp. 372–381, Gold Coast, Australia, 1992.

[24] E. Waingold, et al. Baring it all to software: Raw machines. *IEEE Computer*, pp. 86–93, Sept. 1997.

[25] Y. Yamada. *Data Relocation and Prefetching in Programs with Large Data Sets*. PhD thesis, UIUC, Urbana, IL, 1995.

[26] X. Zhang, A. Dasdan, M. Schulz, R. K. Gupta, and A. A. Chien. Architectural adaptation for application-specific locality optimizations. In *Proc. of the 1997 ICCD*, 1997.

Access Order and Effective Bandwidth for Streams on a Direct Rambus Memory

Sung I. Hong, Sally A. McKee[†], Maximo H. Salinas, Robert H. Klenke, James H. Aylor, Wm. A. Wulf

Dept. of Electrical and Computer Engineering
University of Virginia
Charlottesville, VA 22903

[†]Dept. of Computer Science
University of Utah
Salt Lake City, Utah 84112

Abstract

Processor speeds are increasing rapidly, and memory speeds are not keeping up. Streaming computations (such as multi-media or scientific applications) are among those whose performance is most limited by the memory bottleneck. Rambus hopes to bridge the processor/memory performance gap with a recently introduced DRAM that can deliver up to 1.6Gbytes/sec. We analyze the performance of these interesting new memory devices on the inner loops of streaming computations, both for traditional memory controllers that treat all DRAM transactions as random cacheline accesses, and for controllers augmented with streaming hardware. For our benchmarks, we find that accessing unit-stride streams in cacheline bursts in the natural order of the computation exploits from 44-76% of the peak bandwidth of a memory system composed of a single Direct RDRAM device, and that accessing streams via a streaming mechanism with a simple access ordering scheme can improve performance by factors of 1.18 to 2.25.

1. Introduction

As processors continue to become faster and to consume more bandwidth, conventional DRAM memory systems will have more and more difficulty keeping up. The kinds of applications that are particularly affected by the growing processor-memory performance gap include scientific computations, multi-media codecs, encryption, signal processing, and text searching. Although data caches perform well for some access patterns, the vectors used in these *streaming computations* are normally much too large to cache in their entirety, and each element is typically visited only once during lengthy portions of the computation. This lack of temporal locality of reference makes caching less effective, and performance becomes limited by the speed of the memory system.

The new Direct Rambus DRAMs (RDRAMs) propose to bridge the current performance gap with a pipelined microarchitecture that allows direct control of all DRAM row and column resources concurrently with data transfer operations [21]. The RDRAM memory architecture merits study for several reasons: its interface, architecture, and timing are unique; it advertises a peak bandwidth of 1.6Gbytes/sec, a significant improvement over that of other currently available memory devices; all of the top thirteen DRAM suppliers are actively developing Direct RDRAMS; and Intel has selected the Direct Rambus technology to become its next PC main-memory standard [7].

Like nearly all modern DRAMs, Direct RDRAMs implement a form of *page mode* operation. In page mode, memory devices behave as if implemented with a single line, or *page*, of cache on chip. A memory access falling outside the address range of the current DRAM page forces a new page to be accessed. The overhead time required to do this makes servicing such a request significantly slower than one that hits the current page. The order of requests affects the performance of all such components. Access order also affects bus utilization and how well the available parallelism can be exploited in memories with multiple banks.

These three observations — the inefficiency of traditional, dynamic caching for streaming computations; the high advertised bandwidth of Direct Rambus DRAMs; and the order-sensitive performance of modern DRAMs — motivated our investigation of a hardware streaming mechanism that dynamically reorders memory accesses in a Rambus-based memory system.

This paper explains how the details of the Direct Rambus interface affect sustained, streaming accesses, and presents analytic and simulation results for inner loops of streaming kernels performed on a memory system composed of a single Direct RDRAM device. We evaluate two memory interleaving schemes, deriving bounds on the percentage of available memory bandwidth exploited when accessing streams via (a) cacheline accesses in the natural order of the computation, and (b) streaming hardware that dynamically reorders accesses. We find that the former approach generally fails to exploit much of the potential memory bandwidth. Adding hardware support for streaming improves the performance of these Direct RDRAM systems, allowing computations on streams of a thousand or more elements to utilize nearly all of the available memory bandwidth. A system with streaming support outperforms a traditional Rambus system by factors of up to 2.25 for stride one and 2.20 for strides bigger than a cacheline.

2. Background

To put the analysis and results in Section 5 and Section 6 in perspective, this section describes basic Dynamic Random Access Memory (DRAM) organization and operation, compares and contrasts the timing parameters of several types of current DRAMs, and explains how the new Direct RDRAMs work.

2.1 DRAM basics

DRAM storage cell arrays are typically rectangular, and thus a data access sequence consists of a *row access* (RAS, or *row address strobe* signal) followed by a one or more *column accesses* (CAS, or *column address strobe* signal). During RAS, the row address is presented to the DRAM. In page mode, data in the storage cells of the decoded row are moved into a bank of *sense amplifiers* (the "sense amps" or *page buffer*), which serves as a row cache. During CAS, the column address is decoded and the selected data is read from the sense amps. Consecutive accesses to the current row — called *page hits* — require only a CAS, allowing data to be accessed at the maximum frequency.

Sung Hong's current address: Lockheed Martin Federal Systems, 9500 Godwin Dr. Manassas, VA 20110, sung.hong@lmco.com.

The key timing parameters used to analyze DRAM performance include the row-access time (t_{RAC}), column-access time (t_{CAC}), page-mode cycle time (t_{PC}), and random read/write cycle time (t_{RC}). Typical timing parameter values for various common DRAMs are given in Figure 1 [14][21]. Extended Data Out (EDO) DRAMs are similar to fast-page mode DRAMs, except that *data buffers* are added between the column decoder and the input/output buffer. These buffers permit data transfer to extend beyond the CAS signal de-assertion, allowing a faster page-cycle time. Burst-EDO DRAMs transfer larger blocks of data by incorporating an internal counter. After the memory controller transfers the initial address, this internal counter generates the subsequent memory addresses in the block. SDRAMs synchronize all inputs and outputs to a system clock, allowing an even faster page-cycle time.

		Fast-Page Mode	EDO	Burst-EDO	SDRAM	Direct RDRAM
nsec	t_{RAC}	50	50	52	50	50
	t_{CAC}	13	13	10	9	20
	t_{RC}	95	89	90	100	85
	t_{PC}	30	20	15	10	10*
MHz	max freq.	33	50	66	100	400

*The packet transfer time, since t_{PC} doesn't apply here.

Figure 1 Typical DRAM timing parameters

2.2 Rambus DRAMs

Although the memory core — the banks and sense amps — of RDRAMs is similar to that of other DRAMs, the architecture and interface are unique. An RDRAM is actually an interleaved memory system integrated onto a single memory chip. Its pipelined microarchitecture supports up to four outstanding requests. Currently, all 64 Mbit RDRAMs incorporate at least eight independent banks of memory. Some RDRAM cores incorporate 16 banks in a "double bank" architecture, but two adjacent banks cannot be accessed simultaneously, making the total number of independent banks effectively eight [20].

First-generation *Base RDRAMs* use a 64-bit or 72-bit internal bus and a 64-to-8 or 72-to-9 bit multiplexer to deliver bandwidth of 500 to 600 Mbytes/sec. Second-generation *Concurrent RDRAMs* deliver the same peak bandwidth, but an improved protocol allows better bandwidth utilization by handling multiple concurrent transactions. Current, third-generation *Direct RDRAMs* double the external data bus width from 8/9-bits to 16/18-bits and increase the clock frequency from 250/300 MHz to 400 MHz. A memory system composed of these chips has been observed to operate near 95% efficiency under multimedia PC workloads [7].

The Direct Rambus interface converts the 10 ns on-chip bus, which provides 16 bytes on each internal clock, to a two-byte wide, external, 1.25 ns bus. By transferring 16 bits of data on each edge of the 400MHz interface clock, even a single Direct RDRAM chip can yield up to 1.6 Gbytes/sec in bandwidth.

Figure 2 illustrates timing parameter definitions for Direct RDRAMs. All communication to and from an RDRAM is performed using *packets*. Each command or data packet requires four 2.5 ns clock cycles to transfer. ROW command packets are used for *activate* (ACT) or *precharge* (PRER) operations. COL command packets are used to initiate data transfer between the sense amps and the data bus (via RD or WR commands), or to retire data in the chip's write buffer. In addition, COL packets may also

initiate a precharge operation. The smallest addressable data size is 128 bits (two 64-bit stream elements). The full memory bandwidth cannot be utilized unless all words in a DATA packet are used. Note the distinction between the RDRAM transfer rate (800 MHz), the RDRAM interface clock rate (400 MHz), and the packet transfer rate (100 MHz). All references to cycles in the following sections are in terms of the 400 MHz interface clock.

Timings for a Min -50 -800 Direct RDRAM Part*		
t_{CYCLE}	interface clock cycle time (400 MHz)	2.5ns
t_{PACK}	packet transfer time	4 t_{CYCLE} 10ns
t_{RCD}	min interval between ROW & COL packets	11 t_{CYCLE} 27.5 ns
t_{RP}	page precharge time: min interval between ROW precharge (PRER) & activate (ACT) packets	10 t_{CYCLE} 25 ns
t_{CPOL}	column/precharge overlap: max overlap between last COL packet & start of row PRER	1 t_{CYCLE} 2.5 ns
t_{CAC}	page hit latency: delay between start of COL packet & valid data	8 t_{CYCLE} 20 ns
t_{RAC}	page miss latency: delay between start of ROW ACT request & valid data ($t_{RCD} + t_{CAC} + 1$) extra cycle	20 t_{CYCLE} 50 ns
t_{RC}	page miss cycle time: min interval between successive ROW ACT requests (random read/ write cycle time for single device)	34 t_{CYCLE} 85 ns
t_{RR}	Row/row packet delay: min delay between consecutive ROW accesses to the same RDRAM device	8 t_{CYCLE} 20 ns
t_{RDLY}	Roundtrip bus delay: latency between start of COL packet & valid data (added to read page-hit times, since DATA packet travels in opposite direction of commands; no delay for writes)	2 t_{CYCLE} 5 ns
t_{RW}	Read/write bus turnaround: interval between writing & reading ($t_{PACK} + t_{RDLY}$)	6 t_{CYCLE} 15 n

*These are the key parameters that affect our study. For complete timing parameters and most recent data sheets, see http://www.rambus.com/.

Figure 2 RDRAM timing parameter definitions

The RDRAM has separate pins for row address, column address, and data. Each bank's sense amplifiers can be independently opened, accessed, and precharged. For example, one bank's page can be left open while accessing another bank's sense amps. This independence permits a number of precharge policies. In a *closed-page* policy, the sense amps are always precharged after a data access (or burst of accesses) to a bank. In an *open-page* policy, the sense amps are left open — unprecharged — after a data access to a bank. A closed-page policy works best when successive accesses are expected to be to different pages, and an open-page policy works best when successive accesses are likely to be to the same page. We give more details and examples of RDRAM timing protocols in Section 5; see the Direct RDRAM Data Sheet for complete details [21].

3. Dynamic access ordering

Operating Direct RDRAM chips at peak efficiency requires that the memory requests be issued in an order that exploits the locality of the page buffers and the parallelism provided by the interface and the many banks. The unlikelihood of achieving the optimal order through serendipity (or through the compiler, which seldom knows the details of the memory system) makes RDRAM systems good candidates for *access ordering*, which we define as any technique that changes the order of memory requests from that generated by the issuing program. Here we are specifically concerned with ordering vector-like stream accesses. In earlier work, we proposed a combined hardware/software scheme for implementing access ordering dynamically at run-time, and presented results demonstrating its effectiveness on a single-processor system [16][17]. The interface, architecture, and timing differences between Direct Rambus DRAMs and conventional DRAMs motivated us to investigate the design of dynamic access ordering hardware for RDRAM memory systems.

Our approach augments a general-purpose microprocessor system with a *Stream Memory Controller* (SMC), the logical organization of which is shown in Figure 3. The compiler detects the presence of streams (as in [1]), and generates code to transmit information about those streams (base address, stride, number of elements, and whether the stream is being read or written) to the hardware at runtime. To avoid polluting the cache, we provide a separate *Stream Buffer Unit* (SBU) for stream elements; all stream data — and only stream data — use these buffers. From the processor's point of view, each buffer is a FIFO. Each stream is mapped to exactly one FIFO, the head of which is a memory-mapped register. The processor accesses the next element of a stream by dereferencing the head of the corresponding queue.

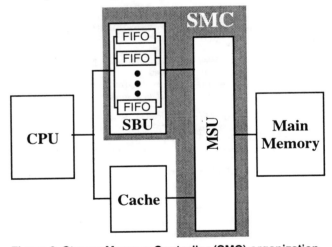

Figure 3 Stream Memory Controller (SMC) organization

To take advantage of the order sensitivity of the memory system, we include a scheduling unit that is capable of reordering accesses. This *Memory Scheduling Unit* (MSU) prefetches the reads, buffers the writes, and dynamically reorders the memory accesses to stream elements, issuing the requests in a sequence that attempts to maximize effective memory bandwidth. Because the stream data is buffered within the SMC, the microprocessor can still issue its memory requests in the natural order of the computation. In principle, the MSU can access the SBU's internal storage in an arbitrary order, and thus the buffers may appear as a small

addressable memory or register file from the memory system's point of view. Note that this model still uses the normal cache hierarchy for non-stream accesses, and for these, the MSU provides the same functionality and performance as a traditional memory controller.

We built two experimental versions of an SMC system in which each proof-of-concept implementation was a single ASIC interfaced to an Intel i860 host processor [12]. We selected the i860 because it provides load/store instructions that bypass the cache. The memory system consisted of two banks of 1 Mbit × 36 fast-page mode components with 1 Kbyte pages. We found that an SMC significantly improves the effective memory bandwidth, exploiting over 90% of the attainable bandwidth for long-vector computations. For a specific set of benchmark kernels, we observed speedups by factors of two to 13 over normal caching and of up to 23 over non-caching accesses issued in the natural order of the computation. The technique is practical to implement, exploiting existing compiler technology and requiring only a modest amount of special purpose hardware [16][17].

Even though the hardware we built and that we model in this study does not cache stream data, the dynamic access ordering described here is equally valid for memory systems such as Impulse [24] that perform intelligent access ordering and/or prefetching and buffering within the memory controller, but transmit data in cacheline increments to a processor chip with a traditional cache hierarchy. *The decision whether or not to cache stream data is orthogonal to the problem of designing an efficient memory controller for modern DRAMs.*

4. Experimental framework

We want to determine the maximum possible bandwidth utilization for inner loops of streaming applications on a range of Direct RDRAM system configurations. To this end, we have developed analytic models of maximum performance for each configuration, both with and without access ordering hardware. We expect that in practice the performance of a traditional memory system on streaming computations will correspond closely to these limits. Performance for dynamic access ordering systems is sensitive to many more parameters, and is thus more variable. Therefore, in addition to mathematically analyzing the performance limits when using the SMC, we perform detailed functional simulations of each system to determine how well the streaming hardware exploits the system's available bandwidth.

We examine two memory configurations:
- a closed-page policy with *Cacheline Interleaving* (CLI), so successive cachelines reside in different RDRAM banks, and
- an open page policy with *Page Interleaving* (PI), so crossing an RDRAM page boundary means switching banks.

These were chosen because they represent two extreme points of the design space for RDRAM memory systems and are both employed in real system designs [20]. Henceforth, references to CLI systems imply a closed-page policy, and references to PI systems imply an open-page policy.

4.1 Modeling assumptions

We assume that the cacheline size is an integer multiple of the packet size, and that the RDRAM page size is an integer multiple of the cacheline size. For simplicity in our equations, we model all vectors in a streaming computation to be of equal stride, length, and size. Each vector is composed of 64-bit elements, is aligned to begin on a cacheline boundary, and is a multiple of the cacheline size in length. Distinct vectors do not share any DRAM pages in common. Within an inner loop, the processor consumes or generates one element of each vector on each iteration. For PI systems, we assume vectors[1] do not share any banks in common, and refresh delays and page miss overheads from crossing page boundaries are ignored, since they can be overlapped with accesses to other banks.

In our analytic models, we assume that the SMC's read FIFOs are completely empty and write FIFOs are completely full whenever the SMC begins servicing them. All bank conflict delays are ignored. These assumptions make the performance bounds more optimistic, and thus harder to achieve in practice.

We assume that the system is matched so that the bandwidth between the microprocessor and the SMC matches the bandwidth between the SMC and memory. In other words, the CPU can consume data items at the memory's maximum rate of supply, and the SMC can keep up with both the CPU and the memory system. We model the processor as a generator of only loads and stores of stream elements. All non-stream accesses are assumed to hit in cache, and all computation is assumed to be infinitely fast. These modeling assumptions stress the memory system as much as possible. A faster CPU would let an SMC system exploit more of the memory system's available bandwidth, but overall performance would be limited by the speed of the memory. A faster CPU would not affect our analysis for random-access cacheline fills.

4.2 Functional simulation environment

We evaluate how much effective bandwidth the SMC could deliver in practice by adapting our cycle-based, functional SMC model for fast-page mode memory systems to model a Direct RDRAM SMC system. Analytic and simulation results for the fast-page mode systems correlate highly with measured hardware performance for our proof-of-concept implementations, validating the simulation and analytic models on which the work presented here is based.

In modeling the SMC, we assume that the MSU considers each FIFO in turn, performing as many accesses as possible for the current FIFO before moving on. This simple round-robin scheduling strategy represents a reasonable compromise between design complexity and performance [16][11], but it prevents the MSU from fully exploiting the independent banks of the RDRAM when a FIFO is ready for a data transfer but the associated memory bank is busy. Hong investigates a more sophisticated scheduling algorithm that attempts to avoid such bank conflicts [11].

We represent the extremes of the performance spectrum with respect to the MSU's scheduling strategy and data placement by modeling two vector alignments: with base addresses aligned to map to the same bank (so the SMC incurs a bank-conflict delay when switching FIFOs), and with base addresses staggered to map to different banks.

4.3 Benchmark kernels

We present results for a subset of the same benchmarks used to evaluate our experimental SMC system with fast-page mode DRAMs. Shown in Figure 4, these kernels were chosen because they are representative of the access patterns found in real codes. *Daxpy* and *copy* are from the Basic Linear Algebra Subroutines (BLAS) [9], *hydro* is from the Livermore Fortran Kernels [18], and *vaxpy* denotes a vector operation that occurs in matrix-vector multiplication by diagonals.

---

1. We use the terms *vector* and *stream* interchangeably, but they are not precisely the same: a read-modify-write vector constitutes two streams, a read-stream and a write-stream.

copy:	$\forall i$	$y_i \leftarrow x_i$
daxpy:	$\forall i$	$y_i \leftarrow ax_i + y_i$
hydro:	$\forall i$	$x_i \leftarrow q + y_i \times (r \times zx_{i+10} + t \times zx_{i+11})$
vaxpy:	$\forall i$	$y_i \leftarrow a_i x_i + y_i$

Figure 4 Benchmark kernels

5. Analytic models

This section presents bounds for effective memory bandwidth on a system composed of Direct RDRAMs when streams are either accessed by cachelines in the natural order of the computation or via an SMC. We use these bounds to compare the performance potential of different accessing schemes and to evaluate our simulation results. Throughout this paper, *effective bandwidth* and *percentage of peak bandwidth* describe the percentage of the total memory bandwidth exploited for a particular configuration and accessing scheme. Peak bandwidth for Direct RDRAM systems is the maximum data transfer rate, 1.6 Gbytes/sec.

Let b be the number of memory banks on an RDRAM, w_p be the number of vector elements (64-bit words) per packet, σ be the vector stride in 64-bit words, and t_{PACK} be the transfer time of one DATA packet. In a CLI organization, the number of contiguous addresses mapped to a single bank of memory is equal to the size (in 64-bit words) of the cacheline (L_c). In a PI organization, the number of contiguous elements mapped to a single bank of memory is equal to the number of 64-bit words in a DRAM page (L_P).

To illustrate the timing differences between the two organizations, consider an inner loop that reads streams x and y, performs some computation on them, and writes a result stream z (so the body of the loop is modeled as {rd x[i]; rd y[i]; st z[i];}). Let each cacheline hold four 64-bit stream elements, and let the organization be CLI. The memory activity for this computation on this system is illustrated in Figure 5. If we assume that the cache controller supports *linefill buffer forwarding*, so that the CPU can read all the data in the line buffer as soon as they are retrieved from memory (as in the PowerPC [8]), then the store request can be initiated as soon as the first data packet is received, t_{RAC} after the last load request. Note that the t_{RAC} delay is a property of the RDRAM's commodity core, not an artifact of the interface. Successive load requests are separated by t_{RR}, the required latency between ROW command packets. Here we model 32-byte lines — for long cachelines, the t_{RR} delay is overlapped with data transfer, and no additional delay between command packets is required. The PRER command packet is sent t_{RAS} cycles after the previous ROW ACT packet, and the next ROW ACT packet must follow by at least t_{RP}. The precharge (not shown in Figure 5) can be completely overlapped with other activity, since $t_{RAS} + t_{RP} < 2t_{RR} + t_{RAC}$.

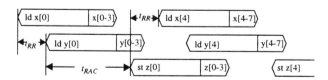

Figure 5 CLI closed-page timing for three-stream loop

If we perform the same loop on a PI system, then we pay the cost for precharging the RDRAM page for the first cacheline accessed for each stream, but subsequent lines for that stream can be accessed quickly, since the data is already in the sense amps. This memory activity is depicted in Figure 6.

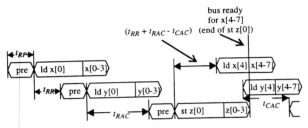

Figure 6 PI open-page timing for three-stream loop

Direct RDRAMs use write buffers to temporarily store data to be written to memory. To properly retire the data in the write buffer, a COL RET packet must be inserted between the last COL WR packet and the next COL RD packet. Thus a t_{PACK} delay occurs between the end of write DATA packet and the start of the read DATA packet. In addition, an interval of t_{RDLY} must be added between the start of a COL RD packet and valid data, since the DATA packet travels in the opposite direction from the command. We combine these two latencies into t_{RW}, which denotes the entire the read/write bus turnaround time.

5.1 Cache performance bounds

We first develop equations to describe the maximum percentage of peak bandwidth delivered by accessing streams in cacheline increments in the natural order of the computation.[1] These bounds ignore the time to write dirty cachelines back to memory, and are thus not necessarily accurate predictors of the performance streaming computations might observe in practice; nonetheless, they provide an optimistic performance bound, and are useful for SMC performance comparisons in this initial study. The impact of cacheline writebacks on performance depends largely on how often these operations generate bank conflicts. If there are few conflicts, then these accesses can be pipelined and overlapped with operations to other banks, hiding their latency.

The performance limit for natural-order cacheline accesses depends on the average time T to access each data word, which in turn depends on the vector stride. We present equations for small-stride streams here; see Hong's master's thesis for analysis of streams whose stride exceeds the cacheline size [11]. Effective bandwidth is:

$$\% \text{ peak bandwidth} = \frac{100}{T \times w_p / t_{PACK}} \quad (5.1)$$

Single stream bandwidth for closed-page policies

For a system implementing a closed-page policy, the time required for one cacheline access is:

$$T_{LCC} = t_{RAC} + t_{PACK} \times \left(\frac{L_c}{w_p} - 1 \right) \quad (5.2)$$

---

1. We cannot cover all possible scenarios for command sequences here. Note also that the RDRAM data sheets are moving targets. Consult the Rambus web pages for complete, up-to-date information.

The average latency of each data word of a single stream with stride less than the cacheline size is simply the total time required to load a cacheline divided by number of useful words fetched:

$$T = \frac{T_{LCC}}{L_c / \sigma} \quad (5.3)$$

Multiple stream bandwidth for closed-page policies

Equation 5.2 and Equation 5.3 describe memory latency when accessing a single stream. When there are multiple streams in the computation, then the pipelining of the Direct RDRAMs comes into play. We model asymptotic performance in terms of overlapped memory requests in cacheline-sized blocks. Let s_r be the number of streams being read, s_w be the number of streams being written, and $s = s_r + s_w$ be the total number of streams in the computation. If L_s denotes the length of the streams, then unit-stride streams generate L_s / L_c cacheline accesses.

Consider the sample loop and timing depicted in Figure 5. For pipelined accesses and 32-byte cache lines, the latency between one cacheline access and the next to the *same* stream (e.g., from the start of ld x[0] to the start of ld x[4]) is $t_{RR} + t_{RAC} + t_{RR}$. If we had another stream in the loop, we would have $t_{RR} + t_{RR} + t_{RAC} + t_{RR}$. For longer cache lines, the remaining data packets delay the issue of each subsequent ROW ACT packet, so that command and data packet activity cannot be completely overlapped. This generalizes to:

$$T_{pipe} = t_{RAC} + \max\left(t_{RR}, \frac{L_c}{w_p} \times t_{PACK} \right)(s - 1) \quad (5.4)$$

The final accesses in the loop are not overlapped with other activity, so from the start of ld x[n-4] to the completion of st z[n-4], we have:

- t_{RR} between the start of ld x[n-4] and the start of ld y[n-4],
- t_{RAC} between the start of ld y[n-4] and the start of st z[n-4], and
- T_{LCC} to complete st z[n-4].

If there were another stream in the loop, the latency would be $t_{RR} + t_{RR} + t_{RAC} + T_{LCC}$. This generalizes to:

$$T_{last} = t_{RR}(s - 2) + t_{RAC} + T_{LCC} \quad (5.5)$$

So for T_{pipe}, one stream requires t_{RAC} and the rest take t_{RR}; for T_{last}, one stream requires t_{RAC}, one requires T_{LCC}, and the rest require t_{RR}. The latency for the whole computation is T_{last} for the last cachelines accessed for the streams, plus one less than the number of cachelines multiplied by T_{pipe}.

$$\text{cycles} = \left(\frac{L_s}{L_c} - 1 \right) T_{pipe} + T_{last} \quad (5.6)$$

For all but very short streams, T_{pipe} will dominate T_{last}. The average access time per element is Equation 5.6 divided by the total number of stream elements accessed.

Single stream bandwidth for open-page policies

PI systems map consecutive cachelines to the same bank of an RDRAM. This means that the initial precharge and page miss latencies cannot be hidden, but that subsequent accesses to cachelines in the current page incur only the t_{CAC} latency (between the COL packet and valid data). The equations to model asymptotic performance for this system are similar to those for CLI, but precharge and bus conflict delays must be taken into account.

The time to perform a cacheline access from a page currently in the sense amps is:

$$T_{LCO} = t_{CAC} + t_{PACK} \times \left(\frac{L_c}{w_p} - 1 \right) \qquad (5.7)$$

Recall that L_p, the RDRAM page size in 64-bit words, is an integer multiple of L_c. If we incur the page miss penalty whenever we switch RDRAM banks, the average latency of each data word of a single stream with small stride is the total time spent accessing the data in one page divided by the portion of useful data in that page (L_p / σ):

$$T = \frac{(T_{LCC} + T_{LCO}((L_p/L_c)-1))}{L_p / \sigma} \qquad (5.8)$$

This is the time to precharge the page (t_{RP}), plus the time to access the first cacheline (T_{LCC}, as in the closed-page policy case), plus the time to access the remaining cachelines from the open pages, adjusted for the portion of data that was actually useful.

Multiple stream bandwidth for open-page policies

For multiple-vector computations, the latency between the start of one cacheline access and the next from the same stream (after the initial precharge) is:

$$T_{pipe} = T_{LCO} + \left(\frac{L_c}{w_p}(s-2) + 1 \right) t_{PACK} \qquad (5.9)$$

The first group of memory requests (the first access to each stream) must perform the precharge operations, and thus they require:

$$T_{init} = (2 \times t_{RP}) + t_{RAC} + T_{LCC} + (t_{RP} + t_{RR}) \times (s-2) \qquad (5.10)$$

Combining Equation 5.9 and Equation 5.10 gives the lower bound on the number of cycles to perform all the stream accesses:

$$\text{cycles} = T_{init} + \left(\frac{L_s}{L_c} - 1 \right) T_{pipe} \qquad (5.11)$$

The average access time per element is Equation 5.11 divided by the total number of stream elements accessed.

5.2 SMC performance bounds

In this section, we develop analytic bounds on the achievable effective bandwidth of a Stream Memory Controller system using Direct RDRAMs. These will then be used to evaluate the simulation performance of our SMC design for Rambus memory systems. For simplicity, the following equations assume unit-stride streams; see [11] for extensions to non-unit strides. Two different bounds govern SMC performance: the *startup delay*, and the *asymptotic bandwidth limit*.

The bound on bandwidth caused by either limit is the minimum time to complete all stream accesses for the computation divided by that minimum plus any extra cycles of delay:

$$\% \text{ Peak Bandwidth} = \frac{L_s(t_{PACK}/w_p) \times s}{\Delta + L_s(t_{PACK}/w_p) \times s} \times 100 \qquad (5.15)$$

Here Δ denotes either the startup delay (from Equation 5.16 for CLI organizations, or from Equation 5.17 for PI organizations) or the bus turnaround delay (from Equation 5.18), both described below.

Startup delay bound

The startup delay bound Δ_1 describes the time that the processor must wait to perform the first iteration of a loop. Since the MSU issues as many accesses as possible for the current FIFO before beginning to service the next, the processor waits for the *first element of the last read-stream* in the computation while the MSU prefetches a FIFO's worth of elements from each of the previous read-streams. The startup delay thus increases with FIFO depth and the number of read-streams, but for long vector computations, this one-time delay has little impact on effective bandwidth.

Recall that s_r denotes the number of read-streams in the computation. If we let f be the FIFO depth (in 64-bit words), t_{PACK} be the transfer time of one DATA packet, and w_p be the number of elements per packet, then the startup delay for CLI systems is:

$$\Delta_{1,CLI} = (s_r - 1) \left(f \times \frac{t_{PACK}}{w_p} \right) + t_{RAC} \qquad (5.16)$$

For PI systems with an open page policy, we need to add the precharge time associated with the first vector access:

$$\Delta_{1,PI} = (s_r - 1) \left(f \times \frac{t_{PACK}}{w_p} \right) + t_{RAC} + t_{RP} \qquad (5.17)$$

Asymptotic bandwidth bound

If a computation's vectors are long enough to make startup costs negligible, the limiting performance factor becomes the read-write *bus turnaround* delay. Whenever the RDRAM data bus cycles from write back to read mode, a delay of t_{RW} — the bus turnaround time — must be inserted. Because the CPU is draining or filling the FIFOs while the MSU is accessing memory, the MSU can perform more than f consecutive requests for a FIFO. Given our modeling assumptions of matched bandwidths between the CPU, SMC, and memory, if a read FIFO is completely empty when the MSU starts to fill it, as many as $F = fs/(s-1)$ elements can be fetched before the FIFO will be full (see [16] or [11] for details). The MSU will service this particular FIFO at least L_s/F times during the computation. The total bus turnaround latency Δ_2 for both CLI and PI is t_{RW} multiplied by the minimum number of times the bus switches direction for the entire computation. If all read FIFOs are serviced before any write FIFOs each time the MSU performs its round-robin cycle, then we incur the bus turnaround delay once every tour of service:

$$\Delta_2 = \frac{t_{RW} \times L_s}{F} = \frac{t_{RW} L_s (s-1)}{fs} \qquad (5.18)$$

For sufficiently deep FIFOs, the asymptotic bound (Equation 5.18 substituted into Equation 5.15) approaches 100% of peak. Increasing the speed of the processor relative to the memory would raise this limit towards the full system bandwidth for shallower FIFOs. Note that this asymptotic bound differs significantly from that for an SMC system with fast-page mode memory [17]. In fast-page mode systems, performance is limited by the number of DRAM page misses that a computation incurs. Since Direct RDRAM page miss times can be overlapped with pipelined memory operations, the limiting factor for long-stream computations becomes bus turnaround time.

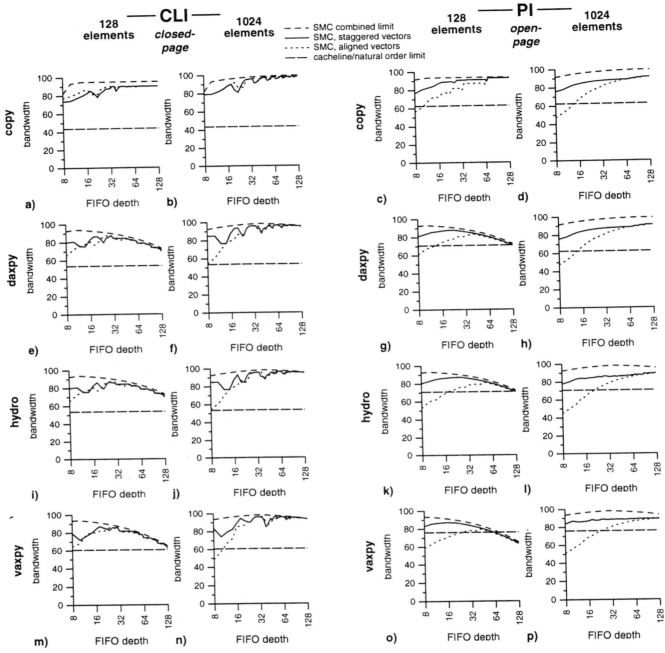

Figure 7 Percentages of peak bandwidth

6. Results

In our experiments, we model memory systems composed of Direct RDRAMs with eight independent banks and 1Kbyte pages (128 64-bit words, L_p). The vectors we use are either 128 (short), or 1024 (medium length) 64-bit elements in length, and are unit-stride unless otherwise stated. Two 64-bit stream elements (w_p) fit in a

DATA packet, and four elements (L_c) fit in a cacheline. We consider FIFO depths from eight to 128 stream elements.

Figure 7 illustrates our results for each of the four multi-vector benchmark kernels and the two memory interleaving schemes. Graphs in a given row show results for the same benchmark. Those on the left side of the figure indicate performance for CLI systems (with cacheline interleaving and a close-page policy), and those on the right, PI systems (with page interleaving and an open-page policy). The long-dashed lines in these graphs indicate the maximum bandwidth that can be exploited when accessing streams via cachelines in the computation's natural order. Even though this performance bound has nothing to do with FIFO depth, we represent it as a line in our graphs to facilitate comparisons with SMC performance. This limit is optimistic in that it ignores potential delays from writing dirty lines back to memory and assumes an optimal data placement such that the computation encounters no bank conflicts (so the bank conflict time in our cache models (BC_t) is merely the minimum time between accesses to different pages (t_{RC})). The dotted lines labeled "SMC, aligned vectors" show simulated SMC performance when the vector data layout causes the maximal number of bank conflicts, and the solid lines labeled "SMC, staggered vectors" illustrate results for a more advantageous data placement. The dashed lines show the combined SMC asymptotic and startup-delay bounds: ascending portions represent the asymptotic bound, and descending or flat portions represent the influence of the startup delay.

Our results for cacheline accesses of streams in Figure 7 are lower than the 95% efficiency rate that Crisp reports [7]. This difference is due to the fact that we model streaming kernels on a memory system composed of a *single* RDRAM device, whereas Crisp's experiments model more random access patterns on a system with *many* devices. For kernels with four or fewer streams, we find that effective bandwidth is limited to less than 76% for PI systems and less than 61% for CLI systems. Maximum effective bandwidth increases with the number of streams in the computation: loops with more streams exploit the Direct RDRAM's available concurrency better by enabling more pipelined loads or stores to be performed between each bus-turnaround delay. A computation on eight, independent, unit-stride streams (seven read-streams and one write-stream, aligned in memory so that there are no bank conflicts between cacheline accesses) incurs a performance bound of 88.68% of peak bandwidth for stride-one vectors on a PI system, and 76.11% of peak on a CLI system. When the vector stride increases to four or more — so that three-fourths of the data in the cacheline goes unused — this performance drops to 22.17% and 19.03% of peak bandwidth for PI and CLI systems, respectively. Even though PI organizations perform better than CLI organizations for streaming, they should perform much worse than CLI for more random, non-stream accesses, where successive cacheline accesses are unlikely to be to the same RDRAM page.

Although performance for accessing cachelines in the computation's natural order is sensitive to the number of streams in the computation, performance for the SMC is uniformly good, regardless of the number of streams in the loop or the order in which the processor accesses them. An SMC always beats using natural-order cacheline accesses for CLI memory organizations, and an SMC with deep FIFOs on unit-stride, long-vector computations delivers between 2.11 (for *vaxpy*) to 2.94 (for *copy*) times the maximum potential performance of the naive approach. The improvement is smaller for shorter vectors or shallower FIFOs, particularly for an unfavorable vector alignment.

For PI organizations and appropriate FIFO depths, an SMC still beats the natural order every time, although the improvements here are smaller than for CLI systems. The best FIFO depth must be chosen experimentally, since the SMC performance limits developed in Section 5.2 do not help in calculating appropriate FIFO depths for a computation *a priori* (this differs from the SMC that we built with a fast-page mode memory system, for which we derived a compiler algorithm to calculate appropriate FIFO depth according to the number, length, and type of streams).

Note that in the graphs for the *copy* kernel, shown in Figure 7(a)-(d), the startup-delay bound does not decrease with increasing FIFO depth. The startup delay here results entirely from the additional latency for the first cacheline access (t_{RAC} for CLI systems, $t_{RAC} + t_{RP}$ for PI systems), since there is only one stream being read. For this kernel, the processor does not have to wait for elements of other read-streams to be prefetched during its first loop iteration. For *copy* using 128-element vectors, this small delay limits effective bandwidth to about 95% of peak, but for longer vector computations, the effects are barely detectable. For *copy* with streams of 1024 elements, the SMC exploits over 98% of the system's peak bandwidth.

Vector alignment has little impact on effective bandwidth for SMC systems with CLI memory organizations, as evidenced by the nearly identical performances for the simulations of maximal and minimal numbers of bank conflicts on systems with FIFOs deeper than 16 elements (shown on the left side of Figure 7). A larger performance difference arises between the maximum and minimum bank-conflict simulations for SMC systems with PI memory organizations and FIFO depths of 32 elements or fewer. With deep FIFOs (64-128 elements) and long vectors, the SMC can deliver good performance even for a sub-optimal data placement, yielding over 89% of the *attainable bandwidth* (defined by the analytic SMC performance bounds) for all benchmarks.

SMC performance approaches the bandwidth limits in all cases except for computations on 1024-element vectors on PI systems with an open-page policy, shown in the right-hand column of Figure 7. This difference in the SMC's ability to exploit available bandwidth results from our simple MSU scheduling policy. When the MSU's current request misses the RDRAM page, it must initiate a precharge operation before it can access the data. This means that we incur a precharge delay (t_{RP}) for the first access of each stream, and every time the stream crosses an RDRAM page boundary. We also incur a precharge delay whenever a bank conflict occurs. Furthermore, when we switch pages, the MSU must issue a row-activation command packet, in addition to the column access packet. These overhead costs occur frequently, and thus have a significant impact on long-stream performance. A scheduling policy that speculatively precharges a page and issues a ROW ACT command before the stream crosses the page boundary would mitigate some of these costs, as would an MSU that overlaps activity for another FIFO with the latency of the precharge and row activate commands. We are still investigating the design and performance tradeoffs of such policies. For computations on shorter streams, the SMC can deliver nearly the effective bandwidth defined by the startup-delay bound.

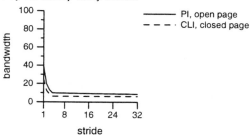

Figure 8 Cacheline fill performance for strided accesses

As stride increases, any RDRAM controller becomes hampered in its ability to deliver peak performance. Data types and strides that do not densely occupy the 128-bit DATA packets can only exploit a fraction of the RDRAM's bandwidth. To put this in perspective, Figure 8 shows the maximum percentage of peak bandwidth that using cacheline accesses in the computation's natural order can deliver when reading single streams of various strides. The solid and dotted lines indicate performance bounds for CLI and PI systems, respectively. The effective bandwidth drops as vector stride increases up to the cacheline size, and remains constant once the stride exceeds the number of words in the cacheline. For these larger strides, the natural-order cacheline accesses only deliver 10% or less of the Direct RDRAM's potential bandwidth.

Increasing the number of non-unit-stride streams accessed increases the potential to exploit the parallelism supported by the Direct RDRAM interface, just as it did for unit-stride streams of Figure 7. To illustrate this, Figure 9 compares performances for the *vaxpy* kernel on vectors of length 1024. The FIFO depth in these experiments is 128 elements. The y-axis in Figure 9 indicates the percentage of *attainable* bandwidth, which for non-unit strides is 50% of the peak system bandwidth. Performance for the SMC systems is sensitive to the stride of the computation, which determines the number of bank conflicts that the MSU will suffer. For PI systems and computations with strides over about 40, using cacheline accesses in the computation's natural order may beat using an SMC with the current, simplistic reordering scheme. For smaller strides, and for some advantageous strides larger than 40, the SMC delivers significantly better performance than the cache can — up to 2.2 times the maximum effective bandwidth of the naive approach. For CLI systems, the SMC delivers up to 1.6 times the bandwidth of the naive approach, but performs worse for strides that are multiples of 16. Note that using natural-order cacheline accesses for these strides is likely to generate many cache conflicts, because the vectors leave a larger footprint. Measuring the negative performance impact of these conflicts is beyond the scope of this study.

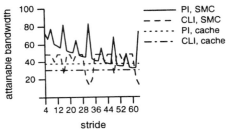

Figure 9 Performance for *vaxpy* with non-unit strides

7. Related work

The recent literature abounds with arguments that traditional caching, no matter how hard we push it, cannot bridge the growing processor-memory performance gap. Burger, Goodman, and Kagi demonstrate that dynamic caching uses memory inefficiently, postulating that pin bandwidth will be a severe performance bottleneck for future microprocessors [3][4]. They calculate cache efficiency, traffic ratios, traffic inefficiencies, and effective pin bandwidths for different levels of the memory hierarchy, finding that the percentage of live data in the cache is generally under 20%, and that current cache sizes are often thousands of times larger than an optimal cache.

McCalpin examines effective memory bandwidth for streaming computations on existing architectures, measuring machine balance for a range of systems [15]. In his experiments, cache miss latency is the key determinant to sustainable memory bandwidth.

Swanson, Stoller, and Carter [22] propose an adaptable main memory controller that increases processor cache utilization and reduces memory bus contention. The Impulse memory system dynamically remaps physical memory to support scatter/gather operations to sparse or non-contiguous data structures, creates shadow superpages that can be mapped to a single TLB entry from non-contiguous physical pages, and prefetches non-unit stride streams into dense cache regions. Our dynamic access ordering approach can be adapted to further improve bandwidth utilization between the Impulse controller and main memory.

Valero et al. propose efficient hardware to avoid bank conflicts dynamically in vector processors [23], and del Corral and Llaberia analyze a related hardware scheme for avoiding bank conflicts among multiple streams in complex memory systems [5]. Memory systems for vector processors are generally composed of SRAMs (which have uniform access times), and so this access-ordering hardware does not reorder requests to individual banks, since it does not need to exploit locality of reference to get better performance. The recently proposed Command Vector Memory system [6] resembles the SMC in its attempts to exploit locality and bank parallelism: the out-of-order vector processor sends command packets (with base, length, and stride information for a single vector) to the memory controller, which uses this information to schedule bursts of stream accesses to the SDRAMs.

Many others have investigated memory hierarchies that incorporate stream buffers. Most of these focus on non-programmable buffers to perform hardware prefetching of consecutive cachelines, such as the prefetch buffers introduced by Jouppi [13]. Since these schemes prefetch cachelines speculatively, the stream buffers may decrease effective bandwidth by fetching unneeded data. Palacharla and Kessler investigate the use of such stream buffers to replace the L2 cache [19], and Farkas et al. identify performance trends and relationships among the various components of the memory hierarchy (including stream buffers) in a dynamically scheduled processor [10]. Both studies find that dynamically reactive stream buffers can yield significant performance increases, but can also increase bandwidth requirements. Farkas et al. mitigate this problem by implementing an incremental prefetching technique that reduces stream buffer bandwidth consumption by 50% without decreasing performance. To the same end, Brooks describes source-program transformations to increase the effective bandwidth delivered by the read-ahead stream buffers implemented in the Cray T3D [2].

8. Conclusions

In this paper, we have investigated how access order affects the effective bandwidth delivered by Rambus memory systems. We present analytic and simulation results for inner loops of streaming computations performed on a memory system composed of a single Direct Rambus DRAM. We find that for systems that access cachelines in the natural order of the computation, a page-interleaved (PI) memory organization is capable of delivering higher effective bandwidth for streams than a cache-line interleaved (CLI) organization, although the latter should deliver better performance for non-stream accesses. By adding hardware support for streaming in the form of a Stream Memory Controller (SMC), we improve the performance of both memory organizations, allowing computations on long streams to utilize nearly all of the available memory bandwidth.

The SMC delivers a larger performance boost on CLI systems, but it can still provide a significant advantage on PI systems. Furthermore, SMC performance is robust: an SMC's ability to exploit memory bandwidth is relatively independent of the processor's access pattern or the number of streams in the computation. An SMC configured with appropriate FIFO depths can always exploit available memory bandwidth better than natural-order cacheline accesses. When we take non-unit strides, cache conflicts, and cache writebacks into account, the SMC's advantages become even more significant.

The SMC described here is integrated onto the processor chip and implements a fairly simple scheduling scheme, albeit one that performs well under most circumstances. More sophisticated access ordering mechanisms are certainly possible, and we have begun investigating a few. These policies warrant further study to determine how robust their performances are, and whether they justify the additional hardware complexity. Other placements of the access ordering hardware are possible, too: an SMC implemented as a separate ASIC, as in the experimental system we built, can deliver most of the performance benefits of the on-chip version.

If stream data bypasses the cache, some mechanism must ensure data coherence between the different components in the memory hierarchy. This could be accomplished by mapping stream pages as non-cacheable, or might require more sophisticated support from the compiler, the hardware, or some combination thereof. We are investigating the performance tradeoffs of using dynamic access ordering to stream data into and out of the L2 cache, which simplifies the coherence mechanism, but which opens up the possibility for cache conflicts to evict needed data prematurely.

Acknowledgments

Thanks go to Tito Autrey, Chenxi Wang, Steve Woo, and the anonymous reviewers for their many helpful comments for improving the content and presentation of this work. Thanks also go to the Oregon Graduate Institute Department of Computer Science and Engineering for providing resources to conduct a portion of this work while the second author was in residence as a visiting scholar.

References

[1] M.E. Benitez and J.W. Davidson, "Code Generation for Streaming: An Access/Execute Mechanism", Proc. 4th Architectural Support for Programming Languages and Operating Systems, April 1991.

[2] J. Brooks, "Single PE Optimization Techniques for the Cray T3D System", Proc. 1st European T3D Workshop, September 1995.

[3] D.C. Burger, J.R. Goodman, and A. Kägi, "The Declining Effectiveness of Dynamic Caching for General-Purpose Microprocessors", Univ. of Wisconsin-Madison Computer Science Dept. Technical Report 1261, January 1995.

[4] D. Burger, J.R. Goodman, A. Kägi, "Quantifying Memory Bandwidth Limitations of Current and Future Microprocessors", Proc. 23rd International Symposium on Computer Architecture, May 1996.

[5] A.M. del Corral and J.M. Llaberia, "Access Order to Avoid Inter-Vector-Conflicts in Complex Memory Systems", Proc. 9th International Parallel Processing Symposium, April 1995.

[6] J. Corbal, R. Espasa, and M. Valero, "Command Vector Memory Systems: High Performance at Low Cost", Proc. International Conference on Parallel Architectures and Compilation Techniques, October 1998.

[7] R. Crisp, "Direct Rambus Technology: The New Main Memory Standard", IEEE Micro, November/December 1997, pp. 18-28.

[8] M. Denman, P.Anderson, and M.Snyder, "Design of the PowerPC 604e Microprocessor", Proc. of IEEE Compcon'96, 1996, pp. 126-131.

[9] J.J. Dongarra et al., "A Set of Level 3 Basic Linear Algebra Subprograms", ACM Trans. Mathematical Software, March 1990, pp. 1-17.

[10] K.I. Farkas, P. Chow, N.P. Jouppi, Z. Vranesic, "Memory-System Design Considerations for Dynamically-Scheduled Processors", Proc. 24th International Symposium on Computer Architecture, June 1997.

[11] S.I. Hong, "Evaluation of Stream Computation Performance for Rambus DRAM", master's thesis, University of Virginia, Dept. of Electrical and Computer Engineering, July 1998.

[12] "Intel i860XP Microprocessor Data Book", Intel Corp., 1991.

[13] N.P. Jouppi, "Improving Direct-Mapped Cache Performance by the Addition of a Small Fully-Associative Cache and Prefetch Buffers", Proc. 17th International Symposium on Computer Architecture, May 1990, pp. 364-373.

[14] M. Levy, "Souped-Up Memories Boost System Performance", EDN, January 4, 1996, pp. 38-52.

[15] J.D. McCalpin, "Memory Bandwidth and Machine Balance in Current High Performance Computers", IEEE Computer Society Technical Committee on Computer Architecture (TCCA) Newsletter, December 1995, pp.19-25.

[16] S.A. McKee, "Improving Memory Bandwidth for Streamed Computations", Ph.D. dissertation, University of Virginia, May 1995.

[17] S.A. McKee et al., "Design and Evaluation of Dynamic Access Ordering Hardware", Proc. International Conference on Supercomputing, June 1996, pp. 125-132.

[18] J. Owens,"The ASCI LKF Benchmark Code Readme File", http://www.llnl.gov/asci_benchmarks/asci/limited/lfk/README.html, October 1995.

[19] S. Palacharla, R. E. Kessler, "Evaluating Stream Buffers as a Secondary Cache Replacement", Proc. 21st International Symposium on Computer Architecture, April 1994, pp. 24-33.

[20] Rambus Inc., "Direct Rambus Technology Disclosure", DL 0040-00, October 1997. (available from http://www.rambus.com/documentation.html)

[21] Rambus Inc., "64M/72M Direct RDRAM Data Sheet", DL 0035-00.c0.5.28, March 1998. (available from http://www.rambus.com/documentation.html)

[22] M. Swanson, L. Stoller, and J. Carter, "Increasing TLB Reach Using Superpages Backed by Shadow Memory", Proc. 25th International Symposium on Computer Architecture, June 1998.

[23] M. Valero et. al., "Increasing the Number of Strides for Conflict-Free Vector Access", Proc. 19th International Symposium on Computer Architecture, May 1992.

[24] L. Zhang et al., "Impulse: Building a Smarter Memory Controller", Proc. 5th International Symposium on High Performance Computer Architecture, January 1999.

Lightweight Hardware Distributed Shared Memory Supported by Generalized Combining

Kiyofumi Tanaka*, Takashi Matsumoto, and Kei Hiraki
Department of Information Science, Faculty of Science, University of Tokyo
7-3-1 Hongo, Bunkyo-ku, Tokyo 113–0033 Japan
{tanaka, tm, hiraki}@is.s.u-tokyo.ac.jp

Abstract

On a large-scale parallel computer system, shared memory provides a general and convenient programming environment. This paper describes a lightweight method for constructing an efficient shared memory system supported by hierarchical coherence management and generalized combining. The hierarchical management technique and generalized combining cooperate with each other. We eliminate the following heavyweight and high-cost factors: a large amount of directory memory which is proportional to the number of processors, a separate memory component for the directory, tag/state information, and a protocol processor. In our method, the amount of memory required for the directory is proportional to the logarithm of the number of processors. This implies that a single word for each memory block is sufficient for covering a massively parallel system and that the access costs of the directory are small. Moreover, our combining technique, generalized combining, does not expect the accidental events which existing combining networks do, that is, events that messages meet each other at a switching node. A switching node can combine succeeding messages with a preceding one even after the preceding message leaves the node. This can increase the rate of successful combining. We have developed a prototype parallel computer, OCHANOMIZ-5, that implements this lightweight distributed shared memory and generalized combining with simple hardware. The results of evaluating the prototype's performance using several programs show that our methodology provides the advantages of parallelization.

1. Introduction

Shared memory provides a general and convenient programming environment on a parallel and distributed system. Caching of remote data is effective in preventing a large access latency from degrading the overall performance of a large-scale parallel system. However, caching causes a cache consistency problem. Distributed shared memory (DSM) is the most effective method when a Symmetric Multi-Processor (SMP) method is difficult to apply to a system because of a large number of processors. There is a software solution in which a processing element creates data copies, identifies cache misses and hits, and performs the coherence management. In this case, overheads for the software execution of cache management are comparatively large.

There is another scheme that uses a virtual shared memory of the IVY [15]. This scheme uses a hardware page management mechanism (i.e., MMU and TLB in a processing element), and invokes remote memory accesses by page fault trap software. Although this scheme reduces the above software overheads when a processor hits the cache, it still leaves the software execution overheads for maintaining cache consistency and spends a long time on invoking a remote request because the processors execute a trap or system call routine. Moreover, the unit size for caching is fixed to a page size, which causes false sharing and performance degradation.

It is possible to reduce all these overheads by providing hardware mechanisms dedicated to cache management [14, 13, 9]. The implementation costs of the hardware must be considered, however, whereas the software solutions require no special hardware components and can be implemented on commercial PC or workstation clusters. Under present conditions, where the performance of software solutions supported by lazy release consistency models [12, 10] or an optimizing compiler [20] is improving, a hardware system loses its merits if it cannot provide reasonable performance improvements that are proportional to the hardware costs. One factor which makes hardware costs high is the use of the protocol processor used in existing hardware DSM systems. Although a dedicated protocol processor is useful for implementing a complicated coherence

---

*Research Fellow of the Japan Society for the Promotion of Science.

protocol, its sophisticated structure has the disadvantages of high costs and a long development time. It is therefore important to construct a hardware shared memory system that is efficient and inexpensive.

In this paper, we propose a lightweight hardware solution which does not require a large amount of storage space for the directory, a high-speed memory for tag and state information, or a protocol processor. The only extra components that need to be added to the basic distributed memory system are a small amount of additional hardwired logic in a memory controller and a switching node in the interconnection network. Although the simple structure of the hardware brings about redundant inter-node messages, dynamic multicasting and combining techniques prevent them from reducing efficiency.

Section 2 describes our strategy. Section 3 describes the generalized combining that supports our scheme. Section 4 describes an implementation of our method on a prototype system, OCHANOMIZ-5. Section 5 discusses the performance of our system, Section 6 describes the related work on directory schemes and combining networks, and Section 7 concludes the paper.

2. Lightweight DSM Architecture

2.1. Design Policy

Our design eliminates the following heavyweight and high-cost factors in conventional hardware DSM systems: a large amount of directory memory which is proportional to the number of processors, a separate memory component for the directory, tag and state information, and a dedicated protocol processor. In order to reduce the amount of directory memory, we use a rough directory management scheme, called a hierarchical coarse directory, which indicates a superset of the members sharing a memory block. The amount of memory required for the directory is proportional to the logarithm of the number of processors. We locate the directories, tag, and state information in main memory rather than in a separate directory memory. A memory controller manages the information without any software execution according to memory access requests from processing elements or from outside the processing node. As a result, there is no need for a protocol processor.

The simplicity of the directory and absence of a protocol processor make it possible to increase the volume of network communications. Dynamic multicasting and combining techniques prevent the communications from causing inefficiency. The next subsections describe our directory scheme, multicasting and combining technique.

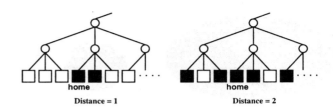

Figure 1. Hierarchical coarse directory.

2.2. Hierarchical Coarse Directory

To provide both a small requirement for memory space and the low access costs, we use hierarchical coarse directory management which is a simplified version of pseudo fullmap directory [16, 17].

We assume that a tree structure is physically embedded in the interconnection network. A home processor[1] is statically assigned to each memory block and manages the directory which records data-sharing information by using the "maximum shared distance". Here, the term "maximum shared distance" means half of the number of hops between the home processor and the most distant sharing processor. In other words, the distance is the height of the minimum subtree which includes all the processors caching the block copy. Figure 1 illustrates the hierarchical coarse directory. The black leaves in the figure represent processors which have a shared copy, and the gray areas indicate shared areas. The distance is 1 in the left figure and 2 in the right figure.

The amount of memory required is proportional to the logarithm of the number of processors. This logarithmic relationship implies that a single 16 or 32 bit word for each memory block is sufficient for covering a massively parallel system. The small amount of memory required eliminates the necessity for multiple access and can hide the overheads of accessing the directory stored in main memory (DRAM).

The number of shared copies is overestimated because all processors within the shared area indicated by the distance are regarded as sharing members of the memory block. In Figure 1, for example, white leaves inside a gray space are regarded as a holder of the block. On invalidation of the shared copies, invalidation messages are broadcasted to all processors in the shared area. As a result, there are redundant transmissions. Processors that do not have a copy receive the invalidation message. Such processors return a dummy acknowledgement message. The next subsection describes the mechanisms for reducing the amount of this wasteful communication.

---

[1]When a processing node is a multiprocessor cluster with a shared bus, the term "processor" is replaced with "cluster".

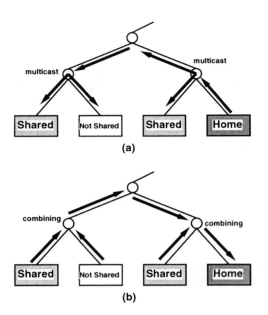

Figure 2. Multicasting and combining.

2.3. Hierarchical multicasting and combining mechanism

Transportation of identical requests to many processors is frequently required during consistency processing such as invalidating and updating. The transport performance can be improved by utilizing hierarchical multicasting. For example, when invalidation of shared copies is processed, the home processor assigned in advance to the memory block issues only one invalidation message. Each switching node in the network that receives the message multicasts it in all the directions within the shared area. Figure 2(a) shows the multicasting when the maximum shared distance is 2.

When more than one message is sent to the same processor, the messages are combined hierarchically into a single message. This reduces the need for serialized processing at the destination processor. For example, every processor receiving the above invalidation message returns an acknowledgement message which indicates the completion of invalidation within the processor, even if it does not have a shared copy. All the acknowledge messages are directed toward the home processor. Each switching node forwards one message after it confirms all the arrivals from the directions in which it multicasted the preceding invalidation. The process is shown in Figure 2(b).

In a directory scheme such as a fullmap directory that manages sharing information precisely, it is necessary for a home processor to issue coherence messages serially and receive and process acknowledgement messages one by one.

The hierarchical multicasting and combining scheme require no serialized processings at a home processor. It takes only one round-trip latency for the home processor to complete the coherence transaction. This combining of acknowledge messages is accomplished by using the generalized combining described in the next section.

3. Generalized Combining

The simplicity of the directory, absence of a protocol processor, and management per cache line size increase the number of inter-processor communications, and therefore increase the network traffic and cause hotspot contentions [18]. Combining [8] is effective for alleviating this contention. It dynamically combines more than one request destined for the same destination into a single request and thus reduces the total number of network communications. The technique, however, requires a large amount of hardware within a network switching node [18], and it cannot work sufficiently since it expects the accidental events that requests meet each other at a switching node. In other words, combining does not occur if a request arrives at the switching node after the preceding request has departed from the node.

We propose a flexible combining technique called *generalized combining* to prevent the increase in traffic from reducing efficiency. The combining of acknowledge messages is one instance. Generalized combining consists of three generalizations: generalization of arrival requirement, generalization of processing function, and generalization of matching requirement.

Generalization of arrival requirement

The matching points for combining are grouped into four categories according to the time a message arrives at a switching node. The four categories are in the past, at the present, during the delayed time, and in the future. Matching in the past means that matching has been already done when the message arrives at the node. Matching at the present means that matching happens at the same time as the arrival. Matching during the delayed time means that a message matches with other subsequent messages during its stay at the node; existing combinings perform only this type of matching. Matching in the future means that matching will be completed after a message leaves the node. Figure 3 illustrates these matching points for combining.

We enable the delayed time to be set up to any length from zero to eternity. In the case of zero, a message passes through a switching node without waiting for other subsequent messages. This message is not combined during the delayed time, although it may be combined in the past, at the present, or in the future. Setting the delayed time to eternity ensures that a message stays at the node until all

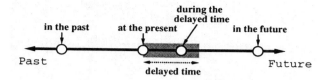

Figure 3. Time frame of matching points for combining.

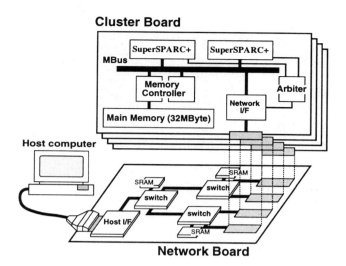

Figure 4. Block diagram of OCHANOMIZ-5.

of the messages that should be combined with each other arrive there. The combining of acknowledge messages is accomplished by a delayed time of eternity. Other time values between zero and eternity make a message depart from the node after waiting there for the specified time.

This generalization eliminates the restriction that matching chances occur only while a message is staying at a node, that is, only while a message is passing through a combining queue [8]. As a result, it can cope with time gaps between the arrivals of messages and can increase the rate of successful matching.

Generalization of processing function

In generalized combining, a switching node supports a variety of functions with messages. This generalization makes it possible not only to combine identical read or Fetch&Ops requests, but also perform other operations such as the combining of acknowledge messages, barrier synchronization, and numerical reduction using the interconnection network as a systolic array like a sorting network [3]. Although each switching node must contain all the function units to make this generalization possible, we select only the functions needed for realizing a lightweight hardware DSM. These selected functions make use of a common combining unit.

Generalization of matching requirement

The matching requirement is generalized in two ways.

a) Combining of any number of messages

The number of combinable messages is any number from zero to infinity. The number is specified for every combining. A combined message is forwarded only after the specified number of messages have arrived. The departure time of a combined message thus depends on the specified number; however, when the delayed time expires, the forwarding is done even if some of the messages have not arrived. To ensure that all messages are combined, the delayed time is set to eternity.

b) Any matching key

Any matching key can be selected as a matching requirement. In addition, we allow a message to have any number of matching keys. In our DSM system, we use network addresses as keys for memory access requests and processor IDs as keys for barrier synchronization.

4. Implementation: OCHANOMIZ-5

4.1. The architecture

OCHANOMIZ-5 [22] is a prototype parallel computer for verifying the lightweight hardware DSM mechanism proposed in this paper. It consists of processing elements, main memories, memory controllers, bus arbiters, network interfaces, switching nodes in a network, and a host computer. Figure 4 shows the block diagram of OCHANOMIZ-5. The system consists of four clusters and a network board interconnecting those clusters. The main memories are distributed over all of the clusters.

In each cluster there are two SuperSPARC+ processors [21] with secondary cache memories connected by a shared bus. The main memory in each cluster consists of 32 Mbytes DRAMs. The memory controller, bus arbiter and network interface are implemented using FPGA (Xilinx XC4010 for the memory controller and arbiter, XC4025 for the network interface) [25].

OCHANOMIZ-5 has a hierarchical binary tree interconnection network. Each internal switching node is designed with FPGA (XC4025). There are two separate paths between a parent and a child node, one upward and the other

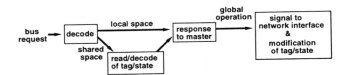

Figure 5. Control sequence of the memory controller.

Table 1. Device utilization of a memory controller.

	Non cacheable	Cacheable DSM	Max. available
F&G Function Generators	217	305	800
H Function Generators	42	82	400
CLB Flip-Flops	135	157	800

downward. The width of each path is 8 bits. Each switching node has two SRAMs (total: 128 Kbytes) that are used as the wait-buffers for generalized combining.

4.2. Processing of the memory controller

Cluster-level cache blocks can be in one of three states: private, shared, or invalid.

- **Private**
  In the private state the memory block is cached only in the cluster and is not cached in any other clusters. This cache copy may be clean or dirty.

- **Shared**
  In the shared state the memory block is shared among multiple clusters. There is no shared&dirty state because a memory block in the home cluster becomes shared state whenever it is shared. That is, a home cluster is always one of the sharing members.

- **Invalid**
  In the invalid state the cluster does not have a valid copy of the memory block.

The physical memory address space is divided into local and shared spaces. The memory controller receives bus requests and then reads the corresponding tag and state information when the request is for access to a shared address space, and replies to the requester with valid data or a retry message according to the information. In the case of a retry, the memory controller makes the network interface start a network transaction as the need arises and modifies the tag and state. Figure 5 illustrates the control flow.

It takes 11 bus clock cycles (0.5 μ seconds) to complete a memory transaction requiring access to a 32-byte block in a local address space. An access to a shared address space takes four extra cycles for reading and decoding tag and state information. Cache hits within a processor conceal the cycles after the first cache miss.

We designed a memory controller that manages cluster-level cache coherence. It requires about 40% more gates than a memory controller which does not have cache management logic. This amount is not large because the design

of the original non-coherent controller is simple. The memory controller was designed using a FPGA, Xilinx XC4010 whose capacity is equal to 10,000 gates. Table 1 shows the device utilization.

4.3. Functions of a network switching node

The network of OCHANOMIZ-5 implements a part of the generalized combining.

- Combining of acknowledgement messages [16]

  Management of cache consistency requires the use of acknowledge messages. If a home cluster receives all acknowledge messages from all clusters in the shared area serially, communication latency grows undesirably high. This latency can be reduced by combining the messages. The acknowledge messages are combined by setting the delayed (waiting) time to eternity and dynamically setting up the combining number when the corresponding multicast occurs.

- Hierarchical hardware barrier

  The conventional hardware barrier mechanism requires an amount of hardware proportional to the number of processing elements and therefore cannot be used in a large system. An effective way to reduce the hardware cost is to use a hierarchical hardware barrier. Each switching node in the network combines barrier request signals from its children and sends one signal to its parent, a root node sends completion signals to its children after it receives the barrier request signals from them, and then each switching node multicasts the completion signal downward. Because the name space of a hardware barrier is processor space, the matching key is the processor group ID. The waiting time is eternal because of the nature of barrier synchronization.

- Combining of atomic requests

  The generalization of processing function makes it possible to combine atomic requests such as Fetch&Add [8] or Test&Set. Doing so can reduce the occurrence of tree saturations caused by hot-spot

Table 2. Types of waiting time.

Type	Waiting time	Purpose	Remark
0	zero	Invalidate multicast message	no-combining
1	zero	Read, Invalidate, Test&Set request	future combining
2	specified time	Fetch&Add	four different prepared times
3	eternity	Acknowledgement, Barrier	complete combining

contentions. Generalization of arrival requirement increases the rate of successful matching.

- Combining of read or invalidate requests

    Combining of read or invalidate requests sent to the same memory address reduces the total number of messages. Future matching increases the rate of successful matching. For these combinings, the matching key is a memory address.

We implement the generalization of arrival requirement as follows. Network packets are divided into four types:

- **Type-0**

    This type indicates that the delayed (waiting) time is zero and a message does not wait at a node. Type-0 messages do not pass through a combining unit, and no combinings occur.

- **Type-1**

    This type indicates that the waiting time is zero. An arrival message passes through a combining unit in a switching node. If the message is the first request access to the address, an entry is set in the wait-buffer and the message is forwarded immediately. If the message is not the first and can be combined with a preceding message, it is not forwarded. At the same time, The corresponding entry is modified for the reply message to find that combining has been occurred. When a reply message reaches the node, it is multicasted if the entry has been modified. At the same time, the entry is cleared. Type-1 messages are used to implement future matching, and all combinable messages can be combined as long as the entry exists in the wait-buffer.

- **Type-2**

    This type indicates that a message waits at a node for the specified time. We can select the delayed time out of four times specified in advance.

- **Type-3**

    This type indicates that the waiting time is eternal. A combined message is forwarded only after all the related messages have arrived there. When a message

Table 3. Device utilization of a switching node.

	Switching circuit	Combining unit	Max. available
F and G Function Generators	682	281	2048
H Function Generators	74	85	1024
CLB Flip-Flops	184	110	2048

arrives at a switching node, a corresponding entry in the wait-buffer is modified. The entry is cleared and the message is forwarded only if the arriving message is the last of the intended messages.

Table 2 shows the correspondence of operations to the above types. Messages other than those listed in the table are of Type-0.

Our combining mechanism does not include a combining queue [8]. Our switching node is implemented using simple wired-logic and memory for the wait-buffer. It is built within the capacity of a single FPGA, xc4025, of which contents are equivalent to about 25,000 gates. Table 3 shows the device utilization.

4.4. Example of network transaction

As an example of a network transaction, we show the operations required for a coherent invalidation of shared cache blocks. The following shows the steps of the transaction, and Figure 6 shows the series of operations in the transaction.

1. When a processor issues a coherent invalidate request to a shared block, the network interface in the cluster issues an invalidate request by sending a **Type-1** message to the home cluster of the block.

2. When this request arrives at an internal switching node, the wait-buffer is searched. If there is no entry for preceding requests sent to the same address, an entry is set and the request is forwarded to the next node because it is sent as a Type-1. If an entry is found, it is modified to indicate that the final reply acknowledgement message should be multicasted.

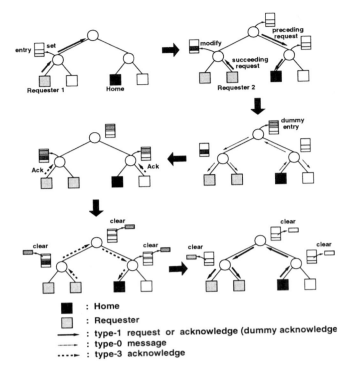

: Home
: Requester
⟶ : type-1 request or acknowledge (dummy acknowledge
----➤ : type-0 message
····➤ : type-3 acknowledge

Figure 6. Series of operations during invalidate transaction.

3. When this request reaches the home cluster, the network interface issues a single invalidate message by sending a **Type-0** message toward the subtree determined by the maximum shared distance.

4. When this Type-0 message arrives at an internal switching node, it is multicasted in all directions within the shared subtree. At the root node of the subtree, the message is forwarded only to another child node, and a **Type-3** dummy acknowledgement entry is inserted into the wait-buffer. The entry is used later during the collection of acknowledge messages.

5. Each cluster receiving this message performs invalidation of the block and returns an acknowledge message by sending a **Type-3** message. If the block copy is not in the cluster or the cluster is the original requester of the invalidation, the cluster returns a dummy acknowledgement message.

6. When this Type-3 (dummy) message arrives at an internal node, the wait-buffer is searched. If an entry for a preceding acknowledge message is not found, an entry is set. If an entry is found, one message is forwarded and the entry is cleared.

Table 4. Latency of remote memory access.

Distance	Type	Size (Bytes)	System clock cycles	μs
1	Write	1–8	33	1.50
	Write	32	60	2.73
	Read	1–8	47	2.14
	Read	32	74	3.36
	Invalidate	32	76	3.45
2	Write	1–8	41	1.86
	Write	32	68	3.09
	Read	1–8	63	2.86
	Read	32	90	4.09
	Invalidate	32	110	5.00

Table 5. Bandwidth of remote memory access.

Number of PEs	Type	Bandwidth (Mbytes/s)
1	Write	15.2
	Read	7.3
4	Write	58.3
	Read	24.5
8	Write	47.8
	Read	30.8

7. When the combined acknowledge message reaches the home cluster, the network interface returns a final acknowledge message by sending a **Type-1** message to the original requester.

8. When this message arrives at an internal node, it is forwarded (multicasted if necessary), and the corresponding entry is cleared.

9. When all of the requesters receive this acknowledgement, the transaction finishes.

5. Performance Evaluation

5.1. Performance of network communication

The CPU in OCHANOMIZ-5 runs at 60 MHz, and the other systems run at 22 MHz. The data width of a network path is eight bits. The remote memory access latency and bandwidth are shown in Tables 4 and 5. Distance in Table 4 denotes the height of the minimum subtree which includes a source and a destination cluster. Invalidate in the table denotes the time needed for a home cluster to complete the invalidation of the shared area.

In Table 5, the specified number of PEs repeatedly issue 32-byte write or read requests to the next cluster. When the number of PEs is four, one PE in each cluster executes the

Table 6. Impact of combining read requests.

Combining ON/OFF	Bandwidth (Mbytes/s)
OFF	19.3
ON	30.0

Table 7. Execution time of lock acquisition loop.

Combining ON/OFF	Total time (seconds)
OFF	119.1
ON	85.7

write or read requests. With regard to write executions, the four-PE case is better than the eight-PE case because of the bus contention in each cluster.

The network performs combinings of read requests, Test&Set, or the hardware barrier. The impact of combining read requests is shown in Table 6, which shows what happens when eight PEs repeatedly issue read requests to the same address. The combining network exhibits a higher bandwidth in this undesirable situation.

We used the Test&Set request for lock acquisition. Each processor repeatedly increments a counter variable in the critical section. The following shows the program model.

```
for (i=0; i<LOOP_COUNT; i++) {
    while(Test&Set(LockVar) != 0);
    counter += 1;
    LockVar = 0;    /* unlock */
}
```

Table 7 shows the results for eight PEs when the number of iterations is 2^{20}.

5.2. Effect of combining

We will now illustrate the impact of combinings by using a numerical computation: the nth power of the matrix A[N][N] when $N = 128$ and $n = 32$.

Each processor is given an element number for every execution trial. An element number is the value of a shared variable which indicates the value of $i \times N + j$ for the element $A[i][j]$ ($0 \leq elemNo < N \times N$). The shared variable is protected by a critical section. Then it executes $\sum_{i=0}^{N} A[elemNo/N][i] \times A[i][elemNo\%N]$. There are barrier synchronizations at the beginning and end of each increment of the power. We used a software barrier or a hierarchical hardware barrier. The former is implemented with

a critical section and a counter variable. When the counter value equals the number of PEs, the barrier is completed. The algorithm is as follows:

```
shared double A[N][N];
local  double AA[N][N];    // copy of matrix A
for(k=0; k<nthpower; k++) {
  counter = 0;
  copy(A,AA);                // copy from A to AA
  barrier();
  while(1) {
    while(Test&Set(LockVar) != 0);//lock acquire
    elemNo = counter;
    counter = elemNo + 1;
    LockVar = 0;                  //lock release
    if (elemNo < N*N) {
      double d = 0.0;
      for (i=0; i<N; i++)
        d += AA[elemNo/N][i] * AA[i][elemNo%N];
        A[elemNo/N][elemNo%N] = d;
    }
    else {
      barrier();
      break;
    }
  }
}
```

The execution times when the number of PEs are 1, 2, 4, and 8 are listed in Table 8. When the number is 2, two PEs in one cluster execute. When the number is 4, four PEs in two clusters execute. NC in the table means that the execution uses no combining. Executions in the HC column use the hierarchical hardware barrier. HLC means the additional use of Test&Set combining, and HLRC means the use not only of those two but also of read request combining.

In the case of 4-PE execution, Test&Set and read request combinings do not contribute to the execution. This is because network packets must pass through a combining unit in every switching node. The extra latency degrades the effect of the combinings. In 8-PE execution, HLRC provides the best result. The gains from combinings exceed the losses due to the increase in latency. HLRC is 7.7% faster than NC.

Table 8. Execution time (seconds) for computing the nth power of a 128×128 matrix.

Number of PEs	NC	HC	HLC	HLRC
1	19.9	19.9	19.9	19.9
2	10.1	9.9	9.9	9.9
4	7.3	6.5	6.6	6.7
8	6.5	6.4	6.3	6.0

Table 9. Execution time (seconds) of LU-Contig.

Number of PEs	NCC	CC
1	149.36	10.57
2	64.39	4.96
4	72.32	2.71
8	47.18	1.97

5.3. Effect of hardware cache coherence DSM

We employed LU-Contig of SPLASH-2 [24] using 1, 2, 4, and 8 PEs in order to evaluate the performance of the hardware cache coherence DSM. When the number is 2, two PEs in one cluster execute. When the number is 4, four PEs in two clusters execute. LU-Contig performs blocked LU factorization of a dense matrix. The size of a matrix is 512×512 and it has 16×16 sub-blocks. Table 9 shows the results of LU-Contig. We used a hierarchical hardware barrier for barrier synchronization. In the table, NCC means non-use of caches (processor's cache or cluster cache). CC means computation with all caches. Execution with two PEs is more than twice as fast as execution with a single PE. This is the effect of the superlinear when the total data size exceeds the capacity of a single PE's internal cache. As a whole, the result shows that CC is much faster than NCC and also provides the advantages of parallelization.

6. Related Work

The amount of memory a system uses for directory, tag, and state information increases with the scale of the system. The storage size is most sensitive to the directory structure. Since a fullmap directory [6] requires an amount of memory proportional to the number of processors in the DSM systems, it is not scalable for a large-scale system. Moreover, it requires multiple accesses to the directory memory when the number of processors exceeds the width of a single access. Although the use of a chained directory [11, 23] decreases the directory size, it also results in the inefficiency of multiple accesses.

The hierarchical bit-map directory in COMA [9] requires $\sum_{k=1}^{m} n^k$ bits for each memory block in an n-ary tree of height m. The resultant amount of memory is larger than that required by a fullmap directory, and the scheme requires a directory access at every level in the hierarchy.

The limited directory [2] allows only a limited number of shared copies, and requires cache replacement or broadcasting when there are more copies than the limited number. The LimitLESS directory [7] removes this limitation by in-

terrupting a processor when an overflow occurs. The processor emulates a fullmap directory by software execution, which becomes an overhead.

In our method, the amount of memory required is proportional to the logarithm of the number of processors. The logarithm implies that a single word for each memory block is sufficient for covering a massively parallel system and that the access costs of the directory are small, that is, a single access is adequate.

Hardware DSM systems are classified roughly into two categories: those which have a dedicated protocol processor and those which do not have it. For example, DASH [14], Alewife [1] and KSR1 [5] have not a protocol processor. DASH adopts a fullmap directory scheme and has separate memories for caches of remote data and the directory. Alewife adopts a LimitLESS directory. A processing element executes software emulation of a fullmap directory when the number of copies exceeds a limited number. The system has separate memories for the directory. KSR1 provides a hardware DSM by a COMA scheme. The scheme requires a directory access at every level in the hierarchy.

On the other hand, FLASH [13] and Typhoon [19] have a protocol processor. FLASH stores the directory information in main memories and therefore does not have separate memories. The protocol processor, MAGIC, executes protocol management. Typhoon has a protocol processor which includes SPARC-core and implements a LimitLESS directory.

The DSM scheme in this paper stores the directory information in main memories, and additional hardwired logic in a memory controller performs coherence management.

In our distributed shared memory system, we use generalized combining. Originally, the combining technique was established on the NYU Ultracomputer [8]. In the design, combining can occur only while combinable messages are passing through a combining queue. Each switching element has the same number of comparators as there are entries in the combining queue. This is complicated. Pfister and Norton [18] showed that the cost and size of the hardware of the combining switch are 6 to 32 times that of a non-combining switch.

To raise the combining rate, Philip Bitar [4] proposed the "combining window". In the paper of Ref. [4], he claims that if each combinable message temporarily stayed in a buffering space at a switching node, the occurrence of combinings increases. The concept for implementing this waiting time at the switching node is the combining window. This approach might increase the success rate of combining, but there might be a danger that if enough combinings do not occur, each combinable message will receive an extra latency because of the waiting time.

In contrast with the above combinings, our technique requires only a small amount of extra logic, and a switching node can combine succeeding messages with a preceding one even after the preceding one leaves the node. This can improve the success rate of combining.

7. Conclusion

We have described a lightweight hardware solution supported by hierarchical coherence management and generalized combining. The hierarchical management and generalized combining cooperate with each other. We eliminate the following heavyweight and high-cost factors: a large amount of directory memory which is proportional to the number of processors, a separate memory component for the directory, tag and state information, and a protocol processor.

We have developed a parallel computer prototype, OCHANOMIZ-5, which implements the lightweight distributed shared memory and generalized combining. We evaluated its performance using several programs.

In parallel calculation of the nth power of a matrix, our combining techniques reduced the calculation time by about 8%. The results of the execution of the LU-Contig program of SPLASH-2 show that a lightweight distributed shared memory system supported by generalized combining provides the advantages of parallelization.

Acknowledgements

This work is supported in part by Real World Computing (RWC) project in the Ministry of International Trade and Industry (MITI).

References

[1] A. Agarwal, R. Bianchini, D. Chaiken, and K. Johnson. The mit alewife machine: Architecture and performance. In *Proc. of ISCA*, pages 2–13, June 1995.

[2] A. Agarwal, R. Simoni, J. Hennessy, and M. Horowitz. An Evaluation of Directory Schemes for Cache Coherence. In *Proc. of ISCA*, pages 280–289, June 1988.

[3] K. Batcher. Sorting networks and their applications. *AFIPS Spring Joint Computing Conference*, pages 307–314, Apr. 1968.

[4] P. Bitar. Combining Window: The Key to Managing MIMD Combining Trees. *The Workshop on Scalable Shared Memory Multiprocessors*, May 1990.

[5] H. Burkhardt III, S. Frank, and J. Rothnie. Overview of the ksr1 computer system. *Technical Report KSR-TR-9202001, Kendall Square Research*, Feb. 1992.

[6] L. Censier and P. Feautrier. A New Solution to Coherence Problems in Multicache Systems. *IEEE Transactions on Computers*, pages 1112–1118, Dec. 1978.

[7] D. Chaiken, J. Kubiatowicz, and A. Agarwal. LimitLESS Directories: A Scalable Cache Coherence Scheme. In *Proc. of ASPLOS*, pages 224–234, Apr. 1991.

[8] A. Gottlieb, R. Grishman, C. Kruskal, K. McAuleffe, L. Rudolph, and M. Snir. The NYU Ultracomputer–Designing and MIMD Shared Memory Parallel Computer. *IEEE Transactions on Computers*, pages 175–189, Feb. 1983.

[9] E. Hagersten, A. Landin, and S. Haridi. DDM–A Cache-Only Memory Architecture. *IEEE Computer*, pages 44–54, Sept. 1992.

[10] L. Iftode, C. Dubnicki, E. Felten, and K. Li. Improving Release-Consistent Shared Virtual Memory using Automatic Update. In *Proc. of the 2nd HPCA*, Feb. 1996.

[11] D. James, A. Laundrie, S. Gjessing, and G. Sohi. Distibuted–Directory Scheme: Scalable Coherent Interface. *IEEE Computer*, pages 74–77, June 1990.

[12] P. Keleher, A. Cox, and W. Zwaenepoel. Lazy Release Consistency for Software Distributed Shared Memory. In *Proc. of ISCA*, pages 13–21, May 1992.

[13] J. Kuskin, D. Ofelt, M. Heinrich, J. Heinlein, R. Simoni, K. Gharachorloo, J. Chapin, D. Nakahira, J. Baxter, M. Horowitz, A. Gupta, M. Rosenblum, and J. Hennessy. The Stanford FLASH Multiprocessor. In *Proc. of ISCA*, pages 302–313, Apr. 1994.

[14] D. Lenoski, J. Laudon, K. Gharachorloo, A. Gupta, and J. Hennessy. The Directory-Based Cache Coherence Protocol for DASH Multiprocessor. In *Proc. of ISCA*, pages 148–159, May 1990.

[15] K. Li. IVY: A Shared Virtual Memory System for Parallel Computing. In *Proc. of ICPP*, pages 94–101, Aug. 1988.

[16] T. Matsumoto and K. Hiraki. A Shared Memory Architecture for Massively Parallel Computer Systems. *IEICE Japan SIG Reports*, 92(173):47–55, Aug. 1992. (In Japanese).

[17] T. Matsumoto, T. Kudoh, E. Nishimura, K. Hiraki, H. Amano, and H. Tanaka. Distributed Shared Memory Architecture for JUMP-1 a General-Purpose MPP Prototype. In *Proc. of ISPAN*, pages 131–137, June 1996.

[18] G. Pfister and V. Norton. Hot Spot Contention and Combining in Multistage Interconnection Networks. *IEEE Transactions on Computers*, pages 943–948, Oct. 1985.

[19] S. Reinhardt, J. Larus, and D. Wood. Tempest and typhoon: User-level shared memory. In *Proc. of ISCA*, Apr. 1994.

[20] D. Scales, K. Gharachorloo, and C. Thekkath. Shasta: A Low Overhead, Software–Only Approach for Supporting Fine–Grain Shared Memory. In *Proc. of ASPLOS*, pages 174–185, Oct. 1996.

[21] Sun Microsystems, Inc. *SuperSPARC & MultiCache Controller User's Manual*, 1994.

[22] K. Tanaka, J. Tsuiki, T. Matsumoto, and K. Hiraki. Parallel Computer Prototype OCHANOMIZ-5. In *The 3rd FPGA/PLD Design Conference & Exhibit*, pages 505–514, July 1995. (In Japanese).

[23] M. Thapar and B. Delagi. Distributed–Directory Scheme: Stanford Distributed Directory Protocol. *IEEE Computer*, pages 78–80, June 1990.

[24] S. Woo, M. Ohara, E. Torrie, J. Singh, and A. Gupta. The SPLASH-2 Programs: Characterization and Methodological Considerations. In *Proc. of ISCA*, pages 24–36, June 1995.

[25] XILINX, Inc. *The Programmable Logic Data Book*, 1994.

Controversial Panel

Yale Patt

University of Michigan, Ann Arbor

Keynote Address II

Software and HPCA

Ken Kennedy

National Academy of Engineers

Session 4

Instruction Scheduling & Speculation

Exploiting Basic Block Value Locality with Block Reuse

Jian Huang
Dept. of Computer Science and Engineering
Minnesota Supercomputing Institute
University of Minnesota
Minneapolis, MN 55455
huangj@cs.umn.edu

David J. Lilja
Dept. of Electrical and Computer Engineering
Minnesota Supercomputing Institute
University of Minnesota
Minneapolis, MN 55455
lilja@ece.umn.edu

Abstract

Value prediction at the instruction level has been introduced to allow more aggressive speculation and reuse than previous techniques. We investigate the input and output values of basic blocks and find that these values can be quite regular and predictable, suggesting that using compiler support to extend value prediction and reuse to a coarser granularity may have substantial performance benefits. For the SPEC benchmark programs evaluated, 90% of the basic blocks have fewer than 4 register inputs, 5 live register outputs, 4 memory inputs and 2 memory outputs. About 16% to 41% of all the basic blocks are simply repeating earlier calculations when the programs are compiled with the -O2 optimization level in the GCC compiler. We evaluate the potential benefit of basic block reuse using a novel mechanism called a block history buffer. This mechanism records input and live output values of basic blocks to provide value prediction and reuse at the basic block level. Simulation results show that using a reasonably-sized block history buffer to provide basic block reuse in a 4-way issue superscalar processor can improve execution time for the tested SPEC programs by 1% to 14% with an overall average of 9%.

Keywords*: block history buffer, block reuse, compiler flow analysis, value locality, value reuse*

1 Introduction

Speculative execution has been introduced to extend the limits of instruction-level parallelism since dependences between instructions limit the instruction execution rate of a typical superscalar processor to an average of only about 1.7 to 2.1 instructions per cycle (IPC) [2]. To speculate beyond control and data dependences, Lipasti *et al* [4, 5] introduced the concept of *value locality*, which is a measure of how often an instruction regenerates a value that it has produced before. They discovered that the values produced by an instruction are actually very regular and predictable.

Tyson and Austin [9] further found that 29% of the load instructions in the SPECint benchmarks and 44% of the loads in the SPECfp benchmarks reload the same values as the last time the loads were executed. This *value locality* allows processors to predict the actual data values that will be produced by instructions before they are executed. Several techniques have been proposed to improve value prediction accuracy. These include a history-based predictor, a stride-based predictor, a hybrid predictor [10], and a context-based predictor [7]. All of these schemes work at the level of a single instruction, and try to predict the next value that will be produced by an instruction based on the previous values it has already generated.

The scope of all these techniques can be too limited, however, and the values predicted can be wrong. By determining actual values instead of simply predicting them, the processor could throw away redundant work and simply jump directly to the next task. For example, dynamic instruction reuse [8] saves the input and output register values for each instruction to allow the execution of the instruction to be skipped when the current input values match a previously cached set of values. We observe, however, that the inputs and outputs of a chain of instructions are highly correlated. Thus, a natural coarsening of the granularity for value reuse is the basic block. A basic block can be viewed as a *superinstruction* [6] that has some set of inputs and produces some set of live output values. Using the basic block as the prediction and reuse unit may save hardware compared to previous instruction-level schemes in addition to reducing execution time.

We investigate the input and output value locality of basic blocks to determine their predictability and their potential for reuse. The basic block boundaries are determined dynamically at run-time with the upward-exposed inputs of each basic block, as well as its live outputs, stored in a new hardware mechanism called a *block history buffer*. The pro-

---

*This work was supported in part by National Science Foundation grant nos. MIP-9610379, CDA-9502979, and CDA-9414015.

cessor uses these stored values to determine the output values a basic block will produce the next time it is executed. If the current inputs to a block are found to be the same as the last time the block was executed, all of the instructions in the block can be skipped. This technique is called *block reuse* in contrast to instruction reuse [8]. To prevent the register outputs that are dead after a block's execution from occupying limited *block history buffer* resources, and to prevent dead outputs from poisoning a block's value locality, we use the *GCC* compiler to mark dead register outputs, and pass this information to the hardware. Our simulation results show that block reuse can boost performance by 1% to 14% over existing superscalar processors with reasonable hardware assumptions.

2 Basic Block Value Locality

Each instruction in a program belongs to a basic block, which is a sequence of instructions with a single entry and a single exit point. Instructions within a basic block are correlated in that some inputs to an instruction may be produced by previous instructions within the same block. An input which is not produced within the same block is called an *upward-exposed input*. The set of all upward-exposed inputs compose the input set of a basic block. This set includes both registers and memory references. When a basic block is executed a second time and the set of input values are the same as the last time the block was executed, we say that this block is demonstrating *block-input value locality*. *Block-output value locality* is defined similarly. However, some values produced inside a basic block may not be needed by the following blocks, since they may be either unused or overwritten by the following blocks. These types of outputs are termed *dead outputs*, similar to the concept of a dead definition in a compiler. The output value locality of a block refers only to its live outputs. The input and output value locality of a block that has only a single instruction is the same as that instruction's value locality [4]. We use the terms input and output value locality in later discussions to refer to block input and output value locality.

We construct basic blocks and their input and output sets dynamically at runtime as discussed in Section 3. We store up to four sets of input and output values for a block from its previous four executions. The values that were read or produced by the immediately previous execution of the block are called its *depth-1 inputs* or *outputs*, with the values in *any* of the previous n executions called the *depth-n inputs* or *outputs*. The value locality corresponding to depth-n inputs or outputs is called *depth-n input* or *output value locality*. All programs are compiled with the *GCC* compiler using the *-O2* optimization flag.

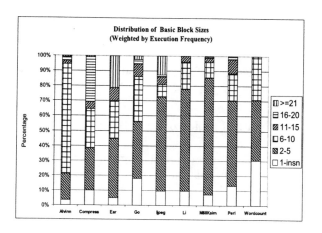

Figure 1: Distribution of executed instructions for different basic block sizes.

2.1 Characteristics of Basic Block Inputs and Outputs

A basic block can consist of an arbitrary number of instructions, although typical values range between 1 and 25. Table 1 shows the average number of instructions in a basic block for a subset of the SPEC benchmark programs. The corresponding cumulative execution frequencies are shown in Figure 1. We see that for 5 of the 9 programs, approximately 70% of the blocks have no more than 5 instructions. For 6 out of the 9 programs, 90% of the blocks have fewer than 15 instructions. For most programs, roughly 10% of the basic blocks have only 1 instruction, and fewer than 5% have more than 20 instructions. For *Ijpeg* and *Ear*, however, about 15 to 20% of the blocks have more than 20 instructions.

Since most of the basic blocks are not very large, we expect to see relatively few inputs and outputs for each block. As shown in Figure 2, roughly 90% of the blocks have fewer than 4 upward-exposed register inputs and fewer than 4 memory inputs for all programs except *Ear*. We have modified the *GCC* compiler to mark the dead register outputs in each instruction using the SimpleScalar [1] instruction annotation tool. The hardware interprets this information to exclude the marked registers from the set of live outputs of each basic block. From this analysis, we find that the number of live register outputs in a block tends to be slightly larger than the number of inputs. About 90% of the basic blocks have fewer than 5 live register outputs. Roughly 10% to 15% of the basic blocks have no live register outputs, which is very close to the percentage of blocks that contain only 1 instruction. Usually these single-instruction basic blocks contain only a single branch or jump instruction. The number of memory outputs per basic block is very small due to the infrequent use of store instructions.

Most of the values written to memory are used by later basic blocks. Hence, we assume all of the memory writes are live. We find that 85% to 95% of the basic blocks have at most 1 store, while 25% to 75% of all blocks actually have no stores at all.

2.2 Ideal Value Locality of Basic Blocks

How repetitive or determinable are a block's input values? To answer this question, we studied the behavior of 9 SPEC benchmark programs using the SimpleScalar tool set [1]. We first assume unlimited hardware resources and record all of the input and output values for all basic blocks. The basic blocks themselves are constructed on the fly at run-time with a value history of depth one to four stored for each block. This information is adequate to summarize the overall determinability. The *depth-n input value locality* for each block is calculated as the number of times a block finds the same input values in the depth-n input history table divided by the number of times the block is executed. Then the overall depth-n input value locality is weighted by the block's execution frequency. The overall *depth-n output value locality* is obtained in a similar fashion. Table 2 listed the block value locality for the 9 SPEC programs tested

We find that the input value locality varies from 2.21% to 41.44%, and the output value locality ranges between 3.09% and 51.63%. *Ear* has the worst basic block value locality for both input and outputs. In this program, most of the blocks with high execution frequencies are large with many register inputs and possibly some memory inputs. Furthermore, its loops often update induction variables within frequently executed basic blocks. As a result, these blocks tend to have low input locality. From the relatively small differences between the input and output value locality numbers, we infer that most basic blocks produce repeated outputs only when they have repeated inputs. However, these differences may indicate an opportunity to predict the output values for speculative execution.

Increasing the history depth tends not to produce a significant increase in the input or output value locality, except for *M88Ksim*, which is a processor simulator with a well-defined input domain (a fixed instruction set). For the other programs, the set of inputs to a basic block has a large domain, so that even a tiny change in any input values will cause the basic block to lose its value locality. As a result, individual basic blocks tend to exhibit either very good value locality or almost none at all. A depth-one history is sufficient to capture most of the essential value locality behavior of a block for most of the tested programs. Consequently, if the goal is simply to identify redundant basic block executions, a history depth of one is adequate.

2.3 Determinable Locality

The unlimited resource assumption will not help us to understand the potential benefits of exploiting basic block input and output value locality. We thus assume the number of input register values the hardware can store is 4, and the number of memory input values is at most 4. The corresponding numbers for outputs are 5 register values and 2 memory values. Based on the results in Figure 2, these parameters are sufficient to cover the requirements of 90% of all of the basic blocks. If the hardware configuration is too small to store all inputs and outputs of a block, it must be assumed that there is no value locality. The updated locality values with this resource limitation are shown in Table 3. The block value locality observed in this case is quite close to the unlimited resource case, suggesting that we may be able to exploit basic block value locality with realistic hardware configurations.

An actual processor could not store the necessary input and output values for all basic blocks all the time. This is too expensive and practically impossible. Instead, we next examine the effect on value locality of restricting the number of entries that are stored. Since this buffer acts like a value history buffer for basic block data, we call it a *block history buffer*. This *block history buffer* is indexed with the address of the first instruction in a basic block, shifted right 2 bits. We evaluated history buffer sizes of 512, 1024, 2048 and 4096 entries. The miss rate for each configuration is plotted in Figure 3. *Word-count, Compress* and *Alvinn* have the smallest number of basic blocks (see Table 1) and consequently have the lowest miss rates in the *block history buffer*. For large programs, such as *Perl* and *Go*, the miss rates are 20.50% and 28.63% when the buffer is small, and 4.51% and 6.37% when the buffer is as large as 4K entries. A buffer size of 2K entries is sufficient to cover the block execution window for most programs. Even *Go*, which has 8969 unique basic blocks, has a miss rate of only 11.28% with the 2K buffer. As shown in Table 4, the input and output value locality for these programs is still substantial in this case. Hence, we decide to use the 2048-entry configuration in all of the subsequent experiments.

The previous experiments all used *GCC*'s -*O2* optimization level. This optimization level does not include loop-unrolling or function inlining, which could possibly change the size of the basic blocks, as well as their input and output value localities. We studied the effects of applying each optimization individually and together and found that these optimization strategies do not consistently produce the same effect, nor do they drastically change the basic block's value locality [3]. Hence we use only the -*O2* optimization flag in the subsequent experiments.

Metric	Alvinn	Compress	Ear	Go	Ijpeg	Li	M88Ksim	Perl	Wordcount
Arithmetic Mean(AM)	4.82	4.35	4.81	5.72	5.95	4.15	4.68	4.15	4.14
Weighted Mean(WM)	8.89	9.80	10.09	6.03	14.03	4.00	4.16	4.76	3.35
Number of Blocks (NB)	1071	760	1632	8969	2755	1462	2388	3285	487

Table 1: Average size and number of basic blocks in the test programs (WM = execution frequency weighted mean).

Depth/programs	Alvinn	Compress	Ear	Go	Ijpeg	Li	M88Ksim	Perl	Wordcount
Input Locality									
1	16.21	19.68	2.21	28.80	21.16	30.52	39.68	41.44	32.84
2	20.22	20.54	2.42	34.43	22.33	32.96	53.54	44.52	33.57
3	21.80	21.20	2.45	38.94	23.54	34.83	54.89	48.24	34.15
4	23.85	21.65	2.81	42.33	24.36	35.62	69.24	49.42	34.52
Output Locality									
1	18.85	23.47	3.15	46.27	31.90	39.70	51.63	42.26	37.40
2	21.59	24.10	3.18	50.65	33.62	44.58	64.95	45.92	37.41
3	23.19	24.79	3.29	54.50	35.03	50.66	65.77	51.06	37.41
4	24.71	25.20	3.78	57.62	36.14	59.96	80.58	52.15	37.41

Table 2: Input and output value locality for different history depths (percentage).

Value Locality	Alvinn	Compress	Ear	Go	Ijpeg	Li	M88Ksim	Perl	Word-count
Input	13.85	19.08	1.87	27.37	17.91	29.00	28.67	34.33	32.83
Output	17.01	23.16	2.87	45.60	34.35	39.50	57.66	41.92	37.40

Table 3: Block value locality with a limited number of input and output values stored (percentage).

Value Locality	Alvinn	Compress	Ear	Go	Ijpeg	Li	M88Ksim	Perl	Wordcount
Input	11.87	18.72	1.75	23.47	14.28	30.13	25.73	31.43	32.83
Output	18.54	23.40	3.15	44.91	34.61	39.61	57.06	41.52	37.40

Table 4: Value locality (percentage) with 2K block history buffer entries.

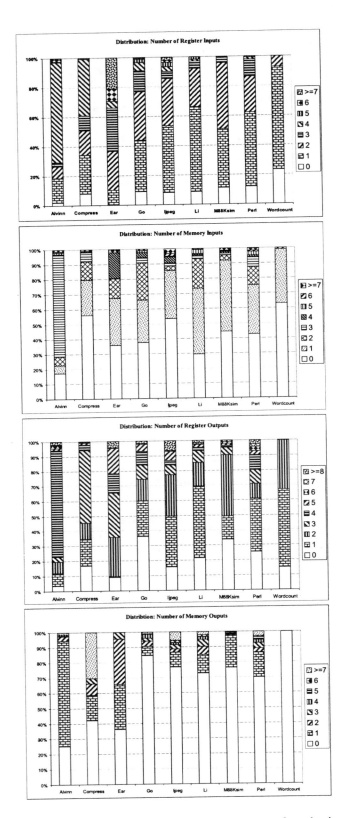

Figure 2: Distribution of the number of outputs for a basic block weighted by execution frequency.

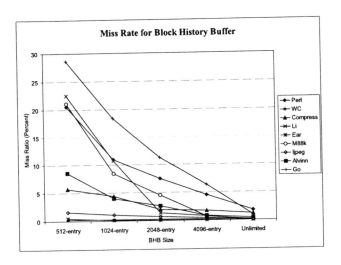

Figure 3: Miss rates for different sizes of the BHB.

3 The Performance Potential of Block Reuse

Good input value locality for a basic block provides opportunities to improve the performance of a processor. The instruction value prediction table in a superscalar processor could be replaced with a *block history buffer* (BHB) that can be used for both value prediction and block reuse. Specifically, when the current input values to a basic block are identical to those stored in the *BHB*, the stored output values can be passed to the inputs of the next basic block to be executed, thereby allowing the processor to skip the execution of all of the instructions in the current block. [1] Furthermore, when one block sees a repetition of its input values, its successors are likely to have duplicated input values in the same execution path. We call this program behavior a *flow of input value locality*. The number of basic blocks involved in a flow before a block in the sequence sees differing inputs is called the *run-length* of input value locality. When a series of blocks demonstrate input locality together, the processor can skip all of the work that is included in this series of blocks and directly update the output registers and memory. Hence, the sizes of the blocks involved in a flow are very important. We call the total number of instructions included in this type of flow of basic blocks the *Task Redundancy* (TR) of the sequence of blocks. The larger the TR, the greater the performance potential of block reuse.

---

[1] More aggressive implementations could use the history buffer to predict block output values even when the input values have changed. This speculative use of the *BHB* is beyond the scope of this paper, however.

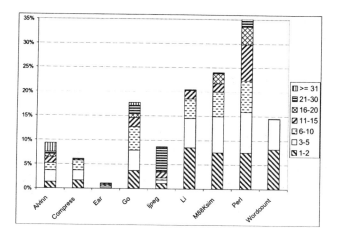

Figure 4: Distribution of skippable instructions for different block sizes.

The average run-length with uninterrupted input locality ranges between 1.15 and 3.65 basic blocks, but the average TR varies from 1.70 to 18.33 instructions, as shown in Table 5. The average size of the basic blocks involved in a run is larger than the average size of all basic blocks shown in Table 1. *Wordcount*, however, is a short program that repetitively executes several switch statements, which makes it consist of many small basic blocks, as shown in Figure 1. As a result, the average size of basic blocks in the run is actually smaller than the overall average block size for *Wordcount*. The other programs typically have TR values of around 4-9 instructions. The average TR for a locality flow is large for floating point programs like *Alvinn* and *Ear*, although *Ear* exhibits little input value locality.

If the task redundancy in a program is not large enough, skipping the execution of the basic blocks cannot offset the time required to access the *BHB* and update the processor state. Figure 4 depicts the distribution of skippable instructions for different basic block sizes. About 2% to 35% of the executed instructions are redundant, and hence are skippable. For *Wordcount*, most of the skippable instructions belong to one-instruction basic blocks. Thus, the benefit of block reuse cannot be large for this program. *Ear* has very low input locality, and the total number of instructions that are skippable is less than 3%, which means block reuse will not be effective for *Ear*, either. For the other programs, skippable instructions that belong to basic blocks of 3 or more instructions comprise 5% to 28% of the total instructions executed. Skipping the execution of these blocks may compensate for the time required to interrogate the *BHB* and the data cache, and the time required to update the processor state.

3.1 Hardware Implementation

To evaluate the potential performance benefit of block reuse, we propose one possible design. The input and live output values must be stored for each basic block in the *block history buffer* (BHB) along with the starting address of the next basic block. When the entry point to a block is encountered in the execution of a program, the *BHB* is checked to see if the output of this block is determinable. That is, if all of the input values to the block (including any memory inputs stored in the data cache) match the stored values in the *BHB*, the processor jumps to the subsequent block and skips all of the work in the current block. If it is not determinable, however, the processor issues instructions to the functional units as usual. When any instruction in a basic block commits, the *BHB* is updated. Figure 5 shows the processor model we use.

Basic blocks are constructed dynamically as follows:

1. Any instruction after a branch is identified as the entry point of a new block. The first instruction of a program is the entry point of a block automatically. Note that subroutine calls and returns are treated exactly as any other type of branch instructions.

2. A branch instruction marks the end of a basic block.

3. A branch to the middle of a basic block splits the current block into two separate blocks. (A performance optimization could duplicate the instructions after the split point to create a new block entry in the *BHB* instead of splitting the current block.)

Each *BHB* entry contains the 6 fields shown in Figure 6. The *Tag* stores the starting address of a basic block. The *Reg-In* field contains several subfields. The *input mask* subfield maintains one valid bit for each logical register in the instruction set architecture and n sub-entries to store up to n actual data values with the corresponding register numbers. The *Reg-Out* field is organized in the same fashion. Each subentry in the *Mem-In* and *Mem-Out* fields has a *tag* that stores the program counter (PC) of the memory reference instruction, an *Addr* field that stores the memory address for the reference, and a *Data* field to store the actual value. Each data field has a full/empty bit to indicate if that field is currently storing a valid value. The *Next_Block* field records the starting address of the block that follows when the current block is involved in a flow of input value locality. When an instruction is fetched, the *BHB* is queried. If this instruction matches an entry for a block in the BHB, the current input values to this basic block are compared with the stored values. When any entry in the *Mem-In* field of a basic block is valid, the data cache must be accessed. If the

Metrics	Alvinn	Compress	Ear	Go	Ijpeg	Li	M88Ksim	Perl	Word-count
run-length (blocks)	3.65	1.65	2.08	1.57	1.48	1.74	2.57	2.02	1.15
task redundancy (instructions)	18.33	5.05	11.16	5.83	9.24	4.69	8.37	8.23	1.70

Table 5: Average run-length of input locality flow and average task redundancy for basic blocks.

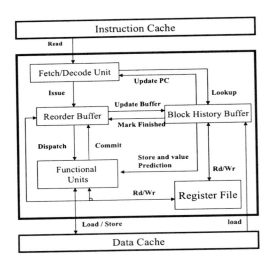

Figure 5: The processor model used for evaluating the performance potential of block reuse.

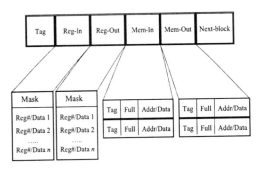

Figure 6: A possible design of a *block history buffer* entry

access produces a hit, the value from the data cache is compared with the stored value. If the cache access is a miss, the memory contents are assumed to be different and value locality is lost.

The hardware collects the input and output values of the basic blocks dynamically. When an instruction is executed, the *input mask* bits for all logical input registers are set, and the appropriate *output mask* bits are set for the block's live output registers, as previously determined by the compiler. The memory input and output fields are used in a first-come-first-served manner, and the full/empty-bit is set when any entry is taken. If the *output mask* bit is set for a register that

the current instruction is trying to read, this read is not an upward-exposed input. In this case, the *input mask* is left unchanged. Also, if a load instruction finds that the address it is trying to read already resides in the *Mem-Out* field, the load is not upward-exposed. Consequently the memory input field is left untouched.

When the *BHB* determines that all of the instructions in the block are redundant and can be skipped, it will perform one of the two following actions depending on the type of exception processing desired.

- For precise exceptions, the instructions are issued as in normal processing. They are marked as completed when they reserve a reorder buffer entry, which prevents them from consuming any functional unit resources. Note that store instructions actually access the cache when they commit.

- For imprecise exceptions, the branch target stored in the *Next_Block* field for the block is retrieved from the *BHB* and used as the next PC. This effectively skips the entire block of instructions.

If the input values stored in the *BHB* do not match those in the processor's current state, or if there is no entry for this block in the *BHB*, the processor core will take control and issue the instructions to the functional units for normal execution. The processor core will continue to update the *BHB* whenever an instruction in a block commits.

3.2 Indirect Memory Referencing

In load-store architectures, memory addresses change only if the corresponding input registers also change. Therefore, if the register inputs to a basic block differ, then the memory addresses calculated from these registers will also differ. Furthermore, recall that the *BHB* checks the contents of the data cache as well as the addresses being referenced. Consequently, even if the user program uses multiple levels of pointers, the *BHB* still detects the repetition of block inputs correctly.

3.3 Simulation Methodology

We use execution-driven simulations to investigate the performance potential that could be obtained by using the

BHB to skip around the execution of all of the instructions in a basic block with repeating inputs. While there could be many different *BHB* implementations, our purpose is to illustrate the potential of a novel mechanism instead of comparing different design options. We modified the SimpleScalar Tool Set [1] for all of our experiments. The SimpleScalar processor has an extended MIPS-like instruction set architecture with modified versions of the *GCC* compiler (version 2.6.2), the *gas* assembler, and the *gld* loader.

The base superscalar processor used in this study contains 4 integer ALUs, 1 integer multiply/divide unit, 4 floating-point adders, and one floating-point multiply/divide unit. It can issue and commit up to four instructions per cycle with dynamic instruction reordering. The execution pipeline, the branch prediction unit, and a two-level cache are simulated in detail. All programs are compiled with the -*O2* optimization level. The resulting programs are simulated on an SGI Challenge cluster with MIPS R10000 processors running version 6.2 of the IRIX operating system.

Three programs from SPEC92, *Alvinn, Ear*, and *Word-count*, and 6 programs from SPEC95, *Compress, Go, Ijpeg, Li, M88Ksim* and *Perl*, were evaluated. The *test* input sizes were used for most of the programs. However, *Go* was driven with the *train* input size. *Word-count* used an input text file of 9871 lines, containing over 40,000 words.

3.4 Compiler Support

The *GCC* compiler saves all dead register information in the *REG_NOTE* field of its *RTX* structure in the flow analysis step. However, this information is inaccurate after it does register allocation. We added another flow analysis step to encode dead register information in each instruction's annotation field [1]. The *block history buffer* can interpret the annotation field to identify the register number for each dead register output. While dead register outputs of a block are common, dead memory outputs are very rare. Consequently, we chose not to mark dead memory outputs so that all memory outputs are considered live at the end of a basic block.

3.5 Performance Results

To obtain a coarse upper bound on the performance benefit of the *block history buffer* mechanism, the initial simulations assume that it takes one cycle to query the *BHB* and another cycle to update the registers and data cache. Also, each entry in the *BHB* can store any number of input and output values, but it is limited to 2048 entries with 2 read/write ports. The resulting speedup values shown in

Table 6 are calculated by dividing the base execution time with the execution time obtained using the *BHB*. The resulting speedup values range from 1.01 to 1.37 with a typical value of 1.15. *Ear* has approximately 2% input locality and, consequently, shows almost no speedup using the *BHB*. *Compress, Wordcount* and *Ijpeg* have good input locality but small skippable basic blocks. Hence, the speedup for these programs is relatively low (1.04-1.11). *Alvinn, Go, Li, M88Ksim*, and *Perl* have larger skippable basic blocks and large *task redundancy* (Figure 4 and Table 5) which together produce speedup values for these programs between 1.15 and 1.37.

We next test the sensitivity of these speedup results to the number of fields available in each entry of the *BHB*, based on the cumulative distributions of the number of block inputs and live outputs. For example, Figure 2 showed that 85% of all basic blocks have fewer than four register inputs, four live register outputs, three memory inputs, and two memory outputs. Thus, this configuration is used for the 85-percentile case. Table 7 shows the hardware configurations tested with the corresponding speedups listed in Table 6. We see that the performance improves gradually for all of the programs as the number of input and output values that can be stored increases. For the 95-percentile configuration, the speedup values are between 1.01 and 1.16 with a typical value of 1.10, which is close to the unlimited case.

Since each entry in the *BHB* records more than one register number and value pair, the time required to check the *BHB* and update the processor state may be longer than the 2 cycles assumed above. Figure 7 shows the speedup obtained when varying the total time in cycles required to access the *BHB* and data cache, and to update the processor state. Here each entry in the BHB can hold 4 register inputs, 5 register outputs, 4 memory inputs, and 2 memory outputs, which corresponds to the 90-percentile case. We see that the performance potential of the *BHB* is not overly sensitive to the time required to interrogate the *BHB* and the data cache when a block is entered and to then update the processor state. For example, even if the delay takes 5 cycles, the speedup of block-reuse is still about 1.03 to 1.09, with a typical value of 1.06. This robust performance is due to the relatively large amount of time saved when a block's execution is skipped compared to the *BHB* overhead.

4   Conclusion

While current prediction and reuse approaches use the instruction as the base unit, we have extended these ideas to the granularity of the basic block. The relatively high

Programs	4/4/3/2	4/5/4/2	5/6/4/3	Unlimited
Alvinn	1.04	1.05	1.05	1.15
Compress	1.06	1.06	1.06	1.07
Ear	1.01	1.01	1.01	1.01
Go	1.08	1.09	1.09	1.18
Ijpeg	1.01	1.08	1.08	1.11
Li	1.09	1.09	1.10	1.14
M88k	1.09	1.09	1.10	1.21
Perl	1.12	1.14	1.16	1.37
WC	1.04	1.04	1.04	1.04

Table 6: Speedups for different hardware settings as listed in Table 7.

Percentile	R-In	R-Out	M-In	M-Out	Label
85	4	4	3	2	4/4/3/2
90	4	5	4	2	4/5/4/2
95	5	6	4	3	5/6/4/3
100	-	-	-	-	Unlimited

Table 7: Hardware settings to cover different basic block input and output requirements (in number of entries).

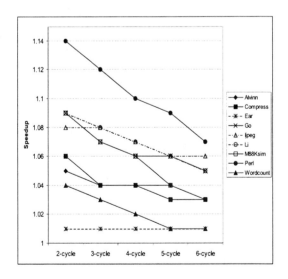

Figure 7: Potential speedup with different *BHB* delays.

input and output value locality of basic blocks, as well as their limited numbers of inputs and outputs, provides the basis for our block reuse mechanism. The *block history buffer* records the input and output values of basic blocks to thereby skip the execution of blocks with repetitive upward-exposed inputs. Simulation results using a subset of the SPEC benchmarks and the SimpleScalar Tool Set showed that block reuse with a 2048-entry *block history buffer* and enough input and output fields to cover the requirements of 90% of the basic blocks can improve the performance of the tested programs by 1% to 14% with an overall average improvement of 9% when using reasonable hardware assumptions.

References

[1] D. Burger, T. Austin, S. Bennett. *The Simplescalar Tool Set, Version 2.0.* Technical Report 1342, Computer Science Department, University of Wisconsin, Madison.

[2] A. Gonzalez and M. Valero. "Virtual Physical Registers". In the *4th Int'l Symposium on High Performance Computer Architecture* (HPCA-4), Las Vegas, February, 1998, Page 175-184.

[3] J. Huang, D.J. Lilja. *Exploiting Basic Block Value Locality with Block Reuse.* University of Minnesota Supercomputing Institute Research Report UMSI98/145, August, 1998.

[4] M. Lipasti, C. Wilkerson and J. Shen. "Value Locality and Load Value Prediction", In the *Proceedings of 8th Int'l Conf. on Architecture Support for Programming Languages and Operating Systems* (ASPLOS VII), October 1996, Page 138-147.

[5] M. Lipasti and J. Shen. "Superspeculative Microarchitecture for Beyond AD 2000". In *IEEE Computer* September, 1997, volume 30, number 9, Page 59-66.

[6] S. Melvin and Y. Patt. "Enhancing Instruction Scheduling with a Block-Structured ISA". In the *Int'l Journal of Parallel Programming*, Volume 23, Number 3, 1995. Page 221-243.

[7] Y. Sazeides, J. Smith. "The Predictability of Data Values". In the *30th Annual Int'l Symposium on Microarchitecture* (MICRO'30), December 1997, Page 248-258.

[8] A. Sodani and G. Sohi. "Dynamic Instruction Reuse". In the *24th Int'l Symposium on Computer Architecture* (ISCA), June, 1997, Page 194-205.

[9] G. Tyson, T. Austin. "Improving the Accuracy and Performance of Memory Communication Through Renaming". In the *Proceedings of the 30th Annual Int'l Symposium on Microarchitecture* (MICRO'30), December, 1997, Page 218-227.

[10] K. Wang, and M. Franklin. "Highly Accurate Data Value Prediction using Hybrid Predictors". In the *30th Annual Int'l Symposium on Microarchitecture* (MICRO'30), December 1997, Page 281-290.

A Study of Control Independence in Superscalar Processors

Eric Rotenberg*, Quinn Jacobson, Jim Smith
Computer Sciences Dept.* and Dept. of Electrical and Computer Engineering
University of Wisconsin - Madison

Abstract

Control independence has been put forward as a signifi-cant new source of instruction-level parallelism for future generation processors. However, its performance potential under practical hardware constraints is not known, and even less is understood about the factors that contribute to or limit the performance of control independence.

Important aspects of control independence are identi-fied and singled out for study, and a series of idealized machine models are used to isolate and evaluate these aspects. It is shown that much of the performance potential of control independence is lost due to data dependences and wasted resources consumed by incorrect control dependent instructions. Even so, control independence can close the performance gap between real and perfect branch prediction by as much as half.

Next, important implementation issues are discussed and some design alternatives are given. This is followed by a more detailed set of simulations, where the key imple-mentation features are realistically modeled. These simula-tions show typical performance improvements of 10-30%.

1. Introduction

In order to expose instruction-level parallelism in sequential programs, dynamically scheduled superscalar processors form a "window" of fetched instructions. Each cycle, the processor selects and issues a group of indepen-dent instructions from this window. Maintaining a suffi-ciently large window of instructions is essential for high instruction-level parallelism -- the more instructions in the window, the greater the chance of finding independent ones for parallel execution.

Branch instructions are a major obstacle to maintaining a large window of useful instructions because they intro-duce *control dependences* -- the next group of instructions to be fetched following a branch instruction depends on the outcome of the branch. Typically, high performance pro-cessors deal with control dependences by using branch pre-diction. Then instruction fetching and speculative issue can proceed despite unresolved branches in the window. Unfor-tunately, branch mispredictions still occur, and current superscalar implementations squash all instructions after a mispredicted branch, thereby limiting the effective window size. Following a squash, the window is often empty and

several cycles are required to re-fill it before instruction issuing proceeds at full efficiency. Furthermore, we are fast approaching the point where the hardware window that can be constructed exceeds the average number of instructions between mispredictions.

There are three ways of dealing with the conditional branch problem. The first, and most widely studied, is to improve branch prediction. This approach has received considerable (successful) research effort for many years. The second is to fetch and execute both paths following a branch, and keep only the computation of the correct path. Of course this can lead to exponential growth in hardware, so recently, more selective approaches have been advo-cated, where multi-path execution is only used for hard-to-predict branches [1-6]. Predicated execution is a software method for achieving a similar effect [7, 8]. The third approach is aimed at reducing the penalty after a misprediction occurs. This approach exploits the fact that not all instructions following a mispredicted branch have performed useless computation.

The third approach is probably less well understood than the other two, and in this paper we explore its poten-tial. The key point is that only a subset of dynamic instruc-tions immediately following the branch may truly depend on the branch outcome. These instructions are *control dependent* on the branch. Other instructions deeper in the window may be *control independent* of the mispredicted branch: they will be fetched regardless of the branch out-come, and do not necessarily have to be squashed and re-executed [9, 10]. This can be illustrated with a simple example.

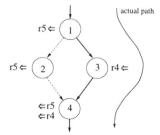

FIGURE 1. An example of control independence.

Figure 1 shows a control flow graph (CFG) containing four basic blocks. Basic blocks are used for simplicity and may be substituted with arbitrary control flow. The branch terminating block 1 is mispredicted, with dashed arrows indicating the mispredicted path 1, 2, and 4. Two data dependences, through registers r4 and r5, are also shown.

At the time the misprediction is detected, blocks 1, 2, and 4 have already been speculatively fetched and some of their instructions may have already started executing. Because only block 2 is control dependent on the mispredicted branch, it is the only block whose instructions must be squashed. Immediately after the misprediction is found, the fetch unit goes back and fetches block 3 to replace the squashed instructions of block 2.

Control independent instructions following the mispredicted branch, specifically block 4, are not squashed, but they do need to be inspected for data dependence violations caused by the mispredicted control flow, and some instructions may have to be re-executed. The value identified with r5 must be corrected so that block 4 uses the value produced earlier in block 1 instead of the one incorrectly produced in block 2. Likewise, when block 3 is eventually inserted into the window, the data dependence through register r4 must also be established. Note that data dependences through memory must similarly be repaired. After the instructions using r4 and r5 in block 4 correct their data dependences and reissue, all subsequent data dependent instructions must also reissue. Hence, selective instruction reissue [11, 12] in some form is necessary.

Lam and Wilson's limit study on control independence [9] showed that substantial performance improvements may be possible. However, as a limit study, most implementation constraints were not considered. Further, important aspects of programs themselves were not modeled; in particular, a significant subset of data dependences were ignored due to the trace-driven nature of the study. Several microarchitecture implementations have since been proposed that incorporate control independence in some form [10,12-19]. In these studies, however, either the impact of control independence is not isolated, or insight into the reported performance gains is limited and obscured by artifacts of the particular design.

In this paper we have three primary objectives and contributions. The first objective is to *establish new bounds on the performance potential of control independence under implementation constraints*. The study focuses on two fundamental constraints that characterize superscalar processors: instruction window size and instruction fetch/issue bandwidth. Other aspects of the study remain ideal and aggressive to avoid artificial design limitations.

The second objective is to *provide insight into the factors that contribute to or limit the performance of control independence*. Data dependences between control dependent and control independent instructions play an important role. In Figure 1, there is a **true data dependence** (register r4) between the **correct control dependent instructions** in block 3 and subsequent control independent instructions in block 4. Similarly, there is a **false data dependence** (register r5) produced by the **incorrect control dependent instructions** in block 2. Resolving both types of data dependences is delayed by the branch misprediction in spite of control independence. Another important factor is the waste of fetch and execution resources by incorrect control dependent instructions. Having to first fetch the misspeculated instructions delays filling the instruction window with correct, control independent instructions. Also, if there are more incorrect control dependent instructions than correct ones, e.g. block 2 is larger than block 3, window space is wasted that might have gone to more control independent instructions.

The third objective is to *assess the complexity of implementing aggressive control independence mechanisms in superscalar processors*. Although it is beyond the scope of this paper to put forth detailed designs, implementation requirements are identified and hardware/software alternatives for meeting the requirements are proposed. We have also developed a detailed execution-driven simulator that implements the outlined requirements.

Several conclusions emerge from our study. First, the performance gap between branch prediction with conventional speculation and oracle branch prediction is quite large, but control independence holds the potential for closing the gap by as much as half. Second, the effects of incorrect control dependent instructions -- both wasted resources and false data dependences -- significantly limit the benefits of control independence, with wasted resources being the chief problem. The impact of true data dependences is slightly smaller than that of false data dependences. Third, for the chosen design alternatives in the detailed execution-driven model, performance improvements ranging from 10% to 30% are measured.

In order to keep the study manageable, we limit our scope to one of two major schemes for exploiting control independence. In particular, the study targets processors that use a single flow of control, i.e. a single fetch unit, as in today's superscalar processors. Other schemes, using multiple flows of control, are not studied here.

1.1 Prior work

Lam and Wilson's limit study [9], and a similar study by Uht and Sindagi [1], demonstrates that control independence exposes a large amount of instruction-level parallelism, on the order of 10 to 100. Although these results are important, full interpretation is obscured for both technical and practical reasons. As pointed out in an analysis by Sundararaman and Franklin [20], the limit study makes certain assumptions that may inflate the apparent benefits of control independence. Static branch prediction based on profiling is used, as opposed to more accurate dynamic branch predictors. More importantly, because the simulation is fully trace-driven, it does not account for false data dependences created on mispredicted paths, thus allowing incorrect-data dependent instructions to be scheduled earlier than they would be in practice. Furthermore, limit studies, by definition, are unconstrained in order to measure *inherent parallelism* in programs, and do not consider fundamental processor features. There is no concept of a limited instruction window or instruction fetch bandwidth, whether considering a single or multiple flows of control. The entire dynamic instruction stream is scheduled at once; exposing the observed parallelism may require buffering speculative state for thousands of instructions and using an impractical number of parallel fetch units.

Multiscalar processors [10,13] and other speculatively multithreaded architectures [14-17,19] exploit control independence by pursuing multiple flows of control. In the case of multiscalar, the compiler partitions the program into tasks, or subgraphs of the CFG, which may contain arbitrary control flow. Branch mispredictions within a task may not cause subsequent tasks to squash if they are control independent of the branch. To date, however, there has been no study that separates the impact of control independence and determines its contribution to performance in the multiscalar paradigm.

Trace processors [12,21] are a variant of multiscalar processors where the dynamic instruction stream is divided into traces -- frequently executed dynamic instruction sequences. An internal mispredicted conditional branch causes its trace to be squashed, but subsequent traces are not squashed if, after repairing the mispredicted branch and predicting a new sequence of traces, the new traces are the same as those already residing in the processing elements [12]. Only modest improvements are reported because no optimization in trace selection or processor assignment was done to expose control independence.

The instruction reuse buffer [18] provides another way of exploiting control independence. It saves instruction input and output operands in a buffer -- recurring inputs can be used to index the buffer and determine the matching output. In the proposed superscalar processor with instruction reuse, there is complete squashing after a branch is mispredicted. However, control independent instructions after the squash can be quickly evaluated via the reuse buffer. Overall speedups due to reuse are on the order of 10%, over half of which is due to squash reuse.

1.2 Paper organization

In Section 2, we consider a series of idealized machine models in order to better understand the relative importance of some of the bigger issues affecting control independence. Section 3 lists the key features in a superscalar processor for exploiting control independence and dis-

cusses implementation alternatives for each of the features. Next, in Section 4, we study performance considering timing constraints imposed by practical implementations.

2. The potential of control independence

In this section we begin evaluating the performance potential of control independence in superscalar processors. It is an idealized study in the sense that some of the models have oracle knowledge so that (1) performance bounds can be established and (2) aspects that limit the performance of control independence can be isolated. The latter has important implications: by understanding the limiting aspects, techniques may be developed to overcome them. On the other hand, the study is *not* an unconstrained "parallelism limit study" -- a particular class of implementations is targeted, and fundamental resources are limited.

2.1 Control independence models

In the models given below, the performance impact of three important aspects of a control independent design are singled out for study.

- The first aspect concerns true data dependences between correct control dependent instructions and control independent instructions. In such cases, issuing the control independent instructions is delayed until after the misprediction is resolved and the correct control dependent instructions are fetched/issued.

- The second aspect is the handling of false data dependences created by incorrect control dependent instructions. As discussed earlier, these cause the selective reissue of some control independent instructions. Delays brought on by this repair and selective reissue can inhibit performance gains.

- The third aspect is the use of machine resources by instructions on an incorrect path that are eventually squashed. Even if control independence is ideally implemented otherwise, this waste of resources and time will reduce performance.

Six different models are evaluated. Figure 2 illustrates the differences among these six models, using the example CFG in Figure 1. Only two resources, instruction fetch and issue, are shown. Time progresses downward in the fetch/ issue schedules. Fetching each basic block consumes fetch bandwidth; this is shown using basic block labels within their respective fetch slots. Likewise, instructions consume issue bandwidth, and are labeled first with the corresponding basic block, followed by the production/consumption of a value. For clarity, only instructions that ultimately retire (i.e. correct instructions) are shown; for these, only the final issue time is shown. The labels "M" and "D" in the diagrams indicate the time of the branch misprediction (M) and the time that the misprediction is detected (D).

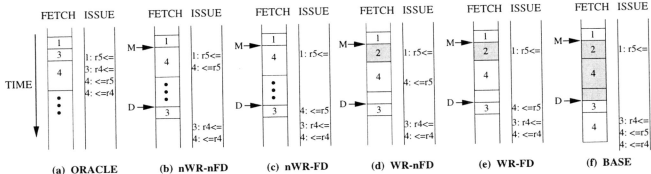

FIGURE 2. Fetch and issue timing for the six models, corresponding to the example CFG in Figure 1.

The *oracle* model (Figure 2(a)) uses oracle branch prediction and therefore the branch terminating block 1 is not mispredicted. Blocks 1, 3, and 4 are fetched in correct dynamic program order.

The next four models use real branch prediction coupled with complete knowledge of control dependences to exploit control independence. The following notations are used.

- *WR* ("Wasted Resources"): Misspeculated instructions consume window resources and bandwidth, thus delaying other, correct instructions.

- *FD* ("False Data Dependences"): The effects of false data dependences between incorrect control dependent instructions and control independent instructions are modeled.

The inverse notations, *nWR* and *nFD*, indicate the corresponding factor is *not* modeled. Thus, there are four possible models: *nWR-nFD*, *nWR-FD*, *WR-nFD*, and *WR-FD*.

In the *nWR-nFD* model (Figure 2(b)), mispredicted branches delay fetching the correct control dependent instructions. But between the time that a branch is mispredicted and the misprediction is detected, fetch and window resources are kept busy with control independent instructions. Incorrect control dependent instructions are not considered (for example, block 2 is not fetched into the window), thereby eliminating false dependences and devoting resources solely to control independent work while the misprediction is resolved.

The only difference between this model and *oracle* is that instructions are fetched in a different order following mispredicted branches. This has a negative performance impact only when true data dependences are delayed with respect to *oracle*. For example, instruction "4: <=r4" issues later because the producer instruction in block 3 is delayed by the misprediction.

Interestingly, there are situations where performance of *nWR-nFD* may actually exceed that of *oracle*. For example, instruction "4: <=r5" issues slightly earlier with respect to *oracle*, because block 4 is fetched out-of-order and earlier. If this instruction is on the critical path, scheduling it earlier may improve overall performance.

The *nWR-FD* model, shown in Figure 2(c), also does not waste time with misspeculated instructions, however their effects on data dependences are felt. For example, we do not know the true producer of "r5" until the misprediction is resolved, delaying instruction "4: <=r5" until that time. The repair of false data dependences is assumed to occur in a single cycle, at the time a misprediction is resolved -- this is the best that can be achieved.

The dual of this model is *WR-nFD* (Figure 2(d)): misspeculated instructions take up time and resources (indicated by shaded regions), but false dependences are hidden. Performance degradation with respect to *nWR-nFD* is caused by an underutilized window and delayed fetching of correct (control independent) instructions.

The *WR-FD* model (Figure 2(e)) uses no oracle knowledge regarding misspeculated instructions -- they waste both time and resources, and interfere with data dependences. This model represents an upper bound on the performance of superscalar processors exploiting basic control independence.

Finally, the *base* model (Figure 2(f)) squashes all instructions after a branch misprediction.

2.2 Hardware constraints and assumptions

We are interested in the performance impact of instruction window size and machine width (peak fetch, issue, and retire rate) on control independence. In our study, the machine width is 16 instructions per cycle for all simulations, and window size is varied. We implement the following additional hardware constraints and assumptions:

- Instruction fetch is ideal: up to 16 instructions, including any number of branches, can be fetched every cycle.

- Instruction fetch, dispatch, issue, execute, and retire stages are modeled. Fetch and dispatch take 1 cycle each. Issue takes at least 1 cycle, possibly more if the instruction must stall for operands. Execution takes a fixed latency based on instruction type, plus any time spent waiting for a result bus. Address generation takes 1 cycle, and all data cache accesses are 1 cycle (i.e. perfect data cache). Instructions retire in order.

- Any 16 ready instructions may issue in a cycle.
- Output and anti-dependences for both registers and memory are eliminated (i.e. perfect renaming).
- Oracle memory disambiguation is used. (However, stores fetched down the wrong control path may still interfere with subsequent, control independent loads.)
- A 2^{16}-entry *gshare* predictor [22] is implemented for predicting the direction of conditional branches. All direct target addresses are assumed to be predicted correctly. For indirect calls and jumps, a 2^{16}-entry correlated target buffer [23] is used. Returns are predicted using a perfect return address stack [24].

2.3 Benchmarks

Dynamic instruction traces, including both correctly speculated and misspeculated instructions, are generated by the Simplescalar simulator [25]. Five integer SPEC95 benchmarks -- chosen to reflect a variety of prediction accuracies (Table 1) -- were simulated to completion.

TABLE 1. Benchmark information.

benchmark	input dataset	dyn. instr. count	misp. rate
gcc	-O3 genrecog.i	117 M	8.3%
go	9 9	133 M	16.7%
compress	400000 e 2231	104 M	9.1%
ijpeg	vigo.ppm	166 M	6.8%
vortex	modified train input	101 M	1.4%

2.4 Results

Results of simulating the six machine models are in Figure 3. Performance is measured in instructions per cycle (IPC) and is shown as a function of window size.

First of all, a performance upper bound is established with the *oracle* results. These results, assuming perfect branch prediction, are typically over 10 IPC for window sizes of 256 to 512. The machine width upper bound is 16, and most of the benchmarks come close to this mark. Comparing the *oracle* and *base* results indicates a large performance loss due to branch mispredictions with a complete squash (but otherwise ideal) model. For a 512 instruction window, the loss is between 40% and 70% for four of the five benchmarks. The benchmark that has the least performance loss is *vortex* -- but its prediction accuracy is quite high. Performance for the *base* model typically saturates at a window size of 128 or 256. There is no such saturation point for the *oracle* model. These results are consistent with those produced by others and indicate the importance of branch mispredictions on overall performance.

The difference between *oracle* and *nWR-nFD* illustrates performance losses from deferring instructions on a correct control dependent path until after a mispredicted branch is resolved. In *nWR-nFD*, however, machine resources do not sit idle while the mispredicted branch is resolved -- all machine resources are kept as busy as possible fetching and executing the control independent path. The performance loss is typically only 1 to 2 IPC for the medium to large windows.

The *base* model also defers execution of the correct control path following a misprediction, but it gets no benefit from the machine resources before the mispredicted branch is resolved -- any work done after the branch is squashed. Viewed in this way, *nWR-nFD* indicates that the otherwise wasted resources in *base* can lead to large performance benefits. In terms of the way control flow is managed, *nWR-nFD* is most similar to Lam and Wilson's model [9], because misspeculated instructions are ignored.

With *nWR-FD*, the impact of false data dependences is isolated. For four of the five benchmarks, the performance drop is significant, another 1 to 2 IPC below *nWR-nFD*. *Compress* experiences a much larger drop in performance. False dependences in *compress* limit IPC to under 5 for all window sizes.

With *WR-nFD*, we isolate the effects of wasting resources by executing incorrect control dependent instructions until the branch is resolved. Some resources are still used for the control independent path -- but not until and unless the fetch unit reaches the control independent region. This results in a major drop in performance, bigger than the drop caused by *nWR-FD*. For all benchmarks except *compress*, the effect of wasted time and resources dominates that of false dependences, by about a factor of 2.

With *WR-FD*, we see the combined impact of wasted resources and false dependences caused by incorrect control dependent instructions. Fortunately, the effects are not additive. The *WR* component already dominates, so there is little additional penalty caused by repairing and reissuing false data dependent instructions in the control independent stream (except for *compress*). At this point performance gains are about 100% over the *base* machine.

2.5 Summary and applications of the study

This initial study has established performance bounds for control independence in the context of superscalar processors. The *WR-FD* model reduces the gap between the *oracle* and *base* models by half, and a realistic implementation will fall somewhere between *base* and *WR-FD*.

The other three control independence models also have interesting implications. A major performance limiter is the incorrect control dependent path, primarily because of wasted fetching and window space (*WR-nFD*), but also false data dependences (*nWR-FD*). If these limitations

119

could be mitigated in some way, performance of the *nWR-nFD* model indicates the remaining problem is less significant, i.e. the problem of true data dependences between the deferred, correct control dependent path and control independent instructions.

A possible approach to mitigating the effects of incorrect control dependent instructions is to design instruction windows and fetch units that are less sensitive to wasted resources. The multiscalar architecture is a candidate due to its multiple program counters and "expandable, split-window" [10]. Although strictly speaking our study is only applicable to processors with a single flow of control, we at least get a hint of the control independence potential for *some* multiscalar design points. For example, Vijaykumar's thesis [26] indicates average task sizes on the order of 15 instructions (comparable to the fetch width of 16 instructions) and effective window sizes of under 200 instructions for integer benchmarks. Given a multiscalar processor with aggressive resolution of inter-task data dependences and selective reissuing capability, the *nWR-FD* model rather than *WR-FD* gives the more appropriate performance bound due to the expandable window.

The large performance drop between *nWR-nFD* and *WR-nFD*, the result of wasted fetch and execution resources, tends to indicate that both hardware and software forms of multi-path execution should be performed carefully. These techniques are applied to both correctly predicted and incorrectly predicted branches. We have shown that wasted resources caused by incorrect predictions alone is a problem; adding some fraction of correct predictions worsens the problem.

3. Implementation issues

In this section we discuss important implementation issues for exploiting control independence in superscalar processors. This discussion allows us to better understand, qualitatively, where implementation complexities may lie. We do not mean to suggest that the methods we describe are the only ones possible, but we feel the approaches outlined here are adequate for highlighting the major implementation issues that must be considered, and they form a basis for our later performance simulations in Section 4.

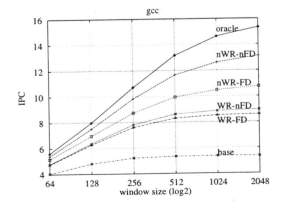

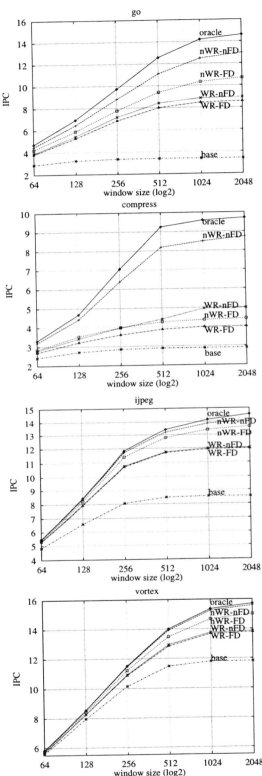

FIGURE 3. Performance of the six models.

120

3.1 Handling of branch mispredictions

When a branch misprediction is detected in a traditional superscalar processor, the processor performs a series of steps to ensure correct execution. Instructions after the mispredicted branch are squashed and all resources they hold are freed. Typically, freeing resources includes returning physical registers to the freelist and reclaiming entries in the instruction issue buffers, reorder buffer, and load/store queues. In addition, the mapping of physical registers is backed up to the point of the mispredicted branch. The instruction fetch unit is also backed up to the point of the mispredicted branch and the processor begins sequencing on the correct path.

Exploiting control independence requires modifications to the recovery sequence, as illustrated in Figure 4 and described below. Steps 1-3 below constitute the *restart sequence*, and step 4 the *redispatch sequence*.

1. After detecting a branch misprediction, the first control independent instruction (if it exists) must be found in the window. We call this the **reconvergent point**, because, in general, control independence exists when control flow diverges and subsequently re-converges.

2. Instructions are selectively squashed, depending on whether they are incorrect control dependent instructions or control independent instructions. Squashed instructions are removed from the window, and any resources they hold are released.

3. Instruction fetching is redirected to the correct control dependent instructions, and these new instructions are inserted into the window which may already hold subsequent control independent instructions.

4. Based on the new, correct control dependent instructions, data dependences must be established with the control independent instructions already in the window. Any modified data dependences cause already-executed control independent instructions to be reissued.

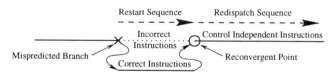

FIGURE 4. Misprediction recovery sequence.

3.2 Key microarchitecture mechanisms

To support the above recovery steps, we have identified four underlying microarchitecture mechanisms. These are: detecting the reconvergent point, supporting arbitrary insertion and removal of instructions within the window, establishing correct data dependences following a misprediction, and selectively reissuing instructions.

3.2.1 Detecting the reconvergent point

Ideally, one would find reconvergent points by associating with every branch instruction its **immediate post-dominator**: the basic block nearest the branch which lies on every path between the branch and the CFG exit block [27]. In Figure 1, for example, block 4 is the immediate post-dominator of the mispredicted branch. Although the post-dominator does not directly specify the program's control dependences, it is sufficient for identifying all reconvergent points. Finding immediate post-dominators could be difficult using hardware alone. Software can aid the hardware by encoding this information. For example, the compiler could encode this information by including in each branch instruction a small offset to its post-dominator instruction. A second option is to incorporate post-dominator registers into the architecture. Software can load these registers with the addresses of post-dominator instructions for soon-to-be-executed branches and then specify a post-dominator register in each branch instruction.

Hardware-only solutions for detecting reconvergent points probably require imprecise heuristics. One alternative is to exploit easily-identified control flow constructs such as loops and functions. The targets of subroutine return instructions and backward branches are detectable by hardware, and they may serve as "global" reconvergent points. While these points are not the precise, i.e. nearest, reconvergent point of any particular branch, they often identify a subset of control independent instructions common to many branches in a region. Hardware can easily detect and record the location of such points in the window, and when a misprediction is detected, the nearest such point is assumed to be the correct reconvergent point.

3.2.2 Instruction removal/insertion

The restart sequence requires selectively removing and inserting instructions while maintaining a correct ordering. The reorder buffer (ROB) of a traditional superscalar processor can be augmented to support this. One option is to have the ROB support arbitrary physical shifting of instructions to collapse and expand the window for restart sequences. This first option causes the physical ROB slots to move, and any instruction tags in the pipelines pointing to them will become out-of-date.

A second option is to implement the ROB as a linked list. Then, any outstanding instruction tags do not change as the ROB is repaired, but dispatch and retirement will be complicated by multiple linked list operations being done in parallel. The complexity of manipulating the linked list can be reduced by implementing it at a granularity larger than a single instruction. That is, ROB space can be partitioned into multi-instruction blocks. For example, a 256 instruction ROB can be implemented as 16 blocks of 16 instructions each. Then, a block at a time can be inserted or removed from the ROB in a more-or-less conventional way. This reduces complexity but also reduces full utilization of the window as ROB blocks will often not be fully utilized. For example, when the processor needs to insert eight instructions into the middle of the ROB, it will allocate a full block of 16 but use only half the entries.

During the restart sequence, resources (physical registers and load/store buffers) of squashed control dependent instructions are iteratively reclaimed. In parallel, as the correct control dependent path is fetched, new instructions may acquire the resources freed by the old instructions. If there are more correct control dependent instructions than incorrect ones, the resources of control independent instructions, youngest first, are reclaimed to make room.

3.2.3 Forming correct data dependences

Although instructions may be *control* independent with a preceding block of instructions, they may not be *data* independent. Consequently, both register and memory dependences of control independent instructions must be repaired after a misprediction.

When the restart sequence completes, the register rename maps reflect state up to the re-convergent point. Control independent instructions are redispatched [12] using the up-to-date register maps. During redispatch, source operands are remapped while destination operands maintain their original assignments. If an instruction's source operand is mapped to a new physical register, the instruction reissues with new data.

To repair memory dependences, the memory-ordering mechanism detects when a preceding store is removed or inserted by a restart sequence and directs affected loads to reissue. An implementation can be found in [12].

3.2.4 Selective reissuing of instructions

If a control independent instruction reissues due to incorrect register/memory dependences, then subsequent data dependent instructions will also need to reissue.

Ultimately, instructions may issue and execute multiple times before they eventually retire. Reissuing, therefore, becomes a common case and the microarchitecture must be modified to reflect this. To reduce the complexity and latency of reissuing instructions, they remain in the instruction issue buffers until they retire [11,12]. Instruction issue buffers can be built to reissue their instructions autonomously when they observe a new value being produced for a source operand. This functionality can be built into the normal issue logic. Thus, the redispatch logic need only identify instructions directly affected by incorrect data dependences, and the following data dependent chain of instructions will automatically reissue.

4. Performance of control independence in a superscalar processor

The idealized studies of Section 2 provide insight into the factors that govern performance of control independence. We now proceed with a more refined analysis, focusing on an implementation of the model *WR-FD*. The analysis is based on a detailed, fully-execution driven simulator, and reflects the performance impact of implementing the basic mechanisms outlined in Section 3.

4.1 Simulator detail

Many of the basic hardware constraints are the same as in Section 2. The machine width is 16 instructions and the underlying pipeline is similar. Instruction fetching remains ideal, but a more realistic data cache is modeled. The data cache is 64KB, 4-way set associative. The cache access latency is two cycles for a hit instead of one, and the miss latency to the perfect L2 data cache is 14 cycles. Also, realistic, but aggressive, address disambiguation is performed. Loads may proceed ahead of unresolved stores, and any memory hazards are detected as store addresses become available [12] -- recovery is via the selective reissuing mechanism. Lastly, the branch predictor, while identical to that in the ideal study, may have lower accuracy due to delayed updates and temporarily incorrect global history.

The key mechanisms for supporting control independence, outlined in Section 3, are modeled as follows.

Detecting the reconvergent point is done via software analysis of post-dominator information.

Instruction removal/insertion is implemented via the linked list approach, using single-instruction granularity.

Forming correct data dependences is delayed a variable number of cycles after the misprediction is detected, unlike the ideal study, because (1) the redispatch sequence cannot proceed until after the restart sequence completes and (2) redispatch proceeds at the maximum dispatch rate.

Selective reissuing is modeled in detail, whereas the ideal study models only the *delay* caused by repaired dependences, i.e. only the final instruction issue. The source of reissuing includes both register rename repairs and loads squashed by stores, followed by a cascade of reissued instructions along the dependence chains.

4.2 Performance results

Figure 5 shows the instructions per cycle (IPC) for three different machines: a superscalar processor that squashes all instructions after branch mispredictions (BASE), a processor with control independence capability (CI), and one with the added capability to instantaneously repair data dependences and redispatch all control independent instructions after the restart sequence completes (CI-I). Measurements are made for three window sizes, 128, 256, and 512 instructions.

For less predictable workloads, control independence offers a significant performance advantage over complete squashing, although less than the ideal study indicated. The relative performance improvement of CI over BASE for each of the window sizes is summarized in Figure 6. *Go*, *compress*, and *jpeg* show improvements on the order of 20% to 30%. While *jpeg* is fairly predictable, it is also rich in parallelism and any misprediction cycles result in a large penalty. *Go* on the other hand is a very control-intensive workload with frequent mispredictions, and it demonstrates the most performance benefit.

Gcc also shows a substantial performance gain, about 10%. Statistics presented in the next section show that approximately 60% of *gcc*'s mispredictions have a corresponding reconvergent point in the window, while for *go*, *jpeg*, and *compress* the same statistic is over 70%. The fact that less control independence is exposed in *gcc* may partially account for the lower performance gain.

From Figure 5 we see that CI-I, as expected, gives better performance than CI. However, the gain is small -- between 1% and 4% -- meaning the time spent during redispatch sequences has less impact than anticipated.

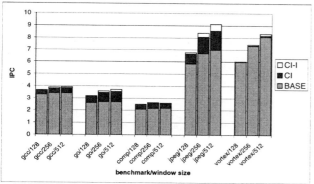

FIGURE 5. Performance of the three models.

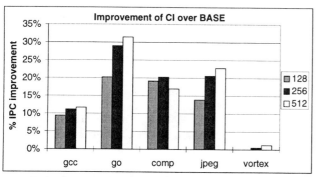

FIGURE 6. Percent improvement in IPC.

4.3 Other control independence measures

This section explores the behavior of control independence in a superscalar processor to better understand the

performance results given in the previous section. The results in this section are for a 256-instruction window.

The first row of Table 2 shows how often a control independent reconvergent point is in the window at the time a misprediction is detected. Except for *vortex*, a reconvergent point is present for over 60% of mispredictions.

The second and third rows of Table 2 show the average number of instructions removed and inserted *for those restart sequences that reconverge in the window*. On average, fewer than 14 incorrect control dependent instructions are removed, and fewer than 20 correct control dependent instructions are inserted. For over 80% of the restarts that reconverge in the window, both the number of instructions inserted and removed is fewer than 32 (not shown in table).

The fourth row in Table 2 shows that the average number of control independent instructions after the reconvergent point is greater than 50 for all the benchmarks. The fifth row in Table 2 shows that on average, only 2 to 3 of the control independent instructions will acquire new physical register names during redispatch, requiring them to reissue (as well as subsequent data dependent instructions).

The last row in Table 2 shows the amount of useful work that can be saved with control independent instructions. Ignoring *vortex*, 11% (*jpeg*) to 39% (*compress*) of all retired instructions issue and have their final value before a preceding mispredicted branch is resolved. Without using control independence this work would be lost.

TABLE 2. Control independence measures.

statistic	gcc	go	comp	jpeg	vortex
% of misp. that reconverge	62%	71%	91%	82%	47%
# removed ctl. dep. instr.	13.2	13.5	6.8	9.0	9.2
# inserted ctl. dep. instr.	16.5	18.1	6.6	10.7	12.8
# control indep. instr.	51.8	62.4	122	79.8	81.5
# instr. w/ new reg. names	2.8	2.2	1.7	2.2	2.1
work saved	20%	30%	39%	11%	4%

5. Conclusions and future work

This research refines our understanding of control independence, perhaps the least understood solution to the conditional branch problem. The study establishes new performance bounds that account for practical implementation constraints and incorporate all data dependences. To gain insight, the study identifies three important factors and isolates their impact on performance: true data dependences between correct control dependent instructions and control independent instructions, false data dependences created by incorrect control dependent instructions, and wasted resources consumed by incorrect control dependent instructions. A conclusion is that both types of data dependences limit the potential of control independence in perhaps unavoidable ways, but the biggest performance limiter is wasted resources consumed by incorrect control dependent instructions. This limitation may be reduced in designs capable of "absorbing" wasted instruction fetch and execution bandwidth.

This paper also discusses important implementation issues and provides some design alternatives. Simplified alternatives are proposed to address some of the more complex aspects, such as the segmented ROB for arbitrary insertion/removal of instructions, and hardware heuristics for identifying reconvergent points. Detailed simulations of a superscalar processor implementing the key features show typical performance improvements of 10-30%, derived from the 20% of retired instructions whose computation is saved as a result of control independence.

The purpose of this work is not so much to advocate control independence in conventional superscalar processors as to promote other control independence architectures. This research is a necessary step towards improving control independence in trace processors, whose hierarchical structure provides a simpler implementation in many respects, including arbitrary instruction insertion/removal. Further, the abstract *nWR-FD* model suggests combining the expandable window model of multiscalar processors with the aggressive data dependence resolution and recovery model of trace processors.

A much more comprehensive treatment of control independence can be found in [28], an extension of this paper.

Acknowledgments

This work was supported in part by NSF Grant MIP-9505853 and by the U.S. Army Intelligence Center and Fort Huachuca under Contract DABT63-95-C-0127 and ARPA order no. D346. The views and conclusions contained herein are those of the authors and should not be interpreted as necessarily representing the official policies or endorsements, either expressed or implied, of the U.S. Army Intelligence Center and Fort Huachuca, or the U.S. Government. Eric Rotenberg is supported by an IBM Fellowship, and Quinn Jacobson by an Intel Fellowship.

References

[1] A. Uht and V. Sindagi. Disjoint eager execution: An optimal form of speculative execution. *28th Intl. Symp. on Microarchitecture*, Dec 1995.

[2] T. Heil and J. Smith. Selective dual path execution. Technical report, Univ. of Wisc., ECE Dept., Nov 1996.

[3] G. Tyson, K. Lick, and M. Farrens. Limited dual path execution. Technical Report CSE-TR-346-97, Univ. of Michigan, EECS Dept., 1997.

[4] A. Klauser, A. Paithankar, and D. Grunwald. Selective eager execution on the polypath architecture. *25th Intl. Symp. on Comp. Arch.*, June 1998.

[5] S. Wallace, B. Calder, and D. Tullsen. Threaded multiple path execution. *25th Intl. Symp. on Comp. Arch.*, June 1998.

[6] P. Ahuja, K. Skadron, M. Martonosi, and D. Clark. Multipath execution: Opportunities and limits. *Intl. Conf. on Supercomputing*, July 1998.

[7] S. Mahlke, R. Hank, J. McCormick, D. August, and W. Hwu. A comparison of full and partial predicated execution support for ilp processors. *22nd Intl. Symp. on Comp. Arch.*, June 1995.

[8] H. Ando, C. Nakanishi, T. Hara, and M. Nakaya. Unconstrained speculative execution with predicated state buffering. *22nd Intl. Symp. on Comp. Arch.*, June 1995.

[9] M. S. Lam and R. P. Wilson. Limits of control flow on parallelism. *19th Intl. Symp. on Comp. Arch.*, May 1992.

[10] M. Franklin. *The Multiscalar Architecture*. PhD thesis, Univ. of Wisc., Nov 1993.

[11] M. Lipasti. *Value Locality and Speculative Execution*. PhD thesis, Carnegie Mellon University, April 1997.

[12] E. Rotenberg, Q. Jacobson, Y. Sazeides, and J. Smith. Trace processors. *30th Intl. Symp. on Microarchitecture*, Dec 1997.

[13] G. S. Sohi, S. Breach, and T. N. Vijaykumar. Multiscalar processors. *22nd Intl. Symp. on Comp. Arch.*, June 1995.

[14] P. Dubey, K. O'Brien, K. M. O'Brien, and C. Barton. Single-program speculative multithreading (spsm) architecture: Compiler-assisted fine-grained multithreading. *PACT*, 1995.

[15] J.-Y. Tsai and P.-C. Yew. The superthreaded architecture: Thread pipelining with run-time data dependence checking and control speculation. *PACT*, 1996.

[16] J. Oplinger, D. Heine, S.-W. Liao, B. Nayfeh, M. Lam, and K. Olukotun. Software and hardware for exploiting speculative parallelism in multiprocessors. Technical Report CSL-TR-97-715, Stanford University, CSL, Feb 1997.

[17] J. Steffan and T. Mowry. The potential for using thread-level data speculation to facilitate automatic parallelization. *4th Intl. Symp. on High Perf. Comp. Arch.*, Feb 1998.

[18] A. Sodani and G. S. Sohi. Dynamic instruction reuse. *24th Intl. Symp. on Comp. Arch.*, June 1997.

[19] H. Akkary and M. Driscoll. A dynamic multithreading processor. *31st Intl. Symp. on Microarchitecture*, Dec 1998.

[20] K. Sundararaman and M. Franklin. Multiscalar execution along a single flow of control. *ICPP'97*, Aug 1997.

[21] S. Vajapeyam and T. Mitra. Improving superscalar instruction dispatch and issue by exploiting dynamic code sequences. *24th Intl. Symp. on Comp. Arch.*, June 1997.

[22] S. McFarling. Combining branch predictors. Technical Report TN-36, WRL, June 1993.

[23] P. Chang, E. Hao, and Y. Patt. Target prediction for indirect jumps. *24th Intl. Symp. on Comp. Arch.*, June 1997.

[24] D. Kaeli and P. Emma. Branch history table prediction of moving target branches due to subroutine returns. *18th Intl. Symp. on Comp. Arch.*, May 1991.

[25] D. Burger, T. Austin, and S. Bennett. Evaluating future microprocessors: The simplescalar toolset. Technical Report CS-TR-96-1308, Univ. of Wisc., CS Dept., July 1996.

[26] T. Vijaykumar. *Compiling for the Multiscalar Architecture*. PhD thesis, Univ. of Wisc., Jan 1998.

[27] R. Cytron, J. Ferrante, B. Rosen, M. Wegman, and F. Zadeck. An efficient method of computing static single assignment form. *Symp. on Principles of Prog. Languages*, Jan 1989.

[28] E. Rotenberg, Q. Jacobson, and J. Smith. A study of control independence in superscalar processors. Technical Report 1389, Univ. of Wisc., CS Dept., Nov 1998.

Instruction Pre-Processing in Trace Processors

Quinn Jacobson and James E. Smith

Department of Electrical & Computer Engineering
University of Wisconsin - Madison
{qjacobso, jes}@ece.wisc.edu

Abstract

In trace processors, a sequential program is partitioned at run time into "traces." A trace is an encapsulation of a dynamic sequence of instructions. A processor that uses traces as the unit of sequencing and execution achieves high instruction fetch rates and can support very wide-issue execution engines. We propose a new class of hardware optimizations that transform the instructions within traces to increase the performance of trace processors. Traces are "pre-processed" to optimize the instructions for execution together. We propose three specific optimizations: instruction scheduling, constant propagation, and instruction collapsing. Together, these optimizations offer substantial performance benefit, increasing performance by up to 24%.

1. Introduction

Trace Processors [11] are based on a microarchitecture that encapsulates dynamic instruction sequences into *traces* at run time. Each trace contains on the order of 16 dynamic instructions and commonly spans multiple basic blocks. The traces are cached [10][8] and become the fundamental unit of work for the rest of the processor. A fetch unit predicts the sequence of traces [4] and dispatches them as units to distributed processing elements. Each processing element is a modest superscalar execution engine capable of a high clock rate.

Because traces are cached, fetched, and executed as a unit, they provide a new opportunity for hardware-based optimization – at the trace-level. That is, a trace of instructions can be optimized via a "pre-process" phase prior to being placed in the trace cache.

There are a number of inherent characteristics of traces that enable pre-processing optimizations. First, each trace sequence contains basic blocks within a specific context, and optimizations applied across basic block boundaries must be valid only for that specific context. Second, the overhead of relatively complex optimizations can be amortized over many uses of a trace. Finally, pre-processing can target new, internal instructions which are not supported in the external instruction set.

In this paper we examine a number of trace optimizations. These optimizations have been chosen to exhibit the diversity of optimizations possible, and the specific ones we study improve performance by 4% to 24% across the benchmarks we studied.

1.1. Trace-Level Optimizations

The following examples illustrate the variety of optimizations that are possible. In later sections, we will discuss specific implementations and performance improvements for each.

- **Scheduling instructions** to take into account extra latency for inter-trace communication.
- **Performing constant propagation** that can not be implemented at compile time, by taking advantage of a single dynamic path and a powerful internal instruction set.
- **Collapsing data dependent chains of computation to single instructions** by adding new internal instructions that make use of very powerful execution units.

Note that pre-processing is intended to complement, not substitute for, good optimizing compilers. The dynamic nature of traces and implementation dependence allows additional transformations that would be impossible, or at least very difficult, in compile-time optimizations.

125

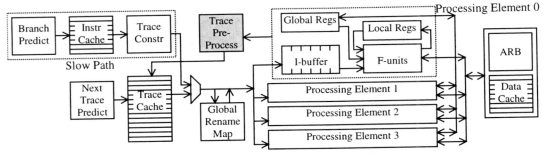

Figure 1 Trace processor hardware with pre-processing.

1.2. Trace Processor Overview

The main components of the trace processor frontend are the next-trace predictor and the trace cache (see Figure 1). Next-trace prediction [4] implicitly performs branch prediction and branch target prediction with sufficient bandwidth to take advantage of the potentially high fetch rate of the trace cache. During normal operation, the next-trace predictor and the trace cache provide a stream of instructions to the processor's execution engine. When the trace cache can not provide the needed instructions, the *slow path* is used.

We model a trace processor with a distributed backend, based on the design proposed in [11]. It is composed of 8 processing elements (PEs) each with a register file, instruction window and execution units. In trace processors, the unit of work dispatched to each processing unit is a trace. Each processing element has full bypasses internally and can support back-to-back dependent operations. It takes a full cycle for register values to be broadcast to other processing elements. Synchronizing of dependences through memory is enforced by special hardware [2] in the memory subsystem. We model a 2-cycle, 4 ported, 64Kbyte level-one data cache and a 10-cycle level-two data cache.

The maximum trace length is 16 instructions. Traces are forced to end at all jump indirect or return instructions. The trace cache has 2K entries and there is a 64Kbyte instruction cache.

1.3. Previous Work

This work is similar to recent work done independently by Friendly et. al. [3]. It builds on the work in trace caches [8][10] and trace processors [11][15].

The optimizations of scheduling and constant propagation are well studied in the context of compilers [1]. Dynamically scheduling groups of instructions was also studied in [7]. The optimization of data collapsing builds on a large body of work [5][9][12][13][14] in this area.

2. Implementing Trace Pre-Processing

When the next trace of a program is not in the trace cache, the slow-path hardware constructs it. This newly constructed trace is dispatched to an idle processing element to be executed and is also placed in the trace cache (in non-optimized form). Most of the work of pre-processing is performed in parallel with the initial execution of the trace. When the trace is completed, the pre-processor performs the final transformations on the trace. We assume a two-cycle latency for this transformation. The new optimized trace is then inserted into the trace cache. Using this model, the latency of trace pre-processing is not on the critical path.

2.1. Instruction Scheduling

The first optimization considered is instruction scheduling. As a practical matter, we do not schedule by literally moving the instructions within the trace. Rather, we assign priorities to instructions in a trace and rely on out-of-order issue logic to complete the scheduling task. When an instruction is identified for increased priority, instructions it depends on must also be increased in priority.

There are many possible heuristics that could be incorporated into assigning priorities. We focus on trace-level communication. Instructions that use values generated in previous traces are decremented in priority and instructions that produce values used in other traces are incremented in priority (incrementing priority has precedence over decrementing). This is an optimization that can not be performed at compile time.

2.2. Constant Propagation

The second pre-processing optimization considered is constant propagation within traces. There are many cases where computation chains with no inputs are used to generate constant values. These can occur because of encoding limitations in the instruction set and because of control dependences that affect the value being produced. With traces, both of these restrictions can be overcome.

Constant propagation leads to performance improvement in two ways. First, there are some instructions that do not need to be executed after constant propagation. Second, constant propagation reduces the length of dependence chains.

Constant propagation can be incorporated into the initial execution of a trace. This is performed by adding a bit to the local register file indicating whether a value was generated from constant operands only. Instructions propagate the bit to their destination if all their sources have the bit set. Instructions producing a constant value record the value and are marked to inhibit their execution in the future. Register source operands with the constant bit set are replaced by the constant value for future execution.

2.3. Instruction Collapsing

The third pre-processing optimization considered is instruction collapsing. Recently, there has been much discussion about the impact of the increase in wire delays relative to gate delay [6]. The flip side of the relative increase in wire delays is the relative decrease in gate delays. While much current research is motivated by the problems posed by long wire delays, there has been little work performed to investigate the opportunities posed by short gate delays. Developing more sophisticated execution resources can significantly reduce the latency of executing a program. With the relative decrease in the delays of gates, adding a few levels of logic to execution resources may not impact the cycle time.

More complex operations can be used to collapse small chains of dependent operations into a single operation, thus reducing the latency. In general, data collapsing turns a chain of dependent operations into a single operation with more operands.

Most of the benefits of collapsing can be obtained by adding a new operation described below. This operation still has two register source operands and a single register destination operand. This is very important as it does not change the demands on the register file and data bypassing configurations, both of which are communication intensive and are usually timing critical. The new operation consists of shifting each of the register source operands left by a small immediate amount (0 to 3), inverting either or both operands, and adding the two values to a third immediate value to produce the result. This operation is extremely powerful but adds only a couple of gate delays over the traditional two-operand add instruction.

After collapsing is performed, an instruction may become redundant, as all instructions that depend on its result have been replaced with a compound instruction that encompasses the redundant instruction. We investigate the performance impact of either executing or not executing these redundant instructions. Executing the redundant instruction simplifies maintaining precise state for recovering from control mispredictions or traps.

Dependence collapsing is implemented in two phases. The first phase is implemented during the initial execution of the trace. A small type field is added to the local register file specifying the type of the instruction that creates the register value. Dependent instructions detect whether they can be collapsed with producing instruction(s). In this way the candidates for collapsing are determined. The second phase takes dependent chains of instructions and forms a new compound instruction that captures the same functionality but has lower total latency.

3. Performance Results

Five of the SPECint95 benchmarks (compress, gcc, go, list and m88ksim) are used to study the benefits of incorporating pre-processing. Each benchmark is run for 100 million instructions. We study the benefit of incorporating each optimization in isolation as well as in conjunction with the other optimizations.

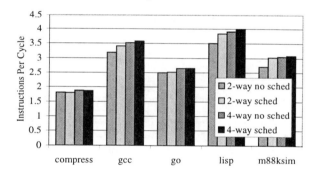

Figure 2 Performance gains from scheduling.

The performance benefit of instruction scheduling for trace-level communication is studied for two processor configurations (2-way issue per PE and 4-way issue per PE). Three of the five benchmarks see a notable performance gain from instruction scheduling in the case of the narrower issue configuration (see Figure 2). With narrower issue there is a greater chance that more instructions will be ready to issue then there are issue slots, so priorities can influence the order of execution. The benefit of scheduling is not significant with the wider issue processors. Scheduling becomes more important when applied in conjunction with collapsing.

Table 1 Instructions removed by constant propagation.

Benchmark	% of insns removed by constant propagation
Compress	4.8
Gcc	9.2
Go	12.0
Lisp	4.1
M88ksim	9.5

Constant propagation removes computation that need not be performed each time a trace is reused. A significant fraction of instructions can be optimized away (see Table 1). This reduces the demand for execution resources in the processor.

Although a significant fraction of instructions are removed by constant propagation the speedup is minimal, less than 1%. The reason is that with the large instruction window and accurate prediction, computation based only on constants can usually be computed before the values are needed. This is especially true in the trace processor configuration where execution resources are dedicated to traces. Constant propagation may have a larger impact if small pools of execution resources are shared by multiple processing elements.

Table 2 Breakdown of instructions effected by instruction collapsing.

Benchmark	% of instruction removed by collapsing			% of instructions replaced by collapsed instruction		
	Agr	Mod	Con	Agr	Mod	Con
Compress	28.5	27.8	0.0	16.4	14.4	14.4
Gcc	20.8	20.4	0.0	9.0	8.3	8.3
Go	21.2	20.6	0.0	10.4	9.9	9.9
Lisp	18.9	18.9	0.0	5.3	5.3	5.3
M88ksim	20.7	17.5	0.0	8.1	4.9	4.9

Instruction collapsing removes data dependence delays by replacing instructions with new compound instructions. We consider three policies for collapsing instructions. The first case, labeled "Aggressive," allows any dependent chain of logical operations (AND, OR,…) to be collapsed together as long as the total number of register operands is four or fewer. Also, any chain of additions and subtractions, including address calculations and set instructions, can be collapsed together as long as the total number of register operands is four or fewer. For chains of either logical or arithmetic operations, left shifts of immediate counts of 3 or fewer are allowed anywhere in the computation chain. Instructions no longer needed after collapsing is performed are not executed unless there is a branch mispredict or an exception within the trace.

The second case, labeled "Moderate," limits collapsed instructions to addition/subtraction of up to two register operands and one immediate operand. Either of the register operands can be shifted left by an immediate counts of 3 or fewer. This restriction limits the needed hardware support to a relatively simple arithmetic unit and requires no additional register ports or bypass logic. This

new instruction can encode a number of possible chains of additions and left shifts. As before, instructions no longer needed after collapsing is performed are not executed unless there is a branch mispredict or an exception within the trace.

The third case, labeled "Conservative," is similar to the Moderate case except that instructions no longer needed after collapsing are still executed. This simplifies the logic for branch mispredict recovery and traps. This also simplifies the logic for performing the pre-processing, as it does not require the analysis of which instructions can be safely removed after collapsing.

Table 2 gives the breakdown of instructions effected by pre-processing. The first three columns present the fraction of instructions that do not need to be executed after collapsing for each of the collapsing policies. The next three columns present the fraction of instructions replaced by a new compound instruction.

A significant amount of collapsing takes place in all the benchmarks, with 5% to 16% of instructions being replaced by new compound instructions. The aggressive and moderate approaches, which remove unnecessary computation after collapsing, remove about 20% of instructions for all the benchmarks. The simpler approaches can capture a majority of the collapsing that the aggressive model can. Only in one benchmark, m88ksim, does the number of instructions replaced by compound instructions vary substantially between the aggressive and the simpler approaches. Even in this case, the simpler approaches get 60% of the collapsing of the aggressive approach.

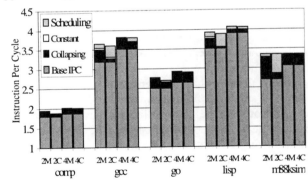

Figure 3 Performance gains from pre-processing
(2M = 2-way issue PEs and moderate collapsing,
2C = 2-way issue PEs and conservative collapsing,
4M = 4-way issue PEs and moderate collapsing,
4C = 4-way issue PEs and conservative collapsing).

Figure 3 gives the performance of the processor as successive pre-processing optimizations are added. Four processor configurations are studied, 2-way and 4-way issue per processor with both the conservative and moderate collapsing approaches. There is a notable benefit, up to a 20% increase in performance, by incorporating the collapsing optimization. When constant propagation is incorporated in addition to collapsing, there is no significant increase in performance.

The scheduling optimization has a large effect when it is applied in conjunction with instruction collapsing. Instruction collapsing increases the amount of instruction level parallelism and therefore increases the chances of exceeding available issue bandwidth. Even with the wider issue processor, instruction scheduling is important. Instruction scheduling has a significantly larger effect with conservative instruction collapsing, where redundant instructions are not removed. With instruction scheduling, the conservative collapsing policy performs almost as well as the moderate collapsing policy.

The proposed pre-processing optimizations enable the processor to make the best utilization of available issue bandwidth. The narrower issue configuration with conservative collapsing and instruction scheduling optimizations perform as well as, or better than, the wider issue configurations without pre-processing. By better utilizing limited resources, intelligent pre-processing can significantly improve the price/performance of a processor.

4. Summary

We have proposed a new set of hardware optimizations for processors with trace caches. These optimizations take advantage of the intermediate program representation encoded in traces. The instructions within traces are pre-processed to optimize them for execution as a group. Three optimizations are studied: instruction scheduling, constant propagation and instruction collapsing. Together, these optimizations can increase performance by 4% to 24% across the benchmarks we studied.

The trace pre-processing optimizations allow for better utilization of execution resources. Trace pre-processing enables a given performance level to be achieved by a trace processor implementation with reduced total issue bandwidth. Trace pre-processing can therefore significantly improve not only the performance, but also the price/performance of a processor.

Acknowledgments

Quinn Jacobson is supported by a Graduate Fellowship from Intel. This work was supported in part by NSF Grant MIP-9505853 and the U.S. Army Intelligence Center and Fort Huachuca under Contract DAPT63-95-C-0127 and ARPA order no. D346. The views and conclusions contained herein are those of the authors and should not be interpreted as necessarily representing the official policies or endorsement, either expressed or implied, of the U.S. Army Intelligence Center and For Huachuca, or the U.S. Government.

References

[1] A. Aho, R. Sethi, J. Ullman, *Compilers: Principles, Techniques and Tools*, Addison-Wesley Publishing Co., 1986.

[2] M. Franklin, G. S. Sohi, "ARB: A Hardware Mechanism for Dynamic Memory Disambiguation," *IEEE. Transactions on Computing*, pp. 552-571, Feb. 1996.

[3] D. Friendly, S. Patel, Y. Patt, "Putting the Fill Unit to Work: Dynamic Optimizations for Trace Cache Microprocessors," To appear in the *Proceedings of the 31st International Symposium on Microarchitecture*, Nov. 1998.

[4] Q. Jacobson, E. Rotenberg, J. E. Smith, "Path-Based Next Trace Prediction," *Proc. of the 30th Int'l Symposium on Microarchitecture*, pp. 14-23, Dec. 1997.

[5] N. Malik, R. Eickemeyer, S. Vassiliadis, "Interlock Collapsing ALU for increased Instruction-Level Parallelism," in *Proceedings of the 25th International Symposium on Microarchitecture*, Sept 1992.

[6] D. Matzke, "Will Physical Scalability Sabotage Performance Gains," *IEEE Computer* Volume 30, Number 9, pp. 37-39, Sep. 1997.

[7] R. Nair and M. Hopkins, "Exploiting Instruction Level Parallelism in Processors by Caching Scheduling Groups," in *Proc. of the 24th Int'l Symposium on Computer Architecture*, pp. 13-25, June 1997.

[8] S. Patel, D. Friendly and Y. Patt, "Critical Issues Regarding the Trace Cache Fetch Mechanism." University of Michigan Technical Report CSE-TR-335-97, 1997.

[9] J. Phillips, S. Vassiliadis, "High Performance 3-1 interlock collapsing ALU's," *IEEE Transactions on Computers*, pp. 825-839, March 1994.

[10] E. Rotenberg, S. Bennett and J. E. Smith, "Trace Cache: a Low Latency Approach to High Bandwidth Instruction Fetching," in *Proceedings of the 29th International Symposium on Microarchitecture*, pp. 24-34, Dec. 1996.

[11] E. Rotenberg, Q. Jacobson, Y. Sazeides and J. E. Smith, "Trace Processors," *Proc. of the 30th Int'l Symposium on Microarchitecture*, pp. 138-148, Dec. 1997.

[12] Y. Sazeides, S. Vassiliadis, J. E. Smith, "The Performance Potential of Data Dependence Speculation & Collapsing," in *Proceedings of the 29th International Symposium on Microarchitecture*, Dec 1996.

[13] S. Vassiliadis, B. Blaner, R. Eickemeyer, "Scism: A Scalable, Compound Instruction Set Machine Architecture," *IBM Jounal of Research and Development*, pp. 59-78, Jan 1993.

[14] S. Vassiliadis, J. Phillips, B. Blaner, "Interlock Collapsing ALU's," *IEEE Transactions on Computers*, pp. 825-839, July 1993.

[15] S. Vijapeyam, T. Mitra, "Improving superscalar instruction dispatch and issue by exploiting dynamic code sequences," *Proc. of the 24th Int'l Symposium on Computer Architecture*, pp. 1-12, June 1997.

Distributed Modulo Scheduling

Marcio Merino Fernandes
University of Edinburgh, UK
Department of Computer Science
mmf@dcs.ed.ac.uk

Josep Llosa
Universitat Politècnica de Catalunya, Spain
Department d'Arquitectura de Computadors
josepll@ac.upc.es

Nigel Topham
University of Edinburgh, UK
Department of Computer Science
npt@dcs.ed.ac.uk

Abstract

Wide-issue ILP machines can be built using the VLIW approach as many of the hardware complexities found in superscalar processors can be transferred to the compiler. However, the scalability of VLIW architectures is still constrained by the size and number of ports of the register file required by a large number of functional units. Organizations composed by clusters of a few functional units and small private register files have been proposed to deal with this problem, an approach highly dependent on scheduling and partitioning strategies. This paper presents DMS, an algorithm that integrates modulo scheduling and code partitioning in a single procedure. Experimental results have shown the algorithm is effective for configurations up to 8 clusters, or even more when targeting vectorizable loops. [1]

Keywords: ILP, VLIW, Clustering, Software Pipelining

1. Introduction

Current microprocessor technology relies on two basic approaches to improve performance. One is to increase clock rates, resulting in faster execution of machine operations. The other is *instruction-level parallelism (ILP)*, a set of hardware and software techniques that allows parallel execution of machine operations. ILP can be exploited by VLIW architectures [8, 16]. In this case all data dependence analyses and scheduling of operations are performed at compile time, which simplifies the hardware and allows the inclusion of a large number of functional units in a single chip.

Loop structures usually found in DSP or numeric applications can take advantage of the available processing power of a wide-issue machine. In many cases they account for the largest share of the total execution time of a program. Several loop optimizations have been developed targeting ILP machines. One of them is *software pipelining* [2], a scheduling technique that allows the initiation of successive loop iterations before prior ones have completed. Modulo scheduling is a class of software pipelining algorithms that produces a basic schedule for a single iteration [15]. The basic schedule is structured in order to preserve data dependencies and avoid machine resource conflicts if it is issued every *Initiation Interval (II)* cycles [14].

The drawback of these techniques is that they increase *register requirements* [10]. The number of storage positions alone can be a problem in the design of a register file (RF). Furthermore, the number of ports required by a VLIW machine may compromise the RF access time, causing a negative impact on the machine cycle time [4]. Hence, wide-issue unclustered VLIW architectures may not deliver the expected performance, which has motivated us to develop a clustered VLIW architecture [7]. However, the effectiveness of such an organization also depends on the code partitioning strategy, as data dependent operations must communicate results between them. We have developed a scheme to produce software pipelined code for a clustered VLIW machine aiming to achieve performance levels similar to an unclustered machine without communication constraints. It is called **Distributed Modulo Scheduling (DMS)**, *integrating* in a single phase both scheduling and partitioning of operations. The remaining of this paper includes an overview of the architecture model targeted by DMS, presents the algorithm, and shows some experimental results along with related conclusions.

---

[1] Research work partially supported by Capes (Brazil)

2. A Clustered VLIW Architecture

The structure of the clustered VLIW architecture targeted by DMS is shown in figure 1. It comprises a collection of clusters connected in a *bi-directional ring* topology. In this paper we focus exclusively on the performance of the VLIW compute-engine, as it should determine the performance of execution of the target applications for this kind of architecture.

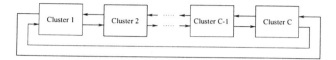

Figure 1. Clustered VLIW architecture

Each cluster contains a set of functional units (FUs) capable of executing a statically compiled loop schedule. They connect to a *Local Register File (LRF)*. We have shown in [5] that loop variant lifetimes produced by a modulo scheduled loop can be allocated to a *queue register file*, resulting in some advantages over a conventional RF. Hence, all *intra-cluster* communication takes place via the LRF, while *inter-cluster* communication takes place via one of the *Communication Queue Register Files (CQRFs)*. A CQRF is a queue register file located between two adjacent clusters, providing read-only access to one of them, and write-only access to the other. Sending a value from one cluster to another requires only a pair of write/read operations to the appropriate CQRF. Thus, no explicit instruction is necessary for near-neighbour communication. This is done by the code generator, which maps lifetimes that span a cluster boundary onto the corresponding CQRF. One of the advantages of this communication mechanism is to allow *fixed timing* in the communication process between two clusters, a desirable feature for static schedulers. Another motivation for using queues is the possibility of implementing asynchronous data transfer across clusters, which might be necessary due to clock skewing.

In spite of the distribution of functional units among clusters, the proposed architecture model still assumes a single thread of control. This will almost certainly involves data exchange among FUs located in distinct clusters. Compiling for a clustered architecture involves *code partitioning* in order to meet communication constraints. An optimal partitioning would yield in the same performance that would be otherwise achieved by an unclustered architecture. However, communication constraints may require a group of operations to be scheduled in a given cluster, which may not have enough resources for that. In this case, the only alternative is to increase the II, reducing the net execution rate.

A number of previous works have dealt with problems similar to this. The Multiflow Architecture [11] performs code partitioning and then scheduling of operations in two separate steps. The Limited Connectivity Model also performs these phases in sequence, though the other way around [1]. A two-phase approach to partitioning and modulo scheduling for a clustered architecture is proposed in [6]. The idea is to partition prior to scheduling, ensuring that no communication conflicts arise when operations are scheduled. This problem can be described as a *k*-way graph partitioning in which the II is to be minimized. Once the partitioning is completed, the scheduling can proceed, taking into account the assignment of operations to clusters. A similar scheme was also reported in [12]. Experiments with an algorithm integrating in a single phase both modulo scheduling and code partitioning was presented in [7]. Although effective for machine models with up to 5 clusters, the scheme is inappropriate for larger configurations because it cannot consider communication between indirectly-connected clusters. That algorithm originated DMS, which addresses this problem. Another algorithm combining both tasks in a single phase is UAS [13]. In that scheme cluster assignment is integrated into a list scheduler, although software pipelining is not performed.

3. DMS Algorithm Description

We have used the Iterative Modulo Scheduling (IMS) algorithm [14] as the basic structure to develop DMS, a scheme able to deal with distributed functional units and register files. As defined in [14], we assume that a *data dependence graph (DDG)* is used to represent the dependencies between operations of the innermost loop to be scheduled. A clustered machine model introduces communication constraints to the scheduling algorithm, in addition to resource and dependence constraints. We say that a **communication conflict** occurs when two operations with a *true data dependence* are scheduled in indirectly-connected clusters.

IMS has one basic strategy to find a *valid slot* to schedule a given operation *OP*, which takes into account its scheduled predecessors and resource conflicts. The later can lead to *backtracking* in order to unscheduled operations to release a slot for *OP*. Eventually, successor operations of *OP* might also be unscheduled, if a dependence conflict arises. On the other hand, the DMS algorithm has three basic strategies to schedule an operation, as seen in figure 2.

Initially DMS tries to find a valid slot to schedule *OP* in such a way that no communication conflict arises with its scheduled *predecessors* and *successors* (strategy 1). In this case a slot is considered valid to schedule *OP* only if the communicating operations in the resulting partial schedule are located in *directly* connected clusters.

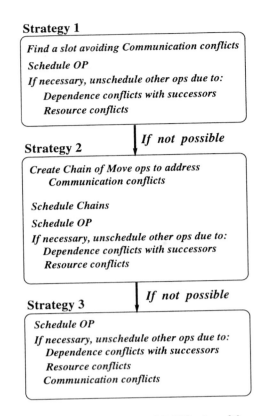

Strategy 1

Find a slot avoiding Communication conflicts
Schedule OP
If necessary, unschedule other ops due to:
Dependence conflicts with successors
Resource conflicts

If not possible

Strategy 2

Create Chain of Move ops to address
Communication conflicts

Schedule Chains
Schedule OP
If necessary, unschedule other ops due to:
Dependence conflicts with successors
Resource conflicts

If not possible

Strategy 3

Schedule OP
If necessary, unschedule other ops due to:
Dependence conflicts with successors
Resource conflicts
Communication conflicts

Figure 2. Overview of DMS algorithm

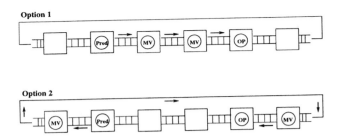

Figure 3. Options to create a chain

If that is not possible, strategy 2 is attempted. In this case DMS tries to insert **move** operations between *OP* and all of its *scheduled predecessors*, using a structure called **chain**. A chain is a string of move operations scheduled in the clusters between *OP* and one of its predecessors. This makes possible to transfer operands between a pair of producer/consumer operations located in indirectly-connected clusters. In the particular architecture model considered in this paper, a move operation simply read one value from a CQRF and write it back to another one. Thus, given a candidate cluster to schedule *OP*, and the cluster of its predecessor, there are two possibilities to create a chain, each of them following *opposite* directions (figure 3). The bidirectional ring of queues used to connect clusters allows this flexibility.

Initially any cluster can be considered to schedule *OP*. More than one chain might be necessary to schedule *OP* in a given cluster because multiple predecessors may be already scheduled. However, these chains can be built only if there are enough machine resources to schedule *all* move operations in the respective clusters. As above discussed, more than one option to schedule a chain might exist to address a given communication conflict. In this case, the selected option is the one that maximizes the number of free slots left

available to schedule move operations in *any* cluster. If two or more possibilities are equivalent regarding this criteria, the smallest number of move operations defines the choice. These conditions determine the cluster in which *OP* will be scheduled.

Once a valid set of chains is chosen, it can be scheduled straightforward as the availability of machine resources has already been verified. The first step involves updating the DDG to include the new move operations and related data dependencies. Then move operations are sequentially scheduled, starting from the first one after the original producer operation. This ordering must be enforced to determine the correct scheduling time of each of them.

If resource conflicts prevent the use of chains to overcome communication conflicts, *OP* is scheduled in a arbitrarily chosen cluster using a process similar to the one employed by IMS. The only difference is that the backtracking process must also unschedule some operations due to communication conflicts (strategy 3).

Special attention must be paid in the implementation of the backtracking procedures. It might happen that an operation ejected from the partial schedule is part of a chain. In this case it may also be necessary to unschedule other operations and update the DDG in order to prevent communication conflicts with the remaining scheduled operations. Distinct actions must be taken when the unscheduled operation is the original producer, a move operation, or the original consumer, respectively.

It is expected that the additional constraints used by DMS may increase the backtracking frequency. However, we have found through experimental analysis that the overhead on the II due to partitioning is tolerable in most of the cases (section 4). Those results suggest that on average the backtracking frequency of IMS and DMS are of the same order. When the backtracking frequency increases it is usually due to insufficient number of slots to schedule the required move operations, rather than a lengthy search across the space of solutions.

Although DMS has been specially developed for the architecture model described in section 2, we believe it could also be used with other clustered VLIW architectures. We understand that other candidate architectures should possess three basic characteristics in order to use DMS efficiently:

- Directly-connected clusters should communicate through a mechanism able to ensure fixed timing constraints, known at compile time.

- The number of possible paths to create a chain should be small, in order to avoid searching through an excessive number of options.

- Some sort of DDG transformation should be made in order to limit the number of immediate data dependent successors of an operation.

The CQRF used in the architecture model presented in section 2 allows a value to be read only once from any of its FIFO queues. Thus, prior to modulo scheduling, all multiple-use lifetimes are transformed into single-use lifetimes using *copy* operations, as reported in [7]. This transformation has also the effect of limiting the number of immediate successors of any operation to 2, which simplifies the code partitioning among clusters with limited connectivity. Multiple-use lifetimes would concentrate the number of move operations around the original producer, possibly requiring more scheduling slots than available within the sough II.

4. Experimental Results

We have used an experimental framework to perform modulo scheduling and register allocation of loops for several architecture configurations, some of them presented in this section. Two architecture models have been considered: unclustered and clustered, which were scheduled using IMS and DMS, respectively. The machine configurations range from 1 to 10 clusters, each of them having 3 functional units: 1 L/S, 1 ADD, and 1 MUL. In addition, each cluster has also a Copy FU to perform copy and move operations. However, these functional units and operations are not considered to estimate performance figures, as they do not perform any useful computation, All eligible innermost loops from the Perfect Club Benchmark have been used, a total of 1258 loops suitable for software pipelining. The original body of many of those loops do not present enough parallelism to saturate the FUs of wide-issue machines. Hence, *loop unrolling* was performed to provide additional operations to the scheduler whenever necessary [9].

As already discussed, a good scheduling/partitioning algorithm should minimize an eventual increase of the II in relation to the value otherwise achieved for the corresponding unclustered machine. The data in figure 4 shows the fraction of loops presenting any increase in the II due to DMS partitioning. Overheads for machines with 2 and 3

clusters are only due to the introduction of copy operations in the DDG, as no communication conflicts occurs in these cases. Over 80% of the loops do not present any overhead for machine models up to 8 clusters (24 FUs). When the II increases it is mainly because the Copy FUs became the most heavily used resources, due to an excessive number of move operations. That could be improved with additional hardware support.

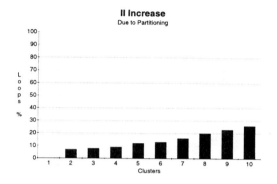

Figure 4. Overhead on II due to partitioning

Performance analyses regarding the execution of two sets of loops were done. Set 1 comprises *all* loops of the benchmark, while set 2 contains only loops without recurrences [14]. The second set was considered because those loops are highly vectorizable, having characteristics similar to the ones usually found in DSP applications [3]. Hence, they can take more advantage of additional machine resources.

The data in figure 5 shows the total number of cycles (in relative values) required to execute the modulo scheduled loops in each machine configuration. The difference between clustered and unclustered machines shows that the partitioning process results only in small performance degradation for up to 21 FUs when the set 1 is used. However, the difference is more accentuated when wider-issue machines are used. On the other hand, very small differences are observed if only loops without recurrences are considered. Furthermore, the results suggest that DMS may be effective with these loops for even wider-issue machines.

The data in figure 6 shows the number of instructions issued per cycle (IPC). It was measured taking into account the iteration counter, including operations from the kernel code, prologue, and epilogue phases. If all loops are considered, the IPC value improves for machines up to 21 FUs (7 clusters), however it levels beyond that point. Loops without recurrences allow improvements for the whole range of machine models, which confirms that they are better suited to exploit ILP in this kind of architecture.

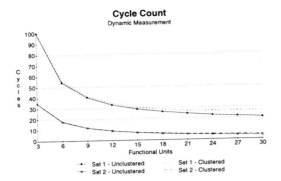

Figure 5. Execution time

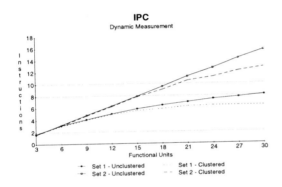

Figure 6. IPC-Instruction per cycle

5. Conclusions

The proposed DMS algorithm is effective for machine configurations up to 8 clusters, resulting in low overhead due to partitioning. A larger overhead was observed for wider-issue machine, although that could be minimized by using additional FUs to schedule move operations. In most of the cases, the use of a few move operations is enough to avoid dead-end states due to communication conflicts. DMS can produce efficient software pipelined code for clustered VLIW machines comprising a number of clusters not previously considered in other works, to the best of our knowledge. Hence, it can significantly extend the potential for ILP exploitation in this kind of architecture, which may be particularly suitable for DSP and numeric applications.

References

[1] A. Capitanio, N. Dutt, and A. Nicolau. Partitioned register files for VLIWs: A preliminary analysis of trade-offs. In *Proceedings of the MICRO-25 - The 25th Annual International Symposium on Microarchitecture*, 1992.

[2] A. Charlesworth. An approach to scientific array processing: The architectural design of the AP120B/FPS-164 family. *Computer*, 14(9), 1981.

[3] P. Faraboschi, G. Desoli, and J. Fisher. The latest word in digital and media processing. *IEEE Signal Processing Magazine*, March 1998.

[4] K. Farkas, N. Jouppi, and P. Chow. Register file design considerations in dynamically scheduled processors. Technical Report 95/10, Digital Western Research Laboratory, 1995.

[5] M. Fernandes, J. Llosa, and N. Topham. Allocating lifetimes to queues in software pipelined architectures. In *EURO-PAR'97, Third International Euro-Par Conference*, Passau, Germany, 1997.

[6] M. Fernandes, J. Llosa, and N. Topham. Extending a VLIW architecture model. Technical Report ECS-CSG-34-97, University of Edinburgh, Department of Computer Science, 1997.

[7] M. Fernandes, J. Llosa, and N. Topham. Partitioned schedules for clustered VLIW architectures. In *IPPS'98, 12th International Parallel Processing Symposium*, Orlando, USA, 1998.

[8] J. Fisher. Very long instruction word architectures and the ELI-512. In *Proceedings of the 10th Annual International Symposium on Computer Architecture*, 1983.

[9] D. Lavery and W. Hwu. Unrolling-based optimizations for modulo scheduling. In *Proceedings of the MICRO-28 - The 28th Annual International Symposium on Microarchitecture*, 1995.

[10] J. Llosa, M. Valero, and Ayguadé. Quantitative evaluation of register pressure on software pipelined loops. *International Journal of Parallel Programming*, 26(2):121–142, 1998.

[11] P. Lowney, S. Freudenberger, T. Karzes, W. Lichtenstein, and R. Nix. The multiflow trace scheduling compiler. *The Journal of Supercomputing*, July 1993.

[12] E. Nystrom and A. Eichenberger. Effective cluster assignment for modulo scheduling. In *Proceedings of the MICRO-31 - The 31th Annual International Symposium on Microarchitecture*, 1998.

[13] E. Ozer, S. Banerjia, and T. Conte. Unified assign and schedule: A new approach to scheduling for clustered register file microarchitectures. In *Proceedings of the MICRO-31 - The 31th Annual International Symposium on Microarchitecture*, 1998.

[14] B. Rau. Iterative modulo scheduling. *The International Journal of Parallel Programming*, February 1996.

[15] B. Rau and C. Glaeser. Some scheduling techniques and an easily schedulable horizontal architecture for high performance scientific computing. In *14th Annual Workshop on Microprogramming*, 1981.

[16] R. Rau and J. Fisher. Instruction-level parallel processing: History, overview and perspective. *The Journal of Supercomputing*, July 1993.

Hardware for Speculative Parallelization
of Partially-Parallel Loops in DSM Multiprocessors[1]

Ye Zhang[†], Lawrence Rauchwerger[‡] and Josep Torrellas[†]

[†]University of Illinois at Urbana-Champaign, http://iacoma.cs.uiuc.edu
[‡]Texas A&M University, http://www.cs.tamu.edu/faculty/rwerger/

1 Introduction

Compiler-driven parallelization of codes has advanced significantly in this decade. Unfortunately, there is still a large body of potential fully- or partially-parallel codes that compilers cannot parallelize because they can not fully analyze the codes' dependence structure. The dependence structure may be too complicated to analyze for current compiler technology or simply not available at compile time. In any case, the code is forced to run sequentially.

Consider, as an example, the loop shown in Figure 1, where arrays f and g depend on the input data. The compiler cannot let the execution of the iterations proceed in parallel because there may be a cross-iteration dependence: two different iterations may access the same array element and one access may be a write. Consequently, the code executes serially.

```
do i = 1,n
   A((f(i)) = ...
   ... = A(g(i))          A: Array under test
enddo
```

Figure 1: Loop that cannot be compiler analyzed.

Unfortunately, these types of codes are common in many application domains, including sparse matrix computations, domain decomposition, molecular dynamics, molecular biology and image processing. Furthermore, many times, these codes have loops that have huge iteration counts and are fully parallel or have only a few cross-iteration dependences. If these codes could be run fully or partially in parallel in an effective manner on Distributed Shared-Memory (DSM) multiprocessors, some important codes would benefit significantly.

To run these codes in a fully- or partially-parallel manner, software approaches based on a *inspector-executor* pair have been proposed ([6] for example). An inspector loop analyzes the data access patterns at run time and yields a partitioning of the iteration space into subsets called wavefronts. Each wavefront is then executed in parallel by the *executor*, with synchronization separating the wavefronts. In general, however, the inspector may be computationally expensive and have side-effects.

Recently, we have introduced a new framework for speculative parallelization in hardware [8]. The scheme is based on a software-based run-time parallelization scheme that we proposed earlier [4]. The idea is to execute the code (loops) speculatively in parallel. As parallel execution proceeds, extra hardware added to the directory-based cache coherence of the DSM machine detects if there is a dependence violation. If such a violation occurs, execution is interrupted, the state is rolled back in software to the most recent safe state, and the code is re-executed serially from that point. The safe state is typically established at the beginning of the loop.

Such a scheme is somewhat related to speculative parallelization inside a multiprocessor chip [1, 2, 3, 5], which also relies on extending the cache coherence protocol to detect dependence violations. Our scheme, however, is targeted to

large-scale DSM parallelism. In addition, it does not have some of the limitations of the proposed chip-multiprocessor schemes. Such limitations include the need to bound the size of the speculative state to fit in a buffer or L1 cache, and a strict in-order task commit policy that may result in load-imbalance among processors [1, 2, 3, 5]. Unfortunately, our scheme has higher recovery costs if a dependence violation is detected, because execution has to backtrack to a safe state that is usually the beginning of the loop.

Although this issue is not a problem in fully-parallel codes, it is an important concern in loops with cross-iteration dependences. Consequently, the contribution of this paper is to extend our previous hardware scheme to effectively handle codes (loops) with a modest number of cross-iteration dependences. With the proposed extensions, when a dependence violation is encountered, the state is quickly repaired on the fly and parallel execution is resumed from that point on. Simulation results suggest that this form of DSM speculative parallelization is promising: a 16-processor parallel execution of 4 important loops runs 4.2 and 31 times faster than two different serial executions of the loops.

In the following, we briefly describe the speculative parallelization scheme that was introduced in [8], then present the new extensions for loops with dependences, and finally evaluate these new extensions.

2 DSM Hardware for Speculative Parallelization

In previous work, we proposed a scheme to speculatively execute non-analyzable loops in parallel in a DSM machine [8]. The idea is to extend the directory-based cache-coherence protocol of the machine to detect, in hardware, any violation of a cross-iteration dependence. The loop is executed in parallel. If the hardware detects such a violation, then the state is rolled back to a safe state and the execution is retried on a single processor. Otherwise, parallel execution completes successfully. For fully-parallel loops, the scheme is shown to deliver speedups between 4 and 11 for 16 processors [8].

The scheme can be fleshed out into different hardware algorithms with different cost and performance. We envision the DSM machine to support a few such algorithms mapped to the same hardware, and the compiler to select the algorithm on an array-by-array basis [8].

First, there are the privatization and the non-privatization algorithms. The latter should be used when the compiler can prove that the array under test is not privatizable. This is because privatization, while requiring extra storage, uncovers more parallelism because it eliminates output- and anti-dependences [8]. Among the privatization algorithms, we focus here on the most general one, namely the Advanced Privatization Algorithm (APA) presented in [8]. Among the non-privatization ones, we focus here on the equivalent to APA, namely the Advanced Non-Privatization Algorithm (ANPA). The ANPA is more general than the non-privatization algorithm of [8]. It was not presented there for lack of space. In the rest of this section, we summarize the ANPA and APA. See [7, 8] for details. We assume the general case of a dynamically-scheduled loop. The non-analyzable variables that may cause a dependence violation we call *arrays under test*.

[1]This work was supported in part by NSF under grants Young Investigator Award MIP-9457436, ASC-9612099, MIP-9619351 and CAREER Award CCR-9734471, DARPA Contract DABT63-95-C-0097, NASA Contract NAG-1-613, NCSA grant ASC980006N and gifts from Intel and IBM.

135

2.1 Advanced Non-Privatization Algorithm (ANPA)

In this algorithm, the arrays under test are backed up in software before the loop starts. In case of a dependence violation during loop execution, the recovery to a safe state will consist of restoring the arrays to their original values in software.

The intuition behind ANPA is to keep two shared pieces of information for each element of the array (or arrays) under test: the highest iteration that has read the element so far ($MaxR$) and the highest iteration that has written the element so far ($MaxW$). When a processor executing iteration $Curr$ reads or writes the element, the hardware performs the algorithms of Figure 2-(a) or 2-(b) respectively. These algorithms check if the element has been accessed by out-of-order iterations, causing a write-after read (WAR), read-after-write (RAW) or write-after-write (WAW) violation. If so, a FAIL cross-processor interrupt is broadcasted.

```
if (Curr < MaxW)                if (Curr<MaxR
    FAIL /* WAR */                  || Curr<MaxW)
else                                FAIL /* RAW or WAW */
    read data                   else
    MaxR = max(Curr, MaxR)          write data
    /* out-of-order rds OK */       MaxW = Curr
```

(a): Processor read.   (b): Processor write.

Figure 2: Compact form of the ANPA.

Ideally, out-of-order execution of iterations that write would be fine as long as we skipped the second update to the data and $MaxW$. In practice, however, all writes must be performed and recorded in order if, as shown in Section 3, we want to repair dependence violations on the fly.

The actual implementation of the ANPA is as follows. The $MaxR$ and $MaxW$ arrays are kept in the directory controller of the home node (or nodes) of the corresponding array under test. If the array under test is distributed, so are the $MaxR$ and $MaxW$ arrays. $MaxR$ and $MaxW$ are operated upon by the directory controller only. When a processor accesses an element of the array under test, the directory controller is prompted to operate on the corresponding $MaxR$ or $MaxW$ entry.

Since elements of the array under test can be cached, the scheme described potentially involves much extra traffic between processor caches and directories. To reduce this traffic, we add some state in the tags of each cache in the machine. Note that the directory only needs to be informed of the first read and the first write to each element in the iteration. Consequently, we add a $Read$ and a $Write$ bit per cache line word. These bits are set by the hardware the first time in the iteration that the corresponding element is read or written respectively. Cache read hits to words with the $Read$ bit set do not generate directory accesses. The same occurs for writes. The $Read$ and $Write$ bits of all the lines in the cache are cleared in hardware at the beginning of every iteration. The bits for a cache line are lost if the line is displaced from the cache. These algorithms, plus further possible optimizations, are described in detail in [7].

2.2 Advanced Privatization Algorithm (APA)

In this algorithm, each processor makes a private copy of the array under test and operates on it. In case of dependence violation during loop execution, the recovery to a safe state simply consists of discarding the private arrays.

To understand the APA, we define $read$-$first$ iterations. Given an array element, if an iteration reads it before the same iteration may write it, we call the iteration a $read$-$first$ iteration for the element. A loop with a privatized array under test is fully parallel if each of the elements of the array satisfies one of the following conditions: (i) it is read-only,

(ii) every read to it is preceded by a write to it in the same iteration or (iii) no $read$-$first$ iteration for the element is preceded by an iteration that writes the element. An iteration that writes the element is called a $writing$ iteration. Figure 3 shows examples of fully-parallel loops.

It 1	It 2	It 3		It 1	It 2	It 3		It 1	It 2		It 1	It 2		It 1	It 2
Rd	Rd	Rd		Wr	Wr	Wr		Rd	Wr		Rd	Rd		Rd	Wr
Rd	Rd	Rd		Rd	Rd	Rd			Rd			Wr		Wr	Rd
												Rd			

Figure 3: Examples of loops that are fully parallel if the element that is read and written is privatized.

The combination of a $writing$ iteration and a $read$-$first$ iteration that, in the sequential loop execution, consumes the data generated by the $writing$ iteration, we call a $pair$ (Figure 5-(a)). From the above definitions, the existence of a $pair$ is a necessary condition for a loop not to be fully parallel. Consequently, APA simply tries to detect the second iteration of a $pair$, and trigger a failure when it finds it. Note that the two iterations of a $pair$ may actually be executed in-order or out-of-order.

Our algorithm implementation involves adding state to the directories of both the shared copy of the array and its privatized copies. The directory of the shared array maintains two timestamps for each array element. One keeps the number of the highest $read$-$first$ iteration for the element executed so far by any processor ($MaxR1st$). The other keeps the number of the lowest $writing$ iteration for the element executed so far by any processor ($MinW$). The parallelization fails when $MaxR1st$ is larger than $MinW$.

During execution, processors operate on private data. Consequently, to identify $read$-$first$ iterations, the directories of the private copies of the array keep, for each element, two timestamps: the highest $read$-$first$ iteration for the element executed so far by the processor ($PMaxR1st$, where P stands for private), and the $highest$ $writing$ iteration for the element executed so far by the processor ($PMaxW$).

Finally, to reduce overhead, the tags of the caches keep a summary of the private directory state. For each word, they keep 2 bits to indicate whether the current iteration is $read$-$first$ for the element ($Read1st$) and/or $writing$ ($Write$). $Read1st$ and $Write$ are cleared at the beginning of each iteration. When an iteration reads an element of the array under test, if both $Read1st$ and $Write$ are zero, $Read1st$ gets set.

The algorithm proceeds as follows. When a processor reads an element of the array under test, it checks whether this is a $read$-$first$ iteration for the element. For the check, it can use the state of the cache tags (both $Read1st$ and $Write$ are zero) or, if the line is not in the cache, the state of the directory for the private array ($PMaxR1st$ and $PMaxW$ are both lower than the current iteration number). If the iteration is $read$-$first$, the directory for the shared array is notified. In the directory, the current iteration number is compared to $MinW$. If the former is larger, the parallelization fails; otherwise, $MaxR1st$ is updated.

When a processor writes to an element of the array under test, it checks whether this is the first write to the element in this iteration. For the check, it can use the state of the cache tags ($Write$ is zero) or, if the line is not in the cache, the state of the directory for the private array ($PMaxW$ is less than the current iteration number). If this is the first write, $PMaxW$ is updated to the current iteration number. $PMaxW$ needs to be kept up-to-date because, in conjunction with $PMaxR1st$, identifies $read$-$first$ iterations. In addition, if this is the very first write of this processor to this element ($PMaxW$ was still zero), the directory for the shared array is notified. In the directory, the current iteration number is compared to $MaxR1st$. If the former is lower, the parallelization fails; otherwise, $MinW$ is updated. More details can be found in [8].

3 Parallelizing Loops with Dependences

The algorithms presented thus far target loops that are fully parallel in most of the invocations. Now, we extend the algorithms to handle loops that often have cross-iteration dependences. With the new extensions, when a dependence violation is detected, the state of the loop is quickly repaired on the fly and *parallel execution* is resumed from that point on. In the following, we first extend ANPA and then APA.

3.1 Extending ANPA: Sliding Commit

The new ANPA does not need to back up the array under test at the beginning of the loop. Instead, it saves a trace of writes on the fly into an undo log as the execution of the loop proceeds. If a dependence violation is detected, the undo log is used to repair the state. The space of the undo log is continuously recycled as iterations commit. At any point in time, only a window of iterations use the undo log space and, therefore, are uncommitted. This window slides as execution proceeds. This concept we call the *Sliding Commit Algorithm* (SCA). In the following, we describe how the undo log is created, the iterations committed, and the dependence violations handled.

3.1.1 Creating an Undo Log on the Fly

Since the unit of work is one iteration, the log needs to record, for each iteration, the initial value of all the array-under-test elements that are updated in the iteration. Consequently, we generate a log entry at every first update to an element in an iteration. The information that we need to store is the iteration number, the physical address of the array-under-test element and the value of the element before it was written.

Because logging occurs frequently, log record generation and maintenance must be supported in hardware. In our implementation, the cache coherence protocol identifies the first update to each array-under-test element in each iteration. This is done using the *Write* bit in the cache tags described in Section 2.1, which is set when its corresponding element is written for the first time in the iteration. At that time, we extend the protocol with a log message to the home directory of that element. The message contains the iteration number, physical address of the element and, if the cache had the element, the old value of the element. In a cache miss, the directory obtains the old value of the data from other caches or memory.

All this information is handled in hardware by the directory controller using the data structures of Figure 4: the Pointer Cache, the Free Sector Stack and the Undo Buffer. The latter is allocated in memory and divided into logical chunks called Sectors. For every iteration that requests space in this node, we assign an entry in the Pointer Cache to keep the iteration number, and a sector in the Undo Buffer to store all the data and address log records.

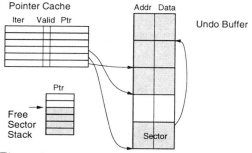

Figure 4: Directory data structures for undo logs.

The Pointer Cache is fully associative. The number of entries is a small multiple of the number of processors. This is

the maximum number of iterations that can be uncommitted at any point in time. If the number of uncommitted iterations reaches the maximum value, the scheduler that provides iterations to processors stops supplying iterations until some iterations commit.

The fixed size of the Undo Buffer sectors is set before execution. It can be easily set based on a compiler estimation of the maximum number of distinct write references per iteration. However, an iteration may write to elements from different home nodes and, therefore, allocate space in several nodes. Consequently, to save space, we aggressively reduce the size of the sectors to a fraction of our initial estimate. This may result in sector overflow, which we handle by linking sectors as shown in Figure 4. The Free Sector Stack is used to identify free sectors. Overall, sector allocation, log storage, and sector overflow handling are all done in hardware for performance reasons. Undo Buffer overflow, however, is handled in software by the node's processor to reduce hardware costs. It is described in [7].

3.1.2 Committing Iterations on the Fly

When an iteration finishes, it cannot be committed until all the lower-numbered iterations are also finished and committed. To keep track of the state of each iteration, processors share three data structures. One of them is *ItSt* (for iteration state), an array which, in a simple approach, has as many elements as iterations, and holds the state of each iteration. An iteration can be *unfinished* or *finished* (FIN). To avoid initializing *ItSt*, we toggle the code associated with *finished* between consecutive loops. The other data structures are a scalar with the last committed iteration (*LstCmtIt*), and a lock *L* that protects them all.

When a processor finishes an iteration, it tries to commit it by updating *ItSt* and *LstCmtIt*. While it could use a simple and intuitive algorithm to do it, we propose a more advanced and efficient one. In both algorithms, when a processor finishes an iteration, it sets the corresponding *ItSt* element to *finished*. In the simple algorithm, it then checks if this is the iteration that follows *LstCmtIt*. If so, the processor checks consecutively increasing iterations, committing them until it finds the first *unfinished* one. Committing iterations is done by updating *LstCmtIt*. All accesses are protected by the lock.

Simple Algorithm:	Advanced Algorithm:
ItSt(this) = FIN	ItSt(this) = FIN
lock(L)	this = LstCmtIt + 1
if(LstCmtIt == this-1)	while(ItSt(this) == FIN)
while(ItSt(this) == FIN)	this++
this++	if(- -this > LstCmtIt)
LstCmtIt = - -this	if(*test&set*(L) == 0)
unlock(L)	if(this > LstCmtIt)
	LstCmtIt = this
	reset(L)

In the advanced algorithm, instead, the processor always checks consecutively increasing iterations starting from the *LstCmtIt* one. This is done without lock protection. In addition, when it later tries to commit iterations, if it fails to grab the lock in the first try, it skips the commit (see the advanced algorithm). Therefore, the lock contention is low. This low lock contention more than compensates for the higher traffic caused and the fact that the commit may be delayed a bit.

After a processor advances *LstCmtIt*, it passes the new value to all directory controllers. The latter, in hardware, deallocate the Pointer Cache entries and Undo Buffer sectors of the committed iterations. The space can now be reused. In our experiments, we optimize this operation to reduce the number of messages sent to directory controllers and to handle the possible deallocation of overflowed Undo Buffers in software. The details are presented in [7].

3.1.3 Dependence Violation and Restart

If a directory controller detects a dependence violation, it sends a cross-processor interrupt to all processors, passing, as argument, the ID of the smaller iteration involved in the violation. Then, the processors executing iterations with IDs higher than the argument, squash the iterations; the others finish off and commit their iterations. Then, all processors synchronize. The system is ready for data restoration.

Data restoration is performed in software by several processors concurrently. If the array under test is allocated in pages from different nodes, then the undo log is also distributed across multiple nodes. Therefore, each processor can restore the data from the Undo Buffer in its own node. There is no overlap between the locations stored in Undo Buffers in different nodes. However, the restoration of the data from a given Undo Buffer is necessarily done in decreasing order of iteration number. This is required to ensure that the newer updates are overwritten by the older updates. The restoration stops when we reach the sector of an iteration whose ID is lower than the argument of the cross-processor interrupt. At this point, the whole Pointer Cache and Undo Buffer can be recycled.

For the data restoration to work well, two issues must be addressed. Recall that the undo log contains physical, not virtual, addresses. Consequently, for lowest overheads, the restoration must be performed by processes that can write directly to physical addresses. This ordinarily implies some type of supervisory mode. In addition, the mapping of the pages that hold the array under test must not change from the time that the undo log is generated until the time that it is read. Otherwise, the restoration would be updating wrong locations. One way to solve this problem is to pin the array-under-test pages in memory during the execution of the loop.

Finally, once the restoration is completed, all processors synchronize. The iteration scheduler is modified to give out the two dependent iterations to one processor at the same time. Such a small change will prevent the same dependence violation from occurring again. Then, parallel execution restarts, starting with the iteration that follows *LstCmtIt*.

3.2 Extending APA

As indicated in Section 2.2, the APA fails when a directory controller detects the second iteration of a *pair* of iterations. That second iteration can either be the *read-first* or the *writing* one. In any case, the repair action will simply be to supply the correct value to the *read-first* iteration, namely the value generated by the *writing* iteration. The actual recover operations performed vary slightly depending on whether the second iteration executed is the *writing* or the *read-first* one. We consider each case in turn. In no case, however, does the extended APA need an undo log like the ANPA to enable the recovery. This is because, except for the *pair* of iterations, no transfer of information from iteration to iteration ever occurs. Consequently, iterations can be freely re-executed without first having to undo past updates.

3.2.1 The Writing Iteration is Executed Last

A directory controller detects the *writing* iteration of a *pair* when an array-under-test element receives a write with an iteration ID lower than element's *MaxR1st*. At that point, the controller sends a cross-processor interrupt to all processors passing, as argument, the iteration ID of the write. The processors executing iterations with higher IDs squash the iterations; the others finish off their iterations. All processors then synchronize. The system is now ready for repair.

The repair starts by flushing private copies of the array element from all the caches. Flushing means line write back and cache line invalidate. Then, the update that caused the ex-

ception is propagated to the copy of the element in the shared array and, from there, to all the copies of the element in private arrays. In reality, we would only need to update the copy in the private array that will be used by the *read-first* iteration. However, we may avoid future dependence violations if we update all private copies. In addition, we also clear the *MaxR1st* and *MinW* fields of the element in the shared array and the *PMaxR1st* and *PMaxW* fields of the element in all private arrays. In effect, we are re-initializing that array element.

Ideally, the only remaining thing to do is to re-execute the corresponding *read-first* iteration of all the *pairs* that the *writing* iteration belongs to. Unfortunately, it may be impossible to identify all such *read-first* iterations. The reason is that each processor keeps in *PMaxR1st* only the *highest* ID of any *read-first* iteration for that element that the processor has executed. Lower IDs have been lost.

Consider, for example, Figure 5-(b), where processor *P1* executes *writing* iteration 2 after *PMaxR1st* for *P1*, *P2* and *P3* have already been set to 0, 6 and 5 respectively. We know that iterations 2-5 and 2-6 form *pairs*. However, we do not know whether any processor executed a *read-first* iteration in 3 or 4, creating *pairs* 2-3 or 2-4. Consequently, our solution is to be conservative and restart the *parallel execution* from the iteration that follows the *writing* one.

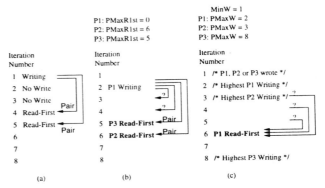

Figure 5: Examples of pairs (Chart (a)). In reality, the system keeps only limited information that we can use to identify the pairs (Charts (b) and (c)).

3.2.2 The Read-First Iteration is Executed Last

A directory controller detects the *read-first* iteration of a *pair* when an array-under-test element receives a read with an iteration ID higher than element's *MinW*. At that point, the controller sends a cross-processor interrupt to all processors, passing as argument the iteration ID of the read. As usual, the processors executing iterations with higher IDs squash their iterations while the others finish off their iterations. All processors then synchronize.

Ideally, the repair would involve what we described in Section 3.2.1: cache flushing and global state update for the array element that was written in the *writing* iteration. Then, we would re-execute the *read-first* iteration. Unfortunately, we may not know what the correct *writing* iteration is. The reason is that each processor keeps in *PMaxW* only the *highest* iteration ID of any *writing* iteration for that element that the processor has executed. Lower IDs have been lost.

Consider, for example, Figure 5-(c), where processor *P1* executes *read-first* iteration 6. *MinW* is 1, and *PMaxW* for *P1*, *P2* and *P3* is 2, 3 and 8 respectively. We do not know whether the *pair* is 3-6, 4-6 or 5-6 because we do not know whether *P3* wrote in iterations 4 or 5. We only keep the highest *writing* iteration for each processor.

Application	Loop Name	Time (% of Tseq)	Number of Invocations	Iterations/ Invocation	Array Size (Kbytes)	Algorithm
Track	*nlfilt_do300*	40.9	56	480	72.4	Extended ANPA
Euler	*dflux_do[100,200], psmoo_do20 eflux_do[100,200,300]*	89.9	120	59,863	703.1	Extended ANPA
Dsmc3d	*move3_goto100*	32.8	80	383,107	158.4	Extended ANPA
Adm	*run_do[20,30,40,50,60,100]*	20.6	900	32 or 64	803.1	Extended ANPA and APA

Table 1: Loop characteristics.

Consequently, the *writing* iteration is identified based on the following rule. We compute the highest *PMaxW* for the element across all processors. Let us call this value *mxw*. We have two cases: *mxw* is smaller than the *read-first* iteration or not. In the first case, the *writing* iteration is *mxw*. In this case, as described in Section 3.2.1, we perform the cache flushing and the global state update for the array element that must be communicated from *mxw* to the *read-first* iteration. Then, all processors synchronize and parallel execution resumes starting from the *read-first* iteration.

In the second case, the potential *writing* iterations are: the highest *PMaxW* that is smaller than the *read-first* iteration, and all the iterations that follow it until the *read-first* iteration. We call these iterations that follow it, the *hidden* ones. In Figure 5-(c), the *hidden* iterations are 4 and 5. In this case, the *hidden* iterations are re-executed *in parallel*. After that, based on the *PMaxW* values, we can determine which iteration was the true *writing* one, and can perform the cache flushing and correct global state update of the array element as in Section 3.2.1. Then, all processors synchronize and parallel execution resumes starting from the *read-first* iteration.

4 Experimental Results

We have evaluated the proposed hardware through simulations. Due to space constraints, we only present a summary of the results here. Full details are in [7]. We use MINT to perform execution-driven simulations of a 16-node CC-NUMA shared-memory multiprocessor. Each node has a 200-MHz 4-issue dynamic superscalar with 4 integer, 2 load-store and 2 floating-point functional units and a 32-entry instruction queue. Each node has a 32-Kbyte L1 cache and a 512-Kbyte L2 cache. Both caches are direct-mapped and have 64-byte lines. The cache sizes are selected so small to match the scaled-down working sets of the applications we run. The caches are kept coherent with a DASH-like cache coherence protocol. Each node has part of the global memory and directory. Contention is modeled in the whole system except in the global network, which is abstracted away as a constant latency. The unloaded round-trip latencies to access the L1 cache, L2 cache, local memory, 2-hop remote memory and 3-hop remote memory are 1, 12, 60, 208 and 291 cycles on average respectively. Finally, shared pages are allocated round-robin across the different memories, while private pages are allocated locally.

For the simulations, we have extracted and measured important loops from well-known codes. Table 1 lists the loops with their weight relative to the total *sequential execution time* of their respective complete application on an SGI PowerChallenge (% of Tseq). The table also shows the number of times that the loops are invoked, their average number of iterations per invocation, the size of the arrays under test and the algorithm used. *Track* and *Adm* are Perfect Club codes, while *Euler* and *Dsmc3d* are HPF-2 applications. They all have been pre-processed with the Polaris parallelizing compiler. All these loops have cross-iteration dependences except *Adm*, which turns out to be fully parallel. *Adm* uses the extensions to both the ANPA and APA.

Figure 6 compares the execution time of the loops under various algorithms. *Serial1* and *Serial16* correspond to the plain serial execution of the loops with the application data allocated in 1 node or in 16 nodes respectively. Since these loops

are part of applications to be executed on a parallel machine, *Serial16* is arguably more realistic. *ANPA* corresponds to the base ANPA. Since *Adm* uses both ANPA and APA, we label it *A(N)PA*. Finally, *Extended* corresponds to the extended ANPA and APA. Time is divided into instruction execution (*Useful*), stall due to pipeline hazards and synchronization (*Haz+Sync*) and stall due to memory latency (*Mem*). The bars that are higher than 200 are broken and labeled with the correct height. All bars are normalized to *Serial1*. From the figure, we see that the extended ANPA/APA perform better than the base ANPA/APA and much better than the serial execution. Overall, the extended algorithms deliver average speedups of 4.2 over *Serial1* and 31 over *Serial16*. More in-depth analysis can be found in [7].

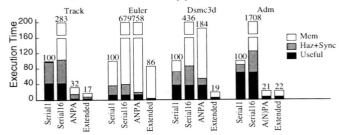

Figure 6: Execution time under various algorithms.

5 Summary

Hardware-based speculative parallelization of non-analyzable codes on DSM multiprocessors is challenging. In this paper, we have extended past work by proposing a scheme to parallelize codes (loops) that have a modest number of cross-iteration dependences. Simulation results suggest that the scheme is promising: a 16-processor parallel execution of 4 important loops runs 4.2 and 31 times faster than two different serial executions of the loops.

References

[1] S. Gopal, T. N. Vijaykumar, J. E. Smith, and G. S. Sohi. Speculative Versioning Cache. In *HPCA-4*, February 1998.

[2] L. Hammond, M. Willey, and K. Olukotun. Data Speculation Support for a Chip Multiprocessor. In *ASPLOS-VIII*, pages 58–69, October 1998.

[3] V. Krishnan and J. Torrellas. Hardware and Software Support for Speculative Execution of Sequential Binaries on a Chip-Multiprocessor. In *ICS-1998*, July 1998.

[4] L. Rauchwerger and D. Padua. The LRPD Test: Speculative Run-Time Parallelization of Loops with Privatization and Reduction Parallelization. In *PLDI-1995*, June 1995.

[5] J. Steffan and T. Mowry. The Potential for Using Thread-Level Data Speculation to Facilitate Automatic Parallelization. In *HPCA-4*, February 1998.

[6] J. Wu, J. Saltz, S. Hiranandani, and H. Berryman. Run-time Compilation Methods for Multicomputers. In *ICPP-1991*, pages 26–30, August 1991. Vol. II - Software.

[7] Y. Zhang. DSM Hardware for Speculative Parallelization. Ph.D. Thesis, University of Illinois, January 1999.

[8] Y. Zhang, L. Rauchwerger, and J. Torrellas. Hardware for Speculative Run-Time Parallelization in Distributed Shared-Memory Multiprocessors. In *HPCA-4*, February 1998.

Cache Coherence

Design and Performance of Directory Caches for Scalable Shared Memory Multiprocessors

Maged M. Michael   Ashwini K. Nanda

IBM Research
Thomas J. Watson Research Center
Yorktown Heights, NY 10598
{michael,ashwini}@watson.ibm.com

Abstract

Recent research shows that the occupancy of the coherence controllers is a major performance bottleneck for distributed cache coherent shared memory multiprocessors. A significant part of the occupancy is due to the latency of accessing the directory, which is usually kept in DRAM memory. Most coherence controller designs that use protocol processors for executing the coherence protocol handlers use the data cache of the protocol processor for caching directory entries along with protocol handler data. Analogously, a fast Directory Cache (DC) can also be used by the hardwired coherence controller designs in order to minimize directory access time. However, the existing hardwired controllers do not use a directory cache. Moreover, the performance impact of caching directory entries has not been studied in the literature before.

This paper studies the performance of directory caches using parallel applications from the SPLASH-2 suite. We demonstrate that using a directory cache can result in 40% or more improvement in the execution time of applications that are communication intensive. We also investigate in detail the various directory cache design parameters: cache size, cache line size, and associativity. Our experimental results show that the directory cache size requirements grow sub-linearly with the increase in the application's data set size. The results also show the performance advantage of multi-entry directory cache lines, as a result of spatial locality and the absence of sharing of directories. The impact of the associativity of the directory caches on performance is less than that of the size and the line size.

Also, we find a clear linear relation between the directory cache miss ratio and the coherence controller occupancy, and between both measures and the execution time of the applications, which can help system architects evaluate the impact of directory cache (or coherence controller) designs on overall system performance.

1 Introduction

Previous research has shown convincingly that scalable shared-memory performance can be achieved on directory-based cache-coherent multiprocessors such as the Stanford DASH [5] and MIT Alewife [1] machines. A key component of these machines is the coherence controller on each node that provides cache coherent access to memory that is distributed among the nodes of the multiprocessor. Each coherence controller is responsible for keeping track of the state and location of memory lines in a part of the global shared memory, typically the part residing in the same node as the coherence controller. The state information necessary for such a task is stored in the *directory*, which is usually implemented in DRAM memory either separately or along with the local node's main memory.

Designs for coherence controllers fall in two broad categories: designs which use programmable protocol processors to implement the coherence protocols and designs which hardwire the coherence protocol in custom hardware finite state machines. The former designs such as in the Stanford FLASH [3] and Wisconsin Typhoon [10] architectures, use the data cache of the protocol processor to cache directory entries in order to reduce directory access latency. The Sequent NUMA-Q [6] architecture uses a programmable engine, but includes only a small Tag Cache used only for transactions in progress.

The custom hardware designs of the Stanford DASH [5], MIT Alewife [1], Sun S3.mp [9], and SGI Origin [4] use DRAM directories and do not include DCs. The HAL S1 [11] architecture uses a sparse directory implemented in SRAM and therefore is in less need of directory caching. However, almost all of the other recent commercial distributed shared memory architectures use full directories, which are too large to be implemented in SRAM. It seems that these architecture would benefit from reducing the directory access time by using a directory cache (DC).

Recent research results [2, 7] show that the occupancy of the coherence controller can be the performance bottleneck for applications with high communication requirements. Motivated by these results and the fact that a major part of coherence controller occupancy is due to directory access latency, we study in this paper the performance impact of using DCs on distributed shared memory multiprocessors. The performance of caching directory entries has not been studied before in the literature.

In addition to determining the performance impact of DCs, we examine in detail the interaction between the main DC parameters: size, line size, and associativity, and system and application parameters that would influence their performance such as the data set size and the coherence unit size. We base our experimental evaluation of DC performance on realistic hardware parameters of system components. We simulate applications from the SPLASH-2 benchmark suite [12] to identify the common trends in DC performance.

We find that DCs have significant impact on the performance of applications with high communication requirements. We also find that DC size requirements grow sub-linearly with data set size. We show that DC line size is a major factor in DC performance, with multi-directory-entry DC lines benefitting from spatial locality. We

142

also show the effect of DC size and coherence unit size on the choice of the DC line size.

DC associativity plays a minor role in DC performance relative to DC size and DC line size, and the largest gain in performance with respect to DC associativity is from 1-way to 2-way associativity. Also, a 4-way set associative DC almost shadows the performance of a fully associative DC.

By relating DC miss ratio to coherence controller occupancy and execution time of the applications, we find a clear linear relation between these measures. This result emphasizes the importance of DCs, and also provides a helpful tool for systems designers in relating coherence controller performance, including the DC, to overall system performance.

The main contributions of this paper are: (1) it demonstrates the significant impact of DCs on the performance of distributed shared memory multiprocessors, (2) it identifies and characterizes the most important DC parameters and their synergy with each other and the impact of other system parameters on them, and (3) it determines an important relation between coherence controller occupancy and execution time.

The rest of this paper is organized as follows. Section 2 presents the multiprocessor system and details coherence controller and DC design alternatives and parameters. Section 3 describes our experimental methodology and presents the experimental results and their implications. Finally, Section 4 presents our conclusions and recommendations for DC designs in future architectures.

2   System Description

The CC-NUMA multiprocessor system model used in this paper is composed of 16 SMP nodes connected by a 16 byte-wide fast switch. Each SMP node includes four 400 MHz PowerPC processors with 32 KB L1 and 1 MB L2 4-way-associative LRU caches. We vary the cache line size in our experiments. The SMP bus is a 133 MHz 16 byte-wide fully-pipelined split-transaction bus. The memory is interleaved and the memory controller is a separate bus agent from the coherence controller. Figure 1 shows a block diagram of an SMP node.

In this paper we consider a custom hardware coherence controller (CC) design as shown in Figure 2. Duplicate directories are used to allow fast response to common requests on the pipelined SMP bus (one directory lookup per 2 bus cycles). The bus-side copy is abbreviated (2-bit state per cache line) and uses fast SRAM memory. Since the controller-side copy of the directory is full-bit-map, SRAM memory is too expensive, therefore a dedicated DRAM directory memory is used.

A directory cache (DC) is used for reducing the directory read latency. We use a DC on the CC chip, except for one set of experiments where we also consider an off-chip DC implementation using SRAM with an optimized data path. We vary the DC size, line size, and associativity. We use the directory entry as the unit of DC size and DC line size. A directory entry consists of a presence bit vector, a modified bit, and a pending bit. The first time a directory entry is accessed by the protocol engine, the DC line containing that entry is cached in the DC. Any changes made to the cached copy of the directory is written through only to the bus side two-bit copy of the directory. A DC line continues to be in the DC until it gets replaced by another DC line due to DC capacity or conflict misses. Note that, since there is only a single writer to a particular directory entry, there

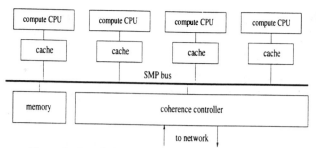

Figure 1: A node in a SMP-based CC-NUMA system.

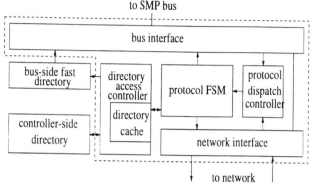

Figure 2: A custom-hardware-based coherence controller (CC) design with directory cache (DC).

are no sharing misses in the DC. The CC keeps using the locally cached copy until the line gets replaced. The controller side DRAM directory is updated only when a DC line gets replaced. For the 16 node system used in this paper, each directory entry will be 18 bits wide (presence vector + modified + pending). For example, a DC containing 4K directory entries requires 9KB (plus tag storage) of memory to store the DC lines.

The CC design includes a custom protocol dispatch controller for arbitration between the request queues from the local bus and the network. The CC runs at 133 MHz. Table 1 shows the no-contention latencies of key system and CC events.

3   Experimental Results

In this section, we present simulation results of the effect of various system and DC parameters on performance. First we demonstrate the impact of DCs on application performance. Then we investigate the main factors in DC design. We conclude this section with investigating the relation between DC performance and overall system performance. We start with the experimental methodology.

3.1   Experimental Methodology

We use execution-driven simulation (based on a version of the Augmint simulation toolkit [8] that runs on the PowerPC architecture) to evaluate DC performance. Our simulator includes detailed contention models for SMP buses, memory controllers, interleaved memory banks, protocol engines, directory DRAM, and external point contention for the interconnection network, in addition to accurate timing of the interaction between the coherence controller

Event	Latency
L1 hit	1
L2 hit (L1 miss)	13
L2 miss to address strobe on bus	6
Bus address strobe to bus response	21
Bus address strobe to start of cache-to-cache data response	27
Bus address strobe to next address strobe	6
Bus address strobe to start of data transfer from memory	30
Network point-to-point	54
CC issue request to bus	3
CC detect response from bus	3
CC issue network message	3
CC read special bus interface associative registers	6
CC write special bus interface registers	3
CC directory read (on-chip DC hit)	3
CC directory read (off-chip SRAM DC hit)	6
DRAM directory read	30
CC directory write	3
CC handler dispatch	3
CC condition	3
CC loop (per iteration)	3

Table 1: No-contention latencies in processor cycles (2.5 ns.).

Application	Type	Problem size
FFT	FFT computation	256K complex doubles
Ocean	Study of ocean movements	258×258 ocean grid
Radix	Radix sort	1M integer keys, radix 1K
Water-Nsquared	$O(n^2)$ study of forces and potentials in water molecules	512 molecules
Water-Spatial	Study of forces and potentials of water molecules in a 3-D grid	512 molecules

Table 2: Benchmark types and data sets.

and the SMP bus, memory, directory, and network interface.

We use five benchmarks from the SPLASH-2 suite [12], to evaluate the performance of directory caches. Unless otherwise mentioned, the data set sizes for the applications are as in Table 2. These applications have high communication requirements except for Water-Spatial which is included as an example of applications with low communication requirements. All the benchmarks are written in C and compiled using the IBM XLC C compiler with optimization level -O2. All experimental results reported in this paper are for the parallel phase only of these applications. We use a round-robin page placement policy. We ran all the applications with data sizes and systems sizes for which they achieve acceptable speedups.

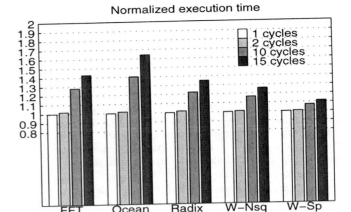

Normalized execution time

Figure 3: Effect of DC on execution time.

3.2 Performance Results

First, we determine the impact of DCs on overall system performance, then we investigate the design of each of the main DC parameters: size, line size, and associativity, and their synergy with each other and with other communication-related parameters such as the coherence unit size (L2 cache line size) and the data set size.

3.2.1 Impact of Directory Caches

Figure 3 shows the execution times for four different designs: (1) perfect (100% hit) on-chip DC with 1 cycle (7.5 ns.) access time, (2) perfect off-chip SRAM DC with 2 cycle access time, (3) DRAM directory without DC with 10 cycle (75 ns.) access time, and (4) a slower DRAM directory without DC with 15 cycle access time. The execution times are normalized to that of the first design. The L2 cache line size is 128 bytes.

We notice a significant increase (up to more than 40%) in execution time for the case with 10 cycle DRAM directory without DC over a perfect on-chip DC, indicating the possible significant performance gains of using DCs. We also notice more significant increase (up to more than 63%) in the relative execution time for the case with 15 cycle DRAM directory without DC, emphasizing the importance of using DCs in future systems as the gap between DRAM speed and processor, bus, and network speeds increases.

We also observe a minor increase in execution time for the 2 cycles SRAM DC relative to the on-chip DC (less than 2%), indicating the minor performance loss of using custom off-chip DC in cases where a large DC is needed, but cannot be accommodated on-chip.

3.2.2 Directory Cache Size

We examine the main factors in determining the effect of DC size on DC performance. We consider data set size and L2 line size (coherence unit size). For these experiments, we use 4-way set associative DCs and 4 directory entries per DC line.

Effect of Data Set Size

Figure 4 shows the DC miss ratios for a range of DC sizes with different ratios of data set size to DC size for each application. The L2 line size is 128 bytes. For FFT, Ocean, and Radix, we vary the data set size. For Water-Nsquared and Water-Spatial we

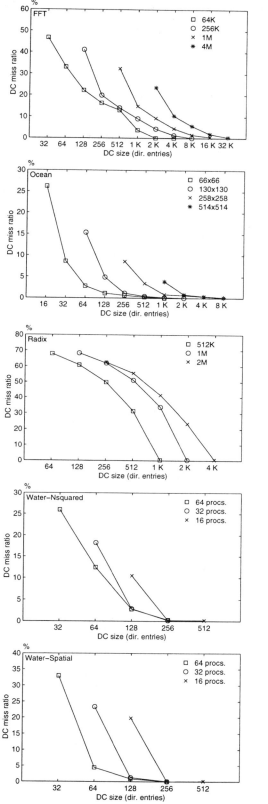

Figure 4: Effect of DC size on DC miss ratio with different data set sizes.

varied the data set size to DC size ratio by using the same data set size (512 molecules) on systems with 64 processors (16 nodes × 4 processors), 32 processors (8 nodes), and 16 processors (4 nodes). This was forced by the prohibitively large simulation time of the next larger data set size that can be evenly distributed on 64 processors.

From the graphs we observe a clear trend of decrease in DC size requirements relative to the data set size with the increase in the data set size for the same level of DC performance. This implies the potential effectiveness and sufficiency of feasible directory cache sizes (e.g. 64KB on-chip or 4MB off-chip) for the requirements of real systems with large data sets. This is due to the sub-linear growth of the working sets of these applications with the data set size, which holds true for most applications [12].

We also observe that for all applications except Radix, the DC miss ratio drops rapidly (super-linearly) with the increase in DC size because the primary working sets for these applications are significantly smaller than the data set, while Radix has a relatively large primary working set [12].

Effect of Coherence Unit Size

Figure 5 shows the DC miss ratios for a range of DC sizes with different L2 cache line sizes (coherence unit size). As the L2 cache line size increases, the same DC size covers more memory, thus a proportional decrease in the DC size requirement is expected.

From the graphs we observe that with keeping the amount of memory covered by the DC constant, the performance of the DC drops with the increase in L2 line size, with varying degrees from one application to another. That is, if we double the L2 cache line size, cutting the DC size in half, we do not maintain the same DC performance. This is primarily due to the the facts that increasing the L2 line size reduces the communication traffic sub-linearly, and that reducing the DC size increases the possibility of capacity misses, even when covering the same amount of memory. However, if the DC size remains constant, as expected, increasing the L2 line size improves the performance of the DC.

This observation is not intended for influencing the choice of the coherence unit size, which undoubtedly has greater impact on performance than the DC, but to help designers adapt DC size to changes in L2 line size in different generations of a system.

The inferior performance of small DC sizes with the larger L2 lines in the case of Radix is because larger L2 lines (128 and 256 bytes) cause more false sharing than 64 byte L2 lines, and accordingly causes more demand on the directory, yielding higher miss ratios. This effect is less evident for larger DC sizes as the higher capacity of the DC balances the effect of the higher demand.

3.2.3 Directory Cache Line Size

By increasing the DC line size (i.e. the number of directory entries per DC line), the DC can benefit more from the spatial locality of directory access without concern for the conventional communication drawbacks of large cache lines due to sharing, as directories are not shared. However, if increasing DC line size implies reducing the number of DC sets (i.e rows), large DC lines can cause more DC fragmentation (more capacity and conflict misses). In this case, we expect the balance between these two opposite factors to be mostly affected by DC size and L2 line size. We also consider the case where the number of sets remains constant with various DC line sizes in order to study the case where the number of sets in the DC

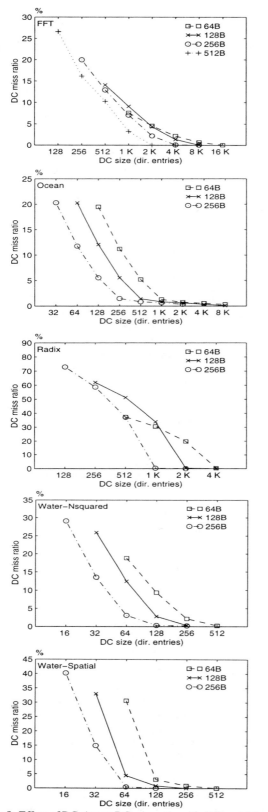

Figure 5: Effect of DC size on DC miss ratio with different L2 cache line sizes.

is more of a design constraint than the total DC size, for example by requiring one-cycle DC access latency, and to separate the effect of spatial locality from that of DC fragmentation.

Effect of Directory Cache Size

As in the previous subsection, we assume 4-way set associative DCs. Figure 6 shows the DC miss ratios for a range of DC line sizes with different DC sizes (total number of directory entries). The L2 line size is 128 bytes.

From the graphs we observe a significant impact of DC line size on DC miss ratio for all applications except Radix, and a wide range of optimal DC line sizes for different applications.

With larger DC sizes, we expect better performance for larger DC lines, as the DC becomes more tolerant to fragmentation and benefits more from spatial locality. We observe this effect with FFT and Ocean. For the other applications, DC size almost has no effect on the optimal DC line size.

Effect of Number of Directory Cache Sets

Figure 7 shows the DC miss ratios for a range of DC line sizes with different DC set numbers (number of rows in the DC). The L2 line size is 128 bytes. From the graphs we observe that larger DC lines clearly improve DC performance for all applications due to spatial locality, and that, in general, the benefits appear to diminish as the DC line sizes increase. A DC line size of 4 to 8 directory entries appears to be at the knee of the size-performance curve for DC lines.

Effect of Coherence Unit Size

Figure 8 shows the DC miss ratios for a range of DC line sizes with different L2 cache line sizes. The DC size is chosen for each application to be at the knee of the size-performance curve for 256 byte L2 lines.

From the graphs we observe a a significant impact of DC line size on DC miss ratio for all applications, and a variation in optimal DC line sizes from one application to another. The variation of optimal DC line sizes with different L2 line sizes is not as large as their variation with different DC sizes. In general a DC line size of 4 or 8 directory entries appears to be the range with best performance in general.

3.2.4 Directory Cache Associativity

We examine the effect of DC associativity on DC performance. We show the results with various DC sizes and DC line sizes to evaluate the importance of DC associativity in comparison to the other DC parameters. The L2 line size is set to 128 bytes.

Figure 9 shows the the DC miss ratios for a range of DC associativities with different DC sizes and a DC line size of 4 directory entries. Figure 10 shows the same relation with different DC line sizes, in order to determine the relative importance to DC performance of DC associativity vs. DC line size.

From the graphs we observe that, in general, DC associativity plays a minor role in DC performance in comparison to DC size and DC line size, and that it has more impact on performance with smaller DC sizes, as the chances of conflict misses are larger. We also observe that the largest differences in DC performance, with respect to associativity, are between 1-way and 2-way DCs, and that a 4-way DC almost shadows the performance of a fully-associative DC.

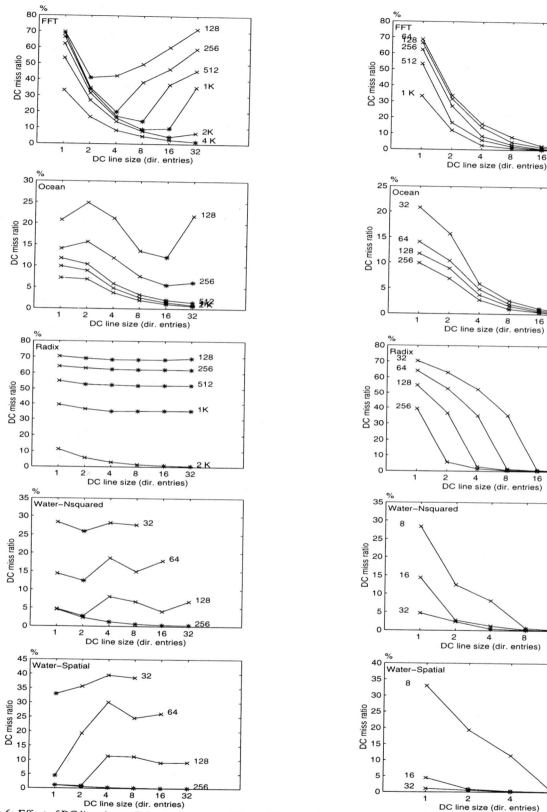

Figure 6: Effect of DC line size on DC miss ratio with different DC sizes (noted to the right of each curve).

Figure 7: Effect of DC line size on DC miss ratio with different DC set numbers (noted to the left of each curve).

147

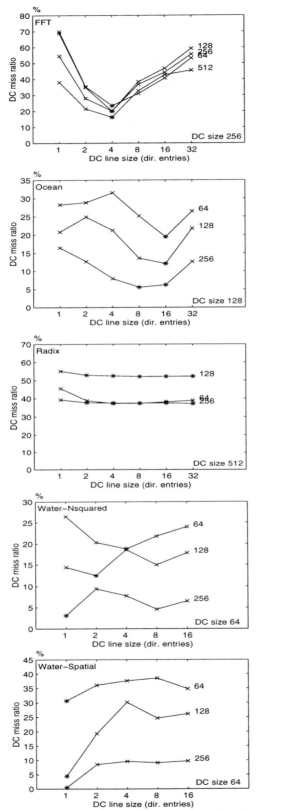

Figure 8: Effect of DC line size on DC miss ratio with different L2 cache line sizes (noted to the right of each curve).

In comparison to DC line size, DC associativity appears to be less critical for performance. Therefore, in cases where the width of DC sets has to be limited in order to simplify the CC chip design, DC set width is better used in widening DC lines rather than in increasing associativity from 2-way to 4-way, for example.

3.3 Relations between Performance Measures

In order to gain more insight into quantifying the impact of DC performance on coherence controller (CC) performance and the whole multiprocessor system, we investigate the relation between three performance measures: (1) DC miss ratio, which is the main performance measure for a DC, (2) CC occupancy which is the most important CC parameter in affecting overall system performance [2, 7], and (3) execution time, which is the primary performance measure for a computing system.

Figure 11 shows the DC miss ratio versus the increase in CC occupancy relative to the case of a CC with a perfect (100% hit) DC [1] for the points with 128 byte L2 lines.

The graphs show a clear linear relationship between the two measures implying that any improvement in DC miss ratio translates directly into an improvement in CC occupancy. The slopes in the graphs for the different applications are more or less equal, since we are using the same coherence protocol and the same CC parameters. The minor variations in the slopes is due to the variations in sharing patterns between the applications creating different mixes of protocol handler frequencies, which result in differences in directory access patterns.

Figure 12 shows the relation between the increase in CC occupancy relative to the case of a CC with a perfect DC and the increase in execution time relative to the case of a CC with a perfect DC, for the points with 128 byte L2 cache lines. The graphs show a clear linear relationship [2] between CC occupancy and execution time, for all the applications with high communication requirements. The slopes vary among applications, depending on their inherent communication characteristics as well as other system and application parameters such as the data set size.

The linear relationship not only emphasizes the impact of CC occupancy on multiprocessor systems performance as shown in previous research [2, 7], but also means that any improvement in CC occupancy counts directly into improving the overall system performance. Besides supporting the use of DCs, this result also supports any reduction in CC occupancy, for example by pipelining the CC, favoring custom-hardware over slower programmable protocol engines, or using multiple protocol engines that can execute multiple protocol handlers concurrently [7, 9].

The linear relationship between CC occupancy and execution time is attributed to the fact that the coherence controller is the bottleneck for applications with high communication requirements. This is supported by the slightly super-linear (or the increase in slope) for Water-Spatial, the application with lower communication requirements. Therefore, the relation between the two measures, most likely, starts super-linear (or with a low slope) until the CC becomes the bottleneck. At which point, the relation grows linearly with a higher slope.

---

[1] The *increase in CC occupancy relative to the case with perfect DC* remains a *pure* representation of *CC occupancy*. We are just dividing it by a constant and subtracting a constant from it, for the sake of producing a quantity that can be related across applications and system configurations than absolute CC occupancy. The same argument applies to the increase in execution time relative to the case with perfect DC.

[2] We find a clear linear relationship between DC miss ration and execution time. We do not include the graphs in this paper as they are derivatives of Figures 11 and 12.

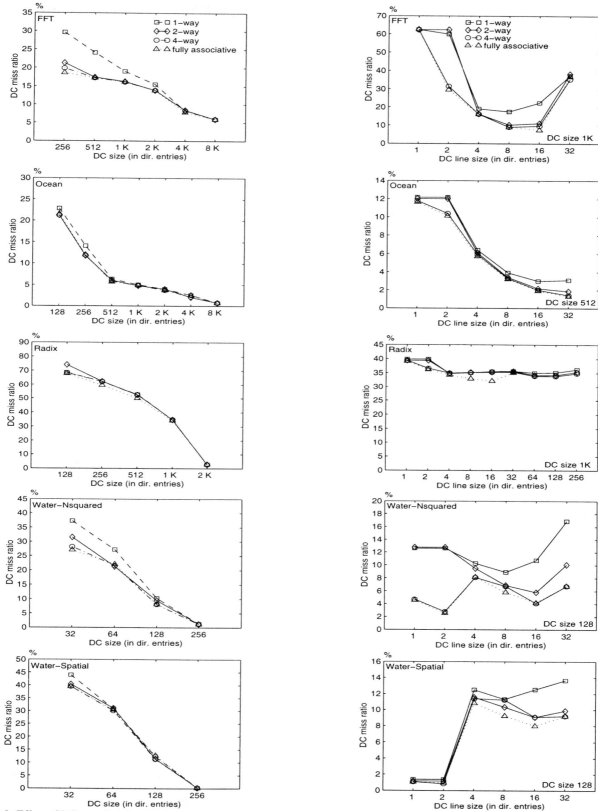

Figure 9: Effect of DC associativity on DC miss ratio with different DC sizes.

Figure 10: Effect of DC associativity on DC miss ratio with different DC line sizes.

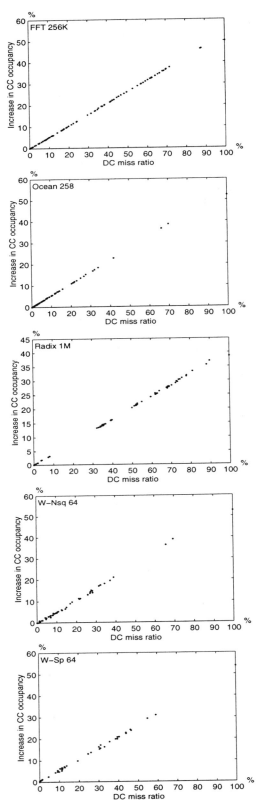

Figure 11: Relation between DC miss ratio and change in coherence controller occupancy relative to that with a perfect DC (0% miss ratio).

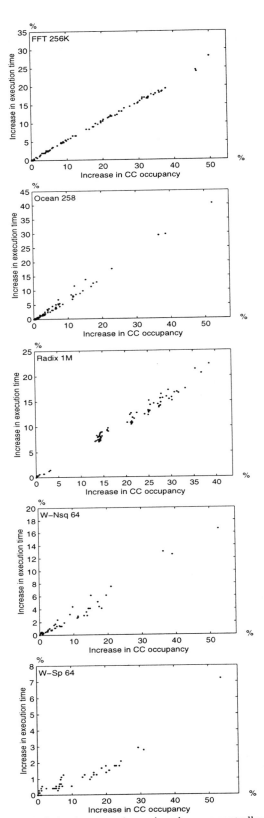

Figure 12: Relation between change in coherence controller occupancy vs. change in execution time relative to those with a perfect DC.

4 Conclusions

The main focus of this paper is on characterizing the performance impact of directory caches on distributed shared memory multiprocessors, and characterizing the DC parameters with the most impact on system performance and the system and application variables with the most influence on the choices for these parameters. We find that for applications with high communication requirements, such as FFT, Ocean, Radix, and Water-Nsquared, using a DC has significant impact on reducing the execution time. Moreover, using an off-chip SRAM directory if an on-chip DC is infeasible still yields most of the performance gains of a DC on-chip. Therefore, we recommend using on-chip DCs in future coherence controllers, and if necessary they can be implemented in off-chip SRAM.

Our results also show that DC size requirements grow sublinearly with the increase in the data set of the application, implying the potential performance benefits of using a DC on real systems with large workloads. We also show that DC line size has significant effect on DC performance and that the optimal DC line size varies from one application to another and with different DC sizes and L2 line sizes. However, a DC line size of 8 or 4 directory entries appears to be the best choice in general.

Associativity has a relatively small impact on the performance of DCs, The largest differences in DC performance, with respect to associativity, are between 1-way and 2-way DCs, and that a 4-way DC almost shadows the performance of a fully-associative one. Also we find that if a choice arrises between increasing DC line size and DC associativity due to limited DC set width, then the former parameter is of greater importance to performance than the latter.

We also investigate the relation between the miss ratio of the DC, the occupancy of the coherence controller, and execution time. We find a clear linear relationship between these three measures, indicating a clear and direct performance benefit for the whole system performance with any reduction in directory access time, by using a DC, and any reduction in coherence controller occupancy. This result can help system architects evaluate the expected performance gains (or losses) as a result of design variations affecting coherence controller occupancy.

In summary, the results of our research imply the importance of using DCs in future coherence controller designs, and help designers select DC parameters and evaluate the impact of these choices on overall system performance.

References

[1] A. Agarwal, R. Bianchini, D. Chaiken, K. Johnson, D. Kranz, J. Kubiatowicz, B.-H. Lim, K. Mackenzie, and D. Yeung. The MIT Alewife Machine: Architecture and Performance. In *Proceedings of the 22nd International Symposium on Computer Architecture*, pages 2–13, June 1995.

[2] C. Holt, M. Heinrich, J. P. Singh, E. Rothberg, and J. Hennessy. The Effects of Latency, Occupance, and Bandwidth in Distributed Shared Memory Multiprocessors. Technical report, Stanford University, January 1995.

[3] J. Kuskin, D. Ofelt, M. Heinrich, J. Heinlein, R. Simoni, K. Gharachorloo, J. Chapin, D. Nakahira, J. Baxter, M. Horowitz, A. Gupta, M. Rosenblum, and J. Hennessy. The FLASH Multiprocessor. In *Proceedings of 21st International Symposium on Computer Architecture*, pages 302–313, April 1994.

[4] J. Laudon and D. Lenoski. The SGI Origin: A ccNUMA Highly Scalable Server. In *Proceedings of the 24th International Symposium on Computer Architecture*, pages 241–251, June 1997.

[5] D. Lenoski, J. Laudon, K. Gharachorloo, W.-D. Weber, A. Gupta, J. Hennessy, M. Horowitz, and M. Lam. The Stanford DASH Multiprocessor. *IEEE Computer*, pages 63–79, March 1992.

[6] T. Lovett and R. Clapp. STiNG: A CC-NUMA Computer System for the Commercial Marketplace. In *Proceedings of the 23rd International Symposium on Computer Architecture*, pages 308–317, May 1996.

[7] M. M. Michael, A. K. Nanda, B.-H. Lim, and M. L. Scott. Coherence Controller Architectures for SMP-Based CC-NUMA Multiprocessors. In *Proceedings of the 24rd International Symposium on Computer Architecture*, pages 219–228, June 1997.

[8] A.-T. Nguyen, M. M. Michael, A. D. Sharma, and J. Torrellas. The Augmint Multiprocessor Simulation Toolkit for Intel x86 Architectures. In *Proceedings of the 1996 IEEE International Conference on Computer Design*, pages 486–490, October 1996.

[9] A. Nowatzyk, G. Aybay, M. Browne, E. Kelly, M. Parkin, B. Radke, and S. Vishin. The S3.mp Scalable Shared Memory Multiprocessor. In *Proceedings of 1995 International Conference on Parallel Processing*, August 1995.

[10] S. K. Reinhardt, J. R. Larus, and D. A. Wood. Tempest and Typhoon: User-Level Shared Memory. In *Proceedings of the 21st International Symposium on Computer Architecture*, pages 325–336, April 1994.

[11] W.-D. Weber, S. Gold, P. Helland, T. Shimizu, T. Wicki, and W. Wilcke. The Mercury Interconnect Architecture: A Cost-Effective Infrastructure for High-Performance Servers. In *Proceedings of the 24rd International Symposium on Computer Architecture*, pages 98–107, June 1997.

[12] S. C. Woo, M. Ohara, E. Torrie, J. P. Singh, and A. Gupta. The SPLASH-2 Programs: Characterization and Methodological Considerations. In *Proceedings of the 22nd International Symposium on Computer Architecture*, pages 24–36, June 1995.

Switch Cache: A Framework for Improving the Remote Memory Access Latency of CC-NUMA Multiprocessors*

Ravi Iyer and Laxmi Narayan Bhuyan

Department of Computer Science
Texas A&M University
College Station, TX 77843-3112, USA.
E-mail: {ravi,bhuyan}@cs.tamu.edu

Abstract

Cache coherent non-uniform memory access (CC-NUMA) multiprocessors continue to suffer from remote memory access latencies due to comparatively slow memory technology and data transfer latencies in the interconnection network. In this paper, we propose a novel hardware caching technique, called switch cache. *The main idea is to implement small fast caches in crossbar switches of the interconnect medium to capture and store shared data as they flow from the memory module to the requesting processor. This stored data acts as a cache for subsequent requests, thus reducing the latency of remote memory accesses tremendously. The implementation of a cache in a crossbar switch needs to be efficient and robust, yet flexible for changes in the caching protocol. The design and implementation details of a* **CA**che **E**mbedded **S**witch **AR**chitecture, CAESAR, *using wormhole routing with virtual channels is presented. Using detailed execution-driven simulations, we find that the CAESAR switch cache is capable of improving the performance of CC-NUMA multiprocessors by reducing the number of reads served at distant remote memories by up to 45% and improving the application execution time by as high as 20%. We conclude that the switch caches provide a cost-effective solution for designing high performance CC-NUMA multiprocessors.*

1. Introduction

To alleviate the problem of high memory access latencies, shared memory multiprocessors employ processors with small fast on-chip caches and additionally larger off-chip caches. To build high performance systems that are highly scalable, several current systems [1, 9, 11, 12] employ the CC-NUMA architecture. In such a system, the shared memory is distributed among all the nodes in the system to provide a closer local memory and several remote memories. While the layers of caches provide data at low latencies and local memory access latencies can also be tolerated, the few remote memory accesses generated during the execution can bring down the performance of applications drastically.

To reduce the impact of remote memory access latencies, researchers have proposed improved caching strategies [13, 15, 22] within each cluster of the multiprocessor. These caching techniques are primarily based on data sharing among multiple processors within the same cluster. Nayfeh et al. [15] explore the use of shared L2 caches to reduce communication misses between processors within the

cluster. Another alternative is the use of network caches or remote data caches [13, 22]. The HP Exemplar [1] implements the network cache as a configurable partition of the local memory. Sequent's NUMA-Q [12] dedicates a 32MB DRAM memory for the network cache. The DASH multiprocessor [11] has provision for a network cache called the remote access cache. Moga et al.[13] explore the use of SRAM network caches integrated with a page cache. Our goal is to reduce remote memory access latencies by implementing a global shared cache abstraction central to all processors in the CC-NUMA system. By incorporating a small fast SRAM cache within each switch in the interconnection network, called *switch cache*, we capture shared data as it flows through the interconnect and provide it to future accesses from processors that re-use this data. Such a scheme can be considered as a multi-level caching scheme without inclusion property. Our studies on application behavior indicate that there is enough spatial and temporal locality between requests from processors. The request-combining technique employed in the NYU Ultracomputer [8] was also based on such an observation. However, their technique relies heavily on requests being generated simultaneously and is suitable more to synchronization traffic. The use of a switch cache relaxes the time constraint, enables several memory read requests to be satisfied in the switch and avoids the need to access the slow main memory. Our recent study [3] indicates that increasing the buffer size beyond a certain value in a switch does not have much impact on the application performance for a shared memory multiprocessor. Thus we think that the large amount of buffers in current switches, such as SPIDER [7], is an overkill. A better utilization of these buffers can be accomplished by organizing them as a switch cache.

The contribution of this paper is the detailed design and performance evaluation of a switch cache interconnect employing CAESAR, a **CA**che **E**mbedded **S**witch **AR**chitecture. The CAESAR switch cache is a dual-ported SRAM cache operating at the same speed as a wormhole routed crossbar switch with virtual channels [6]. The switch design is optimized to maintain crossbar bandwidth and throughput, while at the same time providing sufficient switch cache throughput and improved remote access performance. The performance evaluation of the switch cache interconnect is conducted using six scientific applications. Our experiments show that switch caches offer a great potential for use in future CC-NUMA interconnects for some of these applications.

The rest of the paper is organized as follows. Section 2 introduces the switch cache framework to take advantage of the sharing patterns of several applications. The perfor-

---

*This research has been supported by NSF grants MIP CCR-9622740 and CCR-9810205.

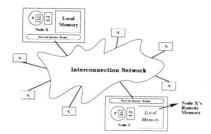

Figure 1. CC-NUMA system & memory hierarchy

mance of an ideal global cache is analyzed and design issues for a hardware switch cache interconnect are also presented in Section 2. Section 3 covers a detailed design and implementation of our crossbar switch cache called CAESAR. Performance benefits of the switch cache are evaluated and analyzed in Section 4. Finally, Section 5 concludes the paper.

2. The Switch Cache Framework

Several current distributed shared memory multiprocessors have adopted the CC-NUMA architecture (Figure 1) since it provides transparent access to data. Figure 1 shows the disparities in proximity and access time in the CC-NUMA memory hierarchy of such systems. A load or store issued by processor X can be served in a few cycles upon L1 or L2 cache hits, in less than a hundred cycles for local memory access or incurs few hundreds of cycles due to a remote memory access. While the latency for stores to the memory (write transactions) can be hidden by the use of weak consistency models, the stall time due to loads (read transactions) to memory can severely degrade application performance.

2.1. Global cache benefits: A trace analysis

To reduce the impact of remote read transactions, we would like to exploit the sharing pattern of the processors. Figure 2 plots the read sharing pattern for six applications with 16 processors using a cache line size of 16 bytes. The x-axis represents the number of sharing processors (X) while the y-axis denotes the number of accesses to blocks shared by X number of processors. From the figure, we observe that for four out of the six applications (FWA, GAUSS, GS, MATMUL), multiple processors read the same block between two consecutive writes to that block. These shared reads form a major portion (35 to 85%) of the application's read misses. To take advantage of such read-sharing patterns across processors, we introduce the concept of an ideal global cache that is centrally accessible to all processors. When the first request is served at the memory, the data sent back as a reply is stored in the global cache. Since the cache is accessible by all processors, subsequent requests to the data item can be satisfied by the global cache at low latencies. There are two questions that arise here:

- *What is the time lag between two accesses from different processors to the same block?* This is identified by *temporal read sharing locality* between the processors, somewhat equivalent to temporal locality in a uniprocessor system.

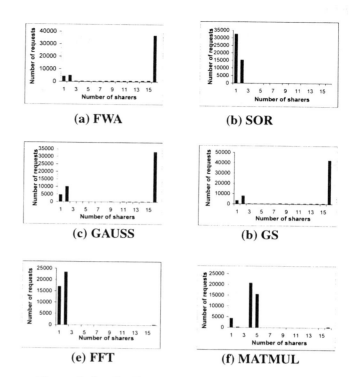

Figure 2. Application read sharing characteristics

- *Given that a block can be held in a central location, how many requests can be satisfied by this cached block?* We call this term *attainable read sharing* to estimate the performance improvement by employing a global cache.

To answer these questions, we instrumented the simulator to generate an execution trace with information regarding each cache miss. We then feed these traces through a trace analysis tool (*SILA* - Sharing Identifier and Locality Analyzer). In order to evaluate the potential of a global cache, SILA generates two different sets of data: temporal read shared locality (Figure 3), and attainable sharing (Figure 4). The data sets can be interpreted as follows.

Temporal Read Sharing Locality: Figure 3 depicts the temporal read sharing locality as a function of different block sizes. A point $\{X,Y\}$ from this data set indicates that Y is the probability that two read transactions (from different processors) to the same block occur within a time distance of X or lower. (i.e. $Y = P(x \le X)$ where x is the average inter-arrival time between two consecutive read requests to the same block). As seen in the figure, most applications have an inherent temporal re-use of the cached block by other processors. The inter-arrival time between two consecutive shared read transactions from different processors to the same block is found to be less than 500 processor cycles (pcycles) for 60-80% of the shared read transactions for all applications. Ideally, this indicates a potential for atleast one extra request to be satisfied per globally cached block.

Attainable Read Sharing: Figure 4 explores this probability of multiple requests satisfied by the global caching technique termed as attainable sharing degree. A point $\{X,Y\}$ in this data set indicates that if a shared block can be held for X cycles in the global cache, the average number of subsequent requests that can be served is Y. The figure

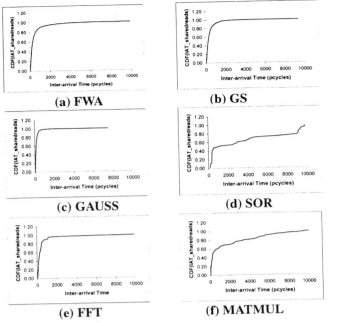

Figure 3. The temporal locality of shared accesses

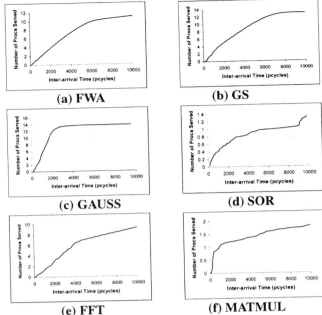

Figure 4. The attainable sharing degree

depicts the attainable read sharing degree for each application based on the residence time for the block in the global cache. The residence time of a cache block is defined as the amount of time the block is held in the cache before it is replaced or invalidated. From Figure 2 we observed that FWA, GS and GAUSS have high read sharing degrees close to the number of processors in the system (in this case, 16 processors). However, it is found that the attainable sharing degree varies according to the temporal locality of each application. While GAUSS can attain a sharing degree of 10 in the global cache with a residence time of 2000 processor cycles, GS requires that the residence time be 5000 and FWA requires that this time be 7000. The MATMUL application has a sharing degree of approx. 4-5, whereas the attainable sharing degree is much lower. SOR and FFT are not of much interest since they have a very low percentage of shared block accesses (see Figure 2).

2.2. The Switch Cache Interconnect

In this section, we present a distributed hardware realization of the ideal global caching solution in the form of a switch cache interconnect. The ideal topology for a switch cache interconnect is the global bus. However, the global bus is not a scalable medium and bus contention severely affects the performance when the number of processors increase beyond a certain threshold. Consequently, interconnect topologies based on tree structures can be considered to be the next best alternative to global caching schemes. Tree-based networks like the fat tree [10] , the hierarchical bus network [20] and the multistage interconnection network (MIN) [14] provide hierarchical topologies suitable for global caching. While offering an inherent tree-structure, the MIN is also highly scalable, and it provides a bisection bandwidth that scales linearly with the number of nodes in the system. These features of the MIN make it

very attractive as scalable high performance interconnects for commercial systems. Existing systems such as Butterfly [2], CM-5 [10] and IBM SP2 [19] employ a bidirectional MIN. In this paper, the switch cache interconnect is a bidirectional MIN to take advantage of the inherent tree structure. Note, however, that logical trees can also be embedded on other popular direct networks like the hypercube used in SGI Origin [9]. The baseline topology of the 16-node bidirectional MIN (BMIN) is shown in Figure 5a. In general, an N-node system using a BMIN comprises of N/k switching elements (a $2k \times 2k$ crossbar) in each of the $\log_k N$ stages connected by bidirectional links. We chose wormhole routing with virtual channels [6] as the switching technique because it is prevalent in current systems such as the SGI Origin[9].

In a shared memory system, communication between nodes is accomplished via read/write transactions and coherence requests/acknowledgements. The read/write requests and coherence replies from the processor to the memory use the forward links to traverse through the switches. Similarly, read/write replies with data and coherence requests from memory to the processor traverse the backward path, as shown in bold in Figure 5a. Separating the paths enables separate resources and reduces the possibility of deadlocks in the network. At the same time, routing them through the same switches provides identical paths for requests and replies for a processor-memory pair that is essential to develop a switch cache heirarchy. The BMIN tree structure that enables this heirarchy is shown in Figure 5b.

The basic idea of our caching strategy is to utilize the tree structure in the BMIN and the path overlap of requests, replies, and coherence messages to provide coherent shared data in the interconnect. By incorporating small, fast caches in the switching elements of the BMIN, we can serve sharing processors at these switching elements. We use the term *switch cache* to differentiate these caches from the processor caches. An example of a BMIN employing switch caches that can serve multiple processors is shown in Fig-

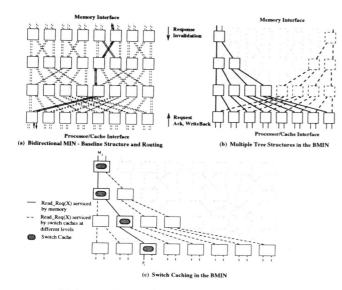

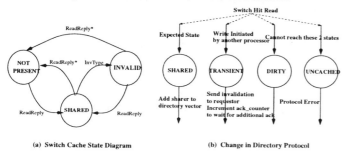

Figure 5. The switch cache interconnect

(a) Switch Cache State Diagram

(b) Change in Directory Protocol

Figure 6. Switch Cache Protocol Execution

ure 5c. An initial shared read request from processor P_i to a block in a remote memory is served at the remote memory M_j. When the reply data flows through the interconnection network, the block is captured and saved in the switch cache at each switching element along the path. Subsequent requests to the same block from sharing processors take advantage of the data blocks in the switch cache at various stages, thus incurring reduced latencies than the initial request.

2.3. The Caching Protocol

The introduction of processor caches in a multiprocessor introduces the cache coherence problem. Many hardware cache-coherent systems employ a full-map directory scheme [5], In this scheme, each node maintains a bit vector to keep track of all the sharers of each block in its local shared memory space. On every write, an ownership request is sent to the *home node*, invalidations are sent to all the sharers of the block and the ownership is granted only when all the corresponding acknowledgements are received. At the processing node, each cache employs a three-state (MSI) protocol to keep track of the state of each cache line. Incorporating switch caches comes with the requirement that these caches remain coherent and data access remain consistent with the system consistency model.

Our basic caching scheme can be represented by the state

diagram in Figure 6 and explained as follows: The switch cache stores only blocks in a shared state in the system. *When a block is read to the processor cache in a dirty state, it is not cached in the switch.* Effectively, the switch cache needs to employ only a 2-state protocol where the state of a block can be either SHARED or NOT_VALID. The transitions of blocks from one state to another is shown in Figure 6a. To illustrate the difference between block invalidations (Inv_Type) and block replacements ($ReadReply*$), the figure shows the NOT_VALID state conceptually separated into two states INVALID and NOT_PRESENT respectively.

On Read Requests: Each read request message that enters the interconnect checks the switch caches along its path. In the event of a *switch cache hit* , the switch cache is responsible for providing the data and sending the reply to the requestor. The original message is marked as switch hit and it continues to the destination memory (ignoring subsequent switch caches along its path) with the sole purpose of informing the home node that another sharer just read the block. Such a message is called a *marked* read request. This request is necessary to maintain the full-map directory protocol. Note that memory access is not needed for these *marked* requests and no reply is generated. At the destination memory, a *marked* read request can find the block in only two states, SHARED, or TRANSIENT (see Figure 6b). If the directory state is SHARED, then this request only updates the sharing vector in the directory. However, it is possible that a write has been initiated to the same cache line by a different processor and the invalidation for this write has not yet propagated to the switch cache. This can only be due to false sharing or an application that allows data race conditions to exist. If this occurs, then the *marked* read request observes a TRANSIENT state at the directory. In such an event, the directory sends an invalidation to the processor that requested the read and waits for this additional acknowledgment before committing the write.

On Read Replies: Each read reply enters the interconnect following the backward path and checks the switch caches along this path. If the line is not present in a switch cache, the data carried by the read reply is written into the cache. The state of the cache line is marked SHARED.

On Writes, Write-backs and Coherence Messages: These requests flow through the switches, check the switch cache and invalidate the cache line if present in the cache.

The caching technique is implemented at the send module of the network interface where messages are prepared to be sent over the network. In a wormhole-routed network, messages are made up of flow control digits or flits. Each flit is 8 bytes as in Spider [7] and Cavallino [4]. The message header contains the routing information, while data flits follow the path created by the header. The format of the message header is shown in Figure 7. To implement the caching technique, we require that the header consist of 3 additional bits of information. Two bits ($Reqtype - R_1 R_2$) are encoded to denote the switch cache access type as follows:

- *00 - sc_read* - Read a cache line from the switch cache. If present, mark read header and generate reply message.
- *01 - sc_write* - Write cache line into the switch cache.
- *10 - sc_inv* - Invalidate the cache line, if present in the cache.
- *11 - sc_ignore* - Ignore switch cache, no processing required.

Note from the above description and the caching protocol that read requests are encoded as *sc_read* requests, read replies are encoded as *sc_write*, while invalidations,

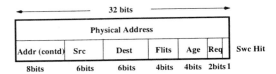

Figure 7. Message Header Format

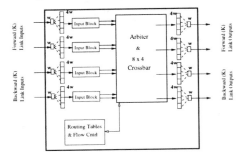

Figure 8. A conventional crossbar switch

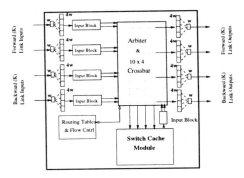

Figure 9. Crossbar Switch Cache Organization

write ownership requests and write-back requests are encoded as *sc_inv* requests. All other requests can be encoded as *sc_ignore* requests. An additional bit is required to mark *sc_read* requests as earlier switch cache hit. Such a request is called a *marked* read request. This is used to avoid multiple caches servicing the same request.

3. Crossbar Switch Cache Design

Crossbar switches provide an excellent building block for scalable high performance interconnects. Crossbar switches mainly differ in two design issues: *switching technique* and *buffer management*. As mentioned earlier, we use wormhole routing as the switching technique and input buffering with virtual channels [6] since these are prevalent in current commercial crossbar switches [4, 7].

3.1. The Switch Cache Organization

Our base bi-directional crossbar switch has four inputs and four outputs as shown in Figure 8. Each input link in the crossbar switch has two virtual channels thus providing 8 possible input candidates for arbitration. The arbitration process is the *age* technique, similar to that employed in the SGI Spider Switch [7]. At each arbitration cycle, a maximum of 4 highest age flits are selected from 8 possible arbitration candidates. The internal switch core and link transmission operates at 200MHz like Cavallino [4]. The wire width at the link is $w = 16$ bits. The 8×4 crossbar takes 4 cycles to arbitrate and move flits from the input to the link transmitter at the output. Since the delay within the switch is 4 cycles, we chose a flit size of 8 bytes ($4w$). Thus, it takes four cycles for the link to transmit a flit from one switch to another. The resultant throughput of the switch is 1 flit served per cycle. Note that the wire width and flit size parameters are the same as in the Cavallino switch[4]. Buffering in the crossbar switch is provided at the *input block* at each link. The input block is organized as a fixed size FIFO buffer for each virtual channel that stores flits belonging to a single message at a time. The virtual channels are also partitioned based on the destination node. This avoids out-of-order arrival of messages

originating from the same source to the same destination. We also provide a bypass path for the incoming flits that can be directly transmitted to the output if the input buffer is empty.

While organizing the switch cache, we are particularly interested in maximizing performance by serving flits within the cycles required for the operation of the base crossbar switch. We follow an arbitration dependent cache organization where only the requests that are passed by the crossbar arbiter are allowed to enter the switch cache. The basic changes to the crossbar switch is to provide the inputs to the switch cache and to arbitrate and transmit the replies from the switch cache. The reply messages from the switch cache are stored in another *input block* as shown in Fig 9. With two virtual channels per input block, the crossbar switch size now expands to 10×4. The switch cache performs the cache operations in parallel with the transmission of the flit over the output link. The cache access time is limited to 4 cycles of wire transmission delay. In a single arbitration cycle, the crossbar arbiter can have a maximum of 8 flits that are ready to be transmitted. However since only 4 physical links are available, the number of flits passed are only 4. Thus the maximum number of switch cache inputs are 4 requests, as can be seen in Figure 9.

The cycle time and access time of an SRAM cache depends on several factors such as associativity, cache output width, number of wordlines, number of bitlines and cache size [21]. The CACTI model [21] shows that direct mapped caches have low cycle times since a direct indexing method is used to locate the line, but have poor hit ratios due to mapping conflicts in the cache. Set-associative caches provide improved cache hit ratios, but have a longer cycle time due to a higher data array decode delay. We found that the increase in cycle time from a direct mapped cache to a 2-way set-associative cache was minor. Thus, we chose a 2-way set associative design that operates within the required 200MHz. Furthermore, most current processors employ multi-ported two-way set associative $L1$ caches operating within a single processor cycle.

Cache output width is also an important issue that primarily affects the data read/write delay. As studied by Wilton et al. [21], the increase in data array width increases the number of sense amplifiers required. The organization of the cache can also make a significant difference in terms of chip area. Narrower caches provide data in multiple cycles, thus increasing the cache access time for an average read request. For example, a cache with 32-byte blocks and a width of 64 bits decreases the cache throughput to one read in four cycles. Within the range of 64 to 256

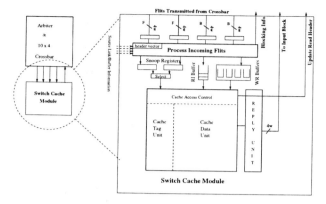

Figure 10. Implementation of CAESAR

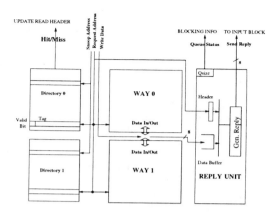

Figure 11. Design of the $CAESAR$ **Cache Module**

bits of data output width, we know that 64 bits will provide the worst possible performance scenario. We designed our switch cache using a 64-bit output width and show that the overall performance is not affected by this parameter.

3.2. CAESAR: CAche Embedded Switch ARchitecture

In this section, we present the hardware design for our crossbar switch cache called $CAESAR$, (CAche Embedded Switch ARchitecture). A block diagram of the $CAESAR$ implementation is shown in Figure 10. As shown in the figure, a maximum of 4 flits transmitted through the crossbar are also latched into switch cache registers at the end of every arbitration cycle. The operation of the $CAESAR$ switch cache can be divided into *(1) process incoming flits, (2) switch cache access, (3) switch cache reply generation,* and *(4) switch cache feedback.* In this section, we cover the design and implementation issues for each of these operations in detail.

Process Incoming Flits: Incoming flits stored into the registers can belong to different request types (based on R_1R_0). Header flits of each request contain the relevant information including memory address required for processing reads and invalidations. Subsequent flit belonging to these messages carry additional information not essential for the switch cache processing. Write requests to the switch cache require both the header flit for address information and the data flits to be written into the cache line. Finally *ignore* requests need to be discarded since they do not require any switch cache processing. An additional type of request that does not require processing is the *marked* read request. This read request has the *swc_hit* bit set in the header to inform switch caches that it has been served at a previous switch cache. Having classified the types of flits entering the cache, the switch cache processing can be broken into two basic operations.

The first operation performed by the flit processing unit is that of propagating the appropriate flits to the switch cache. As mentioned earlier, the flits that need to enter the cache are read headers, invalidation headers and all write flits. Thus, the processing unit masks out *ignore* flits, *marked* read flits and the data flits of invalidation and read requests. This is done by reading the R_1R_0 bits from the header vector and the *swc_hit* bit. To utilize this header information for the subsequent data flits of the message, the switch cache maintains a register that stores these bits.

Flits requiring cache processing are passed to the request queue one in every cycle. The request queue is organized as

two buffers, the RI buffer and the set of WR buffers shown in Figure 10. The RI buffer holds the header flits of read and invalidation requests. The WR buffers store all write flits and are organized as $num\_vc \times k/2$ different buffers. Here multiple buffers are required to associate data flits with the corresponding headers. When all data flits of a write request have accumulated into a buffer, the request is ready to initiate the cache line fill operation.

The second operation to complete the processing of incoming flits is as follows. All unmarked read header flits need to snoop the cache to gather *hit/miss* information. This information is needed within the 4 cycles of output transmission to be able mark the header by setting the last bit (*swc_hit*). To perform this snooping operation on the cache tag, the read headers are also copied to the snoop registers (shown in Figure 10). We require two snoop registers because a maximum of two read requests can enter the cache in a single arbitration cycle.

Switch Cache Access: Figure 11 illustrates the design of the cache subsystem. The cache module shown in the figure is that of a 2-way set associative SRAM cache The cache operates at the same speed as the network links and the processor (200MHz). The set associative cache is organized using two sub-arrays for tag and data. The cache output width is 64 bits, thus requiring 4 cycles of data transfer for reading a 32 byte cache line. The tag array is dual ported to allow two independent requests to access the tag at the same time. We now describe the switch cache access operations and their associated access delays. Requests to the switch cache can be broken into two types of requests: *snoop requests* and *regular requests*.

Snoop Requests: Read requests are required to snoop the cache to determine hit or miss before the outgoing flit is transmitted to the next stage. As seen in Figure 8, it takes 4 cycles to transmit a 64-bit header on a 16-bit output link after the header is loaded into the 64-bit (4w) output register. From the message format in Figure 7, the phit containing the *swc_hit* bit to be marked is transmitted in the fourth cycle. Thus it is required that the cache access be completed within a maximum of 3 cycles. From Figure 10, copying the first read to the snoop registers is performed by the flit processing unit and is completed in one cycle. By dedicating one of the ports of the tag array primarily for snoop requests, each snoop in the cache takes only an additional cycle to complete. Since a maximum of 2 read headers can arrive to the switch cache in a single arbitration cycle, we can complete the snoop operation in the cache within 3 cycles. Note from Figure 11 that the snoop operation is done in parallel with the pending requests in the RI buffer and the WR buffers. When the snoop operation completes, the hit/miss information is propagated to the output transmitter to update the read header in the output register. If the snoop operation results in a switch cache miss, the request is also dequeued from the RI buffer.

Regular Requests: A regular request is a request chosen from either the RI buffer or the WR buffers. Such a request is processed in a maximum of 4 cycles in the absence of contention. Requests from the RI buffer are handled on a $FCFS$ basis. This avoids any dependency violation between read and invalidation requests in that buffer. However, we can have a candidate for cache operation from the RI buffer as well as from one or more of the WR buffers. In the absence of address dependencies, the requests from these buffers can progress in any order to the switch cache. When a dependency exists between two requests, we need to make sure that cache state correctness is preserved. We identify two types of dependencies between a request from the RI buffer and a request from the WR buffer:

- An invalidation (from the RI buffer) to a cache line X and a write (from the the WR buffer) to the same cache line X. To preserve consistency, the simplest method is to discard the write to the cache line, thus avoiding incorrectness in the cache state. Thus, when invalidations enter the switch cache, write addresses of pending write requests in the WR buffer are compared and invalidated in parallel with the cache line invalidation.

- A read (from the RI buffer) to a cache line X and a write (from the WR buffer) to a cache line Y that map on to the same cache entry. If the write occurs first, then cache line X will be replaced. In such an event, the read request cannot be served. Since such an occurrence is rare, the remedy is to send the read request back to the home node destined to be satisfied as a typical remote memory read request.

Switch Cache Reply Generation: While invalidations and writes to the cache do not generate any replies from the switch cache, read requests need to be serviced by reading the cache line from the cache and sending the reply message to the requesting processor. The read header contains all the information required to send out the reply to the requester. The read header and cache line data are directly fed into the reply unit shown in Figure 11. The reply unit gathers the header at the beginning of the cache access and modifies the source/destination and request/reply information in the header in parallel with the cache access. When the entire cache line has been read, the reply packet is generated and sent to switch cache output block. The reply message from the switch cache now acts as any other message entering a switch in the form of flits and gets arbitrated to the appropriate output link and progresses using the backward path to the requesting processor.

Switch Cache Feedback: Another design issue for the CAESAR switch is the selection of queue sizes. In this section, we identify methods to preserve crossbar switch throughput by blocking only those requests that violate correctness. As shown in Figure 10 and 11, finite size queues exist at the input of the switch cache (RI buffer and WR buffer) and at the reply unit (virtual channel queues in the switch cache output block). When any limited size buffer gets full, we have two options for the processing of read/write requests. The first option is to block the requests until a space is available in the buffer. The second option, probably the wiser one, is to allow the request to continue on its path to memory. The performance of the switch cache

Multiprocessor System - 16 processors			
Processor		Memory	
Speed	200MHz	Access time	40
Issue	4-way	Interleaving	4
Cache		Network	
L1 Cache	16KB	Switch Size	4x4
line size	32bytes	Core delay	4
set size	2	Core Freq	200MHz
access time	1	Link width	16 bits
L2 Cache	128KB	Xfer Freq	200MHz
line	32bytes	Flit length	8bytes
set size	4	Virtual Chs.	2
access time	4	Buf. Length	4 flits
Switch/Network Caches			
Switch Cache	128bytes-8KB	Network Cache	4KB
Application Workload			
FWA	128x128	GE	128x128
GS	92x128	MATMUL	128x128
SOR	512x512	FFT	$16K$ pts

Table 1. Simulation parameters

will be dependent on the chosen scheme only when buffer sizes are extremely limited. Finally, invalidate messages have to be processed through the switch cache since they are required to maintain coherence. These messages need to be blocked only when the RI buffer gets full. The modification required to the arbiter to make this possible is quite simple. To implement the blocking of flits at the input, the switch cache needs to inform the arbiter of the status of all its queues. At the end of each cycle, the switch cache informs the crossbar about the status of its queues in the form of *free_space* available in each queue. The modification to the arbiter to perform the required blocking is minor. Depending on the *free_space* of each queue, appropriate requests (based on $R_1 R_0$) will be blocked while others will traverse through the switch in a normal fashion.

4. Performance Benefits

In this section, we present a detailed performance evaluation of the switch cache multiprocessor based on execution driven simulation.

4.1. Simulation Methodology

To evaluate the performance impact of switch caches on the application performance of CC-NUMA multiprocessors, we use a modified version of Rice Simulator for ILP Multiprocessors (RSIM) [16]. RSIM is an execution driven simulator for shared memory multiprocessors with accurate models of current processors that exploit instruction-level parallelism.

The base system configuration consists of 16 nodes. Each node consists of a 200MHz processor capable of issuing 4 instructions per cycle, a 16KB L1 cache a 128KB L2 cache, a portion of the local memory, directory storage and a local bus interconnecting these components. The L1 cache is 2-way set associative and an access time of a single cycle. The L2 cache is 4-way set associative and has an access time of 4 cycles. The raw memory access time is 40 cycles, but it takes more than 50 cycles to submit the request to

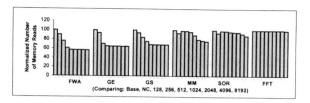

Figure 12. Percentage Reduction in Memory Reads

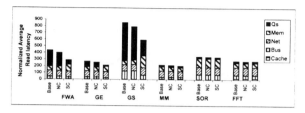

Figure 13. Average Read Latency

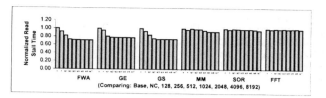

Figure 14. Application Read Stall Time

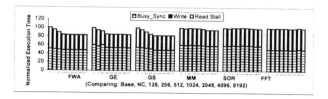

Figure 15. Impact on Execution Time

the memory subsystem and read the data over the memory bus. The system employs the full-map three-state directory protocol [5] and the MSI cache protocol to maintain cache coherence. The system uses a release consistency model. The system employs a wormhole routed bidirectional MIN using 4×4 switches organized in 4 stages as shown earlier in Figure 5. The crossbar switch operation is similar to the description in Section 3.1. Each input link to the switch is provided with 2 virtual channel buffers capable of storing a maximum of 4 flits from a single message. A detailed list of simulation parameters is also shown in Table 1. To evaluate switch caches, we modified the simulator to incorporate a model of switch caches (similar to CAESAR) in each switching element in the IN.

We have selected some numerical applications to investigate the potential performance benefits of the switch cache interconnect. These applications are Floyd-Warshall's all-pair-shortest-path algorithm, Gaussian elimination (GE), QR factorization using the Gram-Schmidt Algorithm (GS) and the multiplication of 2D matrices (MATMUL), successive over-relaxation of a grid (SOR) and the six-step 1D fast fourier transform (FFT) from SPLASH [18]. The input data sizes are shown in Table 1 and the sharing characteristics were discussed in Section 2.1.

4.2. Simulation Results and Analysis

In this subsection, we present and analyze the results obtained through extensive simulation runs to compare three systems: *Base*, network cache (*NC*) and switch cache (*SC*). The *Base* system discussed in the previous subsection does not employ any caching technique beyond the L1 and L2 caches. We simulate a system with *NC* by enabling $4KB$ switch caches in all the switching elements of stage 0 in the MIN. Note that stage 0 is the stage closest to the processor, while stage 3 is the stage closest to the remote memory in Figure 5. The *SC* system employs switch caches in all the switching elements of the MIN. We vary cache size to evaluate their impact of performance of switch caches.

The main purpose of switch caches in the interconnect is to serve read requests as they traverse to memory. This

enhances the performance by reducing the number of read misses served at the remote memory. Figure 12 presents the improvement in the number of read misses to memory by employing network caches (NC) and switch caches over the base system (Base). From the figure, we observe that network caches reduce remote read misses by 7-10% for all applications, except FFT. The switch cache results are denoted by the size of the cache. The size is varied from a mere 128 bytes to a large $8KB$. When compared to the base system, the switch cache system improves the read misses by as high as 45%. As the cache size is increased, we find that a switch cache size of 512 bytes seems to provide the maximum performance improvement. Increasing the switch cache size beyond 512 bytes has a negligible effect on the number of read misses served at the distant remote memory. When compared to the network cache system, we find that a small switch cache of 512 bytes in 4 stages works better than a single $4KB$ cache as the network cache for three (FWA, GAUSS and GS) of the six applications. For the MATMUL application, a larger switch cache of size 1KB or higher is required to improve the performance over a 4KB network cache. The FFT application is unaffected by the use of network and switch caches. SOR, on the other hand, shows a minor reduction in the number of reads serviced at remote memories. These results relate to the amount of read-sharing accesses shown earlier in Figure 2.

Figure 13 shows the improvement in average latency for reads for each application when $1KB$ switch caches are employed in the interconnect. For each application, the figure consists of three bars corresponding to the Base, NC and SC systems. The average read latency is further broken down into processor cache access delay, bus delay, network data transfer delay, memory service time and queueing delays at the network interface. From the figure, we observe that the network cache system improves on the average latency to a certain extent by providing data at the stage 0 level. By using switch caches in all stages of the interconnect, the average read latency is further reduced significantly for three of the six applications. SOR and FFT are unaffected by the use of switch caches.

Figure 14 presents the application read stall time for different system configurations. For three of the six applications, the use of switch caching reduces the stall time by as high as 35% over the base system. We observe that a small cache size of 512 bytes is sufficient to provide a reasonable performance benefit. For the MATMUL application, we find that the read stall time does not reduce tremendously. There are two reasons for such a behavior. The first is a high processor cache hit rate that produces very few memory accesses. The second reason is a significantly lower difference between the base system memory access latency and the switch cache access latency when compared to other applications. However, it should be noted that the improvement in stall time for this application using larger ($> 1KB$) switch caches is still 4% higher than for a network cache and approximately 7% over the base system. Finally, SOR and FFT have negligible changes in stall time.

Figure 15 presents the normalized execution time for each application under different system configurations. The normalized execution time is divided into read stall time, write stall time and processor computation and synchronization time. As expected, the write stall time in a release consistent system is negligible. However, read stall time represents more than 50% of the execution time. We have seen that improvements in read stall time due to switch caching range from 7% to 35%. This directly affects the application execution time and improves the base execution time by as high as 20% with 4KB switch caches.

5. Conclusions

In this paper, a novel hardware caching framework called switch cache was presented to improve the remote memory access performance of CC-NUMA multiprocessors. We started with the concept of an ideal global cache that is centrally accessibly by all processors. We showed that such a shared abstraction can improve the performance substantially for applications with high read sharing degrees. We realized this abstraction by incorporating small caches within each switching element of the MIN and captured shared data as they flowed from the memory to the processor. We dealt with several issues when designing such a distributed caching framework. The main hindrance was that of maintaining cache coherence and full map directory information. We organized the caching technique in a hierarchical fashion by storing the most recently used data in a non-inclusive manner. The data was kept coherent in a transparent fashion using the regular processor invalidations and other control information generated at the home node. To maintain full-map directory information, read requests that hit in the switch cache were marked and they progress to memory for the sole purpose of updating the directory.

The design of crossbar switch caches involved incorporating a cache within typical crossbar switches (like SPIDER) such that messages are not additionally delayed due to switch cache processing. A detailed design of a cache embedded switch architecture (CAESAR) was presented and analyzed. Design parameters included cache access time, set associativity and cache size. We chose a 2-way set associative cache structure to guarantee low cache access time and sufficient cache hits. In order to determine a suitable cache size, we varied this parameter in our execution driven simulations. Our results indicated that a small cache of size 512 bytes is sufficient to provide up to 45% reduction in memory service and thus a 20% improvement in execution time. Current switches such as SPIDER maintain large buffers that are under-utilized in shared memory multiprocessors. By organizing these buffers as a switch cache, the system performance can be tremendously improved.

References

[1] G. Astfalk et al., "An Overview of the HP/Convex Exemplar Hardware," *http://www.convex.com/tech_cache/ps/hw_ov.ps*.

[2] BBN Laboratories Inc., "Butterfly Parallel Processor Overview, version 1," Dec. 1985.

[3] L. Bhuyan, et al., "The Impact of Switch Design on the Application Performance of Shared Memory Multiprocessors," *International Parallel Processing Symposium*, Mar 1998.

[4] J. Carbonaro and F. Verhoorn, "Cavallino: The Teraflops Router and NIC," *Proc. Symp. High Performance Interconnects (Hot Interconnects 4)*, Aug. 1996.

[5] L. M. Censier and P. Feautrier, "A New Solution to Coherence Problems in Multicache Systems," *IEEE Transactions on Computers*, vol. C-27, no. 12, pp. 1112–1118, December 1978.

[6] W. J. Dally, "Virtual-Channel Flow Control," *IEEE Transactions on Parallel and Distributed Systems*, vol. 3, no. 2, pp. 194–205, March 1992.

[7] M. Galles, "Scalable Pipelined Interconnect for Distributed Endpoint Routing: The SGI SPIDER Chip," *Proc. Symp. High Performance Interconnects (Hot Interconnects 4)*, Aug. 1996.

[8] A. Gottlieb et al., "The NYU Ultracomputer: Designinga MIMD Shared-Memory Parallel Computer," IEEE Transactions on Computers, vol. C-32, no. 2, pp. 175-189, Feb. 1983.

[9] J. Laudon and D. Lenoski, "The SGI Origin: A ccNUMA Highly Scalable Server," *Proceedings of 24th Annual International Symposium on Computer Architecture*, pp. 241-251, 1997.

[10] C. E. Leiserson etal, "The Network Architecture of the Connection Machine CM-5," *Symposium on Parallel Algorithms and Architectures*, pp. 272-285, 1992.

[11] D. Lenoski et al., "The Stanford DASH Multiprocessor," IEEE Computer, 25(3), pages 63-79, Mar. 1992.

[12] T. Lovett and R. Clapp., "STiNG: A CC-NUMA Computer System for the Commercial Marketplace.," *Proceedings of the 23rd Annual International Symposium on Computer Architecture.*, pages 308-317. May 1996.

[13] A. Moga and M. Dubois., "The Effectiveness of SRAM Network Caches on Clustered DSMs," *Proceesings of the 4th International Symposium on High Performance Computer Architecture*, pages 103-112, Feb. 1998.

[14] A. Nanda and L. Bhuyan, "Design and Analysis of Cache Coherent Multistage Interconnection Networks," *IEEE Transactions on Computers*, vol. 42, no. 4, April 1993.

[15] B. Nayfeh, et al., "The Impact of Shared-Cache Clustering in Small-Scale Shared-Memory Multiprocessors," *Proceesings of the 2nd International Symposium on High Performance Computer Architecture*, pages 74-84, Feb. 1996.

[16] V. Pai et al., "RSIM Reference Manual. Version 1.0," *Department of Electrical and Computer Engineering, Rice University. Technical Report 9705*. July 1997.

[17] T. Shanley, "Pentium Pro Processor System Architecture," *MindShare Inc., Addison-Wesley Publishing Company*, April 1997.

[18] J. P. Singh, W.-D. Weber, and A. Gupta. "SPLASH: Stanford Parallel Applications for Shared-Memory," *ACM SIGARCH Computer Architecture News*, 20(1):5–44, March 1992.

[19] C. B. Stunkel et al., "The SP2 High Performance Switch," *IBM Systems Journal*, vol. 34, no. 2, pp. 185-204, 1995

[20] A.W. Wilson, "Hierarchical cache/bus architecture for shared memory multiprocessors," *Proc.14th Ann. Int'l. Symp. on Comp. Arch.*, pp. 244-252, 1987.

[21] S. Wilton and N. Jouppi, "An Enhanced Access and Cycle Time Model for On-Chip Caches," *Technical Report #93/5, DEC-Western Research Lab*, 1994.

[22] Z. Zhang and J. Torellas., "Reducing Remote Conflict Misses: NUMA with Remote Cache versus COMA," *Proceedings of the 3rd International Symposium on High Performance Computer Architecture*, Jan. 1997.

Improving CC-NUMA Performance Using Instruction-Based Prediction

Stefanos Kaxiras

Bell Laboratories, Lucent Technologies
600 Mountain Ave., Murray Hill, NJ 07479
kaxiras@cs.bell-labs.com

James R. Goodman

University of Wisconsin-Madison
1210 W. Dayton St., Madison, WI 53706
goodman@cs.wisc.edu

Abstract

We propose Instruction-based Prediction as a means to optimize directory-based cache coherent NUMA shared-memory. Instruction-based prediction is based on observing the behavior of load and store instructions in relation to coherent events and predicting their future behavior. Although this technique is well established in the uniprocessor world, it has not been widely applied for optimizing transparent shared-memory. Typically, in this environment, prediction is based on data-block access history (address-based prediction) in the form of adaptive cache coherence protocols. The advantage of instruction-based prediction is that it requires few hardware resources in the form of small prediction structures per node to match (or exceed) the performance of address-based prediction. To show the potential of instruction-based prediction we propose and evaluate three different optimizations: i) a migratory sharing optimization, ii) a wide sharing optimization, and iii) a producer-consumer optimization based on speculative execution. With execution-driven simulation and a set of nine benchmarks we show that i) for the first two optimizations, instruction-based prediction, using few predictor entries per node, outpaces address-based schemes, and (ii) for the producer-consumer optimization which uses speculative execution, low mis-speculation rates show promise for performance improvements.

1 Introduction

Hardware-based shared-memory architectures are becoming prominent with the popularity of bus-based symmetric multiprocessors (SMPs). Larger shared-memory machines are also advancing in the marketplace. For economic reasons, larger shared-memory machines are built by connecting SMP nodes with high speed interconnects. Typically, in such architectures a directory-based coherence protocol is employed to maintain cache coherence (CC) among the SMP nodes. Examples of such architectures include the HP/Convex Exemplar [8] and Sequent STiNG [24] that use Scalable Coherent Interface (SCI) networks and cache coherence [15], and the SGI Origin 2000 [22] that uses a directory-based cache coherence protocol originating in Stanford's DASH [23].

The widespread use of SMPs is an opportunity to promote shared-memory parallel programming to a much larger audience of programmers than ever before. However, for widespread use of shared-memory we need standardization: a single view of shared-memory should be presented regardless of whether the underlying architecture is SMP-based (with a snoopy-bus CC-protocol) or cluster-based (with a directory-based CC-protocol). Recently, Hill argued that hardware-based shared-memory should be kept as simple as possible, presenting a sequentially consistent transparent shared-memory model to the programmer [14]. Hill argues that speculation could be used to offer transparently high performance while preserving programmers' sanity.

Thus, there is compelling reason to examine transparent hardware optimizations. Indeed, many adaptive cache coherence protocols that optimize various sharing patterns at run-time have been proposed: for migratory data [9,33], for pairwise sharing and producer-consumer sharing [15,16], and for widely shared data [19]. Recently Mukherjee and Hill [26] showed that address-based prediction in coherence protocols can be generalized using two-level adaptive predictors—which were proposed in the context of branch prediction by Yeh and Patt [36]. However, it is not clear at this point whether the gains of this generalized address-based prediction outweigh its costs which involve a predictor entry per memory and cache block.

In this work we propose *Instruction-based Prediction* as a general technique to optimize various aspects of hardware shared-memory. The main idea is to examine—at run-time—the behavior of load and store instructions in relation to coherence events. In every node, the past behavior of its load and store instructions is stored in a *small* predictor structure. Whenever dynamic instances of load and store instructions generate coherence events (such as cache misses, or write-faults on read-only cache blocks) we consult the predictors for optimization hints.

Instruction-based prediction optimizations affect the behavior of the processor toward the CC-protocol (e.g., on a load-miss the processor may ask for permission to write). In contrast address-based prediction optimizations affect the behavior of the CC-protocol toward the processor (e.g, the CC-protocol may decide to return a writable block to a processor that asks for a read-only block). The benefits of instruction-based prediction can be significant because it offers a concise representation of history. Code is much smaller than datasets—static load and stores can be only so many while the dataset can be arbitrarily large—and keeping track of the history of load and store instructions rather than memory blocks and/or cache blocks consumes far fewer resources.

Instruction-based prediction is not new in the uniprocessor world: it is established research and it already appears in commercial processors. Branch prediction is the pioneering instruction-based prediction studied extensively by many researchers including Smith [32] and Yeh and Patt [36]. Abraham et al. showed that very few loads are responsible for most cache misses [1] and subsequently Tyson et al. proposed instruction-based prediction to bypass selectively the cache for such loads [34]. Gonzalez, Aliagas, and Valero used instruction-based prediction to steer data on caches optimized differently for spatial and temporal locality [12]. Moshovos, Breach, Vijaykumar and Sohi introduced memory dependence prediction [25]. They proposed dependence predictors accessed using the address of memory instructions. Chen and Baer were the first to propose prefetching based on instruction-based prediction for parallel systems [7]. Although we believe that instruction-based optimizations can be generally applicable (from bus-based cache coherence to software based coherence) we restrict this presentation to hardware-based, directory-based coherence [15,5,2] (e.g., CC-NUMA).

Contributions of the paper—We propose instruction-based prediction as a general technique to optimize hardware shared-memory architectures. We believe that this technique has the potential to optimize effectively many different aspects of shared-memory using few hardware resources. To support this claim we apply instruction-based prediction to optimize *transparently* three sharing patterns. The optimizations affect performance but not correctness. These three optimization schemes are intended to provide proof-of-concept and we expect that with future research in this area more instruction-based prediction optimizations will emerge. The three schemes implement the following predictions:

- **Predict whether a load-miss will be followed by a store-write-fault.** This prediction can lead to optimization of migratory sharing patterns. The reasoning is that migratory sharing patterns often generate load-misses closely followed by store-write-faults. The optimization we propose (inspired by the work of Cox and Fowler [9], and of Stenström et al. [33]) is to convert the coherent read to a coherent write. We compare the instruction-based scheme to previously proposed adaptive migratory protocols and show that it matches or exceeds their performance using less than 128 predictor entries.

- **Predict whether a load will access widely shared data.** We evaluate two schemes to predict whether a load instruction will access widely shared data. The optimization is to convert the coherent read to a special form that is recognized and handled by scalable extensions to our base CC-protocol (SCI) designed to offer scalable reads and writes [17,18]. The instruction-based schemes consistently outperform an address-based adaptive scheme proposed for wide sharing [19], using less than 128 predictor entries per node.

- **Predict which nodes are going to consume a value generated by a store (Producer-Consumer prediction).** We examine store instructions that generate write-faults and keep track of the potential readers of the newly written cache-blocks. Upon encountering a known store we can *speculatively pre-send* the newly created value to the predicted consumers who can use these values *speculatively* at miss-time but they have to *verify* them through the normal cache coherence protocol. Using few prediction resources, many pre-send messages are verified as correct.

Structure of this paper—Section 2 discusses implementation issues for instruction-based prediction in shared-memory. Section 3 discusses our evaluation methodology. We propose and evaluate instruction-based prediction for optimizing migratory sharing patterns in Section 4. In Section 5 we evaluate instruction-based prediction for wide sharing. Section 6 describes instruction-based prediction for producer-consumer sharing. Finally, Section 7 wraps up this work.

2 Implementation issues

In contrast to previous work where various schemes try to learn the coherence history of a data block at the directories and/or caches, our approach is based on observing the history of load and store instructions in relation to coherence events.

In this paper we emphasize prediction on coherence events since it is a technique whose implementations stand between the processor core and the cache coherence mechanisms—and as such it is a natural point to study first. That we probe and update the predictors on coherence events calls for a tighter integration of the processor core and the cache coherence mechanisms implemented at the coherent cache. In particular our technique requires that both the program counter (PC) of an instruction that generates a coherence event (e.g., cache miss, write fault, etc.) and information from the cache coherence mechanisms be available to the predictors. If the coherent cache and the processor core are on the same chip then implementing instruction-based prediction will not be difficult: both the instruction PC and all the coherency information are readily available in the same place. In the future, with hundreds of millions of transistors on a single chip, we may see devices that are stand-alone CC-NUMA or COMA [13] nodes complete with caches, directories and local memory (such as the new Compaq ALPHA 21364 [3] or such as those studied by Saulsbury, Pong, and Nowatzyk [30] in the context of IRAM [27]). These devices would be an ideal platform in which to implement instruction-based prediction. In the case where there is a boundary between the processor core and the coherence mechanisms, implementation of our techniques becomes difficult: a channel through which information can flow among the processor core, the coherent mechanisms, and the predictors must be established.

With respect to the uniprocessor/serial-program context where predictors are updated and probed continuously with every dynamic instruction instance, we only update the prediction history and only probe the predictor to retrieve information in the case of coherent events. Three events are relevant in this paper: i) cache miss, ii) write fault, and iii) external cache read/invalidation. Upon these coherent events we can trigger optimizations according to the information we get from the predictors. Since we do not probe or update the predictors continuously, the prediction mechanisms are infrequently accessed. Their latency can be hidden from the critical path since we only need their predictions on events which are of significant latency anyway. Thus, we believe that the predictors are neither a potential bottleneck nor add cycles to the critical path.

3 Evaluation setup

In this section we describe the simulator, the base coherence protocol, and the benchmarks we use for all evaluations that appear in following sections.

Wisconsin Wind Tunnel—A detailed study of the methods we propose requires execution driven simulation because of the complex interactions between the program's instructions and the coherence mechanisms. The Wisconsin Wind Tunnel (WWT) [29] is a well-established tool for evaluating large-scale parallel systems through the use of massive, detailed simulation. For speed WWT uses *direct execution* but this also poses certain limitations: only instructions that generate coherence events are observable; the coherent caches are blocking; the cache block size must be a power-of-two multiple of the hardware cache block size (in our case 32 bytes); speculative execution is not supported. Despite these limitations our work provides considerable evidence for the potential of the techniques we propose.

SCI—We have chosen to use SCI as the underlying cache coherence protocol. We chose SCI because it has a rich set of options that can be used to implement optimizations and in addition we have extended it to handle widely shared data [17,18]. In our initial attempt in this area [20], we found the complexity of the SCI protocol impedes simplicity in some of the mechanisms we previously considered. Here, the various instruction-based prediction schemes we propose are not dependent on the specifics of SCI and they can be applied equally well to other directory-based cache coherence protocols.

Hardware parameters—We simulated SCI systems made of readily available components such as SCI network and workstation nodes. For the evaluation in Section 5, which requires detailed network simulation, we have simulated K-ary 2-cube systems (2 dimensions). We simulate contention throughout the network but messages are never dropped since we assume infinite queues. For the evaluation of Section 4 and Section 6 we simulated a constant latency network (which takes 100 processor cycles to transfer any message) with contention at the endpoints. The nodes comprise a processor, an SCI cache, memory, memory directory, and a network interface. The processors run at 500MHz and execute one instruction per cycle in the case of a hit in their caches. Each processor is serviced by a 64KB 4-way set-associative cache with a cache line size of either 32 or 64 bytes. The cache size of 64KB is intentionally small to reflect the size of our benchmarks. Processor, memory and network interface communicate through a 1.2GB/sec, 166 MHz 64-bit bus. The SCI K-ary N-cube network of rings uses a 500 MHz clock; 16 bits of data can be transferred every clock cycle through every link (1GB/sec).

Benchmarks—For this study we use nine benchmarks taken from various sources (see Table 1). We will avoid repeating a detailed description of the benchmarks since they have been described in detail in other work [31,6,11]. Instead, we discuss why we chose them for this study: We chose the CHOLESKY, MP3D, and PTHOR benchmarks to study our first prediction scheme. These benchmarks have migratory sharing and they were also used by Cox and Fowler [9], and by Stenström, Brorsson, and Sandberg [33]. We use the same input for comparisons. For optimization of wide sharing we use the following benchmarks: GAUSS, SPARSE, All Pairs Shortest Path (APSP) and Transitive Closure (TC) [18], and BARNES (taken from the SPLASH benchmark suite [31]). These benchmarks (except BARNES) were used to evaluate scalable extensions to SCI in both static [18] and adaptive flavors [19]. For these benchmarks we use a block size of 64 bytes since this gives better performance for the base case (SCI). Finally, to study the producer-consumer optimizations we use OCEAN (taken from SPLASH [31]), BARNES, GAUSS and SPARSE. For the first two cases we use "control" benchmarks that do not exhibit the desired sharing patterns to study potential negative effects of the optimizations.

Bench.	Input Size	Cache /Block	Sharing			Ref.
			Migr	Wide	P-C	
CHOLESKY	bsstk14	64K/32	Yes	—		[31,9,33]
MP3D	10K/10 iter	64K/32	Yes			[31,9,33,16]
PTHOR	risc	64K/32	Little			[31,9,33,16]
GAUSS	512x512	64K/64	—	Yes (dyn.)	Yes	[6,18]
SPARSE	512x512	64K/64		Yes (static)	Yes	[18]
APSP	256x256	64K/64	—	Yes (dyn.)		[18]
TC	256x256	64K/64		Yes (dyn.)		[18]
BARNES	4K part.	64K/64	—	Yes (static)	Yes	[31,18,16]
OCEAN	130x130	64K/32	—	—	Yes	[31,16]

Table 1: Benchmarks used in this paper.

4 Migratory sharing prediction

In this section we describe an instruction-based prediction that can handle migratory sharing patterns. Migratory data, defined by Weber and Gupta [35], are accessed by one processor at a time. Typically, these data are protected by locks and are accessed inside critical sections.

The idea of our scheme is to detect when a load-miss is followed by a store-write-fault on the same cache block. If such a load/store pair is recurring often we can predict, upon seeing the load-miss, that a write-fault is soon to follow. This mechanism can be classified as **cache block anti-dependence** prediction since it detects writes after reads on the same cache blocks. Let us examine why this optimization is related to migratory sharing patterns. Migratory data are continuously read-modified-written but each time by a different processor [35]. Each processor brings them into its cache as *Read-Only* (RO) cache block, tries to modify them, generates a write fault, converts them to a *Read-Write* (RW) cache block, writes them, and subsequently loses them to another processor that will go through the same cycle. The connection to the instruction-based prediction is straightforward: migratory data are likely to generate load-misses closely followed by store-write-faults.

The optimization is to convert the coherent read to a coherent write ending up with a RW cache block and thus avoiding the write fault. The optimization comes from the work of Carter et al. (Munin) [4] and from the adaptive CC-protocols proposed independently by Cox and Fowler [9], and by Stenström, Brorsson, and Sandberg [33]. In general, in invalidation-based cache coherence protocols the optimization is to "migrate" the data whenever a new processor access them by giving it both read and write permissions, even if it first accesses the data with a read. To give the new processor exclusive access to the data the previous copy (in the processor that last accessed them) is invalidated. The optimization works well because it folds two coherent transactions into one: both the latency and the transaction traffic of the store-write-fault are completely eliminated.

The folding of the two transactions can be initiated either by the home node directory when it decides to return a RW cache block in response to a read request [9,33], or by the processor when, upon a read, it asks for a RW block knowing that it accesses migratory data [4]. SCI originally required three non-overlapping transactions for the folded transaction (directory access, attach to previous node, invalidation of previous node) but we have upgraded it to support an *attach&invalidate* transaction thus making it equivalent to Dir$_i$NB protocols [2]. Also, in SCI a head node is not required to communicate with the directory to write a cache block, but to implement the address-based optimization we modified it (with negligible effects on performance) to behave like Dir$_i$NB or the DASH protocol [23].

4.1 Cache block anti-dependence prediction

The idea of this scheme is simple: if we observe a load-miss/store-write-fault pattern a few times then every time we encounter the load-miss we will bring in a RW cache block to prevent the write-fault. The predictor is a small fully associative table accessed by the load program counter (PC). Each predictor entry contains the PC of the load, the address of the last cache block on which the load missed, a small *n*-bit saturating counter used to make predictions, and a prediction bit (P-bit) that indicates unconfirmed predictions and provides the means for adapting back. Thus, the size of each entry is about 9 bytes (assuming 32-bit addressing). To further reduce the size of the predictor entries, the PC field can be truncated to a few bits or omitted altogether. In the latter case, the predictor is a direct mapped structure indexed by the PC. The address field can also be truncated. Although truncating or eliminating fields may introduce mistakes in accessing or updating the predictor, the smaller size of each predictor entry translates to many more entries for a fixed transistor budget. This may be preferable for large programs. For clarity, in this paper we only discuss full, non-truncated predictor entries.

We only use load PC in the predictor entries and not the store PC. This means that unique load/store pairs are not tracked but all the pairs that have a common load PC are lumped together. A predictor entry, therefore, refers to a single load but it can be affected by multiple distinct stores. We examined alternative implementations where the predictor entry contains both the load PC and the store PC but we did not find enough evidence for their usefulness.

A working example—Figure 1 shows how the predictor is updated by load-misses, stores and store-write-faults, and by external events. On a load-miss the predictor is probed and at first it is empty. A new entry is allocated and includes the load PC and the address of the cache block (Figure 1a). The counter is initialized to zero and the prediction bit (P-bit) is reset since no positive prediction has been made yet (Figure 1a). When a store generates a write-fault the predictor is searched (associatively) using the address of the cache block to find the corresponding load (Figure 1b). Note that the store PC is not needed. A store-write-fault increments the counter of the corresponding entry (Figure 1b). This load-miss/store-write-fault scenario repeats until the counter exceeds a prediction threshold (Figures 1c and 1d). The next time the load-miss occurs (Figure 1e) a positive prediction is made and the coherent read is converted to a coherent write.

Implementation details—In the above description each predictor entry has an address field which holds the address of the last cache block loaded by the corresponding load. This is the "meeting" point, the point that establishes the correspondence of a load-miss and subsequent store-write-faults. Since, more than one load might miss on the same cache block (at different times) the address of the cache block could exist in multiple predictor entries. To avoid this situation, only one instance of a cache block address is allowed in the predictor and specifically only for the load that missed last on this cache block—if another entry contains the same address its address field is purged. More elaborate implementations that can handle concurrent instances of the same load instruction are described elsewhere [19].

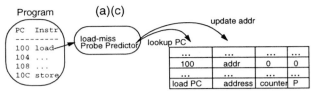

The first load-miss allocates a predictor entry and initializes it.

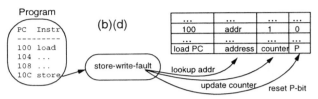

A subsequent store-write-fault on the same cache block (addr) increments the counter. The P-bit is reset.

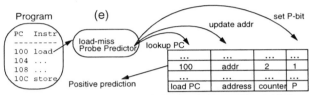

When the counter exceeds the prediction threshold a positive prediction is returned, engaging the migratory optimization. Because of the positive prediction the P-bit is set.

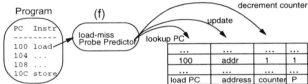

If P-bit is not reset by an intervening store-write-fault the counter is decremented.

Figure 1. Cache block anti-dependence prediction mechanism.

Adapting back—The prediction bit (P-bit) provides the method for adapting back. Its purpose is to confirm the prediction that the cache-block will be written by an ensuing store. When a positive prediction has been made the P-bit is set. To confirm the prediction, the P-bit must be reset when a store writes the block. The next time the load probes the predictor it will find the P-bit either set or reset. If it is set the cache block was not written. In this case (shown in Figure 1f), the prediction counter is decremented and the P-bit is reset (if, however, the counter did not fall below the threshold a new positive prediction will set the P-bit again). On the other hand, if a load finds the P-bit reset a previous positive prediction has been confirmed.

Special care is needed for a store to reset the P-bit. Because of the positive prediction no write-fault will occur to trigger a predictor update. To circumvent this problem, we can update the predictor with any dynamic store instance (regardless of whether it generates a write-fault or not). The disadvantage of this method is the increased pressure on the predictor. Alternatively, we can trap stores that write on cache-blocks brought in with positive predictions. This can be accomplished by bringing in the cache block to an intermediate state which enjoys write privileges but denotes unmodified data. Such state exists in many protocols and it commonly referred to as "Exclusive." Thus, the transition from "Exclusive" to "Modified" (which can be considered as a soft write-fault) triggers a predictor update and resets the P-bit. This is the scheme implemented for the evaluation.

External events—A simple-minded implementation of this instruction-based prediction scheme can be fooled by other-than migratory sharing patterns (e.g., when more than one node read the data block before it is written). To avoid such complications, we only consider read-modify-write operations on cache blocks that are the only copies in the system (i.e., exclusive) and are not affected in any other way throughout the operation. If the cache block is read by another node between the time of the load-miss and the time of the store-write-fault we disable the update of the predictor. This is accomplished by deleting the cache block address field of the corresponding predictor entry. Thus, the correspondence of a load-miss and a store-write-fault cannot be established through the address of a cache block that was externally read. Cache block replacements and invalidations also have a similar effect because they lead to subsequent misses—not store-write-faults.

Prediction threshold—The prediction threshold provides hysteresis in adapting to migratory sharing and back. A low threshold allows the optimization to be applied soon after the load-miss store-write-fault behavior is detected, but it delays adapting back in the face of unconfirmed predictions when the saturating counter has reached its highest value. The opposite behavior is obtained by using a high threshold. In this work we used a 2-bit saturating counter with a prediction threshold of 1.

4.2 Results

We have studied the instruction-based prediction optimizations on CHOLESKY, and MP3D that exhibit migratory sharing and on five other benchmarks (PTHOR, GAUSS, APSP, BARNES and OCEAN). Table 2 shows the speedups of instruction-based prediction (**Instr.**) and of the address-based adaptive protocol (**Address**) over SCI. In addition, we show results applying the migratory optimization for all accesses (denoted by **All** in Table 2). Using the migratory optimization indiscriminately (instead of selectively as the other schemes do) ranges from positive (CHOLESKY), to harmless (MP3D), to disastrous (all other programs).

Bench.	SC model				Relaxed model r1 [16]	
	SCI	Instr.	Address	All	SCI	Instr.
CHOLESKY		1.13	1.12	1.08	1.01	1.14
MP3D		1.16/1.30	1.21	1.02	1.22	1.29
PTHOR		1.02	1.00	0.69	1.07	1.10
GAUSS	1.00	1.00	1.00	0.42	1.01	1.01
APSP		1.03	1.00	0.45	1.03	1.04
BARNES		0.99	1.00	0.73	1.06	1.05
OCEAN		1.02	1.00	0.83	1.05	1.06

Table 2: Simulation results for migratory sharing optimizations (32 nodes, speedup over SCI).

Results show that instruction-based prediction works better than the address-based scheme for CHOLESKY (speedup of 1.13 vs. 1.12). For MP3D, the instruction-based method lags behind the address-based method (speedup of 1.16 vs. 1.21) but we discovered that disabling the adapt-back mechanism increases the speedup to 1.30. In MP3D some migratory

accesses (to the particle array) are *not* protected by locks. Thus, although they are migratory "in spirit," in reality external events (e.g., reads, invalidations) interfere with the adapt-back mechanism, which rules out quite a few. The rest of the programs (PTHOR, GAUSS, APSP, BARNES, and OCEAN) do not exhibit migratory sharing and instruction-based prediction provides small performance improvements.

Under a relaxed memory model that hides write latency, the instruction-based prediction still offers performance improvements albeit smaller than the sequentially consistent memory model case. We have used the relaxed memory model for SCI, called **r1**, described by Kägi et al. [16]. These results are consistent to the results reported by Stenström, Brorsson and Sandberg. With a relaxed memory model the argument for the migratory optimization (regardless of how it is applied) becomes primarily an argument of traffic: the migratory optimization reduces coherent traffic in proportion to the amount of migratory sharing in the program [33].

Our results are comparable to those reported previously for address-based prediction [9,33] given the differences in the simulated systems and in particular the cache coherence protocols (e.g., SCI vs. DASH), the number of cache nodes and the block size. Cox and Fowler reported that the block size has significant effects on the performance of their adaptive protocol for migratory data: increasing block size leads to smaller performance improvements. They reported speedups of 1.23 for CHOLESKY and 1.11 for MP3D in 16 nodes and with a block size of 16 bytes. Similarly, Stenström, Brorsson and Sandberg report good speedups (1.54 for MP3D and 1.25 for CHOLESKY) again in 16 nodes and for a small block size (16 bytes). WWT does not allow a block size smaller than 32 bytes but we briefly examined larger blocks (64 bytes) and observed similar effects for the instruction-based prediction scheme: large block sizes (64 bytes) reduce the performance benefit. The effects of the block size on prediction mechanisms merit further investigation. The instruction-based prediction mechanism could be protected from the adverse effects of larger block sizes by relying on the exact word addresses of the load and store instructions rather than the coarse-grain cache-block addresses.

Statistics		CHOLESKY	MP3D	PTHOR
Static loads considered	all 32 nodes	1844	2264	6309
	average per node	58	71	197
Active predictor entries	all 32 nodes	597	751	1687
(loads followed by	average per node	19	24	53
stores)	maximum	46	34	71

Table 3: Statistics for instruction-based prediction

The most striking results, however, are presented in Table 3 (for the migratory sharing benchmarks). The number of predictor entries allocated is very low. On average, 19 predictor entries are needed for CHOLESKY, 24 for MP3D and 53 for PTHOR. In comparison, the adaptive protocols for migratory data (i.e., address-based prediction) require storage in proportion to the size of the directories. The maximum number of predictor entries was allocated in node 0 (which also executes initialization code) for all three benchmarks.

5 Large-scale sharing prediction

Widely shared data (that are accessed by many processors and are frequently updated) can be a serious performance bottleneck in larger shared-memory systems [17,18]. We have proposed extensions to SCI (called GLOW extensions) that provide scalable reads and writes for widely shared data [17,18]. However, these extensions should not be invoked for other than widely shared data because the overhead may outweigh the benefit. Thus, there are two options for making effective use of these extensions: either wide sharing should be defined statically (undesirable because it is not transparent) or dynamically. Besides request combining in the network, which we do not study here, an adaptive method where the directory identifies widely shared data has been proposed [19]. In this method the directory detects widely shared data (by keeping track of the number of readers) and subsequently informs the nodes in the system to use the GLOW extensions for such data.

Here, we examine instruction-based prediction to predict which load instructions are likely to access widely shared data. The prediction is based on previous history: if a load accessed widely shared data in the past then it is likely to access widely shared data in the future. This behavior can be traced to the way parallel programs are structured. For example, in Gaussian elimination the pivot row—which changes in every iteration—is widely shared and it is always accessed in a specific part of the program. Therefore, once the load instruction that accesses the pivot row has been identified, it can be counted on to continue to access widely shared data. We have found that this prediction is very accurate for all our benchmarks.

We have identified two citeria for making a determination of whether a load accessed widely shared data:

- **Latency**: Whether a load accessed widely shared data can be judged by its miss latency: very large miss latency is interpreted as an access to widely shared data. Using latency as the basis for the prediction is not as farfetched as it sounds: access latency of widely shared data is significantly larger than the average access latency of non-widely shared data. This is because of network contention and most importantly because of contention in the home node directory which becomes a "hot spot" [28]. The latency threshold for widely shared data is a *tuning* parameter that can be set independently for different applications. For this work we set the threshold latency to double the average miss latency of the benchmark.

- **Directory feedback**: This scheme is inspired by the address-based scheme proposed in [19]. Information about the nature of the data is supplied by the directory. The directory counts the number of reads between writes and if this number exceeds a certain threshold the directory's responses indicate that the data block is widely shared. The threshold is again a *tuning* parameter and for this work we set it to a low number of 4 (i.e., more than 4 out of the 32 nodes reading is considered wide sharing). We believe that this scheme is more focused on wide sharing than the latency-based scheme which could be fooled by random long latency operations.

As in Section 4 the predictor is a small fully associative table. Each predictor entry contains the PC of a load and a 2-bit saturating counter to make predictions. Each predictor entry is about 5 bytes. Positive predictions are made when the counter exceeds a threshold value of 1.

A working example:—Figure 2 depicts instruction-based prediction for wide sharing. Upon a load-miss the predictor is probed for information. At first the predictor is empty (predictor miss). The load-miss generates a coherent read. The response to this read will update the predictor according to the criterion used (latency or directory feedback). A new entry is allocated in the predictor and its counter is reset to 0, if the read latency exceeds the latency threshold or if the response from the directory indicates that the block is widely shared. This will happen twice more before the counter exceeds the threshold. At this point a predictor probe returns a positive prediction for wide sharing and instead of an ordinary read a special GLOW read is issued. The GLOW read will trigger the creation of sharing trees in the network [18].

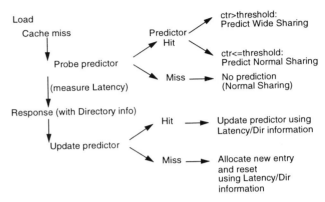

Figure 2. Instruction-based prediction for wide sharing.

5.1 Adapting back

The simple instruction-based prediction described above adapts easily to wide sharing but it is not trivial to adapt the opposite way. Using the GLOW extensions for non-widely shared data (e.g., when only very few nodes share the data simultaneously) results in lower performance since very few nodes incur all the overhead of building scalable sharing trees in the network without any other nodes benefiting [18]. Thus we need to detect when wide sharing has ceased and refrain from using GLOW. Here, we briefly describe two such schemes to adapt back.

It is virtually impossible to obtain reliable feedback for the latency-based prediction because a low miss latency can be attributed either to *lack* of wide sharing or *success* of the GLOW extensions in handling wide sharing. To adapt back in this situation we use an expiration counter for each predictor entry. To use this feature we set the counter to a non-zero value and each time the predictor entry is used we decrement it. When the counter hits zero the predictor entry is deleted. Such expiration counters can also be used in the directory-feedback prediction scheme.

The problem with the directory-feedback prediction is that the actual number of sharers cannot be reliably tracked by the directories when GLOW is in use because of GLOW's read-combining [18]. To solve this problem once a directory discovers a widely shared block it continuously indicates this in its responses until it is directed to do otherwise. The writers are responsible to verify (and correct if necessary) the directory's claim that a data block is widely shared by counting the number of nodes they invalidate (in SCI the writer node invalidates all other sharing nodes rather than the directory) [19].

For the benchmarks that *do have* widely shared data we found no benefit in using the schemes for adapting back. In fact, the performance benefit diminishes slightly. These schemes are mainly intended for situations where the wide sharing prediction can have harmful effects on performance.

5.2 Results

We present results for the two instruction-based prediction schemes (latency-based and directory-feedback). To compare against an address-based scheme we use the adaptive "directory detection" scheme [19]. Since the negative performance impact of wide sharing is more pronounced in larger machines we present results for both 32 and 64 nodes. Table 5 shows the speedups for the five benchmarks with wide sharing and for the two control benchmarks. The two instruction-based prediction schemes (**IL** using the latency criterion and **ID** using directory feedback) perform almost identically yielding speedups of up to 1.30 for BARNES in 32 nodes and up to 1.54 for TC in 64 nodes. They both outperform the address-based scheme (**A-DD**) in all benchmarks (and in the case of APSP and TC by a significant margin). Only the performance of one of the control benchmarks (CHOLESKY) suffers from instruction-prediction optimizations and in particular from the directory-feedback scheme. However, when the mechanism to adapt back is enabled the negative performance impact is minimized (shaded cells in Table 4). The other control benchmark (OCEAN) is affected negatively by the address-based scheme.

	32 nodes			64 nodes		
	IL	**ID**	**A-DD**	**IL**	**ID**	**A-DD**
GAUSS	1.20	1.19	1.13	1.66	1.64	1.43
SPARSE	1.06	1.04	1.13	1.32	1.28	1.25
APSP	1.11	1.12	1.00	1.53	1.52	1.00
TC	1.14	1.14	1.01	1.53	1.54	1.02
BARNES	1.30	1.29	1.27	1.13	1.14	1.13
OCEAN	1.00	1.00	0.91	1.00	1.00	0.95
CHOLESKY	1.00	0.91/0.99	0.96	1.00	0.92/0.99	1.02

Table 4: Results for wide sharing optimizations (speedup over SCI).

N.	Statistics	GAUSS	SPARSE	APSP	TC	BARNES	CHOLESKY
32	Total entries	249	643	94	91	1555	349
	Average per node	8	20	3	3	49	11
	Maximum	9	25	3	3	54	35
64	Total entries	557	1238	180	185	3251	711
	Average per node	9	20	3	3	51	11
	Maximum	11	24	3	3	56	39

Table 5: Statistics for wide sharing prediction (Directory-feedback scheme).

Table 5 contains predictor statistics for the directory-feedback scheme (results for the latency-based scheme are similar). Again, the striking result is the very small number of predictor entries allocated for each benchmark. The number of predictor entries required depends on the number of points in the program which access widely shared data (such as counters, global variables, pivot rows, etc.) and not on the size of the code. Unless many points in the source code access widely shared data, even in much larger programs this number is likely to remain low.

6 Producer-Consumer sharing prediction

Finally, we present instruction-based prediction for producer-consumer sharing. The producer is a store instruction that generates misses or write-faults. Its potential consumer(s) are tracked using information from the CC-protocol. The prediction can take the following two forms: i) a binary prediction for the existence of stable producer-consumer sharing, and ii)

prediction of the identity of potential consumers. Using the first form we can invoke pairwise sharing optimization [15,16] or switch to an update protocol. Using the second form we can *pre-send* data *speculatively* to consumers.

Pairwise sharing allows two nodes to communicate without going to the home-node directory. The pairwise sharing optimization is very well implemented in SCI and even if it is heavily misused it does not affect performance [16]. Thus, using instruction-based prediction to apply selectively pairwise sharing does not offer significant advantage over indiscriminate use of this optimization for all accesses [20].

An update protocol would not constitute a *transparent* optimization in the case of a sequentially consistent memory system because such protocols can violate sequential consistency and therefore need support from the programmer/compiler to guarantee correctness. Because of this reason and because SCI does not yet support an update protocol we did not study this optimization. However, we do believe that it is an interesting future direction for instruction-based prediction.

Subsequently, we propose a new optimization for producer-consumer sharing and apply it using instruction-based prediction.

6.1 Prediction with speculative execution

The most advanced prediction scheme we propose predicts the identity of the consumers and sends the data speculatively to the consumers. The prediction is influenced by the work of Moshovos et al. [25] on optimizing producer-consumer communication in uniprocessors. The optimization (to send the data speculatively to potential consumers) is influenced by the work of Koufaty, Chen, Poulsen, and Torrellas on Data Forwarding [21] and prompted by Hill's views on speculative execution in shared-memory [14].

Evaluation of this scheme presents considerable difficulties because our current tools do not support speculative execution. Thus, we are unable to provide execution time measurements. Instead—analogous to studying branch prediction—we study this scheme by presenting prediction accuracies and hit rates for the speculative pre-sends. Finally, we discuss possible implementations of this scheme, including how to read speculative data external to the processor.

In search of the consumers—Before we describe the prediction scheme we need to explain how to identify possible consumers. The following discussion is dependent on the idiosyncrasies of SCI—in other directory-based CC-protocols the directory itself keeps track of the consumers (using a full bitmap) and can supply all the relevant information to a producer. In SCI, a node that wishes to write a cache block is responsible for invalidating the sharing list. Thus, any nodes that are invalidated by a node (the "producer") are considered consumer nodes. As an option, any node that at a later point attaches in front of the producer (i.e., reads the producer's cache block) can be considered a consumer.

Prediction—We use a predictor structure similar to the predictors described previously but in each prediction entry we use a bit-map (32 bits) to track multiple consumers (a total of about 13 bytes per entry). We examined two simple predictor schemes: Last-prediction that predicts the last set of consumers to be the new set, and Intersection-prediction that predicts the intersection of the last two sets of consumers to be the new set. The two schemes work as follows:

1. **Last-prediction**: The predictor is both updated and probed on a store-miss or a store-write-fault. The predictor is updated when the producer node invalidates a sharing list. The update collects the identities of the invalidated nodes on a temporary bit-map and compares it to the bit-map stored in the predictor entry. If there is significant overlap between the bit-maps the entry's 2-bit saturating prediction counter is incremented; otherwise it is decremented. The temporary bit-map (new) is then installed in the predictor entry. The predictor is then probed and if the counter exceeds a threshold the bit-map containing the possible consumers is returned. This predictor has two *tuning* parameters: the counter threshold and a parameter that defines what is "significant overlap" between bit-maps. In this work the threshold is 1 and the overlap parameter requires at least 2 common consumers (in bit-maps that *do* have 2 or more consumers).

2. **Intersection-prediction**: The predictor is again updated when the producer invalidates a sharing list. Again, the identities of the consumers are collected in a temporary bit-map. The logical AND of the temporary bit-map and the predictor entry bit-map (that contains the consumers of the previous store-miss or store-write-fault) constitutes the prediction bit-map. After the prediction bit-map is calculated, the temporary bit-map is installed over the predictor entry's bit-map.

Speculative pre-send—After obtaining a prediction about the identity of the consumers we can send them the data on condition that they use them speculatively until they verify the data's correctness through the coherence protocol. We call this *speculative pre-send*. The hope is that the data will arrive at the consumer(s) before they even ask for them. Speculative pre-send is not an update: (i) it is *outside the coherence domain*, (ii) the set of the predicted consumers is not cumulative (as in the update) but it changes dynamically, (iii) it allows feed-back through the coherence protocol. Since everything has to be verified through the CC-protocol, speculative pre-sends affect only performance but not correctness.

There are two questions concerning pre-sends: what to send and when to send. Regarding the first question we must decide whether to send just the new value written by the store or the whole cache block, while for the second question we must decide whether to send it immediately (at the end of the write fault) or wait until a later time. In this work, we accumulate pre-sends in a small buffer which is emptied on synchronization operations (i.e., barriers and unlocks) and we send the whole cache line (if it is available at the time of the actual send). This scheme is based on the concept of *write caches,* that improve the performance of update protocols by coalescing writes on the same cache blocks [10]. The same reasoning applies in our case.

On the consumer side pre-sends are accumulated in the cache by taking advantage of invalid cache blocks. A speculative pre-send is only accepted if an invalid cache block with the same address exists in the consumer's cache. We impose this restriction for two reasons: (i) a correct pre-send is likely to encounter a corresponding invalid cache block since the producer previously invalidated all the consumers—assuming a stable producer-consumer relationship—and (ii) it provides a cost-effective implementation since no additional resources (to store pre-sends) are required at the consumers.

How can a processor read speculative data?—To make a convincing argument for the feasibility of the speculative schemes we sketch a method for a processor to read speculative data from outside. Our proposal is compatible (at a high level) with existing memory speculation mechanisms in advanced processor designs. In modern microprocessors that support speculative execution, loads can speculatively bypass stores that issued earlier and whose target address is unknown. If at a later time the address of the store is resolved and there is no dependence to the speculative load then the latter is committed; otherwise, if there is a dependence the speculative load is "squashed" along with all speculative instructions that followed (or in the case of *selective invalidation* along with all speculative instructions dependent on the speculative load).

To read speculative data from the outside world, the processor creates a hypothetical *shadow store* whose address is unknown. The purpose of this shadow store (which never really executes) is to control the fate of the load that reads external speculative data. This load is executed speculatively, pending confirmation of absence of dependence to the shadow store. After the load reads the external speculative data, the address of the shadow store remains to be resolved. The outside mechanisms control the speculative execution by supplying the appropriate address for the shadow store (an additional *shadow load* can be used to read this address). Eventually, the validity of the speculative data will be verified by the CC-protocol. If the data were correct the outside mechanisms supply to the shadow store an irrelevant address (e.g. 0x0000) that does not affect the execution of the program. If, however, the data were found to be wrong their address is supplied to the shadow store thereby squashing all incorrect execution.

6.2 Results

In this section we present preliminary results for the producer-consumer prediction using the pre-send optimization. We implemented all the mechanisms described in the preceding sections in the WWT except speculative execution. Thus, the producers use the predictors to send cache blocks to the consumers; the pre-send messages are accepted in the consumer nodes only if there is available space in their cache in the form of invalid cache blocks; the consumers upon a miss access their caches to read speculative data. However, they cannot execute speculatively so they wait until they obtain a coherent cache block through the CC-protocol. When the coherent cache block is brought into the cache the consumers compare the speculative data to the coherent data to determine mis-speculations.

Table 6 and 7 show the results gathered using this setup for four benchmarks (OCEAN, BARNES, GAUSS, and SPARSE) using the Last-prediction scheme and the Intersection-prediction scheme. These tables list the number of static stores that generated misses or write-faults and the number of entries in the prediction tables. These two numbers are the same since all stores encountered are tracked. Similar to the other two instruction-based predictions described in previous sections, the number of predictor entries required is very low for all programs. The total number of predictor probes gives an indication of the usage of the predictors (equivalent to the number of coherence events generated by stores). The percentage of the probes that return a prediction is a metric that depends on the prediction scheme employed.

For the first scheme, Last-prediction, a saturating counter is used to indicate whether the successive store instances have

Statistics	LAST PREDICTION			
	OCEAN	BARNES	GAUSS	SPARSE
Static Stores considered (all)	2499	1636	471	310
Average per node	79	51	15	10
Predictor entries allocated (all)	2499	1636	471	310
Average per node	79	51	15	10
Total number of predictor probes	1378698	106535	175564	813815
% returned non-null prediction	56%	63%	54%	3%
Total pre-send messages sent	402404	100696	87930	81756
% of non-null predictions	52%	150%	93%	335%
Pre-sends as % of data messages.	10%	3%	12%	1%
pre-sends rejected at consumers	168463	60106	2466	24085
% of total pre-sends	42%	60%	3%	29%
pre-sends accessed in consumers	158103	24984	85183	56421
% of total sent	39%	25%	97%	70%
Correct pre-sends accessed	135866	19439	85123	55032
% of total accessed	86%	78%	100%	98%
% of total sent	34%	19%	97%	67%
Incorrect pre-sends accessed	22237	5545	60	1390
% of accessed	14%	22%	0%	2%
% of total sent	5%	6%	0%	3%

Table 6: Statistics for producer-consumer Last-Prediction with speculative pre-send (32 nodes).

Statistics	INTERSECTION PREDICTION			
	OCEAN	BARNES	GAUSS	SPARSE
Static Stores considered (all)	2500	1644	471	310
Average per node	78	51	15	10
Predictor entries allocated (all)	2500	1644	471	310
Average per node	78	51	15	10
Total number of predictor probes	1378658	106263	175564	813960
% returned non-null prediction	100%	97%	100%	100%
Total pre-send messages sent	247428	36530	87809	39480
% of non-null predictions	18%	34%	50%	5%
Pre-sends as % of data messages.	7%	1%	12%	1%
Pre-sends rejected at consumers	57268	15636	2032	10480
% of total pre-sends	23%	43%	2%	26%
pre-sends accessed in consumers	129465	14142	85612	28025
% of total sent	52%	39%	97%	71%
Correct pre-sends accessed	109501	11227	85567	26745
% of total accessed	85%	79%	100%	95%
% of total sent	44%	31%	97%	68%
Incorrect pre-sends accessed	19964	2915	45	1280
% of accessed	15%	21%	0%	5%
% of total sent	8%	8%	0%	3%

Table 7: Statistics for producer-consumer Last-Prediction with speculative pre-send (32 nodes).

common consumers. When the predictor is probed and the counter is below the threshold a null prediction is returned. The percentage of a non-null prediction ranges from 3% for SPARSE to 63% for BARNES. This percentage can be changed by tuning the threshold of the saturating counter and the parameter that defines the overlap in the consumer bit-maps. For the second scheme, Intersection-prediction, we do not employ a saturating counter. A null prediction is returned the first two times a store is encountered.

For both schemes, the non-null predictions can generate from zero to 32 pre-send messages (depending on the number of consumers predicted). However, a prediction may be nullified if the cache block is not available at the time of the pre-send. Because the pre-send can be delayed until a synchronization point, many times cache blocks are lost before they can be sent. Under these conditions the total number of pre-sends is

shown in the corresponding columns. The total number of pre-sends is also expressed as a percentage of the non-null predictions.

A number of these pre-sends is rejected in the consumer nodes because there is no free space in their cache in the form of invalid cache-blocks. This number is quite high (e.g., 60% for BARNES). A possibility here is to implement a speculative pre-send cache that holds the pre-sends that do not fit in the main cache. To read speculative data, the processor would access this cache in parallel with its main cache. Such a cache is additional hardware but it would increase the number of pre-sends accessed and verified as correct.

Finally, the percentage of pre-sends accessed in the consumer nodes and the percentage of them verified as correct determine the mis-speculation rate and ultimately affect the performance. For OCEAN and GAUSS these numbers are comparable for the two prediction schemes. For BARNES and SPARSE the second prediction scheme (Intersection-prediction) performs better. The percentage of the accessed pre-sends ranges from 25% (BARNES) to 97% (GAUSS) for the first scheme and from 39% (BARNES) to 97% (GAUSS) for the second scheme. The percentage of the accessed pre-sends that are verified through the CC-protocol as correct is high: for Last-prediction it ranges from 78% for BARNES (22% mis-speculations) to 100% for GAUSS (0% mis-speculations); for Intersection-prediction it ranges from 79% for BARNES to 100% for GAUSS. For all programs the percentage of correct pre-sends is comparable for the two schemes ranging from 19% to 97% for Last-prediction and 31% to 97% for Intersection-prediction. More sophisticated prediction schemes (e.g., two-level adaptive predictors [36,26]) have the potential to increase these percentages.

The optimization based on speculative execution is a tradeoff between bandwidth and latency: in hope of reducing the apparent latency of reads we send more data that, nevertheless, will be re-sent for verification. Our results show that: i) a significant number of pre-sends will allow processors to go ahead and execute useful work and ii) the pre-send traffic is low ranging from 1% to 12% of the total data traffic (see Table 6, "Pre-sends as % of data messages"). If these pre-sends are in the critical path of the program execution, then we could considerably reduce latency consuming a small amount of bandwidth.

7 Conclusions

In this paper we explore instruction-based prediction to optimize transparently hardware shared memory. Instruction-based prediction is well established in the uniprocessor world but fairly novel in the world of parallel shared-memory architectures (where it has been used only for prefetching [7]). The compelling advantage of instruction-based prediction—compared to address-based prediction—is that it requires *very few* prediction resources.

We propose and study instruction-based prediction that *logically* stands between the processor and the CC-protocol mechanisms. It requires two streams of information to converge to the prediction structures: from the processor we require the PC of the load and store instructions that generate coherence events; from the CC-mechanisms we require coherence information. Thus, we can track the history of loads and stores in relation to coherence events such as cache misses or write-faults. Subsequently, each time a known instruction generates a new coherence event we can take action to optimize it.

To make the case that instruction-based prediction is a serious competitor both in terms of resource usage (in most cases using less than 128 predictor entries) and in terms of performance to previously proposed address-based prediction mechanisms we propose optimizations for three different sharing patterns:

- **Migratory sharing.** This prediction/optimization works well for three benchmarks (CHOLESKY, MP3D, and PTHOR) that exhibit migratory sharing and it is competitive to previously proposed address-based adaptive protocols. Equipped with safeguards to avoid applying the optimization to non-migratory sharing it shows no negative performance impact on four other control benchmarks (GAUSS, APSP, BARNES, OCEAN).

- **Wide sharing.** This prediction/optimization works very well and consistency outperforms an address-based scheme on five benchmarks which exhibit wide sharing (GAUSS, SPARSE, APSP, TC, and BARNES). With appropriate mechanisms for adapting back to non-wide sharing there is no negative performance impact on two other control benchmarks (CHOLESKY and OCEAN).

- **Producer-consumer sharing.** We found that prediction can be accurate especially for some programs and a significant number of speculative pre-sends can be successful. However, the optimization trades bandwidth for latency and further research is needed to quantify its performance.

Future directions—We believe that this work will be a starting point for novel instruction-based prediction optimizations. Similarly to work that examined the coherence behavior of data [35] we need to examine the behavior of the instructions in relation to the coherency events and in relation to hardware parameters such as cache and block size.

Regarding the instruction-based predictions we study here, we considered them a starting point. In future work, we intent to examine alternative implementations (using other directory-based protocols), sophisticated predictors, and the combined effects of the different prediction schemes. Finally, we are investigating novel instruction-based predictions, such as the prediction of producers at consumer nodes as an alternative method to reduce access latency.

8 Acknowledgments

We would like to thank Alain Kägi, Doug Burger, Ravi Rajwar, David Wood, Mark Hill, and Guri Sohi for their helpful comments on drafts of this paper.

9 References

[1] S. G. Abraham, et al. "Predictability of Load/Store Instruction Latencies" *26th Micro*, November 1993.

[2] A. Agarwal, M. Horowitz and J. Hennessy, "An evaluation of Directory schemes for Cache Coherence." *15th ISCA*, June 1988.

[3] Peter Bannon, "Alpha 21364: A Scalable Single-chip SMP," Microprocessor Forum, Oct 1998. www.digital.com/alphaoem/present/index.htm

[4] John Carter et al. "Munin: Distributed Shared Memory Based on Type-Specific Memory Coherence." *Proceedings of the Conference on the Principles and Practices of Parallel Programming*, 1990.

[5] Lucien M. Censier and Paul Feautrier, "A New Solution to Coherence Problems in Multicache Systems." *IEEE Trans. Computers*, Vol. 27, No. 12, pp. 1112-1118, Dec. 1978.

[6] S. Chandra et al., "Where is Time Spent in Message-Passing and Shared-Memory Programs?" *ASPLOS VI*, Oct. 1994.

[7] T.-F. Chen, J-L Baer, "A Performance Study of Software and Hardware Data Prefetching Schemes." *21st ISCA*, April 1994

[8] Convex Computer Corp., "The Exemplar System" 1994.

[9] Alan L. Cox, Robert J. Fowler, "Adaptive Cache Coherency for Detecting Migratory Shared Data." *20th ISCA*, 1993.

[10] F. Dahlgren, P. Stenström, "Reducing the Write Traffic for a Hybrid Cache Protocol." *ICPP*, Aug. 1994

[11] B. Falsafi et al., "Application-Specific Protocols for User-Level Shared Memory." *Supercomputing '94*, Nov. 1994.

[12] A. Gonzalez et al. "A Data Cache with Multiple Caching Strategies Tuned to Different Types of Locality." *ICS*, 1997.

[13] E. Hagersten et al., "DDM — A Cache-Only Memory Architecture." *IEEE Computer*, Vol 25. No 9, September 1992.

[14] Mark D. Hill, "Multiprocessors Should Support Simple Memory Consistency Models", *IEEE Computer*, Vol. 31 No. 8, Aug. 1998.

[15] IEEE Standard for Scalable Coherent Interface (SCI) 1596, IEEE 1993.

[16] Alain Kägi et al., "Techniques for Reducing Overheads of Shared-Memory Multiprocessing." *ICS*, July 1995.

[17] S. Kaxiras, "Kiloprocessor Extensions to SCI." *10th IPPS*, Apr. 1996.

[18] S. Kaxiras, J. R. Goodman "The GLOW Cache Coherence Protocol Extensions for Widely Shared Data." *ICS*, May 1996.

[19] S. Kaxiras, "Identification and Optimization of Sharing Patterns for High-Performance Scalable Shared-Memory." Ph.D. Thesis, University of Wisconsin-Madison, August 1998.

[20] S. Kaxiras, "The Use of Instruction-Based Prediction in Hardware Shared-Memory." *Univ. of Wisconsin CS TR-1368*, April 1998.

[21] D. A. Koufaty et al, "Data Forwarding in Scalable Shared-Memory Multiprocessors." *ICS*, July 1995

[22] James Laudon, Daniel Lenoski. "The SGI Origin: A cc-NUMA Highly Scalable Server," *24th ISCA*, June 1997.

[23] Daniel Lenoski et al., "The Stanford DASH Multiprocessor." *IEEE Computer*, Vol. 25 No. 3, March 1992.

[24] Tom Lovett and Russell Clapp, "STiNG: A CC-NUMA Computer System for the Commercial Marketplace." *23rd ISCA*, May 1996.

[25] A. Moshovos at al., "Dynamic Speculation and Synchronization of Data Depenences." *24th ISCA*, 1997.

[26] Shubhendu S. Mukherjee and Mark D. Hill "Using Prediction to Accelerate Coherence Protocols", ISCA, 1998.

[27] David Patterson et al., "The case for Intelligent RAM," *IEEE Micro*, Vol 17, No. 2, March/April 1997.

[28] G. F. Pfister and V. A. Norton, "Hot Spot Contention and Combining in Multistage Interconnection Networks." *ICPP*, Aug. 1985.

[29] Steven K. Reinhardt et al., "The Wisconsin Wind Tunnel: Virtual Prototyping of Parallel Computers." *Proceedings of the 1993 ACM SIGMETRICS*, May 1993.

[30] A. Saulsbury et al., "Missing the Memory Wall: The Case for Processor/Memory Integration." *23rd ISCA*, May 1996.

[31] J.P. Singh, W-D. Weber, A. Gupta. "SPLASH: Stanford Parallel Applications for Shared Memory." *Computer Architecture News*, 20(1):5–44, March 1992.

[32] James E. Smith, "A Study of Branch Prediction Strategies." *8th ISCA*, 1981.

[33] P. Stenström, M. Brorsson, L. Sandberg, "An Adaptive Cache Coherence Protocol Optimized for Migratory Sharing," *20th ISCA*, 1993.

[34] G. Tyson et al., "A New Approach to Cache Management" *28th Micro*, Nov 28 - Dec 1, 1995.

[35] W-D. Weber and Anoop Gupta, "Analysis of Cache Invalidation Patterns in Multiprocessors." *ASPLOS III*, April 1989.

[36] T.-Y. Yeh and Yale Patt "Alternative Implementations of Two-Level Adaptive Branch Prediction." *19th ISCA*, 1992.

Session 5B

SMP Clusters

WildFire: A Scalable Path for SMPs

Erik Hagersten and Michael Koster
Sun Microsystems, Inc.
901 San Antonio Road
Palo Alto, CA 94303

Abstract

Researchers have searched for scalable alternatives to the symmetric multiprocessor (SMP) architecture since it was first introduced in 1982. This paper introduces an alternative view of the relationship between scalable technologies and SMPs. Instead of replacing large SMPs with scalable technology, we propose new scalable techniques that allow large SMPs to be tied together efficiently, while maintaining the compatibility with, and performance characteristics of, an SMP. The trade-offs of such an architecture differ from those of traditional, scalable, Non-Uniform Memory Architecture (cc-NUMA) approaches.

WildFire is a distributed shared-memory (DSM) prototype implementation based on large SMPs. It relies on two techniques for creating application-transparent locality: Coherent Memory Replication (CMR), which is a variation of Simple COMA/Reactive NUMA, and Hierarchical Affinity Scheduling (HAS). These two optimizations create extra node locality, which blurs the node boundaries to an application such that SMP-like performance can be achieved with no NUMA-specific optimizations.

We present a performance study of a large OLTP benchmark running on DSMs built from various-sized nodes and with varying amounts of application-transparent locality. WildFire's measured performance is shown to be more than two times that of an unoptimized NUMA implementation built from small nodes and within 13% of the performance of the ideal implementation: a large SMP with the same access time to its entire shared memory as the local memory access time of WildFire.

1. Introduction

There has been a concentrated effort in academia to find a scalable replacement for the SMP architecture. There still seems to be a wide-spread belief that SMPs will not scale over time. Many, including the authors of this paper, have claimed for a decade that the bandwidth limitations of the SMP "backplane" would eventually prevent the implementation of yet another generation of scalable SMPs. When we wrote this in 1988, the backplane of the state-of-the-art Sequent Symmetry had an effective bandwidth of about 40 MB/s. Today, some 10 years later, the passive backplane has been replaced by an active switch in Sun's E10000 "Starfire" capable of 12.5 GB/s [4]. SMP bandwidth has improved by roughly a factor of 300 over a time period of

10 years. This is faster than doubling every 18 months, as predicted by Moore's law for CPU development, which yields a factor of 128 improvement over the same time period. Thus, SMP bandwidth has scaled faster than Moore's law over the past 10 years.

Meanwhile, some companies have abandoned their SMP product lines and instead offer implementations of cc-NUMA architectures. While cc-NUMA architectures have the potential for greater scalability, they are less optimal for access patterns caused by "real" communication, such as producer-consumer and migratory data [1]. They also require substantial application and operating-system optimization in order to handle capacity and conflict misses well. Nor is the scheduling algorithm for cc-NUMA trivial. A process migrated to a different node may perform much worse than if it had stayed in the same node, because of a higher ratio of remote traffic.

SMPs provide a simpler model than NUMA for several architectural reasons. The SMP's uniform access time to shared memory provides a simple programming and performance model. An SMP does not require data and code to be placed in any special way for the application to run well. Popular code and data structures are easily shared by all the CPUs. This simplifies algorithms for managing resources, such as memory, processors and I/O devices. A suspended process may be re-scheduled on any other processor at a relatively small cost, even though running it on the CPU where it last ran has an advantage (affinity), leveraging its hot cache. Managing the memory is also easier; any free physical memory can be utilized when a page gets paged in. Non-uniform memory makes all these tasks more difficult. SMPs are also more efficient in handling communication misses (coherence misses), which are common in

Figure 1: WildFire connects up to four E6000 by inserting one WildFire Interface Board (WFI) in each node.

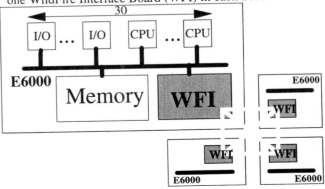

commercial applications [1, 3]. The SMP's current implementation style, often based on some kind of broadcast interconnect, is best served when fit into one cabinet. Physical constraints on the size of the cabinet, such as the size of an elevator or the cargo hold of an airplane, put an upper bound on the scalability of SMPs. Today, there are several SMP implementations scaling between 16 and 30 CPUs [2, 17] and one that scales all the way to 64 CPUs [4]. Our experience and several benchmark world records show these systems' bandwidths to be more than sufficient for the most important and fairly bandwidth-hungry commercial applications. Actually, published benchmarks for commercial workloads show that SMPs often scale better than cc-NUMAs [18].

SMPs are definitely alive and thriving. There is no apparent reason why they will suddenly disappear in a few years.

2. Scalability goal of MSMP

If we accept the fact that SMPs remain one of the primary alternatives for commercial server systems up to a certain scale for many years to come, the question of how to build "scalable" systems needs to be reformulated. The SMP's major limitation is not its viability, but rather that it is difficult to build an SMP with a huge number of CPUs spanning several physical boxes. The question is not how to replace SMPs with a new technology, such as cc-NUMA, but rather how to create a technology that allows high-end SMPs to be part of a scalable family of products providing growth beyond the box limit. We would simply like to ride the SMP curve for as long as it is technically and economically feasible and extend the SMP with a scalable technology such that SMP applications would also be able to run on configurations larger than a single SMP. We call such a scalable technology multiple SMP (MSMP).

The rules for designing an MSMP differ somewhat from other scalable systems. The MSMP should coexist with the SMP, which can be expected to account for far more revenue than the MSMP. The MSMP must, therefore, impose minimal additional complexity and cost on the SMP. Since running on an MSMP should have no impact on the application, it must run the same operating system as the SMP and cannot expect substantial OS modifications to accommodate its special needs. These constraints can often necessitate less optimal DSM solutions than traditional cc-NUMA implementations and add to the remote latency.

There are also several advantages to using large SMP nodes in an MSMP architecture. Large nodes reduce the number of nodes in a large-scale configuration which allows for simple, nonscalable approaches in the cache-coherence protocol. The DSM protocol only needs to keep a handful of nodes coherent and can avoid scalable and complicated solutions, such as SCI's linked lists. The complexity and latency of the interconnect is also reduced by a smaller number of nodes. Furthermore, each large node contains more memory banks, thereby allowing a higher degree of memory interleaving within a node. Large nodes also have a positive impact on node locality. Having fewer nodes implies that a larger fraction of random accesses will be local. Large popular data structures can also be more cheaply replicated in all the nodes of a system built from few nodes. Further, a node-aware load balancer is more likely to find an idle local processor if the nodes are large.

3. WildFire system overview

WildFire is an internal code name for a prototype shared-memory multiprocessor developed by Sun Microsystems. WildFire supports up to 112 UltraSPARC I or II processors, runs a slightly modified version of Solaris 2.6, and is 100% application-binary-interface (ABI) compatible with Sun's SMP multiprocessors. WildFire first booted in February 1997. This paper has been edited using a WildFire running Solaris 2.6. WildFire connects two to four unmodified Sun Enterprise E6500/E5500/E4500/E3500™ SMP servers. Supporting the entire SMP family can allow for flexibility in choosing the system's node size. The rest of this paper assumes nodes built from the largest SMP member, E6500, supporting up to 30 CPUs.

Each E6500 has a GigaPlane™ bus connecting up to 16 dual-processor or I/O boards. Boards are interchangeable so a system with minimal I/O (one I/O board) can have up to 30 processors (15 dual CPU boards). GigaPlane supports 50 M transactions/sec, 112 outstanding transactions, a peak data bandwidth of 3.2 GBytes/s, and an lmbench latency today of 252 ns to the entire shared memory [17, 15]. A WildFire Interface (WFI) board replaces a dual-processor or I/O board. Up to four E6500 nodes can be connected through their WFI board. WildFire supports full cache coherence and Total Store Order (TSO), like other Sun systems. By default, WildFire is a "Cache-Coherent Non-Uniform Memory Access" machine (cc-NUMA) built from unusually large nodes.

Wildfire appears as a single system to most layers of the operating system. Remote program-controlled I/O and DMA are transparently handled by the WFI; a process need not know whether an I/O device is connected to its local SMP node or a remote SMP node. Inter-node interrupts are handled uniquely on WildFire, but differences are invisible to processes and drivers. Only the low-level machine-specific layers of Solaris need know of Wildfire's hierarchical structure. Memory allocation is also segregated by node. Wherever possible, local memory is used to satisfy process memory allocation requests.

Shared memory across the system is supported both through multithreading of individual processes and explicit sharing of memory between processes. Wherever possible, threads of a multithreaded process are kept together on the same node. Only when a process has more threads than there are processors on a node does the process begin to span multiple nodes, causing process memory to be shared across the WildFire interconnect.

To reduce remote-memory traffic and improve average memory latency, WildFire also supports "Coherent

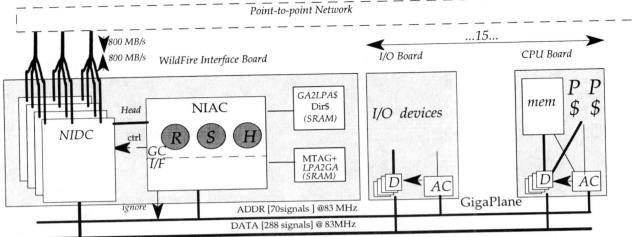

Memory Replication" (CMR). CMR is a version of a "Simple Cache-Only Memory Architecture" (S-COMA) [8], but cannot be called a true COMA since the coherence protocol assumes a fixed home location for each address. Specifically, CMR allows an SMP to allocate local "shadow" physical pages to correspond to remote physical pages. The operating system allocates and reclaims pages for replicated data. Coherence, however, is maintained by hardware at the 64-byte block level.

To avoid performance problems related to memory pressure [16], WildFire can switch between cc-NUMA and CMR at page-by-page and node-by-node granularity. All new pages are created as cc-NUMA pages. The Solaris operating system makes use of integrated hardware counters to determine which pages to switch from cc-NUMA to CMR. The selection is done using a variant of the Reactive NUMA (R-NUMA) algorithm [6]. This adaptive algorithm responds to memory-access patterns in order to dynamically decide when CMR can improve performance over cc-NUMA, and vice versa. Early evaluations showed this to be more useful for long-running commercial applications than starting all pages in CMR and converting some of them to cc-NUMA, as proposed for the PRISM architecture [5] based on SPLASH simulations.

WildFire's has a fairly conservative replication strategy in order to avoid situations where its associated overhead would increase the execution time rather than help. Excessive communication to a remote page will initially result in page migration. Page replication is only used for pages for which the migration does not help. The amount of local memory used for replication is dynamically adjusted and depends on the current memory pressure.

The Solaris 2.6 port that runs on Wildfire does include a number of changes to optimize performance. A hierarchical affinity scheduler tries to schedule a process first on the processor it last ran, then on some processor on the same node. Only when load imbalance exceeds a specified threshold is the process scheduled on a remote node. This scheduler increases the time each process spends in a node, increasing the benefit from the state built up in the large

CMR memory. The first version of the WildFire operating system has some limitations in its CMR algorithm. Memory-resident pages and "large" physical pages cannot be replicated. These types of pages may still be "explicitly" replicated when created.

4. WildFire implementation

WildFire's interface is divided into two different ASICs: the Network Interface Address Controller (NIAC), which implements the coherence protocol, and the bit-sliced Network Interface Data Controller (NIDC), which provides a fat connection to/from the interconnect, as shown in the figure above. The four NIDC chips are controlled by the NIAC chip. Each WFI board exports three high-speed links of 800 MB/s in each direction, allowing construction of a four-node system without introducing the extra cost and latency of a switched network. Each link is bit-sliced and connected to all four NIDC chips, providing a fat and fast connection for the data transactions between the node's data bus and the interconnect. Interfacing a large SMP node puts a higher bandwidth demand on the coherence interface than a traditional DSM implementation; this is what prompted our bit-sliced solution. The smaller address transactions and the header part of a data transaction are detoured through the NIAC and its coherence protocol.

NIAC functionality is divided into two parts: the bus interface (I/F) and the global-coherence layer (GC). I/F acts as a proxy in the node's SMP protocol. It detects transactions which need attention from the global coherence protocol and asserts an "ignore" signal for those transactions. This signal, which effectively removes the transaction from the local snoop order, is one of the few hooks included in E6500's protocol in order to allow for MSMP implementations. Adding the WFI board slows down the access time to local memory by up to two cycles compared to the E6500, since the WFI board does not support the "fast arbitration mode" of the E6500 [17].

WildFire supports a global physical address space where higher-order address bits determine the node on which home memory resides. Remote cc-NUMA requests appear as GigaPlane transactions to memory physically residing on another SMP node; the I/F detects this by checking the higher-order bits. The memory tag (MTAG) data structure contains 2 bits of MOSI state per 64-byte block in the local physical memory. The I/F performs a lookup in the MTAG for each local access to the node's memory. If the state is inadequate (e.g., a "read exclusive" to a "shared" block), WFI asserts the "ignore" signal and invokes the global coherence layer (GC). Otherwise, the transaction proceeds as in a single SMP.

The global cache-coherence protocol is implemented in the GC layer of the NIAC, similarly to the Dash implementation [13]. Three protocol agents (Request, Home, and Slave) exchange messages over the global interconnect. The GC protocol is efficiently implemented directly in hardware and supports up to 40 simultaneous ongoing transactions in each WFI. A directory cache tracks the necessary coherence-directory state needed by the GC protocol, similarly to the FLASH prototype [9]. The SMP's memory is used to back the directory cache.

Part of the SMP's memory can be used to cache remote data by using the CMR technique. A remote page (backed by local CMR memory) is referenced on the local bus by using the CMR page's local physical address. Upon an access miss to the CMR page (insufficient MTAG state), the ignore signal is asserted and the transaction removed from the node's snoop order. The local physical address needs to be translated to the corresponding global address of the remote page before a remote request can be sent by the local WFI. To support CMR, WFI provides a data structure to translate between local physical CMR addresses and the global (remote) physical addresses in the home node. We call this translation Local Physical Address to Global Address, LPA2GA. The second address translation needed to support CMR, the reverse address translation (GA2LPA), is stored in an SRAM cache backed by memory. Unlike traditional S-COMA, the GA2LPA translation is only needed by the slave agents. The greater part of the extra hardware needed to implement CMR comes from these two address translation tables. All other hardware support needed to implement CMR is negligible.

The WFI has associative counters to monitor capacity and conflict behavior of accesses to remote pages and provide input to the operating-system policy deciding which pages should use CMR. This policy is similar to R-NUMA [6]. Software initializes a counter as "free." The first remote access which is identified as a capacity or conflict miss, a so-called excess misses (E-miss), initializes the address part of the counter with its page number. All subsequent E-misses to the same page will cause the counter to increment. Software periodically monitors and frees these counters. Pages showing an appropriate sharing pattern for a long duration will get replicated. This fairly conservative way of choosing CMR pages keeps the software overhead associated with setting up coherently shared pages low. WildFire's software also supports interfaces for placement and replication of pages under user control.

The "scalability" requirements for MSMP architectures are quite different from other DSM systems. Here, only a handful of nodes need be connected and simplicity is the guiding principle. Scalable directory approaches, such as linked lists, are not needed. WildFire uses a fairly traditional MOSI write-invalidate coherence protocol with a full-mapped directory representing each node in the system with one bit, and two bits identifying one node as the owner. This allows for very compact representation in the directory cache. WildFire implements a three-hop protocol to minimize latency to remote dirty data in nodes other than the home node or request node. The extra throughput requirement prompted by the large nodes precluded us from implementing a programmable protocol [9]. Instead, we designed a simple coherence protocol with no corner cases. This allowed for a fairly straightforward verification strategy and gave us the confidence to implement the protocol directly in hardware. The protocol was bug-free in first silicon. We call the approach a "deterministic directory." Unlike most other coherence-directory protocols, this protocol's directory state and the state of the caches are always in agreement. This is achieved by two separate features: the blocking directory and three-phase writebacks. The blocking directory only allows for one outstanding transaction per cache line; in other words, the protocol guarantees that all previous read requests to the same cacheline have been completed before new requests to the cache line are serviced. Nor are writebacks started until all previous requests to the cache line have been serviced. This guarantees that the cache line's state as represented by the directory always corresponds to the cache state in the different nodes and corner cases are avoided. Two simplified examples can be found in the Appendix. As can be seen from those examples, most global accesses will involve a total of three bus transactions; two in the requesting node and one in either the home node or the owning node. This may create a bandwidth problem for applications with poor memory locality, the effects of which are discussed further in Section 8. On the other hand, applications with poor locality will experience a latency problem in DSMs anyhow (as shown in Figure 6.)

5. Simple latency comparison

How does WildFire's MSMP approach compare to other system families? That question cannot be answered by looking at a single latency or bandwidth number since it involves a wide range of system sizes. We have elected to compare our DSM approach with the two commercially available systems: Origin 2000™ from SGI and NUMA-Q™ from Sequent. The three systems represent three very different approaches to building DSM systems, as shown in Figure 2. In order to compare technology from the same timeframe we use the data from Sun's previous generation SMPs, E6000, here.

Origin is a DSM-optimized architecture focused on reducing the remote latency to clean remote data. Each DSM

Table 1 The latency of some scalable architectures measured by the lm-bench benchmark [15]

	Origin[1]	NUMA-Q[1]	WildFire
CPU	R10000	P6	UltraSPARC I/II
CPU cache	1-4 MB	.5 MB	.5 - 4 MB[2]
#CPUs/node	2	4	28
Node cache	None	32 MB	0-6 GB (CMR)
Page replication	Read	Read	Read/Write
Local memory Latency	472 ns	250 ns	330 ns (252 ns)[3]
Local cache2cache Latency	1036 ns	300 ns	470 ns (400ns)[3]
Remote memory latency (nearest node)	704 ns	2000 ns	1762 ns
Remote cache2cache (3hop nearest nodes)	1272 ns	2500 ns	2150 ns
Latency for extra router hop	50 ns	20 ns	No router
Memory overhead replicating 10% of the data in all the nodes (~100 CPUs)	490%	240%	30% (3 extra copies)
# router hops grows	Log	Linearly	No router

node consists of two R10000 CPUs connected to a memory controller (Hub in Figure 2). The directory state is co-located with the data in the DRAM banks, allowing the large directory state to be accessed cheaply if the data are clean in the home node. However, the directory lookup in DRAM also will be on the critical path for accesses to dirty data in the cache of another node. Each CPU has a fairly large cache, but there is no node cache (a.k.a. remote access cache [13]) to help create extra node locality. Instead, a high-bandwidth interconnect of hypercube type is implemented by distributed routers (R) to handle the increased global traffic. The bisectional bandwidth of a system with 32 CPUs is 6.4 GB/s [10, 12].

NUMA-Q is built from small proprietary SMP building blocks with four P6 processors in each node. Each node has a node cache of 32 MB (N$), shared by all the CPUs. Since the nodes are built from SMP nodes, each with its own memory controller, the directory could not be co-located with the data. However, the directory is still implemented using SDRAM. The coherence protocol is a

variation of the SCI, with a four-hop dirty-data protocol. It is implemented in two chips (here called: I/F and GC) in a programmable fashion to lower the risk of protocol bugs. Nodes are connected using an SCI ring of 1 GB/s, implemented with Datapump™ chips by Vitesse (DP) [14].

Table 1 lists some properties of the compared systems. WildFire's local latency is shorter than Origin's and longer than NUMA-Q's. For remote traffic, the order is reversed with Origin as the fastest, followed by WildFire and NUMA-Q. Origin's and NUMA-Q's remote latency are more dependant on system size than WildFire. WildFire's larger nodes also incurs a lower cost to replicate data.

The remote-latency numbers in Table 1 are fairly hard to compare out of context. A system built from large nodes will not experience any remote latency until the system size is larger than its node size, which is at 28 CPUs for Wild-Fire. Even above 28 CPUs, a comparison is not straightforward. At this size, traditional DSMs will experience, on average, a much longer latency than the quoted latency in the table, which is to "nearest node."

A normal SMP application is not optimized for an architecture with non-uniform memory-access time. If the application and the operating system are not rewritten, we can assume that the access pattern is randomly distributed over the entire shared address space.

$$avg\_latency = locality*local\_latency + (1-locality)*remote\_latency \quad \text{[F1]}$$

For random accesses with no extra optimizations, the locality is approximately 1/N, where N is the number of nodes in the system. As N grows, this locality-for-free effect diminishes. Figure 3 shows the average access time to clean data from memory, assuming random distribution of accesses. In the 4 to 28 CPU range, traditional DSMs have an access time 2 to 8 times that of WildFire's. This is not surprising since WildFire simply behaves as an E6000 for this system size. It should be noted that this is really the sweet spot of the market for servers. Origin shows a slightly better latency than WildFire for systems above 28 CPUs.

In systems with large caches, a large fraction of accesses is to migratory-shared data structures. Typically, such data structures will not be found clean in the home memory and

Figure 2 A simplified view of the three compared architectures.

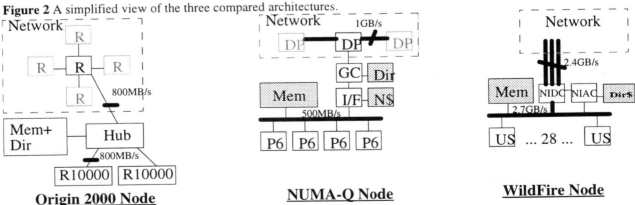

Origin 2000 Node   **NUMA-Q Node**   **WildFire Node**

---

[1] The NUMA-Q number are not explicitly published and have been extracted from [14], the Origin 2000 numbers are from [10]

[2] UltraSPARC I of 167 HMz and 0.5 Mbyte caches are used in this study.

[3] This is the current access time for E6500, the number used for the comparison and in Section 8 are based on the older E6000 with 167 MHz CPUs.

Figure 3. The average latency to shared memory for cache misses, assuming random distribution.

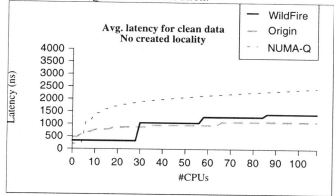

Figure 4. The average access time to satisfy a migratory cache miss, assuming random distribution.

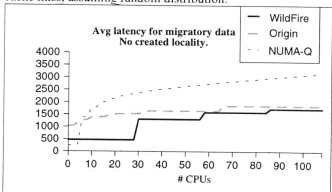

Figure 5. The average latency to satisfy a cache miss assuming 50% cache-to-cache misses and average distribution of memory accesses to the shared address space.

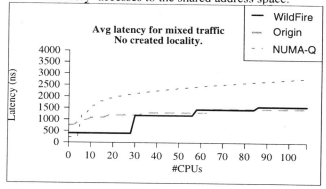

Figure 6. The effect of created locality on the average access time assuming 50% cache-to-cache misses

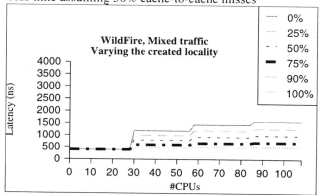

will be satisfied from some other cache. In a NUMA system, that cache will typically be in a node other than the requesting node or home node. Figure 4 shows the average latency for this type of accesses. The figure shows an even larger latency difference between WildFire and other DSMs for systems with less than 28 CPUs. The reason for this is the rather efficient cache-to-cache implementation within a single WildFire SMP node supported by a broadcast snooping protocol. In a DSM system, a cache-to-cache transfer most often involves a so-called three-hop or four-hop transaction: a remote access to the home node, a lookup in the directory, a remote access to a third node where the dirty data resides and, finally, a remote data packet sent back to the home node. Both NUMA-Q and Origin implement their directory structure in SDRAM. WildFire has a large directory cache implemented in SRAM. The data set size for migratory data tends to be fairly small and fits in the directory cache. This reduces the directory-lookup overhead for systems larger than 28 CPUs.

Another factor that reduces the random cache-to-cache latency is the 1/N effect of WildFire's rather large nodes. This makes up for WildFire's long latency to remote nodes and makes it the overall fastest solution for migratory data.

A real application would experience an access mix of the two access types discussed above. The ratio between the two categories varies widely with applications. We have

seen many commercial applications with 40--60% cache-to-cache accesses, which have also been reported by others [1]. Figure 5 shows the average access time for the three systems assuming 50% of each kind. The figure shows that the WildFire approach is very advantageous in systems up to 28 CPUs. Above 28 CPUs, WildFire is roughly on par with Origin, but still far ahead of NUMA-Q.

If the application and the operating system are altered, or large node cache added, more locality can be created. The total locality will have a component caused by this optimization. We call it "created locality" and define it as the fraction of accesses that are made local to a node due to some extra measure. The remaining transactions will still be randomly distributed and experience the 1/N locality:

$$locality = created\_locality + (1\text{-}created\_locality)\,/\,N \quad \textbf{[F2]}$$

This way we isolate the locality effect caused by the large nodes from the forced locality effect, which is less dependant on the number of nodes in the system.

One way of creating locality is by adding a third-level node cache, such as in the NUMA-Q, or by adding support for migration and read-only replication with a page granularity, as done by Origin. WildFire's CMR can be viewed as a large node cache, but will also effectively support page migration and read-only or read/write replication of pages with a coherence unit of one cache line. The effect of WildFire's average latency as a function of its created locality can be studied in Figure 6. This figure assumes that the created locality is independent of the number of nodes in the system.

It is apparent that DSMs, regardless of the efficiencies of their implementations, require a substantial amount of created locality in order to run applications well. The OLTP application studied in this paper resulted in 75% created locality. A 75% created locality (highlighted in the picture) keeps the average latency in the range of 1.5 times the SMP's latency.

6.   Application-transparent optimizations

To successfully exploit WildFire as a large SMP, it should not be required that user processes be aware of their locations, or the node locations of their memory regions, to get good performance and scalability. WildFire uses additional kernel modules for Coherent Memory Replication and Hierarchical Affinity Scheduling control. CMR and HAS policies are implemented by daemon processes which periodically sample CPU load and the excess-remote-cache-miss counters. Set-aware load balancing moves processes from one node to another to balance CPU load, and the CMR daemon will migrate or replicate memory pages to minimize the frequency of remote memory cycles. In this way, WildFire transparently and continuously optimizes the location of both processes and their favorite memory regions for best application performance. Additionally, the system will attempt to optimize the initial placement of processes and memory for improved locality. The kernel itself is replicated transparently on all nodes at boot time; but, the prototype OS used in the tests described below does not replicate many of its data structures.

To analyze the application-transparent optimizations, the following questions were asked:

1. Is MSMP as implemented in WildFire viable for commercial workloads running unmodified SMP applications?

2. What operating system features can be used to effectively hide the latency of remote memory from the application?

3. How close to an SMP's performance characteristics is an MSMP?

7.   Application example

We have chosen to study two of the key features and their impact on performance in more detail: the coherent memory replication and the scheduling policies. A large commercial OLTP benchmark workload is used. It exhibits intense shared-data update activity, stressing the ability of the system to deal with migratory data sharing. Cache-miss ratios and memory traffic are high, even for commercial workloads, and this workload imposes a unique demand for a very large, shared-memory region.

The system was scaled to 900 warehouses on 240 disks connected to one of the nodes through 8 fiber- channel interfaces. WildFire's I/O architecture does not add significant performance penalties for inter-node programmed I/O or DMA operations. The shared memory was configured to be approximately 2 GB in size, and 4 GB of physical memory were configured on each node so as to have enough memory for both the Shared Global Area (SGA) and process private memory.

Database testing was done on a 16 CPU E6000 and on a two-node E6000 WildFire with 8 CPUs in each node. For the two-node tests, the second node was connected to the existing system and half the CPU boards (including their memory) were moved over. As mentioned before, the I/O was left connected to only one of the nodes. This small-scale evaluation using only 16 CPUs allowed us to compare our results with an equivalent "ideal" SMP system as a standard for comparison and to avoid software contention which would impose an artificial limit on the performance of both configurations. We wanted to focus primarily on the effect of remote-memory latency in these experiments.

8.   Experimental results

The effects of the different optimizations were studied by first turning them on one by one, and later turning them all on, while measuring the execution time and the ratio of memory accesses staying local in one node. The following configurations are compared:

NUMA fat nodes represents the expected performance of a NUMA system built from hardware identical to WildFire's, but running a completely unmodified operating system resulting in random distribution of accesses. Still, 50% of the memory accesses are local since the system is built from only two nodes. However, no completely unoptimized WildFire operating system exists, so this performance number had to be modelled based on the number of L2 cache misses measured on a real WildFire system, and the average access time assuming 50% local accesses [F1].

NUMA thin nodes is modelled similarly to the NUMA fat nodes, but assumes a system built from eight nodes with two CPUs in each node, i.e., 12.5% local accesses, and a local and remote latency equal to WildFire's. The performance of this system is set to 1.0 in Figure 7. The increased memory locality of NUMA with fat nodes gives it a 35% performance edge over the NUMA built from thin nodes.

WildFire base is the real WildFire system with as many optimizations as possible turned off. The allocation of memory is locality aware and some kernel text and data structures are statically replicated by this kernel. This version of the kernel has a flat affinity scheduler. WildFire base runs 21% faster than NUMA fat. It can be expected that a NUMA thin would experience a similar speedup if a similarly optimized kernel was used.

HAS only is running WildFire base with the hierarchical affinity scheduling turned on. This will maximize the time a process stays within a node; it also introduces some overhead in the scheduler and adds some extra imbalance to the system. On the positive side there is an increased likelihood of finding requested data in a cache local to the node.

Figure 7. Relative OLTP performance from different DSM and SMP implementations.

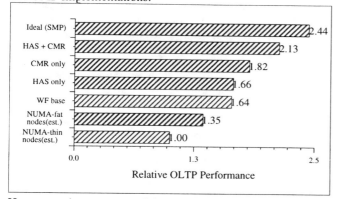

However, the state stored in the local caches is not large enough to make this a huge advantage and the measured performance gain is very small compared to WildFire base.

CMR only is running WildFire base with the coherent memory replication turned on. Some pages will be replicated in both nodes. Processes frequently migrate between nodes; but, since much of the important read-mostly data is replicated in both nodes, the memory locality is increased enough to give this system an 82% performance advantage over a NUMA built of thin nodes.

HAS and CMR has both the hierarchical affinity scheduler and the coherent memory replication turned on. The combination of rare process migration between nodes and the huge read/write caches supported by CMR result in a multiplication effect compared to using only one of the two techniques at a time. The net result is a 113% performance increase compared to the plain NUMA built from thin nodes.

Ideal SMP is built from a single SMP with 16 processors, as discussed earlier, and thus experiences "100% memory locality." This represents the upper bound for these kinds of locality optimizations. The performance of the HAS and CMR system is only 13% slower than this ideal system when running this unaltered commercial SMP application on the WildFire port of the Solaris operating system.

The most performance-critical property of the different systems is the amount of memory locality. Memory locality was measured as the ratio of local memory accesses to total

memory traffic (L2 cache misses and DMA traffic) using hardware counters on the WFIs, as shown in Figure 8. Expected locality for the modeled fat/thin NUMA systems is also shown as a reference. Kernel replication and initial placement policy together accounted for 71% of the local memory cycles, up from an expected 50% for random placement. Coherent Memory Replication increased the measured locality to 87%.

A measured locality of 87% in a two-node system implies a "created locality" of 75%. This is a measure of the effectiveness of the kernel replication and CMR. With a created locality of 75%, the remaining 25% will be distributed equally among the two nodes, resulting in a 75% + (100% - 75%)/2 equals the 87.5% measured locality on a two node system.

As mentioned before, a global transaction will generate a total of three bus transactions while local transaction only generates one transaction. This increase in bus traffic is the bandwidth bottleneck in WildFire. However, good locality will limit the negative effect. The SMP equivalent bandwidth, SysBW, can be derived as:

$SysBW * (locality+3*(1-locality))= BusBW*\#Nodes \quad ==>$
$SysBW = BusBW *\#Nodes/(3-2*Locality) = \qquad (using\ [F2])$
$= BusBW*\#Nodes/(3-2*(created\_locality+(1-created\_locality)/N))$ **[F3]**

$SysBW(2\ Nodes,\ 75\%\ created\ locality) = 4.3\ GB/s.$

E6000's CPUs share 2.7 GB/s. In WildFire, each CPU runs at 87% the speed in E6000, so each CPU requires only 87% of the bandwidth. The number of CPUs we can we put in each of the two node while maintaining the equivalent per-CPU bandwidth can be calculated as:

$CPUsPerNode = 4.3/(2*0.87*2.7) = 0.91$

Thus, for this kind of application, each WildFire node should be able to have about 91% as many CPUs as a single E6000 while maintaining the same bus utilization.

To evaluate the effect of replicating only the frequently accessed region of the SGA, we conducted a crude experiment, relying on the known characteristics of the layout of the SGA in memory. In particular, many of the "hot" data structures reside in the lower address range of the SGA. Thus, limit the replication of the SGA to the lower end of its address range is an approximation of the performance achieved if only 25% of SGA could be replicated. Results are shown in Figure 9.

Figure 8. The locality of traffic, i.e., what ratio of cache misses is satisfied locally in a node.

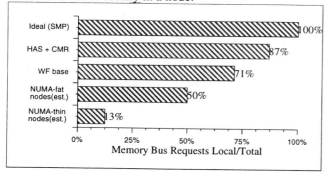

Figure 9. Graph showing the importance of large data replication.

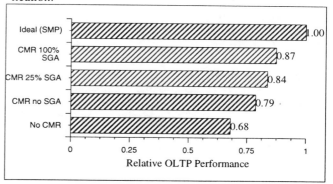

Limiting replication to 25% of the SGA, or approximately 450 MBytes out of 1.8 GBytes, resulted in some 3% performance degradation. These results imply that dynamic replication for special memory regions such as database SGAs could result in a savings of physical memory (less physical replication across nodes). Fat nodes are a definite advantage here; where the two-node system uses 450 MBytes extra physical memory (450 MB * 1 nodes), an eight thin-node system would need to use 3.1 GB of extra physical memory (450 MB * 7 nodes) to replicate 25% of the SGA region.

9.   Related work

COMA [7] and S-COMA [8, 16] are similar to, and have inspired, the creation of WildFire. However, WildFire hardware has been simplified and does not allow the home to migrate between nodes and is not a true COMA. Home migration is instead supported through the software for page migration. WildFire also has a sophisticated algorithm for deciding which data structures should be replicated, while COMA and S-COMA have no support for such a selection strategy.

KSR-1 was architecturally very similar to WildFire in that groups of processors, connected by a ring, formed large nodes. Several nodes were connected together using yet another ring structure. However, rather than using a high-volume tight nonscalable technology to form the large nodes, the rather ineffective ring structure was used also at this level. KSR claimed to be a COMA; but, since each page required space to be allocated all the time in a "home node," it actually only implemented memory replication. Similarly to COMA and S-COMA, KSR only supported replication and cannot dynamically switch to/from the cc-NUMA strategy.

The R-NUMA [6] and the ASCOMA [11] algorithm for page caching strategy is very similar to the one used in WildFire; but, here WildFire chose a simplified implementation strategy based on associative counters. We have also added a scheduling strategy and shown it to be vital to good performance when using an algorithm such as R-NUMA. PRISM [5] presents yet another alternative approach to switching between cc-NUMA and S-COMA. These three simulation studies are based on fairly short-running technical applications. The performance study presented here is based on a real hardware implementation and a long-running commercial application.

10.   Conclusion

In conclusion, MSMP, as implemented in Sun's WildFire prototype, appears to be a viable architecture for OLTP workloads. Application-transparent locality and load balancing are able to relieve the burden of memory-locality awareness from the database application. Coherent Memory Replication and Hierarchical Affinity Scheduling are effective kernel features and are able to manage processes and memory pages for good locality.

These results on the WildFire prototype demonstrate that MSMP with Coherent Memory Replication can effectively hide the locality issue from user processes for the studied application, extending the SMP model beyond the SMP box. The performance results demonstrate 2.13 times that of a NUMA implementation with no optimizations. While the ideal implementation, an even larger SMP with the same memory access time as the local memory access time of WildFire shows 2.44 times. WildFire's applications-transparent optimizations bring it within 13% of the ideal performance.

WildFire is a prototype installed at number of external beta sites. It is not a product offered by Sun Microsystems, Inc.

11.   Acknowledgments

The WildFire architecture was developed by Sun's High-End Server Engineering group, based in Massachusetts. We would like to thank the entire team for tireless and enthusiastic work during the WildFire hardware and software implementation. Cathy Melior-Benoit, Anders Landin, Ken Won, Alan Mandel, Jon Wade, Brad Carlile, Andy Phelps, Alan Charlesworth and Ashok Singhal provided helpful comments on early drafts of this paper. Mark Hill and David Wood added valuable help during the development of the WildFire architecture as well as this paper.

REFERENCES

[1] L. Barroso, K. Gharachorloo, and E. Bugnion. *Memory System Characterization of Commercial Workloads.* ACM/IEEE International Symposium on Computer Architecture (ISCA), June 1998.

[2] T. Brewer and G. Astfalk. *The Evolution of the HP/Convex Exemplar.* In Proceedings of COMPCON Spring 1997.

[3] B. Carlile. *Seeking the Balance: Large SMP Warehouses.* Database Programming & Design, August 1996.

[4] A. Charlesworth. *STARFIRE: Extending the SMP Envelope.* IEEE Micro Jan/Feb 1998. (http://www.sun.com/servers/enterprise/10000/wp/)

[5] K. Ekanadham, B-H. Lim, P. Pattnaik, and M. Snir. *PRISM: An Integrated Architecture for Scalable Shared Memory.* In Proc. HPCA 1998.

[6] B. Falsafi, D. Wood. *Reactive NUMA: A Design for Unifying S-COMA with CC-NUMA.* ACM/IEEE International Symposium on Computer Architecture (ISCA), June 1997.

[7] E. Hagersten, A. Landin, and S. Haridi. *DDM - A Cache-Only Memory Architecture.* IEEE Computer, 25(9):44-54, Sept. 1992.

[8] E. Hagersten, A. Saulsbury, and A. Landin. *Simple COMA Node Implementations.* In Proceedings of Hawaii International Conference on System Science, January 1994.

[9] M. Heinrich, et al. *The Performance impact of flexibility in the Stanford FLASH multiprocessor.* Proceedings of the 6th *International Conference on Architectural Support for Programming Languages and Operating Systems* (ASPLOS) 1994.

[10] C. Hristea, D. Lenoski, and J. Keen. *Measuring Memory Hierarchy Performances of Cache-Coherent Multiprocessors Using Micro Benchmarks.* In Proceedings of *Supercomputing* 1997.

[11] C-C. Kou, J. Carter, R. Kuramkote, and M. Swanson. *AS-COMA: An Adaptive Hybrid Shared Memory Architecture.* ICPP Aug 1998.

[12] J. Laudon and D. Lenoski. *The SGI Origin: A ccNUMA Highly Scalable Server.* ACM/IEEE *International Symposium on Computer Architecture (ISCA),* June 1997

[13] D. Lenoski, J. Laudon, K. Gharachorloo, A. Gupta, and J. Hennessy. *The directory-based protocol for the DASH multiprocessor. International Symposium on Computer Architecture (ISCA),* 1990.

[14] T. Lovett and R. Clapp. *STiNG: A cc-NUMA computer system for the commercial marketplace.* ACM/IEEE *International Symposium on Computer Architecture (ISCA),* June 1996.

[15] L. McVoy and C. Staelin. *lmbench: Portable tools for performance analysis.* USENIX January 1996.

[16] A. Saulsbury, T. Wilkinson, J. Carter, A. Landin, and S. Haridi. *An Argument for Simple COMA.* In *Proceedings of* HPCA 1995.

[17] A. Singhal, D. Broniarczyk, F. Cerauskis, J. Price, L. Yaun, C. Cheng, D. Doblar, S. Fosth, N. Agarwal, K. Harvery, E. Hagersten, and B. Liencres. *A High Performance Bus of Large SMPs.* In *Proceedings of IEEE Hot Interconnects,* P 41-52, Aug 1996.

[18] *TPC-C and TPC-D Results.* http://www.tpc.com/

APPENDIX

Example: Read-to-own (RTO) access, data shared in two remote non-home nodes

1. The I/F detects an RTO which cannot be satisfied locally. It asserts the ignore signal and queues the transaction for the GC. If the accessed page is CMR, do an LPA2GA translation.

2. Send an R_RTO request to the home node.

3. The cache line address is marked as "blocked" in the blocking logic in the home node; a home agent is allocated and performs a directory-cache lookup. The directory entry identifies the two nodes with a shared copy, one of them is identified as the "owner."

4a. The home agent sends H_INV demands to the shared node's slave agent. If the accessed page is CMR in the slave node, do GA2LPA.

4b. The home agent sends an H_RTO demand to the owner's slave agent. If the accessed page is CMR in the slave node, do GA2LPA.

5a. The shared slave agent initiates an invalidate SMP transaction (RTO) and sends a S_ACK reply to the request agent once the SMP transaction has been queued.

5b. The owned slave agent initiates invalidate-retrieve SMP transactions and sends a S_DATA reply to the request agent.

6. The replies carries the "number-of-replies" which tells the request agent to expect two replies before it reissues the RTO transaction on its SMP bus and provides the data.

7. After receiving both replies, the request agent sends an R_CMP to the home node's blocking logic, which now will allow new transactions to the cache line.

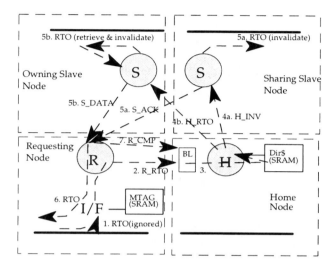

Example: Writeback (WB) NUMA, not canceled

1. The I/F detects an WB to remote memory. It asserts the ignore signal and queues the transaction for the GC. The effect is that the issuing device has still not seen its WB.

2. A request-agent instance is allocated in the GC and sends an R_WB request to the home node.

3. The cache line address is marked as "blocked" in the blocking logic; a home agent is allocated and performs a directory-cache lookup. If the requesting node is not the "owner," the writeback is canceled.

4. The home agent sends H_ACK demands to the shared node's slave agent.

5. The request agent reissues the WB transaction on its SMP bus.

6. The issuing device now sees its own WB and will provide the data to the request agent if it is still the owner. If it is no longer the owner, it will cancel the writeback operation.

7. The request agent sends a data packet to the home node, which unblocks the cache line

8. The home agent reissues the WB transaction on its SMP bus and updates the memory.

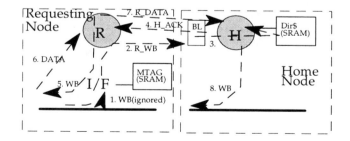

Parallel Dispatch Queue:
A Queue-Based Programming Abstraction To Parallelize Fine-Grain Communication Protocols

Babak Falsafi

School of Electrical & Computer Engineering
Purdue University
1285 EE Building
West Lafayette, IN 47907
babak@ecn.purdue.edu

David A. Wood

Computer Sciences Department
University of Wisconsin–Madison
1210 West Dayton Street
Madison, WI 53706
david@cs.wisc.edu

Abstract

This paper proposes a novel queue-based programming abstraction, Parallel Dispatch Queue (PDQ), that enables efficient parallel execution of fine-grain software communication protocols. Parallel systems often use fine-grain software handlers to integrate a network message into computation. Executing such handlers in parallel requires access synchronization around resources. Much as a monitor construct in a concurrent language protects accesses to a set of data structures, PDQ allows messages to include a synchronization key protecting handler accesses to a group of protocol resources. By simply synchronizing messages in a queue prior to dispatch, PDQ not only eliminates the overhead of acquiring/releasing synchronization primitives but also prevents busy-waiting within handlers.

In this paper, we study PDQ's impact on software protocol performance in the context of fine-grain distributed shared memory (DSM) on an SMP cluster. Simulation results running shared-memory applications indicate that: (i) parallel software protocol execution using PDQ significantly improves performance in fine-grain DSM, (ii) tight integration of PDQ and embedded processors into a single custom device can offer performance competitive or better than an all-hardware DSM, and (iii) PDQ best benefits cost-effective systems that use idle SMP processors (rather than custom embedded processors) to execute protocols. On a cluster of 4 16-way SMPs, a PDQ-based parallel protocol running on idle SMP processors improves application performance by a factor of 2.6 over a system running a serial protocol on a single dedicated processor.

This work is supported in part by Wright Laboratory Avionics Directorate, Air Force Material Command, USAF, under grant #F33615-94-1-1525 and ARPA order no. B550, NSF PYI Award CCR-9157366, NSF Grants MIP-9225097 and MIP-9625558, an IBM graduate fellowship, and donations from A.T.&T. Bell Laboratories, Hewlett Packard, IBM Corporation, and Sun Microsystems. The U.S. Government is authorized to reproduce and distribute reprints for Governmental purposes notwithstanding any copyright notation thereon. The views and conclusions contained herein are those of the authors and should not be interpreted as necessarily representing the official policies or endorsements, either expressed or implied, of the Wright Laboratory Avionics Directorate or the U.S. Government. This research also greatly benefited from computing resources purchased by NSF Institutional Infrastructure Grants No. CDA-9623632.

1 Introduction

Clusters of symmetric multiprocessors (SMPs), have emerged as a promising approach to building large-scale parallel machines [23,22,15,14,5]. The relatively high volumes of small- to medium-scale SMP servers make them cost-effective as building blocks. By connecting SMPs using commodity off-the-shelf networking fabric, system designers hope to construct large-scale parallel machines that scale with both cost and performance.

To program these clusters, researchers are studying a variety of parallel programming abstractions. Some of these abstractions—such as shared virtual memory [5]—communicate data at coarse granularity (e.g., a 4-Kbyte page) using conventional high-overhead legacy TCP/IP protocols. Many abstractions, however, rely on low-overhead messaging—as in Active Messages [25]—and employ fine-grain protocols to exchange small amounts of data (e.g., 8~256 bytes) over the network [23,22,15]. Protocol handlers in such systems, typically execute a small number of instructions to move data between the application's data structures and the network message queues, and optionally perform a small amount of computation and book-keeping and send a reply message.

Fine-grain parallel abstractions traditionally targeted uniprocessor-node parallel computers. As such, the protocol handlers either executed on the node's commodity processor along with computation or an embedded processor on the network interface card. Multiple SMP processors, however, increase the demand on fine-grain protocol execution on a node [23,16,14,6]. To maintain the balance between computation and communication, protocol execution performance must increase commensurate to the number of SMP processors.

One approach to increase software protocol performance is to execute protocol handlers in parallel. Legacy stack protocols (e.g., TCP/IP) have long been parallelized to execute on multiple SMP processors [21,1,10,11]. These protocols synchronize and coordinate handler accesses to system resources—e.g., messaging queues, and protocol and application data structures—using software spin-locks. Fine-grain parallel systems, however, have short handler running times. Acquiring and releasing software locks around individual resources would incur prohibitively high overheads and may result in busy-waiting in these systems, thereby offsetting the gains from parallel handler execution. As such, executing fine-grain protocol handlers in parallel requires efficient synchronization support [15].

Recent research on networking technology for clusters has primarily focused on virtualizing the network interface with no support for fine-grain handler synchronization. Both U-Net [24] and the Virtual Interface Architecture [4] provide multiple pairs of message send/receive queues per node with protected low-overhead access to the network. To avoid fine-grain synchronization, many fine-grain parallel systems [15,22] using these networks partition the node's resources (e.g., memory) among the SMP processors treating each processor as a stand-alone node in a uniprocessor-node parallel computer.

A significant shortcoming of the multiple protocol queues model is that individual processors do not take advantage of the tight coupling of resources within an SMP. Michael et al., recently observed that static partitioning of messages into two protocol queues leads to a significant load imbalance [16]. Rather than partition the resources among protocol queues, processors on one node can collaborate handling messages from a single queue. It follows from a well-known queueing theory result that single-queue/multi-server systems inherently outperform multi-queue/multi-server systems [13].

In this paper we propose *Parallel Dispatch Queue (PDQ)*, a set of mechanisms that allow protocol handlers to synchronize in a single queue prior to dispatch. Much as a monitor synchronization variable in a concurrent language provides mutual exclusion for a set of data structures [7], PDQ allows a message to specify a synchronization *key* corresponding to a *group* of resources a protocol handler accesses when handling the message. By synchronizing messages prior to dispatch and executing handlers in parallel only for messages with distinct keys, PDQ obviates the need for explicit fine-grain synchronization around individual resources within protocol handlers. PDQ can significantly improve performance by not only eliminating the overhead of acquiring/releasing a synchronization primitive but also preventing busy-waiting within handlers. Busy-waiting offsets the gains from parallel handler execution and wastes processor cycles that could otherwise contribute to handling messages.

To fully exploit the potential for parallel handler execution, PDQ requires a protocol programmer/designer to organize resources into fine-grain groups so that frequently executing handlers can access resources in mutual exclusion. Fine-grain protocol handlers, however, occasionally may require access to a larger group of resources—e.g., to migrate an entire application data structure from one node to another. PDQ provides mechanisms to temporarily serialize handler execution so that a handler can access all of the available resources at the cost of a lower protocol performance.

We evaluate PDQ's impact on fine-grain protocol performance in the context of fine-grain distributed shared memory (DSM) [23,22]. As a programming abstraction, however, PDQ has potential for much wider applicability and can be used to efficiently synchronize threads in any fine-grain parallel computing environment. We propose

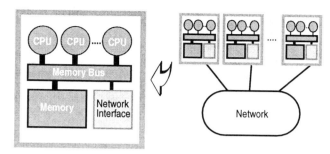

FIGURE 1. An SMP cluster.

and evaluate three fine-grain DSM systems loosely derived from the Wisconsin Typhoon family of DSMs [20]:

- *Hurricane,* is a high-performance system that tightly integrates PDQ, fine-grain sharing hardware, and multiple embedded protocol processors into a single custom device interfacing the network,

- *Hurricane-1,* is a less hardware-intensive system that integrates PDQ with fine-grain sharing hardware into a custom network interface device, but uses dedicated SMP-node processors for protocol execution,

- *Hurricane-1 Mult,* is most cost-effective and is much like *Hurricane-1* but schedules the protocol handlers on idle SMP processors thereby eliminating the extra dedicated SMP processors.

To gauge the performance impact of PDQ on software DSM protocol performance, we compare the Hurricane systems to Simple COMA (S-COMA) [8], an all-hardware DSM protocol implementation. Our model for S-COMA conservatively assumes that all protocol actions are executed in one processor cycle and only accounts for handler memory access times. Results from simulating the Hurricane and S-COMA systems running shared-memory applications indicate that:

- parallel protocol execution using PDQ significantly increases software protocol performance,

- Hurricane with multiple embedded processors offers performance competitive to or better than S-COMA,

- Hurricane-1 Mult benefits most from parallel protocol execution especially for clusters of fat SMPs (i.e., SMPs with a large number of processors), in which many idle processors contribute to protocol execution. Hurricane-1 Mult on a cluster of 4 16-way SMPs increases application performance on average by a factor of 2.6 over a system with a single dedicated SMP protocol processor per node.

The rest of the paper is organized as follows. Section 2 presents an overview of the fine-grain parallel systems we study. Section 3 describes fine-grain synchronization using PDQ in detail and discusses the implementation issues. Section 4 presents an application of PDQ in the context of fine-grain software DSM. Section 5 presents a discussion of the performance results. Finally, Section 6 concludes the paper.

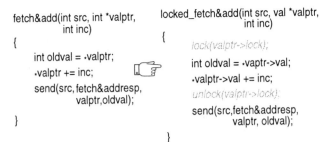

```
fetch&add(int src, int *valptr,
           int inc)
{
    int oldval = ·valptr;
    ·valptr += inc;
    send(src, fetch&addresp,
         valptr,oldval);
}
```

```
locked_fetch&add(int src, val *valptr,
                  int inc)
{
    lock(valptr->lock);
    int oldval = ·vaptr->val;
    ·valptr->val += inc;
    unlock(valptr->lock);
    send(src,fetch&addresp,
         valptr, oldval);
}
```

FIGURE 2. Fine-grain communication protocols: (left) a simple fine-grain protocol handler, (right) protecting handler data structures using locks.

2 Fine-Grain Communication Protocols

Figure 1 illustrates the general class of parallel machines that we study in this paper. Each node consists of an SMP connected to a low-latency, high-bandwidth network via a network interface card residing on the memory bus. A high-level parallel programming abstraction—such as Split-C [3] or coherent distributed shared memory—provides fine-grain communication among processors. Low-level communication occurs *within* a node using the snoopy cache coherent memory bus. A software protocol implements communication *across* SMP nodes using a fine-grain messaging abstraction—such as Active Messages [25]. The software protocol executes either on embedded network interface processors [16,14] or on the SMP commodity processors [15,23].

Figure 2 (left) depicts an example of a simple active-message based protocol which performs a fetch&add operation on a memory word. The handler takes as input parameters the message source node id (src), the address of the memory word (valptr), and the fetch&add increment (inc). The handler reads the current content of the memory word, increments it, and subsequently sends the appropriate reply message. In general, fine-grain protocol handlers are more complex than our simplistic fetch&add handler and access more than just a single resource. For instance, coherent DSM protocols maintain a memory block's sharing status in a directory which is additionally accessed by the protocol handlers.

In this paper, we study parallel execution of fine-grain protocol handlers. Parallel handler execution requires synchronization around the protocol resources. A simple approach to synchronizing handler accesses is to use software spin-locks (e.g., as in parallel TCP/IP protocols [21,1,10,11]). Figure 2 (right) depicts the use of a spin-lock in our fetch&add handler to prevent simultaneous fetch&add operations on the same memory word by parallel handlers. The figure indicates that the lock doubles the number of memory accesses in the fetch&add handler. Moreover, synchronizing within the handler may result in busy-waiting if multiple processors simultaneously access the same memory word. Instead, we propose a technique to synchronize handlers prior to dispatch to obviate the need for synchronizing within handlers.

Message Receive Queue

synchronization key	message data	dispatch status
⋮	⋮	
0x300	fetch&add(....)	dispatched
0x100	fetch&add(....)	*waiting*
0x200	fetch&add(....)	dispatched
0x100	fetch&add(....)	dispatched

Handler dispatch to processors

FIGURE 3. Parallel fetch&add handler dispatch.

3 PDQ: Synchronization in a Queue

Parallel dispatch queue (PDQ) is a set of mechanisms that unify access synchronization to protocol resources (e.g., data in memory) with protocol handler dispatch. Rather than perform fine-grain synchronization (using software spin-locks) around individual resources, PDQ allows a message to request access to a *group* of resources and performs the synchronization at handler dispatch time. A PDQ message specifies a synchronization *key* indicating the set of resources accessed by the message much as a monitor variable in a concurrent language [7] provides mutual exclusion around a group of data structures. A PDQ implementation then dispatches handlers with distinct synchronization keys in parallel while serializing handler execution for a specific synchronization key.

Figure 3 illustrates an example of how a PDQ implementation may dispatch our fetch&add handler (from Figure 2 (left)) in parallel. Assume that the protocol programmer specifies the fetch&add memory word address as the PDQ synchronization key. There are four (active) messages in the queue requiring invocation of the fetch&add handler. The PDQ implementation dispatches fetch&add handlers for messages with memory addresses 0x100, 0x200, and 0x300 in parallel. A fetch&add handler for a second message with memory address 0x100 can not execute due to a first message being handled with the same key. However, other incoming messages with distinct keys will continue to dispatch as long as there are processors waiting to execute handlers.

Fine-grain synchronization in a dispatch queue has two advantages. First, it obviates the need for explicit synchronization within handlers and thereby eliminates the corresponding overhead. Because of the fine-grain nature of resource accesses (e.g., reading a small memory word or block), the overhead of acquiring and releasing a lock may prohibitively increase handler execution time.

Second, without in-queue synchronization, multiple handlers may dispatch and contend for the same resource. Because only one handler succeeds in acquiring the lock, the rest of the dispatched handlers must wait spinning on the lock. An example of handler synchronization after dispatch is address interlocks in the Stanford FLASH [12]. The interlocks guarantee mutual exclusion among messages entering the handler execution pipeline and freeze the pipeline (i.e., busy wait) when two messages have the same address. Busy-waiting, however, wastes cycles that could otherwise contribute to handling messages for which resources are available.

Rather than busy wait, some fine-grain messaging systems (like Optimistic Active Messages (OAM) [26]) postpone handling a message and invoke a light-weight thread to re-execute the handler after the lock is released. Resource contention in such a system, however, may severely impact performance due to the high thread management overhead. Synchronization in a queue eliminates busy waiting by only dispatching and executing handlers that access mutually exclusive resources.

To fully realize the potential for parallel handler execution, PDQ only requires protocol programmers to organize the resources into fine-grain groups which frequently executing handlers can access in mutual exclusion. Fine-grain parallel systems, however, may occasionally execute protocol handlers that require access to a large set of protocol resources. In fine-grain DSM, for instance, the majority of executed protocol handlers implement coherence on fine-grain shared-memory blocks. Occasionally, a protocol handler may manipulate multiple blocks—e.g., to migrate a page of shared memory from one node to another. PDQ also provides mechanisms by which the system can temporarily revert back to sequential handler execution at the cost of lower protocol performance.

3.1 PDQ Programming Model

Much like other queue-based abstractions (e.g., Remote Queues [2]), PDQ provides a programming interface to store and remove entries into a queue. An *enqueue* operation includes at least three parameters specifying a queue name, a synchronization key, and a pointer to a buffer containing the handler dispatch address and the message data. As a high-level synchronization abstraction, the PDQ programming interface does not associate a specific syntax with the queue name. The queue name, for instance, can be an id corresponding to the machine node on which the queue resides, or a global address in a shared-memory system. A *dequeue* operation specifies the queue from which a processor wishes to handle messages. The dequeue operation either returns successfully with a synchronization key and a pointer to a buffer with the message data, or with a flag indicating there are no messages to be dispatched.

Besides synchronization keys used by the protocol programmer to allow in-queue synchronization, PDQ also provides two pre-defined synchronization keys. A *sequential* synchronization key indicates that a handler must execute in isolation. The implementation simply stops dispatching handlers, waits for all handlers to complete, and subsequently dispatches the handler for the message with the sequential key. Once the handler completes, PDQ can resume dispatching handlers in parallel.

PDQ also provides a pre-defined *nosync* key that indicates handler synchronization is not required. A message with a nosync key may invoke a handler at any time. Such a message can be used in a fine-grain parallel system to access remote read-only data structures. Similarly, applications with inherent data races (e.g., using SOR-based algorithms [27]) in which data coherence is not a requirement for correct execution can use nosync messages to perform remote writes to data.

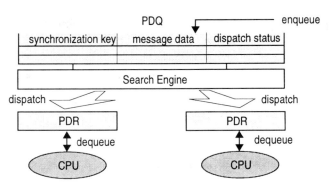

FIGURE 4. Parallel handler dispatch in PDQ.

3.2 PDQ Implementation

In the simplest form, a PDQ implementation (Figure 4) provides a queue of incoming messages, a search engine to perform an associative search through the messages to match synchronization keys, and a per-processor protocol dispatch register (PDR) through which the protocol processors receive dispatched PDQ entries. The implementation also provides per-processor message send queues (not shown) so that processors can send messages without requiring synchronization. The PDQ also keeps track of an entry's dispatch status so that the search engine can determine which keys are currently dispatched.

In this paper, we only consider PDQ implementations in which every machine node includes a single PDQ for incoming messages, and a single PDR and message send queue per protocol processor. Virtualizing the PDQ hardware to provide multiple protected message queues per processor is an active area of research and beyond the scope of this paper [4,24].

Message queues can generally be large and may sometimes spill to memory to remove back pressure from the network [17]. As such, an associative search on the entire queue may not be feasible. The search, however, can be limited to a small number of entries in the PDQ. The implementation can use a small buffer to store PDQ entries that are ready to be dispatched and perform the search in the background while the handlers are executing. The search engine can continue inserting entries from the PDQ into the buffer. The dispatch logic can meanwhile simply remove entries from the small buffer and store them in the PDRs upon demand.

Similarly, for message queues that partially reside in memory, a PDQ implementation may use a buffer to cache several entries at the head of the PDQ. The buffer allows the search engine to proceed without frequently accessing the memory. Such a scheme allows the entire PDQ to spill to memory much like a cachable queue [17]. Buffer entries can be prefetched from memory upon a message dispatch to hide the latency of the memory access.

4 Hurricane: Parallelizing Fine-Grain DSM

We evaluate the impact of parallel handler execution on software protocol performance in the context of fine-grain DSM. Our results, however, are applicable to a wide

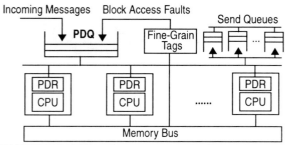

FIGURE 5. A Hurricane custom device.

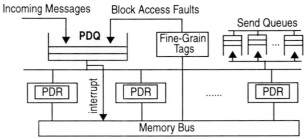

FIGURE 6. A Hurricane-1 custom device.

variety of fine-grain parallel systems and programming abstractions that require efficient fine-grain synchronization and can take advantage of PDQ to execute in parallel. We propose and evaluate three fine-grain DSM systems— *Hurricane*, *Hurricane-1*, and *Hurricane-1 Mult*—loosely derived from the Wisconsin Typhoon family of DSMs [20]. The systems vary in the level of hardware support for fine-grain sharing and result in a spectrum of system cost and performance.

All systems execute a modified version of the Stache coherence protocol [19] written to comply with the PDQ protocol programming interface. Stache is a full-map invalidation-based cache coherence protocol that caches remote data into the node's main memory. To implement caching, Stache allocates memory at page granularity but maintains coherence at a fine-grain cache block granularity (e.g., 32~128 bytes).

Our modified protocol uses cache block shared-memory addresses as the PDQ synchronization key and organizes all protocol data structures (e.g., DSM directory) so that data structure accesses for distinct cache blocks are mutually exclusive. Protocol handlers manipulating data structures for a group of cache blocks—such as page allocation/deallocation handlers—use a special PDQ synchronization key corresponding to an invalid address to guarantee serialization semantics (Section 3.1).

In the rest of this section, we describe in detail the Hurricane fine-grain DSMs. Section 5 presents the performance evaluation and the results of this study.

4.1 Hurricane

Hurricane, like Typhoon [20], is a high-performance hardware-centric implementation that integrates the fine-grain access control logic, messaging queues, and embedded protocol processors into a single custom device that interfaces the network. A Hurricane custom device differs from Typhoon in that it includes multiple embedded processors (rather than one) and provides the PDQ hardware to dispatch protocol handlers to the protocol processors.

Figure 5 illustrates the architecture of a Hurricane custom device. In fine-grain DSM, there are two types of events that invoke protocol handlers. A *block access fault* (generated locally on a node) corresponds to a request to fetch and access a remote shared-memory block. A *message* (from other nodes) typically carries fetched shared data or coherence information such as an invalidation. A PDQ collects all block access faults and incoming messages. Both protocol event types use a global shared-memory address (corresponding to a cache block) as the PDQ

synchronization key. The PDQ dispatches block access faults and messages into a per-processor PDR upon demand. A protocol processor indicates the completion of a handler by writing into its PDR. Upon handler completion, the PDQ dispatches a new entry into a processor's PDR. As in Typhoon, the PDRs reside on the cache bus and can be accessed in a single cycle [20].

4.2 Hurricane-1 & Hurricane-1 Mult

Hurricane-1 is a less hardware-intensive implementation and combines the fine-grain access control logic with the messaging queues on a single device but uses SMP commodity processors to run the software protocol. As in Hurricane, a single PDQ gathers information about all block access faults generated on the node and all of the incoming messages. Hurricane-1 also provides a PDR per SMP processor to implement handler dispatch.

Figure 6 illustrates the architecture of a Hurricane-1 custom device. To provide efficient polling between SMP processors and the PDRs across the memory bus, each PDR is implemented as a cachable control register [17]. By allowing a PDR to be cached in the processor cache, a cachable control register turns polling into a cache hit in the absence of protocol events, thereby eliminating polling traffic over the memory bus. Upon dispatching a protocol event, a Hurricane-1 device invalidates the cached copy of the PDR forcing a protocol processor to read the new PDR contents. A protocol processor indicates completion of a handler by performing an uncached write into its PDR.

A Hurricane-1 device allows both dedicated and multiplexed protocol scheduling on SMP processors [6]. Multiple SMP processors can be dedicated to only execute protocol handlers for the duration of an application's execution. Dedicated protocol processors save overhead by not interfering with the computation, result in a lower protocol occupancy [9]—i.e., the time to execute a protocol handler, and consequently increase protocol performance. Dedicated processors, however, waste processor cycles that could otherwise contribute to computation. In the rest of this paper, we use the term *Hurricane-1* to refer to a fine-grain DSM with the Hurricane-1 custom device and dedicated SMP protocol processors.

A Hurricane-1 device also supports multiplexed protocol scheduling where all SMP processors perform computation and execute protocol handlers whenever idle. To guarantee timely message handling when all processors are busy computing, a Hurricane-1 device provides a mechanism for invoking interrupts on the memory bus (Figure 6). Whenever an SMP processor resumes computation, it signals the device by performing an uncached write into its PDR. An interrupt arbiter on the memory bus distributes interrupts round-robin among SMP processors. To reduce the interrupt frequency and eliminate extra scheduling overhead, a Hurricane-1 device only delivers an interrupt when all SMP processors are busy. Such a policy assumes that interrupts are infrequent and are only invoked to prevent long protocol invocation delays. In the rest of this paper, we use the term *Hurricane-1 Mult* to refer to a fine-grain DSM with the Hurricane-1 custom device and multiplexed SMP processor scheduling.

5 Performance Evaluation

We use the Wisconsin Wind Tunnel II (WWT-II) [18] to simulate SMP cluster implementations of the Hurricane systems (Figure 1). Each node consists of 400 MHz dual-issue statically scheduled processors—modeled after the Ross HyperSPARC—interconnected by a 100 MHz split-transaction bus. We model a highly-interleaved memory system, characteristic of high-performance SMP servers. A snoopy MOESI coherence protocol—modeled after SPARC's MBus protocol—keeps the caches within each node consistent. Our fine-grain DSM software protocol (Section 4) extends the SMP shared memory abstraction across a cluster. Unless specified otherwise, we assume a 64-byte DSM protocol.

WWT-II assumes perfect instruction caches but models data caches and their contention at the memory bus accurately. WWT-II further assumes a point-to-point network with a constant latency of 100 cycles but models contention at the network interfaces. Interrupt overheads are 200 cycles, characteristic of carefully tuned parallel computers.

To gauge the impact of PDQ on software protocol performance we compare the Hurricane systems to a simple all-hardware protocol implementation, Simple-COMA (S-COMA) [8]. S-COMA is an invalidation-based full-map directory protocol much like Stache. The simulation model for S-COMA assumes minimum protocol occupancies accounting for only memory access times. As such, S-COMA's performance numbers in this study are optimistic, making the comparison to S-COMA conservative.

In the rest of this paper, we use the term *protocol processor* to refer to either S-COMA's finite-state-machine (FSM) hardware protocol implementation, an embedded processor on Hurricane, or a commodity SMP processor in Hurricane-1 and Hurricane-1 Mult. Following this terminology, S-COMA is a single-processor device, and Hurricane and Hurricane-1 are either single-processor or multiprocessor devices.

5.1 Protocol Occupancy

Parallel protocol execution improves communication performance by reducing queueing at the protocol processor. Queueing is a function of both application communication characteristics and protocol occupancy [9]. Latency-bound applications primarily benefit from low-occupancy implementations (such as hardware DSM) because a lower occupancy directly reduces roundtrip miss times and thereby communication time. Bandwidth-bound

	Action	S-COMA	Hurricane	Hurricane-1
	detect miss, issue bus transaction	5	5	5
Request	dispatch handler	12	16	87
	get fault state, send	0	36	141
	network latency	100	100	100
Reply	dispatch handler	1	3	51
	directory lookup	8	61	121
	fetch data, change tag, send	136	140	205
	network latency	100	100	100
Response	dispatch handler	1	4	50
	place data, change tag	8	50	63
	resume, reissue bus transaction	6	6	178
	fetch data, complete load	63	63	63
	Total	440	584	1164

TABLE 1. Remote read miss latency breakdown (in 400-MHz cycles) for a 64-byte protocol.

applications, however, may eventually saturate a single protocol processor even in a low-occupancy implementation due to a large number of outstanding protocol events which lead to queueing. Such applications will most likely benefit from parallel protocol execution.

Table 1 compares the minimum protocol occupancies in S-COMA, Hurricane, and Hurricane-1 (Hurricane-1 Mult). The table depicts the breakdown of time for various system events on a simple remote read of a 64-byte block. The table groups the system events into three categories. A request category on the caching node accounts for all the events from the arrival of the bus transaction upon a block access fault to sending a request message to the home node. A reply category on the home node consists of all events from the detection and dispatch of the request message to sending the 64-byte block to the caching node. A response category on the caching node accounts for all events from the dispatch of the reply message to resuming the computation.

Hurricane and S-COMA both tightly integrate the protocol resources on a single custom device. The key source of overhead in Hurricane as compared to S-COMA is the time to execute the handler instructions. Instruction execution overhead in Hurricane results in a significant increase in request/response protocol occupancies of 315%, but only increases the total roundtrip miss time by 33% as compared to S-COMA. Therefore, applications which rely on high request/response bandwidth—e.g., processors on one SMP node access data on several other nodes—can significantly benefit from parallel protocol execution in Hurricane.

In addition to software execution overhead, Hurricane-1 (Hurricane-1 Mult) also incurs the overhead of traversing the memory bus to receive handler dispatch information (i.e., to access the PDR), and moving fine-grain data blocks between the protocol processor caches and message queues [20]. These additional overheads increase the request/response occupancies and total roundtrip latency in Hurricane-1 by 518% and 165% as compared to S-COMA respectively. Because of the large overall protocol occupancies, applications executing on Hurricane-1 can benefit from both higher request/response bandwidth and reply bandwidth through parallel protocol execution.

5.2 Results

Comparing minimum protocol occupancies and roundtrip times helps analyze the latency and bandwidth characteristics of S-COMA and the Hurricane systems for simple DSM operations (e.g., a remote read miss). Real applications, however, exhibit more complex interactions between the memory system and the protocol resulting in an increase in protocol occupancies and roundtrip times. Remote misses, for instance, can result in messages among three nodes in a producer/consumer relationship if neither the producer nor the consumer are the home node for the data. Real data sets also typically do not fit in caches and produce additional memory traffic on the bus. The performance impact of parallel protocol execution also highly depends on how much queueing there is at the protocol processor. Moreover, parallel execution using PDQ is only beneficial when there are multiple independent protocol events (i.e., corresponding to distinct memory blocks) in the queue. In this section, we evaluate our DSMs' performance using shared-memory applications.

Table 2 presents the applications we use in this study and the corresponding input parameters. *Barnes, cholesky, fft, fmm, radix* and *water-sp* are all from the SPLASH-2 [27] benchmark suite. *Em3d* is a shared-memory implementation of the Split-C benchmark [3].

The table also depicts application speedups for a cluster of 8 8-way SMPs interconnected by S-COMA hardware. The speedups are calculated with respect to application running times on a uniprocessor. *Water-sp* is primarily computation-intensive and achieves near-linear speedups. *Cholesky* is primarily communication-bound, suffers from a severe load imbalance [27], and does not speed up much. *Barnes, fmm,* and *em3d* have moderate communication-to-computation ratios and achieve a 50% efficiency with 64 processors. *Fft* and *radix* are communication-bound and exhibit poor speedups. In the rest of the section, we present performance results normalized to our base S-COMA system.

Baseline System Performance

Figure 7 depicts a performance comparison of the base case systems. Our baseline system corresponds to a cluster of 8 SMPs. The S-COMA and Hurricane, and Hurricane-1 Mult systems use 8-way SMPs. The Hurricane-1 systems use 8 SMP processors per node for computation and extra dedicated SMP processors for protocol execution. Performance results are normalized to S-COMA. The figure indicates that S-COMA improves performance over a software protocol running on an embedded processor (Hurricane 1pp) on average by 32%. The figure also indicates that S-COMA significantly improves performance (by up to 89%) over a software protocol implementation

Benchmark	Description	Input Set	Speedup
barnes	Barnes-Hut N-body simulation	16K particles	31
cholesky	Sparse cholesky factorization	tk29.O	5
em3d	3-D wave propagation	76K nodes, 15% remote	34
fft	Complex 1-D radix-$\sqrt{n}$ FFT	1M points	19
fmm	Fast Multipole N-body simulation	16K particles	31
radix	Integer radix sort	4M integers	12
water-sp	Water molecule force simulation	4096 molecules	61

TABLE 2. Applications, input sets, and S-COMA speedups on a cluster of 8 8-way SMPs.

running on a commodity SMP processor (Hurricane-1 1pp). These results are consistent with those of Reinhardt et al. comparing Typhoon and Typhoon-1 (which are similar to single-processor Hurricane and Hurricane-1) against S-COMA [20].

The graphs indicate that there are three classes of applications. The first class is *water-sp* which is primarily computation-intensive and not sensitive to protocol execution speed. All systems perform within 91% of S-COMA for *water-sp*.

The second class consists of *barnes* and *fmm* which are primarily latency-bound and do not substantially benefit from parallel protocol execution. In these applications, much of the execution time is spent in a force calculation phase between bodies in a galaxy. Communication in this phase is sporadic and evenly distributed among the nodes. These applications benefit more from a lower protocol occupancy than parallel protocol execution.

A single-processor Hurricane system performs well (within 90% of S-COMA) running *barnes* and *fmm*. Two-processor and four-processor Hurricane systems improve performance over a single-processor configuration by at most 11% and 13% respectively. A single-processor Hurricane-1 system reduces the performance to approximately within 60% of S-COMA making room for performance improvement. Nevertheless, adding protocol processors to Hurricane-1 increases the performance to at most within 84% of S-COMA. Furthermore, a Hurricane-1 with four dedicated protocol processors improves performance over Hurricane-1 Mult; handler scheduling and the resulting cache interference in Hurricane-1 Mult incur overhead and increase protocol occupancy (Section 4.2). The parallelism in handler execution is not high enough to offset the extra scheduling overhead.

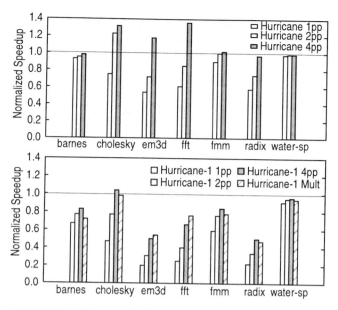

FIGURE 7. Comparing baseline system performance.
The figure compares Hurricane's (above) and Hurricane-1's (below) performance with S-COMA on a cluster of 8 SMPs. The Hurricane, Hurricane-1 Mult, and S-COMA systems use 8-way SMPs. The Hurricane-1 systems use additional dedicated protocol processors per SMP. The graphs plot application speedups in one- (1pp), two- (2pp), and four-processor (4pp) Hurricane and Hurricane-1 systems, and Hurricane-1 Mult system. The speedups are normalized to S-COMA. Values appearing under the horizontal line at 1 indicate a better performance under S-COMA.

The third class consists of *cholesky, em3d, fft,* and *radix* which are all bandwidth-bound applications. *Cholesky* incurs a large number of compulsory misses to data that is not actively shared. As such, the reply handlers in *cholesky* frequently involve reading data from memory and have high occupancies. Multiprocessor Hurricane devices substantially improve performance over single-processor devices by parallelizing the memory accesses thereby increasing the reply bandwidth. A two-processor Hurricane actually improves performance over S-COMA by 23%. Limited parallelism in protocol execution, however, limits Hurricane's performance improvement over S-COMA to at most 32% with four protocol processors.

In *cholesky,* Hurricane-1's performance also extensively benefits from multiple protocol processors. Adding protocol processors significantly improves performance even up to four processors. The high protocol occupancy in Hurricane-1 results in large queueing delays at the protocol processor. Parallel protocol processors reduce queueing delays and thereby improve performance. The four-processor Hurricane-1 outperforms S-COMA, and the Hurricane-1 Mult system both performs very close to S-COMA and improves cost by eliminating the extra dedicated protocol processors.

Communication and computation in *em3d, fft,* and *radix* proceed in synchronous phases. Communication in these applications is highly bandwidth-intensive, bursty, and of a producer/consumer nature. In *em3d,* communication involves reading/writing memory blocks from/to neighboring processors. *Fft,* and *radix* both perform all-to-all communication with every processor exchanging its

produced data with other processors. The large degrees of sharing in *em3d, fft,* and *radix,* result in frequent coherence activity. Coherence events often involve executing protocol handlers that only modify state and send control messages (e.g., an invalidation). Because the handlers do not transfer data between the memory and the network, the handlers' occupancy in a software protocol is primarily due to instruction execution. Software protocol implementations, therefore, have a much higher occupancy for control messages than hardware implementations. The figure indicates that the single-processor Hurricane systems at best perform within 61% of S-COMA. The single-processor Hurricane-1 systems exhibit extremely poor performance and at best reach within 25% of S-COMA's performance.

Multiprocessor Hurricane systems help mitigate the software protocol execution bottleneck in *em3d, fft,* and *radix.* The two-processor Hurricane systems improve performance over a single-processor system by at most 40% because parallel protocol execution at a minimum incurs the additional overhead of protocol state migration among the protocol processor caches. The four-processor Hurricane systems' performance ranges from slightly worse than S-COMA (in *radix*) to 36% better than S-COMA (in *fft*). Hurricane-1's performance also significantly improves with multiple protocol processors but at best reaches within 76% of S-COMA (in *fft* under Hurricane-1 Mult).

To summarize the results, a four-processor Hurricane system on average increases speedups by 12% over S-COMA, and a four-processor Hurricane-1 on average performs within 76% of S-COMA. More importantly, the most cost-effective Hurricane-1 Mult system performs within 74% of an all-hardware S-COMA system without requiring extra dedicated protocol processors. Previous research indicated that static partitioning of resources among protocol processors results in a load imbalance rendering parallel protocol execution less beneficial [16]. These results indicate that fine-grain handler synchronization using PDQ can realize the full potential of parallelism in fine-grain protocol execution.

Impact of Clustering Degree

This section evaluates the impact of clustering degree—i.e., the number of processors in every SMP node—on the relative performance of the systems while maintaining the number of processors and the total amount of memory in the system constant.

Clustering typically increases the total amount of protocol traffic generated per machine node [23]. The increase in protocol traffic, however, depends on an application's sharing patterns. On the one hand, clustering allows processors to share a single cached copy of remote data, reducing protocol traffic generated per processor. On the other hand, in the absence of sharing, clustering may linearly increase protocol traffic in/out of a node with the increase in the number of processors per node. Clustering also reduces the number of network interfaces in the system, placing higher demands on the protocol processors favoring parallel protocol execution.

Figure 8 compares Hurricane's performance against S-COMA for a cluster of 16 4-way SMPs (above) and a cluster of 4 16-way SMPs (below). The graphs indicate that a higher clustering degree increases the performance

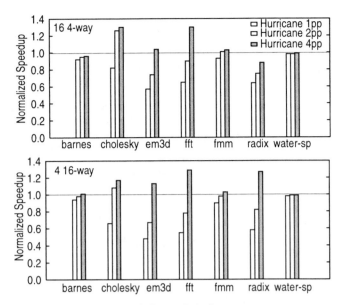

FIGURE 8. Impact of clustering degree on Hurricane's performance.

The figure compares performance in S-COMA and Hurricane on a cluster of 16 4-way SMPs (above), and a cluster of 4 16-way SMPs (below). The graphs plot application speedups in one- (1pp), two- (2pp), and four-processor (4pp) Hurricane systems. The speedups are normalized to S-COMA. Values appearing under the horizontal line at 1 indicate a better performance under S-COMA.

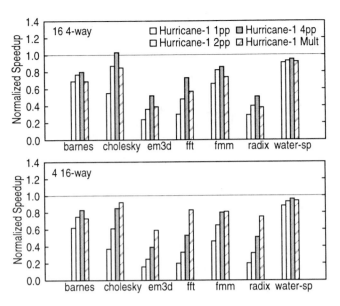

FIGURE 9. Impact of clustering degree on Hurricane-1's performance.

The figure compares performance in S-COMA and Hurricane-1 on a cluster of 16 (above) and 4 (below) SMPs. The S-COMA and Hurricane-1 Mult systems use 4-way (above) and 16-way (below) SMPs respectively. The rest of the Hurricane-1 systems use additional dedicated protocol processors per SMP. The graphs plot application speedups in one- (1pp), two- (2pp), and four-processor (4pp) Hurricane-1, and Hurricane-1 Mult systems. The speedups are normalized to S-COMA. Values appearing under the horizontal line at 1 indicate a better performance under S-COMA.

gap between the single-processor Hurricane systems and S-COMA in most of the applications. This result indicates that queueing delays due to a smaller number of network interface devices in the system has a higher impact on performance than the gains from sharing remote data.

Multiple protocol processors in Hurricane systems help close the performance gap between software and hardware implementations. With a clustering degree of 16, a four-processor Hurricane system outperforms S-COMA in all the applications except for *water-sp*; Hurricane's performance in *water-sp* is within 99% of S-COMA. An increase in the clustering degree from 4 to 16 increases a four-processor Hurricane's performance on average from 7% to 13% over S-COMA's.

Figure 9 illustrates the impact of clustering degree on Hurricane-1's performance. A high clustering degree has a large impact on the single-processor Hurricane-1's performance. Because of the poor performance of the single-processor system, even the large performance improvements due to four protocol processors fail to make Hurricane-1 competitive with S-COMA. Not surprisingly, Hurricane-1 Mult substantially benefits from a high clustering degree and outperforms a four-processor Hurricane-1 system in all bandwidth-bound applications. Increasing the clustering degree from 4 to 16 also allows Hurricane-1 Mult to improve performance from 65% to 80% of S-COMA.

Impact of Block Size

An increase in the protocol block size increases the overall protocol bandwidth out of a node. Large block sizes also increase the fraction of protocol occupancy due to data transfer time between memory and the network.

Amortizing the software protocol overhead over a larger overall occupancy reduces the performance gap between software and hardware protocol implementations.

Large blocks, however, result in false sharing in applications with very fine sharing granularity thereby increasing protocol activity. Higher protocol activity intensifies queueing at the protocol processors and results in a larger performance gap between software and hardware protocol implementations. Parallelizing protocol execution alleviates the performance loss due to false sharing by reducing queueing at the protocol processors.

Figure 10 compares Hurricane's performance against S-COMA's for a 32-byte protocol (above) and a 128-byte protocol (below). The graphs corroborate the intuition that an increase in the block size reduces the performance gap between the single-processor Hurricane systems and S-COMA in some applications, and increases the gap in others. With a 128-byte block, *cholesky, em3d, fft, radix, water-sp* all exhibit better performance under single-processor Hurricane systems relative to S-COMA. *Barnes* and *fmm* share data at very fine granularity, suffer from false sharing with 128-byte blocks, and therefore experience a larger performance gap between the single-processor Hurricane and S-COMA.

The graphs also indicate that a large block size not only favors the single-processor Hurricane system, but also the multiprocessor systems. Two protocol processors make a Hurricane system competitive with S-COMA in all the applications. A four-processor Hurricane system on average speeds up application execution time by 20% over

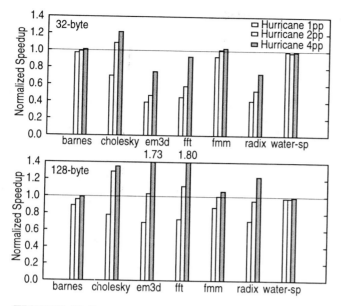

FIGURE 10. Impact of block size on Hurricane's performance.

The figure compares performance in S-COMA and Hurricane for a 32-byte (above) and a 128-byte (below) block protocol. The graphs plot application speedups in one- (1pp), two- (2pp), and four-processor (4pp) Hurricane systems. The speedups are normalized to S-COMA. Values appearing under the horizontal line at 1 indicate a better performance under S-COMA.

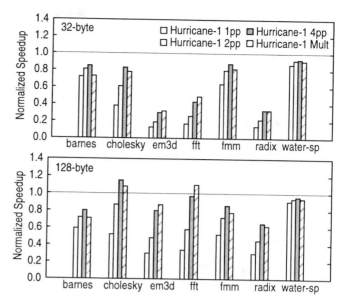

FIGURE 11. Impact of block size on Hurricane-1's performance.

The figure compares performance in S-COMA and Hurricane-1 for a 32-byte (above) and a 128-byte (below) block protocol. The graphs plot application speedups in one- (1pp), two- (2pp), and four-processor (4pp) Hurricane-1, and Hurricane-1 Mult systems. The speedups are normalized to S-COMA. Values appearing under the horizontal line at 1 indicate a better performance under S-COMA.

S-COMA. These results, indicate that pipelining protocol handler execution to allow for multiple outstanding memory requests may enable single-processor devices to achieve a high protocol bandwidth with large blocks.

Figure 11 illustrates the impact of protocol block size on Hurricane-1's performance. A large block size has a higher impact on a single-processor Hurricane-1's performance as compared to Hurricane. Large blocks benefit systems with high software protocol overheads (as in Hurricane-1) allowing the system to amortize the overhead over a larger protocol occupancy. Much as in the Hurricane systems, multiprocessor Hurricane-1 systems close the performance gap between Hurricane-1 and S-COMA. A four-processor Hurricane-1 system, and a Hurricane-1 Mult system both reach approximately within 88% of S-COMA's performance.

6 Conclusions

Many parallel applications and programming abstractions rely on low-overhead messaging and employ fine-grain communication protocols to exchange small amounts of data over the network. Traditionally, fine-grain parallel systems targeted uniprocessor-node parallel computers and executed the fine-grain protocol handlers on either the node's single commodity processor or an embedded network interface processor. With the emergence of cluster of SMPs, however, multiple SMP processors increase the demand on software protocol execution. One approach to provide communication performance commensurate to the number of SMP processors, is to execute fine-grain protocol handlers in parallel.

In this paper, we proposed a novel set of mechanisms, Parallel Dispatch Queue (PDQ), to efficiently execute fine-grain protocol handlers in parallel. Much as a monitor synchronization variable protects a set of data structures in a concurrent programming language, PDQ requires protocol programmers/designers to partition protocol resources into mutually exclusive groups and annotate protocol messages with a corresponding synchronization key. A PDQ implementation then dispatches and executes handlers for messages with distinct synchronization keys in parallel and only serializes handler execution for a given key. In-queue synchronization at handler dispatch time obviates the need for explicit fine-grain synchronization around individual resources within handlers, eliminates busy-waiting, and increases protocol performance.

We studied PDQ's impact on software protocol performance in the context of fine-grain DSM implemented on a cluster of SMPs. Simulation results running shared-memory applications indicated that: (i) parallel protocol execution using PDQ significantly improves the communication performance in a software fine-grain DSM, (ii) tight integration of PDQ and embedded processors in a single custom device can offer performance competitive or better than an all-hardware DSM, and (iii) PDQ best benefits cost-effective systems that use idle SMP processors (rather than custom embedded processors) for protocol execution. Application performance on a cluster of 4 16-way SMPs using PDQ and idle SMP processors for protocol execution on average improved by a factor of 2.6 over a system with a single dedicated SMP protocol processor.

References

[1] M. Bjoerkman and P. Gunningberg. Locking effects in multiprocessor implementations of protocols. In *SIG-COMM '93*, pages 74–83, September 1993.

[2] E. A. Brewer, F. T. Chong, L. T. Liu, S. D. Sharma, and J. Kubiatowicz. Remote queues: Exposing message queues for optimization and atomicity. In *Proceedings of the Seventh ACM Symposium on Parallel Algorithms and Architectures (SPAA)*, pages 42–53, 1995.

[3] D. E. Culler, A. Dusseau, S. C. Goldstein, A. Krishnamurthy, S. Lumetta, T. von Eicken, and K. Yelick. Parallel programming in Split-C. In *Proceedings of Supercomputing '93*, pages 262–273, Nov. 1993.

[4] D. Dunning, G. Regnier, G. McAlpine, D. Cameron, B. Shubert, F. Berry, A. M. Merritt, E. Gronke, and C. Dodd. The virtual interface architecture. *IEEE Micro*, 18(2):66–76, 1998.

[5] A. Erlichson, N. Nuckolls, G. Chesson, and J. Hennessy. SoftFLASH: Analyzing the performance of clustered distributed virtual shared memory supporting fine-grain shared memory. In *Proceedings of the Seventh International Conference on Architectural Support for Programming Languages and Operating Systems (ASPLOS VII)*, Oct. 1996.

[6] B. Falsafi and D. A. Wood. Scheduling communication on an SMP node parallel machine. In *Proceedings of the Third IEEE Symposium on High-Performance Computer Architecture*, pages 128–138, Feb. 1997.

[7] C. Ghezzi and M. Jazayeri. *Programming Language Concepts*. Wiley, 2/e edition, 1987.

[8] E. Hagersten, A. Saulsbury, and A. Landin. Simple COMA node implementations. In *Proceedings of the 27th Hawaii International Conference on System Sciences*, Jan. 1994.

[9] C. Holt, M. Heinrich, J. P. Singh, E. Rothberg, and J. Hennessy. The effects of latency, occupancy, and bandwidth in distributed shared memory multiprocessors. Technical Report CSL-TR-95-660, Computer Systems Laboratory, Stanford University, January 1995.

[10] N. C. Hutchinson and L. L. Peterson. The x-Kernel: An architecture for implementing network protocols. *IEEE Transactions on Software Engineering*, 17(1):64–76, Jan. 1991.

[11] M. Kaiserswerth. The parallel protocol engine. *IEEE/ACM Transactions on Networking*, 1(6):650–663, December 1993.

[12] J. Kuskin et al. The stanford FLASH multiprocessor. In *Proceedings of the 21st Annual International Symposium on Computer Architecture*, pages 302–313, Apr. 1994.

[13] E. D. Lazowska, J. Zahorjan, G. S. Graham, and K. C. Sevcik. *Quantitative System Performance: Computer System Analysis Using Queueing Network Models*. Prentice Hall, 1984.

[14] T. Lovett and R. Clapp. STiNG: A CC-NUMA compute system for the commercial marketplace. In *Proceedings of the 23rd Annual International Symposium on Computer Architecture*, May 1996.

[15] S. S. Lumeta, A. M. Manwaring, and D. E. Culler. Multiprotocol active messages on a cluster of SMP's. In *Proceedings of Supercomputing '97*, November 1997.

[16] M. Michael, A. K. Nanda, B.-H. Lim, and M. L. Scott. Coherence controller architectures for SMP-based CC-NUMA mulitprocessors. In *Proceedings of the 24th Annual International Symposium on Computer Architecture*, May 1997.

[17] S. S. Mukherjee, B. Falsafi, M. D. Hill, and D. A. Wood. Coherent network interfaces for fine-grain communication. In *Proceedings of the 23rd Annual International Symposium on Computer Architecture*, pages 247–258, May 1996.

[18] S. S. Mukherjee, S. K. Reinhardt, B. Falsafi, M. Litzkow, S. Huss-Lederman, M. D. Hill, J. R. Larus, and D. A. Wood. Wisconsin Wind Tunnel II: A fast and portable parallel architecture simulator. In *Workshop on Performance Analysis and Its Impact on Design (PAID)*, June 1997.

[19] S. K. Reinhardt, J. R. Larus, and D. A. Wood. Tempest and Typhoon: User-level shared memory. In *Proceedings of the 21st Annual International Symposium on Computer Architecture*, pages 325–337, Apr. 1994.

[20] S. K. Reinhardt, R. W. Pfile, and D. A. Wood. Decoupled hardware support for distributed shared memory. In *Proceedings of the 23rd Annual International Symposium on Computer Architecture*, May 1996.

[21] J. D. Salehi, J. F. Kurose, and D. Towsley. The effectiveness of affinity-based scheduling in multiprocessor networking. *IEEE Transactions on Networking*, 4(4), Aug. 1996.

[22] D. J. Scales, K. Gharachorloo, and A. Aggarwal. Fine-grain software distributed shared memory on SMP clusters. In *Proceedings of the Fourth IEEE Symposium on High-Performance Computer Architecture*, Feb. 1998.

[23] I. Schoinas, B. Falsafi, M. D. Hill, J. Larus, and D. A. Wood. Sirocco: Cost-effective fine-grain distributed shared memory. In *Proceedings of the Sixth International Conference on Parallel Architectures and Compilation Techniques*, October 1998.

[24] T. von Eicken, A. Basu, V. Buch, and W. Vogels. U-net: A user-level network interface for parallel and distributed computing. In *Proceedings of the 15th ACM Symposium on Operating System Principles (SOSP)*, pages 40–53, Dec. 1995.

[25] T. von Eicken, D. E. Culler, S. C. Goldstein, and K. E. Schauser. Active messages: a mechanism for integrating communication and computation. In *Proceedings of the 19th Annual International Symposium on Computer Architecture*, pages 256–266, May 1992.

[26] D. A. Wallach, W. C. Hsieh, K. L. Johnson, M. F. Kaashoek, and W. E. Weihl. Optimistic active messages: A mechanism for scheduling communic ation with computation. In *Fifth ACM SIGPLAN Symposium on Principles & Practice of Parallel Programming (PPOPP)*, July 1995.

[27] S. C. Woo, M. Ohara, E. Torrie, J. P. Singh, and A. Gupta. The SPLASH-2 programs: Characterization and methodological considerations. In *Proceedings of the 22nd Annual International Symposium on Computer Architecture*, pages 24–36, July 1995.

Limits to the Performance of Software Shared Memory: A Layered Approach

Angelos Bilas[1], Dongming Jiang[2], Yuanyuan Zhou[2], and Jaswinder Pal Singh[2]

[1]Department of Electrical and Computer Engineering
10 King's College Road
University of Toronto
Toronto, ON M5S 3G4, Canada
bilas@eecg.toronto.edu

[2]Department of Computer Science
35 Olden Street
Princeton University
Princeton, NJ 08544, USA
{dj, yzhou, jps}@cs.princeton.edu

Abstract

Much research has been done in fast communication on clusters and in protocols for supporting software shared memory across them. However, the end performance of applications that were written for the more proven hardware–coherent shared memory is still not very good on these systems. Three major layers of software (and hardware) stand between the end user and parallel performance, each with its own functionality and performance characteristics. They include the communication layer, the software protocol layer that supports the programming model, and the application layer. These layers provide a useful framework to identify the key remaining limitations and bottlenecks in software shared memory systems, as well as the areas where optimization efforts might yield the greatest performance improvements. This paper performs such an integrated study, using this layered framework, for two types of software distributed shared memory systems: page-based shared virtual memory (SVM) and fine-grained software systems (FG).

For the two system layers (communication and protocol), we focus on the performance costs of basic operations in the layers rather than on their functionalities. This is possible because their functionalities are now fairly mature. The less mature applications layer is treated through application restructuring. We examine the layers individually and in combination, understanding their implications for the two types of protocols and exposing the synergies among layers.

1 Introduction

As clusters of workstations, PCs or symmetric multiprocessors (SMPs) become important platforms for parallel computing, there is increasing interest in supporting the attractive, shared address space (SAS) programming model across them in software. The traditional reason is that it may provide successful low-cost alternatives to tightly–coupled, hardware–coherent distributed shared memory (DSM) machines. A more important reason, however, is that clusters and hardware DSMs are emerging as the two major types of platforms available to users of multiprocessing. Users would like to write parallel programs once and run them efficiently on both types of platforms, and programming models that do not allow this may be at a disadvantage. Thus, despite (and in fact, because of) the success of hardware–coherent DSM, software shared memory on clusters remains an important topic of research.

Supporting a programming model gives rise to a layered communication architecture that is shown in Figure 1. The lowest layer is the *communication layer*, which consists of the communication hardware and the low level communication library that provide basic messaging facilities. Next is the *protocol* layer that provides the programming model to the parallel application programmer. We assume all–software DSM protocols in this paper, and focus on two well-studied approaches: page–based shared virtual memory (SVM) and fine–grained DSM (FG). Finally, above the programming model or protocol layer runs the *application* itself.

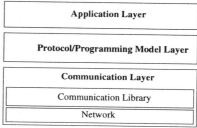

Figure 1: The layers that affect the end application performance in software shared memory.

The last decade has seen a lot of excellent research in the individual layers, especially the lower two system layers [4, 3, 5, 13, 11, 12, 21, 18, 17]. Still, software shared memory systems currently yield performance that is, for several classes of applications, far behind that of hardware–coherent systems even at quite small scale.

This paper uses a layered framework to examine where the major gains (or losses) in the parallel performance of applications can or cannot come from in the future, both in the individual layers and through combinations of them, and to help cluster software and hardware designers determine where best to spend their energy for the goal of supporting software shared memory.

In the application layer, the main variable is how an application is structured or orchestrated for parallelism. The two system layers (communication and protocol) however, have both functionality and performance characteristics, all of which contribute to end application performance. It is this space that we need to navigate. This paper treats the functionality of the system layers as fixed (since it is now quite mature), and varies only their basic performance costs. Results obtained by varying costs can suggest modifications in functionality that can reduce or avoid the critical costs. The less mature, application layer is treated by examining the impact of application restructuring, as performed for SVM in [10], starting from programs that are optimized for moderate-scale hardware coherent systems. We examine the impact of the layers individually and in combination, and also isolate the impact of different costs in each layer. Solving problems or reducing costs at each layer has its own advantages, disadvantages, and potential for being realizable, and is under the control of different forces. Knowledge of actual trends in the layers (application or system) can be used to draw implications for the future of different approaches.

While some individual aspects of this work have been studied in the past (see Section 4), the contributions of this paper are: (i) the layered approach in which it investigates performance issues, which we believe is generally useful, (ii) studying the effects of each layer for both *FG* and *SVM*, (iii) studying the synergies among layers, and (iv) providing detailed results and analysis for a wide range of applications.

Our highest level conclusions are: (i) With currently achievable system parameters the *FG* and *SVM* approaches are competitive in performance, at least at the scale we examine, with the tradeoffs depending on particular application characteristics. (ii) For *FG*, other than access control costs the most important layer to improve is the communication layer (especially overhead and occupancy), and the impact of access control costs are relatively independent. (iii) *SVM* exhibits a much richer story: All three layers are important and exhibit a lot of synergy, and no one or even two of them will suffice for a wide range of applications: in general, the order of importance is application, communication, protocol. While the set of demands is broader, this may be an advantage since there is less dependence on particular aspects of one layer that may be very difficult to control. (iv) Overall, if only one system layer can be improved, it should be the communication layer, though different aspects of it matter for different protocols.

Section 2 describes the protocols and the methodology we use. Section 3 presents our main results for each layer individually as well as for the synergy among them. Section 4 briefly discusses some closely related work, and Section 5 provides a discussion and concludes the paper.

2 Methodology

Although real *SVM* systems are available, a study that varies (and especially reduces) costs in the manner done here can only be done through simulation. We therefore use a detailed execution–driven simulator which we validate carefully against real systems as discussed later. While computational clusters are moving toward using SMP rather than uniprocessor nodes, we perform this study assuming uniprocessor nodes, primarily because protocols for SMP nodes are not so mature and there are many more interactions in the nodes that can affect performance in subtle ways.

Protocols: Since we use well known, state-of-the-art protocols, we describe them only briefly. Page–based coherence protocols use the virtual memory mechanism of microprocessors for access control at page granularity [13]. Fine–grained access control can be provided by either hardware support or by code instrumentation in software [18]. In both cases, we assume the coherence protocol runs in software handlers rather than in hardware, and on the main processor rather than on co–processors.

For *SVM*, we use the Home–based Lazy Release Consistency (HLRC) protocol [21], which implements the lazy release consistency (LRC) model [11] to reduce the impact of false sharing. Both HLRC and older LRC protocols use software *twinning* and *diffing* to solve the multiple–writer problem, but with different schemes for propagating and merging

diffs (updated data). Traditional LRC schemes maintain distributed diffs at the writers, from where they must be fetched on a page fault [11]. In HLRC, the writer sends the diffs eagerly to a designated home node for the page, and the diffs are applied there to the home copy which is always kept up to date according to the consistency model. On a page fault, instead of fetching diffs from previous writers, the whole page is fetched from the home.

Fine–grained protocols are able to reduce the occurrence of false sharing by virtue of their fine granularity of coherence, so they do not rely heavily on relaxed consistency models. However, they require support for fine–grained access control. Our fine–grained implementation (*FG*) uses sequential consistency, is based on the Stache protocol [15], and is similar in protocol structure to many directory–based hardware implementations [1]. Access control is assumed to be provided at any fixed power of two granularity for a given application. The fact that we use the best–performing granularity for each application in the *FG* case requires some programmer intervention. The granularities used are 64 bytes in all other cases than the regular applications: FFT (4 KBytes), LU (4 KBytes) and Ocean (1 KByte).

Simulation environment: Our simulation environment is built on top of augmint [19], an execution driven simulator using the *x86* instruction set, and runs on *x86* systems. It models a cluster of 16 uniprocessor nodes connected with a commodity Myrinet-like interconnect [4] (Figure 2). Contention is modeled in great detail at all levels, including the network end–points, except in the network links and switches themselves. Thus, when we change protocol or communication layer costs, the impact on contention is included as well. The processor has a P6–like instruction set, and is assumed to be a 1 IPC processor. Details about the simulator can be found in [1].

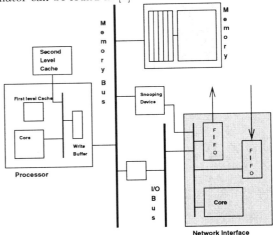

Figure 2: Simulated node architecture.

The fine-grained access control needed for *FG* can be provided via either code instrumentation [18, 17] or hardware support [16]. Code instrumentation is also used for polling to handle asynchronous incoming messages, which would otherwise cause expensive and frequent interrupts (interrupts are much less frequent in the coarser-grained *SVM*, so the tradeoffs between interrupts and polling are less clear

---

[1]Protocols using more complex, delayed consistency or single-writer eager release consistency were found to perform only a little better in [22].

there). Since we do not have access to high-performance instrumentation for the x86 instruction set, and since it is unclear what cost to ascribe to hardware access control which can be implemented in various ways, we assume access control and polling are free in the *FG* protocol (access control is already built in to the processor for *SVM*). In fact, due to our lack of instrumentation, the simulator uses an interrupt-like mechanism for asynchronous message handling, but charges costs based on those of invoking a handler in polling. Actual instrumentation costs can likely be simply added to execution time to first order, since they are just additional compute instructions. We quote some instrumentation overhead data from the Shasta system, which are probably optimistic for x86 machines and hence are provided only to give a very rough idea. Directly, the results we obtain can only be used to compare *SVM* with software *FG* assuming very efficient hardware access control. The cost of each protocol handler is computed according to the protocol task it performs.

The simulator has been validated against real system implementations for both *FG* (by setting parameters close to those of the Typhoon–zero system [16] and comparing with it) and *SVM* for our real cluster [1]. The results, omitted for space reasons, are surprisingly accurate.

Applications: Table 1 shows the applications and the problem sizes we use in this work. These applications are written for hardware DSM and they are known to deliver excellent parallel speedups for hardware cache coherent systems at the 16–processor scale we assume in this paper. They are taken from the SPLASH–2 suite (and from the restructured versions in [10]), and will not be described further here.

Application	Problem Size	Instrum. cost
Barnes	8K particles	8%
FFT	1M points	29%
LU	512x512 matrix	29%
Ocean	514x514 grid	12%
Radix	1M keys	33%
Raytrace	car	29%
Volrend	256x256x256 CT head	5%
Water-Nsquared	512 mols	14%
Water-Spatial	512 mols	18%

Table 1: Applications, problem sizes and instrumentation costs. The last column is the instrumentation cost in the aggressive, Alpha-based Shasta system, which we quote from [17].

Protocol layer parameters: The protocol costs we vary and their achievable values that are assumed for the base system are shown in Table 2. The page protection cost is the cost of mprotect. A single mprotect call may be made to the kernel for a range of contiguous pages; it incurs a startup processing overhead, that is simulated, plus this per–page cost. This cost is aggressive for current operating systems but achievable with existing technology (we verified that using a somewhat larger cost does not change the results much). The effects of twinning and diffing on the cache (and the misses incurred) are simulated. Protocol handlers themselves cost a variable number of cycles. The basic handler cost parameter is set to 100 cycles for both *SVM* and *FG*; additional costs for diffing or traversing lists (e.g. write notice lists) are added to this cost. The cost for traversing lists depends on processor speed and is set to 20 cycles per list element. The cost for diffing is varied to allow for studying the importance of diffing in *SVM*. All these costs closely approximate those of our real implementation. The set of values we consider for the protocol layer costs are: the *achievable* set, the *best* (idealized) set, where all costs are set

to zero, and the *halfway* set, where all costs are halfway between achievable and best. We do not examine a worse set of costs than the achievable set since these costs are quite closely linked to processor speed.

Parameter	Achievable	Best	Halfway	Units
Page Protection	50	0	25	cycles/page
Diff creation	10,10	0,0	5,5	cycles/word
Diff Application	10	0	5	cycles/word
Twin Creation	10000	0	5000	cycles/word
Handler Cost	100+x	0+x	50+x	cycles

Table 2: Protocol layer parameter values. The diff creation cost incurs a cost per word that is compared (first number) and an additional cost per word that is put in the diff (second number). The handler cost is composed of a basic cost and any additional cost for operations that may be executed by the handler.

Communication layer parameters: The parameters of the communication layer that are of most interest are the following *Host overhead* is the time the host processor itself is busy sending a message, i.e. placing it in a buffer for the NI (we assume asynchronous send operations). *NI occupancy* is the time spent in the NI processor or state machine to prepare each packet of the message and place it in an output queue for transmission. Packets are of variable size, depending on how much of the message data is available to the NI at the time, and are up to 4 KBytes long. *I/O bus bandwidth* is the main determinant of the host to network bandwidth, since network links and memory buses tend to be much faster. Finally, *message handling cost* models the time from the moment a message reaches the head of the NI incoming queue to the moment the handler for the message starts to execute on the main processor; time and contention before reaching the head is simulated in detail and is not included in this parameterized cost. Incoming data messages (as opposed to requests) do not invoke a handler, and are deposited directly in host memory by the NI without causing an interrupt or requiring a receive operation on the processor [3, 5]. Hardware link latency is kept fixed at 20 processor cycles since it is usually small compared to the other costs.

All costs we discuss for the communication architecture and the protocol are normalized to processor cycles. Table 3 shows the parameter values we use in the base system. The sets of values we consider for the communication layer are: The *achievable* set, which is modeled after a cluster of Intel PentiumPro nodes connected by a Myrinet interconnect. Occupancy per packet is high because the processor in the Myrinet and most other commercial network interfaces is slow. However, since packets can be as large as 4 KBytes, occupancy can often be amortized. Recall that all contention in the system is modeled in detail, so when costs are changed the effects on contention are simulated as well. The *best* set, where all protocol costs are set to zero. The *halfway* set, where all values are halfway between the first two sets (more realistic than the best set). The *worst* set, where all values are doubled compared to the achievable set (i.e. worse, relative to processor speed).

Presentation of results: We use the following nomenclature to refer to the parameter configurations in the two system layers. *C* and *P* refer to the communication and protocol layers, respectively. The set of values used for each layer is denoted as a subscript. The achievable set is denoted with the digit 0, the best set with the symbol +, the halfway set between achievable and best with $\frac{1}{2}$, and the "worse" set with −. Thus the configuration corresponding to what is

Parameter	Achievable	Best	Worse	Real
Host Overhead	600	0	1200	600–800
I/O Bus Bandwidth	0.5	2	0.25	0.45
NI Occupancy	1000	0	2000	1000
Message Handling Cost	200	0	400	N/A

Table 3: Communication parameter values. The first three columns describe the values we use in our study as the Achievable, Best and Worse sets of values. Units are in cycles (and bytes/cycle for bandwidth). If we assume a 1 IPC, 200 MHz processor the achievable values are from top to bottom $3\mu s$, 100 MBytes/s, $5\mu s$ and $1\mu s$. The fifth column contains the values measured using a real communication library (VMMC [5] on a network of Intel Pentium nodes connected with Myrinet). The message handling cost is obtained from the polling–based Blizzard–S and Shasta systems (Personal communications).

achievable today is C_0P_0, and the zero–cost configuration for both the communication and protocol parameters discussed earlier is C_+P_+.

Figure 3 presents all the main speedup results in this paper. Breakdowns of execution time are presented in Figure 4. As we go through the next few sections, we shall focus on portions of the data in these figures.

For every application, there is a graph in Figure 3 with bars depicting speedups for different combinations of settings for the three layers. Each application graph has two major sets of bars, on the left for the SVM protocol and on the right for the FG protocol. When an application has two versions, there are two sets of bars for each protocol, separated by a space: original and restructured. For ease of comparison, speedups are always measured with respect to the same best sequential version, and the order of arrangement of the bars for the restructured version is a mirror image of the order for the original version.

The color of the bars in the speedup graphs encodes some information as well. The bars with the same color represent configurations with the same communication parameter values, with only the protocol layer parameters being modified across them. Thus, black bars represent varying protocol layer parameter sets while keeping communication parameters fixed at the achievable set, uniformly shaded bars with communication layer parameters fixed at the worse set, and striped bars with those parameters fixed at the best set. Unshaded bars show "ideal", 16-fold speedup as a reference point, which is close to the algorithmic (PRAM) speedup for these applications.

The breakdown graphs (Figure 4) divide the time into components, such as busy time, local cache stall time, data wait time or time spent waiting for communicated data, lock wait time, barrier wait time, and protocol overhead. Breakdowns are shown averaged over all processors for a given execution, to save space. However, in analyzing the results we refer to per–processor breakdowns and more detailed per–processor statistics gathered in the simulator to understand imbalances as well. The averaging may sometimes lead to discrepancies between the heights of the breakdown bars and the speedup bars; however, the alternative of showing the worst or last–to–finish processor instead is often unrepresentative in terms of the breakdowns.

3 Results

Let us first look at the results on only the base or achievable system C_0P_0, to make some basic comparisons and place the results in context with previous work. This includes comparing SVM with FG with our system assumptions, and validating the application restructuring results for SVM from [10].

Then, we will examine new application restructuring results for FG, the impact of the system layers, and the synergy between layers.

3.1 Results for Base Architecture

Consider only the base C_0P_0 bars (the black bars to which the arrows point in Figure 3). For both the original and the restructured applications, we see that FG either equals or outperforms SVM. FG is especially better in applications that use locks frequently, like Barnes-Original and to a lesser extent Water-Spatial and Volrend, and those like Radix or Ocean-Contiguous in which coarse granularity causes a lot of false sharing or fragmentation (false sharing is also a problem with the image and task queues in Volrend due to intervening synchronization). The only case in which SVM does better is the restructured version of Barnes (Barnes-Spatial). Note, however, that this comparison does not account for access control costs in FG. Even with Shasta's aggressive software instrumentation costs (see Table 1 with all caveats of Section 2), performance would be much closer, with each protocol outperforming the other in different applications. Applications with more complex pointer references may incur higher instrumentation overheads. These results for FG versus SVM would also be similar to the results obtained on the Typhoon–zero platform, which provides commodity-oriented hardware support [22]. (The communication parameters here are different than on Typhoon–zero: the C_0P_0 platform has somewhat more bandwidth relative to processor speed, helping SVM, but much more efficient access control, helping FG.) If we disallow application-specific granularities, using 128 bytes or 256 bytes (the best overall granularity found in [22]) in all cases, we find (not shown) that several of regular applications perform better under SVM.

Qualitatively, it appears that the protocols are similar at this scale with realistic access control, differing based on application. For both protocols however, the speedups on C_0P_0 are clearly far from ideal, so there is a lot that can be gained from optimizing the layers.

3.2 Impact of the Application Layer

The original versions of the applications we use (Table 1) are described in [20]. If evolutionary communication trends hold relative to processor speed, and hardware support to reduce protocol costs is not forthcoming, application restructuring may be the only way to improve performance. For SVM, the result of comparing the two black C_0P_0 bars for each application agrees with that of [10]. The sources of the often large and sometimes dramatic improvements, described in [10] include: (i) making actual access granularities to remote data larger in the application (e.g. writing to a local buffer first in Radix or using rowwise instead of square partitioning in Ocean), (ii) reducing locking and fine–grained synchronization (at perhaps some cost in load balance (e.g. in the tree building phase of Barnes), and (iii) in some cases improving the initial assignments of tasks so there is less need for task stealing (which is now very expensive due to synchronization and protocol activity, e.g. in Volrend: note that in Volrend restructuring also greatly improves false sharing and fragmentation in the image at page granularity, and hence data wait time). Many characteristics of the applications relevant to SVM, including sharing patterns, message frequencies and message sizes, are described in [9, 22, 2].

For FG, not examined in [10], restructuring helps significantly in cases where application access granularity is made larger (e.g. Ocean), since it allows a larger granularity to be

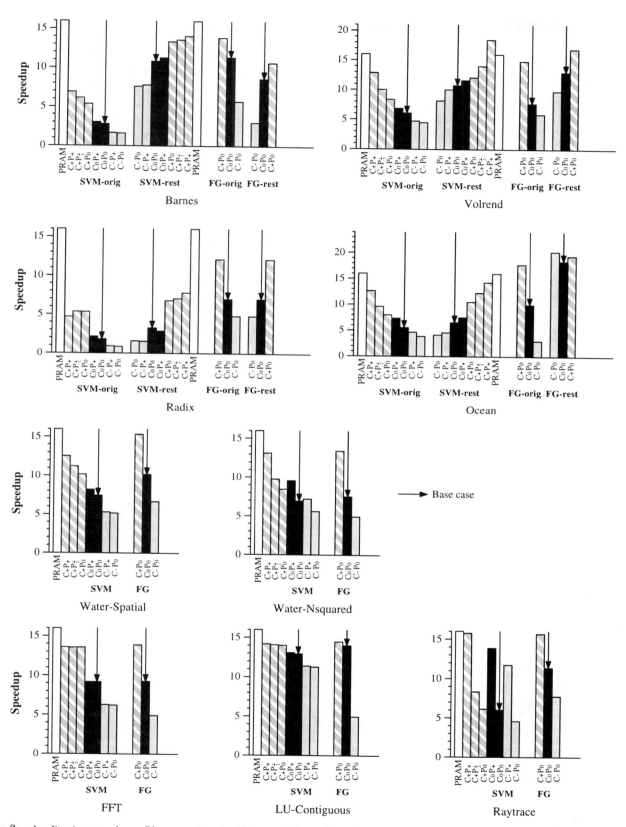

Figure 3: Application speedups. Please see text in **"Presentation of results"** in Section 2 for how to interpret the bars and focus attention on some of them.

used successfully in the system, and when the need for task stealing is reduced (Volrend). However, restructuring that helps SVM can sometimes hurt FG, such as in cases where load balance is compromised to reduce lock wait time (e.g. Barnes). Locks are not so problematic in FG as in SVM protocols: protocol activity is not postponed till synchronization points, and satisfying finer–grained block faults within critical sections is less costly than satisfying page faults, so there is less serialization.

Instead, load imbalance matters more. Overall, restructuring is not beneficial in as many situations as in SVM because the FG protocol and granularities look a lot more like the hardware–coherent protocols for which the original applications are optimized.

3.3 Impact of the Protocol Layer

Even with restructuring, performance of software DSM is still far from hardware DSM for many classes of applications and improvements in the lower layers are clearly needed. This section first examines the impact of idealizing protocol costs (Table 2), i.e. moving from C_0P_0 to C_0P_+. Protocol costs may be improved by selectively adding hardware support or by altering the protocol.

Impact for FG: Focusing only on the black C_0P_0 bar and the C_0P_+ bar just next to it for only the original versions of the applications for FG in Figures 3, we see that improving protocol costs does not have a significant impact on FG. FG does not have diffs or complicated protocol operations at synchronization points. There are only two protocol–related costs for FG: access control and protocol handlers. A rough idea of the impact of instrumentation costs for software access control (which we do not simulate, as discussed earlier) can be gleaned from Table 1. Since protocol handlers are very simple in FG, the cost of running the handlers is very small compared to the communication layer costs associated with handling the messages and invoking the handlers. Instrumentation of the original runs for FG shows that changing the cost of handlers (within a reasonable range) will not really affect performance, so we do not simulate different costs for FG protocol handlers.

Impact for SVM: In SVM, protocol costs have greater impact. However, even the complete elimination of protocol costs usually does not lead to dramatic improvements in performance if the underlying communication architecture is kept the same (with the exception of Raytrace). For coarse–grained–access, single–writer applications like FFT and LU, there is very little expensive protocol activity to begin with. Several of the other applications that use a lot of locks (especially) or have irregular access and invalidation patterns benefit to varying extents: Barnes-original, Water-Spatial and Volrend-original about 10%, and Radix 20%. Greater improvements are seen in Ocean-Contiguous, Water-Nsquared and especially Raytrace.

Table 4 shows the percentage of the protocol time spent in diff computation and application. The rest of the protocol time is mostly spent in executing protocol handlers. The other protocol cost components are very small. Regular, single–writer applications spent very little time in handlers and there is almost no diffing at all. Water-Nsquared is a regular application but not single-writer: it computes many diffs for a lot of migratory data when it is updating forces. For many irregular applications, diff–related computation at synchronization points, such as frequent locks, usually dominates. Raytrace does not have much synchro-

nization (and hence diff activity) but has a very large number of fine–grained messages due to irregular access, so protocol handler cost is a large fraction of data wait time and processors spend a lot of time in the handlers themselves. Ocean-contiguous behaves similarly, although it is a regular application, due to fine-grained (one-element) remote accesses at column-oriented partition boundaries in the near-neighbor calculations. When diff cost is a problem, hardware support for automatic write propagation [3] can eliminate diffs [12, 8, 9], at the potential cost of contention and/or code instrumentation; we might expect it to help substantially in Water-nsquared and Radix. Finally, improving protocol costs halfway ($C_0P_{\frac{1}{2}}$, not shown in the figures) usually provides about half or less of the benefit of eliminating them (more on this in Section 3.5).

Application	Protocol (%)	Diff Compute (%)
Barnes-Original	7.2	68
FFT	0.5	0
LU-Contiguous	0.6	20
Ocean-Contiguous	3.0	10
Radix-Original	7.0	85
Raytrace	58	31
Volrend-Original	13.2	85
Water-Nsquared	10.7	80
Water-Spatial	3.2	94

Table 4: Percentage of total execution time spent by processors in protocol activity, and percentage of this protocol activity time that is spent in diff computation and application.

We see from the restructured applications (black bars in Figures 3), that even idealizing protocol costs together with application restructuring is insufficient to approach the desired levels of performance that these applications can achieve on hardware-coherent machines. The large page granularity usually does not compensate for a less aggressive communication architecture even if protocol costs are magically made zero.

3.4 Impact of the Communication Layer

In recent times, overheads and bandwidths have scaled just a little bit slower than effective processor speed (about 50% per year versus about 70%) and NI occupancy can be assumed to scale with processor speed. It is useful to examine both what might be gained if thresholds or breakthroughs occur in communication performance and what might be lost in parallel speedups if it degrades relative to increasing processor speeds. Let us now return to the original protocol and examine the impact of improving the communication architecture only. In the best set of parameters, only the I/O bus bandwidth is finite or non-zero, being set to the same value as the memory bus bandwidth. Note that contention is still modeled in all parts of the system.

Impact for FG: Figure 3 shows that the best communication layer makes a dramatic difference to speedups (C_+P_0 versus C_0P_0), bringing them quite close to the ideal for the original applications. Except for the (small) protocol handler cost, the FG system becomes like hardware cache coherence with a very fast communication architecture. Of course, adding in instrumentation costs for software access control would make the speedup worse, but the impact of the communication architecture is clear. The cases where C_+P_0 speedups are substantially less than ideal (Barnes cases) are due to load imbalance and the still significant synchronization cost.

Impact for SVM: For SVM, the effects of the best communication architecture alone are substantial but less dramatic than for *FG*. Applications that have little protocol activity, coarse–grained remote access and few or no locks, like FFT and LU, are constrained only by communication layer costs, so they now achieve close to ideal performance just as with *FG*. The irregular applications are helped substantially, but speedups with C_+P_0 are still as low as 5–7 on 16 processors for some of them. The breakdowns (Figure 4) show that the data wait time is mostly eliminated, but time waiting at locks is often still high. Imbalances in this time cause time waiting at barriers to be high too. Overall, starting from C_0P_0, communication costs generally seem to have greater impact than protocol costs even for *SVM* (with exceptions like Water-spatial, Raytrace, and some restructured versions); but as we shall see in Section 3.5, once communication costs are improved even to halfway (or restructuring is performed), protocol costs begin to gain in importance.

Effects of Individual Parameters: Figure 5 shows the impact of varying only one communication parameter at a time for some applications. These data for *SVM* were discussed in detail in [2], but the data for *FG* and the comparison is new. *FG* clearly depends mostly on overhead and occupancy, whereas *SVM* depends mostly on bandwidth (overhead and occupancy do not matter much, and interrupts which dominated in [2] are not used). These data also show the points where crossovers in protocol performance might happen (ignoring access control). Together with access control costs and technology trends (e.g. bandwidth is increasing more rapidly than overhead is dropping), they can help draw conclusions about choices among the protocols for specific architectures or in the future.

Overall, we conclude that dramatic improvements in communication relative to processor performance will dramatically improve data wait time and *FG* performance; for *SVM*, performance improves substantially (usually more than for just improving protocol costs, at least starting from C_0P_0) but is not enough since part of the problem in irregular applications is due to fine–grain lock synchronization. Since I/O bandwidth remained finite in C_+P_0, we experimented with doubling the I/O bandwidth compared to the C_+P_0 configuration. Applications that exhibit contention in the network interface (e.g. FFT) benefit substantially and the performance improves to halfway between C_+P_0 and the PRAM speedup for the application.

3.5   Synergy between Layers
Finally, let us examine both how improvements in the system layers affect the benefits of application restructuring and are affected by them, as well as the synergy between pairs of layers.

Synergy in *FG*: Application restructuring for *FG* helps primarily due to the ability to use coarser granularity. Directly improving the communication architecture therefore reduces the impact of restructuring. When instrumentation is used for access control, its cost may also improve with restructuring (due to coarser access granularity and spatial locality), but this effect is much smaller.

For example, in Barnes, where the restructured version hurts rather than helps due to increased load imbalance, per–process execution–time breakdowns reveal that the key load imbalance is that among data wait times. A faster communication architecture reduces this imbalance, leading to less damage from restructuring. Improving instrumentation costs does not interact much with communication layer performance since the two are quite orthogonal. Thus, in *FG*

there is not much to be gained from the synergy between layers, especially if the communication layer is aggressive.

Synergy in *SVM*: In *SVM* we find a lot of interesting interactions and a lot more synergy among layers. First, how application restructuring affects, and is affected by the two system layers depends on the application. In Barnes-original, restructuring reduces the amount of locking and serialization, and while its importance diminishes as system layers improve, it remains important all the way to C_+P_+ and even beyond. This is because some costs within the node (that are kept fixed) remain, and bandwidth on the I/O bus is still not infinite. Although protocol processing at synchronization points is free, some cost for communication (whether all needed or due to fragmentation) remains and hence so does some serialization at locks. This is especially true for Barnes-Original because every critical section incurs more than one page miss and a lot of fragmentation within it. The $C_{++}P_+$ (Table 5) case does much better. Because reducing communication costs had a dramatic impact on lock serialization in Barnes-original, the communication layer affects the impact of restructuring more than the protocol layer. As for protocol costs, they take on greater relative significance after restructuring than before it because a major other bottleneck has been removed; however, even in the restructured version communication costs are more important than protocol costs. In Ocean, on the other hand, protocol costs impact the benefits of restructuring more than communication costs; also, the relative importance of the two system layers is reversed in the restructured version compared to the original. This is because the restructured version greatly reduces the number of messages but not the amount of useful data transferred, so the impact of message handling (protocol) cost is reduced relative to that of communication. Volrend and Radix behave similarly to Barnes in this respect (only less so): restructuring remains important as lower layers improve, and the impact of restructuring is reduced more by communication costs than by protocol costs (increasing the importance of protocol costs in the restructured version). In Volrend, C_+P_+ finally allows the critical sections used for task stealing to be efficient enough for stealing to be successful at load balancing. While Radix continues to have low performance due to high communication and contention, restructuring makes a substantial difference (66%) even at C_+P_+. It takes $C_{++}P_+$ to deliver good speedups, as in Barnes-Original but for a different reason.

In *SVM*, the two system layers themselves show substantial synergy as well. While protocol costs are limited in the improvement they can provide in the original C_0 case in many applications, once communication costs are dramatically reduced (even halfway) the impact of reducing protocol costs becomes much greater (Figure 3), and vice versa when protocol costs matter (e.g. Ocean-Contiguous, Volrend).

Overall, in *SVM* no two layers are enough to improve performance to rival hardware coherence for all applications, and all three layers are important to improve. The application layer and either of the lower layers combine to give a much greater improvement than any system layer does individually. In most cases, the order of impact is application followed by communication followed by protocol. For both *SVM* and *FG*, the communication layer appears to be more important to making the programmer's job easier (i.e., making application restructuring less important). Restructuring changes the balance between the relative importance of protocol and communication costs, usually making the

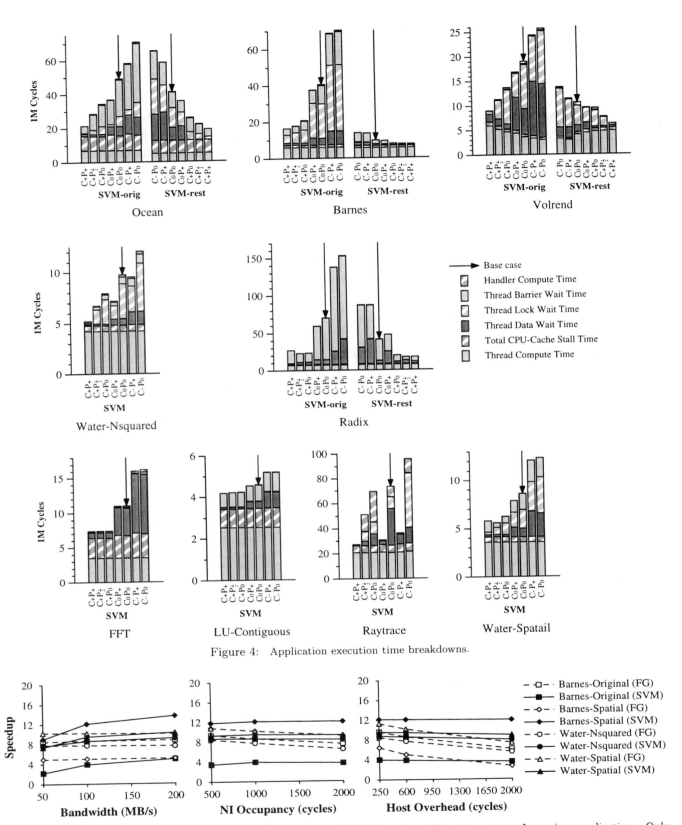

Figure 4: Application execution time breakdowns.

Figure 5: Speedups with communication architecture parameters. Each figure is a different parameter for various applications. Only four applications are shown; for some of the more regular ones *FG* uses a coarse granularity too and the behavior of the two protocols is very similar. The curves with dashed lines are for *FG*, and with solid lines are for *SVM*.

protocol costs more important than they were before. Protocol costs also become more important once communication costs are improved (to say halfway), and vice versa. Table 5 summarizes for SVM, for each application, whether communication cost or protocol cost is initially more important, whether $C_{\frac{1}{2}}P_+$ is better than $C_+P_{\frac{1}{2}}$, and what combinations of parameter values does it take to achieve about 10–fold speedup on 16 processors, which tells us both what is more important and what is needed. The need for improvement in all layers, whether through basic performance characteristics as examined here or through altered functionality to avoid some of these costs [1] is apparent from the last category. More detailed trends can be obtained from the graphs.

4 Related Work

The impact of individual communication architecture parameters on performance has been studied for SVM [2], hardware coherence [7], and a non–coherent SAS [14]. However, it has not been studied for FG, or by varying parameters simultaneously, or by examining the protocol layer as well. Various hardware supports to accelerate protocols have been examined for SVM in [8] and [12], and for FG in the Typhoon–zero prototype [16].

A previous study [6] compared the performance of several non-home-based SVM protocols; it examined two network bandwidths and varied a unified software overhead cost. The study included only three small kernels and one application. Both FG and SVM were compared on a particular hardware platform with a fixed set of cost parameters in [22], with a focus on the impact of consistency models and coherence granularity. Its results are qualitatively similar to the ones we observe here for FG versus SVM. This is the first study we know of that examines the impact of all these protocol and communication cost issues in an integrated framework for a wide range of applications (as well as including the impact of the application layer too).

5 Discussion and Conclusions

We have presented a framework for studying the limitations on the performance of software shared memory systems, in terms of the layers of software and hardware that can be improved and how they impact the end performance of a wide range of applications. We have studied the limitations and performance effects through detailed simulation, treating the system layers (protocol and communication layer) through only their cost parameters. The main limitations of the present work include the fact that it does not simulate true instrumentation–based fine–grained software shared memory, but rather a system with very efficient hardware access control but software protocols. Our main conclusions can be summarized as follows.

First, for currently achievable architectural values the variable–grained FG and page–grained SVM protocols appear to be quite comparable overall, especially if we factor in aggressive but realistic access control costs. This assumes that FG is allowed to choose the best granularity of communication and coherence for each application; for cases like FFT where FG benefits from coarse granularity, we have found using a finer granularity to perform substantially worse. In general, FG will be worse when access control (e.g. instrumentation) costs are high or when it causes too many small messages to be transferred; SVM is worse when applications have a lot of fine-grained synchronization or a lot of fragmentation in page-grained communication (or especially both, as in Barnes-Original).

Second, for FG the communication layer is key; protocol layer costs are not very significant, except for instrumentation cost when software access control is used. Application restructuring is also not so widely important, at least when starting from applications that are well tuned for hardware–coherent DSMs. Exceptions are when restructuring enables a coarser granularity of communication to be used effectively (as in Ocean), and when it reduces the frequency of task stealing (Volrend). As might be expected, the communication parameters that matter most are overhead and NI occupancy, while bandwidth matters only when a coarser granularity is used.

Third, for SVM, contrary to our results for FG, we find a much richer set of interactions. (i) Improvements in all three layers are often necessary to achieve performance comparable to efficient hardware–coherent systems. No one layer or even pair of layers is enough across the range of applications. (ii) There is synergy among the layers in that improving one system layer (even halfway) allows the other to have greater impact, so that realistic improvements to both system layers relative to processor speed may go a good way, and improving the applications often does not substantially diminish the further impact of system layers. (iii) Application restructuring is used both to make access patterns to communicated data more coarse grained and to reduce the frequency of synchronization: when applicable, it usually outperforms the gains from idealizing any one other layer. Thus, if useful guidelines can be developed for programming SVM systems, they can be extremely helpful. (iv) If only one system layer is targeted for improvement, it should be the communication layer; among these parameters, the greatest dependence of performance is on bandwidth, and it is quite insensitive to improvements in the other parameters (when interrupts are used instead of polling, interrupt cost is a key bottleneck [2]). (v) Among protocol costs, the sensitivity is usually greatest to the costs associated with diffs, primarily diff creation. Handler cost can matter substantially in applications that are more constrained by data message count than by synchronization. Table 5 summarizes the key results for SVM in terms of relative importance and what is needed for good performance.

At a higher level, many interesting tradeoffs remain between FG and SVM. For SVM, the fact that it needs synergistic improvements in multiple layers rather than just the communication layer may appear intimidating, and restructuring applications in fact is difficult (although recent results show that similar restructurings are often needed for hardware-coherence at larger scale). But it is in some ways a promising sign, especially since the communication layer may be difficult to improve relative to processor speed, and is not so much under the control of the SVM architect. Also, the communication parameter it relies on most, bandwidth, is the most likely to improve. FG requires overhead and occupancy to improve further, which may be more challenging under current memory and network speed trends. For SVM, while the heretofore major challenge of false sharing appears relatively easy to overcome in applications with today's protocols, the large page granularity of communication seems to get in the way of applications that suffer fragmentation in communication or fine-grained locking (often associated with true sharing as well).

Acknowledgments: We thank the members of the PRISM group at Princeton for useful discussions, and Rudrajit Samanta additionally for help with graphs. We gratefully

Application	Original					Restructured				
	$C_+P_0 >$ C_0P_+	$C_+P_{\frac{1}{2}} >$ $C_{\frac{1}{2}}P_+$	Min Levels			$C_+P_0 >$ C_0P_+	$C_+P_{\frac{1}{2}} >$ $C_{\frac{1}{2}}P_+$	Min Levels		
			Com.	Prot.	Comb.			Com.	Prot.	Comb.
FFT	**Yes**	**Yes**	$\frac{1}{2}$	N/P	$C_{\frac{1}{2}}P_0$	N/A	N/A	N/A	N/A	N/A
LU	Yes	Yes	0	0	C_0P_0	N/A	N/A	N/A	N/A	N/A
Ocean	Yes	No	N/P	N/P	$C_+P_{\frac{1}{2}}/C_{\frac{1}{2}}P_+$	**Yes**	Yes	$\frac{1}{2}$	N/P	$C_{\frac{1}{2}}P_+/C_+P_{\frac{1}{2}}$
Barnes	**Yes**	**Yes**	N/P	N/P	$C_{++}P_+$	**Yes**	Yes	0	0	C_0P_0
Radix	**Yes**	**Yes**	N/P	N/P	$C_{++}P_+$	**Yes**	Yes	N/P	N/P	$C_{++}P_+$
Volrend	Yes	Tie	N/P	N/P	$C_+P_{\frac{1}{2}}/C_{\frac{1}{2}}P_+$	Yes	Tied	0	0	C_0P_0
Raytrace	**No**	**No**	N/P	+	C_0P_+	N/A	N/A	N/A	N/A	N/A
Water-Nsquared	No	No	N/P	+	$C_0P_+/C_+P_{\frac{1}{2}}$	N/A	N/A	N/A	N/A	N/A
Water-Spatial	**Yes**	Yes	+	N/P	$C_+P_0/C_{\frac{1}{2}}P_+$	N/A	N/A	N/A	N/A	N/A

Table 5: Summary of system layer impact for *SVM*. $C_{++}P_+$ means that the communication architecture is even more aggressive than in C_+P_+ by further doubling the I/O bandwidth. *N/P* stands for *not possible*, and *N/A* for *not applicable*. Bold font is used when the difference is large. The columns for each version of each application are: (i) Is C_+P_0 better than C_0P_+, i.e. is communication more important than protocol. (ii) Is $C_+P_{\frac{1}{2}}$ better than $C_{\frac{1}{2}}P_+$. (iii) What minimum set of parameter values for each system layer is necessary, with the base level of the other layer, to get about 10–fold or greater speedup on 16 processors? What combination of levels does it take to achieve the same performance? For example, an $\frac{1}{2}$ under the entry called "Com." says that the halfway or better communication costs, together with any protocol costs starting from the original, is enough to obtain 10–fold speedup. ($C_{++}P_+$ is excluded since it is too unrealistic).

acknowledge the support of NSF and DARPA.

References

[1] A. Bilas. *Improving the Performance of Shared Virtual Memory on System Area Networks*. PhD thesis. Dept. of Computer Science. Princeton University. August 1998. Available as technical report TR-586-98.

[2] A. Bilas and J. P. Singh. The effects of communication parameters on end performance of shared virtual memory clusters. In *In Proceedings of Supercomputing 97, San Jose, CA*, November 1997.

[3] M. Blumrich, K. Li, R. Alpert, C. Dubnicki, E. Felten, and J. Sandberg. A virtual memory mapped network interface for the shrimp multicomputer. In *Proceedings of the 21st Annual Symposium on Computer Architecture*, pages 142–153, Apr. 1994.

[4] N. J. Boden, D. Cohen, R. E. Felderman, A. E. Kulawik, C. L. Seitz, J. N. Seizovic, and W.-K. Su. Myrinet: A gigabit-per-second local area network. *IEEE Micro*, 15(1):29–36, Feb. 1995.

[5] C. Dubnicki, A. Bilas, K. Li, and J. Philbin. Design and implementation of Virtual Memory-Mapped Communication on Myrinet. In *Proceedings of the 1997 International Parallel Processing Symposium*, pages 388–396, April 1997.

[6] S. Dwarkadas, P. Keleher, A. Cox, and W. Zwaenepoel. An evaluation of software distributed shared memory for next-generation processors and networks. In *Proceedings of the 20th Annual International Symposium on Computer Architecture*, May 1993. To Get.

[7] C. Holt, M. Heinrich, J. P. Singh, , and J. L. Hennessy. The effects of latency and occupancy on the performance of dsm multiprocessors. Technical Report CSL-TR-95-xxx, Stanford University, 1995.

[8] L. Iftode, C. Dubnicki, E. W. Felten, and K. Li. Improving release-consistent shared virtual memory using automatic update. In *The 2nd IEEE Symposium on High-Performance Computer Architecture*, Feb. 1996.

[9] L. Iftode, J. P. Singh, and K. Li. Understanding application performance on shared virtual memory. In *Proceedings of the 23rd Annual International Symposium on Computer Architecture*, May 1996.

[10] D. Jiang, H. Shan, and J. P. Singh. Application restructuring and performance portability across shared virtual memory and hardware-coherent multiprocessors. In *Proceedings of the 6th ACM Symposium on Principles and Practice of Parallel Programming*, June 1997.

[11] P. Keleher, A. Cox, S. Dwarkadas, and W. Zwaenepoel. Treadmarks: Distributed shared memory on standard workstations and operating systems. In *Proceedings of the Winter USENIX Conference*, pages 115–132, Jan. 1994.

[12] L. I. Kontothanassis and M. L. Scott. Using memory-mapped network interfaces to improve t he performance of distributed shared memory. In *The 2nd IEEE Symposium on High-Performance Computer Architecture*, Feb. 1996.

[13] K. Li and P. Hudak. Memory coherence in shared virtual memory systems. *ACM Trans. Comput. Syst.*, 7(4):321–359. Nov. 1989.

[14] R. P. Martin, A. M. Vahdat, D. E. Culler, and T. E. Anderson. Effect of communication latency, overhead, and bandwidth on a cluster architecture. Technical Report CSD-96-925, Berkeley, Nov. 1996.

[15] S. Reinhardt, J. Larus, and D. Wood. Tempest and typhoon: User-level shared memory. In *Proceedings of the 21st Annual Symposium on Computer Architecture*, pages 325–336, Apr. 1994.

[16] S. K. Reinhardt. R. W. Pfile, and D. A. Wood. Decoupled hardware support for distributed shared memory. In *Proceedings of the 23rd Annual International Symposium on Computer Architecure*, pages 34–43, New York, May22–24 1006. ACM Press.

[17] D. Scales, K. Gharachorloo, and C. Thekkath. Shasta: A low overhead, software-only approach for supporting fine-grain shared memory. In *The 7th International Conference on Architectural Support for Programming Languages and Operating Systems*, Oct. 1996.

[18] I. Schoinas and et al. Fine-grain access control for distributed shared memory. In *Sixth International Conference on Architectural Support for Programming Languages and Operating Systems*, pages 297–307, October 1994.

[19] A. Sharma, A. T. Nguyen, J. Torellas, M. Michael, and J. Carbajal. Augmint: a multiprocessor simulation environment for Intel x86 architectures. Technical report, University of Illinois at Urbana-Champaign, March 1996.

[20] S. Woo, M. Ohara, E. Torrie, J. P. Singh. and A. Gupta. Methodological considerations and characterization of the SPLASH-2 parallel application suite. In *Proceedings of the 23rd Annual Conference on Computer Architecture*, May 1995.

[21] Y. Zhou, L. Iftode, and K. Li. Performance evaluation of two home-based lazy release consistency protocols for shared virtual memory systems. In *Proceedings of the Operating Systems Design and Implementation Symposium*, Oct. 1996.

[22] Y. Zhou, L. Iftode, J. P. Singh, K. Li, B. Toonen, I. Schoinas, M. Hill, and D. Wood. Relaxed consistency and coherence granularity in DSM systems: A performance evaluation. In *Proceedings of the 6th ACM Symposium on Principles and Practice of Parallel Programming*, June 1997.

Cache and I/O Systems

RAPID-Cache — A Reliable and Inexpensive Write Cache for Disk I/O Systems *

Yiming Hu, Qing Yang and Tycho Nightingale
Department of Electrical & Computer Engineering
University of Rhode Island
Kingston, RI 02881
e-mail: {hu,qyang,tycho}@ele.uri.edu

Abstract

This paper presents a new cache architecture called **RAPID-Cache** *for Redundant, Asymmetrically Parallel, and Inexpensive Disk Cache. A typical RAPID-Cache consists of two redundant write buffers on top of a disk system. One of the buffers is a primary cache made of RAM or NVRAM and the other is a backup cache containing a two level hierarchy: a small NVRAM buffer on top of a log disk[1]. The backup cache has nearly equivalent write performance as the primary RAM cache, while the read performance of the backup cache is not as critical because normal read operations are performed through the primary RAM cache and reads from the backup cache happen only during error recovery periods. The RAPID-Cache presents an asymmetric architecture with a fast-write-fast-read RAM being a primary cache and a fast-write-slow-read NVRAM-disk hierarchy being a backup cache. The asymmetric cache architecture allows cost-effective designs for very large write caches for high-end disk I/O systems that would otherwise have to use dual-copy, costly NVRAM caches. It also makes it possible to implement reliable write caching for low-end disk I/O systems since the RAPID-Cache makes use of inexpensive disks to perform reliable caching. Our analysis and trace-driven simulation results show that the RAPID-Cache has significant reliability/cost advantages over conventional single NVRAM write caches and has great cost advantages over dual-copy NVRAM caches. The RAPID-Cache architecture opens a new dimension for disk system designers to exercise trade-offs among performance, reliability and cost.*

1 Introduction

Modern disk I/O systems make extensive use of nonvolatile RAM (NVRAM) write caches to allow fast write [2, 3, 4], or asynchronous write, i.e. a write request is acknowledged before the write goes to disk. Such write caches significantly reduce response times of disk I/O systems seen by users, particularly in RAID systems. Large write caches can also improve system throughput by taking advantage of both temporal and spatial localities [2, 5] as well as the burstiness of write workloads. For example, the IBM Ramac disk array subsystem uses 64 MB of battery-backed RAM as the NVRAM cache. Treiber and Menon reported that write caches could reduce disk utilization for writes by an order of magnitude when compared to basic RAID-5 systems [3]. However, the use of write caches introduces two problems: poor reliability and high cost.

Disks are impressively reliable today, with a Mean Time To Failure (MTTF) of up to 1 million hours. Such a low failure rate, coupled with possible redundancy such as RAID, gives a Mean Time To Data Loss (MTTDL) of several hundreds of millions of hours in a typical RAID-5 system [6]. Adding a single cache in front of a disk system creates a single point of failure, which is vulnerable to data loss. Savage and Wilkes pointed out in [6] that because typical NVRAM technology (battery backed RAM) has a quite low MTTF of 15K hours, a single-copy NVRAM cache suffers significantly higher risk of data loss than results from disk failures. To overcome the reliability problem, some high-end RAID systems use dual-copy caches, a primary cache and a backup cache, so that a failure in one cache leaves the other cache intact [2].

Besides the reliability problem, NVRAM is also known to be very costly [6, 7, 8]. For example, Dallas Semiconductor's NVRAM with embedded lithium-cell batteries has the published price of about $120/MB at the end of 1997. The cost of disks, on the other hand, is about 10 cents/MB, which is a difference of three orders of magnitude. For a disk system with a reasonably sized write cache, the NVRAM may dominate the cost of the entire system. For example, in a system with 16 disks (4 GB per disk) and an NVRAM write cache of 64 MB, at $120/MB, the NVRAM costs about $7680, while the total cost of 16 disks is only $6400 (assuming each 4-GB disk costs $400). If we use dual-copy caches to ease the reliability problem of the single-copy cache, the cost becomes prohibitively high, particularly for large caches. As a result, it is only suitable for the upper echelon of the market.

The standard dual-copy write cache system has a *symmetric* structure, where both the primary write cache and the backup write cache have the same size and the same access characteristics — fast read speed and fast write speed. However, the backup cache does not provide any performance benefit to the system during normal operations. Therefore it is wasteful to use a backup cache identical to the primary cache. What is needed is only a backup cache that can be written to very quickly while its read operations are not as critical, since reads from the backup cache occur only during error-recovering periods.

Based on these observations, we propose a new disk cache architecture called *Redundant, Asymmetrically Parallel, Inexpensive Disk Cache*, or **RAPID-Cache** for short, to provide fault-tolerant caching for disk I/O systems inexpensively. The main idea of the RAPID-Cache is to use a conventional, fast-write-fast-read *primary cache* and a non-volatile, fast-write-slow-read *backup cache*. The primary cache is made of normal NVRAM or DRAM, while the backup cache consists of a small NVRAM cache and a disk called a cache-disk. In the backup cache, small and random writes are first buffered in the small NVRAM buffer to form large logs that are written into the *cache-disk* later in large transfers, similar to log structured file systems [9, 10, 11, 12]. Because large writes eliminate many expensive small writes, the buffer is quickly made available for additional requests so that the two level cache appears to the host as a large NVRAM. As a result, the backup cache can achieve the same write speed as the primary cache. The slow-read performance of the backup cache does not affect the system performance since every

---

*This research is supported in part by National Science Foundation under Grants MIP-9505601 and MIP-9714370.

data block in the backup cache has a copy in the primary cache which can be read at the speed of RAM. The dual cache system here is asymmetric since the primary cache and the backup cache have different sizes and structures. The reliability of the RAPID-Cache is expected to be high since disk is very reliable. The system is also inexpensive because the NVRAM in the backup cache can be very small, ranging from hundreds of KB to several MB and the cost of the disk space is significantly less than that of a large NVRAM. We will show that RAPID-Caches provide much higher reliability compared to single-copy NVRAM caches and much lower cost compared to dual-copy NVRAM caches, without sacrificing performance. On the other hand, because of its low cost, with the *same budget*, RAPID-Caches can have significantly higher performance compared to conventional NVRAM cache architectures by affording much larger primary cache sizes, while still maintaining good reliability.

We have carried out trace-driven simulation experiments as well as analytical studies to evaluate the performance and reliability of the RAPID-Cache. Using real-world traces as well as synthetic traces generated based on realistic workloads [13, 14], we analyze the performance of the RAPID-Cache architecture and compare it with existing disk cache architectures. Numerical results show that the RAPID-Cache has significant performance/cost and reliability advantages over the existing architectures.

The paper is organized as follows. The next section presents the detailed architecture and operations of the RAPID-Cache. Section 3 presents our experimental methodology. Simulation results will be presented in Section 4, followed by an approximate reliability and cost analysis in Section 5. We discuss related work in Section 6 and conclude the paper in Section 7.

2 Architecture and Operations

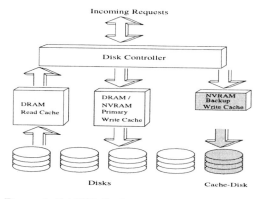

Figure 1: RAPID-Cache on top of a disk system

Figure 1 shows the basic structure of a RAPID-Cache. It consists of a primary RAM cache and a backup cache. The backup cache is a two-level hierarchy with a small NVRAM on top of a cache disk, similar to DCD [1]. In RAPID-Cache, every I/O write operation is sent to both the primary cache and the backup cache while read operations are performed using the primary cache only.

For very high overall reliability, the primary cache can be NVRAM to provide redundant protection during a power failure. On the other hand, for low cost systems, the primary cache can be DRAM. During normal operations, the DRAM primary cache and the backup cache contain redundant data. If any one of the two caches fails, data can be reconstructed

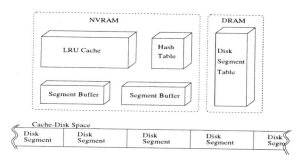

Figure 2: The detailed structure of the backup cache and the cache-disk

from the other. During a power failure, data are retained in the backup NVRAM and the cache-disk.

2.1 Structures of the Backup Cache

Figure 2 shows the detailed structures of the backup NVRAM cache and the cache-disk. The NVRAM cache consists of an *LRU Cache*, two to four *Segment Buffers* and a *Hash Table*. Another related data structure called the *Disk Segment Table* is located in a DRAM buffer.

The frequently-accessed data in the backup cache reside in the LRU cache. The less frequently-accessed data are kept in the cache disk. Data in the cache-disk are organized in the format of *Segments* similar to that in a Log-structured File System such as the Sprite LFS and the BSD LFS [10, 11]. A segment contains a number of *slots* each of which can hold one data block. Data blocks stored in segments are addressed by their *Segment IDs* and *Slot IDs*. Data blocks stored in the LRU cache are addressed by their *Logical Block Addresses (LBAs)*. The Hash Table contains location information for each of the valid data blocks in the backup cache. It describes whether a block is in the NVRAM LRU cache or in the cache-disk, as well as the data address in the LRU cache or the cache-disk. Since data in the backup cache is the exact image of the data in the primary write cache, the total number of valid data blocks in the backup cache is the same as in the primary write cache, regardless of the sizes of the backup NVRAM and the cache-disk. The total hash table size is small and compact enough to be place in the NVRAM. The detailed structure of the hash table can found in [15].

The cache-disk in the backup cache can be a *dedicated physical disk*, as shown in Figure 3(a). It can also be distributed among the data disks of a RAID system, each data disk having a small partition acting as a part of a large *distributed logical cache-disk*, as shown in Figure 3(b). In modern RAID systems, the physical cache-disk can often be implemented without extra cost since many modern RAID systems include one or several spare disks that can be put into service when an active disk fails [16]. However, as pointed out by Wilkes et al. [16], during normal operations the spare disks are not used in many systems [1] and contribute nothing to the performance of the system. It is also hard to tell if the spare disks are still working since they are not in use. Such a spare disk can therefore be used as a physical cache-disk of a RAPID-Cache. A secondary benefit here is that now we are aware of whether the spare disk is in working condition or not, and we are able to replace the failed one before it is too late. When a spare disk becomes an active disk to replace a

---

[1] In a system using *distributed sparing*, the spare disk is utilized during normal operation.

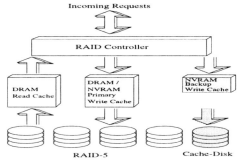

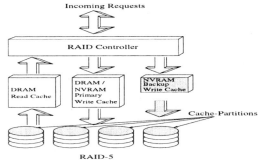

(a) A RAPID-Cache with a dedicated physical cache-disk   (b) A RAPID-Cache with a distributed logical cache-disk

Figure 3: Physical RAPID-Cache and Logical RAPID-Cache

failed one, the RAPID-Cache can be degraded to the logical cache-disk mode by using a partition residing on the spare disk, until the failed disk is replaced and a new spare disk is put into the system. In the case of a logical cache-disk, the data written into the logical cache partitions on the RAID disks do not involve in parity operations.

2.2   Write

When a write request comes, the controller first invalidates any data copy in the read cache. It then sends the data simultaneously to the primary cache and the LRU cache of the backup cache. If there is space available in the caches, the data are then copied to the caches immediately. A hash entry in the backup cache is also created to indicate that the data block is located in the backup LRU cache. Once the data is written into both the primary cache and the NVRAM buffer of the backup cache, the controller sends an acknowledgment to the host signaling that the request is complete.

If there is no space left in the primary cache, the controller first tries to discard a clean block from the cache to make room for the new request. However, if it can not find a clean block, the controller chooses the Least-Recently-Used (LRU) data block and writes it to the RAID. When the LRU block is safely written into the RAID, the space in the primary cache is freed for the incoming request. Meanwhile, the copy of the replaced data in the secondary cache, whether in the LRU cache or in the cache-disk, is also invalidated.

If the LRU cache in the backup cache is full, the RAPID controller picks an empty segment buffer and sets it as the "current" segment buffer. An LRU data block is then copied to the segment buffer and the corresponding entries in the Hash Table and the Disk Segment Table are modified to reflect the fact that the data block is now in the current segment buffer instead of the LRU cache. Since the segment buffer is also in the NVRAM, the cache space used by the LRU data block can now be safely freed to accept the incoming request. The following write requests may continue to evict LRU blocks to the segment buffer until the segment buffer is full. The controller then writes the contents of the segment buffer into a cache-disk segment in one large write. At this point, the controller switches to another empty segment buffer as the current segment buffer and continues operation. Since the entire segment buffer is written in one large write instead of many small writes, the segment buffer is very quickly made available again when the write finishes. Therefore, the small NVRAM cache and the large cache-disk appear to the controller as a large NVRAM write cache.

The dedicated segment buffers allow the data to be transferred to the cache-disk in a single large and continuous transfer. If the I/O systems can support scatter/gather I/O transferring (a hardware technique to assemble data from noncontiguous memory locations), then the dedicated segment buffers are not needed.

2.3   Read

Reading is straightforward in RAPID-Cache. When a request comes, the read cache and the primary write cache are searched. If there is a cache hit, data can be returned immediately. In case of a cache miss, the Least Recently Used (LRU) block in the read cache is discarded and its buffer space is freed. The requested data is then read from the RAID system into the freed LRU block before the data is returned. The backup cache is not involved in read operations.

2.4   Destage

In a traditional RAID system with an NVRAM write cache, dirty data in the write cache is written into the RAID system in a process called *destage* [5] which normally happens in the background. A RAID system with a RAPID-Cache also requires destaging. In our current design, one or several *destaging threads* are initiated when the controller detects an idle period, or when the number of dirty blocks in the primary write cache exceeds a high water-mark, say 70% of the cache capacity. The destaging threads find a dirty LRU block in the primary cache, read the old data and parity of that block from disks or the read cache, compute the new parity, and write the new data and parity to disks. After the new data and parity are written, the dirty block in the primary cache is marked as "clean", and the same data block in the backup cache, whether it is in the NVRAM LRU cache or in the cache-disk, is invalidated. The invalidation of the backup cache block involves releasing the LRU buffer if the block is in the NVRAM LRU cache; marking the corresponding segment slot as "invalid" if the data is in a disk segment or a segment buffer; and deleting the hash entry from the hash table. The destaging threads run continuously until the idle period is over, or until the dirty block count in the primary cache falls below a low water-mark, say 30% of the cache capacity.

Notice that data in the backup cache are never read or written during a destaging process. Therefore the slow-speed of the cache-disk will not affect the destaging performance.

2.5 Garbage Collection

In a RAPID-Cache system, segments in the cache-disk may become fragmented and require garbage collection. However, because of the asymmetrically parallel architecture of the RAPID-Cache, all data in the cache-disk are also in the primary write cache which can be read quickly. There is no need to read data from the cache-disk. To do garbage collection, the RAPID controller simply searches the Disk Segment Table to find several fragmented segments. It then copies the corresponding data from the primary cache to a segment buffer in RAM. Finally the controller writes the whole contents of the segment buffer to a new disk segment and invalidates the old segments. The garbage collection overhead of a RAPID-Cache is only a small fraction of that of LFS. More details of our garbage collection algorithm can be found in [15].

Furthermore, if a sufficently large cache-disk is used, say several hundred MB, the RAPID controller almost never has to call the garbage collector, meaning that the garbage collection overhead has virtually no impact on the overall system performance.

2.6 Error Handling and Availability

A RAPID-Cache system has excellent reliability because of the data redundancy provided by the primary cache and the backup cache. If data in any one of the caches is lost for any reason, the other cache is read to rebuild the data. During a system crash or a power failure, data is retained in the NVRAM or the cache-disk of the backup cache. If the primary cache is also made of NVRAM, it can provide additional protection. It takes only several seconds (tens of seconds at most) to recover all the data from the backup cache, because reading from the cache-disk is done in the large segment size thus is very efficient.

In fact, during a power failure period, data cached in the cache-disk is much safer than in an NVRAM. Disks can retain their data for a long period of time without doing anything. On the other hand, data stored in active devices such as NVRAM or UPS (Uninterrupted Power Supply) backed DRAM are not as safe as data on disks, because NVRAM batteries may leak and UPS may run out of power or fail.

Compared to a single NVRAM write cache, a RAPID-Cache system has excellent availability. If one cache partition of a logical cache-disk crashes, the whole system can operate continuously, since either a spare disk will swap in to replace the failed disk, or the controller can simply skip the failed disk without affecting the system performance significantly. If a dedicated cache-disk crashed, the system can borrow a small partition from each data disk and operate in a logical cache-disk mode. If the NVRAM of the backup cache fails, a small portion of the primary cache can be borrowed so the system can continue its operations until the failed NVRAM is replaced. If the primary write cache fails, the read cache can be switched to a unified read/write cache mode to accept write data. In the case where a RAPID-Cache system uses a unified read/write primary cache, if the entire unified primary cache fails, the system may still operate in a degraded mode with lower performance because of the slow read speed of the backup cache.

3 Simulation Models

3.1 The Simulators

The RAPID-Cache simulator is built on top of a general cached-RAID5 simulator developed by us. The RAID mapping function is borrowed from the Berkeley *raidsim* simulator. The disk model used in our simulator is developed by Kotz et al. [17] that models an HP 97560 disk drive described in [18]. HP 97560 is a 5.25-inch, 1.26 GB disk with an average access time of 23 ms for an 8 KB data block. The disk simulator provides detailed simulation, including SCSI bus contention, built-in cache read-ahead and write-behind, head-skewing, etc. The simulator is quite accurate and is used by several other large scale simulation systems such as Stanford SimOS and Dartmouth STARFISH. However, HP 97560 is slightly out-dated. We have made the following changes to make it closer to the performance ranges of current disks: increasing the rotation speed from 4002 rpm to 7200 rpm; increasing its capacity by increasing the average linear density from 72 sectors/track to 288 sectors/track; increasing the interface bus speed from 10 MB/sec to 40 MB/sec; and decreasing its platter number from 10 to 3. We also assume that the RAID controller has a high-speed 80 MB/sec fibre-channel bus connected to the host. Requests must reserve the bus before starting data transfer. The controller can handle up to 32 pending requests. Additional requests must wait in a FIFO queue. Requests are processed in a First-Come-First-Serve basis, but they may complete out-of-order. The cache block size is 8 KB.

For the RAID-5 simulator, the number of RAID-5 columns is set to be 8 or 16 disks and the number of RAID-5 rows to be 1. The stripe unit is 32 KB and the data layout is Left-Symmetric.

3.2 Workload Models

The purpose of our performance evaluation is to show that the RAPID-Cache can deliver the same performance as very expensive NVRAM caches under various workload environments. In order to provide a fair and unbiased evaluation, we paid special attention in selecting the workload that drives our simulators since it plays a critical role in performance evaluation. Our main objective in choosing the workload models is to make it as close to realistic workloads as possible and to cover as wide a range of parameters as possible. With this objective in mind, two sets of trace files have been selected as discussed below.

3.2.1 Real-world Traces

The first set of traces are real-world traces obtained from EMC Corporation and HP Laboratories. The EMC trace (referred to as *EMC-tel* trace hereafter) was collected by an EMC Symmetrix disk array system installed at a telecommunication customer site. The trace file contains more than 200000 requests, with a fixed request size of 2 KB. The trace is write-dominated with a write ratio of 89%. The average request rate is about 333 requests/second.

The HP traces were collected from HP-UX systems during a 4-month period, and are described in detail in [13]. The name of the trace is called *cello-news* which is a single disk holding the Usenet news database. The news database was updated constantly throughout the day. The trace has been used by Savage and Wilkes to evaluate their AFRAID RAID system [6]. We have chosen 10 days of traces starting from May 1, 1992. Each day has several hundreds of thousand requests.

Careful examination of the HP trace files reveals that I/O requests are very bursty. The request rate in each request burst is very high while there usually exists a very long idle period (up to 30 seconds) between two consecutive bursts of requests. As a result, the average request rate is very low at about several requests per second. With such a low request rate and highly bursty request pattern, the RAPID-Cache will obviously perform very well since it will have enough time to move all data in the NVRAM buffer collected in a burst into the cache disk and to do destaging and garbage collection during an idle period. In order to present a conservative evaluation for the RAPID-Cache, we artificially reduce the idle period to increase the average request rate. We searched the traces and shortened any idle period longer than 50 milliseconds to 50 milliseconds to make the average request rate about 40 requests/second. To further increase the I/O rate, we also overlaid several days of *cello-news* traces into a single trace. The same approach has been used by Varma et al. in [5] in which up to 6 days of *cello* traces were overlaid to study the performance of RAID-5 caches. In this study we overlaid up to 10 days of traces, giving rise to a request rate of 400 requests/second. The numbers of requests in the resulting traces vary from about 200000 requests to about 1 million. The request size is about 8 KB.

3.2.2 Synthetic Traces

While real-world traces give a realistic evaluation of the performance of the systems, they have a limited view of system performance considering the fast changing computer world [19]. In order to observe how the RAPID-Cache performs under a variety of workloads, we generated a set of synthetic traces. Our synthetic traces were generated based on I/O access characteristics of the *cello-news* traces and the traces presented by Zivkov and Smith [14]. We carefully fine-tuned the trace generation parameters such as *request interval times, data access patterns, working-set sizes,* and *read/write ratios* in such a way that the characteristics of generated traces are similar to these real-world traces. Furthermore, in order to provide a fair and comprehensive evaluation, we also vary the workloads over a wide spectrum to cover as many workload situations as possible. Figure 4 shows the cache miss ratios as a function of cache sizes for *EMC-tel, cello-news* and our three synthetic traces on an LRU cache with an 8 KB block size. Table 1 lists the characteristics of all five traces used in this study. The request sizes of these traces are 8 KB except for *EMC-tel*, which has a request size of 2 KB. The details of our trace generation can be found in [15].

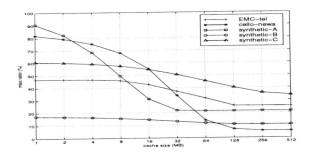

Figure 4: Miss Ratios of Traces with Various Cache Sizes

4 Simulation Results

Our objective here is to show that the RAPID-Cache has the same or similar performance as the conventional cache, with much lower cost and much higher reliability. On the other hand, with the same budget, the RAPID-Cache architecture allows a much larger primary cache because of its low cost to obtain much higher performance compared to a conventional cache. For this purpose we define a baseline system as a conventional read/write cache system with an optional backup NVRAM cache that is of the same size as the primary write cache. The backup NVRAM size of RAPID-Caches is chosen

to be 2 MB. We found through our experiments that using a size larger than 2 MB does not result in significant performance improvement, and using a size smaller than 1 MB may cause performance degradation for some traces. The size of cache-disks of RAPID-Caches is set to 256 MB for all simulation runs. This number was chosen because it is large enough to avoid garbage collection most of time.

4.1 Performance of Real-world Traces

Because the real-world traces (*EMC-tel* and *cello-news*) have only a moderate load, we used a relatively small system for simulation. The number of disks in the RAID-5 system is set to 8. The read cache size is 8 MB for the *EMC-tel* trace and 32 MB for the *cello-news* trace. We varied the primary write cache sizes from 4 to 16 MB for the *EMC-tel* trace and 16 to 32 MB for the *cello-news* trace.

Table 2 lists the read and write response time of the baseline systems and RAPID caches under the *EMC-tel* workload. Because the use of immediate report and the low cache miss ratio of this trace, the average response times are quite low, especially for write requests. The table shows that the baseline system and the RAPID-caches have very similar or almost identical performance.

Figure 5 compares the performance of RAPID-Caches with those of conventional caches under the *Cello-news* trace. In the figure the average I/O response times (of both read and write requests) are plotted as functions of numbers of overlaid traces. The average response times steadily increase as the number of overlaid traces (hence the I/O request rate) goes high because of the increased disk traffic. Eventually, the I/O request rate increases to a point where the system is saturated and the response times increase sharply. At this point the system can not handle any higher workload. We define the throughput at this point as the *maximum system throughput.*

It is clear from the results that the performance of RAPID-Caches is very close to that of baseline systems in terms of maximum system throughput and response time. This confirms that the backup cache of RAPID-Caches performs very well. The small NVRAM and the cache-disk do achieve the similar write performance as that of the large primary write cache.

For a Logical-RAPID-Cache, log writes into disks have to compete with normal data reads and destages, which may cause performance degradation. However it is interesting to note that the Logical-RAPID-Cache performs quite well most of the time. The reason is that the logical cache-disk space is distributed among many data disks, therefore the traffic caused by log-writing seen by each individual data disk is relatively low. In addition, we can use large read caches in our systems because DRAM is inexpensive now. The large read caches significantly reduce the disk read traffic seen by the data disks, thus further reducing the possibility of bandwidth conflicts.

For *EMC-tel*, a Physical-RAPID-Cache always performs better than a Logical-RAPID-Cache. For *cello-news*, a Physical-RAPID-Cache performs better than a Logical-RAPID-Cache at the high workload near the saturation point. However, for this particular trace, the Physical-RAPID-Cache shows slightly higher response times than those of the Logical-RAPID-Cache and the baseline system at low workloads. This can be attributed to the extreme burstiness of the *cello-news* traces as well as the artificially reduced inter-burst periods. Since we have artificially reduced the length of all long inter-burst idle periods to 50 ms to stress the RAPID-Cache system, many large bursts arrive closely, overflowing the small (2 MB) backup NVRAM in the RAPID-Cache. As a result, the contents of the backup NVRAM in the RAPID-Cache have to be log-written into the cache-disk several times during a large burst. This may create a wait-

Trace Name	Read Ratio	Access Pattern	Working set (MB)	Burstiness	Note
EMC-tel	11%	N/A	128	N/A	Write-dominated
Cello-news	40%	N/A	128	N/A	Write-dominated, very bursty
Synthetic-A	40%	normal	32	$\lambda = 32,\ \mu = 1024$	Write-dominated, moderate working-set
Synthetic-B	40%	uniform	1	$\lambda = 128,\ \mu = 1024$	Write-dominated, very small working-set
Synthetic-C	80%	exponential	512	$\lambda = 64,\ \mu = 1024$	Read-dominated, very large working-set

Table 1: Characteristics of Traces. *"Access Pattern" refers to the random function that controls the distance from the top of history table to a selected entry in the table. λ is the mean burst length while μ is the mean interval length, both are in terms of the number of requests.*

Cache sizes Read/Write (MB)	Response Time (ms)											
	Split R/W Cache						Unified R/W Cache					
	baseline		P-RAPID		L-RAPID		baseline		P-RAPID		L-RAPID	
	read	write	read	write	read	write	read	write	read	write	read	write
8/4 (12)	3.44	0.15	3.44	0.16	3.55	0.16	3.03	0.15	3.03	0.16	3.16	0.16
8/8 (16)	2.71	0.15	2.71	0.16	2.84	0.16	2.56	0.15	2.56	0.16	3.16	0.16
8/16 (24)	1.75	0.15	1.75	0.16	1.87	0.16	1.96	0.15	1.96	0.16	2.08	0.16

Table 2: Performance of trace *EMC-tel*. *The size of the NVRAM buffer of the RAPID-Cache is 1 MB. L-RAPID means Logical-RAPID-Cache and P-RAPID means Physical-RAPID-Cache.*

ing queue in front of the physical cache-disk, resulting in a slightly increased write response time therefore a slightly increased average response time. For Logical-RAPID-Caches, the log-write traffic is distributed among multiple disks, so the queuing effect of log-writing is negligible when the workload is low.

We believe that the slightly increased write response time of Physical-RAPID-Caches under such a highly bursty workload is not a major performance concern. The main performance metric here is throughput. As long as the cache-disk has sufficient bandwidth to keep up with the write traffic in the long run (We will discuss the performance of the cache-disk later in this section), the throughput of the entire system in the equilibrium state is limited by the primary cache, not the backup cache. Moreover, because of its low cost, with the *same budget* a RAPID-Cache can use a much larger primary cache to achieve a much higher throughput and lower response time than a baseline system. For example, as shown in Figure 5, for the same backup cache configuration, increasing the size of primary write cache of the RAPID-Cache from 16 MB to 32 MB almost doubles its throughput and reduces the response time.

4.2 Performance of Synthetic Traces

Since the synthetic traces have higher I/O rates, we scaled up the systems by increasing the number of disks in the RAID-5 systems from 8 to 16 and the read cache size from 32 MB to 64 MB. Figures 6 to 8 compare the performance of RAPID-Caches with those of conventional caches. In the figures the average I/O response times are plotted as functions of I/O request rates (throughput).

It is clear from the simulation results that performance of Physical-RAPID-Caches is almost identical to that of baseline systems. Its response-time vs. throughput curves are almost completely overlapped with that of a baseline system most of time. Logical-RAPID-Caches also perform very well. Their performance is similar or close to that of baseline systems.

It is interesting to note that for read-dominated traces such as *synthetic-C* (Figure 8), the performance degrades gracefully when the workload increases, while for write-dominated traces such as *synthetic-A* and *synthetic-B* (Figures 6 and 7) the performance changes relatively abruptly. When the workload increases, the read response times increase rapidly because of the increased disk traffic, while the write response times increase only gradually because of the use of the fast write technique. In write-dominated traces the average response time is largely determined by the write response time therefore the average response times increase only gradually until the system write cache saturates. At this point, the average response times increase abruptly.

5 Reliability and Costs

5.1 Reliability Model

In this subsection, we analyze the reliability of the cache system based on exponentially distributed failures and repairs for both RAM and disks. We will consider four different cache configurations, namely *RAPID-Cache with an NVRAM primary cache*, *RAPID-Cache with a DRAM primary cache*, *Single NVRAM cache*, and *Dual NVRAM caches*.

Consider a RAPID-Cache with an NVRAM primary cache. Assume that the primary cache consists of a number of NVRAM memory modules. Let $MTTF_{NVRAM}$ and $MTTF_{disk}$ represent the mean time to failure of an NVRAM module and the mean time to failure of a disk, respectively. In case of a failure, a repair process can start by replacing a failed memory module or a failed disk. It is reasonable to assume that the mean repair time for both RAM and disk is same denoted by $MTTR$. Recall that each write operation in the RAPID-Cache is performed in both the primary cache and the backup cache. If a memory module in the primary cache fails, the data are lost only if the component containing the same data copy in the backup cache also fails before the repair for the failed module is done. Similarly, if a component in the backup cache fails first, that data is lost if the copy in the primary cache also fails before repair. Let S_{PrimeC}, and $S_{bkupRAM}$ be the size, in terms of memory modules, of primary cache

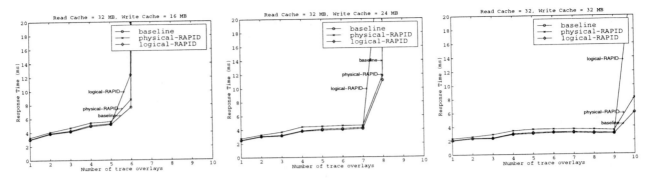

Figure 5: Performance of trace *cello-news*. *Note: A single trace has a request rate of about 40 requests/sec. Overlaying 10 traces results in a request rate of about 400 requests/sec.*

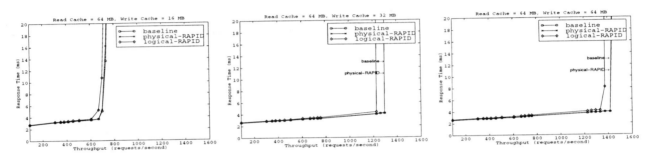

Figure 6: Performance of trace *Synthetic-A*

and the size of the NVRAM in the backup cache, respectively. The mean failure rate caused by both a primary cache failure and a failure of the NVRAM of the backup cache is $S_{PrimeC}S_{bkupRAM}MTTR/(MTTF_{NVRAM})^2$. And the mean failure rate caused by both a primary cache failure and a disk failure is $S_{PrimeC}MTTR/(MTTF_{NVRAM}MTTF_{disk})$. The probability that the mirror copy of a primary cache data resides in the NVRAM of the backup cache is $S_{bkupRAM}/S_{PrimeC}$, and the probability that the mirror copy resides in the disk of the backup cache is $1 - S_{bkupRAM}/S_{PrimeC}$. Therefore, the mean failure rate of the entire cache system is given by

$$\lambda_1 = \frac{S_{PrimeC}S_{bkupRAM}MTTR}{(MTTF_{NVRAM})^2}\left(\frac{S_{bkupRAM}}{S_{PrimeC}}\right)$$
$$+ \frac{S_{PrimeC}MTTR}{MTTF_{NVRAM}MTTF_{disk}}\left(1 - \frac{S_{bkupRAM}}{S_{PrimeC}}\right).$$

It reduces to

$$\lambda_1 = \frac{(S_{bkupRAM})^2MTTR}{(MTTF_{NVRAM})^2} + \frac{(S_{PrimeC} - S_{bkupRAM})MTTR}{MTTF_{NVRAM}MTTF_{disk}}.$$

The *mean time to data loss* ($MTTDL$) of the RAPID-Cache system with an NVRAM primary cache is therefore given by

$$MTTDL_{RAPID1} = \frac{1}{\lambda_1}$$

As mentioned previously, NVRAM is orders of magnitude more expensive than regular DRAM. With the new RAPID-Cache architecture, it is possible to implement the primary cache using DRAM instead of NVRAM. Using DRAM as a primary write cache, on the other hand, may compromise the reliability of the cache. In addition to RAM failures, data may get lost due to several other reasons such as a power failure, hardware failures such as CPU failures, and environment failures etc. To cope with frequent power failures, most systems use an UPS to prevent data loss from sudden power failures. In this case, data loss occurs in the DRAM only when the power fails and the UPS also fails. If a hardware failure such as a CPU failure occurs, replacing the failed hardware usually requires a system shutdown. As a result, all data in a DRAM will be lost and they have to be recovered from the backup cache. The data failure rate at the backup cache is $S_{bkupRAM}/MTTF_{NVRAM} + 1/MTTF_{disk}$. Let $MTTPF$, $MTTF_{UPS}$, and $MTTHF$ be the mean time to power failure, mean time to failure for the UPS, and the mean time to hardware failure, respectively. Assume that the mean time to repair is same for all types of failures ($MTTR$). Then the mean failure rate is given by

$$\lambda_2 = \left(\frac{S_{bkupRAM}}{MTTF_{NVRAM}} + \frac{1}{MTTF_{disk}}\right) \times$$

$$\left(\frac{S_{PrimeC}MTTR}{MTTF_{DRAM}} + \frac{MTTR}{MTTHF} + \frac{MTTR^2}{MTTPF*MTTF_{UPS}}\right),$$

and the mean time to data loss of the RAPID-Cache with a DRAM primary cache is

$$MTTDL_{RAPID2} = \frac{1}{\lambda_2}.$$

210

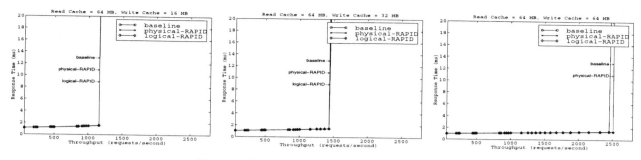

Figure 7: Performance of trace *Synthetic-B*

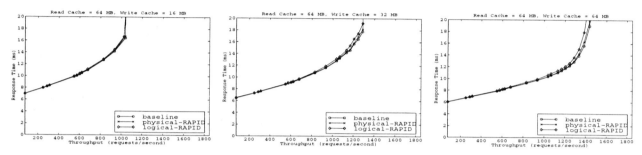

Figure 8: Performance of trace *Synthetic-C*

The reliability analysis of the other two cache architectures is straightforward. For the single NVRAM cache case, the mean time to data loss is simply $MTTF_{NVRAM}/S_{PrimeC}$. The mean time to data loss for the dual NVRAM case is $(MTTF_{NVRAM})^2/(S_{PrimeC}MTTR)$

5.2 Reliability and Costs Comparison

One important factor that determines the reliability of the write cache is the mean time to failure of NVRAM. Unfortunately, remarkably little data is available from literature or data sheets of various RAM products. Savage and Wilkes [6] cited 25-87K hours of data retention lifetimes of Integral Lithium-cell-backed static RAM that are extremely expensive and 15K hours of predicted MTTF for the popular PrestoServe card. With the lack of published data for MTTF, we assume optimistically an MTTF of RAM to be 200k hours, which favors conventional NVRAM cache architectures and represents a conservative evaluation for RAPID-Cache. Our analysis also assumes that the NVRAM cache consists of a number of 2MB modules [20]. Some existing disk systems such as the RAIDs from Storage Computer Co. use independent modules to constitute a write cache. Power failures and UPS failure are another source of possible data loss if DRAM is used. We assume that all the systems considered are backed up by UPS systems. We chose the mean time to power failure (MTTPF) of 4300 hours [21] and the MTTF of UPS ($MTTF_{UPS}$) of 200k hours [6] in our analysis. The mean time to hardware failures and environment failures etc. is assumed to be one month or 720 hours [4]. The MTTF for disks, $MMTF_{disk}$, is assumed to be 1 million hours. The mean time to repair for all types of failures here is assumed to be 48 hours.

Cost figures for semiconductor devices and disks change very rapidly. It is difficult to give an accurate and up-to-date cost evaluation. In order to give a general idea for the cost of the different cache architectures, we made the following assumptions. The cost of DRAM is $5/MB and the cost of NVRAM is $120/MB which was quoted by Dallas Semiconductor recently. The cost of disk space is 10 cents/MB. For a logical cache-disk, it is quite reasonable to use this cost number since the cache space of a logical cache-disk is located in partitions of data disks. In the case of a physical cache-disk the cache space is located in a partition of a hot standby disk as explained previously. Therefore, it is also reasonable to use the per MB cost figure since no additional disk drive is needed. If no spare disk were available in a RAID, a dedicated cache disk would be required that will add to the cost an additional $200 for a minimum size disk drive available in the market.

Table 3 lists the reliability and cost comparison between the baseline cache and our RAPID-Cache for 3 typical configurations. It is clear from the table that the difference between the baseline cache and the RAPID-Cache in terms of reliability and cost is significant. Compared to a single copy NVRAM write cache, the reliability of the RAPID-Cache with an NVRAM write cache is 5 orders of magnitudes higher than that of the baseline cache system while the additional cost introduced by the RAPID-Cache is only between 3% and 12%. Compared to the dual copy NVRAM caches, the RAPID-Caches with an NVRAM primary cache still have higher reliability than the baseline cache system (because disks are more reliable than NVRAM) with approximately half of the cost. For the RAPID-Cache with a DRAM write primary cache, its reliability is 3 orders of magnitude better than a single-copy NVRAM cache. More importantly, the cost of the RAPID-Cache is dramatically lower than both single-copy NVRAM caches and dual-copy NVRAM caches.

Cache sizes	Reliability (MTTDL in hours)				Cost (US Dollars)			
Read/Write (MB/MB)	Single NVRAM	Dual-copy NVRAM	RAPID Cache-DP	RAPID Cache-NP	Single NVRAM	Dual-copy NVRAM	RAPID Cache-DP	RAPID Cache-NP
64/16	$1.25*10^4$	$5.21*10^7$	$6.70*10^5$	$4.53*10^7$	\$2,240	\$4,160	\$905	\$2,746
64/32	$6.25*10^3$	$2.60*10^7$	$6.36*10^5$	$3.86*10^7$	\$4,160	\$8,000	\$986	\$4,666
64/64	$3.13*10^3$	$1.30*10^7$	$5.77*10^5$	$2.98*10^7$	\$8,000	\$15,680	\$1146	\$8,506

Table 3: Reliability and Costs comparison of the different write cache architectures. The size of the NVRAM buffer of the RAPID-Cache is 2 MB. *Note: RAPID Cache-DP refers to a RAPID-Cache with a DRAM primary write cache. RAPID Cache-NP refers to a RAPID-Cache with an NVRAM primary write cache.*

In some cases, the cost of the RAPID-Cache is only 11% of the single-copy NVRAM caches and 6% of the dual-copy NVRAM caches. In other words, the RAPID-Cache comes almost free to provide similar reliability to that of the baseline cache costing over ten thousand dollars can provide. Moreover, a RAPID-Cache can use a much larger primary cache to improve its performance while still maintaining its low cost. For example, a RAPID-Cache with a 64 MB DRAM read cache and a 64 MB DRAM write cache costs only \$905. Yet it provides more than 2 times higher throughput and 3 orders of magnitude better reliability than a single-copy NVRAM write cache of the 16 MB, which costs \$2,240.

6 Related Work

The idea of using a disk-based log to improve system performance or to improve the reliability of RAM has been used in both file systems and database systems for a long time. For example, the Log-structured File System (LFS) [9, 10, 11], the Journal File System (JFS) and other similar systems all use disk-based data/metadata logging to improve file system performance and speed-up crash recovery. Database systems have long been using elaborate logging techniques to improve the reliability of the RAM buffer and to implement the transaction semantics. NVRAM has been used by many database systems to reduce the overhead of logging.

Several RAID systems have implemented the LFS algorithm at the RAID controller level [22, 16]. LFS collects writes in a RAM buffer to form large logs and writes large logs to data disks. While LFS has demonstrated superior performance for many workloads, studies have shown that the garbage collection overhead of LFS can become a major performance bottleneck in transaction-processing environments, decreasing the system performance by 34–40% [11, 23]. The garbage collection overhead becomes very high when the disk utilization reaches 80% of the total disk capacity [11, 22].

eNVy [7] is a large nonvolatile main memory storage system based on flash EPROM. Flash EPROM has some disk-like characteristics, i.e, data must be erased in blocks and the write speed is slow. eNVy solved the write problem by using a battery-backed SRAM in front of the flash-EPROM. Data are first written into the SRAM and then parallelly transferred into the flash EPROM in large blocks. The whole system appears to users as a large high-speed NVRAM.

While the idea of RAPID-Cache is inspired by the previous research, especially LFS and DCD [1], there are several important differences as highlighted below.

- In both LFS and DCD, data are collected in a RAM buffer and logged into disks when the buffer is full. In the backup cache of RAPID-Cache, data are written into an LRU cache made of NVRAM. Active data may be overwritten in the LRU cache frequently. Only the inactive data evicted from the LRU cache are collected in a

segment buffer and logged into the cache-disk. The separation of active data from inactive data significantly reduces the cache-disk traffic and garbage collection cost.

- In DCD, data in the cache-disk must be destaged into the data disk. In RAPID-Cache, there is no need to read the cache-disk during destaging, since all dirty data can be accessed from the primary cache. Therefore the destage overhead of RAPID-Cache is the same as that of a conventional system with a single-copy or a dual-copy NVRAM write cache.

- LFS needs garbage collection which significantly limits the system performance in some cases. The asymmetrically parallel architecture of RAPID-Cache and the separation of active data from inactive data in the backup cache enable us to design a garbage collection algorithm that is much more efficient than the one used by LFS. Moreover, RAPID-Cache seldom requires garbage collection. In fact, the garbage collection overhead of RAPID-Cache is so low that it has virtually no impact on system performance.

7 Conclusions

In this paper, we have presented a new disk cache architecture called RAPID-Cache. The main feature of the RAPID-Cache is its asymmetrically parallel architecture that consists of a fast-write-fast-read primary cache and an inexpensive, fast-write-slow-read hierarchical backup cache. We trade the read performance of the backup cache for economy and reliability. Fortunately, the compromise in read performance of the backup cache does not affect the system performance in any way because read operations from the backup cache are necessary only during error recovery periods. On the other hand, the economy, reliability and performance gained have been shown to be dramatic. Such win-win trading is made possible by exploiting the locality of disk accesses and efficiency of large disk transfers. We have shown through simulation experiments and analysis that it is possible to configure the RAPID-Cache in a number of ways to optimize throughput, reliability, or system cost:

- Compared to a single-copy NVRAM cache, a RAPID-Cache with a DRAM primary cache has much higher reliability and similar performance, with only a fraction of the cost.

- Compared to a single-copy NVRAM cache, a RAPID-Cache with an NVRAM primary cache has much better reliability and similar performance, with only slightly higher cost.

- Compared to a dual-copy NVRAM cache, a RAPID-Cache with an NVRAM primary cache has similar or better reliability and similar performance, with only half of the cost.

- Because its low cost, with the *same budget*, RAPID-Caches can have significantly higher performance compared to conventional NVRAM cache architectures by affording a much larger primary cache size, while still maintaining good reliability.

- The asymmetrically parallel architecture of RAPID-Caches and its algorithm that separates active data from inactive data virtually eliminate the garbage collection overhead, which are the major problems associated with previous solutions such as LFS and DCD.

Furthermore, using DRAM for the primary cache makes it economically feasible to combine the read cache with write cache resulting in a unified cache that has significant performance advantages. Such a unified cache would be very expensive to implement with the existing dual-copy cache architectures because of the requirement of the large read cache that would have to be NVRAM if combined with a write cache. While we have not presented the results of unified RAPID-Cache in this paper because of the space limitation, our simulation results show that a unified RAPID-Cache can achieve 2–4 times higher throughput than a split cache with the same total cache size. The low cost feature of the RAPID-Cache also makes it possible to use a very large primary cache to achieve very high performance for high-end systems. Therefore, a wide range of disk I/O systems can benefit from the RAPID-Cache architecture.

Acknowledgments

We thank Dr. David Kotz of Dartmouth College for letting us use his disk simulator. We also thank HP Laboratories and EMC Corporation for providing us with disk traces. We benefited from discussions with Dr. Jien-Chung Lo of University of Rhode Island on reliability issues of NVRAM. Some algorithms of the synthetic trace generator were initially designed by Qi Zhang.

References

[1] Y. Hu and Q. Yang, "DCD—disk caching disk: A new approach for boosting I/O performance," in *Proceedings of the 23rd International Symposium on Computer Architecture*, (Philadelphia, Pennsylvania), pp. 169–178, May 1996.

[2] J. Menon and J. Cortney, "The architecture of a fault-tolerant cached RAID controller," in *Proceedings of the 20th Annual International Symposium on Computer Architecture*, (San Diego, California), pp. 76–86, May 16–19, 1993.

[3] K. Treiber and J. Menon, "Simulation study of cached RAID5 designs," in *Proceedings of Int'l Symposium on High Performance Computer Architectures*, (Raleigh, North Carolina), pp. 186–197, Jan. 1995.

[4] P. M. Chen, E. K. Lee, G. A. Gibson, R. H. Katz, and D. A. Patterson, "RAID : High-performance, reliable secondary storage," *ACM Computing Surveys*, vol. 26, pp. 145–188, June 1994.

[5] A. Varma and Q. Jacobson, "Destage algorithms for disk arrays with non-volatile caches," in *Proceedings of the 22nd Annual International Symposium on Computer Architecture*, (Santa Margherita Ligure, Italy), pp. 83–95, June 22–24, 1995.

[6] S. Savage and J. Wilkes, "AFRAID — A frequently redundant array of independent disks," in *Proceedings of the 1996 USENIX Technical Conference*, (San Diego, CA), Jan. 1996.

[7] M. Wu and W. Zwaenepoel, "eNVy, a non-volatile, main memory storage system," in *Proceedings of the 6th Symposium on Architectural Support for Programming Languages and Operating Systems*, pp. 86–97, Oct. 1994.

[8] S. Akyürek and K. Salem, "Management of partially safe buffers," *IEEE Transactions on Computers*, vol. 44, pp. 394–407, Mar. 1995.

[9] J. Ousterhout and F. Douglis, "Beating the I/O bottleneck: A case for log-structured file systems," tech. rep., Computer Science Division, Electrical Engineering and Computer Sciences, University of California at Berkeley, Oct. 1988.

[10] M. Rosenblum and J. Ousterhout, "The design and implementation of a log-structured file system," *ACM Transactions on Computer Systems*, pp. 26 – 52, Feb. 1992.

[11] M. Seltzer, K. Bostic, M. K. McKusick, and C. Staelin, "An implementation of a log-structured file system for UNIX," in *Proceedings of Winter 1993 USENIX*, (San Diego, CA), pp. 307–326, Jan. 1993.

[12] D. Stodolsky, M. Holland, W. V. Courtright II, and G. A. Gibson, "Parity logging disk arrays," in *ACM Transactions of Computer Systems*, pp. 206–235, Aug. 1994.

[13] C. Ruemmler and J. Wilkes, "UNIX disk access patterns," in *Proceedings of Winter 1993 USENIX*, (San Diego, CA), pp. 405–420, Jan. 1993.

[14] B. T. Zivkov and A. J. Smith, "Disk caching in large databases and timeshared systems," Tech. Rep. CSD-96-913, Computer Science Division, University of California, Berkeley, Sept. 1996.

[15] Y. Hu, Q. Yang, and T. Nightingale, "RAPID-Cache — a reliable and inexpensive write cache for disk I/O systems," Tech. Rep. 1198-0001, Department of Electrical and Computer Engineering, University of Rhode Island (http://www.ele.uri.edu/Research/hpcl/RAPID/), Nov. 1998.

[16] J. Wilkes, R. Golding, C. Staelin, and T. Sullivan, "The HP AutoRaid hierarchical storage system," *ACM Transactions on Computer Systems*, vol. 14, pp. 108–136, Feb. 1996.

[17] D. Kotz, S. B. Toh, and S. Radhakrishnan, "A detailed simulation model of the HP 97560 disk drive," Tech. Rep. PCS-TR94-220, Department of Computer Science, Dartmouth College, July 1994.

[18] C. Ruemmler and J. Wilkes, "An introduction to disk drive modeling," *IEEE Computer*, pp. 17–28, Mar. 1994.

[19] G. R. Ganger, "Generating representative synthetic workloads – an unsolved problem," in *Proceedings of the Computer Measurement Group (CMG) Conference*, pp. 1263–1269, Dec. 1995.

[20] Dallas Semiconductor, "DS1270Y/AB 16M Nonvolatile SRAM data sheet."

[21] G. A. Gibson and D. A. Patterson, "Designing disk arrays for high data reliability," *Journal of Parallel and Distributed Computing*, vol. 17, pp. 4–27, Jan.-Feb. 1993.

[22] J. Menon, "A performance comparison of RAID-5 and log-structured arrays," in *Proceedings of the Fourth IEEE International Symposium on High Performance Distributed Computing*, pp. 167–178, Aug. 1995.

[23] M. Seltzer, K. A. Smith, H. Balakrishnan, J. Chang, S. McMains, and V. Padmanabhan, "File system logging versus clustering: A performance comparison," in *Proceedings of 1995 USENIX*, (New Orleans, LA), pp. 249–264, Jan. 1995.

Permutation Development Data Layout (PDDL)

Thomas J.E. Schwarz, S.J.
Jesuit School of Theology
1756 LeRoy Avenue
Berkeley, CA 94709
schwarz@scudc.scu.edu

Jesse Steinberg   Walter A. Burkhard
Gemini Storage Systems Laboratory
Department of Computer Science and Engineering
University of California, San Diego
La Jolla, CA 92093-0114
<jsteinbe, burkhard>@cs.ucsd.edu

Abstract

Declustered data organizations in disk arrays (RAIDs) achieve less-intrusive reconstruction of data after a disk failure. We present PDDL, a new data layout for declustered disk arrays. PDDL layouts exist for a large variety of disk array configurations with a distributed spare disk. PDDL declustered disk arrays have excellent run-time performance under light and heavy workloads. PDDL maximizes access parallelism in the most critical circumstances, namely during reconstruction of data on the spare disk. PDDL occurs minimum address translation overhead compared to all other proposed declustering layouts.

1 Introduction

Many applications require high availability and throughput from cost effective storage subsystems. Disk arrays offer higher throughput compared to a single disk since a single, large access is serviced by a number of disks. They store information redundantly so that a single or even multiple disk failure does not leave data inaccessible. By adding a (virtual) spare disk to the ensemble, we increase data availability even more [8]. We propose a novel *data layout,* Permutation Development Data Layout (PDDL), which distributes client data, redundant data and spare blocks throughout the disk array [12]. The layout is implemented without large tables or involved calculations. In addition, its performance is either the best or similar to that of the best of other proposed layouts. In contrast to other layouts, it explicitly provides a virtual spare disk.

2 Disk Array Declustering

Disks arrays store data redundantly. We group a fixed number of consecutive disk blocks into a *stripe unit.* A *stripe* (a.k.a. reliability stripe, reliability group, parity group, or cluster) contains a fixed number of stripe units; in a stripe, all stripe units but one store client data. The remaining stripe unit, the *parity unit,* stores the bit-wise parity of the other stripe units. If we cannot access a stripe unit in a stripe, then we access all the others in the stripe and recalculate the data on the inaccessible stripe unit. For this reason, we position the stripe units of a stripe on different disks. In a RAID Level 5 [11], a stripe contains stripe units on all the disks. If a disk fails, all the other disks must process additional accesses for every read from the failed disk. The surviving disks then carry not only their own load, but also the read load of the failed disk.

In a *declustered* disk array [1, 2, 6, 7, 10], the number of stripe units per stripe is smaller than the total number of disks. Any usable data layout (the assignment of stripe units to stripes) fulfills a number of fairly natural criteria: (1) Each stripe contains the same number k of stripe units. (2) Each disk contains the same number b of stripe units. (3) Single Failure Correction: No two stripe units in a stripe reside on the same disk; otherwise, a single disk failure can cause data loss. (4) Even Reconstruction Load: For any two disks, the number of stripes λ with stripe units on these two disks is independent of the two disks chosen; the workload increase after a disk failure is proportional to λ and evenly distributed accordingly. Properties (1) to (4) characterize a *balanced block design* [5]. We need to impose certain other conditions in order to use balanced block designs for disk array layouts: First, all writes to a single stripe unit also update the parity unit. In order to distribute the write load evenly we demand, that (5) all disks carry the same number of parity units. We frequently insert a virtual spare disk (distributed sparing, [8]) into the disk array. We accomplish this by reserving a set of stripe units, called *spare units,* which will be only used after a disk failure. After a failure, we reconstruct the stripe units including the parity units of the failed disk and place them in this spare space. If no disk has failed, then the spare space on a disk is never accessed,

214

Figure 1. PDDL: Two Virtual RAID Level 4 Stripes with One Virtual Spare Disk

so that the utilization of the disk decreases correspondingly. We demand that this decrease be distributed uniformly or, equivalently, that (6) each disk contains the same number of spare units.

Run-time among different data layouts varies considerably. Since disk arrays derive their performance benefits from the increased throughput, an obvious design goal is to maximize read and write throughput. However, not only are read and write operations different since writes need to update parity, but also the operation conditions of the disk array differ depending on whether we work in the fault free mode, whether we have to reconstruct data and place it in the spare space just after a disk failure, or whether we use spare space after the blocks on a failed disk have been recovered.

The data layout mediates between the file system view of storage, typically a very large virtual disk organized as a linear address space of stripe units, and the actual placement of these stripe units on the various disks in the disk array.

PDDL uses almost no storage or calculation to determine its mapping. Recent declustering schemes PRIME of Alvarez, Burkhard, Stockmeyer and Cristian [2] and DATUM of Alvarez, Burkhard, and Cristian [1] also use straightforward, efficient calculation to map stripe units to disks thereby avoiding table lookup. Previous schemes include *Parity Declustering* of Holland and Gibson [6] which uses table lookup to specify balanced incomplete block design together with parity rotation. The *Random Permutation* scheme of Merchant and Yu [9] uses pseudo-random permutations for data layout.

3 PDDL Data Layout

The PDDL approach assumes there are n disks logically partitioned into g virtual RAID Level 4 stripes each containing k stripe units. Figure 1 present the configuration for $n = 7$ disks with $g = 2$ RAID Level 4 stripes, each consisting of $k = 3$ disks. Each stripe consists of dedicated data disks and a dedicated parity disk. We assume that stripe units are accessed via disk logical block addresses (LBA). PDDL numbers the virtual disks of the virtual RAID from 0 to $n - 1$. To address a virtual stripe unit , we need to have a virtual disk number d_v and a virtual LBA b_v. Since we have n physical disks, we number them similarly. We address a physical stripe unit in the same fashion by a physical disk

number d_v and a LBA b_v. PDDL provides a one-to-one correspondence between physical and virtual stripe units. This mapping fulfills our seven design goals for a data layout.

The PDDL mapping does not change the LBA. Thus, a physical and a virtual stripe unit address under PDDL have only different physical and virtual disk numbers. PDDL uses a *base permutation* as an initial mapping for disk addresses with LBA 0. For all other LBAs, PDDL adds the LBA to the disk address obtained from the base permutation as shown in Figure 2. This code implements the PDDL mapping for the disk array of Figure 1; the mapping is typical and exemplifies the run-time efficiency possible. The mapping is cyclic and repeats after n LBAs.

```
int permutation[ ] = { 0, 1, 2, 4, 3, 6, 5 } ;
int virtual2physical( int disk , int stripeUnit )
{
    return ( ( permutation[disk] + stripeUnit ) % 7 ) ;
}
```

Figure 2. PDDL Address Translation

Suppose we need to access stripe unit 10 of the virtual spare disk 0. We would calculate $(0 + 10)\%7 = 3$ and access stripe unit 10 on disk 3. Suppose we must write to stripe unit 20 on disk 4 of the virtual RAID. A disk array write also updates the parity unit, which is located in our case on disk 6 of the virtual RAID. We first apply the base permutation to the disk numbers 4 and 6 and obtain 3 and 5 respectively. We calculate then $(3 + 20)\%7 = 2$ and $(5 + 20)\%7 = 4$. Thus, we access the data of stripe unit 20 of disk 2 and the parity unit 20 on disk 4.

For each virtual LBA there is exactly one spare unit. Accordingly, every disk has the same number of spare units — $1/n^{th}$ of its stripe units. Similarly, there will be the same number of parity units on each disk. This gives us criteria (1), (2), (3), (5), and (6).

Criteria (4) is not true for every base permutation, and finding suitable base permutations is the challenge to utilize the PDDL approach. Sometimes, the best we can do is to use two (or more) base permutations, where the data layout is generated by rotating through the base permutations [12]. In all cases, the PDDL address translation calculation is efficient and the storage requirements minimal.

Number	Stripe Width					
of Stripes	5	6	7	8	9	10
1	1	1	1	1	1	1
2	1	1	2	1	1	?
3	1	1	1'	2	2	1
4	1	1	1	1'	1	1
5	1	1	1'	1	3	2
6	1	1	1	3	6	1
7	1	1	2	5	?	1
8	1	2	4	?	1	?
9	2	2	5	1	?	?
10	1	1	1	?	?	1

Table 1. PDDL data layouts; an apostrophe denotes a solution for a non-prime number of disks obtained or compiled by Furino [5]

4 Existence of PDDL Base Permutations

The PDDL data layouts implement near resolvable incomplete block designs [5]. The way we generate layouts is known as "permutation development." Bose [3] in 1939 gave a general method to create base permutations when n is a prime number. For n composite, the literature [5] contains some base permutations. We have extended this search to include configurations composed of a small number of base permutations. Our results are summarized in Table 1. Each row is for a particular g and every column for a particular k; the entry designates the number of base permutations generating a PDDL data layout. The question mark entries indicate that we do not have a suitable set of base permutations for this configuration.

If the number of disks n is not a prime number but a prime power, then we can created PDDL layouts using calculations within finite fields. This is very attractive for powers of 2 (e.g. for 32 or 64 disks) since we can implement the virtual to physical address translation using only a few XOR and shift operations. Indeed, we believe this is among the fastest address translation schemes possible, if not the fastest. For other prime powers, the resulting implementation is more complicated, but still very fast.

5 Extensions of PDDL

PDDL has the drawback that the number of disks n and the stripe width k have to satisfy $n = 1 \pmod{k}$. We can combine DATUM with PDDL to extend the PDDL's useful domain in a technique referred to as DATUM *wrapping*. Assume that n is slightly larger than $n_0 = gk + 1$. We then use the DATUM data layout with n disks and stripe width n_0. Since n_0 and n are very close, the DATUM mapping is

very efficient and remains very small even for large n. We number the DATUM stripes units and treat these numbers as virtual disk numbers in a virtual array with n_0 disks. We then arrange data according to PDDL within this virtual array. In effect, the physical disks are the physical disks of the DATUM layout, the stripes units within DATUM replace the physical disks of PDDL, and the virtual disks of PDDL are the interface abstraction.

We assumed tacitly that there is only one *check* (parity) disk in PDDL. However, for high reliability environments, this does not provide sufficient redundancy. PDDL as well as DATUM, PRIME, Parity Declustering, and Pseudo-Random layouts can be extended to include the extra redundant data.

6 Performance Evaluation

We have tested PDDL as well as DATUM, PRIME, Parity Declustering and RAID Level 5. We used RAIDframe [4] simulating a small disk array with 13 HP 2247 (1.03GB) disks; PDDL can be used for large ensembles of disks as we see in Table 1 but DATUM becomes less efficient for larger ensembles. The other schemes accommodate large ensembles. We tested the data layouts with synthetic workloads consisting of random accesses to a fixed number of contiguous disk blocks. PDDL's response times were at least comparable and often better than all others except DATUM operating at very heavy workloads.

As a result of our experiments, we believe that the intuitively attractive goal of maximum parallelism (one of the design goals for a good declustering scheme in [6]) needs to be modified. While a single large data access benefits from being serviced by as many disks as possible under light workloads, as the workload increases the completion of a single job can be actually faster if it is partitioned over fewer disks. This phenomena has been mentioned recently by Triantifillou and Faloutsos [13]. We introduce the notion of the *footprint*, or, disk working-set, the number of disks accessed by accessing a contiguous set of stripe units in the disk array. The size of the footprint should increase only gradually as the number of contiguous stripe units within the query increases.

7 Comparisons

Distributed sparing dramatically increases reliability and performance [8]. Any of the previous schemes can be modified to include distributed sparing. However, only PDDL distributes the spare space over all n disks of the ensemble thereby incurring the smallest loss of client data space penalty. The other declustering schemes require modification; the most obvious approaches require roughly g times as much spare space. PDDL uses almost no extra space within its mapping implementation. As Table 1 shows, PDDL schemes exist for a wide variety of disk array parameters. Using DATUM wrapping, we can find PDDL schemes for most commercially interesting dimensions, namely with stripe width k up to 10 and number of disks n up to about 60.

8 Conclusion

PDDL is a new disk array declustering data layout. PDDL layouts exists for a large number of commercially interesting disk array configurations. PDDL uses very little storage and shows minute overhead as it calculates the data layout. The run-time performance of PDDL is very competitive with all other good declustering schemes except for very heavy workloads when DATUM is the clear winner. However, we note that DATUM is most efficient when used with small ensembles. For situations were light to moderate workloads are expected for small to large disk ensembles, PDDL presents an excellent declustering choice.

References

[1] G.A. Alvarez, W.A. Burkhard, F. Cristian: "Tolerating Multiple Failures in RAID Architectures with Optimal Storage and Uniform Declustering", *Proceedings of the 24th Annual ACM/IEEE International Symposium on Computer Architecture*, pp. 62-72, 1997.

[2] G.A. Alvarez, W.A. Burkhard, L.J. Stockmeyer, F. Cristian: "Declustered Disk Array Architectures with Optimal and Near-Optimal Parallelism", *Proceedings of the 25th Annual ACM/IEEE International Symposium on Computer Architecture*, pp. 109-120, 1998.

[3] R.E. Bose: "On the Construction of Balanced Incomplete Block Designs", *Annals of Eugenics*, vol. 9, pp. 353-399, 1939.

[4] W. Courtright, G. Gibson, M. Holland, J. Zelenka: "A Structured Approach to Redundant Disk Array Implementation", *Proceedings of the International Symposium on Performance and Dependability*, pp. 11-20, 1996.

[5] S. Furino, Y. Miao, J. Yin: **Frames and Resolvable Designs: Uses, Constructions, and Existence**, CRC Press, Boca Raton, 1996.

[6] M. Holland, G.A. Gibson: "Parity Declustering for Continuous Operation in Redundant Disk Arrays", *Proceedings, ASPLOS-V*, pp. 23-35, Sept. 1992.

[7] M. Holland, G.A. Gibson, D.P. Sieworuk: "Architectures and Algorithms for On-Line Failure Recovery in Redundant Disk Arrays", *Journal of Parallel and Distributed Databases,* 2, 1994.

[8] J. Menon, D. Mattson: "Distributed Sparing in Disk Arrays", *Proceedings of the COMPCON Conference 1992*, San Francisco, pp. 410-416, 1992.

[9] A. Merchant, P.S. Yu: "Analytic Modelling of Clustered RAID with Mapping Based on Nearly Random Permutation", *IEEE Transactions on Computers*, vol. 45, no. 3, March 1996.

[10] R. Muntz, J. Lui: "Performance Analysis of Disk Arrays under Failure", *Proceedings of the Conference on Very Large Data Bases*, pp. 162-173, 1990.

[11] D.A. Patterson, G.A. Gibson, R.H. Katz: "A Case for Redundant Arrays of Inexpensive Disks (RAID)", *Proceedings, ACM SIGMOD Conference*, pp. 109-116, July 1988.

[12] T.J.E. Schwarz, W.A. Burkhard, J. Steinberg: "Permutation Development Data Layout (PDDL) Disk Array Declustering," *UCSD technical report CS98-584*, April 1998. www.ucsd.edu/~groups/gemini

[13] P. Triantafillou, C. Faloutsos: "Overlay Striping and Optimal Parallel I/O in Modern Applications," http://www.ced.tuc.gr/Research/Reports/HERMES/Reports/htm, #TR8. 1997.

Dynamically Variable Line-Size Cache Exploiting High On-Chip Memory Bandwidth of Merged DRAM/Logic LSIs

Koji Inoue[†]   Koji Kai[‡]   Kazuaki Murakami[†]

[†] Dept. of Computer Science and Comm. Eng.
Kyushu University
6–1 Kasuga-koen, Kasuga,
Fukuoka 816-8580 Japan.
ppram@c.csce.kyushu-u.ac.jp

[‡] Institute of Systems &
Information Technologies/KYUSHU
2-1-22 Momochihama, Sawara-ku,
Fukuoka 814-0001 Japan.
kai@k-isit.or.jp

Abstract

This paper proposes a novel cache architecture suitable for merged DRAM/logic LSIs, which is called "dynamically variable line-size cache (D-VLS cache)". The D-VLS cache can optimize its line-size according to the characteristic of programs, and attempts to improve the performance by exploiting the high on-chip memory bandwidth. In our evaluation, it is observed that the performance improvement achieved by a direct-mapped D-VLS cache is about 27%, compared to a conventional direct-mapped cache with fixed 32-byte lines.

1 Introduction

For merged DRAM/logic LSIs with a memory hierarchy including cache memory, we can exploit high on-chip memory bandwidth by means of replacing a whole cache line at a time on cache misses [5][10][11]. This approach tends to increase the cache-line size if we attempt to improve the attainable memory bandwidth. In general, large cache lines can benefit some application as the effect of prefetching. Larger cache lines, however, might worsen the system performance if programs do not have enough spatial locality and cache misses frequently take place. This kind of cache misses (i.e., *conflict misses*) could be reduced by increasing the cache associativity[10][11]. But, this approach usually makes the cache access time longer.

To resolve the above-mentioned dilemma, we have proposed a concept of "variable line-size cache (*VLS cache*)"[5]. The VLS cache can alleviate the negative effects of larger cache-line size by partitioning the large cache line into multiple small cache lines. The perfor-

mance of the VLS cache depends largely on whether or not cache replacements can be performed with adequate line-sizes. However, the paper[5] did not have discussed how to determine the adequate cache-line size. Several studies have proposed cache architectures for adjusting the cache-line size to the characteristics of programs. Coherent caches proposed in [1][2] focused on shared-memory multiprocessor systems. For uni-processor systems, cache architectures exploiting varying amount of spatial locality have been proposed in [3][6][7]. These caches need tables for recording the memory access history for evicted data from the cache, or situations of past load/store operations.

This paper proposes a realistic VLS cache architecture, which is referred to as "dynamically variable line-size cache (*D-VLS cache*)". The D-VLS cache changes its cache-line size at run time according to the characteristics of application programs to execute. Line-size determinator selects adequate line-sizes based on recently observed data reference behavior. Since the algorithm for determining the adequate line-sizes is very simple, the D-VLS cache has no large tables for storing the memory access history. This scheme does not require any modification of instruction set architectures. The goal of D-VLS cache is to improve the system performance of merged DRAM/logic LSIs such as PPRAM(Parallel Processing RAM)[8] or IRAM(Intelligent RAM)[9] by making good use of the high on-chip memory bandwidth.

The rest of this paper is organized as follows. Section 2 describes the concept and principle of the VLS cache. Section 3 discusses the D-VLS cache architecture. Section 4 presents some simulation results and shows the performance improvements achieved by the D-VLS cache. Section 6 concludes this paper.

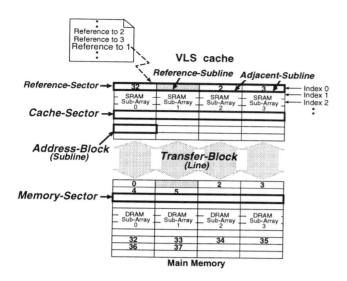

Figure 1. Terminology for VLS Caches

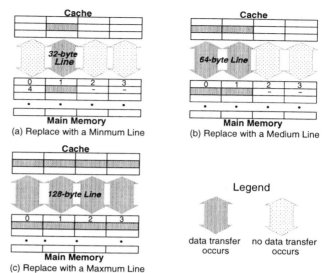

Figure 2. Three Different Transfer-Block Sizes on Cache Replacements

2 Variable Line-Size(VLS) Cache

2.1 Terminology

In the VLS cache, an SRAM(cache) cell array and a DRAM(main memory) cell array are divided into several subarrays. Data transfer for cache replacements is performed between corresponding SRAM and DRAM subarrays. Figure 1 summarizes the definition of terms. *Address-block*, or *subline*, is a block of data associated with a single tag in the cache. *Transfer-block*, or *line*, is a block of data transferred at once between the cache and main memory. The address-blocks from every SRAM subarray, which have the same cache-index, form a *cache-sector*. A cache-sector and an address-block which are being accessed during a cache lookup are called a *reference-sector* and a *reference-subline*, respectively. When a memory reference from the processor is found a cache hit, referenced data resides in the reference-subline. Otherwise, referenced data is not in the reference-subline but only in the main memory. A *memory-sector* is a block of data in the main-memory, and corresponds to the cache-sector. *Adjacent-subline* is defined as follows.

- It resides in the reference-sector, but is not the reference-subline.

- Its home location in the main-memory is in the same memory-sector as that of the data which is currently being referenced by the processor.

- It has been referenced at least once since it was fetched into the cache.

2.2 Concept and Principle of Operations

To make good use of the high on-chip memory bandwidth, the VLS cache adjusts its transfer-block size according to the characteristics of programs. When programs have rich spatial locality, the VLS cache would determine to use larger transfer-blocks, each of which consists of lots of address-blocks. Conversely, the VLS cache would determine to use smaller transfer-blocks, each of which consists of a single or a few address-blocks, and could try to avoid cache conflicts. Since the VLS cache can avoid cache conflicts without increasing the cache associativity, the access time of it (i.e., hit time) is shorter than that of conventional caches with higher associativity[5].

When a memory access takes place, the cache tag array is looked up in the same manner as normal caches, except that every SRAM subarray has its own tag memory and the lookup is performed on every tag memory. On cache hit, the hit address-block has the required data, and the memory access performs on this address-block in the same manner as normal caches. Otherwise, one or more address-blocks are replaced on cache replacement. For the example VLS cache shown in Figure 1, there are three transfer-block sizes as follows:

- Minimum transfer-block size (see Figure 2 (a)).

- Medium transfer-block size (see Figure 2 (b)).

- Maximum transfer-block size (see Figure 2 (c)).

3 Dynamically VLS(D-VLS) Cache

3.1 Architecture

The performance of the VLS cache depends heavily on how well the cache replacement is performed with optimal transfer-block size. However, the amount of spatial locality may vary both within and among program executions. The D-VLS cache changes its cache-line size at run time according to the characteristics of programs. The line-size determinator for the D-VLS cache selects adequate line-sizes based on recently observed data reference behavior.

Figure 3 illustrates the block diagram of a direct-mapped D-VLS cache with four subarrays. The address-block size is 32 bytes, and three transfer-block sizes (32 bytes, 64 bytes, and 128 bytes) are provided. Since it does not be allowed that the medium transfer-block (64-bytes line) could not be beyond 64-byte boundary in the 128-byte cache-sector, the number of combinations of address-blocks to be involved in cache replacements is just seven rather than fifteen. The cache lookup for determining cache hit or miss is carried out as follows:

1. The address generated by the processor is divided into the byte offset within an address-block, subarray field designating the subarray, index field used for indexing the tag memory, and tag field.

2. Each cache subarray has its own tag memory and comparator, and it can perform the tag-memory lookup using the index and tag fields independently with each other.

3. One of the tag-comparison results is selected by the subarray field of the address, and then the cache hit or miss is determined.

The D-VLS cache provides the following for optimizing the transfer-block sizes at run time:

- **A reference-flag bit per address-block** : This flag bit is reset to 0 when the corresponding address-block is fetched into the cache, and is set to 1 when the address-block is accessed by the processor. It is used for determining whether the corresponding address-block is an adjacent-subline. On cache lookup, if the tag of an address-block which is not the reference-subline matches the tag field of the address and if the reference-flag bit is 1, then the address-block is an adjacent-subline.

- **A line-size specifier (LSS) per cache-sector** : This specifies the transfer-block size of the corresponding cache-sector. As described in Section 2.2,

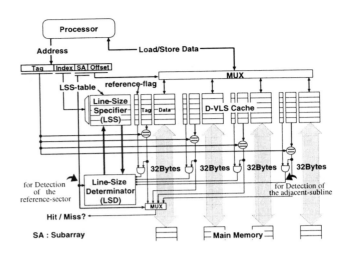

Figure 3. Block Diagram of a Direct-Mapped D-VLS Cache

each cache-sector is in one of three states: minimum, medium, and maximum transfer-block-size states. To identify these states, every LSS provides a 2-bit state information. This means that the cache replacement is performed according to the transfer-block size which is specified by the LSS corresponding to the reference-sector.

- **Line-size determinator (LSD)** : On every cache lookup, the LSD determines the state of the line-size specifier of the reference-sector. The algorithm is given in the next section.

3.2 Line-Size Determinator Algorithm

The algorithm for determining adequate transfer-block sizes is very simple. This algorithm is based on not memory-access history but the current state of the reference-sector. This means that no information of evicted data from the cache need be maintained. On every cache lookup, the LSD determines the state of the LSS of the reference-sector, as follows:

1. The LSD investigates how many adjacent-sublines exist in the reference-sector using all the reference-flag bits and the tag-comparison results.

2. Based on the above-mentioned investigation result and the current state of the LSS of the reference-sector, the LSD determines the next state of the LSS. The state-transition diagram is shown in Figure 4.

220

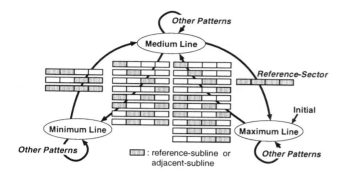

Figure 4. State Transition Diagram

If there are many neighboring adjacent-sublines, the reference-sector has good spatial locality. This is because the data currently being accessed by the processor and the adjacent-sublines are fetched from the same memory-sector, and these sublines have been accessed by the processor recently. In this case, the transfer-block size should become larger. Thus the state depicted in Figure 4 transits from the minimum state (32-byte line) to the medium state (64-byte line) or from the medium (64-byte line) state to the maximum state (128-byte line) when the reference-subline and adjacent-sublines construct a larger line-size than the current line-size.

In contrast, if the reference-sector has been accessed sparsely before the current access, there should be few adjacent-sublines in the reference-sector. This means that the reference-sector has poor spatial locality at that time. In this case, the transfer-block size should become smaller. So the state depicted in Figure 4 transits from the maximum state (128-byte line) to the medium state (64-byte line) when the reference-subline and adjacent-sublines construct equal or smaller line-size than the medium line-size (64-byte or 32-byte line). Similarly, the state transits from the medium state (64-byte line) to the minimum state (32-byte line) when the reference-subline and adjacent-sublines construct minimum line-size (32-byte line)

4 Evaluations

4.1 Evaluation Models

To evaluate the effectiveness of the D-VLS cache, we simulated the following conventional fixed line-size caches and D-VLS caches.

- *FIX32, FIX64, FIX128* : Conventional 16 KB direct-mapped caches, each of which has a fixed transfer-block(line) size of 32 bytes, 64 bytes, and 128 bytes, respectively.

- *FIX32double* : Conventional 32 KB direct-mapped cache with fixed 32-byte line size.

- *S-VLS128-32* : 16 KB direct-mapped VLS cache having three line sizes of 32 bytes, 64 bytes, and 128 bytes. S-VLS128-32 changes its line size program by program. The adequate line-size of each program is determined based on prior simulations.

- *D-VLS128-32ideal* : 16 KB direct-mapped D-VLS caches having three line sizes of 32 bytes, 64 bytes, and 128 bytes. It is an ideal D-VLS cache ignoring the hardware overhead. D-VLS128-32ideal provides a line-size specifier (LSS) for each memory-sector rather than for each cache-sector.

- *D-VLS128-32LSS1, D-VLS128-32LSS8* : 16 KB realistic direct-mapped D-VLS caches having three line sizes of 32 bytes, 64 bytes, and 128 bytes. D-VLS128-32LSS1 provides an LSS for each cache-sector, while D-VLS128-32LSS8 provides an LSS for eight consecutive cache-sectors.

4.2 Methodology

We used the following four benchmark sets, each of which consists of three programs from the SPEC92 and the SPEC95 benchmark suite, as follows:

- *mix-int1* : 072.sc, 126.gcc, and 134.perl.

- *mix-int2* : 124.m88ksim, 130.li, and 147.vortex.

- *mix-fp* : 052.alvinn, 101.tomcatv, and 103.su2cor.

- *mix-intfp* : 132.ijpeg, 099.go, and 104.Hydro2d.

The programs in each benchmark set are assumed to run in multiprogram manner on a uni processor system, and a context switch occurs per execution of one million instructions. Mix-int1 and mix-int2 contain integer programs only, and mix-fp consists of three floating-point programs. Mix-intfp is formed by two integer and one floating-point programs. We captured address traces using QPT[4] of each benchmark set for the execution of three billion instructions.

Average memory-access time ($AMT = HitTime + MissRate \times MissPenalty$) is a popular metric to evaluate the cache performance. Miss penalty in merged DRAM/logic LSIs can be a constant time regardless of the cache-line sizes, because of the high on-chip memory bandwidth. Moreover, the hit time overhead produced by the VLS caches is trivial[5]. As a result, we have decided to use cache miss rate as the performance metrics. We measured miss rate for each benchmark set using two cache simulators written in C: one for conventional caches with fixed line-sizes and the other for D-VLS caches.

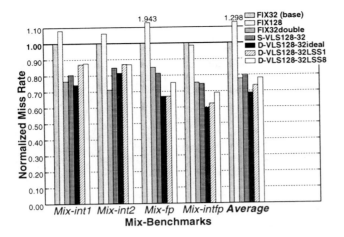

Figure 5. Simulation Results

4.3 Simulation Results

Figure 5 shows the simulation results for all the benchmark sets and the average of them. For each benchmark set, all results are normalized to FIX32.

First, we compare the D-VLS caches (D-VLS128-32LSS1 and D-VLS128-32LSS8) with the conventional caches. The fixed large lines in FIX128 worsen the system performance due to frequent evictions, while the D-VLS caches give remarkable performance improvements by means of the variable line-size. On average, FIX128 worsen the cache performance by about 30% while D-VLS128-32LSS1 and D-VLS128-32LSS8 improve the performance by about 27% and 22%, respectively, compared to FIX32. These performance improvements are equal or better than that of FIX32double with two times larger cache size.

Next, we compare the D-VLS caches with the statically variable line-size cache (S-VLS128-32). On average, D-VLS128-32LSS1 and D-VLS128-32LSS8 are superior to S-VLS128-32. This is because S-VLS128-32 adjusts its line size among programs, while the D-VLS caches can adjust its line size both within and among programs.

Finally, we compare the realistic D-VLS cache (D-VLS128-32LSS1) with the ideal D-VLS cache (D-VLS128-32ideal). The difference of the performance improvements given by the realistic model and the ideal model is only 5% on average. This means that the line-size determinator can select the adequate line-sizes even if it does not accurately track the amount of spatial locality of individual memory-sectors.

5 Conclusions

In this paper, we have proposed the dynamically variable line-size cache (D-VLS cache) for merged DRAM/Logic LSIs. The line-size determinator in the D-VLS cache can detect the varying amount of spatial locality within and among programs at run time, and optimizes its cache-line size. Experimental results have shown that the realistic D-VLS caches, or D-VLS128-32LSS1 and D-VLS128-32LSS8, improve the performance by about 27% and 22%, respectively, compared to a conventional cache.

References

[1] Dahlgren, F., Dubois, M, and Stenstrom, P., "Fixed and Adaptive Sequential Prefetching in Shared Memory Multiprocessors," *Proc. of the 1993 International Conference on Paralled Processing*, pp.56–63, Aug. 1993.

[2] Dubnicki, C., and LeBlanc, T. J., "Adjustable Block Size Coherent Caches," *Proc. of the 19th Annual International Symposium on Computer Architecture*, pp.170–180, May 1992.

[3] Gonzalez, A. Aliagas, C. and Valero, M., "A Data Cache with Multiple Caching Strategies Tuned to Different Types of Locality," *Proceedings of International Conference on Supercomputing*, pp.338–347, July 1995.

[4] Hill, M. D., Larus, J. R., Lebeck, A. R., Talluri, M., and Wood, D. A., "WARTS: Wisconsin Architectural Research Tool Set," *http://www.cs.wisc.edu/˜larus/warts.html*, University of Wisconsin - Madison.

[5] Inoue, K., Koji, K., and Murakami, K., "High Bandwidth : Variable Line-Size Cache Architecture for Merged DRAM/Logic LSIs," *IEICE Transactions on Electronics*, Vol.E81-C, No.9, pp.1438–1447, Sep. 1998.

[6] Johnson, T. L., Merten, M. C, and Hwu, W. W., "Runtime Spatial Locality Detection and Optimization," *Proc. of the 30th Annual International Symposium on Microarchitecture*, pp.57–64, Dec. 1997.

[7] Kumar, S. and Wilkerson, C., "Exploiting Spatial Locality in Data Caches using Spatial Footprints," *Proc. of the 25th Annual International Symposium on Computer Architecture*, pp.357–368, June 1998.

[8] Murakami, K., Shirakawa, S., and Miyajima, H., "Parallel Processing RAM Chip with 256Mb DRAM and Quad Processors," *1997 ISSCC Digest of Technical Papers*, pp.228–229, Feb. 1997.

[9] Patterson, D., Anderson, T., Cardwell, N., Fromm, R., Keeton, K., Kozyrakis, C., Thomas, R., and Yelick, K., "Intelligent RAM (IRAM): Chips that remember and compute," *1997 ISSCC Digest of Technical Papers*, pp.224–225, Feb. 1997.

[10] Saulsbury, A., Pong, F., and Nowatzyk, A., "Missing the Memory Wall: The Case for Processor/Memory Integration," *Proc. of the 23rd Annual International Symposium on Computer Architecture*, pp.90–101, May 1996.

[11] Wilson, K. M. and Olukotun, K., "Designing High Bandwidth On-Chip Caches," *Proc. of the 24th Annual International Symposium on Computer Architecture*, pp.121–132, June 1997.

A Scalable Cache Coherent Scheme Exploiting Wormhole Routing Networks

Yunseok Rhee and Joonwon Lee

Department of Computer Science
Korea Advanced Institute of Science and Technology (KAIST)
E-mail: {rheeys, joon}@camars.kaist.ac.kr

Abstract

Large scale shared memory multiprocessors favor a directory-based cache coherence scheme for its scalability. The directory space needed to record the information for sharers has a complexity of $\Theta(N^2)$ when a full-mapped vector is used for an N-node system. Though this overhead can be reduced by limiting the directory size assuming that the sharing degree is small, it will experience significant inefficiency when a data is widely shared.

In this paper, we propose a new directory scheme and a cache coherence scheme based on it for a mesh interconnection. Deterministic and wormhole routing enables a pointer to represent a set of nodes. Also a message traversing on the mesh performs a broadcast mission to a set of nodes without extra traffic, which can be utilized for the cache coherence problem. Only a slight change on a generic router is needed to implement our scheme. This scheme is also applicable to any k-ary n-cube networks including a mesh.

1 Introduction

Two issues arise in designing a scalable directory-based cache coherent protocol: (1) how to make the directory small, and (2) how to reduce coherence traffic. Some limited pointer protocols [2, 1, 4, 3] need very scalable and economic memory for directories, and are known to work well for many parallel programs with small worker-set sharings. Those protocols, however, cannot avoid considerable performance degradation when a data is shared among many processors (referred to as *wide sharing* [3]), since it causes frequent directory overflows. Such overflows entail many evictions and replacements in the directory which increase the memory access latencies as well as the coherence traffic.

In this paper, we propose a scalable directory-based cache coherence protocol (called *DirQ*) which remedies both of the two issues. The solution is found from an observation on current representative technologies for direct interconnection networks: wormhole routing and dimension-order routing algorithms. Since a router can watch all the passing worms, such mechanisms for broadcast and snooping can be easily implemented as in bus-base machines. For large-scale multiprocessors, parallel programs exploit higher parallelism, which may involve the entire set of processors. In such cases, a shared data is likely to be widely shared by many processors. So far such widely shared objects have been known uncommon in most parallel programs [3, 7]. Our experiments, however, show that some parallel programs severely suffer from such widely sharings as shown in Figure 1.

Figure 1 shows the result of sharing degrees for two parallel programs: BARNES from the SPLASH-2 parallel program suite and APSP which is our parallel implementation of the Floyd-Warshall all-pairs shortest path algorithm. Those programs are executed on a 64 mesh-connected multiprocessor simulator with a full-map directory and a write invalidate protocol which will be illustrated in more details in Section 3. The result is obtained from every access to writable shared variables. In the figure, the positive values at the y-axis denote the distribution of read and write sharing degrees of ordinary variables, and the negative values denote that of synchronization variables used for spin locks and barriers.

Read sharing, in particular, now becomes a major source which activates the coherence transactions. Thus, like the full-map directory, it is required to record as many readers as possible. Most programs also exhibit high sharing degrees even at writes. At those writes, coherence transactions as many as those sharers should be issued and consequently, spend considerable time and network bandwidth.

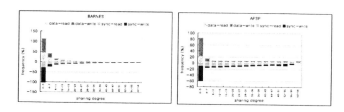

Figure 1. Sharing degree distribution

2 Broadcast Directory-based Cache Protocol

Basic Mechanism: Based on the wormhole routing and a dimension-ordered routing, the invalidation transaction can be realized by *path-broadcast* and *worm-snooping*. The path-broadcast mechanism is to transmit a worm to a destination in an attempt to deliver the same message to all the nodes on the path leading to the destination, called *snoop-path*. For this purpose, a worm must contain additional information to identify whether it is being destined to a specific destination only or being path-broadcast. The worm needs not contain all the sharing locations in its header flit. On the other hand, the worm-snooping is the activity of each router to continuously read every passing worm to accomplish the invalidation transaction using the path-broadcast.

A router must examine the passing header flit to know whether it is being broadcast or coming to itself only. Broadcast flits are forwarded to the next neighbor while being copied to a message buffer (the extra buffers apart from flit buffers) in the router which can be accessed by the cache controller. It is assumed that such a broadcast worm uses *forward-and-absorb* capability at the router interface of each intermediate destinations.

The $DirQ$ protocol can be easily implemented by adding some logic circuits to a current router and reserving two bits in the header flit. A header flit consists of bits for a *broadcast-flag*(1 bit), a *phase-flag*(1 bit), and *destination bits*.

Directory Entry: For a system with N processors, the broadcast directory entry is composed of status bits, and $2\sqrt{N}$ new pointers. Each pointer has $\log_2 N/2$ bits to identify a snoop path. Note that a limited directory entry consists of $\sqrt{N}$ pointers where each pointer needs $\log_2 N$ bits. In a $\sqrt{N} \times \sqrt{N}$ mesh using the X-Y routing algorithm, a set of nodes in a column can be covered by at most two snoop-paths which are formed toward the topmost and the bottommost nodes, respectively. Thus, a node can cover the entire sharers with $2\sqrt{N}$ snoop-paths for all the column. In the $DirQ$ protocol, a fixed pair of pointers is allocated for a column by the ordinal number. A value of each pointer locates the farthest sharer in its dedicated routing path.

Coherence Channels: Two virtual channels are provided for the $DirQ$ protocol. One is for invalidation requests, and conforms to the X-Y routing. The other is for invalidation acknowledgments, and conforms to the Y-X routing which reverses X-Y routing. These two channels with opposite routings allow one worm to complete the acknowledgment phase by going back the request worm's path. Without these two virtual channels, more acknowledgment worms would be generated by many sharing nodes, which would conform to a dedicated routing algorithm. For convenience, hereafter, those channels are called R-channel (for requests) and A-channel (for acknowledgments), respectively.

Coherence Worms: The I-REQ worm is a broadcast worm that delivers the invalidation request from a home node to ll the nodes on a snoop-path over an R-channel. The des-

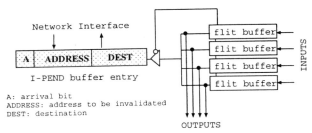

A: arrival bit
ADDRESS: address to be invalidated
DEST: destination

Figure 2. Structure of I-PEND buffers

tination denotes the farthest ordered sharer in the snoop-path. Besides, the header flit is followed by a data flit which contains the address to be invalidated. With the forward-and-absorb capability in the router, the worm is copied to an I-PEND buffer in the router interface of each visited node. The I-PEND buffers are extra buffers implemented in each router in an attempt to keep the invalidation request in progress or being pending.

The I-ACK worm collects acknowledgments from each sharer on its way to the home node over an A-channel. The worm has similar contents to the I-REQ worm except that the phase-bit must be set and the destination field holds the home node of a memory block. An I-ACK worm is initiated by the last node of a snoop-path when the invalidation of its cache copy is completed. Then, the worm traverses all the nodes of the corresponding snoop-path in the opposite direction of the I-REQ worm. When an I-ACK worm arrives at an intermediate node, the router looks up the I-PEND buffer to check if the invalidation of a cache copy corresponding to the I-ACK worm has been completed. If no matching entry is found, i.e., the invalidation at the corresponding node is completed, it is passed on to the next node. Otherwise, this worm should watch at the node until the transaction is completed.

I-PEND buffer: The I-PEND buffer is designed to hold invalidation requests in progress or pending. These buffers are located on the router interface and can be accessed directly by the node processor. As Figure 2 shows, the buffer is directly connected to the flit buffers, and consists of *arrival bit*, *address to be invalidated*, and *destination* fields. An I-REQ worm is allocated one I-PEND buffer entry to notify the invalidate block to its corresponding cache controller using the invalidate block number field.

3 Simulation Environment

We simulate an 8x8 bidirectional mesh-connected multiprocessor with wormhole routing, and the X-Y and the Y-X routing algorithms. Shared memory addresses are evenly distributed among all the processors. For each processor, we assume an infinite cache since our interests are mainly in the coherent cache misses. Such an assumption is justified by current sufficient caches as well as optimization techniques regarding a finite cache capacity which are used for our workload applications. The parameters used in the simulation are as follows: 1 pclock for cache access time, 4 pclocks and 6 pclocks for unicast and multicast message startup times respectively, 4 pclocks for router delay, 32-bit sized flit, 3 flits for a coherence message, 32-byte cache block, 4-entry I-PEND buffer.

Memory access requests to a home node are sequentially forwarded to its memory controller. A request which need invalidate a remote copy is usually completed in a long time. During that time, subsequent requests to the same block are pended blocked. In general, a finite buffer for those pending requests is provided at the home node, and further requests issued after the buffer is full are rejected and they are retried later. But we assume an infinite pending buffer in the simulator, since our concern is mainly the effect of cache coherence.

Based on the baseline architecture, we evaluate the performance of four directory-based protocols: the full-map (**F**), an 8-pointer limited (**L**), a coarse-vector with a region size of 4 (**C**), and the $DirQ$ (**D**) protocols. When a directory entry overflows, the limited directory protocol evicts a cache copy at the least recently referenced node. Results from the limited directory protocol especially concerns us, since the protocol consumes equal directory memory to that of the $DirQ$ protocol. Also, all protocols except the $DirQ$ are based on the multidestination communication which use one message to invalidate multiple cache copies on a feasible routing path. This hardware is expected to need more complexity than that for the $DirQ$, and further the message startup latency to compose a multicast message also increases. But the invalidation acknowledging traffic significantly differs in schemes. The $DirQ$ scheme utilizes a reverse traversed path for the acknowledge phase and thus decreases the acknowledge traffic.

An invalidation cache coherence scheme similar to the Stanford DASH multiprocessor [6] is employed in this simulation. Also, the sequential memory model [5] is simulated, and hence stall time due to write misses is not hidden unlike the relaxed memory models. Synchronization operations related to a barrier or a semaphore are implemented by the *test-test-and-set*.

4 Evaluation Result

Figure 3 shows the normalized traffic volume to that of the full-map protocol. In all figures, the full-map protocol is denoted as **F**, the limited directory protocol as **L**, the coarse-vector protocol as **C**, and the $DirQ$ protocol as **D** respectively. Each traffic is broken down into its individual parts: *read*, *write*, *inv_req*, *inv_ack* and *eviction* traffics. The cache coherence traffic is the sum of the *inv_req*, the *inv_ack*, and the *eviction* traffics. For programs other than RAY-TRACE and BARNES, the cache coherence traffic does not show a large difference in all but the $DirQ$ protocol. This means that the limited directory protocol generates less invalidate traffic than the full-map protocol while it generates

extra eviction traffic. Thus burstiness of traffic is reduced with the limited directory protocol because evictions are less frequent than invalidations. For the full-map and the limited directory protocols, the cache coherence traffic covers a significant part of the overall traffic in most programs, and further, dominates the overall traffic. The result from BARNES means that the limited directory protocol with an eviction scheme show poor performance for widely shared programs. Further such traffic increase makes our scheme more appealing under the circumstance of a limited network bandwidth.

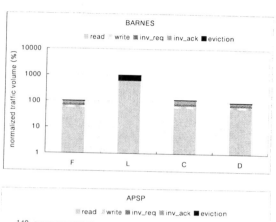

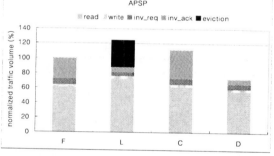

Figure 3. Normalized traffic volume

The execution times are shown in Figure 4. Each time is also normalized to the execution time of the full-map protocol. Further, an execution time is broken down into *busy*, *spin*, *read*, *write*, *pend*, and *block*. The *busy* time is the time executing instructions without cache misses which include memory accesses hit in the cache. The *spin* time is the time spent spinning on synchronization variables at caches which is non-productive time. All but these two times are the times that a processor stalls for. The *pend* time is the pending time at memory modules to obey the sequential memory consistency. The *block* times is due to network channel contention since the bandwidth is finite.

For APSP, the $DirQ$ protocol reduces the overall execution time by 18% compared to the full-map protocol, 28% to the coarse-vector protocol, and 60% to the limited protocol respectively. It is encouraging to outperform the full-map protocol and unexpectedly the coarse-vector protocol shows comparable performance to the full-map protocol. It is deemed due to that the simulated system scale is not so

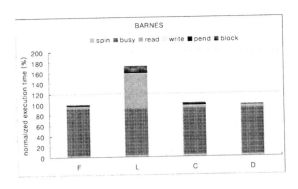

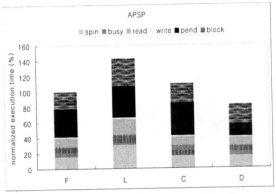

Figure 4. Normalized execution time

large to reflect the disadvantage of the coarse-vector protocol. The speedups of the $DirQ$ protocol are mainly affected by two components: the *pend* and *block* times. Additionally the *read* time affects the speedups of the the $DirQ$ protocol over the limited protocol. As shown in the result on traffic, the $DirQ$ protocol generates much less traffic compared to the other protocols, and thus the channel contention becomes lower. The low contention results in a low *block* time. The *block* time is closely related to the average number of pending requests at a home node. Such pending requests increase as a transaction in progress takes a longer time.

In most programs, invalidations or evictions of a block are shortly followed by read miss requests of the block. As the result, the network is easily saturated with such a burst traffic. The traffic congestion contributes to a long transaction time. The increase in the *spin* time stems from spinning on synchronization variables at caches. This is also affected by the large number of pending requests, since a long pending time can delay a following lock release. The limited directory protocols show longer execution times than the other protocols for all programs. The long execution time is related to the *pend*, the *eviction*, and the *read* times. All the three times are influenced by the limitation of directory pointers. That is, an overflow of a directory entry causes an eviction, and in short time, the victim reads the block again. Thus, such a useless traffic affects the number of pending requests as explained above.

5 Conclusions

This work proposes a new directory cache coherence scheme named broadcast directory protocol (also called $DirQ$) which can be used for large-scale mesh-connected multiprocessors using a deterministic routing algorithm and the wormhole routing. Unlike other precedent works, in particular, we focus on developing the directory-based cache coherence protocol exploiting network features. For a mesh-connected machine, it requires scalable directory memory of $\Theta(N^{3/2} \log N)$ compared to the full-map directory.

Several parallel programs of the SPLASH-2 suite are executed on the simulator which implements the $DirQ$ protocol. The proposed protocol outperforms all the tested protocols in terms of network latency and traffic volume. For widely-shared memory blocks, the network traffic is significantly reduced due to the cache coherence transaction using only two worms for a set of sharers. Though we show an implementation on a mesh interconnection network in this paper, this scheme can be easily applied to all k-ary n-cube direct interconnection networks that employ a deterministic routing and the wormhole routing.

References

[1] A. Agarwal, R. Simoni, J. Hennessy, and M. Horowitz. An Evaluation of Directory Schemes for Cache Coherence. In *Proceedings of the 15th International Symposium on Computer Architecture*, June 1988.

[2] L. M. Censier and P. Feautrier. A New Solution to Cache Problems in Multicache Systems. *IEEE Transactions on Computers*, C-27(12):1112–1118, 1978.

[3] D. Chaiken, J. Kubiatowicz, and A. Agarwal. LimitLESS Directories: A Scalable Cache Coherence Scheme. In *Proceedings of International Conference on Architectural Support for Programming Language and Operating Systems IV*, Apr. 1991.

[4] A. Gupta, W.-D. Weber, and T. Mowry. Reducing Memory and Traffic Requirements for Scalable Directory-Based Cache Coherence Schemes. In *Proceedings of International Conference on Parallel Processing*, 1990.

[5] L. Lamport. How to Make a Multiprocessor Computer That Correctly Executes Multiprocess Programs. *IEEE Transactions on Computer*, C-28(9), 1979.

[6] D. Lenoski, J. Laudon, K. Gharachorloo, W. D. Weber, A. Gupta, J. Hennesy, M. Horowitz, and M. Lam. The Stanford DASH Multiprocessor. *IEEE Computer*, pages 63–79, Mar. 1992.

[7] W. D. Weber and A. Gupta. Analysis of Cache Invalidation Patterns in Multiprocessors. *Proceedings of International Conference on Architectural Support for Programming Language and Operating Systems III*, pages 243–256, Apr. 1989.

Session 6B

Communication Issues I

The Impact of Link Arbitration on Switch Performance *

Marius Pirvu, Laxmi Bhuyan and Nan Ni
Department of Computer Science
Texas A&M University
College Station, TX 77845
E-mail: {pirvum, bhuyan, ninan}@cs.tamu.edu

Abstract

Switch design for interconnection networks plays an important role in the overall performance of multiprocessors and computer networks. In this paper we study the impact of one parameter in the switch design space, link arbitration. We demonstrate that link arbitration can be a determining factor in the performance of current networks. Moreover, we expect increased research focus on arbitration techniques to become a trend in the future, as switch architectures evolve towards increasing the number of virtual channels and input ports.

In the context of a state-of-the-art switch design we use both synthetic workload and execution driven simulations to compare several arbitration policies. Furthermore, we devise a new arbitration method, Look-Ahead arbitration. Under heavy traffic conditions the Look-Ahead policy provides important improvements over traditional arbitration schemes without a significant increase in hardware complexity. Also, we propose a priority based policy that is capable of reducing the execution time of parallel applications. Lastly, we enhance the arbitration policies by a supplemental mechanism, virtual channel reservation, intended to alleviate the hot-spot problem.

1. Introduction

The performance of the interconnection network is critical in multiprocessor systems because the network latency contributes significantly to the overall execution time of an application. The factors that affect network performance are the switching technique, buffer management and physical link arbitration. Most of the research that deals with switch design concentrates either on the switching technique or on the buffer management. The third factor, arbitration, is either briefly mentioned or completely overlooked. In this paper we demonstrate that arbitration can play an important role in the performance of a system. Moreover, this role is expected to increase as current switches become more and more complex, have more virtual channels and more input ports.

In our study we compare several arbitration policies and show how they affect the network latency and throughput.

We design a novel arbitration method, Look-Ahead, which outperforms traditional policies such as First Come First Served or Round Robin, by keeping a better balance among the link loads. We also show how to apply a simple priority based scheme to reduce the execution time of applications in shared memory multiprocessors. Furthermore, we refine our arbitration policies by a supplemental mechanism, virtual channel reservation, intended to alleviate the hot-spot problem. This mechanism works well in conjunction with any arbitration policy and gives performance benefits even in the absence of an explicit hot-spot.

Related arbitration studies most often look into bus arbitration issues [7, 14, 10]. There are only a handful of papers that discuss link arbitration for switches in interconnection networks. However, in these papers the analysis method is typically modeling [1]. To the best of our knowledge this is the first paper to study switch arbitration in more detail using simulations. Our main results are based on simulations with a synthetically generated workload. We further validate our results through execution driven simulation of a few parallel programs. Our simulated architecture reflects the current state-of-the-art interconnect and processors. The switch we use in our simulations is based on wormhole routing with virtual channels [4] and employs a DAFC (dynamically allocated fully connected) [5] design which is known to perform the best compared to other alternatives. We chose this configuration so that the only source of improvement remains a better arbitration scheme. Current state-of-the-art switches use simple, traditional arbitration policies (e.g. first-come-first-served and round robin). We prove that the implementation of alternative arbitration policies, such as shortest message first or our Look-Ahead and Priority schemes, is definitely worthwhile. Each of these arbitration techniques is focused on optimizing a particular performance metric and addresses a different network problem.

Shortest message first, a simple but often ignored arbitration policy, is designed to improve the average message latency. It performs well when the traffic is composed of messages of different sizes. By promoting shorter packets, we achieve a secondary beneficial effect: the virtual channel availability is increased due to the faster rate at which virtual channels are freed.

Our Priority arbitration policy is targeted towards reducing the latency of critical messages. Even if the average message latency may increase, the overall execution time is reduced. This policy builds on priority-based mechanisms commonly used in real-time systems. We use this technique in shared memory multiprocessors giving priority to read

*This research has been supported by NSF Grants CCR 9622740 and CCR 9810205

memory accesses over write accesses.

The Look-Ahead policy we propose attempts to increase the link throughput. It achieves a better load balancing among the physical links by using information provided by the neighbor switches. The information we exchange is the value of the link load. To increase the parallelism of flits, the arbiter will prefer a packet going to a lightly loaded link. This policy can be applied to any topology and is scalable because it involves communication only between neighbor switches.

All of the above policies can be used either as stand alone or as refinements to existing policies. We show that they can be successfully combined into more powerful policies covering a wide range of network traffic conditions.

However, none of them is capable of preventing the lane hogging problem [8] common in hot-spot situations. We introduce an additional mechanism, virtual channel reservation to address this problem. Lane hogging can occur in traditional implementations of wormhole routing with virtual channels because any worm can occupy any virtual channel irrespective of the destination of the packet. This can lead to the case where all the channels are used up by worms going to the same destination, thus blocking the way of other worms. Our reservation mechanism prohibits the arbiter from choosing a worm which could hog the next input port. This method resembles the flow group implementation in ATLAS I chip [9] where identically destined flits (thus belonging to the same flow group) are not allowed to reside at the same time in an input port. In contrast to this method, we restrict the number of worms (not flits) that go to the same destination. More importantly, we demonstrate that this restriction should not be fixed across the whole network, but should vary according to the position of the input port in the interconnect.

To summarize, the paper makes the following original contributions:

- Quantifies the importance of arbitration in the performance of a switch and investigates the conditions under which arbitration has a greater impact on performance

- Evaluates the behavior of several arbitration policies

- Proposes a new arbitration scheme, Look-Ahead, that aims at evenly distributing the load among the physical links

- Shows how to implement a Priority arbitration scheme in the context of shared memory multiprocessors

- Introduces an arbitration enhancement, virtual channel reservation, designed to avoid the performance bottleneck due to lane hogging

The rest of the paper is organized as follows: Section 2 describes our test-bed and other architectural assumptions. Section 3 presents various arbitration policies currently existent and proposes a new policy called Look-Ahead. The arbitration policies are compared in terms of performance in Section 4. Section 5 introduces the idea of virtual channel reservation as a method of preventing the negative effects of the hot-spot. Finally, Section 6 concludes the paper.

2. Simulation Environment

Our simulator is based on RSIM [12], but we completely changed the network part to allow for a cycle by cycle sim-

ulation of various arbitration policies. The architecture we simulate is a shared memory machine with 16 nodes connected by a 4×4 mesh like in Figure 1(a). Each node is

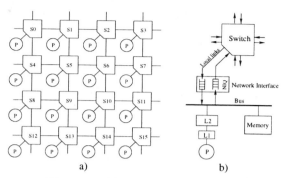

Figure 1. Simulated architecture

composed of a processor, two levels of write-back cache, a memory module, a network interface and a switch (see Figure 1 (b)). We simulate a state-of-the-art 4-way superscalar processor with branch prediction, out-of-order speculative execution, non-blocking reads and release consistency shared memory model. The only simplifying assumption we make is that instructions are considered to always hit in the I-cache of the processor. The instruction window of the processor has 64 entries and the functional units have latencies similar to the UltraSPARC processor. The memory is four way interleaved and has an access time of 18 cycles. The bus connecting the various components is a split transaction bus with a width of 16 bytes; its clock is three times slower than that of the processor. All the other characteristics of our simulated architecture are summarized in Table 1. The size of the L2 cache is smaller than one can find in today's machines to account for the rather small problem size that we run.

To accurately measure the contention in the network we employ a cycle by cycle simulation. The switch at each node is based on our design proposed in [11]. It has 4 input ports, 4 output ports and a pair of local links (1 input, 1 output) for the communication with the processing unit. It

Switch parameters	
flit size	8 bytes
link width	2 bytes
switch cycle	4 pcycles
wire delay	1 pcycle
routing delay	4 pcycles
routing algorithm	X-Y
virtual channels	4 per input
buffer size per port	32 flits
Cache parameters	
L1, L2 size	16 K, 128 K
L1, L2 associativity	2 way, 4 way
L1 latency	1 pcycle
L2 latency	8 pcycles pipelined
L1, L2 cache line	64 bytes
L1, L2 write policy	write back, write allocate

Table 1. Default architectural parameters

uses wormhole routing and has four virtual channels (VC) at each input port. Such a small number of VCs is common. The Spider [6] and Cavallino [2] routers have both four VCs per input while the switch used in Cray T3E network has five. However, in our case the input buffer is dynamically allocated using a circular buffer [11]. Moreover, to improve performance, one flit per VC is reserved and only the rest of the input space is shared. In some experiments the total size of the input buffer is varied between 16 and 64 flits; in others we use the default value of 32 flits. This is only half of the value used in the Spider chip or Cray T3E routers. We think that the dynamic buffer allocation enabled by our switch design justifies the use of a smaller input buffer. The switch is fully connected which permits us to simultaneously read several flits out of an input port and pass them to the corresponding outputs. A secondary benefit deriving from this feature is that the design of the arbiter is simpler.

The physical links between switches are considered to operate at processor frequency, while the core (the switch) is four times slower. Thus, a *switch cycle* is four times the wire cycle. Every packet is divided in flits of 64 bits each. Because the width of the links is only 16 bits, a flit is further divided in four *phits*. Hence, the transmission of a flit is achieved by four consecutive phit transfers. To assemble flits at reception and disassemble flits for transmission two special purpose registers (RxR and TxR) are kept at each input port. The arbitration is performed at flit level, every switch cycle. The flow control is also maintained at flit level and, similar to Spider [6] and ATLAS I [9] chips, is done using credit flow information [3].

In our experiments we employ two simulation methodologies:

A. Synthetic workload. In this case the processor characteristics are irrelevant. The packets are generated with a given frequency and pushed in the network interface queue (NIQ) whose size is large enough to avoid overflow. From the NIQ the packets are absorbed one by one by the network and routed towards their destinations. For each generated packet its destination is randomly determined. The performance metrics we employ are throughput and message latency.

In parallel machines periods of very high levels of traffic are mixed with periods when very few messages are pushed into the network. Thus, it is interesting to analyze the network behavior during congestion phases. In our experiments packets are generated at a saturation rate so that, on average, for each processor a flit is created each cycle. Due to congestion the NIQ has the tendency to build up. If simulations were continued forever the latency would increase without a limit. Instead, we abruptly stop the simulation after 32000 packets have been received. Due to this technique the absolute value of the latency on the graphs is not very meaningful. However, the relative performance between the various arbitration techniques is an accurate indicator of how good an arbitration method is when compared to the others.

B. Execution driven simulation of shared memory applications. In this case the only metric that we employ is the execution time. As applications we use three kernels: FFT and RADIX sort from the SPLASH-2 benchmark suite [13], and MATMUL (matrix multiplication). FFT is run for 2^{16} complex points, RADIX for 2^{18} integers and MATMUL for 128×128 matrices. The time has been measured only for the parallel part of the applications.

The packets pushed into the network are of two types: requests and replies. The requests are usually short. In our case they have a length of two flits. As for the replies, if they carry a cache line, they have 10 flits in length; otherwise they have also two flits (acknowledgments fall in this category for example).

3. Presentation of the Arbitration Policies

In the following we describe some known arbitration policies used in current state-of-the-art switches and propose how to use a priority policy in the context of shared memory multiprocessors. More importantly, we introduce a new and better policy called Look-Ahead.

3.1. Round Robin

One of the most popular arbitration policy is *Round Robin*. Here, the arbiter scans all the channels and the first one that is ready to transmit, say channel i, is selected to send one flit. The next cycle the scanning process starts with channel $i + 1$. This method is evidently fair and no starvation can occur. However, the network latency tends to be uniformly increased for all the worms. To alleviate this negative effect we can make the following amendment: the scanning process will move to the next ready VC only if the current VC has just sent a tail flit. In other words, the arbiter will prefer the worm that is currently flowing out of the switch. When this worm has drained out completely, the simple Round Robin policy is used. We will refer to this scheme as *Round Robin - Keep Flow*. A slightly modified variation of this scheme is used in the routers for the Cray T3E network.

3.2. First Come First Served

In *FCFS* the oldest worm has priority. A possible implementation is the following: an 'age' counter is associated with each VC. When a new worm enters a VC, the age counter is set to 0. Afterwards, the age is incremented at a programmable rate. The arbiter will prefer the worm with the highest age. Inherently this arbitration policy is starvation free. As in the Round Robin case we can have a *FCFS - Keep Flow* method where the worm that is currently flowing out of the switch is given priority. The Spider chip [6] uses an 8-bit age counter to implement FCFS. However, their implementation differs from ours in that the age is carried along by the worm and is not reset when the worm enters a new switch.

3.3. Shortest Message First

From the process scheduling theory it is known that shortest-job-first achieves a very good response time. The equivalent policy for arbitration is *Shortest Message First* (SMF) which tries to promote the worms with the fewest flits still to be transmitted, thus minimizing the message latency. A second motivation of the SMF policy is increased VC availability. This advantage arises when the input buffer is fairly large and only a single worm can use a VC at a time. For such switches there might be situations where, even though there are sufficient buffers available, a header flit is blocked because the next switch does not have a free VC. Hence, the arbiter should try to free virtual channels as fast as possible and this is exactly what SMF does. However, the method is not fair and, if special measures are not taken, starvation can occur. To the best of our knowledge this arbitration method is not used in the current switches.

3.4. Priority Arbitration for Shared Memory Multiprocessors

When arbitration is based on priority, each packet is assigned a priority level. Packets with higher priorities are always selected first. When multiple packets have the same priority, the FCFS method is used to break the tie. To avoid starvation some special measures must be taken. For instance, in the Spider chip [6] when a packet accumulates a certain age, its priority level is increased.

Traditionally, this arbitration policy has been used in the context of real time systems. We will show how it can be applied with success to shared memory multiprocessors that employ relaxed memory consistency models. In such a machine the latency of write operations can be hidden to a large extent. Read operations are more critical because the processors will soon stall in the absence of the desired data. Therefore, it seems natural to give priority to read operations over write operations. In our implementation we use just two levels of priorities. Read requests and read-modify-write (RMW) operations issued by the processor have priority 1. Write requests have priority 0. All the other consistency messages and replies inherit the priority of the message they originated from. For instance, if due to a write request the memory needs to send some invalidation messages, all these invalidations together with their corresponding acknowledgments will inherit the priority of the write (i.e. 0). If the same invalidations are caused by a RMW request they will have priority 1. Such a simple scheme is far from being perfect. For example, the command given to processors to leave a synchronization barrier is essentially a write operation. Delaying this write request can negatively affect the performance of applications. Such subtleties are not the goal of this paper and will not be discussed here. Rather, we keep the implementation simple to show the potential of such an arbitration scheme in the context of shared memory multiprocessors. Its evaluation will be done using execution driven simulation of a few parallel applications. We will not use this arbitration policy with synthetic workload because it is impossible to compare it to other policies: of course, the high priority packets will have a shorter latency while the low priority packets will be delayed. Minimizing the average message latency is not the goal of this policy.

3.5. A New Arbitration Policy: Look-Ahead

The *Look-Ahead* arbitration method proposed in this paper is intended to better distribute the load among the links, and hence, to improve the network throughput. Consider for instance the situation in Figure 2. The numbers in parenthesis represent the number of channels that contend for a particular physical link. We will refer to this number as the

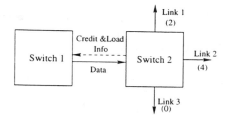

Figure 2. Look-Ahead operation

link load. There are two worms that want to occupy link 1, four worms that want to go on link 2, but no worm for link 3. Therefore, link 3 of switch 2 is unutilized. To maximize the throughput, it is better for switch 1 to try to send a flit which will use link 3 of switch 2. Such a flit, rather than waiting for others in front of him, can immediately proceed on link 3. To make this possible switch 1 must periodically "look-ahead" and collect information about the link loads of switch 2. The link load bits can be easily passed back together with the credit flow information. It must be noted that this *load information* is regarded by the upstream switch as a hint and does not oblige it to strictly take it into account. The ties in arbitration are broken by using the FCFS policy as a backup.

One possible source of overhead in the Look-Ahead scheme is the fact that the arbiter must know the next two hops of a worm. Thus, the routing table used to determine the next switch to be visited must be extended to also contain the identity of the second next switch (like in the Spider chip). This extension is not expected to affect the routing time as the two destinations are read in parallel.

Determining the link load threshold. A first question that arises is under what circumstances a link can be considered lightly loaded. What we need is a threshold value: if the link load exceeds this threshold, then the link is considered to be heavily loaded; otherwise it is lightly loaded. We performed experiments with synthetic workload to determine the optimum value for the threshold. Our results for two different packet sizes are presented in Figure 3. If

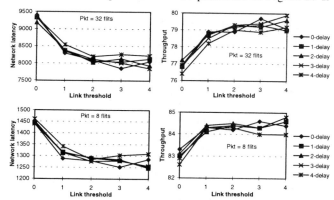

Figure 3. Look-Ahead arbitration method (above: Pkt = 32 flits, below: Pkt = 8 flits)

we look at any curve on the graphs we see that, for good

performance, the threshold should be 2 or greater. As we shall see shortly, to minimize the hardware implementation overhead, a value of 2 is preferred. This value will be used throughout the rest of the paper.

Look-ahead delay. A second implementation issue refers to the inherent time span between the moment of inspecting the link load (by the downstream switch) and the instant the upstream switch can effectively make use of this information. We will refer to this delay as *look-ahead delay*. Suppose that during cycle i the downstream switch collects load information. Then, this information can be passed back in cycle $i+1$, and the arbiter from the upstream switch can use it in cycle $i+2$. Hence, there can be a delay of at most two cycles. In some situations, if the switch is fast enough, the first two steps (load info gathering and transmission) can be combined into one, and the look-ahead delay is reduced to just one cycle. We performed synthetic workload simulations to see how this delay affects the performance of the switch. As Figure 3 shows, the distance between the curves named *x-delay* is very small which suggests that the impact of the look-ahead delay is minimal. The reason is that the link load tends to change very slowly in time. Thus, we can relax the requirements of our switch and use a delay of two cycles. This value will be used in all of our experiments.

Reducing the number of lines for the Look-Ahead policy
Another concern refers to the way the load information is encoded. Of course we want as few bits as possible to minimize the number of lines between two adjacent switches. For an $n \times n$ switch we need to convey information about the load of only $n-1$ links. This is due to the fact that a worm cannot leave the switch using the same port it used for entering. Based on the previous results from Figure 3 we decided to have a link load threshold of 2. With just two bits we can encode four load levels: 0, 1, 2 and more than 2. Hence, for a 2D mesh the total number of bits needed for carrying load information is 8. The number of additional lines between the switches is given by the ratio between the number of bits used for link loads and the number of phits per flit. For example, we use 4 phits per flit, so the number of required lines is $8/4 = 2$. This number can be further reduced by half using one of the following three techniques.

1. Transmit only partial information about the load. In this case we send a bit mask specifying which links have the lowest load under the given threshold. The disadvantage is that there might be no worms that want to occupy one of these very lightly loaded links while there might exist some worms going to moderately loaded links. We will refer to this method as LA1.

2. Transmit 'vague' information about the load. In this variant we send a bit mask that shows which links have the load below the threshold and which are above. The information is vague in the sense that there is no distinction between the links whose load is below the threshold. Hence, the arbiter from the upstream switch might not choose the optimum one. This alternative will be referred to as LA2.

3. Transmit full load info, serially, across two flit cycles. The rationale behind this method is that the load cannot change sharply from one cycle to another. Even

if we send information that is not current, its accuracy is good enough to provide good results. By using two cycles we basically increase the look-ahead delay. As Figure 3 suggests, this approach, called here LA3, is expected to perform very well.

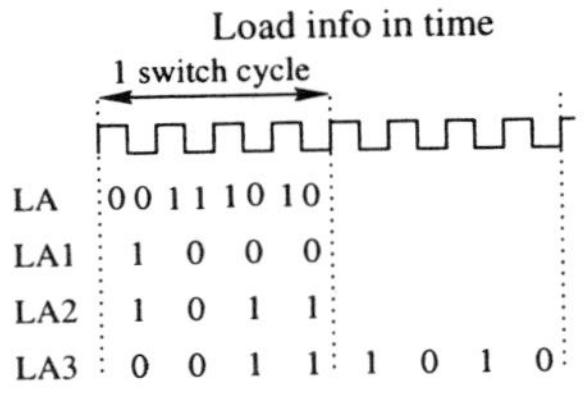

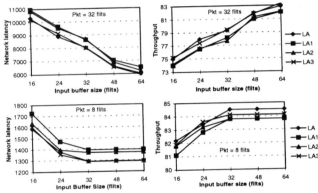

Figure 4. Examples of link load info used in three variations of the LA arbitration method

For a better understanding, Figure 4 shows an example of the link load information passed between the switches for all the variations of the Look-Ahead method introduced above.

Figure 5. Look-Ahead arbitration variations

We evaluated these three variations of the Look-Ahead policy for several input buffer sizes. The results are plotted in Figure 5. On the graphs, LA denominates the original Look-Ahead method as described at the beginning of this section. LA1, LA2, LA3 represent the three look-ahead variations in the order they have been introduced. As we can see, using just partial (LA1) or vague (LA2) information about the link load does not degrade the performance too much (6-8% higher latencies and 0.5-1.5% lower throughput). However, LA3 is even a better alternative as its curve is almost identical with that of LA. This is a direct consequence of the fact that the look-ahead delay affects minimally the performance of LA.

4. Comparison of the Arbitration Policies

The goal of this section is two fold. First, it tries to determine the impact of arbitration on switch performance and to find out the circumstances under which the role of arbitration becomes more prominent. Second, it tries to rank the arbitration policies and to show the provisions that must be met for better performance. For this task we will use both synthetic workload and execution driven simulations.

The policies under examination are:

- First Come First Served (FCFS)
- First Come First Served - Keep Flow (FCFS-KF)
- Round Robin - Keep Flow (RR-KF)
- Shortest Message First (SMF)
- Look-Ahead (LA)

Due to the high latency, the simple Round Robin arbitration policy has been excluded from our results (only Round Robin - Keep Flow is presented). For Look-Ahead we consider a load threshold of 2 and a look-ahead delay of 2 cycles; also, full information (8 bits) about the load is communicated between the switches in just one flit cycle.

4.1. Results for Synthetic Workload Simulations

In Figure 6 (a) and (b) we plot the network latency and throughput of the five policies for packets of 32 flit and 8 flit respectively and for different input buffer sizes. As we can see the arbitration policy is an important factor in the design of a switch. The differences between the worst (RR-KF) and the best (LA) policy can be as high as 35% in network latency and 10% in throughput. These discrepancies become more important as the input buffer is smaller or the messages are larger. The reason is that for small buffers and large packets the network is more congested and the arbitration policy plays a larger role.

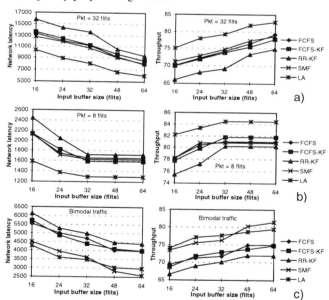

Figure 6. Comparison of arbitration policies

Between FCFS and FCFS-KF there are only minor differences. Of all arbitration policies, RR-KF has the worst performance. This is not surprising. It is already known that FCFS behaves better that RR because it tends to send flits from channels that are full. SMF policy behaves only slightly better than FCFS. Because packets are of same size there are fewer opportunities for SMF to select between various worms. In our experiments, SMF uses FCFS to break a tie. This is the reason why SMF is almost as good as FCFS. The Look-Ahead method clearly outperforms all the others in both network latency and throughput.

So far, we presented experimental results where all the packets had a fixed size of either 8 or 32 flits. For shared memory multiprocessor machines the network traffic is usually composed of two types of packets: read/write memory requests which are short, and reply messages which are often longer because they contain a whole cache line. Therefore, it is interesting to study the behavior of the network when loaded with a mixture of small and large packets. The small packets we use have 8 flits and they account for 50% of the input traffic. The remaining 50% of the traffic is formed by packets of 32 flits in length. Hence, the small packets outnumber the large packets by a factor of 4:1. The input buffer size is varied between 16 and 64 slots. The results are plotted in Figure 6 (c). Under bimodal traffic the SMF method improves considerably. As explained in Section 3.3 by giving priority to short messages we accelerate the process of freeing virtual channels, thus limiting the number of stalls due to unavailable VCs. With small buffers, usually, the switch runs out of buffers before it runs out of available channels. However, for large buffers the main impediment is the lack of free VCs. This is why SMF behaves better for large input buffer sizes, outperforming even the Look-Ahead policy. The ranking between all the other arbitration policies under analysis is maintained. LA method exhibits a latency reduction of 26% and a 6% improvement in network throughput over FCFS.

4.2. Results for Execution Driven Simulations

In this case the set of arbitration policies under analysis is slightly modified. Due to its similarity with FCFS we decided to drop the FCFS-KF scheme from the graphs. On the other hand we added two new policies. One is the Priority arbitration scheme described in Section 3.4. The other is a combination of Look-Ahead, Priority and SMF policies. The normalized execution time (with respect to FCFS) is presented in Figure 7.

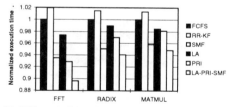

Figure 7. Effect of arbitration policies on execution time

In general, the ranking of the policies follows the pattern for bimodal traffic presented earlier in Figure 6 (c). However, the discrepancies between the policies are reduced because the network load is well beyond saturation (20-30% on average). Still, we can say that even in this situation the arbitration method cannot be neglected: it could lead to a reduction of about 12% in execution time.

The SMF policy proves to be a very effective method. There are two reasons for the good performance of SMF when compared to LA. First, the packet sizes (2 and 10 flits) are small when compared to the input buffer size (32 flits). We already showed that in such circumstances SMF outperforms LA. Second, SMF is more oriented towards latency reduction while LA strives to conserve bandwidth by a better distribution of the link loads. This makes LA an attractive policy when the network is very congested. Such conditions may arise for instance in database applications where the memories are stressed with a large number of requests.

The Priority arbitration policy, even though simple in implementation, achieves a relative good improvement in FFT (7% over FCFS, 9% over RR-KF) and a moderate improvement in MATMUL and RADIX. In MATMUL the number of read operations exceeds by far the number of write operations, so the priority mechanism does not have enough chances to be applied. In RADIX there are plenty of writes, but they are clustered together. For a good improvement we need the read and write operations to be as interspersed as possible.

Because all these three policies, LA, Priority, SMF complement each other we combined them in one powerful method: LA-PRI-SMF. This new policy is expected to perform as good as any of its components in any situation. Indeed, in our experiments it succeeds to outperform all the other policies for all the applications considered.

5. Enhancing the Arbitration Process by Virtual Channel Reservation

In a previous paper [11] we showed that reserving a few flits per virtual channel has a beneficial effect on performance because it eliminates the possibility of one worm occupying all the available slots and blocking the other worms. In this section we will show how a similar reservation idea can be applied with success at virtual channel level.

5.1. The Effect of VC Reservation on Uniformly Destined Traffic

In a traditional implementation of virtual channels, packets going to the same output can occupy more than one, or even all of the virtual channels belonging to an input port. In the latter case, even if there is space available in the shared buffer, these packets can block the way of others packets going to different outputs, because all the virtual channels from a particular input port are used up. Due to the pseudo-random nature of the input traffic, such situations can temporarily appear for a short time at different nodes in the mesh worsening the network latency and throughput. To avoid such a case, we propose to restrict the number of channels that packets going to a particular destination can use. The rest of the channels are said to be *reserved*. For instance, when one VC is reserved, no more than 3 channels can be used by worms going to the same destination (we assume 4 VCs per input port).

So far we have been elusive as to what destination means. It could be the output link to be used in the current switch, or it could mean the final node to be reached by the message. Our experiments (not presented here) indicate that the latter variant is better.

We enhanced the VC reservation process by observing that the number of reserved VCs should not be the same across the whole network. This number should vary according to the position of the link and of the switch in the mesh. For a better understanding lets look at an example where a worm moves from node 4 to node 0 (see Figure 1). Given the X-Y routing algorithm, the worm cannot take any turns because is already moving on the Y direction. Also, on Y direction, node 0 is the last one that can be visited. Therefore, the link between node 4 and node 0 can be used only by worms that have node 0 as their final destination. In this case, reserving any VCs would be totally inappropriate because those reserved VCs will never be used. Starting from this observation, for any given link we must determine the number of nodes that can be reached by worms going on that link. For a deterministic routing algorithm this number is fixed, and upon the placement of the switch in the mesh it can be easily computed and programmed into the router. Still, we have to determine the equation that gives us the number of reserved VCs per input port. We experimented with several choices and empirically found the following formula to perform the best:

$$adj\_\#VCres = min(2 * \#possible\_dest, \#VCres)$$

where $\#VCres$ is what we try to reserve and $adj\_\#VCres$ is the adjusted number based on the position in the mesh. In plain words, the above equation says that for most of the input ports we should try to reserve $\#VCres$, but for some nodes this number should be reduced so that no more than two VCs are reserved for every reachable node. We will refer to this scheme of reservation as *enhanced VC reservation* while the previous one where no adjustment is made will be denoted as *simple VC reservation*.

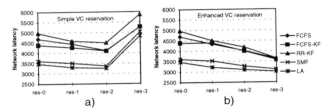

Figure 8. Effect of simple VC reservation (left) and enhanced VC reservation (right) on different arbitration policies for bimodal traffic

The benefits for the two reservation methods, simple and enhanced, are presented in Figure 8 (a) and (b) respectively. With simple reservation the number of channels that must be reserved is two. However, the enhanced reservation scheme is capable of better results, and in this case the optimum number of VCs to be reserved ($\#VCres$) is three. A second conclusion is that VC reservation can successfully be applied in conjunction with any arbitration policy. As expected, the arbitration methods that perform poorer benefit more from reservation. Still, the Look-Ahead method remains the best of all. The improvement in network latency is about 14-22% over the situation where no VC reservation is done. The next section will demonstrate that VC reservation plays an even more important role in case of a hot-spot situation.

5.2. Dealing with Hot-Spot Traffic

In the real world we can not expect the communication pattern of applications to be always perfectly balanced. Hot spots are often observed when processors contend for synchronization variables. In such cases, the buffers of the switches on the path leading to the hot-spot node are saturated with packets and block both hot-spot and regular packets alike. By restricting the number of virtual channels that packets going to one destination can take, we guarantee paths for non-hot packets. Therefore, regular traffic can pass through the network unhindered by the hot traffic.

The goal of this section is two fold: first, we want to show the impact of hot-spot on performance relative to various arbitration policies. Second, we are interested in seeing to what extent the VC reservation idea can prevent the negative effects introduced by the hot-spot. Figure 9 illustrates the variation of the network latency for different arbitration policies, when the input buffer has 32 slots. 90% of the packets are uniformly destined (destination is randomly selected) and 10% go to the hot-spot node (node 4 in our case). For reference, the situation when no hot-spot exists is also presented (NoHS).

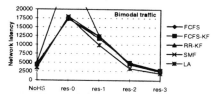

Figure 9. Negative effects of the hot-spot traffic and the effect of enhanced VC reservation on the uniformly destined traffic

Under hot-spot conditions, messages that go to the hot-spot node are substantially delayed. This effect is inevitable. Unfortunately, the hot-spot traffic repercuss on the uniformly destined traffic which is also delayed a great deal. None of the arbitration policies (including LA) is able to limit this negative effect. However, after applying the VC reservation technique the latency of the uniformly destined traffic improves considerably. As we reserve more virtual channels, the latency of UD messages decreases gradually, reaching levels even lower than the case where there is no hot-spot. The explanation for such a more than expected improvement is that, for short periods of time, even UD messages can create small hot-spots. The reservation process not only prevents HS traffic from interfering with UD traffic, but also helps to a better distribution of uniformly destined messages. The ranking between various arbitration policies is maintained even in the presence of the hot-spot.

6. Conclusion

In this paper we used synthetic workload and execution driven simulations to examine the behavior of a broad spectrum of link arbitration policies in the context of switch design. Our results show that link arbitration does play a significant role in the performance of an interconnect and this role is expected to increase as the switches become more complex. The discrepancies between the various arbitration policies can be as high as 35% in network latency, 10% in throughput and 12% in execution time of parallel applications. The arbitration becomes more important when the input buffer is smaller or when the messages are bigger. The Look-Ahead policy proposed in this paper proved to be very effective at high traffic rates. At a cost of just one additional wire between switches it provides significant improvements over traditional arbitration policies. The SMF policy, even though ignored in practice, has a great potential in situations of bimodal traffic and large input buffers. For shared memory multiprocessors the simple priority arbitration scheme introduced in this paper can significantly reduce the execution time for certain applications. We also showed that these arbitration methods can be successfully combined in even more powerful policies, applicable to a wide range of situations. However, none of the policies is able to prevent the negative effects of the hot-spot and therefore a supplemental mechanism is needed. Our solution of reserving a certain number of virtual channels depending on the switch position in the mesh can be added on top of any arbitration policy and is very efficient. Moreover, the VC reservation provides improvements even when there is no explicit hot-spot.

References

[1] L. N. Bhuyan. Analysis of interconnection networks with different arbiter designs. *Journal of Parallel and Distributed Computing*, 9(4):384–403, 1987.

[2] J. Carbonaro and F. Verhoom. Cavallino: The teraflops router and NIC. In *Proceedings of Symposium on High Performance Interconnects*, pages 157–160, August 1996.

[3] W. Dally. Virtual-channel flow control. *IEEE Transactions on Parallel and Distributed Systems*, 3(2):194–205, 1992.

[4] W. J. Dally and C. L. Seitz. Deadlock-free message routing in multiprocessor interconnection networks. *IEEE Trans. on Comp.*, C-36, 5:547–553, 1987.

[5] J. Ding and L. N. Bhuyan. Evaluation of multi-queue buffered multistage interconnection networks under uniform and non-uniform traffic patterns. *International Journal of Systems Science*, 28(11):1115–1128, 1997.

[6] M. Galles. Spider: A high-speed network interconnect. *IEEE Micro*, pages 34–39, January/Febrary 1997.

[7] F. E. Guibaly. Design and analysis of arbitration protocols. *IEEE trans. on comp.*, C-38, 2:161–171, 1989.

[8] M. Katevenis, D. Serpanos, and E. Spyridakis. Credit-flow-controlled ATM for MP interconnection: the ATLAS I single-chip ATM switch. In *Proceedings of the Fourth International Symposium on High-Performance Computer Architecture*, pages 47–56, January 1998.

[9] M. Katevenis, D. Serpanos, and P. Vatsolaki. ATLAS I: a General-Purpose, Single-Chip ATM Switch with Credit-Based Flow Control. In *Proceedings of the Hot Interconnects IV Symposium*, pages 63–73, 1996.

[10] D. J. Kinniment and J. V. Woods. Synchronization and arbitration circuits in digital systems. *IEE Proceedings, Computers and Digital Techniques*, 123(10):961–966, Oct. 1976.

[11] N. Ni, M. Pirvu, and L. Bhuyan. Circular buffered switch design with wormhole routing and virtual channels. In *Proceedings of the 1998 IEEE International Conference on Computer Design*, pages 466–473, October 1998.

[12] V. S. Pai, P. Ranganathan, and S. V. Adve. RSIM: An Execution-Driven Simulator for ILP-Based Shared-Memory Multiprocessors and Uniprocessors. In *Proceedings of the Third Workshop on Computer Architecture Education*, February 1997.

[13] S. C. Woo, M. Ohara, E. Torrie, J. P. Singh, and A. Gupta. The SPLASH-2 programs: Characterication and methodological considerations. In *Proceedings of the 22nd ISCA*, pages 24–37, June 1995.

[14] Q. Yang. Effects of arbitration protocols on the performance of multiple-bus multiprocessors. In *Proceedings of the 1991 ICPP*, pages I–600–I–603, Aug. 1991.

LAPSES: A Recipe for High Performance Adaptive Router Design *

Aniruddha S. Vaidya   Anand Sivasubramaniam   Chita R. Das

Department of Computer Science and Engineering
The Pennsylvania State University
University Park, PA 16802
E-mail: {vaidya,anand,das}@cse.psu.edu

Abstract

Earlier research has shown that adaptive routing can help in improving network performance. However, it has not received adequate attention in commercial routers mainly due to the additional hardware complexity, and the perceived cost and performance degradation that may result from this complexity. These concerns can be mitigated if one can design a cost-effective router that can support adaptive routing. This paper proposes a three step recipe — Look-Ahead routing, intelligent Path Selection, and an Economic Storage implementation, called the LAPSES approach — for cost-effective high performance pipelined adaptive router design.

The first step, look-ahead routing, reduces a pipeline stage in the router by making table lookup and arbitration concurrent. Next, three new traffic-sensitive path selection heuristics (LRU, LFU and MAX-CREDIT) are proposed to select one of the available alternate paths. Finally, two techniques for reducing routing table size of the adaptive router are presented. These are called meta-table routing and economical storage. The proposed economical storage needs a routing table with only 9 and 27 entries for two and three dimensional meshes, respectively. All these design ideas are evaluated on a (16 × 16) mesh network via simulation. A fully adaptive algorithm and various traffic patterns are used to examine the performance benefits. Performance results show that the look-ahead design as well as the path selection heuristics boost network performance, while the economical storage approach turns out to be an ideal choice in comparison to full-table and meta-table options. We believe the router resulting from these three design enhancements can make adaptive routing a viable choice for interconnects.

1 Introduction

Multiprocessor interconnection network designers have always strived to design scalable interconnects with low latency and high throughput. While low message latency helps to reduce the communication overhead in any parallel application, it is particularly beneficial for short messages encountered in shared memory systems. High throughput/bandwidth is essential for bulk data transfer that could occur due to remote page migration, I/O traffic or other data intensive applications. Since low latency in general translates to high throughput, a network should provide minimal latency over the entire, anticipated workload on the system. Moreover, network architectures, designed originally for multiprocessors, are increasingly being accepted in demanding application domains such as web servers and multimedia servers [16]. A more general environment such as a system area network is likely to experience high and fluctuating workloads. Enhancing network performance is thus imperative to fuel continued improvements not only in parallel architectures but also on many other fronts. The building block of a network being its router or switch fabric, the router design should

have the necessary features to aid in building a high performance interconnect, and is the focus of this paper.

Network research over the years has converged towards wormhole switching mechanism and virtual channel flow control to provide improved performance in scalable direct networks. These research ideas have manifested into many commercial switch designs today [12, 20, 21, 13, 19, 3, 26, 18, 1]. Table 1 shows a non-exhaustive list of commercial routers and the features they support. A third component, in addition to switching and flow control, that has a significant impact on network performance is the routing algorithm. Several research studies have shown performance benefits of various adaptive routing schemes compared to oblivious routing [15, 14, 9, 17, 7, 2, 5]. Theoretically, it is known that routing adaptivity is a desirable feature since it can lower average message latency at moderate to high load. Further, the ability to use alternate paths improves fault-tolerance properties of the network. In spite of these advantages, very few commercial router designs have adopted this idea (T3E router [21], Servernet-II [13] and Transputer/C-104 [18] switch to a limited extent).

Complexity and cost are the main reasons attributed to the limited commercial adoption of adaptive routing. We believe that if we can provide a cost-effective solution to implementing adaptive routing in the context of the current router architectures, then adaptive routers will have a better commercial viability. Since adaptivity helps in boosting network performance, we can see its benefit translated to fine grain parallel applications and to emerging applications that are likely to inject high network load.

The two main cost factors associated with providing adaptivity in a router are the number of VCs required and the implementation of the algorithm itself. It was argued in [4] that addition of each VC slows down the router clock by 25–30%. This is only true for a non-pipelined design. Current commercial routers are being designed with increasingly large transistor and area budgets. Also, faster design cycles due to ASIC design approaches and general-purpose applicability of routers (for use in arbitrary topologies and system-area interconnects) have lead to the adoption of programmable routing tables, virtual channels, and increased fault-tolerance features using pipelined router designs [21, 12, 13]. An adaptive router should, therefore, adhere to a pipelined design and should exploit all available facilities such as VCs and table based routing. VCs are thus not considered an additional expense.

Even though these key enabling technology trends set the broad guideline for designing routers to support adaptive routing, there are still a few challenges that need to be addressed for making adaptive routing commercially viable and popular:

- Additional work required for adaptive routing can potentially increase the number of pipe-stages in the router and/or result in a slower router clock cycle as compared to a deterministic router. In particular, the serially dependent operations of table-lookup and path-selection cum arbitration (Fig. 1 shows the pipelined stages in a router.) are a key part of the critical path through the router. Decoupling of table-lookup and path-selection cum arbitration functions through a technique called *look-ahead routing* has the potential to reduce

*This research is supported in part by NSF grant MIPS-9634197, NSF Career Award MIPS-9701475, and equipment grants from NSF and IBM.

236

Router	R-Tbl	Design	Max Nodes	Ports	VCs	Port Type	Routing
SGI SPIDER	Y	ASIC	512	6	4	P	Det
Cray T3D	Y	ASIC	2K	7	4	P	Det
Cray T3E	Y	ASIC	2176	7	5	P	Adpt
Tandem Servernet-II	Y	ASIC	1M	12	No	P	Lim. Adpt
Sun S3.mp	Y	ASIC	1K	6	4	2P + 4S	Adpt
Intel Cavallino	N	Custom	> 4K	6	4	P	Det
HAL Mercury	N	Custom	64	6	3	P	Det
Inmos C-104	Y	Custom	Any	32	Any	S	Lim. Adpt
Myricom Myrinet	N	Custom	Any	8/16	No	P	Det

Table 1: A non-exhaustive list of state-of-the-art commercial wormhole and virtual-cut through routers.

pipeline-latency in adaptive routers.

- When multiple paths are available for routing to a given destination, a unique path has to be selected for the next route [10]. Selection of a good path among the available alternatives is important for improved performance. This issue does not arise in deterministic routers.

- Adhering to a table-based router design, adaptive routing requires multiple path choices to be stored in routing tables, thus increasing table storage cost. Offsetting this cost, especially in the design of routers for large scalable interconnects, may become important.

We investigate these three issues in this paper and propose the design of high-performance, low-latency, table-based routers using the *LAPSES* approach — look-ahead (LA) routing, good path-selection (PS) and economical storage (ES). Look-ahead routing decouples the table lookup and path selection/arbitration stages of the pipelined design and uses the current routing table entry for the next routing step. In essence, by making lookup and arbitration concurrent, we reduce one pipe stage and thus the overall delay. This technique has been implemented in the SGI SPIDER, which uses oblivious routing. We extend the look-ahead technique to adaptive routers by providing the valid path options in the header flit. Next, we propose three path selection strategies, called *least frequently used* (LFU), *least recently used* (LRU) and *maximum credit* (MAX-CREDIT) for selecting one of the available paths provided by the adaptive routing algorithm. Finally, we discuss various options to implement adaptive routing using table-lookup. Since multiple table entries are required for maintaining alternate routing options, increased storage cost is another concern here. We study three different designs - (i) full table implementation, where the table size is proportional to the number of nodes in the network, (ii) a meta-table design that partitions the network into groups (clusters) and uses hierarchical lookup for inter cluster and intra cluster routing and (iii) an elegant economic routing table implementation, which needs only 3^n entries for an n-dimensional interconnect.

All these design options are examined by simulating a (16×16) 2-D mesh network using these routers. As an example, Duato's fully adaptive algorithm [9] is used in this study. We use various synthetic traffic patterns to evaluate the impact on average network latency. The results indicate that the look-ahead feature reduces the average latency at low load while the routing flexibility becomes advantageous at high load, thereby making look-ahead adaptive router a good choice across the entire spectrum. The effect of look-ahead is significant for short messages as the latency could reduce by as much as 15%. The LRU, LFU and MAX-CREDIT path selection strategies outperform previously proposed static-XY [10] and MIN-MUX [9] policies for all of the nonuniform traffic patterns. The LRU and MAX-CREDIT policies seem to be better choices because of their low cost of implementation. Finally, we observe that meta-table implementation is not an appropriate choice for 2-D mesh networks, although it is cost-effective compared to full-table design. The proposed scheme (economical storage) that needs only 3^n entry-tables can provide identical performance as full-table routing, making it attractive for adaptive routers. This scheme needs only 9 and 27 routing table entries for 2-D and 3-D networks, which are the common topologies. These three techniques used in conjunction with todays enabling router design technology can make high-performance adaptive routers a commercially viable and successful design choice.

The rest of the paper is organized as follows. In section 2, a pipelined router model, called PROUD, and the experimental setup are presented. The look-ahead routing scheme is discussed in section 3. The next section introduces the path selection policies and analyzes their performance. Section 5 presents the table implementation details, followed by the concluding remarks in in Section 6.

2 Preliminaries

2.1 Router Architecture

Since this paper is on the design and analysis of router architectures, we begin with a logical description of its building blocks. A typical wormhole router has synchronization and hand-shaking logic at the ports, input/output flit buffers, flit-decoders as well as a crossbar and its control unit (consisting of a routing decision block and arbiter). Message flits enter the router at an input port and eventually exit the router at an appropriate output port as determined by the crossbar setting. The routing information contained in the header flit of a message is used by the routing decision block to determine the appropriate crossbar setting. The crossbar arbitration unit arbitrates between messages contending for the same crossbar output port. Flits of a message that temporarily cannot make progress because of currently unavailable network resources, are held in the flit buffers.

To support VCs, a VC de-multiplexor unit precedes the input flit buffers and a VC multiplexor precedes the output port of the router [6, 24]. In an adaptive router, the routing decision block may have a choice of crossbar output ports to route a message. A *path selection function* is required in the routing decision block to select one of multiple valid output ports. To support flexibility in network designs and routing algorithms, some routers use table-lookup routing (see Table 1). The routing decision block in these routers is implemented as a programmable lookup-table. The table is typically indexed by the destination node address and the corresponding table entry determines the crossbar output port to route the message on. By providing multiple entries in the routing table for every index, the routing table can provide support for adaptive routing. The routing table entries are configured based on the routing algorithm to be used.

2.2 Router Models and Experimental Setup

Router Models: The cumulative delay through the router that is experienced by a message flit is determined by the individual delays of the functional units within the router. However, in order to increase the throughput, modern routers use a pipelined design [12, 21, 8].

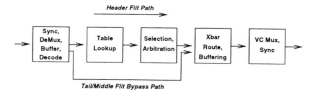

Figure 1: Pipeline stages in the PROUD router

237

The pipelined router models used in this study are called PROUD (for Pipelined ROUter Design) and LA-PROUD (for PROUD with Look-Ahead). The five-stage pipeline for PROUD is given in Fig. 1. In this study, we use the PROUD model to study the performance of deterministic and adaptive routers without lookahead. Note that in deterministic routers, the selection cum arbitration stage simply reduces to arbitration (as no path-selection is required). However, path-selection does not contribute significantly to the delay of this stage and hence we assume identical delays for deterministic and adaptive routers in our analysis.

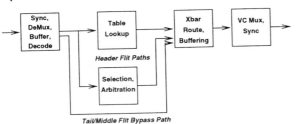

Figure 2: Pipeline stages in the LA-PROUD router

In the PROUD delay model, the routing-table lookup stage and the path-selection cum arbitration stage are serially dependent. The LA-PROUD delay model is a four-stage pipe with table-lookup functions decoupled from path-selection cum arbitration achieved via lookahead routing. This model is shown in Fig 2. Details of look-ahead routing are discussed in Section 3.

Both the PROUD and LA-PROUD models are similar to the pipelined architectures of the SPIDER or T3E routers. Conceptually, a router can be considered as a set of parallel PROUD/LA-PROUD pipes equal to the product of the number of physical input/output ports and the number of VCs per port. Contention for resources between the parallel pipes can occur only in the crossbar arbitration and VC multiplexing stages. In a contention-free environment, the key functional unit delays which determine the router cycle time are the table-lookup delay and the arbitration delay [12]. Our entire study here is confined to improving the design in these two critical stages of the pipelined router to support adaptivity.

Experimental setup: In this study we use the PROUD network simulator to simulate a 256 node two-dimensional (16×16) mesh interconnection network. Each router is modeled as a 5 port bidirectional switch. Four of the ports are connected to up to four neighboring nodes in the mesh and the fifth port is used to communicate to the local processing node network interface. We assume 4 VCs per physical channel as is available in most recent routers. Each stage of the PROUD (or LA-PROUD) is assumed to take unit cycle time under no resource contention. In addition, unit cycle delay is assumed for traversing a link between two connected routers.

Parameter	Value
Mesh Network Size	256 node (16×16)
Message Length	20 flits (unless specified)
Inter-arrival time	Exponential distrib.
Traffic	Uniform, Transpose, Shuffle. Bit-Reversal
In/Out Buffer Size	20 flits
VCs per PC	4
Network Cycle Time	1 unit
Router Latency (contention-free)	5 units (PROUD) 4 units (LA-PROUD)
Link Delay	1 unit

Table 2: Simulation parameters used in performance study

All our performance studies are for a constant message length of 20 flits (unless otherwise indicated). Messages are injected with exponential inter-arrival times for 4 different traffic patterns (uniform, transpose, bit-reversal and perfect-shuffle traffic). These traffic patterns are consistent with standard definitions for synthetic traffic patterns used in interconnection network studies [11]. We

present performance results as the average network latency versus normalized load. Normalized load is defined as the ratio of the message injection rate per-cycle to that injection rate, required to reach the bisection bandwidth of the network under node-uniform traffic [11]. Results are only presented for loads leading up to network saturation. Simulation data was collected by injecting 10000 warm-up messages after which statistics was collected over 400000 message injections. A summary of the simulation parameters used in this study is given in Table 2.

2.3 Adaptive Routing Algorithms

Several adaptive routing algorithms have been proposed for direct networks [15, 14, 9, 22, 2, 5]. These algorithms vary in terms of their performance and hardware (VC) requirements. Since we are interested in a cost-effective implementation, we use a fully adaptive routing algorithm that requires the minimum number of VCs. The algorithms that meet this criteria are those in [14, 2, 9, 22] and they require 2 VCs per physical channel for deadlock-free adaptive routing in a 2-D mesh. In this paper, we use Duato's fully adaptive algorithm [9] for performance analyses, and these discussions are valid for other fully adaptive algorithms as well since they exhibit similar behavior.

3 Look Ahead Routing

3.1 Basic Look Ahead Routing

It was seen in Section 2 that table lookup and path selection cum arbitration operations are serially dependent. First, the table-lookup determines the output port of the router crossbar to be used to route a given message towards its destination. Then, upon determination of the desired output port, the message arbitrates for that port. Fig. 3 (a) illustrates this serial dependency. Also note that, only the destination address is required to be present in the message header-flit for the purposes of routing, and the same header-flit can be used by the message without modification at the next router.

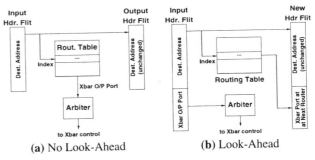

(a) No Look-Ahead   **(b)** Look-Ahead

Figure 3: Input header flit format, usage and new header generation for deterministic routers (a) without, and (b) with lookahead.

Now, if the crossbar output port can be known in advance, then arbitration can be performed directly by eliminating the need for table lookup for routing at the current router. Table lookup can then be performed concurrently with arbitration, for deciding the output port to be taken at the next router along the path to the destination. We refer to such a scheme as *look-ahead* routing. In particular, when such a scheme is used in a deterministic router, we refer to it as *deterministic look-ahead* routing. This scheme is illustrated in Fig. 3 (b). Note that look-ahead routing requires the crossbar output port to be used at the current router to be pre-specified in the header-flit of the message (thus increasing header size), and a partial modification of the header-flit at every router along the path. Deterministic look-ahead routing is used in the SGI SPIDER [12][1]. We extend the concept of look-ahead routing to adaptive routers.

---

[1] This technique is called "table-lookup pipelining" in SGI SPIDER.

3.2 Adaptive Look-Ahead Routing

Adaptive routing implies the possibility of multiple path choices being available at a given router to route a message towards its destination. Routing table entries in an adaptive router thus need to store multiple valid output ports per destination. Further, for enabling look-ahead routing, look-up tables need to contain allowed output-port information for routers along multiple candidate paths out of the current router. This further increases the storage requirement for adaptive look-ahead routing. Note that when multiple candidate paths are available, a unique path has to be picked from amongst the choices. This is called *path selection*. Path-selection and arbitration are both required before a message may be routed through the crossbar. We illustrate the working of adaptive look-ahead routing through the example of a 2-D mesh interconnect.

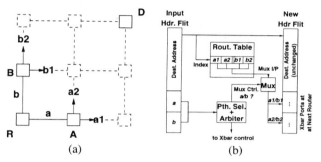

(a)   (b)

Figure 4: (a) Multiple paths to a destination node in a mesh network. (b) Input header flit format, usage and new header generation.

Consider the intermediate router R of Fig. 4 (a). If a message at R needs to be routed toward D, then ports a and b would both take the message in productive directions to routers A and B, respectively. Ports $a1, a2$ and $b1, b2$ at routers A and B, respectively, would take the message further in productive directions. The table entries at router R to route to node D for adaptive lookahead would then have entries for ports $a1$ and $a2$ of node A, which is along port a of R, and entries for ports $b1$ and $b2$ of node B, which is along port b of R. As soon as path-selection and arbitration have been performed at R, it is known which of the port a or b will be uniquely used to route towards destination D. At this point, part of the lookahead table lookup information corresponding to the unused port at R (either $a1, a2$ or $b1, b2$) can be discarded. The rest is used to construct a new header flit containing information for path-selection and arbitration at the next node along the route to D.

The header flit interpretation, table-lookup and new-header flit generation in adaptive look-ahead routers, corresponding to the above example, is shown in Fig. 4 (b). It should be observed that the new header generation based on the outcome of path selection (seen as the Mux-Control line and Mux unit in Fig. 4 (b)) is not on the critical path for the arbitration to proceed and hence does not increase the delay of the path-selection cum arbitration stage. New header generation can be performed concurrently with the header being routed through the crossbar and into the crossbar output buffer.

3.3 Performance of Adaptive Lookahead Routing

Compared to deterministic routing, performance improvement with adaptive look-ahead routers stems from two aspects of their design, viz. their ability to adaptively use multiple candidate paths and to reduce router latency by look-ahead routing. In this section, we quantify the performance improvement due to the above factors using a consistent set of delay models (PROUD and LA-PROUD) and compare the performance of four routers for a 2-D mesh interconnection network — deterministic routers with and without look-ahead, and adaptive routers with and without look-ahead. (As stated in Section 2, the routing table implements Duato's fully adaptive scheme.) Next, we evaluate the impact of message length on the latency of adaptive lookahead routers.

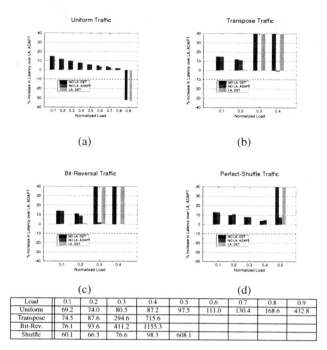

(a)   (b)

(c)   (d)

Load	0.1	0.2	0.3	0.4	0.5	0.6	0.7	0.8	0.9
Uniform	69.2	74.0	80.5	87.2	97.5	111.0	130.4	168.6	432.8
Transpose	74.5	87.6	294.6	715.6					
Bit-Rev.	76.1	93.6	411.2	1155.3					
Shuffle	60.1	66.3	76.6	98.3	608.1				

Figure 5: Comparison of Router performance with or without Look-Ahead and with or without adaptive routing for four traffic patterns on a (16 × 16) mesh. A positive/negative bar in the figures indicates that a given scheme has higher/lower latency than the adaptive router with lookahead. The table provides the actual latency values for the adaptive router with lookahead for each of the traffic patterns.

Figure 5 shows the latency comparison of the four router architectures (NO LA DET, LA DET, NO LA ADAPT, and LA ADAPT) as a function of normalized load on the network. The results are given for a message length of 20 flits and static path selection strategy (explained in the next section) used for simulating the adaptive algorithm. The latency results are normalized with respect to the LA ADAPT router scheme. In all the four figures for the four traffic patterns, it is seen that the LA ADAPT router outperforms both the no look ahead routers (NO LA DET and NO LA ADAPT) by as much as 12-15% when the load is low. The LA DET performs almost identical as the LA ADAPT scheme for light load and hence the latency difference is negligible. For uniform traffic in Fig. 5(a), both the deterministic implementations perform better than the adaptive implementations for high load re-confirming the results that routing adaptivity does not help uniform traffic. The results for the three non-uniform traffic patterns indicate that the adaptive algorithms with or without look-ahead show significant performance improvements against deterministic schemes at high load. The benefits of look-ahead are swamped by the relatively larger benefits of adaptive routing at high loads.

Mesg. Len	Look Ahead	No Look Ahead	% Improv.
5	51.9	63.4	18.0
10	58.9	69.6	15.4
20	74.0	83.6	11.5
50	120.2	128.6	6.5

Table 3: Impact of message length (Uniform traffic, normalized network load of 0.2.)

Effectiveness of the lookahead with respect to varying message length is given in Table 3. The results are for adaptive routers with look-ahead and no look-ahead features. As expected, short messages benefit the most due to look-ahead and the relative improvement reduces with an increase in message length.

In summary, look-ahead helps in reducing message latency at low load while adaptivity takes over for reducing message latency at high load. Thus, a look-ahead, adaptive router is the best choice since it can help over the entire range of workload. In addition, short messages see the maximum reduction in latency by saving one pipe line stage in the router architecture.

4 Path Selection Heuristics

4.1 Path Selection

An adaptive router when presented with multiple path choices to route to a given destination, must select a unique and currently available path from amongst the multiple candidates. The criterion for selection is called the path selection function [10]. Researchers and router designers have commonly used dimension-order selection [10, 2], random selection [17], and first-available-free-path selection [13] for their simplicity. These criteria are static in the sense that they do not make use of current network conditions to select a path, which is likely to experience the lowest contention. In this paper, the dimension-order selection is referred to as STATIC-XY since it prefers the X-dimension first (in the case of a 2D-mesh).

By using port usage history, dynamic or traffic sensitive selection criteria can be used with an attempt to minimize path contention in the network, thereby improving routing performance. We propose three dynamic path selection heuristics (PSHs), called LRU, LFU and MAX-CREDIT, and compare them against STATIC-XY and another dynamic scheme referred to as MIN-MUX in this paper. MIN-MUX uses the physical channel with the minimum degree of VC-multiplexing (For details about the MIN-MUX PSH, see [9]).

Least Frequently Used (LFU) PSH: This PSH selects the output port (among the candidates) with the lowest usage count until that time. It works on the premise that if link utilizations are balanced, it will result in improved network performance. Implementing this PSH would require maintaining a counter for each crossbar output port, incrementing it whenever the corresponding port is used and selecting the port with the lowest counter value.

Least Recently Used (LRU) PSH: Typically, recent history is a better indicator of congestion information than cumulative history. LRU tries to route a message through a candidate crossbar output port that was used farthest in the past. One way to implement this scheme would be to use counters for each output port like in LFU. However, these "age" counters would get incremented every time the output port remains unused and reset when the corresponding crossbar port is used. The oldest port amongst the candidates would be selected.

MAX-CREDIT PSH: The LFU PSH keeps track of all past usage of a channel. However, it does not accurately reflect the current usage of the channel. The MAX-CREDIT PSH tries to remedy this situation.

A majority of wormhole routers use credit-based flow control, where routers credit their neighboring routers with the amount of free buffer space available for that channel with them. These credits are decremented by the upstream router as flits are sent along the link and incremented as acknowledgments are received. Thus, a large credit value for a link is indicative of possibly low congestion at the downstream router. The MAX-CREDIT PSH hence picks the channel with maximum available credits from amongst the available candidate channels. Implementation details of these schemes can be found in [23].

4.2 Performance of Path Selection Heuristics

Figure 6 depicts the average message latency as a function of network load with five PSHs (static-XY, MIN-MUX, LFU, LRU and MAX-CREDIT). The results are for a (16 × 16) network with four different traffic patterns.

As expected, the static path selection performs the best for uniform traffic, although MIN-MUX, LRU and MAX-CREDIT heuristics are comparable except at very high load. For the rest of the three traffic patterns, the four load sensitive selection schemes perform much better than the static path selection. In particular, the

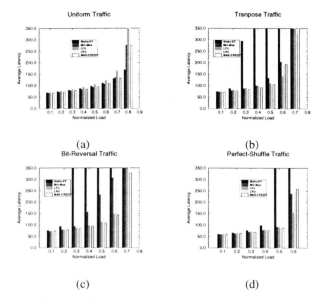

Figure 6: Performance of path-selection heuristics

LRU, LFU and the MAX-CREDIT schemes are the best performers under medium to high load before saturation. The LFU policy has the minimum latency for bit-reversal traffic. In most cases, MAX-CREDIT performance lies in between LFU and LRU. While all these three policies exhibit similar performance, the LRU and MAX-CREDIT implementations need smaller counters.

These results indicate that adaptive router designs should include traffic-sensitive path selection heuristics to utilize the links more efficiently. It is possible to enhance the performance further by implementing the same adaptive algorithm with better, but not necessarily expensive hardware support.

5 Reducing Table Storage Overhead

Table-based routing schemes have become popular due to factors such as the ability to reprogram routers for changes in topology, improving performance (by using more efficient routing algorithms), small and constant table lookup cost (independent of routing algorithm complexity) and fault-tolerance capability. The preferred method of implementing routing tables has been to use complete routing tables, where a distinct routing table entry is available for every destination node in the network (up to the maximum number of nodes to be supported). Such an implementation scheme is referred to as *full-table routing*.

Full-table routing has the flexibility of supporting arbitrary network topologies limited only by the number of ports in the router. This approach is used in the Cray T3D and T3E routers [20, 21], as well as the Sun S3.mp router [19]. However, full-table routing by its nature has storage overhead proportional to the maximum number of nodes in the network and thus limits its scalability to large network sizes. A large table RAM size may also lead to slower lookup times.

Support for adaptive routing require multiple entries per table index, increasing storage requirements over deterministic routers. Lookahead routing further increases these requirements. This motivates the need for economical storage solutions for scalable high performance routers. In this section, we present two-known schemes for reducing routing table sizes, discuss their applicability for adaptive routing and propose an innovative approach for drastically reducing storage requirements for *n*-dimensional mesh-like networks.

5.1 Earlier Schemes for Reducing Routing-Table Size

5.1.1 Hierarchical or Meta-table Routing

In full-table routing, destination addresses are used to index into a flat routing table-structure. Conceptually, hierarchical or meta-table routing differs by maintaining two or more levels of routing tables. Interconnection network nodes are partitioned logically into clusters such that all nodes within a cluster have the same *cluster id* and distinct *sub-cluster ids*. Routing to nodes within the same cluster is performed by means of a full mapped table. Routing information for nodes which are outside the local cluster is restricted to a single entry per cluster maintained in a cluster table. This cluster table could have a flat structure or further hierarchies. This type of storage savings are used in the SGI-SPIDER (2-level) [12] and the Servernet-II router [13] (3-levels). For adaptive routing, the sub-cluster routing table as well as the cluster routing table(s) need to support multiple entries per index.

5.1.2 Interval/Universal Routing

Interval routing [25] reduces table-size on a router to the smallest possible size equal to the number of router ports, thus making the table-size independent of the number of nodes in the interconnection network. This is achieved by a node-labeling scheme, wherein nodes with contiguous labels within a specified interval can be routed to using the same router exit port. The number of such non-overlapping intervals is equal to the number of router exit ports. It has been shown that interval labeling schemes can be derived for any connected network, hence also the name *universal routing*. The Transputer/C-104 switch [18] uses interval routing.

This scheme has significant advantages in terms of the small table size, excellent scalability and applicability to arbitrary topologies. However, in general, it cannot guarantee minimal paths for routing and requires specific labeling schemes, deadlock freedom for routing algorithms is not simple to specify, and this scheme is not readily receptive to adaptive routing.

5.2 Economical Storage for Mesh-like networks

The three schemes, full-table routing, meta-table routing and interval routing schemes do not use topology specific information to optimize routing table size. However, most often such routers are used in fairly regular topologies such as hypercubes, meshes and tori. Here, we propose a scheme, which uses topology-specific optimizations for n-dimensional mesh-like networks, to reduce table size for fully-adaptive routing, while retaining the advantages of programmable routing tables. We call this scheme *economical storage* (ES).

Consider a 2-D mesh network with node labels specified in (X, Y) Cartesian coordinates. Each router in such a network has five exit ports — four in the 4 coordinate directions $+X, +Y, -X, -Y$ and one port to exit the interconnection network if the current node is the destination. From any given node in this network, at most two output port choices exist for routing to any other node using minimal paths. Without loss of generality, let this source node be at the origin. Now, all destination nodes in any one of the four quadrants, say the quadrant $(X > 0, Y > 0)$, can be routed to using one of the two ports choices, $+X$ or $+Y$ in this case. Any destinations on the four axes, say the positive X-axis $(X > 0, Y = 0)$, can be routed to using only one port, which in this case is $+X$ port. Finally, the last case is if the destination port is the current node itself (origin $(0, 0)$), which can be routed to using port 0. Thus, for any arbitrary sized 2-D mesh network, only 9 table entries, each with up to two output-port choices, are required in a router to implement minimal path fully-adaptive routing.

5.2.1 Implementing Economical-Storage Routing Tables

Assume that nodes in the 2-D mesh are labeled with Cartesian coordinates. Let $D = (dx, dy)$ be a destination node specified in the header of a message arriving at an intermediate router $I = (ix, iy)$.

The router computes the sign of the relative coordinates of the destination, by computing

$$sx = sign(dx - ix), \text{ and}$$

$$sy = sign(dy - iy),$$

where, $sx, sy \in \{+, -, 0\}$. The signs sx and sy together are used to index into the 9 entry routing table to determine the output port(s) to be taken to route to destination D.

The actual hardware requirements apart form the routing table are a *node-id* register on the router and two comparators to find sx and sy used to index into the routing table.

Fig. 7 shows an example of a 9-node 2-D mesh, and shows how the router at an intermediate node $4 = (1, 1)$ would be programmed for North-Last partially adaptive routing (based on the Turn Model [15]). It should be noted from this example that although 2 output ports may be available to route to some destination, specific routing algorithms could deny them for guaranteeing deadlock freedom.

The 9 entry table for 2-D meshes stems from the 3 choices $\{+, -, 0\}$ each for sx and sy. Extending the economical storage scheme for 3-D mesh routers requires a 27 entry routing table. In general, for n-dimensional k^n-node meshes, a 3^n size table would suffice while full-table routing would require a k^n node routing table. Implementation concerns usually restrict mesh interconnects to small n (typically 2 or 3) and large k (typically 8 to 12). For example, the 2048 node 3-D interconnect in Cray T3D uses a 2048 entry routing table, which could be reduced to a 27 entry table using the economical storage scheme.

In the interest of brevity, we have only presented a basic implementation for the ES scheme here. It is, however, possible to implement ES with lookahead, provide minimal path routing n-dimensional tori, and support irregular topologies. (See [23].)

5.2.2 Adaptive Routing Performance Comparison with Various Table Storage Schemes

Table storage optimizations come with an associated tradeoff — that of decreased routing flexibility. It is thus, important to study the performance impact of lowering table storage requirements. We analyze this impact on the performance of adaptive routing in two-dimensional meshes. We compare the performance of full-table routing, meta-table routing (with a 2-level hierarchy) and economical storage routing.

Full-table routing offers complete flexibility in routing, where routing paths from each source to every destination can be individually configured. This flexibility is, however, rarely useful. For example, perhaps all the popular adaptive mesh routing algorithms use network symmetry and source-relative directions for routing to the destination for simplicity of the algorithm and proof of deadlock freedom.

In the case of meta-table routing, there is some loss of flexibility. In a (two-level) meta-table implementation an n-bit node-id is partitioned (into 2) to derive a cluster id and a sub-cluster id. For routing to any node in a distinct cluster, the same set of output ports have to be used. This implies that node-ids must be appropriately assigned to provide maximal flexibility in routing. For the sake of performance comparisons, we have used 2 different node-labeling schemes for studying meta-table routing in meshes. These mappings are presented in Fig. 8. The first mapping, Fig. 8 (a) permits minimal flexibility. This is because all nodes within a cluster are in a single row, which implies no-flexibility in routing within the sub-cluster. Similarly, no flexibility exists in routing to other clusters, because clusters are arranged in a single column. This map forces routing to be equivalent to deterministic XY routing. The second mapping, Fig. 8 (b), permits maximal flexibility. This is because, each sub-cluster is a square (4 × 4) mesh, permitting maximal adaptivity within the cluster. Clusters are also arranged in a (4 × 4) configuration which permits flexibility in routing to other clusters.

In economical storage routing, there is no real loss of flexibility as compared to full-table routing. This is because, all the known

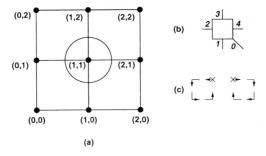

Dest node	Sign sx	Sign sy	Candidate Router Ports	Tbl-Entries North-Last Rout.
(0,0)	-	-	2, 1	2, 1
(1,0)	0	-	1	1
(2,0)	+	-	4, 1	4, 1
(0,1)	-	0	2	2
(1,1)	0	0	0	0
(2,1)	+	0	4	4
(0,2)	-	+	2, 3	2
(1,2)	0	+	3	3
(2,2)	+	+	4, 3	4

(d)

Figure 7: Table programming for a 2-D mesh network router using economical storage. (a) 9-node mesh with node labels in (X,Y) co-ordinates. Node (1,1) is the source router under consideration. (b) Output port labels for 5 port 2-D mesh router. (c) Permitted turns in North-Last routing. Turns with dotted lines in the figure are disallowed for guaranteeing deadlock. (d) Economical Storage Table programming for North-Last routing.

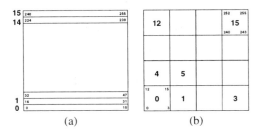

(a)   (b)

Figure 8: Meta-table mapping for a 256 node 2-D mesh for (a) minimal, and (b) maximal adaptivity in routing. In each of the figures the labels in small-type indicate the complete address of a node in the mesh, and the labels in large type indicate cluster labels.

mesh routing algorithms such as those in [15, 9, 22, 2] can be implemented with the economical storage. Hence, performance of full-table routing and economical storage routing are identical.

The results comparing the performance of the two meta-table mapping schemes and the full-table and ES tables are presented in Table 4. As the node labels in the meta-table map for maximal adaptivity differ from the conventional mesh node labeling scheme, we have ensured that when considering the various traffic patterns used for evaluation, source and destination locations (and not labels) are preserved. This makes the performance comparisons meaningful.

Traffic	Load	Meta-Tbl Adp.	Meta-Tbl Det.	Full-Tbl-Adp./ Econ. Storage
Unif.	0.1	71.5	69.2	69.2
	0.2	82.3	74.0	74.0
	0.3	294.1	80.6	80.5
	0.4	Sat.	87.4	87.2
	0.5	Sat.	97.8	97.5
	0.6	Sat.	111.5	111.0
	0.7	Sat.	132.2	130.4
	0.8	Sat.	169.3	168.6
	0.9	Sat.	289.1	432.8
Trans.	0.1	1024.1	74.6	74.5
	0.2	1632.7	88.5	87.6
	0.3	Sat.	746.6	294.6
	0.4	Sat.	1485.0	715.6
	0.5	Sat.	Sat.	853.5
Bit-Rev.	0.1	77.5	76.3	76.1
	0.2	103.3	95.0	93.6
	0.3	1164.8	1033.2	411.2
	0.4	Sat.	Sat.	1155.3

Table 4: Performance Comparison of Table-Storage Schemes. (Sat. indicates that network saturation has occured.)

A counter intuitive result that is seen is that the performance of meta-table routing with the minimal flexibility mapping (Meta-Tbl-Det) performs better than the mapping for maximal flexibility (Meta-Tbl). This behavior occurs because of large link contention at the links at cluster boundaries in the latter mapping. To understand why this behavior is exhibited consider a message being sent from any node in cluster 0 of Fig. 8 (b) to any node in cluster 5. This message could route adaptively until it cross over into cluster 4 at the north boundary or into cluster 1 at the east boundary. When the message reaches either cluster 4 or cluster 1, it can no longer route adaptively until it crosses over into cluster 5. Although, it can once again route adaptively within cluster 5 to reach its destination, the loss of adaptivity at the boundary nodes of cluster 4 or 1 causes unbalanced congestion at these links resulting in high latencies and premature saturation of the network. As a result, despite adaptive routing capabilities, this scheme performs worse than even deterministic routing.

Router Property	Full-Table	m-Level Meta Table	Interval	Economical Storage
Table Size	2^N	$m.2^{N/m}$ (optimal)	#-ports (Indep. of Net. Size)	9 (2-dim), 27 (3-dim)
Scalability	Poor	Better	Great	Great
Adaptivity Possible ?	Yes	Yes (limit.)	Not-direct	Yes
Topology	Arbitrary	Fairly Arbit.	Arbitrary	Meshes. Tori, Irregular
Lookup Time ($\propto$ tbl-size)	Possibly High	Low	Small	Small
Commercial Routers	T3D, T3E, S3.mp	SPIDER ($m=2$), Servernet-II ($m=3$)	C-104 Transputer	None (Proposed here)

Table 5: A summary of the relation between table storage optimizations and router properties considering a 2^N node network. Commercial implementations of various table storage optimizations are also summarized.

Although meta-table based adaptive routing holds the promise of reducing table-storage, it results in poor adaptive routing performance, at least in the case of mesh networks. It is possible, however, that adaptive routing with meta-table implementation may demonstrate good performance for topologies where intra-cluster messages do not interfere with inter-cluster message (due to distinct links being used), such as in the case of hypercubes. On the other hand, we find that the novel economical storage scheme offers all the benefits of table-lookup routing at a small storage cost without affecting performance of adaptive routing. A summary of schemes to reduce table storage in presented in Table 5.

6 Concluding Remarks

With the increasing use of multiprocessor networks in more demanding as well as general purpose application environments, where the workload could be high, fluctuating and may require other service guarantees, latency reduction becomes even more meaningful. While prior research has shown that adaptive routing can help in this regard, very little attention has been paid to their practicality of implementation. Thus, the idea has not been well received in commercial routers. This paper, therefore, considers the feasibility of supporting adaptivity in the context of current wormhole switched, pipelined-router designs and proposes three enhancements, together called as the LAPSES approach, which can supplement each other in providing a cost-effective solution to adaptive routing.

The first solution, known as *look-ahead routing* decouples the table lookup and arbitration stages of the pipelined design and uses the current routing table entry for the next routing step. The second solution proposes three new path selection heuristics, known as *least recently used* (LRU), *least frequently used* (LFU) and *maximum credit* (MAX-CREDIT) for selecting one of the available alternate paths due to routing adaptivity. The third solution attempts to reduce storage requirement for implementing adaptive routing via routing tables. We first show how one can use meta-table routing that can reduce the memory requirement. Next, we propose an economic table-based implementation of adaptive routing that needs only 3^n table entries (9 or 27 entries for a 2-D or 3-D topology) for an n-dimensional mesh. This implementation reduces the storage requirement drastically, can implement all proposed mesh/torus routing algorithms and has identical performance to that of the full-table scheme. The lookahead and path selection policies help network performance while the economic table implementation addresses the storage cost concern.

We analyze the performance implications of these designs via simulation on a (16×16) mesh network that uses this router architecture and several traffic patterns. The lookahead mechanism is shown to benefit the latency at low load while the advantage of adaptivity kicks in at high load. Thus, the combined lookahead adaptive router seems to a good choice for the entire workload. The results further suggest that the look-ahead feature should be more attractive for short message transfer typically encountered in shared memory systems. It is shown that the new path selection strategies can utilize the available paths more prudently than the static-XY scheme and the MIN-MUX scheme [9] and hence can contribute to low message latency. The network latency thus reduces significantly for non-uniform traffic patterns. The two-level, meta-table implementation of adaptive routing algorithm severely affects the performance in a 2-D mesh due to traffic congestion at the boundary nodes between clusters. This suggest that unless the inter-cluster and intra-cluster communications use separate links, meta-table routing is not a good choice. Separate link traversal is feasible in networks such as hypercubes, but not in flat mesh topologies. We plan to evaluate these designs with various application workloads and other service requirements for quantifying the performance improvements more accurately.

Acknowledgments

Discussion on several of the issues regarding implementation of routers and performance enhancement schemes in this paper were possible due to the help and suggestions provided by Mike Galles of SGI, Steve Scott of SGI/Cray, Jose Duato of Universidad Politéchnica de Valencia, Wolf-Dietrich Weber of HAL, Andreas Nowatzyk of Compaq Western Research Labs and Dave Garcia of Compaq/Tandem. The authors gratefully acknowledge the help from all.

References

[1] N. J. Boden, D. Cohen, R. E. Felderman, A. E. Kulawik, C. L. Seitz, J. N. Seizovic, and W.-K. Su. Myrinet: A Gigabit-per-second Local Area Network. *IEEE Micro*, 15(1):29–36, February 1995.

[2] Y. M. Boura and C. R. Das. Efficient Fully Adaptive Wormhole Routing in *n*-dimensional Meshes. In *Proc. Intl. Conf. on Distributed Computing Systems*, pages 589–596, June 1994.

[3] J. Carbonaro and F. Verhoorn. Cavallino: The Teraflops Router and NIC. In *Proc. Symp. High Performance Interconnects (Hot Interconnects 4)*, pages 157–160, August 1996.

[4] A. A. Chien. A Cost and Speed Model for k-ary n-cube Wormhole Routers. In *Proc. Symp. High Performance Interconnects (Hot Interconnects)*, August 1993.

[5] A. A. Chien and J. H. Kim. Planar-Adaptive Routing: Low-cost Adaptive Networks for Multiprocessors. *Journal of the ACM*, 40(1):91–123, January 1995.

[6] W. J. Dally. Virtual-Channel Flow Control. *IEEE Trans. on Parallel and Distributed Systems*, 3(2):194–205, May 1992.

[7] W. J. Dally and H. Aoki. Deadlock-Free Adaptive Routing in Multicomputer Network using Virtual Channels. *IEEE Trans. on Parallel and Distributed Systems*, 4:466–475, April 1993.

[8] W. J. Dally, L. R. Dennison, D. Harris, K. Kan, and T. Xanthopoulos. Arhitecture and Implementation of the Reliable Router. In *Proc. of Hot Interconnects II*, Stanford University, Palo Alto, CA, August 1994.

[9] J. Duato. A New Theory of Deadlock-Free Adaptive Routing in Wormhole Networks. *IEEE Trans. on Parallel and Distributed Systems*, 4(12):1320–1331, December 1993.

[10] J. Duato, S. Yalamanchili, and L. M. Ni. *Interconnection Networks: An Engineering Approach*. IEEE CS Press, 1997.

[11] M. L. Fulgham and L. Snyder. Performance of Chaos and Oblivious Routers under Non-Uniform Traffic. Technical Report UW–CSE–93–06–01, Department of Computer Science and Engineering, University of Washington, Seattle, WA 98195, July 1994.

[12] M. Galles. Scalable Pipelined Interconnect for Distributed Endpoint Routing : The SGI SPIDER Chip. In *Proc. Symp. High Performance Interconnects (Hot Interconnects 4)*, pages 141–146, August 1996.

[13] D. Garcia and W. Watson. Servernet II. In *Proc. of the 1997 Par. Computing, Routing, and Comm. Workshop (PCRCW'97)*, June 1997.

[14] C. J. Glass and L. M. Ni. Maximally Fully Adaptive Routing in 2D Meshes. In *Proc. Intl Conf. on Parallel Processing*, August 1992.

[15] C. J. Glass and L. M. Ni. A Turn Model for Adaptive Routing. In *Proc. Intl. Symp. on Computer Architecture*, pages 278–287, May 1992.

[16] D. Jadav and A. Choudhary. Designing and Implementing High-Performance Media-on-Demand Servers. *IEEE Parallel & Distributed Technology*, pages 29–39, Summer 1995.

[17] S. Konstantinidou and L. Snyder. The Chaos Router. *IEEE Trans. on Computers*, 43(12):1386–1397, December 1994.

[18] M. D. May. The Next Generation Transputers and Beyond. In *Proc. 2nd European Distrinuted Memory Conf.*, pages 7–22, April 1991.

[19] A. G. Nowatzyk, M. C. Browne, E. J. Kelly, and M. Parkin. S-Connect: from Network of Workstations to Supercomputer Performance. In *Proc. of the 22nd Annual International Symposium on Computer Architecture*, pages 71–82, June 1995.

[20] S. L. Scott and G. M. Thorson. Optimized Routing in the Cray T3D. In *Proc. Parallel Computer Routing and Communications Workshop (PCRCW)*, pages 281–294. Springer Verlag Lecture Notes in Computer Science, May 1994.

[21] S. L. Scott and G. M. Thorson. The Cray T3E Network: Adaptive Routing in a High Performance 3D Torus. In *Proc. Symp. High Performance Interconnects (Hot Interconnects 4)*, pages 147–156, August 1996.

[22] C. Su and K. G. Shin. Adaptive Deadlock-Free Routing in Multicomputers Using Only One Extra Channel. In *Proc. Intl. Conf. on Parallel Processing*, volume I, pages 227–231, August 1993.

[23] A. S. Vaidya, A. Sivasubramaniam, and C. R. Das. LAPSES: A Recpie for Adaptive Router Design. Technical Report CSE-98-010, Department of Computer Science and Engineering, The Pennsylvania State University, 220 Pond Lab, University Park, PA, 1997.

[24] A. S. Vaidya, A. Sivasubramaniam, and C. R. Das. The PROUD Pipelined Router Architectures for High Performance Networks. Technical Report CSE-97-007, Department of Computer Science and Engineering, The Pennsylvania State University, 220 Pond Lab, University Park, PA, 1997.

[25] J. van Leeuwen and R. B. Tan. Interval Routing. *The Computer Journal*, 30(4):298–307, 1987.

[26] W.-D. Weber, S. Gold, P. Helland, T. Shimizu, T. Wicki, and W. Wilcke. The Mercury Interconnect Architecture: A Cost-effective Infrastructure for High-Performance Servers. In *Proc. International Symposium on Computer Architecture*, pages 98–107. ACM, 1997.

Sensitivity of Parallel Applications to Large Differences in Bandwidth and Latency in Two-Layer Interconnects

Aske Plaat Henri E. Bal Rutger F. H. Hofman

aske@cs.vu.nl bal@cs.vu.nl rutger@cs.vu.nl

Department of Computer Science, Vrije Universiteit, Amsterdam, The Netherlands

http://www.cs.vu.nl/albatross/

Abstract

This paper studies application performance on systems with strongly non-uniform remote memory access. In current generation NUMAs the speed difference between the slowest and fastest link in an interconnect—the "NUMA gap"—is typically less than an order of magnitude, and many conventional parallel programs achieve good performance. We study how different NUMA gaps influence application performance, up to and including typical wide-area latencies and bandwidths. We find that for gaps larger than those of current generation NUMAs, performance suffers considerably (for applications that were designed for a uniform access interconnect). For many applications, however, performance can be greatly improved with comparatively simple changes: traffic over slow links can be reduced by making communication patterns hierarchical—like the interconnect. We find that in four out of our six applications the size of the gap can be increased by an order of magnitude or more without severely impacting speedup. We analyze why the improvements are needed, why they work so well, and how much non-uniformity they can mask.

1 Introduction

As computer systems increase in size, their interconnects become more hierarchical, resulting in growing bandwidth and latency differences in their interconnects. This trend is visible in NUMA machines and clusters of SMPs, where local memory access is typically a factor of 2–10 faster than remote accesses [17]. The gap in future large-scale NUMAs is larger, and the gap in meta-computers and computational grids is *much* larger.

For NUMAs with a small gap good performance has been reported with conventional numerical applications [17, 21]. On systems with a larger gap, such as clusters of SMPs and networks of workstations, it is harder to achieve good performance [19, 22, 26]. As gaps increase, it is likely that performance will continue to suffer.[1]

There is little insight in how a growing NUMA gap influences application performance, or how good performance

can be achieved on systems with a large gap. This paper studies the performance of six nontrivial parallel applications, Barnes-Hut, Water, FFT, TSP, ASP, and Awari. We have built an experimental testbed using 64 Pentium Pros, a high-speed network (Myrinet) and an ATM network. The testbed can be configured as multiple Myrinet clusters that are interconnected by ATM links with different latencies and bandwidths. In this way, we can emulate a variety of NUMA/meta-computer configurations, where the gap between the fast local network (Myrinet) and the wide-area network (ATM) varies from 0 to 4 orders of magnitude. The parameter settings have been calibrated using a real wide-area system.

The contributions of the paper can be summarized as follows: We analyze the impact of a wide range of gaps between the slowest and fastest links of the interconnect, to see where performance of conventional parallel applications starts to deteriorate. We find that for gaps larger than those of current NUMAs (one order of magnitude) performance rapidly drops to an unacceptable level.

For five out of six applications we describe performance improvements. (Since the applications were originally designed for a machine with a uniform interconnect, it should perhaps not be surprising that there is room for improvement.) The applications are quite diverse, and so are the algorithmic changes, though all have in common that the application's communication pattern is made to fit the hierarchical interconnect—the changes do *not* improve performance on a uniform network. Commonalities between the improvements are described.

For the improved applications, the impact of the same range of gaps in the interconnect is analyzed, to see how the changes influence application behavior, and how well they work. Taking a speedup of 60% of speedup under uniform remote access as our criteria, we find that, for bandwidth, the acceptable NUMA gap is increased to two orders of magnitude, and for latency it is increased to three orders of magnitude.

We conclude that in many applications, with careful optimization there is room for growth to large architectures with highly non-uniform access times. The application im-

---

[1] This has prompted some to claim, perhaps whimsically, that non-uniformity is a bug, not a feature.

provements themselves are straightforward programming techniques—the challenge lies in understanding the interaction between interconnect and communication pattern. Further work is needed to make this easier, by expressing communication with higher level primitives, or by incorporating common traits of the improvements into coherency protocols. The experience with DSMs on SMP clusters suggests, however, that this will be challenging [26].

Gaps of two to three orders of magnitude correspond to differences between local area and wide area links. Most meta-computing projects currently use embarrassingly parallel (job-level) applications that barely communicate. Our results imply that the set of applications that can be run on large scale architectures, such as a computational grid, is larger than assumed so far, and includes medium grain applications. (Further research should study the impact of variations in latency and bandwidth, which often occur on wide area links.)

The remainder of the paper is organized as follows. Section 2 discusses related work. Sections 3 and 4 describe in detail the applications, improvements, and system that have been used in this experiment. Section 5 describes the results of our measurements, and analyzes them. Section 6 concludes the paper and discusses implications of this work.

2 Related Work and Background

In this paper, we try to understand how large differences in bandwidths and latencies in an interconnect influence application performance. For small gaps, several studies report good performance on hardware DSM NUMA systems [9, 17, 21, 29, 35, 28]. These systems have a gap of about a factor of 3 between the slowest and the fastest links. The picture changes for systems with longer access times. Papers by [10, 19, 22, 26, 31, 36] study local area clusters of SMPs, which have a gap of up to an order of magnitude. These studies tend to focus on coherency protocol issues, using software DSMs such as MGS, TreadMarks, SoftFLASH, CashMere and Shasta, to see how the presence of hardware shared memory improves performance. Performance results vary; earlier studies using partial simulation or tightly coupled hardware [10, 36] showed better results than studies using recent stock SMPs [11, 19, 22, 26, 31]. For SPLASH-like numerical applications, the experience with commercial SMPs is that the presence of hardware shared memory helps performance surprisingly little, due to bus contention and the cost of the hardware coherence protocol. Overall performance is somewhat disappointing, especially for applications that synchronize frequently. Soundararajan et al. attempt to improve NUMA performance through better data locality, with migration/replication protocols [30].

False sharing and disappointing performance in general is the reason for work on data structure and algorithm re-

structuring [15, 16]. Jiang et al [16] use a software DSM on top of a network of workstations. Even though here remote access times are uniform, the relatively large network overhead requires application changes for good performance. Their changes exceed simple padding or data-structure rearranging, requiring insight into both the application and key aspects of the SVM. In previous work we have experimented with a still larger gap, of two orders of magnitude, for which we also found that applications need communication pattern changes [3].

Wide-area systems typically have gaps of three to four orders of magnitude, which covers the end of the range that we study here. Compared to SMP clusters, they provide a more challenging environment in terms of latency and bandwidth gap, but also of fault tolerance and heterogeneity. Meta-computing research focuses on the latter two issues [12, 14]. Because of the high (and non-uniform) latencies, applications are typically embarrassingly parallel, unlike ours, which are of medium grain.

As NUMA systems scale up, it is inevitable that memory access times becomes less uniform. There is evidence that applications can be quite sensitive to non-uniform memory access [3, 16, 30], and we want to know how applications perform on such systems. So far, little attention has been paid to the effect of gap size. Previous studies use small, fixed, gaps. We are interested in how performance scales with different gaps; in our interconnect the gap is varied over a large range, from zero to four orders of magnitude. In addition, many studies focus on issues such as DSM protocols or message passing versus shared memory [8, 9, 30]. Again, our focus is the NUMA gap. We investigate where conventional applications break down, how communication patterns can be adapted, and how far performance improvement can be pushed. As an important aside, we want to know how difficult it is to implement such changes.

Differences in link speeds pose interesting challenges to programmers. This paper explores how serious these challenges are, and how we can deal with some of them.

3 Applications

Our application suite consists of six diverse programs. Barnes-Hut, Water, and FFT are numerical programs that originate from the Splash-2 suite [35], TSP and ASP are optimization codes, and Awari is a symbolic artificial intelligence program. The applications have diverse communication patterns. Table 1 summarizes the behavior of the applications on a single Myrinet cluster. For all applications, larger problems give better speedups. We use relatively small problem sizes in order to get medium grain communication. Medium grain is taken here as a total communication volume of at least 100 KByte/s on a single level cluster of 32 processors. All applications and problem sizes run efficiently on a single Myrinet cluster. Five of our six ap-

Program	Speedup 32 p.	Speedup 8 p.	Total Traffic 32 p. MByte/s	Runtime 32 p, in sec
Water	31.2	7.8	3.8	9.1
Barnes-Hut	28.4	7.1	17.8	1.8
TSP	29.2	7.7	0.52	4.7
ASP	31.3	7.8	0.75	6.0
Awari	7.8	4.6	4.1	2.3
FFT	32.9	5.3	128.0	0.26

Table 1: Single-Cluster Speedup on 8 and 32 processors.

plications are written in the Orca parallel programming language [1], for ease of use of the wide-area system, and for ease of debugging (Orca is type-safe). For most programs, serial performance is comparable to serial C performance. Barnes-Hut is written in C with calls to the Panda [1] wide-area/local area messaging layer.

3.1 Application Characteristics

This subsection summarizes key application characteristics. The next subsection describes the improvements that were implemented to achieve good performance on the highly non-uniform system.

Water The Water program is based on the "n-squared" Water application from the Splash suite [35], rewritten for distributed memory [25]. Related distributed memory optimizations are described by [16]. We report on experiments with a medium sized input set of 1500 particles. The serial speed of the distributed memory program is about ten percent better than the original Splash code.

Barnes-Hut Barnes-Hut is an $O(n \log n)$ N-body simulation. The implementation in the Splash-2 suite has a fine coherency unit which causes inefficiencies on coarse grain hardware [1, 16]. In this experiment a new distributed-memory code by Blackston and Suel [4] has been used. Instead of finding out at runtime which nodes and bodies are needed to compute an interaction, this code precomputes where nodes and bodies are needed, and sends them in one collective communication phase at the start of each iteration. Stalls in the computation phase are thus eliminated. Related improvements have been reported by [13, 16, 34]. Using the same input problem, the serial program runs slightly faster than the Splash code (while computing the same answer). We used a set of 64K particles.

ASP The All-pairs Shortest Path program is a parallel version of the classic Floyd-Warshall algorithm. It uses a replicated distance matrix of 1500 by 1500 entries. Each processor iterates over rows in the matrix, and broadcasts result rows as they are computed. These have to be processed in order by the other processors before they can compute their rows. A designated node issues sequence numbers to achieve this ordering.

TSP The Traveling Salesperson Problem computes the length of the shortest path along n cities, by enumerating the possible paths. The program uses a centralized job queue which is filled with partial paths, from which work-

Program	Communication	Optimization
Water	All to Half Multicast	Cluster Cache, Reduct Tree
Barnes	BSP/Pers All to All	BSP-msg Comb Node/Clus
TSP	Centralized Work Queue	Work Q/Cluster + Work Steal
ASP	Totally Ordered Broadcast	Sequencer Migration
Awari	Asynch Unordered Msg	Msg Comb/Clus
FFT	Pers All to All	–

Table 2: Communication Patterns and Optimizations

ers get jobs. A 16 city problem is used as input; jobs consist of a partial tour of 5 cities, creating small jobs and a (for this application) fine communication grain, as Table 1 shows. Deterministic runs are ensured by using a fixed cutoff bound [1].

Awari Awari, a retrograde analysis program, is a symbolic application that computes end game databases, of importance for programs playing games such as checkers. It is based on backwards reasoning and bottom-up search. Here we compute a relatively small 9 stone database for the African board game Awari. The program sends many small, asynchronous, packets of work to other processors [2]. These messages are combined into larger messages for performance reasons. The communication pattern of Awari is irregular asynchronous point-to-point messages.

FFT The FFT application computes a one-dimensional Fast Fourier transform, using the transpose algorithm [20]. The program is a rewrite of the Splash-2 code for distributed memory, and achieves an excellent speedup on a single Myrinet cluster, despite the short run time. The communication part of this program is very simple: it performs three transposes, interspersed by parallel FFTs. The problem size is 2^{20} complex floating point numbers, the largest that would fit in memory. FFT shows a small superlinear speedup, due to cache effects.

Table 2 summarizes the communication patterns and improvements. Figure 1 summarizes inter-cluster traffic of the original applications. The figures show data volumes in MByte/s per cluster and numbers of messages per second per cluster (for 6 MByte/s bandwidth per link and 0.5 ms latency, and 4 clusters of 8 processors, a configuration with

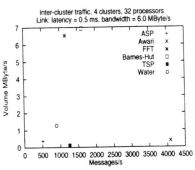

Figure 1: Communication Volume and Messages

12 wide-area links in total). TSP has an extremely low inter-cluster communication volume, 0.1 MByte/s, though a non-negligible number of messages. Barnes-Hut and FFT have a high communication volume of nearly 7 MByte/s (note that the bandwidth limit in this case is 18 MByte/s per cluster, since with 4 clusters there are 3 links of 6 MByte/s out of each cluster). Awari can be found in the opposite corner of the graph, with a high number of tiny inter-cluster messages (more than 4000 per second per cluster). Water and ASP have a modest level of inter-cluster traffic, less than 1000 messages per second and less than 2 MByte/s per cluster.

3.2 Optimizations per Application

The applications are run on an interconnect whose bandwidth and latency difference ranges from small to large. The system consists of 4 clusters of 8 processors each. Inside the clusters the processors are connected by fast Myrinet links (0.020 ms application level latency, 50 MByte/s application level bandwidth). The clusters themselves are fully connected by slow ATM links through additional gateway machines (0.4–300 ms latency, 10–0.03 MByte/s bandwidth). Thus, we have a two level interconnect.

The applications have originally been developed with a uniform network in mind, where all links have the same latency and bandwidth. Performance suffers when the system is highly non-uniform, as in our system, where slow links have latencies up to 5000 times the latency of fast links. This subsection describes which problems have to be resolved to achieve good performance. Some of the improvements have been described previously in [3].

Water The Water program is a classical simulation program of the behavior of n water molecules in an imaginary box. Each of the p processors is assigned an equal number of water molecules. The computation of the $O(n^2)$ inter-molecular forces is the most time-consuming part of the simulation. Forces between two molecules are computed by one of the two processors, the owner of that molecule. At the start of this phase, each processor gets the positions of the molecules of half of the other processors. As a force is calculated it is added locally to determine the total force acting on the local molecule, and is sent to the appropriate other processor so that it can compute the total force for its molecule. All individual molecule updates destined for a processor are combined into one message. The force update phase amounts to two "all-to-half" communications (one to distribute molecule positions, one to send force updates back). The total number of messages approximates $p \cdot \frac{p}{2} = O(p^2)$.

The Water program suffers from a severe performance degradation when inter-cluster links are much slower than intra-cluster links. With 4 clusters, 75% of all messages are between clusters—that is, slow. The two operations, *copying* of molecule positions and *adding* of force updates,

are 1–n and n–1, reduction-like, operations. With the original program, the position of a given molecule is transferred many times over the same inter-cluster link, since multiple processors in a cluster need it. The optimization avoids sending the same data over the inter-cluster link more than once. For every processor p in a remote cluster, we designate one of the processors in the local cluster as the local coordinator for p. If a process needs the molecule data of processor p, it does an intracluster RPC to the local coordinator of p. The coordinator gets the data over the inter-cluster link, forwards it to the requester, and also caches it locally. If other processors in the cluster ask for the same data, they are sent the cached copy. A similar optimization is used at the end of the iteration for the force updates. All updates are first sent to the local coordinator, which does a reduction operation (addition) on the data and transfers only the result over the inter-cluster link.

Barnes-Hut Blackston and Suel's distributed version of the Barnes-Hut algorithm precomputes where nodes and bodies will be needed in each iteration, and sends them in one collective communication phase at the start of the iteration. The program is coded in Valiant's BSP style [33]. Communication takes place in so-called supersteps, which are separated by barriers. In each of these supersteps the program sends many small messages, which incur large overhead if sent indiscriminately over inter-cluster links. All efficient BSP implementations perform message combining of small messages for each recipient. To achieve good performance on the multi-cluster, two more optimizations have been implemented. First, each sender processor combines messages to different recipients in the same target cluster into one message towards the target cluster gateway, using the fact that the code precomputes which parts of the Barnes-Hut tree will be needed on other processors. These messages are dispatched by the receiving cluster gateway to the recipients. Second, the strict barrier synchronization is relaxed by using explicit sequence numbers. (BSP is a relatively young programming model. An active community exists working on efficient implementations of the model, see for example [32].)

ASP In ASP, processors iterate over rows in a distance matrix, generating result rows that are needed by the other processors before they can start new iterations. In the original implementation, a designated sequencer node is used to ensure that rows arrive in order at the processors. The sender of the row has to wait for a sequence number to arrive before it can continue. On a multi-cluster with 4 clusters, 75% of the broadcast requests will thus incur the inter-cluster penalty. This slows down the program significantly.

Communication in ASP is quite regular: first processor 1 computes and broadcasts its rows, then processor 2, etc. On the multi-cluster we take advantage of this regularity by migrating the sequencer to the cluster of the node that does the sending. In this way, sequencer request can be satisfied by a node in the local cluster. In a four cluster system, the sequencer has to migrate only three times, incurring inter-cluster latency only three times. (Another solution would be to drop the sequencer altogether, since processors know who will send which row. Again, this solution exploits the regularity of the ASP algorithm.)

The row broadcasts themselves are asynchronous, so the sender does not suffer from inter-cluster latency. Overall progress is, however, sensitive to inter-cluster bandwidth. Broadcasts are performed using a multicast tree, with point-to-point communication from the sender to the cluster gateways, and multicast primitives inside clusters.

TSP TSP uses a single job queue from which processors retrieve work when their current job is finished. On 4 clusters, 75% of the traffic is between clusters. Even though, compared to the other applications, TSP communicates infrequently, the level of traffic still limits performance considerably. The centralized job queue causes too much inter-cluster traffic. The multi-cluster optimization is to distribute the queue over the clusters. Each cluster now has its own queue, and workers perform work stealing only from their own queue. When the queue becomes empty it tries to steal work from the other cluster queues, to maintain a good load balance. In our system, the number of clusters is small compared to the number of processors. There are only as many queues as there are clusters, and inter-cluster traffic is solely influenced by the number of clusters, not by the number of processors per cluster.

Awari Awari performs a parallel search starting from known end states in a search space (for example, checkmate). States are hashed to processors. The values of all reachable states are computed and sent to the processors owning these positions, which start working on them by generating known values of their reachable states. This process results in many small messages. The original parallel program performs message combining for destination processors, to reduce communication overhead. The search progresses in stages; in each stage, the database for one more stone is computed. Too much message combining results in load imbalance since processors are starved of work at the end of the stages. The high volume of small messages combined with the larger overhead of the inter-cluster links limits performance. To reduce the impact of this overhead, we add another layer of message combining: cross-cluster messages are first being assembled at a designated local processor, are then sent in batch over the slow link, and are subsequently distributed by a designated processor at the other cluster to the final destinations. The extra layer of message combining reduces the impact of the large communication overhead of the inter-cluster links.

FFT The FFT application is renowned for its high communication volume. It is especially ill-suited for a system with long latencies and low bandwidths, or a highly non-uniform interconnect. The communication pattern is a matrix transpose, with little computation. No multi-cluster optimization was found. The purpose of this work is to gain insight in the limits of multi-layer systems with a highly non-uniform architecture. FFT serves as a reminder that there are programs that are unsuited for our interconnects.

3.3 Optimization Overview

Despite the small input problems, all applications except Awari perform well on a single Myrinet cluster (Table 1). Table 2 lists for each program the base communication pattern and its improvement. The main goal of the improvements is to match the communication structure of the application with the hierarchical interconnect; applications should reduce their communication over slow links—or at least reduce their dependency on that communication.

Like the programs, the communication patterns are quite diverse; the optimizations also appear to be quite varied. The general strategy in optimizing for highly non-uniform interconnects is to change the algorithm so that less traffic is sent over the slow links. If that is not possible, then we trade off latency sensitivity at the cost of increased bandwidth requirements. Four types of optimizable communication patterns can be distinguished in our applications; two are of a more algorithmic nature, and two are more related to communication parameters. The first optimization is the reduction operation, which was implemented in Water as a one-level tree. For the multi-cluster interconnect, it is implemented with a two-level tree, the cluster gateways accumulating intermediate results. The second optimization is the work queue, which is implemented in TSP as a single centralized queue. For the multi-cluster interconnect, it is implemented as a distributed queue, one queue per cluster gateway with work stealing among the clusters to maintain load balance. The third optimization is message combining, which is used in Barnes-Hut and Awari to reduce communication overhead for frequent small messages on high-overhead links. The fourth optimization is to exploit asynchrony inherent in the application, which is used in ASP to reduce the number of synchronization points. Furthermore, it can be argued that Blackston and Suel have performed just this kind of optimization in their rewrite of a traditional SPLASH-like shared memory Barnes-Hut code. The communication pattern of FFT is too synchronous and fine grained; no optimization was found.

It is interesting to contrast our changes to the restructuring by Jiang et al [16]. Their work is performed on a software DSM running on a network of workstations, a system with uniform remote access links. They focus on restructuring algorithms to reduce overheads caused by inefficient remote access patterns, fine-grain synchronization, and multiple-writer algorithms. Our system has non-uniform remote access links; we focus on restructuring communication patterns in a two-level system, reducing traffic over the slow links by clustered work stealing, message combining, removing synchronization points, and optimizing reduction operations. Our changes differ from Jiang's in that we make explicit use of the multi-level structure of the interconnect. Indeed, the changes are ineffective on an interconnect with uniform remote access links.

The algorithmic changes are applications of well-known techniques. The novelty lies not so much in the changes themselves as in the magnitude of the performance improvement they cause. The hard part is the understanding of the application behavior, and how it maps to the interconnect (see also [3, 16]). Efforts to express communication constructs on a higher conceptual level [6, 7, 23, 27], or to incorporate them in a cache coherency protocol, would ease this problem (Soundararajan et al describe work on protocol optimizations for a NUMA gap of one order of magnitude [30]). The next two sections describe in detail the impact of the improvements.

4 Experimental Setup

We use an experimental cluster-of-clusters system that consists of four local clusters of 200 MHz/128 MByte Pentium Pro machines connected by Myrinet [5], using LANai 4.1 interfaces. The peak bandwidth of Myrinet is 2.4 Gbit/s, and host-to-host latency is at least 5 μs. In our system, application-level bandwidth is 50 MByte/s, one-way application level latency is 20 μs. The clusters are located at four universities in the Netherlands. They are connected via dedicated gateway machines over ATM by 6 Mbit/s Permanent Virtual Circuits (application-level bandwidth is 0.55 MByte/s over TCP). The round trip latency is 2.5–3 ms. Three sites have 24 compute nodes each, one site has 64. The wide-area network is fully connected, the system-area networks are hypercubes. The operating system is BSD/OS version 3 from BSDI. The wide-area ATM links have a fixed latency and bandwidth. To allow for experimentation with different speeds, 8 local ATM links have been installed in the 64 processor cluster, using the same hardware as in the real wide-area system (ForeRunner PCA-200E ATM boards). The latency and bandwidth of the ATM links can be varied by delay loops in the cluster gateway machines. Except for the local ATM links, this experimentation system is identical to the real wide-area system; the same binaries are run in both setups, and except for the delay loops, there are no simulated parts. When the delay loops are set to the wide area latency and bandwidth, run times differ on average by 3.6% for our applications.

All runs on this experimentaion system showed very reproducible timings, except for Barnes-Hut, whose timings spread more than a factor of two over the runs. Since we suspect the TCP stack of causing this behavior, Barnes-Hut was run on a modified experimentation system where the ATM/TCP links were replaced by Myrinet links. The delay loops for this pure Myrinet system were calibrated to produce exactly the same behavior as the ATM/TCP system. On the pure Myrinet system, the timing anomalies disappeared. Therefore we present the performance on the pure Myrinet system for Barnes-Hut.

The system can be programmed through different libraries and languages, from message passing libraries such as MPI and Panda [1], software DSMs such as TreadMarks and CRL [18], to parallel languages such as Orca [1]. The Panda messaging layer has been adapted to support communication over both Myrinet (using Illinois Fast Messages [24]) and ATM (using BSD's TCP/IP).

5 Results

The goal of this work is charting the sensitivity of application performance to gaps in bandwidth and latency. This section discusses the performance measurements.

The speedup of a multi-cluster machine is bounded by the speedup of a single-cluster machine with the same number of processors, and the same execution schedule. (To put this differently, when some of the fast Myrinet links of the interconnect are changed into slow ATM links, our parallel applications will run more slowly.) Speedups are shown relative to the all-Myrinet upper bound.

5.1 Relative Speedup

Figure 2 shows speedup graphs for the six applications, for 4 clusters of 8 processors: unoptimized on the first and third row, optimized on the second and fourth row. Speedup is shown relative to the speedup of the 32 processor all-Myrinet cluster, for different inter-cluster bandwidths and latencies. It is computed as percentage $\frac{T_L}{T_M}$, where T_L is the run time on the single cluster and T_M is the run time on the multi-cluster. Startup phases are omitted from time and traffic measurements. Myrinet bandwidth is constant at 50 MByte/s, latency is constant at 20 μs. Inter-cluster bandwidth and latency are limited by the local OC3 ATM link of 155 Mbit/s—at the application level, over TCP, this yields 14 MByte/s bandwidth and 0.28 ms latency. On the x-axis the bandwidth of the ATM links is shown. Delays are set so that the resulting bandwidth is 6.3, 2.6, 0.95, 0.3, 0.1, and 0.03 MByte/s. The one-way ATM latency is set to 0.4, 1.3, 3.3, 10, 30, 100, and 300 ms.

The speedup profiles render performance relative to all-Myrinet speedup for latency/bandwidth combinations. The general shape of the graphs is as can be expected: higher inter-cluster bandwidth and lower inter-cluster latency improve performance, and multi-cluster performance is lower than single-cluster Myrinet performance. When we compare the optimized to the unoptimized graphs, the optimizations result in the graphs being shifted upward or to the

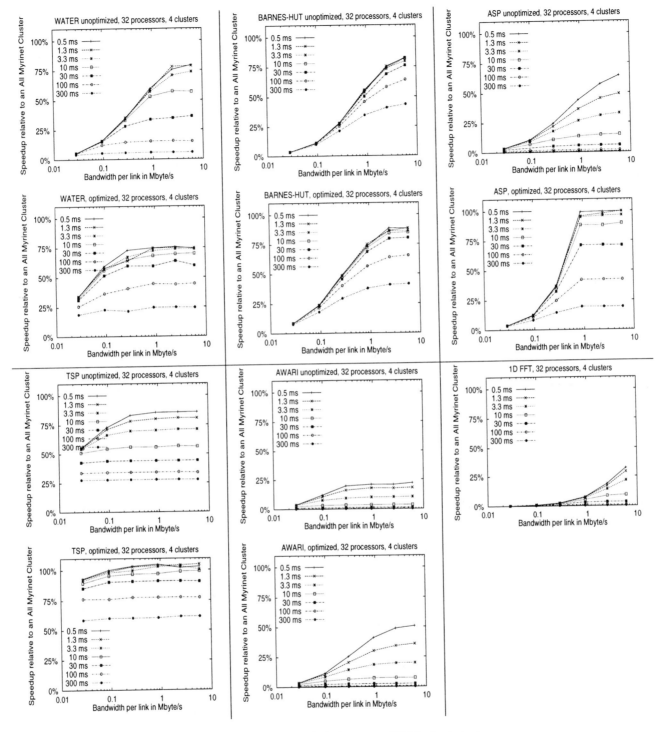

Figure 2: Speedup Relative to an All-Myrinet cluster

left. An upward shift indicates higher performance for the same inter-cluster latency. A shift to the left indicates that the same performance can be achieved at lower inter-cluster bandwidth. (In most applications both effects can be seen.) For Water, the optimizations extend the range of band-width where speedup is better than 60% of all-Myrinet from 1 MByte/s to 0.1 MByte/s. For the original program, perfor-mance decreases steadily from 10 ms latency or 1 MByte/s bandwidth; the performance of the optimized program is much more stable, and deteriorates seriously from 100 ms latency or 0.03 MByte/s. Overall, the NUMA gap for which good performance is achieved is improved by more than an order of magnitude for both inter-cluster latency and bandwidth. For the fastest inter-cluster links, however, the unoptimized program is faster: here, the increase in local communication is not (yet) outweighed by the reduction in remote communication. For Barnes-Hut the improvements have a similar effect, although overall performance is not as good. For Awari the message combining has more than doubled performance for latency up to 3.3 ms; the higher overheads can be masked by message combining, provided that there is enough bandwidth.

The improved version of ASP has a good performance for up to 30 ms latency, against 1 ms for the original program. Speedup shows a sharp sensitivity to bandwidth below 1 MByte/s, as explained in Section 3.2. TSP, on the other hand, is practically insensitive to bandwidth but is sensitive to latency. Its performance is increased by about 25% by the improvements.

For high bandwidth/low latency combinations, performance is good for the improved versions of four of the applications, Barnes-Hut, Water, ASP, and TSP. For inter-cluster latencies of 0.5–3.3 ms and bandwidths of 0.3–6 MByte/s multi-cluster speedup is well above 50% of single-cluster speedup. For bandwidths better than 1 MByte/s speedup reaches 60% for 30 ms latency, and about 40% for 100 ms latency. For extreme bandwidths and latencies (30 KByte/s bandwidth or 300 ms latency) relative speedup drops below 25%, which corresponds to the performance of a single Myrinet cluster of 8 processors. Thus, for these bandwidths and latencies, using extra clusters actually slows down the computation.

Performance for Awari and FFT is significantly lower. For FFT the 25% point is not even reached. The reason for the bad performance of Awari and FFT is that these applications have a higher level of inter-cluster communication. In Awari the extra level of message combining is moderately effective; too much message combining introduces load imbalance. In FFT no optimization has been implemented.

To summarize, for Barnes-Hut, Water, ASP, and TSP, the range for inter-cluster bandwidth and latency at which reasonable speedups are achieved is increased by an order of magnitude or more by the restructuring of the communication pattern. Reasonable speedup starts at an inter-cluster bandwidth of 0.1–0.3 MByte/s and an inter-cluster latency of 30–100 ms. Given a Myrinet bandwidth of 50 MByte/s and a latency of 20 μs, this corresponds to an intra-cluster/inter-cluster performance gap of 167–500 for bandwidth and 1500–5000 for latency, depending on whether 40% or 60% of single-cluster speedup is desired. The optimized applications allow a significantly larger gap for latency than for bandwidth.

In addition to the sensitivity to bandwidth and latency

gaps, we have also performed experiments with different cluster structures. Performance increases as there are more, smaller, clusters: a setup of 8 clusters of 4 processors outperforms 4 clusters of 8 processors. This may seem counterintuitive, since replacing fast links with slow links ought to reduce performance. However, performance is limited by wide-area bandwidth, and our wide-area network is fully connected: in the multi-cluster, bisection bandwidth actually increases as more slow links are added, despite the loss of fast links. This effect can be traced to simple bandwidth sensitivity: speedup decreases as more processors compete for the same wide-area links. (Graphs show a straightforward effect, and are omitted for reasons of space.) In a larger system it is likely that the topology is less perfect. This effect will then diminish, and disappear in star, ring, or bus topologies. Future topologies will in practice be somewhere in between the worst case of a star or ring and the best case of a fully connected network.

5.2 Bandwidth and Latency Sensitivity

This subsection analyzes the inter-cluster traffic in more detail, to complement the speedup picture. We focus on synchronous versus asynchronous communication by examining inter-cluster communication for different bandwidths and latencies.

Performance is influenced strongly by inter-cluster traffic (high-traffic applications have a low speedup and vice versa). The speed of the interconnect influences communication and synchronization overhead of the programs. The left-hand graph in Figure 3 shows the percentage of runtime that is spent in communication over the inter-cluster interconnect as a function of bandwidth, for 4 clusters of size 8; one-way latency is set to 3.3 ms. The right-hand graph in Figure 3 shows the inter-cluster communication time of the interconnect as a function of latency; bandwidth is set to 0.9 MByte/s). The communication time percentage is computed as $\frac{T_M - T_L}{T_M} \cdot 100$, or the difference between multi-cluster run time and single cluster run time as a percentage of multi-cluster run time. These graphs represent no new data compared to Section 5.1, but they offer a different viewpoint to increase understanding of communication behavior.

These graphs indicate where applications are dominated by synchronous communication, and where by asynchronous communication. Purely asynchronous communication is limited by bandwidth (if we disregard startup time); it corresponds to a horizontal line in the latency graph. Purely synchronous communication (i.e., a null-RPC) is limited by latency; it corresponds to a horizontal line in the bandwidth graph. The graphs in Figure 3 show that the communication patterns of the applications contain both streaming of asynchronous communication and request/reply style synchronous communication.

It is interesting to note the differences among the applica-

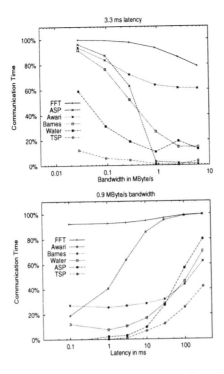

Figure 3: Inter-cluster Traffic—Bandwidth and Latency

tions. In both the bandwidth and the latency graph, communication time for FFT is close to 100%, indicating that run time is almost completely dominated by communication. Awari is a close second, although at latencies lower than 10 ms communication time drops sharply (at 3 MByte/s). For Barnes-Hut, Water, ASP and TSP communication time is significantly less at high bandwidth and low latency.

Latency: Up to 3 ms Barnes-Hut, Water, and ASP are relatively insensitive to latency; their lines are nearly flat. For longer latencies, communication becomes quite sensitive to latency. Apparently, up to 3 ms the data dependencies of the programs allow latency hiding. TSP is quite independent of bandwidth for latencies up to 10 ms.

Bandwidth: For a bandwidth of 10–3 MByte/s, Barnes-Hut, Water, Awari, and ASP are relatively insensitive to bandwidth. TSP is almost completely insensitive to bandwidth; its work-stealing communication pattern comes quite close to the null-RPC.

6 Conclusions

Current NUMA machines yield good performance for many applications [17]; however, there is little insight in application performance on interconnects with a larger gap between slow and fast link speed. Such a large gap will occur in large-scale NUMAs, or when, as in a meta-computer, wide-area links are added to the interconnect. As far as we know, this is the first study to examine performance of non-trivial applications over a large range of gaps, using a real system. Our main contribution is an analysis of when the difference between slow and fast links starts to affect performance. We describe ways to restructure the applications to make performance less sensitive to a large gap, and we analyze how well the improvements work. We do this by examining speedup relative to the gap in bandwidth and latency in the interconnect. We find that when the difference in speed in an interconnect grows larger than in current generation NUMAs, performance suffers dramatically. For these gaps (one order of magnitude and larger) communication becomes limited by the slow links in the interconnect. Once the bottleneck is identified, we can apply changes such as increasing the height of reduction trees, clustering work stealing, combining messages, and removing redundant synchronization points—changes that make explicit use of the multi-level structure of the interconnect, in contrast to the work by Jiang et al, who describe single-level changes [16]. The changes can speed up applications significantly. When acceptable performance is defined as 60% of the speedup on a uniform interconnect, restructuring the communication pattern increases the allowable gap in bandwidth and latency by more than an order of magnitude: in our system gaps of two orders of magnitude for bandwidth, and three orders of magnitude for latency, can be bridged by four of our six applications. However, some communication patterns, such as matrix transpose, resist optimization.

Interconnects are becoming increasingly hierarchical, making it harder to achieve high performance. Nevertheless, we believe that for many real applications it will remain to be possible to do so. We also believe that to achieve this level of performance, more effort is needed to assist programmers in identifying performance problems, to help them better to understand the characteristics of interconnect and program.

Acknowledgements

This research is supported in part by a PIONIER grant from the Dutch Organization for Scientific Research (NWO) and a USF grant from the Free University. NWO has partially supported the DAS project. Aske Plaat is supported by a SION grant from NWO. We are grateful to Torsten Suel for providing us with his n-body code. We thank Andy Tanenbaum and especially Raoul Bhoedjang for insight and inspiration. Together with Thilo Kielmann they also provided valuable feedback on previous versions of this paper. Mirjam Bakker implemented the Awari optimizations. Peter Dozy came up with and implemented the Water and TSP optimizations. Kees Verstoep kept the DAS alive.

References

[1] H. Bal, R. Bhoedjang, R. Hofman, C. Jacobs, K. Langendoen, T. Rühl, and F. Kaashoek. Performance Evaluation of the Orca Shared Object System. *ACM Transactions on Computer Systems*, 16(1), February 1998.

[2] H.E. Bal and L.V. Allis. Parallel Retrograde Analysis on a Distributed System. In *Supercomputing '95*, December 1995. Online at http://www.supercomp.org/sc95/proceedings/.

[3] H.E. Bal, A. Plaat, M.G. Bakker, P. Dozy, and R.F.H. Hofman. Optimizing Parallel Applications for Wide-Area Clusters. In *IPPS-98 International Parallel Processing Symposium*, pages 784–790, April 1998.

[4] David Blackston and Torsten Suel. Highly portable and efficient implementations of parallel adaptive n-body methods. In *SC'97*, November 1997. online at http://www.supercomp.org /sc97/program/TECH/BLACKSTO/.

[5] N.J. Boden, D. Cohen, R.E. Felderman, A.E. Kulawik, C.L. Seitz, J.N. Seizovic, and W. Su. Myrinet: A Gigabit-per-second Local Area Network. *IEEE Micro*, 15(1):29–36, February 1995.

[6] J. Carter, J. Bennett, and W. Zwaenepoel. Techniques for Reducing Consistency-Related Communication in Distributed Shared Memory System. *ACM Transactions on Computer Systems*, 13:205–244, August 1995.

[7] S. Chakrabarti and K. Yelick. Implementing an Irregular Application on a Distributed Memory Multiprocessor. In *ACM Symposium on Principles and Practice of Parallel Programming*, June 1993.

[8] S. Chandra, J. Larus, and A. Rogers. Where is Time Spent in Message-Passing and Shared-Memory Programs. In *ASPLOS-94 Architectural Support for Programming Languages and Operating Systems*, 1994.

[9] F. Chong, R. Barua, F. Dahlgren, J. Kubiatowicz, and A. Agarwal. The Sensitivity of Communication Mechanisms to Bandwidth and Lantency. In *HPCA-4 High Performance Communication Architectures*, pages 37–46, February 1998.

[10] A. Cox, S. Dwarkadas, P. Keheler, H. Lu, R. Rajamony, and W. Zwaenepoel. Software versus hardware shared-memory implementation: a case study. In *Proc. 21st Intern. Symp. Comp. Arch.*, pages 106–117, April 1994.

[11] A. Erlichson, N. Nuckolls, G. Chesson, and J. Hennessy. Soft-FLASH: Analyzing the performance of clustered distributed virtual shared memory. In *Proc. 7th Intern. Conf. on Arch. Support for Prog. Lang. and Oper Systems*, pages 210–220, October 1996.

[12] I. Foster and C. Kesselman. Globus: A metacomputing infrastructure toolkit. *Int. Journal of Supercomputer Applications*, 11(2):115–128, Summer 1997.

[13] A. Grama, V. Kumar, and A. Sameh. Scalable parallel formulations of the barnes-hut algorithm for n-body simulations. In *Supercomputing '94*, November 1994.

[14] A.S. Grimshaw and Wm. A. Wulf. The Legion Vision of a Worldwide Virtual Computer. *Comm. ACM*, 40(1):39–45, January 1997.

[15] T.E. Jeremiassen and S.J. Eggers. Reducing false sharing on shared memory multiprocessors through compile-time data transformations. In *Symposium on Principles and Practice of Parallel Programming*, July 1995.

[16] D. Jiang, G Shan, and J. Singh. Application Restructuring and Performance Portability on Shared Virtual Memory and Hardware-Coherent Multiprocessors. In *PPoPP-97 Symposium on Principles and Practice of Parallel Programming*, June 1997.

[17] D. Jiang and J. Singh. A Methodology and an Evaluation of the SGI Origin2000. In *ACM Sigmetrics / Performance'98*, June 1998.

[18] K. Johnson, F. Kaashoek, and D. Wallach. Crl: High-performance all-software distributed shared memory. In *Symposium on Operating Systems Principles 15*, pages 213–228, December 1995.

[19] L. Kontothanassis, G. Hunt, R. Stets, N. Hardavellas, M. Cierniak, S. Parthasarathy, W. Meira, S. Dwarkadas, and M. Scott. VM-Based Shared Memory on Low-Latency, Remote-Memory-Access Networks. In *ISCA-24, Proc. 24th Annual International Symposium on Computer Architecture*, pages 157–169, June 1997.

[20] V. Kumar, A. Grama, A. Gupta, and G. Karypis. *Introduction to Parallel Computing: Design and Analysis of Algorithms*. Benjamin Cummings, November 1993.

[21] J. Laudon and D. Lenoski. The SGI Origin: A ccNUMA Highly Scalable Server. In *24th Ann. Int. Symp. on Computer Architecture*, pages 241–251, June 1997.

[22] S.S. Lumetta, A.M. Mainwaring, and D.E. Culler. Multi-protocol active messages on a cluster of SMP's. In *SC'97*, November 1997. Online at http://www.supercomp.org/sc97/proceedings/.

[23] MPI Forum. MPI: A Message Passing Interface Standard. *Int. J. Supercomputer Applications*, 8(3/4), 1994. Version 1.1 at http://www.mcs.anl.gov/mpi/mpi-report-1.1/mpi-report.html.

[24] S. Pakin, M. Lauria, and A. Chien. High Performance Messaging on Workstations: Illinois Fast Messages (FM) for Myrinet. In *Supercomputing '95*, San Diego, CA, December 1995.

[25] John W. Romein and Henri E. Bal. Parallel n-body simulation on a large-scale homogeneous distributed system. In Seif Haridi, Khayri Ali, and Peter Magnusson, editors, *EURO-PAR'95 Parallel Processing. Lecture Notes in Computer Science, 966*, pages 473–484, Stockholm, Sweden, August 1995. Springer-Verlag.

[26] D. J. Scales, K. Gharachorloo, and A. Aggarwal. Fine-grain software distributed shared memory on SMP clusters. In *HPCA-4 High-Performance Computer Architecture*, pages 125–137, February 1998.

[27] J. Schaeffer, D. Szafron, G. Lobe, and I. Parsons. The enterprise model for developing distributed applications. *IEEE Parallel and Distributed Technology*, 1(3):85–96, August 1993.

[28] J. Singh, C. Holt, T. Totsuka, A. Gupta, and J. Hennessy. Load balancing and data locality in adaptive hierarchical n-body methods: Barnes-hut, fast multipole and radiosity. *Journal of Parallel and Distributed Computing*, June 1995.

[29] J.P. Singh, W-D. Weber, and A. Gupta. SPLASH: Stanford Parallel Applications for Shared Memory. *ACM Computer Architecture News*, 20(1):5–44, March 1992.

[30] V. Soundararajan, M. Heinrich, B. Verghese, K. Gharachorloo, A. Gupta, and J. Hennessy. Flexible Use of Memory for Replication/Migration in Cache-Coherent DSM Multiprocessors. In *ISCA-98, 25th International Symposium on Computer Architecture*, pages 342–355, June 1998.

[31] R. Stets, S Dwarkadas, N. Hardavellas, G. Hunt, L. Kontothanassis, S. Parthasarathy, and M. Scott. Cashmere-2L: Software coherent shared memory on a clustered remote-write network. In *Proc. 16th ACM Symp. on Oper. Systems Princ.*, October 1997.

[32] T. Suel, M. Goudreau, K. Lang, S. B. Rao, and T. Tsantilas. Towards Efficiency and Portability: Programming with the BSP Model. In *Proceedings of the 8th Annual ACM Symposium on Parallel Algorithms and Architectures SPAA 96*, pages 1–12, June 1996. See also www.bsp-worldwide.org.

[33] L. Valiant. A Bridging Model for Parallel Computation. *Comm. ACM*, 33(8):100–108, August 1990.

[34] M. Warren and J. Salmon. A parallel hashed oct-tree n-body algorithm. In *Supercomputing '93*, November 1993.

[35] S.C. Woo, M. Ohara, E. Torrie, J.P. Singh, and A. Gupta. The SPLASH-2 Programs: Characterization and Methodological Considerations. In *Proceedings of the 22nd International Symposium on Computer Architecture*, pages 24–36, June 1995.

[36] D. Yeung, J. Kubiatowicz, and A. Agarwal. MGS: A Multigrain Shared Memory System. In *Proceedings of the 23rd Annual International Symposium on Computer Architecture*, pages 45–56, May 1996.

Panel Session II

Storage: It Ain't Secondary Any More

A.L. Narasimha Reddy

Texas A&M University

Keynote Address III

The Automation of Computer Architecture: Yet Another Consequence of Moore's Law

Bob Rau

HP Labs

Session 7A

Shared Memory

Comparative Evaluation of Fine- and Coarse-Grain Approaches for Software Distributed Shared Memory

Sandhya Dwarkadas*, Kourosh Gharachorloo[†], Leonidas Kontothanassis[‡],
Daniel J. Scales[†], Michael L. Scott*, and Robert Stets*

*Dept. of Comp. Science	[†]Western Research Lab	[‡]Cambridge Research Lab
University of Rochester	Compaq Computer Corp.	Compaq Computer Corp.
Rochester, NY 14627	Palo Alto, CA 94301	Cambridge, MA 02139

Abstract

Symmetric multiprocessors (SMPs) connected with low-latency networks provide attractive building blocks for software distributed shared memory systems. Two distinct approaches have been used: the *fine-grain* approach that instruments application loads and stores to support a small coherence granularity, and the *coarse-grain* approach based on virtual memory hardware that provides coherence at a page granularity. Fine-grain systems offer a simple migration path for applications developed on hardware multiprocessors by supporting coherence protocols similar to those implemented in hardware. On the other hand, coarse-grain systems can potentially provide higher performance through more optimized protocols and larger transfer granularities, while avoiding instrumentation overheads. Numerous studies have examined each approach individually, but major differences in experimental platforms and applications make comparison of the approaches difficult.

This paper presents a detailed comparison of two mature systems, Shasta and Cashmere, representing the fine- and coarse-grain approaches, respectively. Both systems are tuned to run on the same commercially available, state-of-the-art cluster of AlphaServer SMPs connected via a Memory Channel network. As expected, our results show that Shasta provides robust performance for applications tuned for hardware multiprocessors, and can better tolerate fine-grain synchronization. In contrast, Cashmere is highly sensitive to fine-grain synchronization, but provides a performance edge for applications with coarse-grain behavior. Interestingly, we found that the performance gap between the systems can often be bridged by program modifications that address coherence and synchronization granularity. In addition, our study reveals some unexpected results related to the interaction of current compiler technology with application instrumentation, and the ability of SMP-aware protocols to avoid certain performance disadvantages of coarse-grain approaches.

1 Introduction

Clusters of symmetric multiprocessors (SMP) provide a powerful platform for executing parallel applications. To ease the burden of programming such clusters, software distributed shared memory (S-DSM) systems support the illusion of shared memory across the cluster via a software run-time layer between the application and the hardware. This approach can potentially provide a cost-effective alternative to larger hardware shared memory systems for executing certain classes of workloads.

Most S-DSM systems use virtual memory hardware to detect access to data that is not available locally. Hence, data is communicated and kept coherent at the coarse granularity of a page (e.g., 4-16KB). Early page-based systems [13] suffered from *false sharing* that arises from fine-grain sharing of data within a page. More recent page-based systems [2, 3, 9, 12] address this issue by employing relaxed memory consistency models that enable protocol optimizations such as delaying coherence operations to synchronization points and allowing multiple processors to concurrently write to a page. Page-based systems may still experience overheads due to frequent synchronization or sharing at a fine granularity. Furthermore, the aggressive relaxed memory models and the required use of predefined synchronization primitives limit portability for certain applications developed on hardware multiprocessors [16].

As an alternative, a few S-DSM systems [15, 18] have explored supporting data sharing and coherence at a finer granularity (e.g., 64-256 bytes). Fine-grain access is supported by instrumenting the application binary at loads and stores to check if the shared data is available locally. Such systems provide the highest degree of transparency since they can correctly run all programs (or even binaries) developed for hardware multiprocessors by virtue of supporting similar memory models [16]. In addition, this approach reduces false sharing and the transmission of unnecessary data, both of which are potential problems in page-based systems. Nevertheless, page-based systems can potentially benefit from more optimized protocols and larger transfer granularities, without incurring the software checking overheads associated with fine-grain systems.

The recent prevalence of low-cost SMP nodes has led to extensions to software DSM designs for supporting shared memory across SMP clusters. The key advantage of using SMP nodes comes from supporting data sharing within a node directly via the cache coherence hardware, and only invoking the software protocol for sharing across nodes. Several studies have demonstrated significant gains from exploiting SMP-aware protocols in both coarse-grain [6, 14, 20] and fine-grain [17] S-DSM systems.

As described above, there are important trade-offs between *coarse-grain, page-based* and *fine-grain, instrumentation-based* S-DSM systems, both in the *performance* and the *generality* of the shared-memory programming model. Even though there are a large number of papers that study each approach individually, a direct comparison is difficult due to major differences in the experimental platforms, applications, and problem sizes used in the various studies. Furthermore, only a few studies are actually based on SMP-aware protocols.

This paper presents a detailed comparison of the fine- and coarse-grain approaches based on the same hardware platform and applications. We use two mature systems, Shasta [17] and Cashmere [20], both of which are highly efficient and tuned to run on a state-of-the-art cluster of Digital AlphaServer multiprocessors connected through the Memory Channel network [8]. We study a total of thirteen applications: eight SPLASH-2 applications [21] that have been developed for hardware multiprocessors and five applications that were developed for page-based S-DSM systems. The first part of our study compares the performance of the *unmodified* applications on the two systems. This part allows us to evaluate the portability of applications developed for hardware multiprocessors and to measure the performance gap on applications developed for page-based systems. The second part of the study analyzes the performance of the same applications after modifications that improve their performance on either system. To ensure a fair comparison, we undertook this study as a collaborative effort between the Cashmere and Shasta groups.

Our study quantifies a number of expected trends. Shasta provides robust and often better performance for applications written for hardware multiprocessors and is better able to tolerate fine-grain behavior. Cashmere is highly sensitive to the presence of fine-grain synchronization, but provides a performance edge for applications with coarse-grain behavior. However, we found that the performance gap between the systems can be bridged by program modifications that take coherence granularity into account.

Our study also presents several unexpected results. One interesting result is that Cashmere, due to its SMP-aware implementation, shows very good performance on certain applications known to have a high degree of write-write false sharing at the page level. The regular data layout in these applications leads to page-aligned data boundaries across nodes, thus confining the write-write false sharing to processes on the same SMP node and avoiding the expected software overheads. Another interesting result is that fine-grain false sharing can sometimes favor Cashmere relative to Shasta, due to Cashmere's ability to delay and aggregate coherence operations. Finally, the instrumentation overheads in Shasta were more of a determining factor than we expected in a few cases. This effect is partly due to continued improvements in the Alpha compiler that lead to more efficient code, thus increasing the relative overhead of instrumentation code in some cases.

The only relevant study that we are aware of is by Zhou et al. [22], which also examines performance tradeoffs between fine- and coarse-grain software coherence. However, several critical differences between the studies lead to differing performance results and a number of novel observations in our work. Section 5 contains a detailed comparison of the two studies.

The remainder of this paper is organized as follows. Section 2 presents an overview of the two systems that we compare in this paper. The experimental environment is described in Section 3. Section 4 presents and analyzes the results from our comparison. Finally, we present related work and conclude.

2 Overview of Cashmere and Shasta

This section presents a brief overview of Shasta and Cashmere, and also discusses some portability issues for the two systems. More detailed descriptions of the systems can be found in previous papers [12, 15, 16, 17, 20].

2.1 Shasta

Shasta is a fine-grain software DSM system that relies on in-line checks to detect misses to shared data and service them in software. Shasta divides the shared address space into ranges of memory called *blocks*. All data within a block is always fetched and kept coherent as a unit. Shasta inserts code in the application executable at loads and stores to determine if the referenced block is in the correct state and to invoke protocol code if necessary. A unique aspect of the Shasta system is that the block size (i.e. coherence granularity) can be different for different application data structures. To simplify the inline code, Shasta divides the blocks into fixed-size ranges called *lines* (typically 64-256 bytes) and maintains state information for each line. Each inline check requires about seven instructions. Shasta uses a number of optimizations to eliminate checks, reduce the cost of checking loads, and to batch together checks for neighboring loads and stores [15]. Batching can reduce overhead significantly (from a level of 60-70% to 20-30% overhead for dense matrix codes) by avoiding repeated checks to the same line.

Coherence is maintained using a directory-based invalidation protocol. A *home* processor is associated with each block and maintains a *directory* for that block, which contains a list of the processors caching a copy of the block. The Shasta protocol exploits the release consistency model [7] by implementing non-blocking stores and allowing reads and writes to blocks in pending states.

When used in an SMP cluster, Shasta exploits the underlying hardware to maintain coherence within each node [17]. The SMP-aware protocol avoids race conditions by obtaining locks on individual blocks during protocol operations. However, such synchronization is not used in the inline checking code, since it would greatly increase the instrumentation overhead. Instead, the protocol selectively sends explicit messages between processors on the same node for a few protocol operations that can lead to race conditions involving the inline checks. Because Shasta supports programs with races on shared memory locations, the protocol must correctly handle various corner cases that do not arise in protocols (such as Cashmere's) that only support race-free programs [16].

Messages from other processors are serviced through a polling mechanism in both Shasta and Cashmere because of the high cost of handling messages via interrupts. Both protocols poll for messages whenever waiting for a reply and on every loop backedge. Polling is inexpensive (three instructions) on our Memory Channel cluster because the implementation arranges for a single cachable location that can be tested to determine if a message has arrived.

2.2 Cashmere

Cashmere is a page-based software DSM system that has been designed for SMP clusters connected via a remote-memory-write network such as the Memory Channel [20]. It implements a multiple-writer, release consistent protocol and requires applications to adhere to the data-race-free or properly-labeled programming model [1]. Cashmere requires shared memory accesses to be protected by high-level synchronization primitives such as locks, barriers, or flags that are supported by the run-time system. The consistency model implementation lies in between those of TreadMarks [2] and Munin [3]. Invalidations in Cashmere are sent during a release and take effect at the time of the next acquire, regardless of whether they are causally related to the acquired lock.

Cashmere uses the broadcast capabilities of the Memory Channel network to maintain a replicated directory of sharing information for each page (i.e., each node maintains a complete copy of the directory). Initially, shared pages are mapped only on their associated home nodes. A page fault generates a request for an up-to-date copy of the page from the home node. For a page fault triggered by a write access, a *twin* (or pristine copy of the page) is created and the page is added to a per-processor *dirty list* (a list of all pages modified by a processor since the last release). As an optimization, Cashmere moves the page into *exclusive* mode if there are no other sharers, and avoids adding the page to the dirty list. In addition, the current writer is automatically made the new home node if the current home node is not actively writing the page (home node migration).

At a release, each page in the dirty list is compared to its *twin*, and the differences are flushed to the home node. After flushing the differences, the releaser sends write notifications to the sharers of each dirty page, as indicated by the page's directory entry. Finally the releaser downgrades write permissions for the dirty pages and clears the list. At a subsequent acquire, a processor invalidates all pages for which notifications have been received, and which have not already been updated by another processor on the node.

The protocol exploits hardware coherence to maintain consistency within each SMP node. All processors in the node share the same physical frame for a shared data page and hence see all local modifications to the page immediately. The protocol is also designed to avoid synchronization within a node whenever possible. For instance the protocol avoids the need for TLB shootdown on incoming page updates by comparing the incoming page to the twin if one exists, thereby detecting and applying only the modifications made by remote nodes. This allows concurrent modifications to the page by other processes within the node without the need for synchronization. The correctness of this approach depends on the assumption that programs are race-free.

2.3 Portability Issues

This section briefly discusses differences between Shasta and Cashmere with respect to two important portability issues: (a) the portability of applications to each software system, and (b) the portability of the underlying software system to different hardware platforms.

Application Portability. One of the key goals in the Shasta design is to support transparent execution of applications (or binaries) developed for hardware multiprocessors [16]. Shasta achieves this transparency by supporting memory consistency models that are similar to hardware systems. On the other hand,

Cashmere (like virtually all other page-based systems) opts for a departure from the standard hardware shared-memory programming model in order to achieve better performance. By requiring the use of predefined high-level synchronization primitives to eliminate shared-memory races and using aggressive relaxed memory models, Cashmere can exploit numerous protocol optimizations that are especially important for page-based systems. However, this approach may require extra programming effort to achieve a correct and efficient port of applications that depend on the more general hardware shared-memory programming model.

System Portability. The Cashmere protocol makes heavy use of Memory Channel features, including broadcasting and guarantees on global message ordering. For example, broadcasting is used to propagate directory changes to all nodes. In addition, during a release operation, the processor sending write notifications does not wait for acknowledgements before releasing the lock. Rather, it relies on global ordering of messages to guarantee that causally related invalidations are seen by other processors before any later acquire operation. It is difficult to estimate the performance impact if the protocol were changed to eliminate reliance on broadcasting and total ordering, since the protocol design assumed these network capabilities. In contrast, Shasta was designed for a network that simply offers fast user-level message passing and is therefore more portable to different network architectures.

On the other hand, Shasta is tuned for the Alpha processor and requires detailed knowledge of both the compiler and the underlying processor architecture for efficient instrumentation. It is again hard to estimate the performance impact of moving the system to a significantly different processor architecture (e.g., Intel x86) where potentially a large variety of instructions can access memory.

3   Experimental Methodology

This section describes our prototype SMP cluster and the applications used in our study.

3.1   Prototype SMP Cluster

Our SMP cluster consists of four DEC Alpha Server 4100 multiprocessors connected by a Memory Channel network. Each AlphaServer 4100 has four 400MHz 21164 processors with 512MBytes of shared local memory. Each processor has 8K on-chip instruction and data caches, a 96K on-chip second-level cache (3-way set associative), and a 4MByte board-level cache (direct-mapped with 64-byte lines). The individual processors are rated at 12.1 SpecInt95 and 17.2 SpecFP95, and the system bus has a bandwidth of 1 Gbyte/s.

The Memory Channel is a memory-mapped network that allows a process to transmit data to a remote process without any operating system overhead via a simple store to a mapped page [8]. The one-way latency from user process to user process over Memory Channel is about 3.5 microseconds, and each network link can support a bandwidth of 70 MBytes/sec (with an aggregate bandwidth of 100MBytes/sec). For Shasta, the roundtrip latency to fetch a 64-byte block from a remote node (two hops) via the Memory Channel is 18 microseconds, and the effective bandwidth for large blocks is about 35 MBytes/s. For Cashmere, the roundtrip latency for fetching an 8K page is less than 600 microseconds.

3.2 Applications

We present results for thirteen applications. The first eight are taken from the Splash-2 [21] suite and have been developed and tuned for hardware shared memory multiprocessors. The applications are Barnes-Hut, LU, Contiguous LU (CLU), Ocean, Raytrace, Volrend, Water-nsquared, and Water-Spatial. Five Splash-2 applications are not used: four (Cholesky, FFT, Radiosity, Radix) do not perform well on S-DSM and one (FMM) has not been modified to run under Cashmere (but gets good speedup on Shasta).[1]

The remaining five applications have been developed and tuned for page-based S-DSM systems, and have been shown to have good performance on such systems [12, 20]. These applications are Em3d, Ilink [4], Gaussian Elimination (Gauss), Successive Over-Relaxation (SOR), and the Traveling Salesman Problem (TSP). Descriptions of these applications can be found in a previous paper [20].

4 Results

This section provides an in-depth comparison and analysis of the performance of Shasta and Cashmere. We begin by presenting our overall results for the unmodified applications, followed by a detailed analysis. We next consider minor application and system configuration modifications that improve performance on either Shasta or Cashmere.

4.1 Base Results for Unmodified Applications

Table 1 presents the sequential execution time (without any instrumentation or runtime library overhead), data set size, and memory usage for each application. Wherever possible, we use two dataset sizes — one relatively small, the other larger. This allows us to study performance sensitivity to the size and alignment of data structures relative to the coherence block size. For Shasta, the instrumentation overhead (not shown) increases the single-processor execution time from 9% to 55%, with an average overhead of 27% across all applications and data set sizes. The relative importance of this checking overhead decreases in parallel executions due to the typical increase in communication and synchronization overheads.

Figures 1 and 2 present the speedups on the two systems using their base configurations for the thirteen applications on 8 and 16 processors (two and four SMP nodes each with four processors), for the smaller and larger data sets, respectively. The base configurations used are a uniform block size of 256 bytes for Shasta, and a block size of 8192 bytes (the underlying page size) for Cashmere. The applications were run without any modifications (except for Barnes, as explained in the next section), and are built with the native C compiler (-O2 optimization level). Application processes are pinned to processors at startup. Execution times are based on the best of three runs, and speedups are calculated

with respect to the times of the sequential application without instrumentation or protocol overhead.

Overall, the results in Figures 1 and 2 show that Shasta provides more robust and better performance on average for the eight Splash-2 applications (which have been developed for hardware multiprocessors). Nonetheless, Cashmere provides comparable or better performance on some of the Splash-2 applications, and performs much better than expected on a few applications that are known to exhibit a high degree of fine-grain sharing (e.g., LU, OCEAN). In addition, Cashmere provides superior performance for the other five applications, which have been developed for page-based systems. The next section provides a detailed analysis of these results.

4.2 Detailed Analysis of Base Results

This section presents a detailed comparison and analysis of the performance of the various applications on Shasta and Cashmere. To better understand the reasons for performance differences, we discuss the applications in groups based on their spatial *data access granularity* and temporal *synchronization granularity* (similar to notions used by Zhou et al. [22]). Applications with coarse-grain data access tend to work on contiguous regions at a time, while fine-grain applications are likely to do scattered reads or writes. The temporal synchronization granularity is related to the frequency of synchronization in an application on a given platform. An application has fine-grain synchronization if the average computation time between consecutive synchronization events is not much larger than the cost of the synchronization events themselves.[2]

Throughout this section, we will be referring to Figure 3, which provides a breakdown of the execution time for Shasta and Cashmere (labeled as SH and CSM, respectively) for each of the applications at 16 processors on the smaller data set. Execution time is normalized to that of the fastest system on each application and is split into Task, Synchronization, Data Stall, Messaging, and Protocol time. *Task* time includes the application's compute time, the cost of polling, and the cost of instrumentation in Shasta or page faults in Cashmere. *Synchronization* time is the time spent waiting on locks, flags, or barriers. *Data Stall* time measures the cumulative time spent handling coherence misses. *Messaging* time covers the time spent handling messages when the processor is not already stalled. Finally, *Protocol* time represents the remaining overhead introduced by the protocol.

Additional performance data is available in an extended version of this paper [5], including detailed execution statistics for the two systems (e.g., the number of messages, amount of message traffic, and various protocol-specific measurements) and the execution time breakdown for the larger data set.

4.2.1 Coarse-Grain Access and Synchronization

The applications in this group are CLU, Em3d, Gauss, SOR, TSP, and Water-nsquared. Overall, Cashmere is expected to perform better on these applications given the coarse communication and synchronization granularities.

---

[1]FMM is not "race-free" and requires additional synchronization to work correctly under Cashmere.

[2]Some applications that are classified as exhibiting coarse-grain synchronization in Zhou et al.'s study [22] exhibit fine-grain behavior in our study due to the faster processors of our platform.

Program	Smaller Problem (Data Set) Size	Time (sec.)	Larger Problem (Data set) Size	Time (sec.)
Barnes-Hut	32K bodies (39M)	15.30	131K bodies (153M)	74.69
LU	1024x1024, block: 16 (8M)	14.21	2048x2048, block: 32 (33M)	74.57
CLU	1024x1024, block: 16 (8M)	6.74	2048x2048, block: 32 (33M)	44.40
Ocean	514x514 (64M)	7.33	1026x1026 (242M)	37.05
Raytrace	balls4 (102M)	44.89	—	—
Volrend	head (23M)	3.81	—	—
Water-nsq	4K mols., 2 steps (3M)	94.20	8K mols., 2 steps (5M)	362.74
Water-sp	4K mols., 2 steps (3M)	10.94	8K mols, 2 steps (5M)	21.12
Em3d	64000 nodes (52M)	47.61	192000 nodes (157M)	158.43
Gauss	1700x1700 (23M)	99.94	2048x2048 (33M)	245.06
Ilink	CLP (15M)	238.05	—	—
Sor	3070x2047 (50M)	21.13	3070x3070 (100M)	28.80
TSP	17 cities (1M)	1580.10	—	—

Table 1: Problem and data set sizes and sequential execution time of applications.

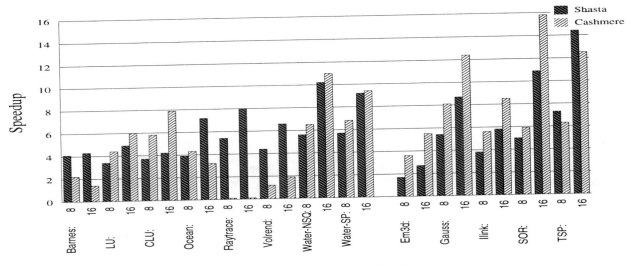

Figure 1: Speedups for the smaller data set at 8 and 16 processors.

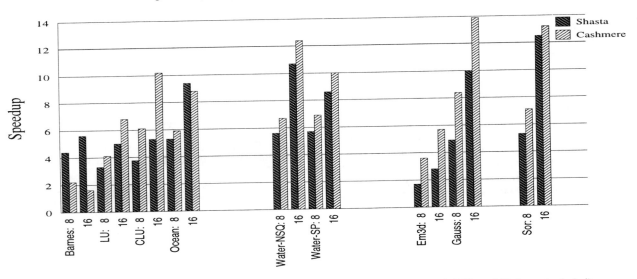

Figure 2: Speedups for the larger data set at 8 and 16 processors (Raytrace, Volrend, TSP, and Ilink not included).

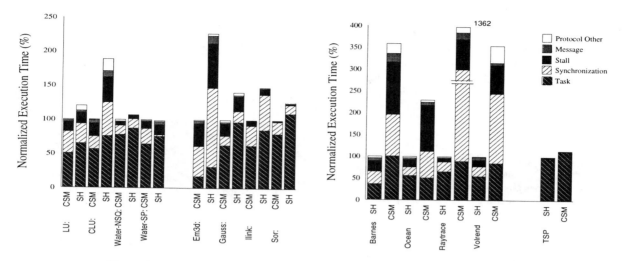

Figure 3: Application execution time breakdown on the smaller data set for 16-processor runs.

CLU uses a tiled data partitioning strategy with each tile of the matrix allocated as a contiguous chunk. Cashmere performs 1.7 times better on average than Shasta for CLU. Data is propagated more efficiently under Cashmere given its large communication granularity. As shown in Figure 3, the Cashmere data stall time component is roughly half that of Shasta. The figure also shows a higher "Task" time under Shasta because of Shasta's checking overhead (as high as 50% for a uniprocessor execution). Section 4.3 presents further results under Shasta with variable granularity and different compiler flags to address the communication granularity and checking overhead issues.

Em3d exhibits nearest-neighbor sharing, though the communication is determined at run-time based on indirection arrays. Cashmere performs two times better than Shasta on Em3d. Because of the coarse granularity of communication in this application, Shasta requires ten times more messages to fetch all the data. As we will see in Section 4.3, Shasta's variable granularity feature can be used to close this performance gap.

Gauss uses a cyclic distribution of matrix rows among processors. Cashmere performs 1.7 and 1.4 times better than Shasta for the larger dataset, and 1.5 and 1.4 times better for the smaller dataset, at 8 and 16 processors respectively. Because the matrix is triangularized, fewer elements are modified in each succeeding row, and Cashmere's large granularity causes communication of unnecessary data. For the 1700x1700 dataset, there is also write-write false sharing, since a row is not a multiple of the page size. However, the effects of false sharing are not as large as one might expect due to the SMP-aware protocol. In effect, the distribution of work becomes block-cyclic, with false sharing only on the edges of each block.

In SOR, each processor operates on a block of contiguous rows and infrequently communicates with its nearest neighbors. The determining factor is the checking overhead in Shasta (as shown by the higher "Task" times in Figure 3). Relative to Shasta, Cashmere performs 1.25 better on average.

TSP has a very coarse work granularity, so communication overheads in either system are largely unimportant. However, the more eager protocol in Shasta can lead to faster propagation of the bound value. This can in turn lead to a more efficient search (given the non-deterministic nature of the branch-and-bound al-

gorithm). Shasta performs approximately 1.15 times better than Cashmere on TSP.

Water-nsquared partitions work such that processors modify contiguous regions of memory. Any false sharing is only at the boundaries of these regions. In addition, there is considerable node locality in the data access; at least half the lock accesses data that was last modified within the same SMP node and is therefore fetched via the node's hardware protocol. Hence, the overheads of false sharing are small in Cashmere. Shasta's performance is primarily affected by the extra checking overhead, and Cashmere performs 1.2 times better than Shasta on average.

Overall, the coarse-grain communication and low frequency of synchronization favors Cashmere in these applications. Furthermore, for Gauss and Water-nsquared, the effect of false sharing on the performance of Cashmere is dramatically reduced by the use of SMP-aware protocols, since the false sharing largely occurs among processors on the same node. The relative performance of Shasta is often determined by the checking overhead and in some cases by its smaller data transfer granularity.

4.2.2 Fine-Grain Access with Coarse-Grain Synchronization

The applications in this group are Ilink, LU, Ocean, and Water-spatial. As we will discuss below, the use of SMP nodes with SMP-aware protocols leads to some surprising results for Cashmere.

Ilink computes on sparse arrays of probabilities and uses round-robin work allocation. The sparse data structure causes Cashmere to communicate extra data on pages that have been modified (since whole pages are communicated on a miss). Shasta's performance on Ilink is affected by three factors: the checking overhead, the small communication granularity, and the use of an eager protocol. The instrumentation overhead (as high as 60% on a uniprocessor) is due to the compiler being unable to verify the commonality of certain high-frequency double indirection operations, and Shasta therefore being unable to batch them effectively. Because the work allocation is round-robin on a per-element basis, there is also much false sharing despite the small block size used by Shasta. Shasta eagerly invalidates all copies of a block whenever any processor writes to the block and generates 10 times more protocol messages than Cashmere, which delays invalidations until synchronization points. These effects outweigh the overheads for Cashmere, and Cashmere performs 1.5 times better than Shasta.

LU uses a tiled partitioning strategy. However, unlike CLU, the matrix is allocated as a single object. Hence, each tile consists of small non-contiguous regions of memory on multiple pages. The small read granularity causes a large amount of extra data to be communicated under Cashmere. In addition, the data layout leads to a large amount of false sharing at the page level. However, LU's 2D scatter distribution leads to an assignment of tiles to processors that confines all false sharing to within each 4-processor SMP node, so all false sharing is handled in hardware. The above effect, along with the checking overheads in Shasta, allows Cashmere to perform better than Shasta by a factor of 1.2 and 1.3 times at 8 and 16 processors respectively.

Ocean also uses tiled data partitioning. For the two datasets, Cashmere performs 1.10 and 1.11 times better than Shasta at 8 processors, while Shasta is 2.25 and 1.07 times better at 16 processors. The communication is nearest-neighbor in both the column and row direction. Hence, while the tiled partitioning reduces true sharing, it increases the amount of unnecessary data communicated when a large coherence unit is used. For example, Cashmere incurs 7 to 8 times more data traffic compared to Shasta at the smaller dataset size. The extra communication generated due to false sharing in Cashmere (incurred on every boundary) increases with the number of processors, which explains Cashmere's lower relative performance at 16 processors. As in LU, the effect of false sharing in Cashmere is greatly reduced because a large portion of the false sharing is confined to individual nodes. Furthermore, both Shasta and Cashmere benefit significantly from the large portion of true sharing communication that is confined to each SMP node [17, 20].

For Water-spatial, Cashmere performs 1.2 times better than Shasta on average, with Shasta's performance being comparable to Cashmere's at the smaller dataset size and 16 processors. In this version of the fluid-flow simulation program (compared to Water-nsquared), a uniform 3-D grid of cells is imposed on the problem domain. Processors own certain cells and only access those cells and their neighbors. Molecules can move between cells during the simulation, creating a loss of locality, but this effect is small in both Cashmere and Shasta. As with Water-nsquared, the performance difference between the two systems can be attributed to the checking overhead in Shasta (as can be seen by the difference in "Task" time in Figure 3).

Overall, the performance of Shasta and Cashmere is comparable for the above set of applications. This is surprising for programs such as LU and Ocean, which exhibit frequent false sharing at the page-level. However, much or all of this false sharing turns out to occur between processors on the same SMP node (due to task allocation policy or nearest neighbor communication behavior) and is handled efficiently by the SMP-aware protocol. In addition, the low frequency of synchronization, along with the lazy protocol employed by the page-based system, allows Cashmere to tolerate any false sharing between nodes. At the same time, Shasta's eager protocol causes extra communication in applications (such as Ilink) that exhibit false sharing even at small block sizes.

4.2.3 Fine-Grain Access and Synchronization

The applications in this group are Barnes-Hut, Raytrace, and Volrend. As we will see, the combination of fine-grain data access and synchronization leads to excess communication and false sharing in page-based systems.

The main data structure in Barnes is a tree of nodes, each with a size of 96 bytes, so there is significant false sharing in Cashmere runs. Furthermore, this application relies on processor consistency in the parallel tree-building phase. Hence, while this application can run correctly on Shasta (which can enforce this form of consistency), it must be modified for Cashmere by inserting an extra flag synchronization in the parallel tree-building phase. The performance presented is for the unmodified Barnes program under Shasta, and with the additional flag synchronization under Cashmere. Shasta performs 2 and 3.5 times better than Cashmere at 8 and 16 processors, respectively. The main reason for this difference is the parallel tree building phase. This phase constitutes 2% of the sequential execution time, but slows down by a factor of 24 under Cashmere because of the fine-grain access, excessive false sharing, and extra synchronization. Shasta also suffers a slowdown in this phase, but only by a factor of 2.

Raytrace shows an even more dramatic difference between the performance of Shasta and Cashmere. Shasta performs 7 and 12.5 times better than Cashmere (which actually has a large slowdown) at 8 and 16 processors, respectively. This result is surprising, since there is little communication in the main computational loop that accesses the image plane and ray data structures. The performance difference can be primarily attributed to a single critical section used to increment a global counter in order to identify each ray uniquely. It turns out the ray identifiers are used only for debugging and could easily be eliminated (see Section 4.3.2). Their presence, however, illustrates the sensitivity of Cashmere to synchronization and data access granularity. Although only a single word is modified within the critical section, an entire page must be moved back and forth among the processors. Shasta's performance is insensitive to the synchronization, and is more in line with the behavior of a hardware DSM platform.

Volrend partitions its image plane into small tiles that constitute a unit of work, and relies on task stealing via a central queue to provide load balance. Shasta performs 3.5 times better than Cashmere for this application. Figure 3 shows that data wait and synchronization time account for 60% of the Cashmere execution time, but only about 35% of Shasta's execution. This difference results from the high degree of page-level false sharing present in the application's task queue and image data. As a result of the false sharing, Cashmere communicates over 10MB of data, as opposed to only 2MB in Shasta. The higher amount of data communication in Cashmere leads to more load imbalance among the processes, thereby triggering more task stealing that compounds the communication costs.

Overall, applications in this category exhibit by far the largest performance gap between the two systems, with Cashmere suffering considerably due to the frequent synchronization and communication.

	selected data structure(s)	block size (bytes)
LU	matrix array	2048
CLU	matrix block	2048
Volrend	opacity, normal maps	1024
EM3D	node and data array	8192
ILINK	all data	1024

Table 2: Variable block sizes used for Shasta.

4.3 Performance Improvements through Program Modifications

The performance results presented in the previous section were for unmodified programs (except to eliminate a race in Barnes for Cashmere) that were taken from either the hardware or software shared memory domain. In most cases, better performance can be achieved by tailoring the application to the latencies and granularity of the underlying software system. In this section, we present the performance of some of the applications that have been modified for either Shasta or Cashmere.

Figure 4 presents the speedups for the modified applications along with the unmodified results for 16 processor runs with the large dataset sizes. The corresponding execution time breakdowns are not shown here, but are available in an extended version of the paper [5].

4.3.1 Modifications for Shasta

The modifications we consider for Shasta are guaranteed not to alter program correctness, and can therefore be applied safely without a deep understanding of the application. This is consistent with Shasta's philosophy of transparency and simple portability. The three types of changes we use are variable granularity hints [15], the addition of padding in data structures, and the use of compiler options to reduce instrumentation overhead.

For variable granularity hints, we use a special shared-memory allocator provided by Shasta that allows one to specify the block size for the corresponding region of memory. By allocating certain regions in this manner, the application can cause data to be fetched in large units for important data structures that are accessed in a coarse-grain manner or are mostly-read. Table 2 lists the applications that benefit from using variable granularity, the data structures on which it was used, and the increased block size. As an example of the benefit of variable granularity, the performance of EM3D improves by a factor of 1.8 and CLU by a factor of 1.2 for the large input set on 16 processors (results labeled as "SH-VG" in Figure 4).

Another change that can sometimes improve performance is padding elements of important data structures. For example, in the Barnes-Hut application, information on each body is stored in a structure which is allocated out of one large array. Since the body structure is 120 bytes, there is some false sharing between different bodies. Shasta's performance improves significantly (by a factor of 1.9 on the large input set for 16 processors) by padding the body structure to 128 bytes (labeled as "Padded" in Figure 4).

A final modification involves using compiler options to reduce instrumentation overhead. Existing compilers typically unroll inner loops to improve instruction scheduling and reduce looping overheads. Batching of checking code is especially effective for unrolled loops, since unrolling increases the number of neighboring loads and stores in the loop bodies. In CLU, instrumentation overhead is still high despite the batching, because the inner loop is scheduled so effectively. The checking overhead is reduced significantly (from 55% to 36% on a uniprocessor with the large input set) by using a compiler option that increases the unrolling of the inner loop from the default four iterations to eight iterations (labelled as "Loop Unroll" in Figure 4).

There are a large class of other optimizations that would improve application performance under Shasta. However, we have limited our investigation to simple hint optimizations to emphasize the ease of portability of applications from hardware multiprocessors to Shasta.

4.3.2 Modifications for Cashmere

The modifications made to tune the applications for Cashmere aim to reduce the frequency of synchronization or to increase the granularity of sharing. Unlike the changes made for Shasta, the Cashmere modifications are not in the form of hints and require some real understanding of the application in order to maintain correctness. We have made changes to three applications that exhibit particularly poor performance under Cashmere (results are labeled as "Restructured/CSM" in Figure 4).

The major source of overhead in Barnes-Hut is in the tree building phase. The application requires processors to position their bodies into a tree data structure of cells, resulting in a large number of scattered accesses to shared memory. In addition, the algorithm requires processors to synchronize in a very fine-grain manner in order to avoid race conditions. The resulting false sharing and fine-grain synchronization cause the tree-building phase to run much slower in parallel under Cashmere than in the sequential execution. While parallel tree-building algorithms suitable for page-based S-DSM [11] exist, we have chosen to use the simple approach of computing the tree sequentially (it constitutes 2% of the total sequential execution time). Building the tree sequentially does, however, have the disadvantage of increasing the memory requirements on the main node and limiting the largest problem size that can be run.

A second source of overhead comes from a parallel reduction in the main computation loop. The reduction modifies two shared variables in a critical section based on per-processor values for these variable. Performance is reduced because of critical section dilation due to page faults. We have modified the code to compute the reduction sequentially on a single processor.

Raytrace is in reality a highly parallel application. There is very little sharing and the only necessary synchronization constructs are per-processor locks on the processor work queues. However, the original version contains some additional locking code that protects a counter used for debugging purposes, as described in Section 4.2.3. Eliminating the locking code and counter update reduces the running time from 71 seconds to 3.7 seconds on 16 processors and the amount of data transferred from 1GByte down to 17MBytes. The magnitude of this improvement illustrates the sensitivity of page-based S-DSM to fine-grain synchronization.

The performance degradation in Volrend comes from false sharing on the task queue data structure as well as the small granularity of work. We have modified the application to change the granularity of tasks as well as to eliminate false sharing in the

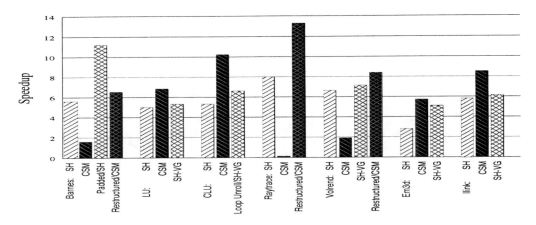

Figure 4: Speedups for the optimized applications on the large data set at 16 processors.

task queue by padding.

Additional optimizations that would improve the performance of these and other applications in our suite on a page-based system can be implemented [11]. In general, if the size of the coherence block is taken into account in structuring the application, most applications can perform well on page-based systems. Restructuring applications tuned for hardware DSM systems does, however, require knowledge of the underlying computation or data structures.

4.4 Summary of Results

This section provided an in-depth comparison and analysis of the performance of two software DSM systems, Shasta and Cashmere. We summarize our results using the geometric mean of the relative speedups on the two systems. For the eight applications (unmodified Splash-2) that were written and tuned for hardware DSM systems, Shasta exhibits a 1.6 times performance advantage over Cashmere. Most of this difference comes from one application (Raytrace) for which the performance of the two systems differs by a factor of 13. Using the same metric, for the five programs that were written or tuned with page-based DSM in mind, Cashmere exhibits a 1.3 times performance advantage over Shasta. After we allow modifications to the applications, Cashmere performs 1.15 times better than Shasta over all 13 applications. However, it is important to emphasize that the modifications we considered for Shasta were in the form of hints that do not affect application correctness or require detailed application knowledge, while the modifications we considered for Cashmere often required changes in the parallelization strategy.

5 Related Work

There is a large body of literature on S-DSM that has had an impact on the design of the Cashmere and Shasta systems. The focus of this paper is to understand the performance tradeoffs of fine-grain vs. coarse-grain software shared memory rather than to design or study a particular S-DSM system in isolation.

Iftode *et al.* [10] have characterized the performance and sources of overhead of a large number of applications under S-DSM, while Jiang *et al.* [11] have provided insights into the

restructuring necessary to achieve good performance under S-DSM for a similar application suite. Our work builds on theirs by providing insight on how a similar class of programs performs under both fine-grain and coarse-grain S-DSM. In addition, we use actual systems implemented on a state-of-the-art cluster, allowing us to capture details not present in a simulation environment.

Researchers at Wisconsin and Princeton [22] have also studied the tradeoffs between fine- and coarse-grain S-DSM systems, but our studies have a number of differences. First, we have studied SMP-aware systems running on clusters of SMPs. Second, the Wisconsin/Princeton platform uses custom hardware not available in commodity systems to provide fine-grain access control. Their fine-grain performance results therefore do not include software checking overhead, which limited performance in several of our applications. In addition, the custom hardware delivers an access control fault in only 5 μs, which is fourteen times faster than the delivery of a page fault on our platform. Third, the processors in our cluster are an order of magnitude faster than those in the Wisconsin/Princeton cluster (400MHz vs 66MHz), while our network is only 3-4 times better in latency and bandwidth, thus increasing the relative cost of communication. All of these differences have manifested themselves in a number of ways in our performance results for both the fine-grain and coarse-grain systems.

Some of the results of our study mirror those of the Wisconsin/Princeton study, but others offer new insight into the granularity issue. For example, both Raytrace and Volrend perform well on the coarse-grain protocol in the Wisconsin/Princeton study, but perform very poorly on Cashmere in our study. The performance gap can be attributed to our fast hardware platform, which causes accelerated synchronization and in turn magnifies the effect of unnecessary data transferred in a coarse-grain protocol. More favorably for coarse-grain protocols, we also found that an SMP-aware implementation can greatly mitigate the effects of false sharing.

We believe that Cashmere and Shasta are among the most efficient S-DSMs in their class. There are still relatively few S-DSMs that are SMP-aware and capable of executing on commodity hardware. The Sirocco system [19] is a fine-grain S-DSM that uses an SMP-aware protocol, but its instrumentation overheads are much higher than Shasta's. SoftFlash [6] was one of the first page-based implementations designed for SMP clusters. The SoftFlash results showed that intra-node synchronization could be excessive. Cashmere-2L [20], however, combines existing techniques with a novel incoming diff operation to eliminate most intra-node synchronization. HLRC-SMP [14] is a more recent protocol that shares several similarities with Cashmere-2L. The Cashmere-2L protocol, however, has been optimized to take advantage of the Memory Channel network and allows home nodes to migrate to active writers, thereby potentially reducing twin/diff overhead.

6   Conclusions

In this paper, we have examined the performance tradeoffs between fine-grain and coarse-grain S-DSM in the context of two state-of-the-art systems: Shasta and Cashmere. In general, we found that the fine-grain, instrumentation-based approach to S-DSM offers a higher degree of robustness and superior performance in the presence of fine-grain synchronization, while the coarse-grain, VM-based approach offers higher performance when coarse-grain synchronization is used.

The performance of applications running under Shasta is most affected by the instrumentation overhead and by the smaller default block size when accessing data at a coarse granularity. Conversely, for Cashmere, the main sources of overhead are critical section dilation in the presence of fine-grain synchronization, and the communication of unneeded data in computations with fine-grain data access. Standard programming idioms such as work-queues, parallel reductions, and atomic counters can cause excessive communication overhead if they are not tuned for coarse-grain systems. However, a number of applications with false sharing at a page-level performed better than expected on Cashmere because its SMP-aware protocol enabled most or all of the false sharing effects to be handled in hardware. Finally, we found that most of the remaining performance differences between Shasta and Cashmere could be eliminated by program modifications that take the coherence granularity into account.

References

[1]   S. Adve and K. Gharachorloo. Shared Memory Consistency Models: A Tutorial. *Computer*, 29(12):66–76, December 1996.

[2]   C. Amza, A. L. Cox, S. Dwarkadas, P. Keleher, H. Lu, R. Rajamony, W. Yu, and W. Zwaenepoel. TreadMarks: Shared Memory Computing on Networks of Workstations. In *Computer*, 29(2):18-28, February 1996.

[3]   J. B. Carter, J. K. Bennett, and W. Zwaenepoel. Implementation and Performance of Munin. In *Proc. of the Thirteenth SOSP*, pages 152–164, October 1991.

[4]   S. Dwarkadas, R. W. Cottingham, A. L. Cox, P. Keleher, A. A. Scaffer, and W. Zwaenepoel. Parallelization of General Linkage Analysis Problems. *Human Heredity*, 44:127–141, July 1994.

[5]   S. Dwarkadas, K. Gharachorloo, L. Kontothanassis, D. J. Scales, M. L. Scott, and R. Stets. Comparative Evaluation of Fine- and Coarse-Grain Approaches for Software Distributed Shared Memory. University of Rochester CS TR 699, October 1998. Also available as Western Research Lab TR 98/7.

[6]   A. Erlichson, N. Nuckolls, G. Chesson, and J. Hennessy. Soft-FLASH: Analyzing the Performance of Clustered Distributed

Virtual Shared Memory. In *Proc. of Seventh ASPLOS*, pages 210–220, October 1996.

[7]   K. Gharachorloo, D. Lenoski, J. Laudon, P. Gibbons, A. Gupta, and J. L. Hennessy. Memory Consistency and Event Ordering in Scalable Shared-Memory Multiprocessors. In *Proc. of the Seventeenth ISCA*, pages 15–26, May 1990.

[8]   R. Gillett. Memory Channel: An Optimized Cluster Interconnect. *IEEE Micro*, 16(2), February 1996.

[9]   L. Iftode, C. Dubnicki, E. W. Felten, and K. Li. Improving Release-Consistent Shared Virtual Memory Using Automatic Update. In *Proc. of the Second HPCA*, February 1996.

[10]   L. Iftode, J. P. Singh, and K. Li. Understanding Application Performance on Shared Virtual Memory. In *Proc. of the Twenty-Third ISCA*, May 1996.

[11]   D. Jiang, H. Shan, and J. P. Singh. Application Restructuring and Performance Portability on Shared Virtual Memory and Hardware-Coherence Multiprocessors. In *Proc. of the Sixth PPOPP*, June 1997.

[12]   L. Kontothanassis, G. Hunt, R. Stets, N. Hardavellas, M. Cierniak, S. Parthasarathy, W. M. Jr., S. Dwarkadas, and M. L. Scott. VM-Based Shared Memory on Low-Latency, Remote-Memory-Access Networks. In *Proc. of the Twenty-Fourth ISCA*, June 1997.

[13]   K. Li and P. Hudak. Memory Coherence in Shared Virtual Memory Systems. *IEEE TOCS*, 7(4):321-359, November 1989.

[14]   R. Samanta, A. Bilas, L. Iftode, and J. Singh. Home-Based SVM Protocols for SMP Clusters: Design and Performance. In *Proc. of Fourth HPCA*, pages 113–124, February 1998.

[15]   D. Scales, K. Gharachorloo, and C. Thekkath. Shasta: A Low-Overhead Software-Only Approach to Fine-Grain Shared Memory. In *Proc. of the Seventh ASPLOS*, October 1996.

[16]   D. Scales and K. Gharachorloo. Toward Transparent and Efficient Software Distributed Shared Memory. In *Proc. of the Sixteenth SOSP*, October 1997.

[17]   D. J. Scales, K. Gharachorloo, and A. Aggarwal. Fine-Grain Software Distributed Shared Memory on SMP Clusters. In *Proc. of the Fourth HPCA*, February 1998.

[18]   I. Schoinas, B. Falsafi, A. R. Lebeck, S. K. Reinhardt, J. R. Larus, and D. A. Wood. Fine-grain Access Control for Distributed Shared Memory. In *Proc. of the Sixth ASPLOS*, pages 297–306, October 1994.

[19]   I. Schoinas, B. Falsafi, M. Hill, J. Larus, and D. Wood. Sirocco: Cost-Effective Fine-Grain Distributed Shared Memory. In *Proc. of PACT '98*, October 1998.

[20]   R. Stets, S. Dwarkadas, N. Hardavellas, G. Hunt, L. Kontothanassis, S. Parthasarathy, and M. L. Scott. CSM-2L: Software Coherent Shared Memory on a Clustered Remote-Write Network. In *Proc. of the Sixteenth SOSP*, October 1997.

[21]   S. C. Woo, M. Ohara, E. Torrie, J. P. Singh, and A. Gupta. Methodological Considerations and Characterization of the SPLASH-2 Parallel Application Suite. In *Proc. of the Twenty-Second ISCA*, June 1995.

[22]   Y. Zhou, L. Iftode, J. P. Singh, K. Li, B. R. Toonen, I. Schoinas, M. D. Hill, and D. A. Wood. Relaxed Consistency and Coherence Granularity in DSM Systems: A Performance Evaluation. In *Proc. of the Sixth PPOPP*, June 1997.

Using Lamport Clocks to Reason About Relaxed Memory Models

Anne E. Condon, Mark D. Hill, Manoj Plakal, Daniel J. Sorin
Computer Sciences Department
University of Wisconsin - Madison
{condon,markhill,plakal,sorin}@cs.wisc.edu

Abstract

Cache coherence protocols of current shared-memory multiprocessors are difficult to verify. Our previous work proposed an extension of Lamport's logical clocks for showing that multiprocessors can implement sequential consistency (SC) with an SGI Origin 2000-like directory protocol and a Sun Gigaplane-like split-transaction bus protocol. Many commercial multiprocessors, however, implement more relaxed models, such as SPARC Total Store Order (TSO), a variant of processor consistency, and Compaq (DEC) Alpha, a variant of weak consistency.

This paper applies Lamport clocks to both a TSO and an Alpha implementation. Both implementations are based on the same Sun Gigaplane-like split-transaction bus protocol we previously used, but the TSO implementation places a first-in-first-out write buffer between a processor and its cache, while the Alpha implementation uses a coalescing write buffer. Both write buffers satisfy read requests for pending writes (i.e., do bypassing) without requiring the write to be immediately written to cache. Analysis shows how to apply Lamport clocks to verify TSO and Alpha specifications at the architectural level.

Keywords: memory consistency models, cache coherence protocols, protocol verification

1 Introduction

Shared-memory multiprocessor systems are increasingly employed both as servers (for computation, databases, files, and the web) and as clients. To improve performance, multiprocessor system designers use a variety of complex and interacting optimizations. These optimizations include cache coherence via snooping or directory protocols, out-of-order processors, and coalescing write buffers. These optimizations add considerable complexity at the architectural level and even more complexity at the implementation level. Directory protocols, for example, require the system to transition from many shared copies of a block to one exclusive one. Unfortunately, this transition must be implemented with many non-atomic lower-level transitions that expose additional race conditions, buffering requirements, and forward-progress concerns. Due to this complexity,

This work is supported in part by the National Science Foundation with grants MIP-9225097, MIPS-9625558, CCR 9257241, and CDA-9623632, a Wisconsin Romnes Fellowship, and donations from Sun Microsystems and Intel Corporation.

industrial product groups spend more time verifying their system than actually designing and optimizing it.

To verify a system, engineers should unambiguously define what "correct" means. For a shared-memory system, "correct" is defined by a memory consistency model. A *memory consistency model* defines for programmers the allowable behavior of hardware. A commonly-assumed memory consistency model requires a shared-memory multiprocessor to appear to software as a multiprogrammed uniprocessor. This model was formalized by Lamport as *sequential consistency* (SC) [12]. Assume that each processor executes instructions and memory operations in a dynamic execution order called *program order*. An execution is SC if there exists a total order of memory operations (reads and writes) in which (a) the program orders of all processors are respected and (b) a read returns the value of the last write (to the same address) in this order. A system is SC if it only permits SC executions.

Our previous work [18,24] proved that abstractions of a SGI Origin 2000-like [5,13] directory protocol and a Sun Gigaplane-like [22] split-transaction bus protocol both implement SC. Instead of asking for the off-line existence of a total memory order, we *pretend* to augment the hardware with logical *Lamport clocks* to construct the needed order dynamically as it executes memory operations (satisfying requirement (a)). We then prove that every load (read instruction) returns the value of the last store (write instruction) in this constructed order. Thus (b) is satisfied. As with any formal method, our Lamport clocks approach cannot replace conventional testing and validation. Nevertheless, it is our premise that Lamport clocks can be valuable when reasoning about the correctness of a specification of memory ordering semantics at the architectural level, thereby aiding in the protocol design process and reducing time spent on validation later.

While work on SC is valuable, many commercial processors implement more relaxed memory consistency models in an effort to improve performance. An example is the insertion of FIFO or coalescing write buffers between the processor and the cache. Processor consistent models, such as SPARC Total Store Order (TSO) [25], relax the SC requirement (a): now, in the total ordering of memory operations, a store (ST) can appear after a load (LD) that follows it in program order. More relaxed models, such as Compaq (DEC) Alpha [23], allow a processor great freedom to re-order memory operations between "memory barriers."

This paper shows that Lamport clocks can be used to verify shared-memory implementations that support the TSO and Alpha relaxed memory models. Towards this end, the paper makes two primary contributions:

1. *We provide clean new memory model definitions, namely Wisconsin TSO and Wisconsin Alpha, that aid in reasoning about correctness of protocols.* We show that protocols satisfying the Wisconsin TSO and Wisconsin Alpha memory models also satisfy TSO [25] and Alpha [23], respectively. We consider the Wisconsin memory models to be more intuitive than the original definitions for the following reasons. Unlike the TSO definition, LDs always get the values of STs that occur earlier in the total order. Unlike the Alpha definition, we use a total order.

2. *We extend our Lamport timestamping scheme to protocols for both the TSO and Alpha memory models.* The key is determining at what point in the protocol an event is timestamped, and it is in this determination that the proofs of this paper differ from our previous work on SC. For example, in the Alpha protocol, a LD that gets its value from a previous ST that is still in the write buffer should be timestamped *after* the ST. But since the ST has not yet been written to the cache, the ST is not yet timestamped when the LD is issued. Our timestamping scheme handles this simply by waiting to timestamp the LD until the ST has actually been written to the cache.

While the details of the timestamping scheme are necessarily different from previous work, a strength of our approach is that, with the timestamping scheme in hand, the proofs of correctness of the protocols are almost identical to the proofs in our previous work on SC. Our protocols for TSO and Alpha are based on the same Gigaplane-like split-transaction bus protocol that we considered in previous work [24]. A similar result could easily be proved for a directory-based implementation, as in Plakal et al. [18].

In the rest of the paper, we assume a *block* to be a fixed-size, contiguous, aligned section of memory (usually equal to the cache line size). Also, LDs and STs operate on *words*, where we assume that a word is contained in a block and is aligned at a word boundary. Our scheme could be extended to handle LDs and STs on sub-units of a word (half-words or bytes) which need not be aligned. However, this makes the specification of the memory models very tedious without any gain in insight or clarity.

The rest of this paper is organized as follows. Section 2 summarizes our previous work that used Lamport clocks to reason about the correctness of shared memory systems, and discusses related work by others. We present our results for TSO and Alpha in Sections 3 and 4, respectively. Section 5 summarizes our contributions and discusses future work.

2 Related Work[1]

2.1 Our Previous Work

Our previous work [18,24] proved that implementations using a SGI Origin 2000-like [5,13] directory protocol and a Sun Gigaplane-like [22] split-transaction bus protocol both implement SC. Both implementations use three-state invalidation-based coherence protocols.

Our reasoning method associates logical timestamps with loads, stores, and coherence events. We call our method *Lamport Clocks*, because our timestamping modestly extends the logical timestamps Lamport developed for distributed systems [11]. Lamport associated a counter with each host. The counter is incremented on local events and its value is used to timestamp outgoing messages. On message receipt, a host sets its counter to one greater than the maximum of its former time and the timestamp of the incoming message. Timestamp ties are broken with host ID. In this manner, Lamport creates a total order using these logical timestamps where causality flows with increasing logical time.

Our timestamping scheme extends Lamport's 2-tuple timestamps to three-tuples: **<global . local . node-id>**, where **global** takes precedence over **local,** and **local** takes precedence over **node-id** (e.g., $3.10.11 < 4.2.1$). Coherence messages, or transactions, carry global timestamps. In addition, global timestamps order LD and ST operations relative to transactions. Local timestamps are assigned to LD and ST operations in order to preserve program order in Lamport time among operations that have the same global timestamp. They enable an unbounded number of LD/ST operations between transactions. Node-ID, the third component of a Lamport timestamp, is used as an arbitrary tie-breaker between two operations with the same global and local timestamps, thus ensuring that all LD and ST operations are totally ordered.

Our prior proofs of SC use two timestamping claims that show that LDs and STs are ordered relative to transactions "as intended by the designer." One of these claims is that for every LD and ST on a given block, proper access is ensured by the most recent transaction on that block in Lamport time. (In contrast, in real time, a processor may perform a LD on a block *after* it has answered a request to relinquish the block.) Roughly, the other claim is that, in logical time, transactions are handled by processors in the order in which they are received. (In contrast, in real time, a processor may receive transaction-related messages "out of order".)

Sequential consistency is established using the concept of *coherence epochs*. An epoch is an interval of logical time during which a node has read-only or read-write access to a block of data. The life of a block in logical time consists of

---

1. This section borrows from material in previous work [18,24].

271

a sequence of such epochs. Our proof shows that, in Lamport time, operations lie within appropriate epochs. That is, each LD lies within either a read-only or a read-write epoch, and each ST lies within a read-write epoch. In addition, the "correct" value of a block is passed from one node to another between epochs. The proofs of these results build in a modular fashion upon the timestamping claims, thereby localizing arguments based on specification details. The differences between the proofs for the bus and directory protocols differ only in the details of the timestamping claims.

2.2 Other Related Work

Our Lamport clock method complements related work on proving protocols correct. First, Lamport clocks are more precise and formal than ad hoc reasoning or simulation.

Second, we find Lamport clocks easier to use and more applicable to larger systems, but less rigorous than approaches that use state-space search of finite-state machines or theorem-proving techniques. These are rigorous methods that can capture subtle errors, but they are often limited to small systems because of the state space explosion for large, complicated systems. For example, the SGI Origin 2000 coherence protocol is verified for a 4-cluster system with one cache block [7], the memory subsystem of the Sun S3.mp cache-coherent multiprocessor system is verified for one cache block [19], and the SPARC Relaxed Memory Order (RMO) memory consistency model is verified for small test programs [16]. Park and Dill [17] propose using transaction aggregation to scale beyond finite-state methods. Our approach can precisely verify the operation of a protocol in a system consisting of any number of nodes and memory blocks.

Another formal approach devised by Shen and Arvind uses term rewriting to specify and prove the correctness of coherence protocols [21]. Their technique involves showing that a system with caches and a system without caches can simulate each other. This approach lends itself to highly succinct formal proofs. We find Lamport clocks easier to grasp, while not lacking expressive power. Term rewriting relies on an ordering of rewrite rules (each of which corresponds to an event) and, as such, may benefit from the Lamport clock technique which can order events.

Third, we find Lamport clocks easier to use and of similar formal power to many of the other methods used to define and verify relaxed memory models [1, 2, 3, 6, 8, 9, 20]. Of particular note are the approaches of Collier [3] and Gharachorloo et al. [8] that model a write as p sub-operations to each of p processors. We find their approaches more general but harder to use than our approach that splits TSO stores (writes) into two components and leaves Alpha stores atomic.

Finally, Lamport Clocks have also been used in other research, including a paper by Neiger and Toueg [15]. They describe a class of problems for which, if a clock-based algorithm is proven correct assuming real-time synchronized clocks, then it must also be correct even if run with logical clocks. One difference between this work and ours is that the protocols we consider are not clock-based. Rather, we attach (logical) clocks to clock-free protocols, in order to prove correctness of the protocols

3 Total Store Order (TSO)

SPARC Total Store Order (TSO) [25] is a variant of *processor consistency* [9,10] that has been implemented on Sun multiprocessors for many years. TSO relaxes SC in that LDs can be ordered ahead of STs which precede them in program order (so long as there are no intervening memory barriers and the two operations are to different locations). We study TSO because it is formally and publicly defined, but we expect that our results can be mapped to the Intel Architecture-32 (IA-32) memory model (Section 7.2 of [4]), the other dominant processor consistency model.

We now define TSO, Wisconsin TSO, a TSO implementation, a Lamport timestamping scheme for that implementation, and its corresponding proof.

3.1 Defining TSO

TSO applies to a system with multiple processors issuing a variety of instructions. For our purposes, we are concerned with word loads (LDs), word stores (STs) and memory barriers (MBs) issued to regular memory (i.e., excluding I/O space). We consider only memory barriers at least as strong as type "MB #StoreLoad," i.e., barriers which guarantee that all prior STs are completed before any future LD, while weaker memory barriers are regarded as no-ops (e.g., "MB #LoadLoad"). Appendix D of the SPARC Architecture Manual Version 9 [25] defines TSO by defining Relaxed Memory Order (RMO) and then adding constraints to form TSO. We give the combined result.

Let $<_p$ denote *program order*. Program order totally orders all LDs, STs, and MBs at the same processor and it is thus a partial order over all processors.

Let $<_m$ be a total ordering of all LD and ST operations.

Then $<_m$ is said to be in *total store order* (TSO) if the following constraints hold. The first two constraints are called "memory order constraints." Let X and Y be a pair of LD or ST operations.

1) If X $<_p$ Y and either X is a LD or Y is a ST, then X $<_m$ Y.

2) If X $<_p$ MB $<_p$ Y then X $<_m$ Y.

The final constraint restricts possible values of LDs:

3) Let X be a LD of word w. Then the value of X is the value of the greatest ST, say Y, to word w in memory order, taken over all STs to word w that either occur before X in memory order or occur before X in program order (but possibly after X in memory order).

Intuitively, constraints 1 and 2 say that memory order may only violate processor order to delay a ST after a subsequent LD when there is no intervening MB. In all other cases, memory order respects program order (i.e., LD $<_p$ LD′, LD $<_p$ ST, and ST $<_p$ ST′ are preserved by memory order). Constraint 3 says that a LD should return the last value written to the same word in memory unless there is a pending ST to the same word (earlier in program order) that has not yet occurred in memory order. In this case, the value from the pending ST should be returned. So if one looks at the memory order, it *appears* as if the LD gets its value from a ST that "happens in the future."

An execution of an implementation satisfies TSO if there exists an ordering of the LDs and STs in the execution that satisfies TSO. An implementation satisfies TSO if all executions of that implementation satisfy TSO.

3.2 Wisconsin TSO

We now define some properties of an ordering which makes verification easier. TSO's condition 3 allows a load to get a value from a "future" store. Wisconsin TSO eliminates this oddity by splitting each store into a $ST_{private}$ and a ST_{public}, both of which have the same value. Each LD gets its value from the past but may return the value of a $ST_{private}$ for which the corresponding ST_{public} has not yet occurred. The goal in this case is to model write buffer bypassing where stores enter the write buffer on a $ST_{private}$ and exit with a ST_{public}.

Let $<_w$ denote an ordering of LDs, $ST_{private}$s and ST_{public}s. We say that $<_w$ is in *Wisconsin total store order* (Wisconsin TSO) if the following conditions hold.

1′) The ordering ($<_w$) of LDs and $ST_{private}$s is consistent with program order. That is, if X and Y are either a LD or a $ST_{private}$, then X $<_p$ Y if and only if X $<_w$ Y.

2′) For each ST, $ST_{private} <_w ST_{public}$.

3′) If X and Y are STs and X $<_p$ Y then $X_{public} <_w Y_{public}$.

4′) If an MB occurs between ST and LD in program order then $ST_{public} <_w$ LD.

5′) Let X be a LD of word w at processor p_i. Then the value of X is the value of the most recent ST to w in $<_w$ that is either:
   a) the most recent $ST_{private}$ to word w at p_i, if for some ST $<_p$ X to word w, the corresponding ST_{public} is after

X in $<_w$, or

   b) the most recent ST_{public} to word w, otherwise.

An execution of an implementation satisfies Wisconsin TSO if there exists an ordering of the LDs, $ST_{private}$s and ST_{public} s in the execution that satisfies Wisconsin TSO. An implementation satisfies Wisconsin TSO if all executions of that implementation satisfy Wisconsin TSO.

Gil Neiger [14] has developed an alternative TSO definition as a total order of LDs and STs in which a LD always get the value of the most recent ST. This is done by moving each LD that returns a value from a $ST_{private}$ to be after the corresponding ST_{public}.

Claim 1: An implementation that satisfies Wisconsin TSO also satisfies TSO.

A proof of this claim can be found in Appendix A.[1]

3.3 TSO Implementation With FIFO Write Buffers

A common TSO implementation approach separates each processor from its cache with a FIFO write buffer. Caches are kept coherent with a write-invalidate coherence protocol sufficient for implementing SC. A MB can be implemented by having a processor flush its write buffer before proceeding past a MB, without the caches or coherence protocol ever seeing MBs. We use this approach here in a manner similar to the Sun Ultra Enterprise 6000 with UltraSPARC II processors.

We begin with a brief summary of the SC implementation that Sorin et al. [24] describe for a Gigaplane-like split-transaction bus (the overall approach would be similar to the directory-based implementation described by Plakal et al. [18]). Memory blocks may be cached as *Invalid, Shared,* or *Exclusive*. The *A-state* (address state) records how the block is cached and is used for responding to subsequent bus transactions. The protocol seeks to maintain the expected invariants (e.g., a block is *Exclusive* in at most one cache) and provides the usual coherence transactions: *Get-Shared* (GETS), *Get-Exclusive* (GETX), *Upgrade* (UPG, for upgrading the block from Shared to Exclusive), and *Writeback* (WB). As with the Gigaplane, coherence transactions immediately change the A-state, regardless of when the data arrives. If a processor issues a GETX transaction and then sees a GETS transaction for the same block by another processor, the processor's A-state for the block will go from Invalid to Exclusive to Shared, regardless of when it obtains the data. In an SC implementation, the processor checks the A-state of a block before executing LDs and STs on that block. On a miss, the processor ensures the

---

1. The converse of this claim can also be proved, but it is not necessary for our proof of correctness, and we omit it here due to space constraints.

appropriate A-state for that block by sending a coherence transaction on the bus.

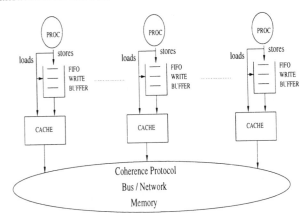

FIGURE 1. Our TSO Implementation

To convert this SC implementation into a TSO implementation, we insert a FIFO write buffer between a processor and its cache (as shown in Figure 1), and we add a MB instruction. The rest of the implementation (external to the processor and write-buffer) obeys the coherence protocol outlined above. The processor issues LDs, STs, and MBs in program order. Below, we specify exactly what happens when the processor issues one of these instructions. The processor completes issuing an instruction before proceeding to issue the next one in program order.

Stores: A ST issues into a FIFO write buffer (considered internal to the processor) in an event denoted as a $ST_{private}$. Entries in the write buffer are the size of processor words. Eventually, these entries are flushed from the write-buffer to the cache in the same order that they entered the write buffer, and this activity is independent of the issuing of STs by the processor. The event whereby an entry is flushed from the write buffer to the cache, once the processor has *established* that the corresponding block's A-state is Exclusive, is called a ST_{public}. By *establish*, we mean that the processor checks the A-state of the block and if it is not Exclusive, then the coherence protocol is invoked to change the A-state to Exclusive. Note that the Exclusive A-state is a prerequisite for a ST_{public} but not for a $ST_{private}$.

Loads: To issue a LD, the processor first checks in its write buffer for a ST to the same word. We refer to this action as a CHECK(LD). If the LD hits in the write buffer, then the LD gets the value of the most recent such $ST_{private}$ in program order. Note that a LD cannot overtake a ST to the write buffer, because the protocol does not start to issue a LD until issuing of all previous STs (in program order) has been completed. If the LD misses in the write buffer, then it is treated just like a LD in the SC protocol and has to go to the cache. That is, the processor establishes that the A-state of the block in the cache is Shared or Exclusive; if necessary, it invokes the coherence protocol (the details of which are as described by Sorin et al. [24]). In this case, the issu-

ing of the LD completes when the processor establishes that the A-state of the block is Shared or Exclusive. We assume that LDs do not overlap with ST_{public}s to the same address, in the sense that the interval during which a LD is issued cannot overlap with the ST_{public} flushing interval, starting when the processor establishes that the A-state is Exclusive and continuing until the flush is completed.

MBs: Upon issuing a MB, our implementation simply flushes all entries in the write buffer to the cache before issuing any more operations. A more aggressive implementation could perhaps mark all the entries in some way and then ensure that subsequent coherence transactions are allowed to happen only when all marked entries have been flushed from the write-buffer.

3.4 Timestamping for TSO Implementation

We now present a scheme that assigns logical timestamps to the events of interest that occur during any execution of a program on our implementation of TSO. We define an *M-operation* (or simply an M-op) to be a LD or $ST_{private}$. M-ops are ordered by program order at a single processor. Our scheme assigns timestamps to M-ops, ST_{public}s and coherence protocol transactions (GETX, GETS, UPG, WB).

We define a notion of *binding* for M-ops and ST_{public}s which is useful for presenting the timestamping scheme. Intuitively, the binding time of an operation is the point in real time when that operation has been "committed" by the processor. $ST_{private}$s are bound when the corresponding entries enter the write buffer. ST_{public}s are bound at the time that the Exclusive A-state of the target block is established by the processor. LDs that hit in the write buffer are bound at the time that the corresponding CHECK(LD) occurs. LDs that miss in the write buffer are bound at the time that the A-state for the corresponding block is established by the processor. Both ST_{public}s and LDs that miss in the write buffer are said to be *bound to* the coherence transaction that obtained the block in the appropriate A-state.

Our timestamps are 3-tuples: <global-time.local-time.processor ID>. We give rules below for assigning global and local times to the various events that we timestamp. The processor ID acts as a tie-breaker. Conceptually, each processor has a global and a local clock which get updated in real time for transactions as well as M-ops and ST_{public}s, respectively.

Transactions are totally ordered by the bus in real time and we define the global time of a transaction to be its rank in this ordering, with the first transaction being assigned a global time of 1. At the moment that the A-state of a processor changes due to a transaction, the global clock of that processor is incremented to equal the global time of that transaction, while the local clock (and the local component of the transaction's timestamp) are set to 0.

Each M-op and ST_{public} is assigned a timestamp at the time that it is bound. If an M-op and ST_{public} happen to be bound at the same moment in real time, we assume that they are assigned timestamps in some arbitrary (but deterministic) ordering (e.g., M-ops are always timestamped first). Note that a LD that misses in the write buffer and a ST_{public} can never be bound at the same time because of the real-time ordering properties of the protocol. The local clock is incremented by 1 to equal the local component of the timestamp assigned. The global timestamp is the value of the global clock at the moment that the M-op or ST_{public} is bound.

3.5 Proof of Correctness of TSO Implementation

We show that for any execution of our implementation, the timestamps of $ST_{private}$s, ST_{public}s, and LDs produce a Lamport ordering $<_w$ that satisfies properties 1′ to 5′ of the Wisconsin TSO definition. That properties 1′ to 4′ are satisfied follows from the real-time ordering properties of the protocol, the timestamping scheme, and the order in which events are bound. Property 5′ is proved as follows. We consider two possible situations for LD X:

1) Suppose that for some $ST <_p X$, both to the same word, $X <_w ST_{public}$. Let $Z_{private}$ be the most recent $ST_{private}$ to word w at p_i (prior to X in $<_w$). It must be that Z_{public} occurs after X in $<_w$, by property 3′ of Section 3.2. We need to show that X's value equals that of $Z_{private}$. Since instructions are issued in program order and issue intervals are non-overlapping, $Z_{private}$ is in p_i's write buffer before p_i performs CHECK(X). We claim that $Z_{private}$ is still present in the write buffer when p_i performs CHECK(X); otherwise, at the moment the check is done, Z_{public} would already be bound, causing X to be bound (to a transaction) in real time AFTER Z_{public} is bound. Since timestamps are consistent with binding order, this would contradict the fact that $X <_w Z_{public}$. Hence, X must get the value of $Z_{private}$.

2) Suppose that for all $ST <_p X$, both to the same word, $ST_{public} <_w X$. It cannot be the case that X takes the value of any $ST_{private}$; if X were to take the value of a $ST_{private}$, say $Z_{private}$, then X would be bound BEFORE Z_{public}, since the interval in which X is issued does not overlap with the interval in which Z_{public} occurs. This contradicts our assumption in the previous sentence because binding order is consistent with $<_w$. Hence X gets the value of some ST_{public} and is bound to some transaction. Let Z_{public} be the most recent ST_{public} before X in $<_w$ (not necessarily at processor p_i). We need to show that X gets the value Z_{public}. The proof of this is identical to the proofs of the main theorems in our SC research [18,24], except that STs need to be replaced by ST_{public}s and the definitions of binding and timestamping there need to be replaced by the definitions of binding and timestamping in Section 3.4.

Hence all executions of the implementation satisfy Wisconsin TSO and so the implementation satisfies Wisconsin TSO. By Claim 1, the implementation also satisfies TSO.

4 Alpha

The Compaq (DEC) Alpha memory model [23] is a weakly consistent model that relaxes the ordering requirements at a given processor between any accesses to different memory locations unless ordering is explicitly stated with the use of a Memory Barrier (MB). We first define the Alpha memory model, introduce a collection of constraints on orderings which we refer to as Wisconsin Alpha, and prove the relationship between Alpha and Wisconsin Alpha. We then describe an Alpha implementation, present a timestamping scheme for the implementation, and prove that the ordering produced by the timestamping scheme satisfies Wisconsin Alpha, thus showing that the implementation correctly implements the Alpha memory model.

4.1 Defining Alpha

As with TSO, we are concerned mainly with a system containing multiple processors issuing word LDs, word STs and MBs (ordered by program order at a single processor) to regular memory (not I/O space). The Alpha memory model is formally defined through the use of two orders that must be observed with respect to memory accesses. The first order, program *issue order*, is a partial order on the memory operations (LDs, STs) issued by a given processor. Issue order relaxes program order in that there is no order between accesses to different locations without intervening MBs. Issue order enforces order between accesses to the same location, order between any access and an MB, and order between MBs. The second order, access order, is a total order of operations on a single memory location (regardless of the processors that issued them).

A third order, the "before" order, is defined to be the transitive closure over all of the issue orders and access orders. An execution of an implementation obeys the Alpha memory model if:

- for every memory location, there exists an access order for which there are no two memory operations A and B (not necessarily to the same address) such that A is before B, and B is also before A.

- a load returns the value of the most recent store to the same location in access order.

An implementation satisfies Alpha if all executions of that implementation satisfy Alpha.

4.2 Wisconsin Alpha

Although the Alpha memory model seems to have little in common with the stricter sequential consistency, we will show that the differences between the two models can be constrained to behavior internal to the processor (i.e., everything not including the cache and the rest of the memory subsystem). An execution of an implementation satisfies the Wisconsin Alpha memory model if there exists a total ordering of all loads, stores, and MBs, such that:

- all of the issue orders are respected.
- a load returns the value of the most recent store to the same location in this total order.

An implementation satisfies Wisconsin Alpha if all executions of that implementation satisfy Wisconsin Alpha.

Claim 2: An implementation that satisfies Wisconsin Alpha also satisfies Alpha.

A proof of this claim can be found in Appendix B.[1]

4.3 An Alpha Implementation Using Coalescing Write Buffers

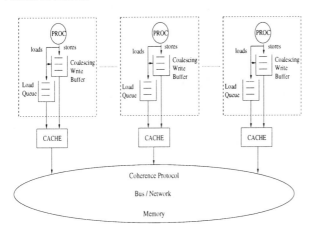

FIGURE 2. Our Alpha Implementation

Each processor in an Alpha implementation internally observes issue order. It can reorder loads and stores to different memory locations as long as there is no intervening MB. The multiprocessor implementation includes some number of these processors connected together either by a shared bus or a network. The cache coherence protocol used in either case is the same as the shared bus protocol [24] or the directory protocol [18] that we described in previous work. Our implementation is loosely modeled after a multiprocessor using the Compaq (DEC) Alpha 21264 microprocessor.

Each processor issues LDs and STs in program order. Stores are issued to a coalescing write buffer which is considered to be internal to the processor. Entries in the write buffer are the size of cache lines. Stores to the same cache line are coalesced in the same entry and if two stores write to the same word, the corresponding entry will hold the value written by the store that was issued later. Entries are eventually flushed from the write buffer to the cache, although not necessarily in the order in which they were issued to the write buffer. Exclusive permission is not

required to issue a store to the write buffer, but it is required to flush the store from the write buffer to the cache.

A LD that hits in the write buffer returns the value that is found there, and this action does not require that line to be flushed from the buffer to the cache. The Alpha model, like most weak memory models, is tailored to include non-blocking caches. This optimization allows the processor to overlap read latency with other useful work, so LDs that miss in the write buffer are issued to a load queue which we consider to be internal to the processor. These LDs are handled by our existing SC coherence protocol with the following difference: a reply from the memory system satisfies all LDs to that location that are in the load queue at the moment that the processor establishes that the A-state is Shared or Exclusive. If the data was already in the cache in the appropriate A-state, then the LD can be satisfied immediately. We assume that there is no overlap between the issuing of LDs and the flushing of STs to the same address once Exclusive permission is obtained.

This implementation uses a simple mechanism for handling MBs, which is to stall the processor until the load queue and the write buffer are empty. Figure 2 illustrates our Alpha implementation, where everything outside of the dotted boxes is exactly the same as in our earlier sequentially consistent implementation.

4.4 Timestamping for Alpha Implementation

The timestamping scheme for the Alpha implementation is quite similar to that used for the TSO implementation. Coherence transactions affect the processors' global clocks in the same fashion. Each LD and ST is timestamped at the moment that it is bound, and it is in this determination of when a LD or ST is bound where Alpha differs from TSO. A ST is considered to be bound when the Exclusive A-state of the target block is established by the processor. Since an entire cache line is written at once, all of the stores in a buffer entry (including coalesced stores to the same word) are bound at the same time, but they are timestamped so as to preserve issue order. A LD that hits in the write buffer is bound exactly when that ST was bound, but it is timestamped after that ST to preserve issue order. If the LD misses in the write buffer, it is bound when the block becomes present in the appropriate A-state. At the moment that each LD or ST is bound, the local clock is incremented by 1 and the local component of the timestamp is set to the updated value. The global timestamp is the value of the global clock at the moment that the event is timestamped.

4.5 Proof of Correctness of Alpha Implementation

We show that each execution of the Alpha implementation satisfies Wisconsin Alpha. In previous work [18,24], we proved that an split-transaction bus protocol and a directory protocol obeyed sequential consistency. Parts of these proofs rely on the processors binding memory accesses in program order. To prove that our target Alpha implementa-

---

1. The converse of this claim can also be proved, but it is not necessary for our proof of correctness, and we omit it here due to space constraints.

tion obeys the Wisconsin Alpha memory model, we can use either proof (depending on whether our interconnect is a bus or a network) as long as we consider that binding order is now a partial order rather than a total order. Specifically, we need to modify the proofs of claims made about the binding of memory operations to coherence transactions so that references to the earliest memory operation are replaced with references to *any* of the earliest memory operations, since there could be more than one that is bound at the same time. Hence all executions of the implementation satisfy Wisconsin Alpha and so the implementation satisfies Wisconsin Alpha. By Claim 2, the implementation also satisfies Alpha.

5 Conclusions and Future Work

High performance shared-memory multiprocessors often incorporate relaxed memory consistency models. These implementations may use many hardware optimizations, such as write buffers and out-of-order issue, and it is difficult to verify that a complex implementation satisfies a given relaxed consistency model. We have extended our Lamport clock verification technique to handle two relaxed consistency models: processor consistency and weak consistency. Reasoning with Lamport clocks, we have shown that two sample implementations satisfy a processor consistent model (Total Store Order) and a weakly consistent model (Alpha), respectively.

Future work with Lamport clocks will extend the method to reason about consistent I/O and the detection of deadlock and livelock. We are interested in automating the verification process.

6 Acknowledgments

This work has benefited from feedback from many people, including Robert Cypher, James Goodman, Erik Hagersten, Daniel Lenoski, Paul Loewenstein, Gil Neiger, and David Wood.

7 References

[1] Sarita V. Adve and Mark D. Hill. Weak Ordering—A New Definition. In *Proceedings of the 17th Annual International Symposium on Computer Architecture*, pages 2–14, Seattle, Washington, May 28–31, 1990.

[2] Hagit Attiya and Roy Friedman. A Correctness Condition for High-performance Multiprocessors. In *Proceedings of the 24th Annual ACM Symposium on the Theory of Computing*, pages 679–690, May 1992.

[3] William W. Collier. *Reasoning About Parallel Architectures*. Prentice-Hall, Inc., 1992.

[4] Intel Corporation. *Pentium Pro Family Developer's Manual, Version 3: Operating System Writer's Manual*. January 1996.

[5] David Culler, Jaswinder Pal Singh, and Anoop Gupta. *Draft of Parallel Computer Architecture: A Hardware/ Software Approach*, chapter 8: Directory-based Cache Coherence. Morgan Kaufmann, 1997.

[6] Michel Dubois, Christoph Scheurich, and Faye Briggs. Memory Access Buffering in Multiprocessors. In *Proceedings of the 13th Annual International Symposium on Computer Architecture*, pages 434–442, June 1986.

[7] Asgeir Th. Eiriksson and Ken L. McMillan. Using Formal Verification/Analysis Methods on the Critical Path in Systems Design: A Case Study. In *Proceedings of the Computer Aided Verification Conference*, Liege, Belgium, 1995. Appears as LNCS 939, Springer Verlag.

[8] Kourosh Gharachorloo, Sarita V. Adve, Anoop Gupta, John L. Hennessy, and Mark D. Hill. Specifying System Requirements for Memory Consistency Models. Technical Report CS-TR-1199, University of Wisconsin – Madison, December 1993.

[9] Kourosh Gharachorloo, Daniel Lenoski, James Laudon, Phillip Gibbons, Anoop Gupta, and John Hennessy. Memory Consistency and Event Ordering in Scalable Shared-memory Multiprocessors. In *Proceedings of the 17th Annual International Symposium on Computer Architecture*, pages 15–26, May 1990.

[10] J. Goodman. Cache Consistency and Sequential Consistency. Technical Report 61, IEEE Scalable Coherent Interface Working Group, 1989.

[11] Leslie Lamport. Time, Clocks and the Ordering of Events in a Distributed System. *Communications of the ACM*, 21(7):558–565, July 1978.

[12] Leslie Lamport. How to Make a Multiprocessor Computer that Correctly Executes Multiprocess Programs. *IEEE Transactions on Computers*, C-28(9):241–248, September 1979.

[13] James P. Laudon and Daniel Lenoski. The SGI Origin: A ccNUMA Highly Scalable Server. In *Proceedings of the 24th International Symposium on Computer Architecture*, Denver, CO, June 1997.

[14] Gil Neiger. Private communication, October 1998.

[15] Gil Neiger and Sam Toueg. Simulating Synchronized Clocks and Common Knowledge in Distributed Systems. *Journal of the Association for Computing Machinery*, 40(2):334–367, April 1993.

[16] Seungjoon Park and David L. Dill. An Executable Specification, Analyzer and Verifier for RMO (Relaxed Memory Order). In *Proceedings of the 7th Annual ACM Symposium on Parallel Algorithms and Architectures*, pages 34–41, Santa Barbara, California, July 17–19, 1995.

[17] Seungjoon Park and David L. Dill. Verification of FLASH Cache Coherence Protocol by Aggregation of Distributed Transactions. In *Proceedings of the 8th Annual ACM Symposium on Parallel Algorithms and Architectures*, pages 288–296, Padua, Italy, June 24–26, 1996.

[18] Manoj Plakal, Daniel J. Sorin, Anne E. Condon, and Mark D. Hill. Lamport Clocks: Verifying a Directory Cache-Coherence Protocol. In *Proceedings of the 10th Annual ACM Symposium on Parallel Architectures and Algorithms*, Puerto Vallarta, Mexico, June 28–July 2 1998.

[19] Fong Pong, Michael Browne, Andreas Nowatzyk, and Michel Dubois. Design Verification of the S3.mp Cache-Coherent Shared-Memory System. *IEEE Transactions on Computers*, 47(1):135–140, January 1998.

[20] Dennis Shasha and Marc Snir. Efficient and Correct Execution of Parallel Programs that Share Memory. *ACM Transactions on Programming Languages and Systems*, 10(2):282–312, April 1988.

[21] Xiaowei Shen and Arvind. Specification of Memory Models and Design of Provably Correct Cache Coherence Protocols. Group Memo 398, Massachusetts Institute of Technology, June 1997.

[22] A. Singhal, D. Broniarczyk, F. Cerauskis, J. Price, L. Yuan, C. Cheng, D. Doblar, S. Fosth, N. Agarwal, K. Harvey, E. Hagersten, and B. Liencres. Gigaplane: A High Performance Bus for Large SMPs. *Hot Interconnects IV*, pages 41–52, 1996.

[23] Richard L. Sites, editor. *Alpha Architecture Reference*

Manual. Digital Press, 1992.

[24] Daniel J. Sorin, Manoj Plakal, Mark D. Hill, and Anne E. Condon. Lamport Clocks: Reasoning About Shared-Memory Correctness. Technical Report CS-TR-1367, University of Wisconsin-Madison, March 1998.

[25] David L. Weaver and Tom Germond, editors. *The SPARC Architecture Manual, Version 9.* Prentice Hall, 1994. SPARC International, Inc.

Appendix A: Proof of relationship between Wisconsin TSO and TSO

<u>Claim 1</u>: An implementation that satisfies Wisconsin TSO also satisfies TSO.

<u>Proof</u>: Suppose that an implementation satisfies Wisconsin TSO, i.e., for every execution on that implementation, there exists a total ordering $<_w$ of the LDs, $ST_{private}$s, and ST_{public}s satisfying Wisconsin TSO. We claim that the implementation satisfies TSO. To show this, we show that each execution that satisfies Wisconsin TSO also satisfies TSO. This is done by defining a new ordering $<_m$ of just LDs and STs by removing all $ST_{private}$s and using the order of ST_{public} to define the order of each ST. We claim that the resulting ordering $<_m$ satisfies TSO. To see this, consider the requirements of TSO:

1. If $X <_p Y$ and X is a LD or Y is a ST, then $X <_m Y$.

- First, suppose that X is a LD. There are two possibilities for Y: (a) Y is a LD. This follows from 1´. (b) Y is a ST. This follows from 1´ and 2´, since by 1´, $X <_w Y_{private}$ and by 2´, $Y_{private} <_w Y_{public}$.

- The other possibility is that X and Y are STs. In this case, $X_{public} <_w Y_{public}$ by property 2' and hence $X <_m Y$.

2. If an MB occurs between X and Y in program order, then $X <_m Y$.

Again, we have separate cases depending what X and Y are:

- X is a LD. Then $X <_p Y$ and so by our argument in 1, $X <_m Y$.

- X is a ST and Y is a ST. Follows from 3´.

- X is a ST and Y is a LD. Follows from 4´.

3. Let X be a LD of word, and Y be the ST to word w in memory order ($<_m$) satisfying the constraints of property 3. Let W be the ST (either a ST_{public} or a $ST_{private}$) to word w in Wisconsin order ($<_w$) satisfying the constraints of property 5'. We need to show that Y = W.

- Suppose that W is a ST_{public}, call it W_{public}. Then, from the constraints in 5´ on W, no ST before X in program order has its ST_{public} after X in Wisconsin order. Therefore, W_{public} is the greatest ST_{public} in Wisconsin order (and hence W is the greatest ST in memory order), taken over all ST_{public}s Z_{public} to word w for which either (i) Z_{public} occurs before X in Wisconsin order (i.e. Z occurs before X in memory order) or (ii) Z

occurs before X in program order (since there are no STs Z in category (ii) that are not already in category (i)). Hence Y = W.

- Suppose that W is a $ST_{private}$, call it $W_{private}$. Since $W_{private}$ satisfies the constraints of 5´, $W_{private}$ must be the most recent $ST_{private}$ at processor p before X in Wisconsin order (and so W must be the most recent ST before X in program order by 1´), and W_{public} must occur after X in Wisconsin order. Since the timestamps of ST_{public}s agree with the order of the corresponding STs in program order (by 3´), W_{public} is the greatest ST_{public} in Wisconsin order, taken over all ST_{public}s Z_{public} to word w for which either (i) Z_{public} occurs before X in Wisconsin order or (ii) Z occurs before X in program order. Therefore, Y = W.

Appendix B: Proof of relationship between Wisconsin Alpha and Alpha

<u>Claim 2</u>: An implementation that satisfies Wisconsin Alpha model also satisfies Alpha.

<u>Proof</u>: Suppose that an implementation satisfies Wisconsin Alpha i.e., for each execution of that implementation, there exists a total ordering of LDs, STs and MBs that satisfies the constraints of Wisconsin Alpha. We show that the implementation also satisfies Alpha by showing that each such execution also satisfies the constraints of Alpha. Given an ordering $<_w$ of LDs, STs and MBs in an execution that satisfies Wisconsin Alpha, let us define the access order for word w to be the ordering of LDs and STs on that word in $<_w$, and the issue order at a processor to be the ordering of LDs, STs and MBs issued at that processor in $<_w$. The "before" ordering is the transitive closure of issue order and access order. We now show that the two constraints of Alpha are met by these definitions of access order and "before":

- Let A and B be any 2 memory operations in the execution. Without loss of generality, suppose that operation A is before operation B. Since the before order is the transitive closure of the access and issue orders, and since $<_w$ respects both access and issue orders, then A $<_w$ B. Hence, it cannot be that B is also before A, because otherwise B $<_w$ A, which is impossible since Wisconsin Alpha order is a total order.

- A LD returns the value of the most recent store to the same location in the $<_w$ ordering which, from our definition of access order above, is also the most recent store to the same location in access order.

A Performance Comparison of Homeless and Home-based Lazy Release Consistency Protocols in Software Shared Memory

Alan L. Cox[†], Eyal de Lara[★], Charlie Hu[†], and Willy Zwaenepoel[†]
[†]Department of Computer Science
[★]Department of Electrical and Computer Engineering
Rice University
{alc, delara, ychu, willy}@cs.rice.edu

Abstract

In this paper, we compare the performance of two multiple-writer protocols based on lazy release consistency. In particular, we compare the performance of Princeton's home-based protocol and TreadMarks' protocol on a 32-processor platform. We found that the performance difference between the two protocols was less than 4% for four out of seven applications. For the three applications on which performance differed by more than 4%, the TreadMarks protocol performed better for two because most of their data were migratory, while the home-based protocol performed better for one. For this one application, the explicit control over the location of data provided by the home-based protocol resulted in a better distribution of communication load across the processors.

These results differ from those of a previous comparison of the two protocols. We attribute this difference to (1) a different ratio of memory to network bandwidth on our platform and (2) lazy diffing and request overlapping, two optimizations used by TreadMarks that were not used in the previous study.

1. Introduction

In this paper, we compare two page-based software distributed shared memory (DSM) protocols based on lazy release consistency. In particular, we compare the behavior of the two most popular multiple-writer protocols, Princeton's *home-based* protocol [9] and TreadMarks' *homeless* protocol [6], on a 32-processor platform. In summary, we found that the difference in performance between the protocols is small for most applications. Thus, our results differ from a previous study in which Princeton's home-based protocol significantly outperformed a homeless protocol [9].

We attribute the difference in our findings to two factors. First, our platform has a different ratio of memory

to network bandwidth. This ratio influences whether it is cheaper to use diffs, which are run-length encodings of the modifications to a page, versus full pages to maintain coherence. On the platform used in the previous study, applying a large diff was more expensive than sending a full page over the network, favoring the home-based protocol. Second, lazy diffing and request overlapping, two optimizations that are possible in a homeless protocol, and are used in TreadMarks, were not used in the previous study. In this paper, we quantify the importance of these optimizations on TreadMarks' performance.

We use seven applications: Red-Black SOR, IS, Gaussian Elimination, 3D FFT, TSP, Barnes-Hut, and Water. For four of these applications, the difference in execution time between the two protocols is less than 4%. For Water, IS and Barnes-Hut the difference is greater than 4%. The TreadMarks protocol performs better for Water and IS, two applications with mostly migratory data. On the other hand, the home-based protocol performs better for Barnes-Hut. The explicit control over the location of data provided by the home-based protocol resulted in a better distribution of communication load across the processors.

We perform our experiments on a network of 32 PCs using switched 100Mbps Ethernet. On this platform the best protocol for each application achieves speedups ranging from a worst case of 7.59 for Barnes-Hut using the home-based protocol to a best case of 25.5 for Red-Black SOR using either protocol. All of the programs achieve better speedups at 16 processors than at 8 processors. Comparing the speedups at 32 processors to the speedups at 16 processors, one program, Gaussian Elimination, slows down on the PCs. In addition, our results show that without lazy diffing and request overlapping TreadMarks' performance declines by as much as 85%.

The rest of this paper is organized as follows. Section 2 provides the necessary background on Lazy Release Consistency and the TreadMarks and home-based multiple-writer protocols. Section 3 describes our methodology, including the details on the platform that we used and the applications that we ran. Section 4 presents the results of our comparison. Finally, section 5 summarizes our conclusions.

2. Background

2.1 Lazy Release Consistency

Lazy release consistency (LRC) [6] is an algorithm that implements the release consistency (RC) [4] memory model. The LRC algorithm [6] delays the propagation of modifications to a processor until that processor performs an *acquire*. An acquire marks the beginning of a critical section. Specifically, LRC insures that the memory seen by the processor after an acquire is consistent with the happened-before-1 partial order [1].

2.2 Multiple-Writer Protocols

With a multiple-writer protocol, two or more processors can simultaneously modify their copy of a (shared) page. The two most popular multiple-writer protocols that are compatible with LRC are the TreadMarks protocol *(Tmk)* [6] and the Princeton home-based protocol *(HLRC)* [9].

In both protocols modifications to (shared) pages are detected by virtual memory faults *(twinning)* and captured by comparing the page to its twin *(diffing)* [5]. The protocols differ, however, in the location where modifications are kept and in the method by which they get propagated. These differences are described in detail below.

2.2.1 Tmk. In Tmk, a diff is not created for a modified (shared) page until a processor requests that diff in order to update its copy of the page. This *lazy* creation of diffs results in greater aggregation of changes, less diffing overhead and a reduced amount of consistency information.

When a processor faults, accessing an invalid page, it examines the write notices for that page. The write notices specify which processors have modified the page. Each write notice contains a vector timestamp that specifies the time of the modification. If one write notice's vector timestamp dominates the others, then the processor that created that write notice has all of the diffs required by the faulting processor to update its copy of the page. Thus, the faulting processor can obtain those diffs with a single request message. If, however, a page doesn't have a dominant write notice, that is, two or more write notices have concurrent vector timestamps, then the faulting processor has to send a request message to each of the

corresponding processors. These request messages are overlapped to reduce the time that the faulting processor will wait.

2.2.2 HLRC. In HLRC, every shared page is statically assigned a home processor by the program. At a *release*, which marks the end of a critical section, a processor immediately generates the diffs for the pages that it has modified since its last release. It then sends these diffs to their home processor(s), where they are immediately applied to the home's copy of the page. The home's copy of a page is never invalid, but it may be write protected.

When a processor faults, accessing an invalid page, it sends a request to the page's home processor. In current implementations, the home processor always responds with a complete copy of the page, instead of one or more diffs. Thus, a diff can be discarded by the creating and home processors as soon as it is applied to the home processor's copy of the page.

2.3 Comparing the Multiple-Writer Protocols

Both protocols have strengths and weaknesses when compared to each other. For migratory data, Tmk uses half as many messages, because it transfers the diff(s) directly from the last writer to next writer. (The current implementation of Tmk avoids the problem of diff accumulation through the methods described by Amza et al. [2].) For producer/consumer data, the two protocols use roughly the same number of messages. Any difference in favor of HLRC is a result of data aggregation. Any difference in favor of Tmk is typically a result of the producer and/or consumer changing. For data in a falsely shared page, that is written by multiple processors and then read by multiple processors, the difference between the protocols is the greatest. HLRC uses significantly fewer messages as the number of readers and writers increases. Specifically, for r readers and w writers, HLRC uses at most $2w+2r$ messages and Tmk uses at most $2wr$ messages.

Regardless of the sharing pattern, the assignment of pages to homes is extremely important to the performance of HLRC. A poor assignment can increase the number of diffs created, messages passed, and bytes transferred by an order of magnitude. On the other hand, a good assignment can have benefits that are not possible with Tmk. For example, in the case of producer/consumer sharing, assigning the page's home to the consumer eliminates any read access faults at the consumer, because the page is always valid. On the other hand, Tmk has its share of advantages: it typically (1) transfers less data because it uses diffs to update faulting processors and (2) creates fewer diffs because their creation is delayed until they are requested by a reader.

Applications	Size / Iterations	Sequential Times (in sec.)
Barnes-Hut	65536, 3	121.6
Water	1331, 10	235.6
IS	26 X 16, 10	150.5
RB SOR	8K x 4K, 20	73.3
Gauss	4096	1547.4
3D FFT	7x7x7, 10	99.2
TSP	19 cities	227.3

Table 1: Applications, input sizes, and sequential execution times.

3 Methodology

3.1 Platform

Our platform was a switched, full-duplex 100Mbps Ethernet of thirty-two 300 MHz Pentium II-based computers. Each computer has a 512K byte secondary cache and 256M bytes of memory. All of the computers were running FreeBSD 2.2.6 and communicating through UDP sockets. The round-trip latency for a 1-byte message is 126 microseconds. The time to acquire a lock varies from 178 to 272 microseconds. The time for a 32-processor barrier is 1,333 microseconds. The time to obtain a diff varies from 313 to 1,544 microseconds, depending on the size of the diff. The time to obtain a full page is 1,308 microseconds.

3.2 Applications

We used seven applications: Red-Black SOR, Gaussian Elimination, and TSP are distributed with TreadMarks; 3D FFT and IS are NAS benchmarks [3]; Barnes-Hut and Water are SPLASH benchmarks [7, 8]. Table 1 displays the input size and sequential execution time for each of the applications.

4 Results

This section has two parts. First, we compare Tmk and HLRC. Second, we quantify the effects of lazy diff creation and request overlapping on Tmk's performance.

4.1 Tmk vs. HLRC

Table 2 presents speedups for all of the applications under Tmk and HLRC. In the rest of this section, we focus on Barnes-Hut, IS, and Water, the only three applications for which the difference in execution time between the two protocols is greater than 4%.

Figures 1, 2 and 3 present the speedups, message counts, and data transferred for Barnes-Hut, IS, and Water on 8, 16, and 32 processors.

Application	Tmk			HLRC		
	8	16	32	8	16	32
Barnes-Hut	4.84	5.83	4.84	4.85	6.51	7.59
Water	5.63	9.18	11.4	5.36	8.09	9.45
IS	7.1	12.7	17.9	6.99	12.3	16.6
RB SOR	7.62	14.8	25.5	7.65	14.5	25.4
Gauss	6.43	8.98	8.32	6.35	8.80	7.98
3D FFT	4.37	8.29	15.1	4.40	8.28	15
TSP	7.41	13.2	21.2	7.36	13.3	21.1

Table 2: Speedups on 8, 16, and 32 processors for Tmk and HLRC.

4.1.1 Barnes-Hut [7] performs an N-body simulation using the hierarchical Barnes-Hut method. There are two shared data structures: a tree used to represent the recursively decomposed subdomain (cells) of the three-dimensional physical domain containing all of the particles; and an array of particles corresponding to the leaves of the tree. Every iteration rebuilds the tree on a single processor followed by a parallel force evaluation on the particles, during which most of the tree is read by all nodes. Updates to the particle array cause a high degree of false sharing. Hence, Barnes-Hut exhibits two different access patterns: the tree is written by a single processor but read by all; while the particle array is written and read by all.

In order to explain the difference in performance between the protocols, we present results for two home assignments: HLRC/all and HLRC/particle. In HLRC/all, the home assignment for the pages containing the tree and the particle array is based on a block distribution. In HLRC/particle only the particle array is distributed in block fashion, while pages containing the tree are assigned to processor 0, the processor that rebuilds the tree.

The purpose of HLRC/particle is to limit the differences between the two protocols' behavior to the multiple-writer pages. By making processor 0 the home for the tree it becomes the source for all tree updates, mimicking the behavior of Tmk, in which updates are kept by the last writer. Hence, Tmk's and HLRC/particle's handling of the producer/consumer tree data is identical, except for the difference of diffs vs. full pages. Thus, any difference in performance must result from the treatment of the falsely shared pages of the particle array.

Our results show that while HLRC/all significantly outperforms Tmk, the speedups for Tmk and HLRC/particle are nearly identical, in spite of the vast difference in message count (1.4 million vs. 130 thousand).

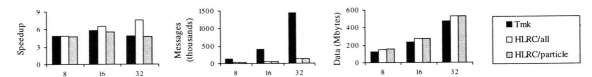

Figure 1: Speedup, messages, and data comparison among HLRC/all, HLRC/particle, and Tmk for Barnes-Hut.

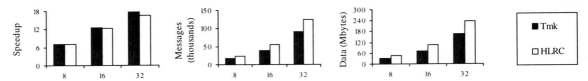

Figure 2: Speedup, messages, and data comparison among HLRC and Tmk for IS.

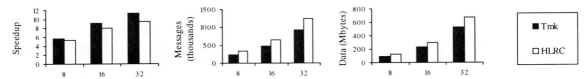

Figure 3: Speedup, messages, and data comparison among HLRC and Tmk for Water.

HLRC/particle demonstrates that HLRC's better performance does not result from a reduction in message count. Hence, the performance advantage of HLRC/all derives from its treatment of producer/consumer data (tree). The block assignment of tree pages lets HLRC/all distribute the responsibility for servicing update requests for the tree. Specifically, if the tree covers *n* pages and every processor reads the whole tree, then Tmk requires the producer of the tree to service *(p-1)*n* page requests. HLRC/all instead distributes the tree in *n*(p-1)/p* messages. After that the load of servicing the tree requests is evenly distributed.

4.1.2 IS [3] ranks a sequence of keys using a counting sort. First, processors count their keys in their private buckets. In the next phase, the values in the buckets are summed.

The sharing pattern in IS is migratory. There is no write-write false sharing, and the pages containing the shared buckets are completely overwritten by each processor. Home assignment in HLRC was done in a block fashion.

HLRC sends more messages and data than Tmk due to the migratory access pattern to the data. In HLRC, after a bucket is written, it is immediately flushed to its home processor. Since in most cases the home is not the next writer, the bucket has to be transferred a second time. In Tmk, the bucket is transferred once from the last writer to the new writer. The diff accumulation problem in Tmk is avoided through the method described by Amza et al. [2].

4.1.3 Water [8] is a molecular dynamics simulation. The main data structure in Water is a one-dimensional array of molecules. During each time step inter-molecular potentials are computed for each molecule. The parallel algorithm statically divides the array of molecules into equally large, contiguous blocks, assigning each block to a processor.

Water exhibits false sharing only for boundary pages between processors. Most of the data is shared in a migratory fashion. In HLRC, we assigned the shared molecule arrays in a block fashion.

HLRC sends more messages and data than Tmk. The reason is that it pushes diffs to their home immediately upon lock release, after a molecule is updated; whereas Tmk waits until a processor actually requests the diff. Consequently, a single diff under Tmk usually contains updates to several molecules by the time it is created. HLRC also suffers from sending whole pages, while updates of a molecule only modify about 100 bytes.

4.2 Lazy Diffing and Request Overlapping

We quantified the impact of lazy diffing and request overlapping on Tmk's performance by running the application suite on two modified versions of Tmk. In Tmk/eager, diffs are created as soon as the processor performs a release. In Tmk/sequential request overlapping is disabled. Table 3 presents the results.

Tmk/eager affected RB SOR the most. The factor of seven increase in execution time is a result of the creation of diffs for the inner rows of the band assigned to each processor. These pages are effectively private so the diffs are not used. Diff creation increased by a factor of 150. Furthermore, the amount of consistency data increased by a factor of 60.

Application	Tmk/eager			Tmk/sequential		
	8	16	32	8	16	32
Barnes-Hut	4.48	5.27	4.25	4.27	4.67	3.56
Water	5.36	fail	fail	5.6	9.09	11.1
IS	7.1	12.7	17.9	7.1	12.7	17.9
RB SOR	1.24	2.60	3.73	7.6	14.6	25.6
Gauss	1.01	1.82	2.35	6.43	8.98	8.3
3D FFT	4.37	8.29	15.1	4.15	8.08	14.8
TSP	7.41	13.1	21.4	7.36	13.2	21.1

Table 3: Effects of eager diff creation and sequential request on Tmk performance

Water would not complete on 16 and 32 processors for Tmk/eager. In both cases, eager diff creation led to a consistency message larger than the 64K byte maximum supported by UDP.

Tmk/sequential affected Barnes-Hut the most. It is the only application with significant false sharing. The disabling of request overlapping caused a 26% drop in performance.

5 Conclusions

Overall, the applications achieved speedups ranging from a worst case of 7.59 for Barnes-Hut using HLRC to a best case of 25.5 for Red-Black SOR using either protocol. All of the programs achieve better speedups at 16 processors than at 8 processors. Comparing the speedups at 32 processors to the speedups at 16 processors, one program, Gaussian Elimination, slows down. Overall, HLRC achieves from 1.6 times better speedup for Barnes-Hut to 1.2 times worse speedup for Water compared to TreadMarks.

We found the performance of the two protocols for four out of seven applications to be within 4% of each other. These results differ from a previous study where HLRC significantly outperformed a homeless protocol, like TreadMarks. We attribute the difference in our findings to two factors: a different ratio of memory to network bandwidth on our platform and lazy diffing and request overlapping, two optimizations used by TreadMarks that were not implemented in the previous study. Our results show that these optimizations are important: Without lazy diffing, RB SOR's execution

time increases by a factor of seven; and without request overlapping, Barnes-Hut's execution time increases by 26%.

Barnes-Hut, IS, and Water, were the only three applications for which the difference in execution time between the two protocols is greater than 4%. TreadMarks performed better for Water and IS; two applications with migratory access patterns. HLRC performed better for Barnes-Hut. Our results show, however, that the performance advantage of HLRC does not result from its lower message count (1.4 million vs. 130 thousand). It is, instead, a result of HLRC's ability to evenly distribute, among the processors, the responsibility for providing the updates for large data structures that are produced by a single processor and consumed by multiple processors. In effect, HLRC's home assignment striped these pages across the processors, thereby spreading the load of servicing updates.

References

[1]   S.V. Adve and M.D. Hill. A united formalization of four shared-memory models. *IEEE Transactions on Parallel and Distributed Systems*, 4(6):613-624, June 1993.

[2]   C. Amza, A.L. Cox, S. Dwarkadas, and W. Zwaenepoel. Software DSM protocols that adapt between single writer and multiple writer. *In Proceedings of the Third International Symposium on High Performance Computer Architecture*, pages 261-271, February 1997.

[3]   D. Bailey, J. Barton, T. Lasinski, and H. Simon. The NAS parallel benchmarks. Technical Report 103863, NASA, July 1993.

[4]   K. Gharachorloo, D. Lenoski, J. Laudon, P. Gibbons, A. Gupta, and J. Hennessy. Memory consistency and event ordering in scalable shared-memory multiprocessors. *In Proceedings of the 17th Annual International Symposium on Computer Architecture*, pages 15-26, May 1990.

[5]   P. Keleher, A. L. Cox, S. Dwarkadas, and W. Zwaenepoel. An evaluation of software-based release consistent protocols. *Journal of Parallel and Distributed Computing*, 29:126-141, October 1995.

[6]   P. Keleher, A. L. Cox, and W. Zwaenepoel. Lazy release consistency for software distributed shared memory. *In Proceedings of the 19th Annual International Symposium on Computer Architecture*, pages 13-21, May 1992.

[7]   J.P. Singh, W.-D. Weber, and A. Gupta. SPLASH: Stanford parallel applications for shared-memory. Technical Report CSL-TR-91-469, Stanford University, April 1991.

[8]   J.P. Singh, W.-D. Weber, and A. Gupta. SPLASH: Stanford parallel applications for shared-memory. Computer Architecture News, 20(1):2-12, March 1992.

[9]   Y. Zhou, L. Iftode, and K. Li. Performance evaluation of two home-based lazy release consistency protocols for shared virtual memory systems. *In Proceedings of the Second USENIX Symposium on Operating System Design and Implementation*, pages 75-88, November 1996.

MP-LOCKs: Replacing H/W Synchronization Primitives with Message Passing

Chen-Chi Kuo, John Carter, and Ravindra Kuramkote*

Department of Computer Science
University of Utah
Salt Lake City, UT 84112

Abstract

Shared memory programs guarantee the correctness of concurrent accesses to shared data using interprocessor synchronization operations. The most common synchronization operators are locks, which are traditionally implemented via a mix of shared memory accesses and hardware synchronization primitives like test-and-set. *In this paper, we argue that synchronization operations implemented using fast message passing and kernel-embedded lock managers are an attractive alternative to dedicated synchronization hardware. We propose three message passing lock (MP-LOCK) algorithms (centralized, distributed, and reactive) and provide implementation guidelines. MP-LOCKs reduce the design complexity and runtime occupancy of DSM controllers and can exploit software's inherent flexibility to adapt to differing applications lock access patterns. We compared the performance of MP-LOCKs with two common shared memory lock algorithms: test-and-test-and-set and MCS locks and found that MP-LOCKs scale better. For machines with 16 to 32 nodes, applications using MP-LOCKs ran up to 186% faster than the same applications with shared memory locks. For small systems (up to 8 nodes), three applications with MP-LOCKs slow down by no more than 18%, while the other two slowed by no more than 180% due to higher software overhead. We conclude that locks based on message passing should be considered as a replacement for hardware locks in future scalable multiprocessors that support efficient message passing mechanisms.*

1 Introduction

To guarantee semantic correctness, shared memory programs must control concurrent accesses to shared data via synchronization operations, the most common of which are *lock* and *unlock*. An inefficient implementation of synchronization impacts the performance of shared memory programs both directly, via the time required to perform the synchronization operations, and indirectly, by increasing the amount of time processes are blocked waiting for other processes to relinquish locks. As a general rule, multiprocessor architects tend to implement primitive operations using custom hardware. For example, lock and unlock operations traditionally have been implemented using a combination of hardware-implemented shared memory and atomic synchroniza-

tion primitives (e.g., *test-and-set* (T&S), *compare-and-swap*, and *load-linked/store-conditional*). Recently, however, the designers of the Cray T3E broke this rule and abandoned the dedicated high performance hardware barrier network that was supported in the T3D. We believe a similar argument applies to locks and that emerging high performance message passing mechanisms make locks based on message passing a viable alternative to hardware locks in future scalable multiprocessors.

Test-and-Set (T&S) locks spin on shared memory locations using hardware T&S instructions. The major problem with T&S locks is that every T&S instruction performed while spinning involves *global* communication. *Test-Test-and-Set* (T&T&S) locks [13] add an extra shared-memory "load" before the T&S primitive to eliminate these unnecessary migrations. However, their performance degrades when multiple nodes are waiting for a lock to be released

Mellor-Crummey and Scott (MCS) [9] locks avoid global spinning entirely by maintaining a distributed queue of processes waiting for a lock. This design can improve performance by reducing global communication and it also guarantees that locks are granted in FIFO order. The downside of MCS locks is that they involve more global operations than T&T&S locks when a lock is free.

Because the performance of T&T&S and MCS locks are heavily dependent on the lock access patterns of cooperative parallel processes, Lim and Agarwal proposed an adaptive scheme called *Reactive* locks [8] that adopts either T&T&S or MCS lock semantics depending on the degree of lock contention.

Finally, the Queue-On-Lock-Bit (QOLB) mechanism [4] associates a special lock bit with cache lines of data. While a complete hardware implementation of QOLB may be the most efficient lock mechanism proposed, it requires significant changes to processor, cache controller, and DSM protocol engine designs. Because they are unsuitable for implementation on multiprocessors based on current commodity microprocessors, we do not consider QOLB locks further.

Conventional shared memory lock mechanisms (T&T&S, MCS, and Reactive locks) were designed based on the performance characteristics of bus-based architectures. On these machines, broadcast invalidations or updates are cheap. However, as remote access becomes increasingly expensive in scalable architectures and as the gap between the speeds of processor and I/O widens, other approaches must be considered.

Many contemporary multiprocessor architectures support efficient message passing in addition to shared memory [5, 7, 12], and an increasing number of high performance of network interfaces and protocols have been proposed [1, 2, 11, 15]. We propose that low latency message passing be exploited to implement synchronization, rather than using hardware synchronization primitives. We call this method of implementing lock primitives via message passing *MP-LOCK*. Instead of using primitive synchroniza-

Email addresses: {chenchi,retrac,kuramkot}@cs.utah.edu.
This research was supported in part by the Space and Naval Warfare Systems Command (SPAWAR) and the Advanced Research Projects Agency (ARPA), under SPAWAR contract No.#N0039-95-C-0018 and ARPA Order No.#B990. The views and conclusions contained herein are those of the authors and should not be interpreted as necessarily representing the official policies or endorsements, either expressed or implied, of DARPA, SPAWAR, or the US Government.

tion operations and shared memory to acquire and release locks, MP-LOCKs send messages to lock managers, which mediate lock requests. In our implementation of MP-LOCKs, the lock managers are embedded inside the operating system kernel to guarantee fast responses to lock requests. In addition to eliminating the design overhead of supporting scalable synchronization primitives in hardware, software's inherent flexibility can be exploited to provide different implementations of locks (e.g., T&T&S style, QOLB style, etc.). MP-LOCKs also can minimize the number of network transfers required to transfer lock ownership, because they do not suffer from unnecessary invalidations and reloads due to the use of general purpose shared memory protocols. Furthermore, MP-LOCKs offload work from the DSM controller to the network controller, thereby reducing DSM controller occupancy. Finally, MP-LOCK's software implementation makes prefetching data (as in QOLB) feasible without the need for non-standard hardware, which should shrink critical sections [4].

To evaluate the tradeoffs of implementing locks in software, we compared the performance of message passing locks with T&T&S and MCS locks on five application programs with fairly heavy synchronization requirements. Although most previous locking studies have concentrated on microbenchmarks, we focused on complete applications to determine the overall impact of using the various locking mechanisms. We found that message passing locks scale better - for machines with 16 to 32 nodes, applications using MP-LOCKs ran up to 186% faster than the same applications with shared memory locks. For small systems (up to 8 nodes), MP-LOCK performance lags shared memory lock performance due to the higher software overhead. However, three of the MP-LOCK applications slow down by no more than 18%, while the other two slowed by no more than 180%.

The remainder of this paper is organized as follows. Section 2 presents three MP-LOCK algorithms. We describe our simulation environment, and test applications in Section 3, and present the results of our experiments in Section 4. Finally, we draw conclusions in Section 5.

2 Design of MP-LOCK

MP-LOCK is a software-based lock mechanism that requires no special-purpose hardware or atomic primitives. The MP-LOCK model has *lock managers* that manage lock ownership. We evaluated three lock manager organizations: (i) a single centralized lock manager (MP-cent), (ii) a set of cooperating lock managers running on each node (MP-dist), and (iii) an adaptive distributed manager that reverts to centralized mode when there is little contention (MP-react). Rather than using shared memory loads/stores and atomic primitives, MP-LOCK synchronization libraries send lock requests to a lock manager. For each request, the lock manager will either queue the request until it can be satisfied or forward it to the lock manager that currently has the lock. We evaluated both user-level and in-kernel lock managers and found that the context switching overhead of user-level lock managers is significant. Therefore, in this paper we restrict our focus to in-kernel lock managers.

To facilitate designing MP-LOCK algorithms, we classify lock acquires into three categories depending on the state the lock is in when the acquire is initiated: *remote idle acquire*, *local idle acquire*, and *remote busy acquire*. A *remote idle acquire* occurs when some node Y attempts to acquire the lock after some other node X has released it. The acquire in this case will succeed immediately after the remote operations required to detect and update the lock status complete. A *local idle acquire* is the same as a *remote idle acquire* state, except X and Y are the same nodes. Both of the idle cases occur frequently when there is little contention. A *remote busy acquire* occurs when an acquire from node Y is issued before the current lock holder, a different node X, releases the lock. This occurs frequently when there is high contention for locks. We found that performance of an implementation primarily depends on two factors: the number of messages (which we call *hops*) that must be sent to acquire or release a lock and the number of interrupts required on all nodes to acquire or release.

In MP-cent, lock managers handle both lock and unlock requests. A node acquires a lock by performing a non-blocking send to a designated lock manager and then spins while waiting for a reply. A releasing node also does a non-blocking send to the central lock manager. An acquire request is granted immediately if the lock is free. Otherwise, the acquire request is queued until lock ownership is returned. Conceptually, MP-cent is similar to T&T&S, which snoops on a global location. However, T&T&S requires up to 8 hops to read a valid lock variable and to acquire exclusive ownership when the lock is free. Acquiring a lock in MP-cent requires only 2 hops and one interrupt at the central lock manager under all circumstances. MP-cent performs well when multiple processes acquire the lock with little contention. However, the lack of support for "caching" and "forwarding" leads to poor performance for local idle or remote busy acquires.

In MP-dist, lock managers cooperate to manage a distributed queue of pending lock requests. When a process wants to acquire a lock, it consults its local lock manager. If the lock is free and the lock ownership is "cached" locally, the local lock manager returns the lock immediately. Otherwise, the process sends the lock request to a designated remote lock manager, which either returns the lock or forwards the request. To release a lock, a process consults its local lock manager. If a request is pending, ownership of the lock is "forwarded" to the requesting process directly in a single message. If no request is pending, the local lock manager caches the lock ownership.

MP-dist performs well for locks that are heavily contested or frequently reused. During periods of heavy contention, lock ownership will be passed between successive owners directly via a single message, and the extra latency and messages required to forward the lock request to the end of the queue is effectively hidden as part of the required stall until the lock is free. When lock reacquisition (local idle acquires) is common, MP-dist's caching of lock ownership makes acquires very cheap. However, when most acquires are remote idle acquires, MP-dist performs relatively poorly - it requires on average 3 hops (messages) and 2 interrupts to transfer the ownership from the current holder and to the requester.

Because different applications have very different lock request patterns, we developed a reactive lock protocol, akin to Reactive locks [8], called MP-react. Since lock managers mediate both lock acquire and release requests, they have accurate knowledge of lock access patterns. A central lock manager initially grants "uncachable" locks so that lock ownership is returned when locks are released. Acquire requests on these locks require two hops to be satisfied, as in MP-cent. If the lock manager detects repeated requests from the same node without intervening requests from other nodes, it grants a "cachable" instance of the lock so that it can be reacquired by the node without performing any remote operations. When a lock is heavily contested, the lock manager will "forward"

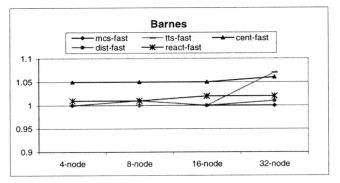

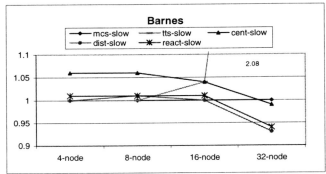

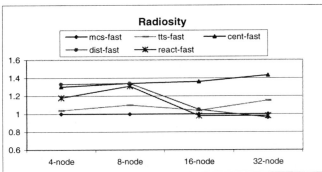

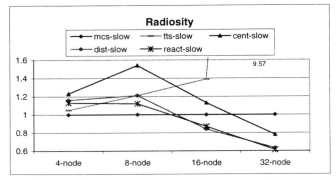

Figure 1. Performance Charts for `barnes` **and** `radiosity` **(execution time relative to MCS).**

acquire requests as in MP-dist so that ownership transfers will take one hop. MP-react has better information about access patterns than Reactive locks because the central lock manager can track all accesses. Thus, MP-react can make more effective decisions about when to switch modes.

To minimize the overhead of MP-LOCK's software implementation, we used a low latency message passing mechanism called *Direct Deposit (DD)* [15] and embedded lock managers in the kernel. We also carefully distributed lock management across nodes to minimize load imbalance effects. The pertinent implementation details can be found in an expanded version of this paper [6]

3 Simulation Methodology and Benchmarks

All experiments were performed using an execution-driven simulation of the Avalanche architecture [3]. The simulation environment includes a kernel based on 4.4BSD that provides scheduling, interrupt handling, memory management, and limited system call capabilities. Simulating the kernel provides a fair accounting for our software-based MP-LOCK overheads. For our interconnect, we modeled a Myrinet network. We ran our experiments with two different switch fall through delays of 4 and 176 cycles to model both high-end commercial DSM systems and DSM systems or clusters of workstations that use less aggressive off-the-shelf interconnects.

We used five programs to conduct our study: `mp3d` from the SPLASH benchmark suite [14], `barnes`, `radiosity`, and `raytrace` from the SPLASH-2 benchmark suite [16], and `spark98` from a sparse matrix kernel suite [10]. We believe a broad set synchronization access patterns are well represented by these five applications.

The detailed simulation parameters, application sizes and the distribution of lock categories for the applications we studied can

be found in the expanded version of this paper [6].

4 Results

Figures 1 and 2 present the performance of MCS, T&T&S, MP-cent, MP-dist, and MP-react relative to the MCS lock version on three of the five applications we studied. We present two graphs for each application. The graph on the left presents the results using the fast interconnect and the graphs on the right present the results using the slow interconnect. Graphs for `raytrace` and `spark98` and detailed breakdown graphs of the execution time can be found in the expanded paper [6].

In `barnes`, most of synchronization occurs while initializing an octree structure that represents 3-D space. Although the average critical section is long, the chance of two processes contending for the same lock is small. Therefore, only 2% of the lock acquires occur when the lock is busy and 73% of the locks are "reused" by the same node in a 4-node system. Since the time spent on synchronization is small compared to the overall execution time, there is little need for special hardware support for locking – MP-LOCKs can provide equal or better performance than shared memory locks. As shown in Figure 1, the shared memory lock implementations (MCS and T&T&S) and MP-LOCK implementations (distributed and reactive) perform equally well in all cases except for the 32-node slow interconnect configuration. The lack of caching penalizes MP-cent, which underperforms the other four implementations by about 5%. As the number of nodes increases from 4 to 32, the degree of lock contention increases from 2% to 25%. The controller occupancy and cache conflicts also increase the user shared memory access time noticeably for the shared memory locks. As a result, MP-dist outperforms MCS by 8% at the 32-node slow interconnect configuration.

In `radiosity`, the degree of contention for locks used to pro-

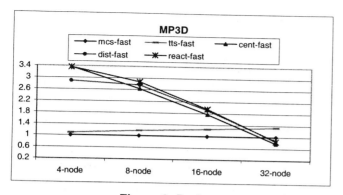
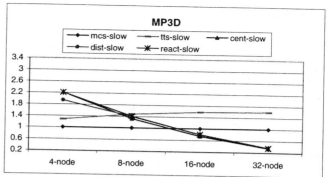

Figure 2. Performance Charts for mp3d **(execution time relative to MCS).**

tect distributed queues, a global barrier, and a buffer pool depends on the number of nodes. For small systems (4 - 8 nodes), most lock acquires are local idle acquires. Locks used to protect image patches show little contention due to their fine granularity. However, the poor temporal locality of these patch locks result in most accesses to them being of the remote idle variety. Due to the low level of contention and MP-LOCK's higher software overhead, MCS locks perform 18% better than MP-LOCKs in the 4-node fast interconnect configuration. However, with a slow interconnect, the increased shared memory access time reduces the performance gap to 13%. As the number of nodes increases, contention increases. This leads to an decrease in the percentage of local idle acquires from 57% to less than 20%, and an increase in the percentage of remote busy acquires from 6% to about 60%. Regardless of configuration, the percentage of remote idle acquires is constant at about 20% because of the large amount number of fine grained patch locks. As a result of these changes in lock access pattern, MP-react starts to outperform MCS at the 16-node configuration and by the time the configuration reached 32 nodes, it outperforms MCS locks by up to 64%. Comparing just the MP-LOCK schemes, when contention is low, MP-cent outperforms MP-dist, as expected. But as the number of nodes and/or network latency increases, MP-dist prevails. MP-react, which is able to adapt to the best of MP-cent and MP-dist, performs up to 10% better than either schemes.

Locks in raytrace are accessed in a manner similar to the locks used in radiosity. In the 4- and 8-node configurations, acquires to the locks that protect a memory pool are mostly remote idle, a category that accounts for 52% of lock requests. In these same small configurations, the locks protecting the distributed task queues are mostly local idle. Thus, for small configurations, shared memory locks perform up to 14% better than MP-LOCKs. As the number of nodes increases, both sets of locks become busy. As a result, 97% of the locks in the 32-node configuration are heavily contested, which causes MP-LOCKs to perform up to 75% better than the shared memory locks for the same reasons as in radiosity.

In mp3d, the degree of contention for locks is extremely low – 2% or fewer of the acquires are to busy locks. In addition, there is very little reuse, so most acquires fall into the remote idle category. In this case, MP-LOCKs require up to two interrupts (one at the lock manager and one at the current lock holder) and three hops to acquire a lock. Thus, for 4 and 8 nodes, shared memory locks outperform the MP-LOCK implementations by up to 180%. The performance gap shrinks as the number of nodes and/or network latency increases due to (i) the tight dependence between shared

memory lock performance and remote memory access latency and (ii) the severe impact on DSM controller occupancy caused by shared memory locks. For example, MP-LOCKs perform better than MCS in the 16-node configuration with a slower network and up to 186% better in the 32-node configuration. Comparing just the MP-LOCK mechanisms, MP-cent outperforms MP-dist in the 32-node configuration because 94% of locks accesses are to remote idle locks. However, only 73% of lock accesses are to remote idle locks in the 4-noode configuration, so MP-dist outperforms MP-cent because of lock caching.

In Spark98, locks have good temporal locality due to the way that processes are assigned work. In the 4-node and 8-node configurations, shared memory locks perform 70% better than MP-LOCKs due to their low-latency lock/unlock routines. As the number of nodes and/or network latency increases, however, MP-LOCKs perform up to 163% better than shared memory locks.

In summary, for applications with high lock contention, the best MP-LOCK algorithm outperforms the best shared memory lock algorithm by up to 186%. In particular, MP-LOCKs tend to outperform shared memory locks once the the system size reaches 16 nodes with a fast interconnect or 8 nodes with a slow interconnect. The superior scalability of MP-LOCKs on these applications occurs for several reasons. First, MP-LOCKs handle remote busy locks better than shared memory locks, because lock ownership can be forwarded in a single message. To achieve similar performance, shared memory locks would require special hardware shared memory protocols not present in modern machines. Second, MP-LOCKs neither increase DSM controller occupancy nor interfere with shared memory data accesses, which can lead to significantly lower average remote memory latency for non-lock shared data. Finally, the software overhead induced by lock managers can be amortized across nodes, which reduces its impact. For applications with low lock contention, MP-LOCKs underperform the best shared memory lock implementation on small systems (4 nodes or 8 nodes) by up to 18% in three applications and no more than 180% in the remaining two applications. Fast hardware shared memory lock implementations can handle low contention locks more efficiently than MP-LOCKs. Given the trends we observed, we expect that MP-LOCKs will scale better than shared memory locks as the number of nodes increases beyond 32 nodes. Thus, we believe that MP-LOCKs are an attractive alternative to hardware synchronization primitives for future scalable shared memory multiprocessors that support efficient message passing.

5 Conclusions

In this paper, we demonstrate that software-based locks are an attractive alternative to hardware-based implementations. The so-called MP-LOCK approach is based on efficient message passing mechanisms that can be supported by most contemporary multiprocessor interconnects. By basing locks on message passing rather than dedicated hardware, MP-LOCK reduces the design complexity and runtime occupancy of DSM controllers. In addition, MP-LOCKs can exploit software's inherent flexibility to support lock protocols that intelligently adapt to differing application lock access patterns.

We evaluated the performance of three MP-LOCK algorithms against that of two efficient hardware-based locks algorithms, test-and-test-and-set[13] and MCS locks[9], on five applications with a variety of lock access patterns. We found that MP-LOCKs scale better than T&T&S or MCS locks because they avoid the use of shared memory and instead support direct point-to-point transfer of lock ownership during periods of high lock contention. As a result, MP-LOCKs consistently perform equal to or better than hardware locks for systems consisting of sixteen or more nodes. In the extreme, the use of MP-LOCKs improved performance by up to 186%. However, for small system sizes, e.g., 4 - 8 nodes, interrupt handling and software overhead caused the performance of the MP-LOCK versions to lag that of shared memory locks. However, the difference was no more than 18% in three applications and no more than 180% in the remaining two applications.

Focusing on the MP-LOCK algorithms in isolation, we found that MP-cent performed best for applications like mp3d with poor lock locality, and thus frequent remote idle accesses. The reason is that for these applications relinquishing locks back to a per-lock centralized lock manager minimizes message traffic. However, when contention is high or locks are reused frequently, MP-dist significantly outperforms MP-cent, because direct lock forwarding and lock caching effectively handle these situations. MP-react exploits global access pattern observations to adaptively switch between centralized and distributed modes, which leads to good overall performance and the best performance for applications that demonstrate a mix of access patterns.

This paper makes several contributions. We present the results of the first study that compares the performance of message passing locks and shared memory locks on macrobenchmarks. We took great pains to conduct a fair comparison by including a detailed 4.4BSD-based kernel in our simulation environment to accurately simulate the software overhead of the proposed message passing mechanisms. Second, we identified the tradeoffs for shared memory locks and message passing locks as system sizes and network latencies vary. These results should assist future architects when designing their synchronization mechanisms. Third, we classified the lock access patterns of five well-known shared memory benchmarks on various number of processors, which will help other researchers understand the locking behavior of these applications. Finally, we provided guidelines for designing synchronization mechanisms in clusters of workstations that are equipped with message passing communication mechanisms. For example, we show that lock caching is essential when designing message-passing based locks.

6 Acknowledgements

We would like to thank Leigh Stoller and Mark Swanson who provided invaluable assistance in using *Direct Deposit* protocol. Al Davis and Michael Scott provided helpful comments on this work. We also thank the members of *Avalanche* project at the University of Utah and the referees for many useful suggestions.

References

[1] A. Basu, V. Buch, W. Vogels, and T. von Eicken. U-net: A user-level network interface for parallel and distributed computing. In *Proc. of the 15th SOSP*, December 1995.

[2] G. Buzzard, D.Jacobson, M. Mackey, S. Marovich, and J. Wilkes. An implementation of the hamlyn sender-managed interface architecture. In *Proc. of the 2nd OSDI*, October 1996.

[3] J. Carter, A. Davis, R. Kuramkot, C.-C. Kuo, M. Swanson, and L. Stoller. Avalanche: A communication and memory architecture for scalable parallel computing. TR UUCS-95-022, Univ. of Utah, 1995.

[4] A. Kagi, D. Burger, and J. Goodman. Efficient synchronization: Let them eat qolb. In *Proc. of the 24th ISCA*, May 1997.

[5] D. Kranz, K. Johnson, A. Agarwal, J. Kubiatowicz, and B.-H. Lim. Integrating message-passing and shared-memory; early experience. In *Proc. of the 1993 PPoPP*, pp. 54–63, May 1993.

[6] C.-C. Kuo, J. Carter, and R. Kuramkote. MP-LOCKs: Replacing h/w synchronization primitives with message passing. TR UUCS-98-021, Univ. of Utah, November 1998.

[7] J. Kuskin and D. O. et al. The Stanford FLASH multiprocessor. In *Proc. of the 21st ISCA*, pp. 302–313, May 1994.

[8] B.-H. Lim and A. Agarwal. Reactive synchronization algorithms for multiprocessors. In *Proc. of the Sixth ASPLOS (ASPLOS-VI)*, pp. 25–35, October 1994.

[9] J. M. Mellor-Crummey and M. L. Scott. Algorithms for scalable synchronization on shared-memory multiprocessors. *ACM Trans. on Computer Systems*, 9(1):21–65, February 1991.

[10] D. O'Hallaron, J. Shewchuk, and T. Gross. Architectural implications of a family of irregular computations. In *Proc. of the Fifth HPCA*, pp. 80–89, Feb. 1998.

[11] S. Paikin, Lauria, and A. Chien. High performance messaging on workstations: Illinois fast messages (fm) for myrinet. In *Proc. of SC '88*, 1995.

[12] S. Reinhardt, J. Larus, and D. Wood. Tempest and Typhoon: User-level shared memory. In *Proc. of the 21st ISCA*, pp. 325–336, Apr. 1994.

[13] L. Rudolph and Z. Segall. Dynamic decentralized cache schemes for mimd parallel processors. In *Proc. of the 11th ISCA*, pp. 340–347, May 1984.

[14] J. Singh, W.-D. Weber, and A. Gupta. SPLASH: Stanford parallel applications for shared-memory. TR CSL-TR-91-469, Stanford Univ., Apr. 1991.

[15] L. Stoller and M. Swanson. Direct deposit: A basic user-level protocol for carpet clusters. TR UUCS-95-003, Univ. of Utah, March 1995.

[16] S. Woo, M. Ohara, E. Torrie, J. Singh, and A. Gupta. The SPLASH-2 programs: Characterization and methodological considerations. In *Proc. of the 22nd ISCA*, pp. 24–36, June 1995.

Session 7B

Communication Issues II

Efficient All-to-All Broadcast in All-Port Mesh and Torus Networks

Yuanyuan Yang*
Department of Computer Science
University of Vermont, Burlington, VT 05405
yang@cs.uvm.edu

Jianchao Wang
GTE Laboratories
40 Sylvan Road, Waltham, MA 02454
jwang@gte.com

Abstract

All-to-all communication is one of the most dense communication patterns and occurs in many important applications in parallel computing. In this paper, we present a new all-to-all broadcast algorithm in all-port mesh and torus networks. Unlike existing all-to-all broadcast algorithms, the new algorithm takes advantage of overlapping of message switching time and transmission time, and achieves optimal transmission time for all-to-all broadcast. In addition, in most cases, the total communication delay is close to the lower bound of all-to-all broadcast within a small constant range. Finally, the algorithm is conceptually simple, and symmetrical for every message and every node so that it can be easily implemented in hardware and achieves the optimum in practice.

Index Terms: Parallel computing, collective communication, all-to-all communication, all-to-all broadcast, routing, interprocessor communication.

1 Introduction

Collective communication [1] involves global data movement and global control among a group of processors in a multicomputer. Many scientific applications exhibit the need of such communication patterns. Collective communication has received much attention in parallel processing community in recent years; see, for example, [1]-[15]. *All-to-all communication* is one of the most dense collective communication patterns and has been extensively studied in the past few years [5]-[15]. In all-to-all communication, every processor in a processor group sends a message to all other processors in the group. Depending on the nature of the message to be sent, all-to-all communication can be further classified as *all-to-all broadcast* and *all-to-all personalized exchange*. In all-to-all broadcast, every node sends the same message to all other nodes, and in all-to-all personalized exchange, every node sends a distinct message to every other node. Clearly, all-to-all broadcast can be viewed as a special case of all-to-all personalized exchange. Although the latter

is functionally more powerful than the former, it can be expected that the former should take less communication time in the same system. In many applications, such as matrix multiplication, LU-factorization, Householder transformations, and basic linear algebra operations, only all-to-all broadcast communication is needed [16, 17]. In this paper, we will be mainly interested in efficient all-to-all broadcasting.

The networks considered in this paper are meshes and tori, which have a simple, regular topology and a bounded node degree. Meshes and tori have become more and more popular for interconnecting the processors in parallel and distributed computing systems due to their better scalability compared with high-dimensional networks such as hypercubes.

In this paper, we assume a communication model where each communication channel is full-duplex and each node has all-port capability. In other words, a node in the network can simultaneously send and receive messages on a channel, and at any time each node can communicate with all its neighboring node simultaneously. We also assume that the messages broadcast from all nodes are of the same length.

There has been much work for all-to-all personalized exchange in meshes and tori, see for example, [5]-[11], and a few for all-to-all broadcast in meshes and tori, see [12] and [15]. Saad and Schultz [12] proposed an all-to-all broadcast algorithm for tori, in which each node first sends a message along horizontal rings and then sends the messages collected in horizontal direction along vertical rings. Calvin, Perennes, and Trystram [15] presented a recursive algorithm for all-to-all broadcast in a torus. In their algorithm, the torus is decomposed into smaller size subnetworks, the center of each subnetwork collects all messages within the subnetwork, then the messages collected are exchanged among the centers of different subnetworks, and finally each center broadcasts the messages from other subnetworks to all nodes in its own subnetwork.

A common idea in designing all-to-all broadcast algorithms is to achieve some degree of parallelism in message transmission. In the existing work, although some degree of parallelism was achieved among the messages passing through different nodes, no time overlap for the messages passing through the same node. This is because that in these designs each node can start to relay one message only after it completes the transmission of the previous message. In this

---

*Research supported by the U.S. Army Research Office under Grant No. DAAH04-96-1-0234 and by the National Science Foundation under Grant No. OSR-9350540.

paper, we adopt a different approach to further explore the parallelism in message transmission. We propose a new algorithm for all-to-all broadcast on 2D meshes and tori, in which some degree of parallelism is achieved among the messages passing through the same node. The newly proposed algorithm is optimal in message transmission time, and in most cases, the total communication delay is close to the lower bound of all-to-all broadcast within a small constant range. In addition, our algorithm is conceptually simple, and symmetrical for every message and every node. The algorithm can be easily implemented in hardware, so that it can achieve the optimum in practice. As can be seen later, the optimal algorithm presented in this paper for all-to-all broadcast on a 2D mesh or torus of size N takes $O(N)$ time, while the algorithms in the literature for all-to-all personalized exchange on a 2D mesh or torus take $O(N^{\frac{3}{2}})$ time.

2 Properties of Meshes and Tori

In this section, we discuss some properties of meshes and tori that are useful in designing our all-to-all broadcast algorithm.

A 2-dimensional mesh or torus we consider in this paper has n^2 nodes, with n nodes along each dimension. Each node is identified by two coordinates (x, y). A node (x, y) in a mesh or torus may have up to four neighbors $(x - 1, y)$, $(x+1, y)$, $(x, y-1)$, and $(x, y+1)$, depending on the type of networks and the location of node (x, y). In an infinite mesh, where each dimension has an infinite number of nodes, each node has exactly four neighbors. In an $n \times n$ mesh, the nodes at four corners of the mesh have a degree of 2, other nodes on the boundary of the mesh have a degree of 3, and the rest of nodes have a degree of 4. In an $n \times n$ torus, each node has four neighbors, but the "plus 1" and "minus 1" operations are performed in modulo n.

The *distance* between two nodes $P_1 = (x_1, y_1)$ and $P_2 = (x_2, y_2)$ in a mesh or torus is defined as the length of the shortest path between these two nodes in the network. In a mesh the distance between P_1 and P_2 is simply

$$dist(P_1, P_2) = |x_1 - x_2| + |y_1 - y_2| \quad (1)$$

while in an $n \times n$ torus, due to the wraparounds in both horizontal and vertical directions the distance is

$$dist(P_1, P_2) = \min\{|x_1 - x_2|, n - |x_1 - x_2|\} + \min\{|y_1 - y_2|, n - |y_1 - y_2|\} \quad (2)$$

Figure 1 shows the distance between two nodes in a mesh. If the distance between two nodes is d, we refer to one node as a *d-neighbor* of the other node. For example, in Figure 1 node $(-1, -1)$ is a 6-neighbor of node $(2, 2)$, and vice versa.

The *diameter* of a mesh or torus is the maximum distance between any two nodes in the network. Thus for an $n \times n$ mesh, the diameter is $2(n - 1)$, and for an $n \times n$ torus, the diameter is $2\lfloor \frac{n}{2} \rfloor$.

Figure 1: The distance between node $(-1, -1)$ and node $(2, 2)$ in a mesh is 6.

The *circle* centered at node P_0 in a mesh or torus is defined as the set of nodes which have an equal distance to P_0, while this distance is called the *radius* of the circle. The *perimeter* of a circle is defined as the cardinality of the node set of the circle. The perimeter of a circle with radius d is denoted as C_d. Next, we explore some useful properties of circles in a mesh or torus. For presentational convenience, we first consider an infinite mesh.

Lemma 1 *In an infinite mesh, the perimeter of a circle with radius d is*

$$C_d = \begin{cases} 1 & \text{if } d = 0 \\ 4d & \text{if } d \geq 1 \end{cases} \quad (3)$$

Proof. By definition, a circle centered at node (x_0, y_0) with radius d in an infinite mesh can be expressed as a set

$$\{(x, y) \mid |x - x_0| + |y - y_0| = d\}$$

Without loss of generality, we can assume $x_0 = y_0 = 0$. That is, C_d is the number of different integer solutions of (x, y) for the equation

$$|x| + |y| = d. \quad (4)$$

Clearly, for $d = 0$, we have a unique solution $x = y = 0$, i.e. $C_d = 1$. We now discuss the cases of $d > 0$,

Case 1: For a given x, $1 \leq |x| \leq d - 1$.
From (4) we have $y = \pm(d - |x|)$. Thus for a given x, there are two possible values for y. Since we have a total of $2(d - 1)$ possible values for x in this case, there are $2 \times 2(d - 1) = 4(d - 1)$ different integer solutions of (x, y) for (4).

Case 2: $x = 0$.
We have $y = \pm d$. Hence, there are two different integer solutions.

Case 3: $x = \pm d$.
We have $y = 0$. There are also two different integer solutions.

In total, there are $4(d - 1) + 2 + 2 = 4d$ different integer solutions of (x, y) for (4). That is, $C_d = 4d$. ∎

Figure 2 depicts the circles centered at the same node with different radii in a mesh, where the number on each node represents the distance between the node and the center.

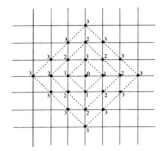

Figure 2: Circles centered at the same node with different radii in a mesh.

Since a torus can be considered as a mesh with wraparound links, all nodes in a torus are topologically symmetric. The following lemma gives the perimeter of a circle in an $n \times n$ torus.

Lemma 2 *In a $(2k + 1) \times (2k + 1)$ torus, the perimeter of a circle with radius d, where $0 \leq d \leq 2k$, is*

$$C_d = \begin{cases} 1 & \text{if } d = 0 \\ 4d & \text{if } 1 \leq d \leq k \\ 4(2k + 1 - d) & \text{if } k + 1 \leq d \leq 2k \end{cases} \quad (5)$$

Proof. Similar to the proof of Lemma 1, we still consider a circle centered at node (x_0, y_0) with radius d in an $n \times n$ torus where $n = 2k + 1$, which can be expressed as a set

$$\{(x, y) \mid \min\{|x - x_0|, n - |x - x_0|\} + \min\{|y - y_0|, n - |y - y_0|\} = d\}$$

Notice that in a torus, we must have that $d \leq 2\lfloor \frac{n}{2} \rfloor = 2k$. Due to the node symmetry of a torus, without loss of generality we can assume $x_0 = y_0 = 0$ and consider all nodes (x, y) for $-k \leq x, y \leq k$. Then C_d is the number of different integer solutions of (x, y) for the equation

$$\min\{|x|, n - |x|\} + \min\{|y|, n - |y|\} = d \quad (6)$$

Since $|x| \leq k$ implies $n - |x| = 2k + 1 - |x| \geq k + 1 > |x|$, we obtain that $\min\{|x|, n - |x|\} = |x|$ and similarly $\min\{|y|, n - |y|\} = |y|$. Therefore, (6) is equivalent to

$$\begin{cases} |x| + |y| = d \\ |x| \leq k \\ |y| \leq k \end{cases} \quad (7)$$

and we only need to find the number of different integer solutions for (7). Clearly, for $0 \leq d \leq k$, equations (7) are equivalent to equation (4). Thus Lemma 1 applies. It remains to prove the case of $k + 1 \leq d \leq 2k$. Since $|x| \leq k$ implies $|y| \geq d - k$ which in turn implies $1 \leq d - k \leq |x|, |y| \leq k$. Similar to Case 1 in the proof of Lemma 1, we have $y = \pm(d - |x|)$. Thus for a given x, there are two possible values for y. Since we have a total of $2(k - (d - k) + 1) =$

$2(2k - d + 1)$ possible values for x in this case, there are $2 \times 2(2k - d + 1) = 4(2k - d + 1)$ different integer solutions of (x, y) for (7), i.e. $C_d = 4(2k - d + 1)$ for $k + 1 \leq d \leq 2k$. ∎

It is interesting to verify that in Lemma 2 if we take a summation of all d-neighbors of a node in a $(2k+1) \times (2k+1)$ torus for all d, $0 \leq d \leq 2k$, we obtain that

$$\sum_{d=0}^{2k} C_d = 1 + 2 \sum_{d=1}^{k} C_d = 1 + 8 \sum_{d=1}^{k} d$$

$$= 1 + 8 \times \frac{k(k + 1)}{2} = (2k + 1)^2$$

which is exactly the total number of nodes in this torus. Figure 3 shows the circles centered at a node with different radii in a torus, where the number on each node represents the distance between the node and the center.

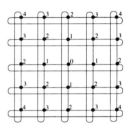

Figure 3: Circles centered at a node with different radii in a 5×5 torus.

We can similarly obtain C_d's for a $2k \times 2k$ torus. Finally, it should be pointed out that for an $n \times n$ mesh, the C_d's of different nodes may differ due to the fact that the nodes in a mesh are asymmetric.

3 Broadcasting in a Mesh or Torus

With the assumptions of full-duplex channels and all-port capability for each node, in Figure 4 we depict the internal structure of a node with the buffers required for all-to-all broadcast in an $n \times n$ mesh or torus. Inside each node, there is an $n \times n$ buffer matrix to store the messages broadcast from all other nodes in the network; in addition, there are four pairs of first-in first-out buffers: four input buffers and four output buffers, with each input buffer associated with an input channel of the node and each output buffer associated with an output channel of the node.

Figure 5 shows the logical format of a message: it includes the source node address of the message and the content of the message. During all-to-all broadcasting, when a message enters a node from an input channel, it is stored into the corresponding location of the buffer matrix indexed by its source address, then it is multicast to some output buffers for broadcasting to other unvisited neighboring nodes of this node.

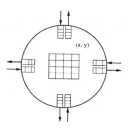

Figure 4: Detailed buffer structure of node (x, y).

Source node address	Message content

Figure 5: The logical format of a message.

3.1 Lower bound for broadcast

Let α be the *startup time* per message, which is the time required for the source node to prepare the message and initialize the communication; δ be the *switching time*, which includes the time to make the routing decision and the time to set a switch at a node; γ be the transmission time per byte; and L be the number of bytes per message. The following theorem gives lower bounds on the maximum communication delays of one-to-all broadcast and all-to-all broadcast in an $n \times n$ mesh or torus.

Theorem 1 *(1) The maximum communication delay of one-to-all broadcast is at least $\alpha + \delta + 2(n - 1)L\gamma$ in an $n \times n$ mesh, and is at least $\alpha + \delta + 2\lfloor \frac{n}{2} \rfloor L\gamma$ in an $n \times n$ torus. (2) The maximum communication delay of all-to-all broadcast in all-port model is at least $\alpha + \delta + \frac{n^2-1}{2}L\gamma$ in an $n \times n$ mesh, and is at least $\alpha + \delta + \frac{n^2-1}{4}L\gamma$ in an $n \times n$ torus.*

Proof. Note that in either one-to-all or all-to-all broadcast, we need a startup time and a switching time for at least one message (e.g. the first message on any path), even when we use a fully overlapped pipeline at message level. Therefore, (1) holds because that in one-to-all broadcast, the message from the source node needs to reach the farthest node and the diameters of a mesh and a torus are $2(n - 1)$ and $2\lfloor \frac{n}{2} \rfloor$, respectively. To obtain (2), we only need to show that the lower bounds on the transmission time in an $n \times n$ mesh and torus in all-port model are $\frac{n^2-1}{2}L\gamma$ and $\frac{n^2-1}{4}L\gamma$, respectively. It is easy to see this is true for a torus because for any node in the network, all other $n^2 - 1$ nodes need to send a message to this node, and there are four input channels at each node in the torus. For a mesh, there may be two to four input channels at each node. In the worst case, there are two input channels at some nodes in the mesh. Thus, the lower bound on the transmission time in a mesh is $\frac{n^2-1}{2}L\gamma$. ∎

3.2 Broadcast pattern

The basic idea of our algorithm is message flooding. To avoid sending the same message twice to a node , the broad-cast is performed on a spanning tree rooted at the source node, which we refer to as a broadcast tree. Thus, the message flooding is a controlled flooding. A broadcast pattern for source node (x_0, y_0) is a broadcast tree shown in Figure 6, which will be formally defined later. The broadcast from node (x_0, y_0) can be logically divided into several phases. In phase d, the message originating from node (x_0, y_0) reaches all its d-neighbors, for $d \geq 1$. Note that the number of phases in broadcast equals to the diameter of the network. In the case of one-to-all broadcast, no channel contention occurs. Thus, each phase takes $O(1)$ time. However, in the case of all-to-all broadcast, each node broadcasts its message to other nodes in a radiant way. In this case we need to take the channel contention into account. The buffers in each node are used to resolve the channel contention. To achieve minimum communication delay, we allow overlapping of the switching time of one message and the transmission time of another message, and ensure that incoming messages arrived at a node are uniformly distributed to its four output buffers so that the lower bound on the total transmission time $\frac{n^2-1}{4}L\gamma$ can be achieved. As can be seen later, the broadcast pattern we use in our algorithm can guarantee these features.

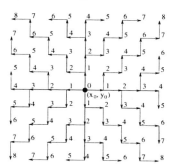

Figure 6: Broadcast pattern from source node (x_0, y_0).

We now formally describe the broadcast pattern of source node (x_0, y_0) shown in Figure 6. For presentational convenience, we first consider an infinite mesh.

When a broadcast message originating from node (x_0, y_0) reaches node (x, y), it continues to broadcast to the neighbors of node (x, y) as follows.

Case 1: $x = x_0$ and $y = y_0$.
(x, y) broadcasts the message to all of its four neighbors $(x, y + 1)$, $(x, y - 1)$, $(x + 1, y)$, and $(x - 1, y)$.

Case 2: Either $x = x_0$ or $y = y_0$ but not both.

    2.1: $x = x_0$ and $y \neq y_0$, i.e. along the y-axis.

        2.1.1: $y - y_0$ is a positive odd number.
        (x, y) multicasts the message to its two neighbors $(x, y + 1)$ and $(x - 1, y)$;

        2.1.2: $y - y_0$ is a positive even number.
        (x, y) multicasts the message to its two neighbors $(x, y + 1)$ and $(x + 1, y)$.

2.1.3: $y - y_0$ is a negative odd number.
(x, y) multicasts the message to its two neighbors $(x, y - 1)$ and $(x + 1, y)$;

2.1.4: $y - y_0$ is a negative even number.
(x, y) multicasts the message to its two neighbors $(x, y - 1)$ and $(x - 1, y)$.

2.2: $x \neq x_0$ and $y = y_0$, i.e. along the x-axis.

2.2.1: $x - x_0$ is a positive odd number.
(x, y) multicasts the message to its two neighbors $(x, y + 1)$ and $(x + 1, y)$;

2.2.2: $x - x_0$ is a positive even number.
(x, y) multicasts the message to its two neighbors $(x, y - 1)$ and $(x + 1, y)$.

2.2.3: $x - x_0$ is a negative odd number.
(x, y) multicasts the message to its two neighbors $(x, y - 1)$ and $(x - 1, y)$;

2.2.4: $x - x_0$ is a negative even number.
(x, y) multicasts the message to its two neighbors $(x, y + 1)$ and $(x - 1, y)$.

Case 3: $x \neq x_0$ and $y \neq y_0$.

3.1: $x > x_0$ and $y > y_0$, i.e. (x, y) is in Quadrant I.

3.1.1: $(x - x_0) + (y - y_0)$ is odd.
(x, y) sends the message to its neighbor $(x, y + 1)$;

3.1.2: $(x - x_0) + (y - y_0)$ is even.
(x, y) sends the message to its neighbor $(x + 1, y)$.

3.2: $x < x_0$ and $y > y_0$, i.e. (x, y) is in Quadrant II.

3.2.1: $(x - x_0) + (y - y_0)$ is odd.
(x, y) sends the message to its neighbor $(x - 1, y)$;

3.2.2: $(x - x_0) + (y - y_0)$ is even.
(x, y) sends the message to its neighbor $(x, y + 1)$.

3.3: $x < x_0$ and $y < y_0$, i.e. (x, y) is in Quadrant III.

3.3.1: $(x - x_0) + (y - y_0)$ is odd:
(x, y) sends the message to its neighbor $(x, y - 1)$;

3.3.2: $(x - x_0) + (y - y_0)$ is even.
(x, y) sends the message to its neighbor $(x - 1, y)$.

3.4: $x > x_0$ and $y < y_0$, i.e. (x, y) is in Quadrant IV.

3.4.1: $(x - x_0) + (y - y_0)$ is odd.
(x, y) sends the message to its neighbor $(x + 1, y)$;

3.4.2: $(x - x_0) + (y - y_0)$ is even.
(x, y) sends the message to its neighbor $(x, y - 1)$.

Clearly, at any time the message is always sent out in the direction leaving the origin (source node). In Case 1, starting from the origin, the message is broadcast to all its four neighbors; in Case 2, starting from a node with the same x-coordinate or y-coordinate as the origin, the message is multicast to two neighbors of the node; in Case 3, starting from a node with a different x-coordinate and y-coordinate from the origin, the message is sent to only one of its neighbors.

For an $n \times n$ mesh, the broadcast pattern is essentially the same as the above except that the pattern is trimmed at the boundary of the mesh. Similarly, for an $n \times n$ torus,

Table 1: Additional checks for a torus

Additional checks for a torus:
For any node (x_1, y_1) which is a neighbor of node (x, y) chosen from the broadcast pattern, if $dist((x_0, y_0), (x, y)) \leq dist((x_0, y_0), (x_1, y_1))$ then remove (x_1, y_1) from the list of the neighbors to which node (x, y) relays the message originating from node (x_0, y_0).

it follows the same broadcast pattern but the additions and subtractions are performed in modulo n. In addition, in the case of a torus, we need to check if a message is sent to a node twice because of the wraparound nature of the torus. To avoid unnecessary traffic in a torus, we can perform the checks in Table 1.

3.3 Simplified form of the broadcast pattern

The broadcast pattern described in the last subsection is regular and easy to understand. However, it is tedious to use when we describe the broadcast algorithm and analyze the performance of the algorithm. We now introduce the following functions to simplify the description of the broadcast pattern.

We define a unit step function $U(\cdot)$ and a polar indicator function $I(\cdot)$ on non-zero integers as

$$U(x) = \begin{cases} 1 & \text{if } x > 0 \\ 0 & \text{if } x < 0 \end{cases} \tag{8}$$

and

$$I(x) = \begin{cases} 1 & \text{if } x > 0 \\ -1 & \text{if } x < 0 \end{cases} \tag{9}$$

We also define a modulo function $mod_2(\cdot)$ on all integers as

$$mod_2(x) = x \bmod 2 \tag{10}$$

The following lemma gives a simplified form for the broadcast pattern described in the last subsection.

Lemma 3 *The broadcast pattern given in the last subsection is equivalent to the following:*

When the broadcast message originating from the source (x_0, y_0) reaches node (x, y), it continues to broadcast to the neighbors of node (x, y) as follows.

Case 1: $x = x_0$ and $y = y_0$.
(x, y) broadcasts the message to all of its four neighbors $(x, y + 1)$, $(x, y - 1)$, $(x + 1, y)$, and $(x - 1, y)$.

Case 2: Either $x = x_0$ or $y = y_0$ but not both.
(x, y) multicasts the message to its two neighbors (x_1, y_1) and (x_2, y_2)

2.1: $x = x_0$ and $y \neq y_0$, i.e. along the y-axis.
$x_1, y_1, x_2,$ and y_2 satisfy

$$x_1 = x + mod_2(y - y_0 + U(I(y - y_0)))$$
$$y_1 = y + I(y - y_0) \times mod_2(y - y_0 + 1 - U(I(y - y_0)))$$

$$x_2 = x - mod_2(y - y_0 + U(-I(y - y_0)))$$
$$y_2 = y + I(y - y_0) \times mod_2(y - y_0 + 1 - U(-I(y - y_0))) \quad (11)$$

2.2: $x \neq x_0$ and $y = y_0$, i.e. along the x-axis. $x_1, y_1, x_2,$ and y_2 satisfy

$$x_1 = x + I(x - x_0) \times mod_2(x - x_0 + U(I(x - x_0)))$$
$$y_1 = y + mod_2(x - x_0 + 1 - U(I(x - x_0)))$$
$$x_2 = x + I(x - x_0) \times mod_2(x - x_0 + U(-I(x - x_0)))$$
$$y_2 = y - mod_2(x - x_0 + 1 - U(-I(x - x_0))) \quad (12)$$

Case 3: $x \neq x_0$ and $y \neq y_0$.

(x, y) sends the message to its neighbor (x_3, y_3) where x_3 and y_3 satisfy

$$x_3 = x + I(x - x_0) \times mod_2((x - x_0) + (y - y_0) + U(I(x - x_0) \times I(y - y_0)))$$
$$y_3 = y + I(y - y_0) \times mod_2((x - x_0) + (y - y_0) + 1 - U(I(x - x_0) \times I(y - y_0))) \quad (13)$$

Proof. First, Case 1 is trivial. We now consider Case 3. In Case 3, we have $x \neq x_0$ and $y \neq y_0$. That is, $I(x - x_0)$ and $I(y - y_0)$ take a value of either -1 or 1, which represent the directions of node (x, y) leaving the origin (x_0, y_0) along the x-axis and the y-axis, respectively. Clearly, based on the broadcast pattern given in the previous subsection, in Quadrants I and III, where condition $I(x - x_0) \times I(y - y_0) = 1$ is satisfied, (x, y) sends the message to its neighbor $(x + I(x - x_0), y)$ when $(x - x_0) + (y - y_0)$ is even, and sends the message to its neighbor $(x, y + I(y - y_0))$ when $(x - x_0) + (y - y_0)$ is odd. In summary, (x, y) sends the message to its neighbor (x_3, y_3), where

$$x_3 = x + I(x - x_0) \times mod_2((x - x_0) + (y - y_0) + 1)$$
$$y_3 = y + I(y - y_0) \times mod_2((x - x_0) + (y - y_0)) \quad (14)$$

Similarly, in Quadrants II and IV, where condition $I(x - x_0) \times I(y - y_0) = -1$ is satisfied, (x, y) sends the message to its neighbor (x_3, y_3), where

$$x_3 = x + I(x - x_0) \times mod_2((x - x_0) + (y - y_0))$$

$$y_3 = y + I(y - y_0) \times mod_2((x - x_0) + (y - y_0) + 1) \quad (15)$$

Combining (14) and (15), we obtain (13).

Finally, we consider Case 2, where either $x = x_0$ or $y = y_0$ but not both. In Case 2.1, where $x = x_0$ and $y \neq y_0$, since $x - x_0 = 0$, function $I(x - x_0) = I(0)$ has no definition. However, we can assume that $I(x - x_0)$ takes two values, 1 and -1, plug the two values of $I(x - x_0)$ into Equation (13) separately, and obtain the two nodes as shown in Equation (11). It is easy to verify that these two nodes are exactly the two neighbors of node (x, y) described in Case 2.1 in the previous subsection. Similarly we can prove Case 2.2. ∎

From the proof of Lemma 3, we can see that Equation (13) can be viewed as a generic form of a node relaying the message of the origin to its neighbors. When $x - x_0 = 0$ or

$y - y_0 = 0$, we can let $I(x - x_0)$ or $I(y - y_0)$ take values 1 and -1 respectively in Equation (13) and obtain multiple neighbors to relay the message in this phase.

We have the following theorem concerning the broadcast pattern.

Theorem 2 *Each node in an infinite mesh can be reached exactly once by using the broadcast pattern in Lemma 3.*

Proof. Since the two-element set, $mod_2((x - x_0) + (y - y_0) + U(I(x - x_0) \times I(y - y_0)))$ and $mod_2((x - x_0) + (y - y_0) + 1 - U(I(x - x_0) \times I(y - y_0)))$ in Equation (13), is always equal to $\{0, 1\}$, we have $dist((x_3, y_3), (x, y)) = |x_3 - x| + |y_3 - y| = 1$. Furthermore, note that from node (x, y) to node (x_3, y_3) is in the direction of leaving the origin (x_0, y_0). Thus, we only need to prove that in phase k every k-neighbor is reached.

By induction on phase k.

It is easy to verify that the argument is true for $k = 1$ and $k = 2$. Now suppose that it is true for phase k. By Lemma 1, there are a total of $4k$ k-neighbors and $4(k + 1)$ $(k + 1)$-neighbors. According to the broadcast pattern, among $4k$ k-neighbors, only four of them multicast the message of the origin to two $(k + 1)$-neighbors and rest of them only relay it to one $(k + 1)$-neighbor. Thus, in total, $4k$ k-neighbors relay the message to $(k + 1)$-neighbors $4 \times 2 + (4k - 4) \times 1 = 4(k + 1)$ times, which is exactly equal to the number of $(k + 1)$-neighbors. It remains to show that among the $4(k + 1)$ relayed messages, no two are sent to the same $(k + 1)$-neighbor, that is, each $(k + 1)$-neighbor receives the message exactly once. Since each of four nodes with the same x-coordinate or y-coordinate as the origin sends the message to two distinct $(k + 1)$-neighbors, we only need to check if two k-neighbors in the same quadrant send the message to two distinct $(k + 1)$-neighbors. Suppose in Quadrant I, two k-neighbors, (x, y) and (x', y'), send the message to (x_3, y_3) and (x_3', y_3') respectively. We have that $x_0 < x, x'$ ($x \neq x'$), $y_0 < y, y'$ ($y \neq y'$), and $dist((x, y), (x_0, y_0)) = dist((x', y'), (x_0, y_0)) = (x - x_0) + (y - y_0) = (x' - x_0) + (y' - y_0) = k$. Thus, from Equation (13), we obtain that

$$x_3 = x + mod_2(k + 1)$$
$$y_3 = y + mod_2(k)$$

and

$$x_3' = x' + mod_2(k + 1)$$
$$y_3' = y' + mod_2(k)$$

Hence, the two $(k + 1)$-neighbors, (x_3, y_3) and (x_3', y_3'), are different since $x \neq x'$ and $y \neq y'$. ∎

4 All-to-All Broadcast Algorithm

In this section, we describe the new all-to-all broadcast algorithm in a mesh or torus.

The basic idea of the algorithm is that the message originating from each node is multicast to one or more neighbors of the current node according to the broadcast pattern described in the last section. Different from one-to-all broadcast, input

Table 2: All-to-all broadcast algorithm

```
All-to-All Broadcast Algorithm:
for each node (x, y) in the network do in parallel
  for each input and output buffer do in parallel
    case of an output buffer:
      repeat
        remove a message from the buffer;
        send it to corresponding neighboring node
          (enter into the input buffer of the neighbor);
      until no more message arrives at the buffer;
    end case;
    case of an input buffer:
      repeat
        remove a message from the buffer;
        extract the source address of the message, say, (x₀, y₀);
        copy the message content to the (x₀, y₀) entry of the
          buffer matrix;
        calculate the addresses of the neighbors to be
          multicast by using the broadcast pattern in Lemma 3;
        for a torus, perform the additional checks in Table 1;
        multicast the message to the output buffers connected
          to the corresponding neighbors;
      until no more message arrives at the buffer;
    end case;
  end for;
end for;
End
```

and output buffers are needed for all-to-all multicast at each node to resolve the possible contention of multiple messages arriving at the same output channel at the same time. In Table 2, we give a higher level description of the algorithm.

In the broadcast algorithm in Table 2, each node is continuously receiving (and sending) messages from (and to) its four neighbors. As mentioned in the previous section, for an easy analysis we logically group the messages into phases such that in phase d the message originated from every node reaches all its d-neighbors. We can see that in each buffer, messages in an earlier phase d' always arrive before those in a later phase d'', for any $d' < d''$. In other words, at any node, the messages originating from the d'-neighbors of this node are always ahead of the messages originating from the d''-neighbors of the node in any buffer of the node for any $d' < d''$. We also know that in phase d, the message originating from node (x_0, y_0) reaches all its d-neighbors, and at the same time, the messages originating from all d-neighbors of node (x_0, y_0) also reach node (x_0, y_0). The remaining question is whether those incoming (and outgoing) messages are uniformly distributed to the four input (and output) buffers at each node. The following theorem gives a positive answer to this question.

Theorem 3 *According to the broadcast pattern given in Lemma 3, in phase d of all-to-all broadcast in an infinite mesh, each node (x_0, y_0) receives $4d$ messages originating from all its $4d$ d-neighbors via the four input channels of node (x_0, y_0), with d messages from each input channel, and at the end of the phase, it will send $4(d + 1)$ messages to its four 1-neighbors via the four output channels, with $d + 1$ messages on each output channel.*

Proof. By induction on phase d.

It is easy to see the theorem holds for phase 0, since at the end of this phase, every node will send its message to its four neighbors. The theorem also holds for phase 1. In fact, in phase 1, node (x_0, y_0) receives four messages from its four neighbors, with one from each neighbor. By applying the broadcast pattern, the message that arrives at node (x_0, y_0) and originates from $(x_0 + 1, y_0)$ will be relayed to two neighbors of node (x_0, y_0), which are

$$(x_0 + I(-1) \times mod_2(-1 + U(I(-1))),$$
$$y_0 + mod_2(-1 + 1 - U(I(-1))))$$

and

$$(x_0 + I(-1) \times mod_2(-1 + U(-I(-1))),$$
$$y_0 - mod_2(-1 + 1 - U(-I(-1)))),$$

that is, $(x_0 - 1, y_0)$ and $(x_0, y_0 - 1)$. Similarly, at node (x_0, y_0), the message originating from node $(x_0 - 1, y_0)$ will be relayed to nodes $(x_0, y_0 + 1)$ and $(x_0 + 1, y_0)$; the message originating from node $(x_0, y_0 + 1)$ will be relayed to nodes $(x_0 + 1, y_0)$ and $(x_0, y_0 - 1)$; and the message originating from $(x_0, y_0 - 1)$ will be relayed to nodes $(x_0, y_0 + 1)$ and $(x_0 - 1, y_0)$. We can see that at the end of phase 1, two messages will be sent to each of the four neighbors, $(x_0 - 1, y_0)$, $(x_0 + 1, y_0)$, $(x_0, y_0 - 1)$ and $(x_0, y_0 + 1)$.

Suppose the theorem holds for phase $k - 1$, we now prove it also holds for phase $k \geq 2$. By induction hypothesis for phase $k - 1$, the four neighbors of node (x_0, y_0) each sends k messages to node (x_0, y_0), thus $4k$ messages in total. Note that node (x_0, y_0) has $4k$ k-neighbors and the messages originating from these nodes arrive at node (x_0, y_0) in phase k. Thus, the $4k$ messages sent by the four 1-neighbors of node (x_0, y_0) are exactly the messages originating from the $4k$ k-neighbors of node (x_0, y_0). Now we show that at the end of this phase, $4(k + 1)$ messages will be sent to the four neighbors of node (x_0, y_0), with each having $k + 1$ messages. First, among the $4k$ k-neighbors only four of them on either the same row or the same column as node (x_0, y_0). Thus the messages originating from these 4 k-neighbors will be relayed to two of the neighbors of node (x_0, y_0) and the messages originating from the rest of k-neighbors will be relayed to one of the neighbors of node (x_0, y_0). Therefore, a total of $4 \times 2 + (4k - 4) \times 1 = 4(k + 1)$ messages will be sent out from node (x_0, y_0) at the end of phase k.

It remains to show that the $4(k + 1)$ messages are uniformly distributed to the four output buffers at node (x_0, y_0). Consider the $4k$ k-neighbors of node (x_0, y_0) depicted in Figure 7. They can be grouped into four groups: in Quadrant I, $(x_0 + l, y_0 + k - l)$; in Quadrant II, $(x_0 - k + l, y_0 + l)$; in Quadrant III, $(x_0 - k + l, y_0 - l)$; and in Quadrant IV,

$(x_0 + l, y_0 - k + l)$; for all l, $0 \le l \le k$. Note that the four special nodes $(x_0, y_0 + k)$, $(x_0 - k, y_0)$, $(x_0, y_0 - k)$ and $(x_0 + k, y_0)$ each is counted twice, and thus each group has $k + 1$ nodes. We now show that node (x_0, y_0) relays the messages originating from the nodes in the same group to the same 1-neighbor of it. It is not surprising that these special nodes reside in two groups, since the messages originating from each of them are relayed to two 1-neighbors of node (x_0, y_0) according to the broadcast pattern. For example, consider node $(x_0, y_0 + k)$ which resides in both Quadrant I and Quadrant II. When calculating the broadcast pattern at node (x_0, y_0) for the message originating from node $(x_0, y_0 + k)$, though $I(x_0 - x_0) = I(0)$ has no definition as in the proof of Lemma 3, we actually treat it as $I(-1)$ and $I(1)$ separately which correspond to Quadrant I and Quadrant II respectively.

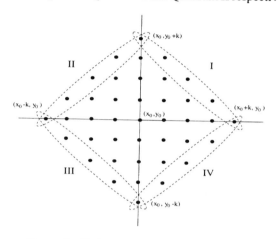

Figure 7: $4k$ k-neighbors of node (x_0, y_0).

Now let's look at the group in Quadrant I: nodes $(x_0 + l, y_0 + k - l)$ for all l, $0 \le l \le k$. Since $x_0 - (x_0 + l) = -l \le 0$, and $y_0 - (y_0 + k - l) = -(k - l) \le 0$, we can let both $I(x_0 - (x_0 + l))$ and $I(y_0 - (y_0 + k - l))$ take a value of -1. Thus using the broadcast pattern in Lemma 3, the 1-neighbor of node (x_0, y_0) that is chosen to relay the message originating from node $(x_0 + l, y_0 + k - l)$ is

$$
\begin{aligned}
& (x_0 - mod_2(-l - (k - l) + U((-1)(-1))), \\
& \quad y_0 - mod_2(-l - (k - l) + 1 - U((-1)(-1)))) \\
= \ & (x_0 - mod_2(-k + 1), y_0 - mod_2(-k)) \\
= \ & \begin{cases} (x_0 - 1, y_0) & \text{if } k \text{ is even} \\ (x_0, y_0 - 1) & \text{if } k \text{ is odd} \end{cases}
\end{aligned}
$$

Through a similar calculation, we can obtain the nodes that are chosen to relay the messages originating from Quadrants II, III, and IV are

$$
\begin{cases} (x_0, y_0 - 1) & \text{if } k \text{ is even} \\ (x_0 + 1, y_0) & \text{if } k \text{ is odd} \end{cases}
$$

$$
\begin{cases} (x_0 + 1, y_0) & \text{if } k \text{ is even} \\ (x_0, y_0 + 1) & \text{if } k \text{ is odd} \end{cases}
$$

and

$$
\begin{cases} (x_0, y_0 + 1) & \text{if } k \text{ is even} \\ (x_0 - 1, y_0) & \text{if } k \text{ is odd} \end{cases}
$$

respectively.

We have now proved that for a given k, the messages originating from $k + 1$ nodes in the same group are relayed to the same 1-neighbor of node (x_0, y_0), and the messages originating from the nodes in different groups are relayed to the different 1-neighbors of node (x_0, y_0). Thus, the theorem holds for phase k. ∎

Furthermore, we can obtain the following corollaries for a mesh and a torus.

Corollary 1 *In all-to-all broadcast using the algorithm in Table 2 in an $n \times n$ torus, each channel between two adjacent nodes in the network relays $\frac{n^2 - 1}{4}$ messages.*

Proof. Similar to the proof for Theorem 3, in phase $d \ge 1$, each node (x_0, y_0) receives C_d messages from all its $\bar{d}$-neighbors via the channels connected to its four 1-neighbors, with $\frac{C_d}{4}$ messages on each channel. By Lemma 2, we have that the total number of messages through a single channel is

$$
\sum_{d=1}^{2\lfloor \frac{n}{2} \rfloor} \frac{C_d}{4} = \frac{1}{4}\left(\sum_{d=0}^{2\lfloor \frac{n}{2} \rfloor} C_d - 1 \right) = \frac{n^2 - 1}{4}
$$

∎

Corollary 2 *In all-to-all broadcast using the algorithm in Table 2 in an $n \times n$ mesh, each channel between two adjacent nodes in the network relays at most $\frac{n^2 - 1}{2}$ messages.*

Proof. The corollary holds by considering the traffic to the nodes at the corner of the mesh. ∎

5 Delay Analysis in All-to-All Broadcast

In this section, we analyze the communication delay of the newly proposed all-to-all broadcast algorithm. Unlike previous algorithms, our algorithm allows switching is overlapped with transmission. In previous algorithms, each node can start to relay one message only after it completes the transmission of the previous message, while in our algorithm, except phase 1, at any time we always has more than one message waiting to be sent out in any direction. Therefore, we can pipeline the messages in all directions. Due to the simplicity and regularity of our algorithm, it is easy to be implemented in hardware to achieve a very short switching time. Our algorithm is optimal in transmission time, and in most cases, the total delay is close to the optimal value within only a small constant range. For a clean presentation, we only analyze the delay for a torus. A similar argument can be made for a mesh.

The following theorem gives the communication delay of the all-to-all broadcast algorithm.

Theorem 4 *The total delay of the all-to-all broadcast algorithm for an $n \times n$ torus is no more than*

$$\alpha + \delta + L\gamma + \left(\frac{n^2-1}{4} - 1\right) \max\{\delta, L\gamma\} + \min\{\delta, L\gamma\} \quad (16)$$

where α, δ, γ and L are the startup time, the switching time, the transmission time per byte, and the number of bytes per message, respectively.

Proof. Each message is prepared once at the source node in the initial phase, then is relayed (unchanged) to neighbors via unicast or multicast (with fanout four in phase 1 and fanout two in other phases) based on the broadcast pattern. By Theorem 3 and Corollary 1, at each node in phase k, each input buffer receives $\frac{C_k}{4}$ messages and each output buffer sends out $\frac{C_{k+1}}{4}$ messages. We assume two messages cannot be simultaneously transmitted on a single channel in the same direction, and the switching times of two messages from the same output buffer cannot be overlapped. However, we allow the transmission time of one message to be overlapped with the switching time of another message. For the first message (in phase 1), the total delay is $\alpha + \delta + L\gamma$. Notice that it cannot have any overlap with the second message (i.e. the first message in phase 2), because the second message relayed from one of its neighbors arrives at the current node right after the transmission of the first message completes. However, starting from the second message, we can have an overlap of the transmission time of one message and the switching time of another message because there are always more than one outgoing messages in any direction. Thus, the message transmission can work in a pipeline fashion. Figure 8 shows the total delay for the first three phases of all-to-all broadcast, where Figure 8(a) and Figure 8(b) are the cases for $\delta \leq L\gamma$ and $\delta > L\gamma$ respectively. By Corollary 1 we know that the number of messages through a channel in each direction is $\frac{n^2-1}{4}$, and except the first message, the switching and transmission of the subsequent messages can be overlapped. Thus, we conclude that the total delay for all-to-all broadcast is no more than $\alpha + \delta + L\gamma + \left(\frac{n^2-1}{4} - 1\right) \max\{\delta, L\gamma\} + \min\{\delta, L\gamma\}$ ∎

When we further consider the relationship between the switching time, δ, and transmission time of a message, $L\gamma$, we can rewrite Theorem 4 as follows.

Corollary 3 *The total delay of the all-to-all broadcast algorithm for an $n \times n$ torus is no more than*

$$\begin{cases} \alpha + 2\delta + \left(\frac{n^2-1}{4}\right) L\gamma & \text{if } \delta \leq L\gamma \\ \alpha + 2L\gamma + \left(\frac{n^2-1}{4}\right) \delta & \text{if } \delta > L\gamma \end{cases} \quad (17)$$

Clearly, our algorithm is optimal in transmission time, since the total transmission time of the algorithm is $\left(\frac{n^2-1}{4}\right) L\gamma$

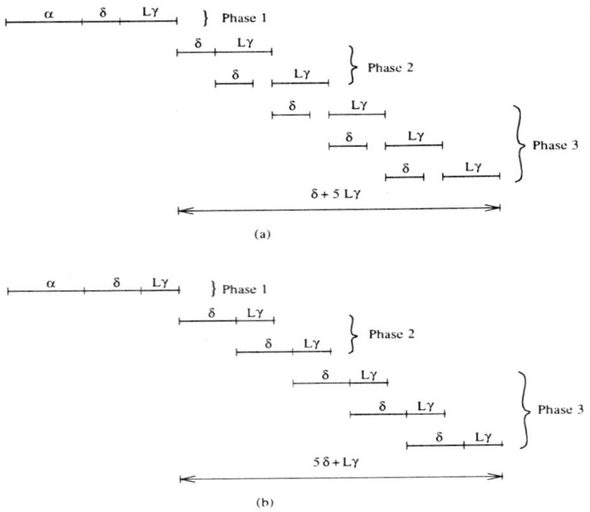

Figure 8: The total delay of the first three phases of all-to-all broadcast. (a) $\delta \leq L\gamma$. (b) $\delta > L\gamma$.

for a torus which matches the lower bound on the transmission time in Theorem 1. In addition, note that by Theorem 1, the lower bound on the communication delay of all-to-all broadcast for a torus is $\alpha + \delta + \left(\frac{n^2-1}{4}\right) L\gamma$. Therefore, Corollary 3 tells us that if $\delta \leq L\gamma$, our algorithm is close to the optimal value within only a small constant δ. Since the broadcast pattern in this paper is simple and regular, and each node uses the same pattern, message switching can be easily implemented in hardware in the router so that we can have a smaller switching time δ than the transmission time $L\gamma$, which enables the algorithm to achieve the optimum in practice.

6 Comparisons

In this section, we compare the communication delay of our algorithm with other existing all-to-all broadcast algorithms. In Saad and Schultz [12]'s horizontal/vertical algorithm for a torus, when we assume full-duplex and all-port model, the total delay should be $2\alpha + 2\lfloor \frac{n}{2} \rfloor \delta + \left(\frac{n^2-1}{2}\right) L\gamma$. In fact, (without loss of generality, let n be an odd number) in the horizontal phase, each node prepares the message (of its own with length L) once, then sends along two horizontal directions to other nodes. This takes $\frac{n-1}{2}$ steps. Thus, switching time is $\frac{n-1}{2}\delta$ and transmission time is $\frac{n-1}{2}L\gamma$ in this phase. In the vertical phase, initially each node needs to prepare a new message (of length nL) once which contains all n messages collected in the previous phase, then sends it along two vertical directions. Therefore, it takes another $\frac{n-1}{2}\delta$ of switching time and $n \cdot \frac{n-1}{2}L\gamma$ of transmission time. Thus, for this algorithm, the total startup time is 2α, the total switching time is $2 \times \frac{n-1}{2}\delta = (n-1)\delta$, and the total transmission time is $n \cdot \frac{n-1}{2}L\gamma + \frac{n-1}{2}L\gamma = \frac{n^2-1}{2}L\gamma$.

Since no overlap among startup time, switching time, and transmission time of the messages going through a single node, the total delay is simply the sum of the above three terms. As can be seen, since the algorithm in [12] does not fully use all channels at each node in the network, its transmission time is twice of that of our algorithm. Also as analyzed in [15], the all-to-all broadcast algorithm for a torus proposed by Calvin, Perennes, and Trystram has a delay of $2 \log_5(n^2)\alpha + \frac{3}{2}(n-1)\delta + \frac{n^2-1}{2}L\gamma$. In each step of a recursive phase in their algorithm, the messages must be prepared since the messages are different. Also its transmission time is still twice as long as that of our algorithm. In addition, both algorithms ([12] and [15]) cannot take advantage of overlapping of the switching time and the transmission time as does our algorithm. Finally, we should point out that when $\delta > 2L\gamma$, there may be the cases that both algorithms take less time than the proposed algorithm. However, as discussed at the end of the last section, in general we can have $\delta < L\gamma$ in our algorithm.

7 Conclusions

In this paper, we have proposed a new all-to-all broadcast algorithm in all-port 2D mesh and torus networks. The algorithm can be implemented in either packet-switched networks or virtual cut-through and wormhole-switched networks. The new algorithm utilizes a controlled message flooding based on a broadcast pattern. Unlike existing all-to-all broadcast algorithms, the proposed algorithm takes advantage of overlapping of message switching time and transmission time, and achieves optimal transmission time for all-to-all broadcast. In addition, in most cases, the total communication delay is close to the lower bound of all-to-all broadcast within a small constant range. Finally, the algorithm is conceptually simple, and symmetrical for every message and every node so that it can be easily implemented in hardware and achieves the optimum in practice. The algorithm can also be extended to multi-dimensional meshes and tori.

References

[1] J. Duato, S. Yalmanchili, and L.M. Ni, *Interconnection Networks: An Engineering Approach,* IEEE Computer Society Press, Los Alamitos, CA, 1997.

[2] Y. Yang and G.M. Masson, "Nonblocking Broadcast Switching Networks," *IEEE Trans. Computers,* vol. C-40, no. 9, pp. 1005-1015, 1991.

[3] Y. Yang and G.M. Masson, "Broadcast Ring Sandwich Networks," *IEEE Trans. Computers,* vol. C-44, no. 10, pp. 1169-1180, 1995.

[4] Y. Yang, "A Class of Interconnection Networks for Multicasting," *IEEE Trans. Computers,* vol. C-47, no. 8, pp. 899-906, 1998.

[5] D.S. Scott, "Efficient All-to-All Communication Patterns in Hypercube and Mesh Topologies," *Proc. of 6th Conference. Distributed Memory Concurrent Computers,* pp. 398-403, 1991.

[6] R. Thakur and A. Choudhary, "All-to-All Communication on Meshes with Wormhole Routing," *Proc. of 8th IEEE International Parallel Processing Symposium,* pp. 561-565, April 1994.

[7] Y.-C. Tseng and S. Gupta, "All-to-All Personalized Communication in a Wormhole-Routed Torus," *IEEE Trans. Parallel and Distributed Systems,* vol. 7, no. 5, pp. 498-505, 1996.

[8] Y.-C. Tseng, T.-H. Lin, S. Gupta, and D.K. Panda, "Bandwidth-Optimal Complete Exchange on Wormhole Routed 2D/3D Torus Networks: A Diagonal-Propagation Approach," *IEEE Trans. Parallel and Distributed Systems,* vol. 8, no. 4, pp. 380-396, 1997.

[9] F. Petrini, "Total-Exchange on Wormhole k-ary n-cubes with Adaptive Routing," *Proc. of the First Merged IEEE International Parallel Processing Symposium & Symposium on Parallel and Distributed Processing,* pp. 267-271, March 1998.

[10] Y.J. Suh and S. Yalmanchili, "All-to-All Communication with Minimum Start-up Costs in 2D/3D Tori and Meshes," *IEEE Trans. Parallel and Distributed Systems,* vol. 9, no. 5, pp. 442-458, 1998.

[11] Y.J. Suh and K.G. Shin, "Efficient All-to-All Personalized Exchange in Multidimensional Torus Networks," *Proc. of 1998 International Conference on Parallel Processing,* pp. 468-475, August 1998.

[12] Y. Saad and M.H. Schultz, "Data Communication in Parallel Architectures," *Parallel Computing,* vol. 11, pp. 131-150, 1989.

[13] S.L. Johnsson and C.T. Ho, "Optimum Broadcasting and Personalized Communication in Hypercubes," *IEEE Trans. Computers,* vol. 38, no. 9, pp. 1249-1268, 1989.

[14] J. Bruck, C.T. Ho, S. Kipnis, and D. Weathersby, "Efficient Algorithms for All-to-All Communications in Muitl-Port Message-Passing Systems, *ACM Symposium on Parallel Algorithms and Architectures,* pp. 298-309, 1994.

[15] C. Calvin, S. Perennes, and D. Trystram, "All-to-All Broadcast in Torus with Wormhole-Like Routing," *Proc. of 7th IEEE Symposium on Parallel and Distributed Processing,* pp. 130-137, 1995.

[16] D. Gannon and J.V. Rosendale, "On the Impact of Communication Complexity in the Design of Parallel Numerical Algorithms," *IEEE Trans. Computer,* vol. C-33, pp. 1180-1194, Dec. 1984.

[17] G.C. Fox, et al., *Solving Problems on Concurrent Processors. Volume I: General Techniques and Regular Problems,* Englewood Cliffs, NJ, Prentice Hall, 1988.

MMR: A High-Performance Multimedia Router - Architecture and Design Trade-Offs

Jose Duato[1], Sudhakar Yalamanchili[2], M. Blanca Caminero[3], Damon Love[2], Francisco J. Quiles[3]

Abstract

This paper presents the architecture of a router designed to efficiently support traffic generated by multimedia applications. The router is targeted for use in clusters and LANs rather than in WANs, the latter being served by communication substrates such as ATM. The distinguishing features of the proposed router architecture are the use of small fixed-size buffers, a large number of virtual channels, link-level virtual channel flow control, support for dynamic modification of connection bandwidth and priorities, and coordinated scheduling of connections across all output channels. The paper begins with a discussion of the design choices and architectural trade-offs made in the current MultiMedia Router (MMR) project. The performance evaluation section presents some preliminary results of the coordinated scheduling of constant bit rate (CBR) traffic streams.

1.0 Introduction

In the past few years we have seen an explosive growth in network-based multimedia applications. Example applications include web servers, video-on-demand servers, telemedicine, immersive environments, interactive simulations, and collaborative design environments. The data are often distributed and these applications individually require substantial bandwidth to meet real-time interactive constraints. The network bandwidth must also be shared by other applications that may not have as demanding constraints.

The physical constraints of cluster/LAN interconnects as well as the applications that utilize them produces differ-

---

1.J. Duato is with the Dept. of Information Systems and Computer Architecture, Universidad Politecnica de Valencia, P.O.B. 22012, 46071 - Valencia, SPAIN, {jduato@gap.upv.es}
2.D. Love and S. Yalamanchili are with the School of Electrical and Computer Engineering, Georgia Institute of Technology, {dlove, sudha}@ece.gatech.edu
3.B. Caminero and F. J. Quiles are with the Dept. of Computer Science, Escuela Politecnica Superior de Albacete SPAIN. {blanca, paco}@info-ab.uclm.es

ent trade-offs in router design from those made in wide area networks (WANs). As a result we arrive at different and more effective architectural solutions for cluster/LAN routers. *The key issue is the ability to provide quality of service (QoS) guarantees at multiprocessor cut-through latencies.* This makes it difficult to use existing substrates such as Gigabit Ethernet and ATM [22]in which message traffic encounters relatively large latencies as compared to networks such as Myrinet [5] or Tandem ServerNet [16,18]. Traditional router technology developed for high-speed multiprocessor networks is optimized for low latency and for best-effort traffic. However, these networks are not designed to permit concurrent guarantees for communication performance for multiple applications.

The primary objective of the Multimedia Router (MMR) project is the design and implementation of a single-chip router optimized for multimedia applications. The goal is to provide architectural support to enable a range of quality of service (QoS) guarantees at latencies comparable to state-of-the-art multiprocessor cut-through routers. To achieve this goal we must provide solutions to many difficult hardware resource management and scheduling problems while constraining required resources to permit effective single-chip implementations. This paper presents some specific trade-offs made in the architecture of the MMR single-chip multimedia router and the results of some preliminary simulation experiments.

2.0 Application Requirements

The main distinguishing features of multimedia communication environments are:

- Very long data streams

- Wide range of bandwidth requirements

- Large number of connections

- Jitter sensitive

- Latency tolerant

300

- Short control messages

Multimedia traffic may also coexist with best-effort traffic generated by other applications. The MMR should handle this hybrid traffic efficiently, satisfying the QoS requirements of multimedia traffic, minimizing the average latency of best-effort traffic, and maximizing link utilization.

Constant bit rate (CBR) connections are relatively easy to handle. Bandwidth requirements can be met by allocating the requested bandwidth while establishing the connection. Variable bit rate (VBR) connections are more difficult to handle. When establishing a VBR coapproximate knowledge of the average and maximum bandwidth requirements. For example, it is possible to compute the average and maximum bandwidth requirements for a stored compressed movie. However, it is not possible to obtain exact values for real-time transmission of compressed video.

Thus, the designer has to carefully select several qualitative and quantitative network design parameters. Qualitative parameters include network topology, switching technique, routing algorithm, admission control strategy, bandwidth allocation algorithm, link/switch scheduling algorithm, buffer organization, buffer management, and crossbar organization. Quantitative parameters include network size, link bandwidth, router degree (number of ports), router clock frequency, buffer size, and number of virtual channels.

VCM - Virtual Channel Memory
LS - Link Scheduler

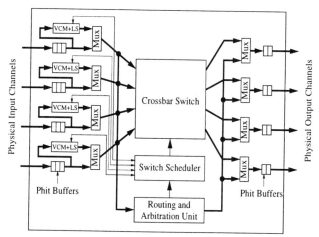

Figure 1. The Architecture of the MultiMedia Router (MMR)

3.0 Router Architecture

Figure 1 illustrates the architecture of the MMR. The following subsections describe some basic trade-offs that were made in the individual components.

3.1 Switching Technique

Multimedia traffic often requires a bounded jitter on long data streams. Switching techniques that reserve resources on the fly, like wormhole switching, are not well suited for such communication because the time a message is blocked waiting for a busy resource is not bounded. Connection oriented schemes with scheduling support within the routers are better suited to meeting jitter requirements over long data streams. On the other hand, control messages and best-effort traffic will benefit from low-latency switching techniques like wormhole or virtual cut-through (VCT) switching. The overhead of connection oriented schemes is excessive for these messages. A good trade-off can be achieved by using a hybrid switching technique [12, 29]. Long data streams can be transmitted by using circuit switching or a variant thereof by first establishing a connection from source to destination and then forwarding the data. Control messages and best-effort traffic can be transmitted by using wormhole or VCT switching. However, we would like both types of messages to use the same pool of link and buffer resources at a node without partitioning of resources among switching classes (e.g., as in [23]).

Among the connection-oriented schemes, we have selected pipelined circuit switching (PCS) because it is simple, can be combined with wormhole or VCT [3], uses flow control to prevent data losses, requires small buffer storage associated with each virtual channel, and the overhead produced by control information is relatively low compared to LAN connection oriented schemes such as ATM. PCS for long data streams is combined with VCT for control and best-effort messages. In both cases the data is organized as a sequence of flow control digits or *flits* [9]. While the use of large flits amortizes flow control and scheduling delays, it also increases latency and buffer storage requirements. Latency can be reduced by pipelining flit transmission at a finer granularity. Pipelining can be done at the phit level, as in the Cray T3D router [25], where a phit is the amount of information that can be transmitted in parallel through a communication link. As serial links are frequent in LAN environments, we assume that pipelining is performed at the word level, where word size is equal to the width of the router internal data paths.

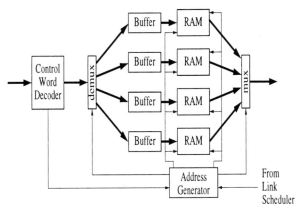

Figure 2. Organization of Virtual Channel Memory

3.2 Buffer Organization

When a connection is established, a virtual channel is reserved at each link in the path from source to destination. In order to support a large number of connections concurrently, buffers at each link must be organized as a large set of virtual channels. Virtual channels have been traditionally organized as a set of queues linked by a multiplexor. As indicated in [8], router delays can increase substantially when a large number of virtual channels are multiplexed onto physical links. This is due in part to the multiplexor and virtual channel controller delays. Moreover fully de-multiplexed crossbars [9] (i.e., one virtual channel per crossbar port) become prohibitively expensive in silicon area as the number of virtual channels increases. Thus, we pursue a different buffer organization to support a large number of virtual channels.

The major buffer organizations that must be considered are central buffers, output buffers, and input buffers. We have considered these organizations and our current analysis [13] argues for input buffers modified as follows to remove head-of-line blocking. The MMR will use virtual channels organized as a set of interleaved RAM modules. Each flit is low-order interleaved across memory modules. Flits belonging to the same virtual channel are stored in adjacent sets of memory locations. The number of memory modules and flit size must be selected to balance memory access time, link speed, and crossbar switching delay, while masking flow control and scheduling delays. The read address required to retrieve flits is supplied by the link scheduler. The write address is obtained from the virtual channel flow control circuitry indicating the virtual channel identifier for the next flit transmission. As shown in Figure 1, small phit buffers are used for link buffers and are deep enough to store all the phits that arrive during a decoding period (i.e., during the computation of the memory address to store those phits). Phit buffers also allow low-latency routing of short messages using VCT, provided that there is no contention (i.e., the requested output link is free). Similarly, phit buffers allow a fast processing of probes and acknowledgments when establishing a connection. There is also some state information stored with each virtual channel that is used for scheduling. The collective resources are referred to as virtual channel memory(VCM).

By designing pipelined memory buffer systems we can match increasing external link speeds to decreasing intra-router delays. The variable parameters that can be adjusted include flit sizes, number of memory banks and the virtual channel depth.

3.3 Switch Organization

In most routers the internal switch is implemented as a crossbar: multiplexed, partially multiplexed and fully de-multiplexed [9]. Although some routers use a fully de-multiplexed crossbar [10], this organization becomes prohibitive when the number of virtual channels is large. Even for a relatively small number of virtual channels, some commercial routers use a multiplexed crossbar [6]. The MMR uses a multiplexed crossbar where the internal switch is a crossbar with as many ports as communication links. It reduces silicon area by V and V^2, respectively, with respect to a partially multiplexed and a fully de-multiplexed crossbar, where V is the number of virtual channels per link.

The main drawback of a multiplexed crossbar is that arbitration is needed every time an input link switches from one virtual channel to another. Arbitration is required at the input side to select a virtual channel from each input link. Arbitration is also required at the output side because several virtual channels may request the same output link although this can be hidden by overlapping with the transmission of a previous flit if flits are large enough. Switch reconfiguration overhead can also be similarly hidden. An interesting feature of multiplexed crossbars is that buffers are not required at the output side. As switch output ports are directly connected to output links, flits are directly transmitted through the switch and the corresponding output link. However, a few phit buffers can be used to pipeline information through the switch and the link. Finally, serialization is required if internal data paths are wider than physical links.

3.4 Packet and Flit Transmission

To fully exploit switch and link bandwidth while simplifying router design, the MMR synchronously assigns switch ports and output links to the requesting virtual channels. Flit transmission is organized as a sequence of flit cycles. During each flit cycle, all the input links with ready flits start by transmitting a control word containing the identifier of the virtual channel to which the next flit belongs. Then they synchronously transmit one flit through the switch and the corresponding output links. Concurrently, arbitration is performed for the assignment of switch ports and output links for the next flit cycle. Once the current flit transmission has finished, the switch is reconfigured. This operation requires one clock cycle. During reconfiguration, no data are transmitted. The MMR uses this cycle to perform pending transmissions of routing probes, backtracking probes, and acknowledgments for connection establishment [1]. Once the switch has been reconfigured, the next flit cycle starts. Although transmission is synchronous inside each router, it should be noted that different routers work asynchronously.

Synchronous flit transmission is efficient for data streams but not for control and best-effort messages. These messages are transmitted asynchronously through the switch using VCT switching. Given the large flit sizes (128-256 bits), the following discussion assumes that packet size is equal to flit size. Note that the unit of flow control and buffer management in VCT is a packet. Therefore, flow control units have the same size in PCS and VCT, thus simplifying router design. Packet headers are routed as soon as they reach a router and are forwarded to the routing and arbitration unit. If the requested switch input port and output link are free (i.e., they are not transmitting any flit during the current flit cycle) and there are free virtual channels in the requested output link, control packets are immediately forwarded because they have a higher priority than data streams. This transmission is not synchronized at flit cycle boundaries. As the transmission of control packets may take longer than the rest of the current flit cycle, the corresponding switch port and output link will be considered busy during link arbitration for the next flit cycle. If the requested switch port and/or output link are busy but there are free virtual channels at the next router, a virtual channel is reserved and the packet is stored in the corresponding buffer at the current router. It will be synchronously scheduled together with flits from data streams. If there are no free virtual channels at the next router, the packet is blocked and stored in the corresponding buffer at the current router.

Best-effort packets are also routed as soon as the header reaches the routing and arbitration unit. However, best-effort packets have lower priority than data streams. If the requested output link has free virtual channels at the next router, a virtual channel is reserved. Otherwise, the packet is blocked. In both cases, the packet is stored in the corresponding buffer at the current router. Best-effort packets are synchronously scheduled together with flits from data streams. When a control or a best-effort packet is completely transmitted, the corresponding virtual channel is released.

3.5 Routing and Arbitration Unit

The routing and arbitration unit executes the routing algorithm. The routing algorithm determines the path followed by the probes when establishing a connection, and the path taken by the best-effort packets. For best effort packets, the MMR uses a fully adaptive routing algorithm that has been proposed for wormhole networks with irregular topology [26,27] and is valid for VCT switching. Exhaustive profitable backtracking (EPB) [17] will be used when establishing connections. This algorithm performs an exhaustive search of the minimal paths in the network until a valid path is found or the probe backtracks to the source node. In order to avoid searching the same links twice, a history store associated with each input virtual channel records all the output links that have already been searched [17]. An implementation of such a protocol has been described in [1].

The routing and arbitration unit keeps the channel mappings between input and output virtual channels for established connections [17]. Virtual channels are specified by indicating the physical link and the virtual channel on that link. Direct and reverse channel mappings are stored. Direct mappings are required to forward data flits. Reverse mappings are used by backtracking headers and returned acknowledgments. Mappings are also used to propagate status information.

4.0 Bandwidth Allocation and Link/Switch Scheduling

The MMR supports QoS for virtual connections realized with virtual channels. Support for QoS guarantees within the MMR takes the form of solutions to three basic problems: bandwidth allocation, link scheduling, and switch scheduling.

The bandwidth allocation scheme allocates bandwidth to each connection when it is established while link and switch scheduling strategies must operate in a tightly coupled manner to make the most effective use of the network bandwidth. The major challenge in a single chip MMR is that these strategies must have compact and fast implementations.

4.1 Link Operation

Link bandwidth and switch port bandwidth are split into flit cycles: the time taken for a flit to be transmitted through the router and across the physical link. Flit cycles are grouped into *rounds* also referred to as *frames*. The number of flit cycles in a round is an integer multiple K ($K > 1$) of the number of virtual channels per link. Bandwidth for a connection is allocated as an integer number of flit cycles/round. Thus, a greater value of K provides a higher flexibility for bandwidth allocation. However, it may increase jitter on a connection since rounds take longer to complete. Therefore, the selected value for K is a trade-off between flexibility and jitter.

The data structures used for supporting fast scheduling decisions are a set of status bit vectors, where each bit in a vector is associated with a single virtual channel. Bit vectors provide information about different conditions for all the virtual channels in the router. Examples of status bit vectors include: *flits_available*, *input_buffer_full*, *CBR_service_requested*, *CBR_bandwidth_serviced*, *VBR_bandwidth_serviced*, etc. A bit on one of these bit vectors is updated every time the status of a virtual channel changes. For example, if a given virtual channel has no flits available to be transmitted and a flit belonging to that virtual channel arrives, the corresponding *flits_available* status bit is updated in the corresponding bit vector. In general status bit vectors are either associated with input or output virtual channels depending on the implementation of the link scheduling algorithm.

The basic idea here is to trade space (silicon) for time (scheduling decisions). Using status bit vectors each physical input link can quickly determine the set of input virtual channels at that link which satisfy some conditions with simple highly parallel bit operations. For example, we can quickly determine the virtual channels with *flits_available* and *credits_available*, by performing the logical AND of the corresponding bit vectors. Similarly, the sets of channels satisfying other more complex conditions can also be quickly obtained.

4.2 Bandwidth Allocation

When a connection is being established in the MMR the source node generates a routing probe that tries to establish a connection by setting up a path from source to destination, reserving link bandwidth and buffer space along that path. If resource reservation is successful the connection is established and the request is granted. If resources cannot be reserved along the whole path, the connection fails and all the resources reserved during the construction of the path are released. Using a backtracking search, alternative paths through the network can be pursued. For CBR connections each probe carries information about the requested bandwidth measured in flit cycles/round. Each output link requires an associated register that keeps track of the total number of flit cycles/round that have been allocated. This register is incremented by the requested number of flit cycles when link bandwidth is allocated and decremented when a connection is removed. A CBR connection can only be allocated if the total number of flit cycles that have been allocated (including the current request) does not exceed the number of flit cycles in a round. Note that it is possible to reserve some bandwidth/round for best-effort traffic in order to prevent starvation of best-effort packets.

For VBR connections, the problem is more difficult to solve since the amount of data varies over time. In order to deal with the varying requirements of different connections, a probe establishing a VBR connection will carry the permanent and peak bandwidth for that connection. These values may be estimates depending on the available knowledge of the connection behavior. To support bandwidth allocation for VBR connections, each output link requires an additional register to that used for CBR connections. This second register stores the total peak bandwidth requested by all of the connections using that link. These two registers are incremented by the permanent and peak bandwidth, respectively, when a connection is established and decremented by those values when a connection is removed. A VBR connection will only be accepted if i) the value of the first register plus the permanent bandwidth of the current connection does not exceed the number of flit cycles in a round, and ii) the value of the second register does not exceed the product of the number of flit cycles in a round and a *concurrency factor*. The concurrency factor is stored in a separate register and is set during power on. Note that the proposed bandwidth allocation mechanism does not guarantee that the connection will be assigned the requested peak bandwidth. Providing such a guarantee could waste a large fraction of link bandwidth especially if peak bandwidths are worst case estimates. The probability that the peak bandwidth will be available at any point in time depends on the concurrency factor. The concurrency factor is a trade-off between the ability to make QoS guarantees, the number of connections that can be concurrently serviced, and link utilization.

During data transmission, a policing protocol operates by limiting the injection of new flits into the network in such a way that each connection does not use higher link bandwidth than that allocated to it when the connection was established. The injection of flits for best-effort packets is automatically limited since it only uses bandwidth that is available after satisfying the requirements of connections that are guaranteed some minimal QoS. The MMR uses flow control to prevent flits from being discarded. Additionally, flit buffers are relatively small, producing a fast propagation of flow control information. Eventually, flow control may propagate backward up to the network interface at the source node, limiting the injection of new flits. Policing within the MMR would only be required if there was no policing at the interface.

4.3 Link Scheduling

As described in the preceding discussion, the basic mechanism to support QoS in the MMR consists of allocating bandwidth to each connection when it is established and guaranteeing that the allocated bandwidth will be available during data transmission via link/switch scheduling.

For CBR connections the link scheduler requires state to store the bandwidth allocated to each virtual channel. The link scheduling algorithm operates on a round basis and ensures that no virtual channel consumes more bandwidth than allocated. For VBR connections, link scheduling becomes more complex. Each virtual channel requires state information storing the permanent and peak bandwidth for that connection, respectively. Additionally, each virtual channel stores the priority associated with the data being transmitted. That priority can be dynamically modified by sending control words from the network interface, for example, based on application specific information. The link scheduling algorithm first assigns all the flit cycles in a round for CBR connections. Then, it assigns the permanent bandwidth to every VBR connection. Note that the bandwidth allocation mechanism guarantees that all the VBR connections can be assigned the permanent bandwidth. Now the link scheduling algorithm considers priorities. Starting from the highest-priority

connection, bandwidth (flit cycles in a round) is allocated to each connection ensuring that no virtual channel consumes more than its peak bandwidth. Thus, at each intermediate router the link scheduler allocates flit cycles/round giving priority to CBR connections and permanent bandwidth on VBR connections followed by VBR connections in priority order. Conflicts at output ports will cause flits on some connections to be delayed.

The MMR link scheduling approach recognizes that low-priority VBR connections may not be able to deliver all flits on time. However the presence of flow control enables delay information to propagate back to the source interface where appropriate action can be taken. For example, an interface may detect that a connection transmitting a low priority compressed video frame makes little progress at some point in time. The network interface may decide to abort the transmission of that frame. By doing so, less bandwidth is wasted in the transmission of a frame that will not meet the deadline. Also, note that the excess bandwidth (difference between peak and permanent bandwidths) requested by VBR connections is serviced in turn, completely servicing the excess bandwidth of one connection before moving to the next one. The idea here is that it is preferable to service the excess bandwidth of most VBR connections completely at the risk of not servicing some of them at all. Certainly other service disciplines are possible.

Finally, we note that using control words along a connection we can dynamically vary the bandwidth requirements of a connection. This may be initiated by the source interface of a connection in response to external (CPU initiated) events or in response to actual performance that is experienced on a connection. The response may involve a change in data rate, selective dropping of data packets, or injection limitation. By using command encodings similar to those used in Myrinet [5] we can encapsulate dynamic bandwidth management in the flow control mechanism. The complex bandwidth control functions can be implemented in the network interfaces or source CPUs where there is a great deal of flexibility and application specific information. In return, the routers remain compact and fast.

4.4 Switch Scheduling

Switch scheduling refers to the process of determining which input ports are connected to which output ports in a flit cycle for the transmission of a single flit per port. Switch scheduling must be tightly coupled with link scheduling. Ideally virtual channels on input links must be selected in such a way that there are no conflicts in the use of switch output ports (note that each switch output port is connected to a physical link). For each round, the scheduling algorithm is invoked every flit cycle servicing connections and best-effort traffic.

Switch scheduling schemes can be classified as input-driven or output-driven. Input-driven schemes first consider the set of virtual channels in each input link. For each set, the link scheduling algorithm determines the virtual channel(s) that should transmit a flit during the next flit cycle. The direct channel mapping store indicates the requested output link for each selected virtual channel. As requests from different input links may contend for the same output link, some arbitration is required at each output port. This is the scheme used in the Intel Cavallino router [6]. On the other hand, output-driven schemes consider the set of input virtual channels requesting a given output link. For each set, the link scheduling algorithm determines the virtual channel that should transmit a flit during the next flit cycle. As contention may occur for the use of switch input ports, some arbitration is required for the assignment of switch input ports.

For fully de-multiplexed switches output-driven schemes provide superior performance [15]. However, for a large number of virtual channels, a fully de-multiplexed crossbar is infeasible. For multiplexed crossbars the choice between input-driven and output-driven scheduling is not clear. In the former the state information associated with competing channels is located in the same router. This potentially enables intelligent decisions in arbitrating between competing requests from input ports. In output-driven schemes the state information associated with competing channels are naturally in distinct routers. Separating the state information from the buffer location would appear to result in more complex flow of control information with the resulting overhead. Therefore, the MMR uses input-driven switch scheduling.

In the MMR we consider switch scheduling algorithms that attempt to schedule all ports concurrently and synchronously set the switch. These scheduling decisions can be classified according to mechanism for arbitrating among multiple requests for an output port. Arbitration can be performed by using static priorities, dynamic priorities or random selection. The MMR utilizes a dynamic priority biasing scheme motivated by the priority biasing scheme proposed in [7,20]. The priorities of the flits at the head of an input virtual channel are updated periodically as often as every flit cycle. The unique aspect of this scheme is that the rate at which these priorities grow is a function of the QoS metric used for the corresponding

connection. The result is a more equitable distribution of bandwidth across connections in a manner that is dependent upon the type of service guarantees rather than simply the time spent by the packet in the network. Dynamic re-computation of priorities can be a time consuming task and the challenge is to develop solutions that can be implemented efficiently in area and time.

Finally, switch scheduling algorithms can be classified according to the number of candidates offered by the link scheduling algorithm from each group of virtual channels on an input link. For example, instead of selecting a single virtual channel from each input link, the router can select a set of candidates. This set is simply obtained as the result of some operations with bit vectors (for instance, the set of input virtual channels at that link with *flits_available*, *credits_available* for flit transmission, *CBR_service_requested* and not *CBR_Completely_Serviced*). Using bit vectors, identification of the set of channels can be quite fast. Having more candidates available per switch port increases the probability of fully utilizing the switch bandwidth in a flit cycle. However, the process of arbitrating among multiple requests is now more complex and time consuming. The challenge is in deciding how many candidates should be considered at an input port to maximize switch bandwidth with minimal impact on switch cycle time.

Concurrently with the transmission of a flit, the scheduling algorithm computes the set of virtual channels that will transmit a flit during the next flit cycle. The switch is then reconfigured according to the computed input-output port assignment and the next flit cycle starts. This process is repeated until the round is completed.

In summary, the MMR scheduler attempts to maximize the probability of assigning virtual channels to every output link during each flit cycle by using sets of candidates (4-8) at each input port and fast priority biasing schemes. Our inclination is to favor simpler, faster schedulers over more complex schedulers that might make better decisions but which lengthen the switch cycle time.

5.0 Simulation Studies

This section provides some preliminary results for link and switch scheduling. The goal here was to determine if the partitioning of scheduling functionality in the MMR (as shown in Figure 1), the use of large flits, and support for a large number of virtual channels could produce good jitter and delay characteristics in a cut-through router architecture. Encouraging results would point us in the directions for further refinement.

Simulation experiments were conducted using a C++ discrete event simulator that models a single router. The following experiments represent an 8x8 router with 256 virtual channels/input port, 1.24 Gbps physical links and 128-bit flits. The behavior for slower links speeds, such as 622 Mbps and 155 Mbps, were qualitatively the same and therefore these latter results are excluded. The simulations were run until steady state was reached and statistics gathered over approximately 100,000 router cycles. Connections were randomly selected from the set (64 Kbps, 128 Kbps, 1.54Mbps, 2Mbps, 5Mbps, 10Mbps, 20Mbps, 55Mbps, 120Mbps) and assigned to random input and output ports on the router. The offered load is computed as the percentage of switch bandwidth demanded by all connections through the router.

These preliminary experiments were conducted on CBR connections and did not include best-effort and control messages. Admission control can guarantee that connections are established only if bandwidth is available on a link and the inter-arrival time on a connection is constant. This study was limited to CBR connections to enable easier interpretation of the interaction between link and switch scheduling and gain some insight into potential bottlenecks.

Delay is computed as difference between the times a flit is ready to be transmitted through the switch and the time it actually leaves the switch. The jitter on a connection is defined as the difference in the delays of successive flits on a connection. The flit cycle time is determined by the physical link speed and the flit size.

5.1 Scheduling Algorithms

We have studied a simple link scheduling algorithm that uses a biased priority based on the ratio of the delay experienced by a flit at the switch and the inter-arrival time on the connection. This priority is recomputed for all connections (head flit) each flit cycle. High speed connections clearly have their priorities grow at a faster rate. For comparison purposes we include results from an algorithm that represents the scheduling in the Autonet switch [2,24]. This algorithm differs in how the candidates are selected at input links and in how conflicts for output ports are arbitrated. To capture ideal performance we also implemented a perfect switch to provide a lower bound on the delay and jitter, and upper bound on switch utilization. When multiple inputs of a perfect switch request the same output port, the flits from these input ports are transmitted to that output port in one flit cycle. Effectively the switch internal bandwidth is N times the link bandwidth for an

NxN switch. There are no port conflicts in a perfect switch and therefore no switch scheduling overheads.

5.2 Simulation Results

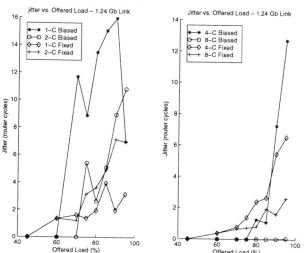

Figure 3. Jitter vs. Offered Load: Fixed and Biased Priorities

In general, we have observed that using a larger number of candidates is effective in increasing switch utilization and is not significantly affected by the priority scheme. This is because while priorities affect which flits are transmitted in a flit cycle they do not directly affect how many inputs can be concurrently transmitting in the same cycle. In contrast the jitter and delay characteristics of individual connections are very sensitive to the priority scheme. The jitter characteristics for fixed and biased priority schemes are illustrated in Figure 3. The vertical axis is represented in router cycles (equivalently flit cycles) which is the time to transmit a flit across the router or link. We chose to represent the jitter in terms of flit cycles since flits emerge from the network at flit cycle boundaries and jitter occurs as an integer number of flit cycles. With 1.24 Gbps links and 128-bit flits a flit cycle is approximately 103 ns. We see that priority biasing consistently performs better especially with a higher number of candidates.

These jitter values are averaged over a large range of connection speeds. Actual jitter values for high-speed connections will be even less and those for low-speed connections will be relatively higher. While we may not be too concerned with relatively higher jitter values on a 64 Kbps connection we expect that jitter values on a 100 Mbps connection will be of more concern. Thus, overall the proposed scheme appears very encouraging for use in multimedia routers.

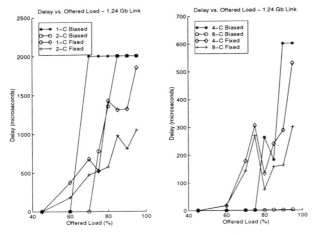

Figure 4. Delay vs. Offered Load: Fixed and Biased Priorities

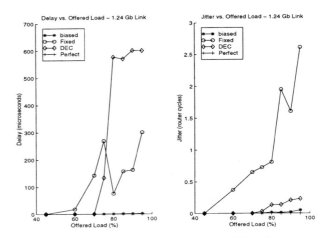

Figure 5. Delay and Jitter vs. Offered Load: Fixed and Biased Priorities, Autonet, Perfect Switch

Figure 4 illustrates the behavior of delay expressed in microseconds as a function of offered load (note the plots for 1 and 2 candidates are clipped to avoid scaling problems). It is apparent that prior to saturation the delay characteristics using a biased priority are consistently better than that of the fixed priority scheme. The differences are particularly pronounced in the region just prior to saturation. For example with two candidates and at 70% load, the biased scheme produces an average delay of 0.82 microseconds while with fixed priority we have ~500 microseconds.

With 8 candidates delays for biased priorities are consistently in the range of 0.4-0.6 microseconds while the fixed priorities realize delays on the order of 100-200 microseconds. Saturation does not appear to occur before 95% load.

Figure 5 compares the delay and jitter characteristics of four algorithms. The plots for biased and fixed priority use 8 candidates. The results are quite favorable with the use of 8 candidates, closely tracking the performance of the perfect switch. While the Autonet algorithm realizes very good jitter characteristics at high loads (>80%), the biased priority scheme maintains extremely low jitter values ranging from 0.0168 router cycles at 80% load to 0.051 router cycles at 95% load.

6.0 Concluding Remarks

The primary (longer term) objective of the Multimedia Router (MMR) project is the design and implementation of a single-chip router optimized for multimedia applications. This paper focused in delineating the initial trade-offs that were made and on the scheduling framework being employed. Targeting 1-2 Gbps links and 128-bit flit sizes, the crossbar must be capable of computing switch settings at a rate of 64 ns-128 ns. At the heart of the proposed algorithm is a dynamic priority update or priority biasing scheme. Other novel features/goals of MMR include use of flow control for dynamic bandwidth management, fixed-size buffers for VBR traffic, cache-like memory design for the virtual channel memory, and the partitioning of switch and link scheduling functionality.

Preliminary performance evaluation results indicate that the use of biased priorities is consistently better below switch saturation. These numbers are predicated on the availability of a router that can schedule a switch in a single cycle. In the example here this would imply a cycle time of 103 ns which is matched to the rate at which 128-bit quantities arrive on a 1.24 Gbps link. The MMR architecture was formulated to permit concurrency and pipelining. The link schedulers can all operate in parallel and be pipelined with the switch scheduler. While we have been concerned with the study of the functional behavior of the switch scheduler, we now turn our attention to supported VBR traffic and best-effort traffic and the hardware implementation to meet these timing constraints.

7.0 References

[1]   J. D. Allen, et al., "Ariadne - an adaptive router for fault-tolerant multicomputers," *Proceedings of the 21st International Symposium on Computer Architecture*, pp. 278--288, April 1994.

[2] T. E. Anderson et. al., "High speed switch scheduling for local area networks," Technical Report SRC research report 99, DEC. Also in *ACM Transactions on Computer Systems*, November, 1993.

[3] B. V. Dao, J. Duato and S. Yalamanchili, "Configurable flow control mechanisms for fault-tolerant routing," *Proceedings of the 22nd International Symposium on Computer Architecture*, pp. 220--229, June 1995.

[4] S. Balakrishnan and F. Ozguner, "A priority-based flow control mechanism to support real-time traffic in pipelined direct networks," *Proceedings of the 1996 International Conference on Parallel Processing*, vol. I, pp. 120--127, August 1996.

[5] N. J. Boden, et al., "Myrinet - A gigabit per second local area network," *IEEE Micro*, pp.~29--36, February 1995.

[6] J. Carbonaro and F. Verhoorn, "Cavallino: The teraflops router and NIC," *Proceedings of Hot Interconnects Symposium IV*, August 1996.

[7] A. Chien and J. H, Kim, "Approaches to Quality of Service in High Performance Networks," *Lecture Notes in Computer Science: Proceedings of the Workshop on Parallel Computer Routing and Communication*, Springer Verlag (pubs.), pp.1-20, June 1997.

[8] A. A. Chien, "A cost and speed model for k-ary n-cube wormhole routers," *Proceedings of Hot Interconnects'93*, August 1993.

[9] W. J. Dally, "Virtual-channel flow control," *IEEE Transactions on Parallel and Distributed Systems*, vol. 3, no. 2, pp. 194--205, March 1992.

[10] W. J. Dally, et. al., "The Reliable Router: A reliable and high-performance communication substrate for parallel computers," *Lecture Notes in Computer Science: Proceedings of the Workshop on Parallel Computer Routing and Communication*, Springer Verlag (pubs.) pp. 241--255, May 1994.

[11] J. Duato, "A new theory of deadlock-free adaptive routing in wormhole networks," *IEEE Transactions on Parallel and Distributed Systems*, vol. 4, no. 12, pp. 1320--1331, December 1993.

[12] J. Duato, P. Lopez, F. Silla and S. Yalamanchili, "A high performance router architecture for interconnection networks," *Proceedings of the 1996 International Conference on Parallel Processing*, vol. 1, pp. 61--68, August 1996.

[13] J. Duato, S. Yalamanchili, B. Caminero, D. Love, F. J. Quiles, "MMR: Architecture and Trade-offs in a High Performance Multimedia Router," Technical Report, Computer Architecture and Systems Laboratory, Georgia Institute of Technology available from *http://www.ece.gatech.edu/research/labs/casl/papers/*.

[14] D. Ferrari, D. Verma "A scheme for real-time channel establishment in wide-area networks," *IEEE Journal on Selected Areas in Communications,* April 1990.

[15] M. L. Fulgham and L. Snyder, "A comparison of input and output driven routers," *Proceedings of Euro-Par'96*, vol. 1, pp. 195-204, August 1996.

[16] D. Garcia and W. Watson, "ServerNet II," *Lecture Notes in Computer Science, Proceedings of the Workshop on Parallel Computer Routing and Communication*, Springer Verlag (pubs.), pp. 119-136, June 1997.

[17] P. T. Gaughan and S. Yalamanchili, "A family of fault-tolerant routing protocols for direct multiprocessor networks," *IEEE Transactions on Parallel and Distributed Systems*, vol. 6, no. 5, pp. 482--497, May 1995.

[18] R. Horst, "TNet: A Reliable System Area Network," *IEEE Micro*, pp. 37--45, February 1995.

[19] M. G. H. Katevenis, et al., "ATLAS I: A single-chip ATM switch for NOWs," *Proceedings of the Workshop on Communications and Architectural Support for Network-based Parallel Computing*, February 1997.

[20] J.H.~Kim, "Bandwidth and latency guarantees in low-cost, high-performance networks," Ph. D. Dissertation, University of Illinois at Urbana-Champaign, 1997.

[21] A. Mekkittikul and N. McKeown, "A practical scheduling algorithm to achieve 100% throughput in input-queued switches," *Proceedings INFOCOM*, pp.792--799, April, 1998.

[22] M. Prycker, *Asynchronous transfer mode: solution for broadband ISDN*, Ellis Horwood Limited, Chichester, West Susex, PO191EB, England, 1991.

[23] J. Rexford, J. Hall and K. G. Shin, "A Router Architecture for Real-Time Point-to-Point Networks," *Proceedings of the International Symposium on Computer Architecture*, May 1996.

[24] M. D. Schroeder et al., "Autonet: A high-speed, self-configuring local area network using point-to-point links," Technical Report SRC research report 59, DEC, April 1990.

[25] S. L. Scott and G. Thorson, "Optimized routing in the Cray T3D," *Lecture Notes in Computer Science: Proceedings of the Workshop on Parallel Computer Routing and Communication*, Springer Verlag (pubs.), pp.281--294, May 1994.

[26] F. Silla, et al., "Efficient adaptive routing in networks of workstations with irregular topology," *Lecture Notes in Computer Science: Proceedings of the Workshop on Communications and Architectural Support for Network-based Parallel Computing*, pp. 46--60, February 1997.

[27] F. Silla and J. Duato, "Improving the efficiency of adaptive routing in networks with irregular topology," *Proceedings of the 1997 Conference on High Performance Computing*, December 1997.

[28] C. B. Stunkel, et al., "The SP2 high-performance switch," *IBM Systems Journal*, vol. 34, no. 2, pp. 185--204, February 1995.

[29] Y. L. Chen and J.-C. Liu, "A hybrid interconnection network for integrated communication services," *Proceedings of the 11th International Parallel Processing Symposium*, pp. 341--345, April 1997.

Communication Studies of Single-threaded and Multithreaded Distributed-Memory Machines
(A Short Summary)

Andrew Sohn, Yunheung Paek, Jui-Yuan Ku
Computer Information Science Department
New Jersey Institute of Technology
{sohn,paek,jku}@cis.njit.edu

Yuetsu Kodama, Yoshinori Yamaguchi
Electrotechnical Laboratory
1-1-4 Umezono, Tsukuba-shi, Ibaraki 305, Japan
{kodama,yamaguti}@etl.go.jp

Abstract

This report explicates the communication overlapping capabilities of three distributed-memory machines, SGI/Cray T3E, IBM SP-2 with wide nodes, and the ETL EM-X. Bitonic sorting and Fast Fourier Transform are selected for experiments. Various message sizes are used to determine when, where, how much and why the overlapping takes place. Experimental results with up to 64 processors indicated that the communication performance of EM-X is insensitive to various message sizes while SP-2 is the most sensitive. T3E stayed in between. The EM-X gave the highest communication overlapping capability while T3E did the lowest. The experimental results are compared with the analytical results based on LogP and LogGP communication models.

1 Background, Experimental Settings and Results

Distributed-Memory Multiprocessors (DMMs) have been regarded as a viable architecture of scalable and economical design in building large parallel machines to meet the ever-increasing demand for high performance computing. The major problem which hinders the performance of distributed-memory machines is remote memory latency. DMMs distribute data in a way that there is no overlapping or copying of major data. Typical distributed-memory machines incur a lot of latency, ranging from a few to tens of microseconds for a single remote read operation. The gap between processor cycle and remote memory access time becomes wider, as the processor technology is advanced using rigorous instruction level parallelism.

Numerous approaches have been taken to study the communication issues of DMMs. Distributed-memory machines such as T3E [9], AP1000+, and SP-2 [1] provide some hardware support to overlap computation with communication in a way to take some of the burden from the main processor. Multithreaded machines EM-4 [8], EM-X [7] and Tera [5] aim at tolerating remote memory latency through split-phase read mechanism and context switch [6]. It is the purpose of this report to investigate the overlapping capabilities of DMMs. Specifically, we identify when, where, how much and why overlapping takes place.

Three DMMs are used in our experiments, including IBM SP-2 with wide nodes, SGI/Cray T3E, and the laboratory prototype EM-X. The multithreading capability of EM-X was turned off in this study by using only one thread. Instead, the remote by-passing mechanism has been used to be fair with the others. The multithreading capabilities of EM-X are described in [10]. The two benchmark problems, fine-grain bitonic sorting [3] and FFT, have been implemented on the three machines. The SP-2 and T3E versions are written in C with Message-Passing Interface (MPI). The EM-X version is written in C with a thread library, which can run only on the EM-4 and EM-X multithreaded machines. Details of the overlapping versions of bitonic sorting and FFT are described in [11].

The terms elements and integers are used interchangeably throughout this paper, as are segments and messages. The unit for sorting is *integers* while that for FFT is *points*. An integer is 4 bytes in EM-X and SP-2 and 8 bytes in T3E. A point consists of real and imaginary parts, each of which is 4 bytes in EM-X and SP-2 and 8 bytes in T3E. The following lists the parameters used in this study:

- P = the number of processors, up to 64.
- n = the total number of data elements, up to 8M (the maximum size which can be run on EM-X).
- s = the number of segments per processor
- $m = n/sP$ = message size

Absolute communication times are plotted in Figure 1. We find from the plots that SP2 is very sensitive to message size, favoring message sizes of 512 to 2K elements. On the other hand, EM-X is less sensitive to message size. T3E generally stays in between. In particular, the machine is very efficient for large-sized messages.

Bitonic sorting shows irregular and often higher communication time than FFT. It forms a valley in the performance curve for EM-X, so does FFT for SP2. On the other hand, the T3E communication times continuously decrease as the segment size increases. Recall that FFT has to send twice as many messages because each element has real and imaginary parts. Hence, the FFT communication times should be halved to make a fair comparison with sorting.

In general, increasing the number of processors increases the communication time for these machines when the data size for each processor is fixed. When the number of processors is increased to 64, SP2 and T3E give consistent behavior over the two problems. EM-X, on the other hand, showed there is little change in the communication time when the number of processors is increased to 64.

2 Comparison with Communication Models

The LogP [4] and LogGP models [2] are designed to capture the communication behaviors of distributed-memory machines. The LogP model defines four parameters, L for latency, o for overhead, g for gap between messages, and P for processors for *short* messages. The LogGP model captures the communication behavior of *long* messages by adding G, where G is the gap between bytes of the same message. Using the five terms, L, o, g, G, and P of the LogGP model, the communication time for a single *long* message with k bytes on a single processor can be defined as $t_{1,1} = o + (k-1)G + L + o$. The communication time for sending *two* consecutive messages with message size k_1 and k_2 on a processor will be $t_{1,2} = o + (k_1 - 1)G + g + (k_2 - 1)G + L + o$. Thus, the communication time for sending s consecutive messages on a single processor will be

$$t_{comm} = 2o + L + (s-1)g + \sum_{i=1}^{s} (k_i - 1)G$$

Let b be the number of bytes per word. Since the message sizes are the same for both benchmarks, we have, $k_1 = k_2 = ... = k_s = mb$. The above formulation for sending s consecutive messages of size m words reduces to

$$t_{comm} = t_{1,s} = 2o + L + (s-1)g + (mb-1)Gs \qquad (1)$$

where b is set to 4 for EM-X and SP2 and 8 for T3E. To compare the analytical results with the experimental results shown in Figure 1, let us consider the case with bitonic sorting on SP2 for $P=64$ and $n=1M$, where we have identified that the maximum communication time occurs when the segment (message) size m is 4 words and the

310

number of messages (segments) is $s = n/P*m = 1\text{M}/64*4 = 4096$ segments. Using Eq. (1), we find the maximum communication time, t_{max}, for $s=4096$, and $m=4$ as

$$t_{max} = 2o + L + (4096 - 1)g + (4*4 - 1)G*4096$$
$$= 2o + L + 4095g + 61440G \qquad (2)$$

G is typically tens to hundreds of nano seconds whereas g is several tens of microseconds. Furthermore, o, L and g are usually on the similar order. We assume $G = 0.001g$ [2,4]. Thus, Eq. (2) reduces to

$$t_{max} = 2g + g + 4095g + 61g \approx 4159g \qquad (3)$$

Note from Figure 1 that the minimum communication time for bitonic sorting with $P=64$ and $n=1\text{M}$ occurred when the message size m is 4K words and the number of messages (segments) is $s = n/P*m = 1\text{M} / 64*4\text{K} = 4$ segments. Using Eq. (1) and the above assumptions on g and G, we approximate

$$t_{min} = 2o + L + (4 - 1)g + (4*4096 - 1)G*4$$
$$= 2o + L + 3g + 65532G = 2g + g + 3g + 66g \approx 72g \qquad (4)$$

Taking the ratio of (3) to (4), we find $t_{max}/t_{min} = 4159g/72g = \mathbf{58}$. The ratio of t_{max} to t_{min} is determined essentially by the number of segments. Note from Table 1 that $t_{max} =8.335$ sec and $t_{min} =0.132$ sec, as highlighted. The empirical ratio is thus $\mathbf{63}$. This analytical result closely matches the experimental result for sorting on SP-2.

For the FFT results with $m = 4$ and 1K, the empirical ratio is $4.370/0.084 = \mathbf{52}$ (Table 2). Using the analytical model, we have $t_{max}/t_{min} = 4159g/83g = \mathbf{50}$ which is also close to the empirical result. From these results, we find that the analytical models can reasonably accurately predict the SP-2 communication times. The empirical results for EM-X and T3E, however, do not agree with the analytical results, as discussed below.

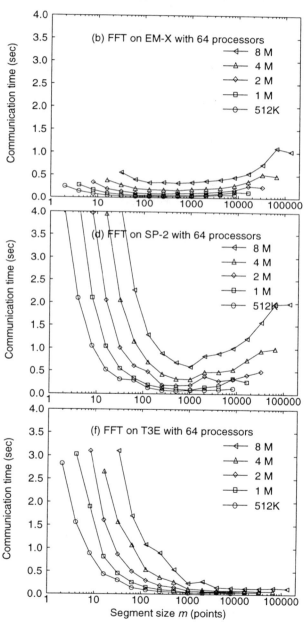

Figure 1: Communication times in seconds on 64 processors.

311

# of seg s	seg size m	EM-X			SP-2			T3E		
		comp	comm	ratio	comp	comm	ratio	comp	comm	ratio
4096	4	0.441	**1.005**	0.44	0.277	**8.335**	0.03	0.131	**5.134**	0.026
2048	8	0.387	0.565	0.69	0.184	4.299	0.04	0.100	2.824	0.035
1024	16	0.360	0.318	1.13	0.148	2.010	0.07	0.085	1.669	0.051
512	32	0.347	0.206	1.68	0.121	1.041	0.12	0.079	1.451	0.054
256	64	0.340	0.155	2.19	0.112	0.585	0.19	0.075	0.564	0.137
128	128	0.337	0.129	2.61	0.103	0.349	0.30	0.072	0.345	0.209
64	256	0.336	**0.124**	2.71	0.100	0.201	0.50	0.072	0.204	0.353
32	512	0.336	0.130	2.58	0.102	0.281	0.36	0.070	0.145	0.483
16	1K	0.338	0.147	2.30	0.097	0.154	0.63	0.070	0.116	0.603
8	2K	0.344	0.163	2.11	0.096	0.142	0.68	0.070	0.114	0.614
4	4K	0.352	0.200	1.76	0.095	**0.132**	0.72	0.069	0.113	0.611
2	8K	0.374	0.255	1.47	0.095	0.179	0.53	0.070	0.080	0.875
1	16K	0.415	0.282	1.47	0.094	0.190	0.49	0.069	**0.079**	0.873

Table 1: Sample execution times(sec) for bitonic sorting with $P=64$, $n=1$M. The highlighted entries represent the t_{min} and t_{max}.

# of seg s	seg size m	EM-X			SP-2			T3E		
		comp	comm	ratio	comp	comm	ratio	comp	comm	ratio
4096	4	1.680	**0.377**	4.46	2.540	**4.370**	0.58	0.271	**3.029**	0.089
2048	8	1.589	0.218	7.29	1.894	2.229	0.85	0.234	1.899	0.123
1024	16	1.553	0.114	13.6	1.058	1.098	0.96	0.218	0.819	0.266
512	32	1.523	0.079	19.3	0.651	0.563	1.16	0.213	0.456	0.467
256	64	1.513	0.058	26.1	0.464	0.311	1.49	0.209	0.262	0.798
128	128	1.508	0.048	31.4	0.390	0.196	1.99	0.207	0.154	1.344
64	256	1.508	**0.047**	32.1	0.323	0.120	2.69	0.207	0.101	2.050
32	512	1.506	0.049	30.1	0.280	0.092	3.04	0.206	0.075	2.747
16	1K	1.504	0.057	26.4	0.265	**0.084**	3.16	0.214	0.041	5.220
8	2K	1.504	0.070	21.5	0.298	0.135	2.21	0.214	**0.040**	5.350
4	4K	1.503	0.092	16.3	0.308	0.134	2.28	0.214	0.048	4.458
2	8K	1.504	0.131	11.5	0.356	0.187	1.90	0.213	0.045	4.733
1	16K	1.513	0.120	12.6	0.393	0.231	1.70	0.213	0.050	4.260

Table 2: Sample execution times(sec) for FFT with $P=64$, $n=1$M.

In EM-X, for sorting with $P=64$ and $n=1$M, the maximum and minimum communication times for EM-X are 1.005 seconds and 0.124 seconds, resulting in the ratio of **8.1**. For FFT, the ratio is 0.377/0.047 = **8.0**. Unlike SP-2, we can see that the communication behavior of EM-X is highly stable since the ratios are essentially the same across the two different problems. However, these ratios do not match with the analytical ratio of 4222/134 = **32**. The T3E results are also different from the EM-X and SP-2 results. The empirical ratios are **64** and **75**, respectively for sorting and FFT. However, the analytical ratios are **32** and **30**. The T3E and EM-X results do not agree with the analytical results.

There are several reasons for the discrepancy. First, our assumptions on L, o, g and G were approximations. It is thus likely that these approximations are not accurate for EM-X and T3E. Indeed, EM-X is a fine-grain machine which communicates with fixed-sized packets. Therefore, the assumptions that o, g and L are on the similar order may not be accurate for EM-X.

Second, the parallel programming paradigms used in the machines are different. EM-X employs *one-sided* communication paradigm based on remote read and write while SP-2 and T3E used *two-sided* communication based on send and receive. The former does not require synchronization while the latter does [11]. Since the overhead associated with one-sided communication is substantially smaller because of no synchronization requirement, the ratios for EM-X were much smaller than those for SP-2 and T3E. The ratios for T3E were larger than the analytical ones and the largest among

the three machines. We found that these results are amplified due to the fact that the MPI implementation incurs very high overhead, almost 10 times the SHMEM one [12]. This high overhead offset the gain by the T3E's high-performance network.

Third, the analytical models do not take into consideration the architectural features for *communication-computation overlapping*, such as communication co-processors, remote by-passing mechanisms, and in turn network contention. EM-X uses a remote by-passing mechanism which does not consume the processor cycles. This misprediction of the analytical models on communication behavior leads us to further investigate the overlapping capabilities embedded in these three machines.

3 Communication Efficiency

Figure 2 identifies the efficiency of overlapping for the three machines. Overlapping efficiency is defined as $(T_{comm,1} - T_{comm,s}) / T_{comm,1}$, where $T_{comm,s}$ is the communication time for s segments. The results indicate that EM-X gave the best communication overlapping capability while T3E did the worst. SP-2 remained in between. To further illustrate these results, we classified the communication times into overhead, barrier synchronization, and latency. *Overhead* refers to the time taken to execute instructions for message preparation. This overhead is fixed and cannot be overlapped with computation since the instructions must be executed to send out packets. *Barrier synchronization* is not part of the original programs but only used at the end of each iteration to synchronize processors and measure various timings. *Latency* is the main target for overlapping. Figure 3 shows the distribution of the communication times for $P=64$, $n=8$ M.

The reason EM-X gave the best performance, despite the fact that the EM-X multithreading capability was turned off, is because of the remote by-passing mechanism coupled with fine-grain fixed-sized packet communication. While other machines use the main processor cycles for communication, EM-X does not. Figure 3 shows that the EM-X curves are essentially flat compared to others. The reason is EM-X treats messages the same in the low execution level, regardless of their sizes, except when the message is less than 32 words. When a message of n words is sent (remote write), the message is broken into n words. Each word is joined by the destination processor number and the target memory address to make an independent packet. Therefore, the difference between a few large messages and many small messages is the number of instructions in the source code level. This is precisely why the overhead curve for EM-X is flat while the overhead for T3E and SP2 forms a valley.

The minimum communication of SP-2 occurs when the message size is 512 to 2K elements. This is obvious because each processor in SP-2 has a 4KB communication buffer. Figure 3 further supports this observation as the sum of the three components are fairly equally weighted in that window. Outside the window, however, SP-2 shows poor communication performance. The reason for the poor performance when the message size is small is because the overhead now becomes the deciding factor. The machine needs to incur very large overhead to generate many small messages. For each small message, some instructions must be executed for message preparation. Overhead is a fixed cost and is not overlapped with computation. When the message size is very large, the overlapping efficiency in SP-2 also drastically reduced because of the small buffer. While there is certainly little overhead, this large-sized messages will occupy the communication channels longer to complete sending/receiving each message, resulting in clogging the bandwidth.

T3E gives essentially no overlapping regardless of the message size. Unlike the other machines, the overall communication time continues to drop even for the largest segment of 1 M words. When the message size is small, the overhead is the dominant factor as in

SP-2. However, for large messages, the latency as well as the overhead continues to drop. The main reason for this little overlapping is its high-throughput network with peak performance of 1.2GB/sec that allows processors to send even fairly large messages with little delay. The plots indicate that T3E gives the lowest latency for large messages among the three because of its high-performance network and large numbers of E-registers dedicated to hide remote memory latency. We believe that the high communication overhead coupled with low latency provides little room to optimize the overall communication time through overlapping.

When the two problems are cross-compared, we find that sorting shows relatively poor overlapping compared to FFT for all three machines. This is due to the *ratio* of computation to communication. The computation time in theory must be at least the same as or larger than the communication time to effectively mask off the communi-

cation time. As we have seen in Table 1, the computation-communication ratios for sorting are on the average 1.5 for EM-X, 0.5 for SP-2, and 0.5 for T3E. These small ratios clearly indicate that there was not enough computation to mask off the communication. However, when the ratios for FFT were increased to 15 (EM-X), 2 (SP-2), and 2 (T3E), the amount of overlapping has improved as the plots indicate. SP-2 has now reached nearly 70% while T3E finally shows a sign of improvement. This increase in overlapping is because the machines can now find the time to mask off some of the communication time.

4 Conclusions

Reducing communication times is key to obtaining high performance on distributed-memory machines (DMMs). This report has examined the communication overlapping capabilities of three

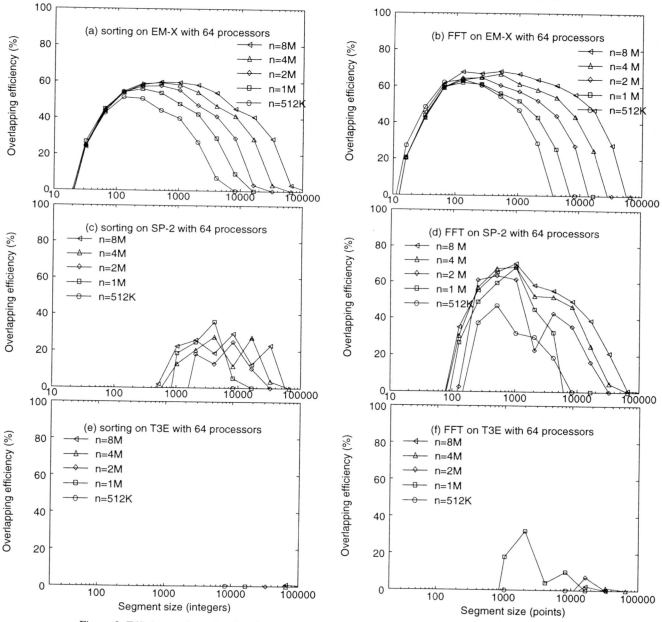

Figure 2: Efficiency of overlapping for bitonic sorting and FFT on three distributed-memory machines.

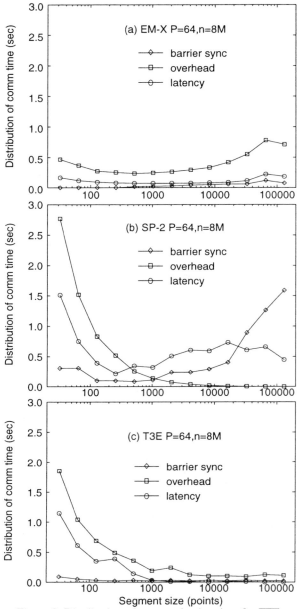

Figure 3: Distribution of communication time for FFT.

DMMs, SGI/Cray T3E, IBM SP-2 and ETL EM-X. Two benchmark problems, bitonic sorting and Fast Fourier Transform, have been selected for experiments. Both problems have been implemented in C with MPI on SP-2 and T3E and with a thread library on EM-X.

Experimental results have indicated that EM-X has showed almost insensitivity to message size because of the remote by-passing mechanism. SP-2 has shown high sensitivity to message size because of the communication buffer of size 4KB. The communication time for T3E has continuously dropped as the message size was increased, showing no size preference, due mainly to the high throughput network and a large of number of external registers.

We have found that the empirical results generally do not agree with the analytical results obtained using the LogP and LogGP models. The reasons include (1) the parallel programming paradigm used in each machine, in particular two-sided versus one-sided communication, (2) the approximation of communication parameters, (3) the lack of incorporating the overlapping capabilities in the analytical models, and (4) the runtime dependent network contention.

Bitonic sorting has been found more difficult to reduce communication time than FFT. The communication times for FFT on SP-2 and EM-X have been reduced to 70% by overlapping. However, communication times for sorting have been reduced to 30% to 60%. The discrepancy is due to the large difference in the ratios of computation to communication. The FFT ratio is almost 10 times larger than the sorting ratio. The performance of T3E, however, has shown very limited, essentially none. This negligible performance has stemmed from the high overhead associated with the MPI implementation. A SHMEM implementation will improve the communication performance at the expense of portability.

Acknowledgments

This work is supported in part by NSF INT-9722545 and NSF INT-9722187. This research used resources of the National Energy Research Scientific Computing Center, which is supported by the Office of Energy Research of the U.S. Department of Energy under Contract No. DE-AC03-76SF00098. Y. Paek is supported in part by Cray Research Inc. and NJIT SBR Program. The T3Es in the Lawrence Berkeley Laboratory and Cray Research Laboratory at Eagan, were used in this work. The SP-2 machines formerly at the NASA Ames and Langley Research Center were used to perform part of the experiments. The authors thank the other EM-X members, Mitsuhisa Sato, Hirofumi Sakane, and Hayato Yamana of the Electrotechincal Laboratory of Japan for various discussions. Andrew Sohn thanks Horst Simon of NERSC, LBL, Joseph Oliger of RIACS at NASA Ames, and Doug Sakal of MRJ Technology Solutions at NASA Ames for their support. The authors thank the referees for their helpful comments.

References

1. T. Agerwala, J. Martin, J. Mirza, D. Sadler, D. Dias, and M. Snir, SP-2 system architecture, *IBM Systems Journal 34*, 1995.
2. A. Alexandrov, M. Ionescu, K. Schauser, and C. Scheiman, LogGP: Incorporating long messages into the LogP model - One step closer towards a realistic model for parallel computation, *ACM SPAA'95*, July 1995, pp. 95-105.
3. K. Batcher, Sorting networks and their applications, in *Proc. the AFIPS Spring Joint Computer Conf. 32*, 1968, pp.307-314.
4. D. Culler, R. Karp, D. Patterson, A. Sahay, K. Schauser, E. Santos, R. Subramonian, and T. von Eicken, LogP: Towards a realistic model of parallel computation, *PPoPP'93*, May 1993.
5. J. Feo and P. Briggs, Tera Programming Workshop, *IEEE/ACM PACT'98*, Paris, France, October 1998.
6. G. Gao, L. Bic and J-L. Gaudiot (Eds.) Advanced topic in dataflow computing and multithreading, IEEE CS Press, 1995.
7. Y. Kodama, H. Sakane, M. Sato, H. Yamana, S. Sakai, and Y. Yamaguchi, The EM-X parallel computer: architecture and basic performance, *ACM ISCA'95*, June 1995, pp.14-23.
8. M. Sato, Y. Kodama, S. Sakai, Y. Yamaguchi, and Y. Koumura, Thread-based programming for the EM-4 hybrid data-flow machine, *ACM ISCA'92*, May 1992, pp.146-155.
9. S. Scott and G. Thorson, The Cray T3E network: adaptive routing in a high performance 3D-Torus, *HOT Interconnects*, 1996.
10. A. Sohn, Y. Kodama, J. Ku, M. Sato, H. Sakane, H. Yamana, S. Sakai, and Y. Yamaguchi, Fine-grain multithreading with the EM-X multiprocessor, *ACM SPAA'97*, pp.189-198.
11. A. Sohn, Y. Paek, J. Ku, Y. Kodama, and Y. Yamaguchi, Communication studies of distributed-memory multiprocessors, NJIT CIS TR 98-3, May 1998. http://www.cs.njit.edu/sohn.
12. T. Welcome, Introduction to the Cray T3E programming environment, http://www.nersc.gov/training/T3E/intro9.html.

Impact of Buffer Size on the Efficiency of Deadlock Detection*

J. M. Martínez, P. López, J. Duato
DISCA, Universidad Politécnica de Valencia
Camino de Vera s/n, 46071 - Valencia, SPAIN
E-mail: {jmmr,plopez,jduato}@gap.upv.es

Abstract

Deadlock detection is one of the most important design issues in recovery strategies for routing in interconnection networks. In a previous paper, we presented an efficient deadlock detection mechanism. This mechanism requires that when a message header blocks it must be quickly notified to all the channels reserved by that message. To achieve this goal, the detection mechanism uses the information provided by flow control.

Some recent commercial multiprocessors use deep buffers, since they may increase network throughput and efficiently allow transmission over long wires. However, deep buffers may increase the elapsed time between header blocking at a router and the propagation of flow control signals, thus negatively affecting the behavior of our deadlock detection mechanism. On the other hand, deeper buffers reduce deadlock frequency. As a consequence, buffer size has opposing effects on deadlock detection. In this paper, we analyze by simulation the influence of these effects on the efficiency of our deadlock detection mechanism, showing that overall performance improves with buffer size.

1. Introduction

Deadlocks are handled in wormhole networks using deadlock avoidance or deadlock recovery [3]. Deadlock avoidance techniques restrict routing so that either there are no cyclic dependencies between channels [1] or some cyclic dependencies between channels are allowed, provided that there exist some escape paths to avoid deadlock [2]. However, deadlocks rarely occur in interconnection networks when sufficient routing freedom is provided [7]. Thus, deadlock recovery strategies appear as an attractive alternative. They allow the use of unrestricted routing, eliminating the need for dedicated resources and potentially outperforming deadlock avoidance techniques. However, recovery strategies require a deadlock detection mechanism that triggers a deadlock recovery mechanism to resolve the deadlock. In [5] we presented a very efficient mechanism for deadlock detection in interconnection networks. This technique reduces false deadlock detection by two orders of magnitude over previous proposals.

The elapsed time between header blocking at a router and the propagation of flow control signals plays an important role in the efficiency of the detection mechanism. The higher this time, the greater the number of false deadlocks detected. This time is closely related to buffer size. With small buffers (i.e., one-flit buffers), when a header blocks, flow control signals are immediately propagated and the remaining data flits are stopped at the channels they are occupying. On the other hand, with large buffers, when a header blocks, the remaining flits continue advancing until the buffer is full. Thus, flow control signals are not immediately propagated. Nowadays, commercial multiprocessors like Cray T3E, SGI Origin 2000, IBM SP2, use deep buffers, leading to increased network throughput. Also, irregular networks used in networks of workstations use pipelined transmission over long wires, requiring the use of buffers deep enough to store all the data that are on the wire at a given time. As a consequence, there may be a performance degradation of our deadlock detection mechanism when it is used in most modern machines. On the other hand, deep buffers also have a positive effect on deadlock frequency [7], reducing the number of deadlocks as buffer size increases. Hence, there are opposing effects, being necessary an in-depth analysis to determine the actual performance of the deadlock detection mechanism as a function of buffer size.

The rest of the paper is organized as follows. Section 2 summarizes the mechanism proposed in [5] to detect deadlocks. In Section 3, the qualitative effect of using large buffers is described. The influence of buffer size on actual deadlock detection rate is evaluated in Section 4. Finally, in Section 5, some conclusions are drawn.

2. Deadlock Detection Mechanism

In this section, we briefly summarize how the deadlock detection mechanism proposed in [5] works. This mechanism will be referred to as FC3D in this paper, which stands for Flow Control-based Distributed Deadlock Detection. Figure 1 shows a fragment of a network with 3 messages crossing it. Assume that the header of message B arrives at node 2 while message A is advancing. Although message B is waiting for channel 2-1 to be freed, it should not detect deadlock unless message A blocks at some node. Then, another message C appears in the scenario. This message blocks at node 3 because it requests channel 3-2, occu-

*This work was supported by the Spanish CICYT under Grant TIC97–0897–C04–01.

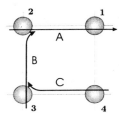

Figure 1. Messages B and C are blocked

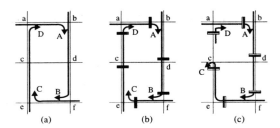

Figure 2. Influence of larger buffer size on the reduction of true deadlocks

pied by message B, which is blocked. The problem is that message C only sees that B is not advancing, but it does not know if B is, in turn, waiting for a channel occupied by a message that is advancing. In order to solve this situation, a control signal could be sent across all the channels reserved by a message, starting from the node that contains the blocked header. Thus, in our example, a signal would be sent from node 2 to node 3. Although this scheme solves the problem, it requires a new control signal that increases the number of channel wires and complicates the control logic.

Fortunately, the same information can be obtained from flow control signals. In wormhole, when a message header blocks, the remaining flits from the same message are also blocked in the network buffers. Thus, the state (blocked or advancing) of a channel is enough to know if a newly arrived message that requests that channel has to detect deadlock. In our example, when message B arrives at node 2, channel 2-1 is occupied by a message that is advancing. Thus, message B becomes eligible to recover from deadlock only if message A blocks. On the other hand, when message C arrives at node 3, the requested channel 3-2 contains a blocked message. Therefore, message C is not eligible to recover from deadlock. Note that at least one message in each cycle will be marked as eligible for deadlock.

FC3D is implemented by using one counter and two flags (*Inactivity* and *Deadlock Threshold*) associated with each physical output channel, and one flag (*Generate/Propagate*) associated with each physical input channel. The counter contains the number of cycles between flit transmissions across the channel. Flags I and DT are set if the counter value exceeds thresholds $t1$ and $t2$, respectively. Flag G/P is set to G if an unsuccessful routing is made and some of the feasible output channels have their I flag reset. If all the feasible output channels have their I flag set then G/P is set to P. A message is presumed to be deadlocked if the input channel it occupies has its G/P flag set to G and all the feasible output channels have their DT flag set. See [5] for more details.

Buffer size may impact the behavior of the deadlock detection mechanism. If buffers are deep, when a header blocks, the remaining flits of the message will continue advancing until the buffer is full or almost full. Thus, the larger the buffer size, the longer the time needed to stop all the flits in the message. In our example, it could happen that when message C arrives at node 3, data flits from message

B are still advancing filling the buffer of channel 3-2. Thus, message C will become eligible to recover from deadlock. When the flits of message B stop, node 3 will detect a false deadlock. The consequence of using deep buffers is that the number of false detected deadlocks increases.

3. Qualitative Effects of Using Large Buffers

Using deeper buffers may increase network throughput, because blocked messages occupy fewer channels, allowing more messages in the network at a given time. In addition, when pipelined transmission is used over long wires, which is the case for NOWs and some multiprocessors, buffers should be deep enough to store at least all the data that can be sent by a source node before flow control stops transmission. Thus, buffers are usually very deep.

Buffer size also has some effects on deadlock frequency [7]. Networks with small buffers lead to substantially higher deadlock frequency, because blocked messages occupy more channels, increasing the number of cycles[1]. Figure 2 shows this behavior qualitatively. Assume that messages A, B, and C are 4-flits long, and D is 2-flits long. Also, assume that the destination nodes are f,e,c, and b, respectively. In Figure 2(b), one-flit buffers are associated with each channel, and the four messages are involved in a deadlocked configuration. In Figure 2(c), two-flit buffers are used and there is no deadlocked configuration because message C can reach its destination.

However, deep buffers can also impact the efficiency of the FC3D mechanism because the elapsed time between header blocking and the propagation of flow control signals increases with buffer size. The number of false deadlock detections may increase as buffer size increases. Let us show this situation by using two examples. Figure 3 shows 4 nodes in a network with one-flit buffers associated with each channel. In cycle $i - 1$, messages A and B arrive at some intermediate nodes b and a, respectively, as shown in Figure 3(a). In cycle i (Figure 3(b)), message A continues advancing and message B arrives at node b, requesting the channel just occupied by message A. As a consequence,

---

[1]In this context, a cycle is a set of messages blocked cyclically

316

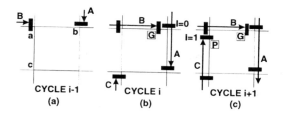

Figure 3. FC3D mechanism with 1-flit buffers

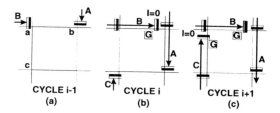

Figure 4. FC3D mechanism with 2-flit buffers

message B blocks. As message A is advancing, the flag I at node b is equal to 0. Thus, the bit G/P of the channel occupied by B is set to G. A new message C also appears in the configuration. In the next clock cycle (Figure 3(c)) message A continues advancing, and message B continues blocked. Message C arrives at node a, setting G/P=P because the channel occupied by B is inactive (B is blocked), flow control signals have been propagated, and hence I=1. Note that we assumed $t1 = 1$ (see Section 2). Thus, using one-flit buffers, in the analyzed configuration only message B is marked with G/P=G. As a consequence, if message A blocks, then threshold $t2$ will be reached, and only message B will be detected as deadlocked.

Consider now the same situation in a network that uses two-flit buffers (Figure 4). The starting point is the same, messages A and B arriving at nodes b and a, respectively (Figure 4(a)). In cycle i (Figure 4(b)), message B arrives at node b, requesting a busy channel, and setting G/P to G because that channel has I=0 (A is advancing). There are no differences with respect to the situation described above. However, in cycle $i + 1$ (Figure 4(c)), when message C arrives at node a and requests the channel occupied by B, the G/P flag is set to G, because B is still advancing filling the channel buffer (the channel flag I is equal to 0). The main problem is that when message B blocks for a number of clock cycles exceeding $t2$, a deadlock will be detected. However, there is no deadlocked configuration, leading to a false deadlock detection and introducing the overhead of the recovery mechanism. Note that the probability of requesting a channel occupied by a blocked message before the corresponding I flag is set to 1 increases with buffer size.

As a consequence, increasing buffer size will negatively affect the accuracy of the FC3D mechanism. However, as deeper buffers also have positive effects on true deadlock frequency, the net effect on the performance of the mechanism is not clear. This effect will be empirically analyzed in the next section.

4. Evaluation

The evaluation methodology used is based on the one proposed in [6]. We will evaluate FC3D for different buffer sizes, measuring the percentage of messages detected as deadlocked with respect to the total number of messages de-

livered during the simulation. Note that this includes both true and false detected deadlocks because our simulator is unable to distinguish between them. In particular, we have considered a uniform message destination distribution and different message lengths (16-flit messages (s), 64-flit messages (l), 256-flit messages (L) and a hybrid load (sl) composed of 60 % of 16-flit and 40 % of 64-flit messages). In all simulations, results have been gathered for 100,000 delivered messages. Finally, we have considered bidirectional k-ary 3-cube networks with 512 and 4096 nodes, respectively.

The network model considered consists of a four-port architecture, a true fully adaptive router [7, 6] with three virtual channels per physical channel, a crossbar switch and some channels. Routing, switch, and channel delays are all equal to 1 clock cycle. Each output virtual channel has a two-flit buffer. Also, each input virtual channel has a variable buffer size. Input buffer size ranges from 2 to 64 flits, taking into account that the maximum buffer size analyzed must not exceed the maximum message length, which in fact corresponds to virtual cut-through switching. We will analyze the influence of the size of this buffer on deadlock detection. FC3D [5] is the deadlock detection technique, with threshold $t1$ and $t2$ equal to 1 and 64 clock cycles, respectively. Finally, the message injection limitation mechanism proposed in [4] is used in order to avoid performance degradation of the network when it reaches saturation and also to decrease the effective deadlock frequency.

We will first present the results for a 512-node network. Figure 5 shows the percentage of messages detected as deadlocked by FC3D mechanism as a function of message injection rate. Note that FC3D detects all true deadlocks, but it may also detect some false deadlocks. For 256-flit messages (L), no deadlocks are detected until the network is close to saturation. At this point, increasing input buffer size leads to an important reduction in the number of detected deadlocks. Thus, the effective reduction in deadlock frequency overcomes the lower effectiveness of the deadlock detection mechanism. However, when the network is just entering saturation (injection rate of 0.55 flits/node/cycle), moving from 16 to 32-flit buffers slightly increases the percentage of detected deadlocks. In this case, increasing buffer size does not significantly reduce true deadlocks, but FC3D detects more false deadlocks. Any-

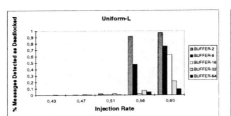 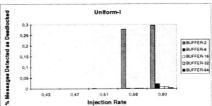 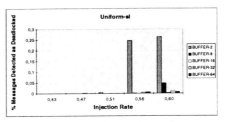

Figure 5. Percentage of messages detected as deadlocked versus injection rate for 512 nodes

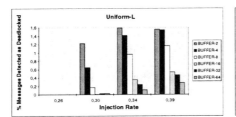 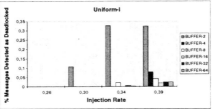 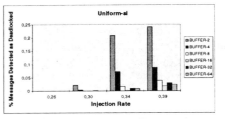

Figure 6. Percentage of messages detected as deadlocked versus injection rate for 4K nodes

way, this increment is negligible when compared with the number of deadlocks detected when load is beyond saturation (0.6 flits/node/cycle). For 64-flit (l) and mixed length messages (sl) the behavior of FC3D mechanism is quite similar. The number of messages detected as deadlocked also decreases when buffer size increases. In this case, we have observed an important reduction on deadlock detection when buffer size is greater than or equal to 8 flits. Additionally, the absolute percentage of messages detected as deadlocked is much lower than for 256-flit messages. The results for 16-flit (s) messages (not shown) only detected as deadlocked a 0.025 % of all the messages when two-flit buffers are used and the network is completely saturated. This percentage was reduced to zero for larger buffer sizes.

Figure 6 shows the results for a network with 4096 nodes. As can be seen, results are qualitatively similar to those for 512-node networks. In summary, increasing buffer size not only increases throughput but also effectively reduces the number of deadlocks detected by our detection mechanism.

5. Conclusions

In this paper we have analyzed the impact of buffer size on actual deadlock detection using the mechanism proposed in [5] (FC3D mechanism) under different load conditions.

Buffer size has a direct impact on deadlock frequency. The use of deep buffers leads to substantially lower deadlock frequency, for the same traffic rate [7]. However, deep buffers also reduce the efficiency of FC3D. Hence, actual deadlock detection rate of FC3D mechanism with large buffers is affected both by the reduction in true deadlock frequency and the increase in false deadlock detection.

The analysis presented in this paper has shown that, for the traffic pattern and message sizes analyzed, the reduction

in true deadlock frequency has a stronger influence than the increase in false deadlock detection. Using large buffers not only increases network throughput but also reduces the effective deadlock detection rate in all the cases. Therefore, we can conclude that the FC3D mechanism can be efficiently used for deadlock detection even if flit buffers are large, following the current trends in router design.

References

[1] W. J. Dally and C. L. Seitz, "Deadlock-free message routing in multiprocessor interconnection networks," *IEEE Transactions on Computers*, vol. C–36, no. 5, pp. 547–553, May 1987.

[2] J. Duato, "A necessary and sufficient condition for deadlock-free adaptive routing in wormhole networks," *IEEE Transactions on Parallel and Distributed Systems*, vol. 6, no. 10, pp. 1055–1067, October 1995.

[3] J. Duato, S. Yalamanchili and L.M. Ni, *Interconnection Networks: An Engineering Approach*, IEEE Computer Society Press, 1997.

[4] P. López and J. Duato, "Deadlock-free adaptive routing algorithms for the 3D-torus: Limitations and solutions," in *Proceedings of Parallel Architectures and Languages Europe 93*, June 1993.

[5] P. López, J.M. Martínez, and J. Duato, "A very efficient distributed deadlock detection mechanism for wormhole networks," in *Proceedings of the Fourth International Symposium on High-Performance Computer Architecture*, February 1998.

[6] J.M. Martínez, P. López, J. Duato and T.M. Pinkston, "Software-based deadlock recovery technique for true fully adaptive routing in wormhole networks," in *Proceedings of the 1997 International Conference on Parallel Processing*, August 1997.

[7] T.M. Pinkston and S. Warnakulasuriya, "On deadlocks in interconnection networks," in *Proceedings of the 24th International Symposium on Computer Architecture*, June 1997.

Session

Workshop Overviews

Fifth Annual Workshop on Computer Education

Organizers:

David Kaeli and Bruce Jacobs

This workshop provides a forum for Computer Architecture educators to share their views, curricula and teaching tools with a wide audience. The goal is to improve the overall quality of Computer Architecture education. The focus of this year's workshop will be on a range of topics, including: curriculum development, simulators, tools, textbooks, and related topics. The workshop will also include panel sessions led by top educators in the field of Computer Architecture Education. The advance program for this workshop will be available at http://www.ece.neu.edu/personal/kaeli/wcae99.html.

Third Workshop on Communication, Architecture, and Applications for Network-Based Parallel Computing (CANPC '99)

Organizers:

Anand Sivasubramaniam and Mario Lauria

Clusters of workstations/PCs connected by off-the-shelf networks have become popular as a platform for cost-effective parallel computing. Hardware and software technological advances have made this network-based parallel computing platform feasible. A large number of research groups from academia and industry are working to enhance the capabilities of such a platform, thereby improving its cost-effectiveness and usability. These developments are facilitating the migration of many existing applications as well as the development of new applications on this platform.

Continuing in the tradition of the two previously successful CANPC workshops, this workshop will bring together researchers and practitioners working in architecture, system software, applications and performance evaluation to discuss state-of-the-art solutions for network-based parallel computing. The advance program for this workshop will be available at http://www.cse.psu.edu/~canpc99.

Multithreaded Execution Architecture and Compilation

Organizers:

Dean M. Tullsen and Guang Gao

Multithreading has become a very important execution model in modern computers, both single and multi-processors. Commercial multithreaded processors now exist, and mainstream multithreaded processors are just around the corner. The focus of this workshop is on multithreading execution techniques and systems, including architecture design and implementation, compilation techniques, system and language support and performance evaluation. The advance program for this workshop will be available at http://www-cse.ucsd.edu/users/tullsen/mteac99.html

Parallel Computing for Irregular Applications

Organizers:

Jacques Chassin de Kergommeaux, Yves Denneulin and Thierry Gautier

Several types of irregularity need to be mastered in order to execute efficiently large scale applications. This includes irregularity of the algorithms as well as the irregularity of the target hardware systems.

The aim of this workshop is to give an opportunity to researchers to present work in progress in the area of runtime systems and compiling techniques to efficiently execute parallel irregular applications. The advance program for this workshop will be available at http://www-apache.imag.fr/manifestations/PCIA/.

Second Workshop on Computer Architecture Evaluation Using Commercial Workloads

Organizers

Russell Clapp, Ashwini Nanda, and Josep Torrellas

It has been widely noted that there is a lack of influence of commercial workloads on new computer architectures and their performance evaluation. This is despite the fact that commercial workloads often consume a large fraction of the cycles in today's machines. The function of this workshop is the discussion of work-in-progress that utilizes commercial workloads for evaluation of computer architectures. By discussing this ongoing research, the workshop will expose participants to the characteristics of commercial workload behavior and provide an understanding of how commercial workloads exercise computer systems. Furthermore, there will be discussion on the difficulties associated with using commercial workloads to drive new computer architecture designs and what can be done to overcome these problems. The advance program for this workshop will be available at http://iacoma.cs.uiuc.edu/caecw99.

Author Index

Notes

IEEE
COMPUTER
SOCIETY

Press Activities Board

8/24/98